Lecture Notes of the Institute for Computer Sciences, Social Informatics and Telecommunications Engineering 169

More information about this series at http://www.springer.com/series/8197

Benny Mandler · Johann Marquez-Barja
Miguel Elias Mitre Campista · Dagmar Cagáňová
Hakima Chaouchi · Sherali Zeadally
Mohamad Badra · Stefano Giordano
Maria Fazio · Andrey Somov
Radu-Laurentiu Vieriu (Eds.)

Internet of Things

IoT Infrastructures

Second International Summit, IoT 360° 2015
Rome, Italy, October 27–29, 2015
Revised Selected Papers, Part I

 Springer

Editors

Benny Mandler
IBM Research
Haifa, Israel

Johann Marquez-Barja
CONNECT Centre, Trinity College
University of Dublin
Dublin, Ireland

Miguel Elias Mitre Campista
GTA/PEE-COPPE/DEL-Poli
Universidade Federal do Rio de Janeiro
  (UFRJ)
Rio de Janeiro, Brazil

Dagmar Cagáňová
Faculty of Materials Science
  and Technology in Trnava
Slovak University of Technology
  in Bratislava
Trnava, Slovakia

Hakima Chaouchi
Institut Télécom SudParis
Evry, France

Sherali Zeadally
College of Communication and Information
University of Kentucky
Lexington, KY, USA

Mohamad Badra
College of Technological Innovation
Zayed University
Dubai, United Arab Emirates

Stefano Giordano
University of Pisa
Pisa, Holy See (Vatican City State)

Maria Fazio
DICIEAMA Department
University of Messina
Messina, Italy

Andrey Somov
CREATE-NET
Trento, Italy

Radu-Laurentiu Vieriu
University of Trento
Trento, Italy

ISSN 1867-8211   ISSN 1867-822X   (electronic)
Lecture Notes of the Institute for Computer Sciences, Social Informatics
and Telecommunications Engineering
ISBN 978-3-319-47062-7   ISBN 978-3-319-47063-4   (eBook)
DOI 10.1007/978-3-319-47063-4

Library of Congress Control Number: 2016954126

Printed on acid-free paper

This Springer imprint is published by Springer Nature
The registered company is Springer International Publishing AG
The registered company address is: Gewerbestrasse 11, 6330 Cham, Switzerland

SaSeIoT 2015

Preface

The Second EAI International Conference on Safety and Security in Internet of Things (SaSeIoT' 2015) was held in Rome, Italy, during October 26–27, 2015, as a collocated event of the IoT 360° Summit 2015.

This international conference attracted submissions from various countries. Each paper went through a rigorous peer-review process, with each submission receiving multiple reviews from the members of the Technical Program Committee. We could only select a few of the highest-quality papers for inclusion in the final program.

The accepted papers, which focus on security and privacy issues, provide great insight into the latest research findings in the area of the Internet of Things. In addition to the technical papers, the workshop program also included two keynote speeches. The first keynote entitled "Contract-Based Design Tailored to Safety Issues for Cyber-physical Systems" was delivered by Dr. Daniela Cancila. The second keynote entitled "Security and Privacy in IoT" was delivered by Dr. Hakima Chaouchi.

We would like to thank all the people who worked hard to make this conference a real success. First and foremost, we thank all authors who submitted their papers for consideration for this conference as well as all Technical Program Committee members for providing rigorous, timely reviews. We would also like to thank the European Alliance for Innovation (EAI) for its sponsorship. Finally, we express our gratitude to Kristina Lukáčová for her continuous administrative support throughout the preparation of this conference.

Hakima Chaouchi
Sherali Zeadally

CYCLONE 2015

Preface

The First EAI International Conference on Cyber Physical Systems, IoT and Sensors Networks (CYCLONE 2015) was held in Rome, Italy, on October 26, 2015, as a collocated event of the IoT 360° Summit 2015.

The conference was an incredible first step on the way to becoming a benchmark in the multidisciplinary fields of CPS, IoT, and sensor networks. The technologies originating from the areas of sensing, networking, control, and processing are enablers for exciting new opportunities for researchers, engineers, and business people to innovate in meaningful ways. And that is who CYCLONE 2015 was created for – the goal was to bring all of these different parties together to share ideas and visions.

It was our great pleasure to host prominent keynote speakers, and authors of all the excellent accepted papers, courtesy of the passionate and dedicated Program Committee members, to whom we would like to extend our warmest thanks. Lastly, this event could not happen without the support of EAI and Kristina Lukáčová, the event manager, who organized CYCLONE 2015 with great effort and expertise; and we wish to extend our sincere gratitude to both.

GOODTECHS 2015

Preface

The GOODTECHS 2015 Conference was the first edition of a conference that aims to become a point of attraction for researchers in the area and it was held in the beautiful city of Rome, a worldwide renowned historical, academic and cultural center. In GOODTECHS we were interested in experiences with the design, implementation, deployment, operation, and evaluation of smart objects and technologies for social good. Clearly, we were not considering only the so-called first world as the scenario for this evolution; we also referred to those areas where ICT is currently less widespread, hoping that it may represent a societal development opportunity rather than a source for further divide.

It was our honor to have prominent international scholars as speakers. The conference program included technical papers selected through peer reviews by the Technical Program Committee members and keynote speakers who provided even more insight into this area. We would like to thank the EAI for the support and all the members of the conference committees and the reviewers for their dedicated and passionate work. None of this would happen without the support and curiosity of the authors who sent their papers to this first event. Finally, we would like to encourage current and future authors to continue working in this direction and to participate in forums like this conference so as to exchange knowledge and experiences and to make ICT actually helpful to society.

Ombretta Gaggi
Pietro Manzoni
Claudio Palazzi

CN4IoT 2015

Preface

The First International Conference on Cloud, Networking for IoT systems (CN4IoT) was held in Rome, Italy, during October 26–27, 2015, as a collocated event of the IoT 360° Summit 2015.

CN4IoT 2015 was conceived to analyze limits and/or advantages in the exploitation of existing solutions developed for cloud, networking, and IoT, and to foster new, original, and innovative contributions. We strongly believe that it is time to link cloud, networking, and IoTs. Nowadays, ICT researchers are looking to improve networking, for example, to effectively improve the quality of life of citizens in smart city scenarios using IoT devices, and to put everything in place trying to improve the experience of common users. There are masses of users who like to use the cloud but it has to be easy to use and it must have a positive impact on their lives. Before, the cloud was an issue only ICT researchers were concerned with. Today, many people are trying to involve professionals in their activities, such as lawyers, doctors, engineers, and so on. They use services like cloud services, small things, and say, "It's amazing, that we can interact with each other, write in the same document, we can make progress in our work and make the workflow better." The workflow has changed. We realize this, and we try to move forward. It is a challenge but it is also time to change how we think, and we are first in the row.

It was our honor to have invited prominent and valuable ICT worldwide experts as keynote speakers. The conference program comprised technical papers selected through peer reviews by the Technical Program Committee members and invited talks. SDWN 2015 would not have been realized without the help and dedication of our conference manager, Kristina Lukáčová, from the European Alliance for Innovation (EAI). We would like to thank the conference committees and the reviewers for their dedicated and passionate work. None of this would have happened without the support and curiosity of the authors who sent their papers to this first edition of CN4IoT.

HealthyIoT 2015

Preface

The Second EAI International Conference on IoT Technologies for Health Care (HealthyIoT 2015) was held in Rome, Italy, during October 26–27, 2015, as a collocated event of the IoT 360° Summit 2015.

Internet of Things (IoT) devices are becoming more powerful every year, and there is an immense amount of information flowing between them in the cloud. By applying the concept of IoT to the health-care sector, it is possible to collect, store, and analyze physiological data and to provide new medical services for citizens based on a constant monitoring and early detection of dangerous situations. IoT offers greater opportunities in the field of health care, allowing for a wider access, a better quality, and a lower cost of health care.

When combining the power of IoT devices and physiological sensors, as well as cloud technology that enables us to work with data in new exciting ways, we can introduce the concept of pervasive health-care systems that provide new health services for chronically ill patients, for people with specific diseases or disorders, and for individuals switching to a healthier lifestyle. The HealthyIoT 2015 workshop produced valuable insights on how the IoT systems, together with new cloud computing and big data capabilities, can help patients, caregivers, and medical personnel to envisage new, value-added health-care solutions for the future.

We wish to extend our great thanks to all the members of the Program Committee for their rigorous effort, dedication, and critical eye. We would also like to thank all of the contributing authors, whose great passion and expertise have produced deep insight into the applications of IoT for health care. Finally, we would like to thank EAI for their support, and Kristina Lukáčová for managing HealthyIoT 2015 with great skill and enthusiasm.

IoTaaS 2015

Preface

It gives us a great pleasure to welcome you to the proceedings of the Second EAI International Conference on IoT as a Service (IoTaaS 2015) held in the beautiful city of Rome, as a part of IoT360, the international summit on Internet of Things. We plan this event as a melting point for researchers, engineers, and business people to meet and exchange ideas and information. IoTaaS is an international venue for publishing innovative and cutting-edge results on the convergence of next-generation technologies and methodologies reshaping our way of living. This conference focuses on the Internet of Things (IoT) in general and in particular on providing innovative and enabling capabilities "as a service." The cloud serves as the central focal point for consumption and delivery of such technologies and applications.

As we are striding into the era of IoT, a key question is how we make the most of IoT for all stakeholders, including platform providers, IoT application developers, end-users, large and small organizations (such as city councils, enterprises) that wish to provide better service, and manufacturers of smart devices. The amount of smart devices immersed in everyday life, from manufacturing to clothing, is growing every day in terms of power, processing, and network connectivity. The sheer size and variety of contextual data that they produce, along with the actions they can take on their environment, is enormous. It remains to be answered how all this potential will come to bear; the Second International Conference on IoT as a Service (IoTaaS 2015) aimed to contribute to the discussion on the challenges posed by these trends.

The conference program comprised technical papers selected through peer reviews by the Technical Program Committee members, invited talks, industrial presentations, and a demo session. We received many good papers. These papers went through a rigorous review process for the selection of papers for the program. The selected papers cover a wide spectrum of topics related to IoTaaS. We had papers on architectures for the IoT, security and privacy, semantics, and testing. Additionally, we were honored to have two prominent keynote speakers: Gabi Zodik from IBM Research discussing "Future Directions in Mobile, IoT and Wearable Enterprise Computing"; and Alfeo Pareschi from Axiros, discussing "IoT Platforms: Security, Identity Management, Ontologies and Interoperability." Finally we were honored to have an invited talk by Afonso Ferreira from the European Commission, who provided the commission's point of view on IoT research and innovation in the European Commission. We believe that this strong program laid a concrete foundation for this conference for years to come.

We would like to thank the EAI for their initiative and support and all the members of the conference committees and the reviewers for their dedicated and passionate work. None of this could happen without the support and curiosity of the authors who sent their papers to this event.

Benny Mandler
Kostas Magoutis

MobilityIoT 2015

Preface

A wide selection of cutting-edge and insightful research papers were presented at the Second EAI International Conference on Mobility in IoT 2015.

The 2015 conference was an IoT co-located event that took place in Rome, Italy, during October 26–27 2015, forming one of the main conferences within the IoT 360 Summit organized by the European Alliance for Innovation, in Trento, Italy, and the European Alliance for Innovation in Slovakia.

The Mobility in IoT 2015 conference was organized by the Faculty of Materials Science and Technology (MTF STU) in Trnava, Institute of Industrial Engineering and Management, in collaboration with the European Alliance for Innovation in Slovakia, and its partner, the European Alliance for Innovation, in Trento, Italy.

It was a great satisfaction to have the opportunity to welcome and meet individuals from around the world, all of whom share a common interest in the area of mobility in IoT. In particular, the organizers would like to thank the presenters, who showcased their latest research, and the audience members, who added to active discussions and debate regarding the recent developments and the outlook for the future for the field.

The goal of the EAI International Conference on Mobility in IoT 2015 was to provide a platform for the cross-fertilization of ideas and to present cutting-edge innovation and technologies for sustainable solutions to the mobility agenda. The focus of the conference reflected the EU thematic priorities for research and innovation to improve the quality of life of citizens and make cities more sustainable with less impact on the environment. The conference presented participants with a unique opportunity to engage with different stakeholders from across Europe and around the world. In doing so, the conference offered an ideal platform to empower the triple helix of university research, industry, and government, while also providing innovative opportunities focusing on the growth and development of mobility in IoT.

A total of 13 research papers are featured in this publication, with contributions by researchers from across Europe and around the world. The publication includes articles that were written and presented by authors from nine countries, including Poland, the Czech Republic, Serbia, Italy, South Korea, Germany, Colombia, India, and Slovakia.

Among the papers presented at the conference were these presented by the conference keynote speakers, Prof. Milan Dado, the Dean of the Faculty of Electronics, TU Zilina, Slovakia, and a coordinator of the project ERA Chair H2020, who discussed the "Internet of Things as Advanced Technology to Support Mobility and Intelligent

Transport," Jaroslav Holeček, vice-president of the Slovak Automotive Industry Association (ZAP), who discussed the topic of "Innovation as Basic Prerequisite of Competitiveness of Automotive Industry in Slovakia," Prof. George Teodorescu, from the International Institute for Integral Innovation, Köln, Germany who presented the topic of "i-WALK, a Different Approach to Urban Mobility," Prof. Dušan Petráš, of the Slovak University of Technology in Bratislava, Slovakia, former vice-rector of STU and former dean of the Faculty of Civil Engineering, who gave a talk on the topic "Smart Cities — Energy-Efficient and Environmentally Friendly Housing," and Dr. Predrag K. Nikolic, Associate Professor at the Faculty of Digital Production, EDUCONS University, Serbia, and visiting professor at the Bergen Academy of Art and Design, Norway, as well as Shenzhen School of Industrial Design, China, who presented the topic of "Multimodal Interactions: Embedding New Meanings to Known Forms and Objects."

The participants were particularly impressed by the wide range of innovative research solutions presented during the conference. As a result, the papers included here, in our opinion, accurately reflect the diversity of content and rapidly developing nature of the IoT agenda. The research not only illustrates the current state of the art in the field but it also helps to contribute to defining the future thematic areas of debate.

In conclusion, the Scientific Committee members and organizers would like to express their sincere thanks to all the authors and audience members who attended the conference in Rome, Italy, and also the authors, who contributed to the creation of this Mobility in IoT publication.

Dagmar Cagáňová
Jana Šujanová

S-Cube 2015

Preface

This volume contains the proceedings of S-Cube 2015, the 6th International Conference on Sensor Systems and Software. The conference took place in Rome, Italy, during October 26–27, 2015. The aim of the conference was to provide a forum in which researchers and practitioners from academia and industry, as well as the "makers," may work together in order to present and debate the different innovative solutions and applications in sensing systems and associated software.

This year the conference was organized in conjunction with the IoT360 Summit and was focused on the Internet of Things (IoT) paradigm. The reason for choosing this topic is that the IoT has slowly but steadily and increasingly permitted what researchers and engineers study and build. "Sensing systems" and "software" play a crucial role for the emerging world of the IoT.

S-Cube received a total of 28 paper submissions of which ten were selected for full publication and presentation. Apart from full papers, six short papers and four invited contributions are published and were presented during the conference. Paper submissions were received from 14 different countries from all over the world. The selection process involved over 90 reviews with all papers being evaluated by at least three independent reviewers. In addition, the reviews were discussed off-line by the chairs and the Technical Program Committee, prior to making final decisions. The final program covered a wide range of topics, which were grouped into six sessions: Sensors, Experimentation and Prototyping, IoT and Cyber Physical Systems, Software, Self-x and Smart Methods, and Evaluation and Analysis.

The conference program included other elements in addition to the presentation of research papers. Two keynotes were given by Andrew Markham, Lecturer in Software Engineering at the University of Oxford, UK, and Fahim Kawsar, Head of IoT Research at Alcatel Lucent Bell Laboratories, Belgium. Dr. Markham and Dr. Kawsar spoke about "Structural Monitoring" and "Innovative Human Centered IoT Systems," respectively.

We would like to thank all authors for their contributions to this volume and in particular the reviewers for their hard work that significantly helped to improve the initial submissions and made our work easier when selecting the papers. We would like to also thank all the volunteers who shared their talent, dedication, and time for the workshop arrangements and for preparing these proceedings.

Andrey Somov
David Boyle

InterIoT 2015

Preface

It is our real pleasure to welcome you to the proceedings of the First EAI International Conference on Interoperability in IoT held in the amazing city of Rome, Italy. Colocated with the IoT360 summit and taking advantage of its attractiveness, InterIoT 2015 offered an exciting technical program consisting of a keynote speech, invited talks, and technical sessions that presented original and fundamental research advances in all aspects of interoperability of these heterogeneous IoT platforms. Indeed, IoT products are now hitting the market across a large variety of segments. Often driven by the fear of "falling behind", small and large companies push their engineering teams to produce solutions quickly. The result is that the market is highly fragmented: A large number of non-interoperable solutions are being installed, eventually leading to increased costs, inefficiencies, customer frustration, and a rate of adoption of the IoT that is much slower than that touted by analysts. The market is now at a state where we ought to think about interoperability. Interoperability appears to a major and new challenge.

The goal of InterIoT is to bring together practicing engineers and advanced researchers to share information on the state of the art around interoperability in the IoT, analyze what is needed, and identify the work that lies ahead to increase the number of interoperable IoT products.

We received high-quality submissions from all parts of the world. After a rigorous review process, eight regular and invited papers were included in the technical program. The program also featured a keynote addressed by Prof. Carsten Bormann from Universität Bremen, Germany.

We would like to thank the Technical Program Committee chair Dr. Thomas Watteyne, who did a remarkable job in the establishment of the technical program. The conference would not have been possible without his help or that of all the TPC members, publicity chair, and external reviewers, who volunteered their time and professional expertise. We would like to take this opportunity to thank all of them for their help. We would also like to thank all the authors for contributing their quality work, and our sponsors and partners for their support, including CREATE-NET and EAI. We received excellent and support from our sponsors, especially from Kristina Lukáčová who managed the conference organization. Sincere and dedicated thanks to her.

Finally, we hope you enjoy the proceedings.

Nathalie Mitton
Thomas Noel

SDWNCT 2015

Preface

The Second EAI International Conference on Software Defined and Virtualized Future Wireless Networks and Cognitive Technologies (SDWNCT 2015) was held in Rome, Italy, on October 26, 2015, as a collocated event of the IoT 360° Summit 2015. SDWNCT aims to explore new design spaces, new challenges and solutions, as well as new applications and services of software-defined virtualized future mobile and wireless networks. At the same time, it targets enthusiastic researchers and practitioners from AI and IoT-related areas sharing the common goal of addressing the challenges posed by the Cognitive aspect of IoT by using new or leveraging existing Artificial Intelligence techniques. All this to bring to the community original and inspiring research contributions from technology experts, designers, researchers, and architects in academia and industry.

It was our honor to have invited prominent scholars as keynote speakers. The conference program comprised technical papers selected through peer reviews by the Technical Program Committee members, invited talks, special sessions, and a demo session. Putting together a workshop of the scope and caliber of SDWN was a challenging and exciting undertaking. We are very grateful for the contributions of each of the members of the Technical Program Committee in selecting the best out of all outstanding work submitted. SDWNCT 2015 would not have been a reality without the help and dedication of our conference manager, Kristina Lukáčová, from the European Alliance for Innovation (EAI), who worked with us and the Technical Program Committee chairs. As Organizing Committee, we hope you enjoy the procedings of SDWNCT 2015 and the IoT 360° Summit 2015, which includes high-quality and exciting research work in SDN and Cognitive Technologies applied to future services in IoT.

Bruno Astuto
Athanasios V. Vasilakos
Frederik Santens
Radu-Laurențiu Vieriu

SaSeIoT 2015

Organization

Steering Committee

Steering Committee Chair

Imrich Chlamtac   Create-Net, EAI, Italy

Steering Committee Members

Hakima Chaouchi   EIT ICT Labs, Institut Mines Telecom-Telecom Sud Paris, France

Organizing Committee

General Chair

Hakima Chaouchi   EIT ICT Labs, Institut Mines Telecom-Telecom Sud Paris, France

Technical Program Chair

Sherali Zeadally   University of Kentucky, USA

Web Chair

Sandrine Bourger   Telecom Sud Paris, France

Workshop Chairs

Anis Laouiti   Telecom Sud Paris, France
Thomas Bourgeau   UPMC, France

Publicity Chairs

Scott Fowler   Linkoping University, Sweden
Wendong Xiao   University of Science and Technology Beijing, China
Mauro Fonseca   Federal Technological University of Paraná, Brazil

Publication Chair

Mohamad Badra   Zayed University, UAE

Conference Manager

Kristina Lukáčová   European Alliance for Innovation, Slovakia

Technical Program Committee

Sergey Andreev	Tampere University, Finland
Cristina Alcaraz	University of Malaga, Spain
Ioannis Anagnostopoulos	University of Thessaly, Greece
Mohamad Badra	Zayed University, UAE
Zubair Baig	Edith Cowan University, Australia
Zorica Bogdanovic	University of Belgrade, Serbia
Thomas Bourgeau	Paris VI University, France
Patrick Capolsini	University of French Polynesia, Tahiti
Ashok Chandra	Indian Institute of Technology Bombay, India
Naveen Chilamkurti	La Trobe University, Australia
Ernesto Exposito	LAAS-CNRS, University of Toulouse, France
Scott Fowler	Linkoping University, Sweden
Alban Gabillon	University of French Polynesia, Tahiti
Zeynep Gurkas Aydin	Istanbul University, Turkey
Jassim Happa	Oxford University, UK
Debiao He	Wuhan University, China
Leila Ismail	United Arab Emirates University, UAE
Arshad Jhumka	Warwick University, UK
Muhammad Khan	King Saud University, Saudi Arabia
Dong-Seong Kim	University of Canterbury, New Zealand
Anis Laouiti	Telcom Sud Paris, France
Albert Levi	Sabanci University, Turkey
Toktam Mahmoodi	King's College, UK
Gregorio Martinez	University of Murcia, Spain
Hassnaa Moustafa	Intel Corporation, USA
Rajarajan Muttukrishnan	City University, UK
Farid Naït-Abdesselam	Paris Descartes University, France
Jalel Othman	University of Paris 13, France
Lotfi Othmane	Fraunhofer Institute for Secure Information Technology (SIT), Germany
Damith Ranasinghe	University of Adelaide, Australia
Sushmita Ruj	Indian Statistical Institute, India
Giovanni Russello	University of Auckland, New Zealand
Khaled Salah	Khalifa University, UAE
Nishanth Sastry	King's College, UK
Faisal Shaikh	Mehran University of Engineering and Technology, Pakistan

Nicolas Sklavos	University of Patras, Greece
Aditya K Sood	Michigan State University, USA
Diego Touceda	University Carlos III de Madrid, Spain
Wei Yu	Towson University, USA
David Yau	Singapore University of Technology and Design, Sinagpore
Wendong Xiao	University of Science and Technology Beijing, China

CYCLONE 2015

Organization

Steering Committee

Steering Committee Chair

Imrich Chlamtac   CREATE-NET, Italy

Steering Committee Members

Periklis Chatzimisios   Alexander TEI of Thessaloniki, Greece
Stefano Giordano   University of Pisa, Italy

Organizing Committee

General Co-chairs

Stefano Giordano   University of Pisa, Italy
Periklis Chatzimisios   Alexander TEI of Thessaloniki, Greece

Technical Program Co-chairs

Honggang Wang   UMass Dartmouth, USA
Athanasios C. Iossifides   Alexander TEI of Thessaloniki, Greece
Gennaro Boggia   Politecnico di Barri, Italy

Publicity and Social Media Chairs

Daniele Mazzei   Research Center E. Piaggio, Univerity of Pisa, Italy
Alessio Botta   Università degli Studi di Napoli Federico II, Italy
Syed Zaidi   University of Leeds, UK

Workshops Chair

Kan Zheng   Beijing University of Posts and Telecommunications
                               China

Special Session Chair

Toktam Mahmoodi   King's College London, UK

Sponsorship and Exhibits Chair

Luca Foschini   University of Bologna, Italy

Panels Chair

Giuliano Manara   University of Pisa, Italy

Tutorial Chair

Charalabos Skianis   University of the Aegean, Greece

Demos Chair

Davide Adami   CNIT, Italy

Posters and PhD Track Chair

Christian Callegari   University of Pisa, Italy

Local Chair

Michele Pegano   University of Pisa, Italy
Raffaele Giaffreda   CREATE-NET, Italy

Web Chair

Christos Klisiaris   Alexander TEI of Thessaloniki, Greece

GOODTECHS 2015

Organization

Steering Committee

Steering Committee Chair

Imrich Chlamtac — Create-Net Trento, Italy

General Co-chairs

Ombretta Gaggi — Università degli Studi di Padova, Italy
Pietro Manzoni — Universitat Politècnica de València, Spain
Claudio Palazzi — Università degli Studi di Padova, Italy

Organizing Committee

Technical Program Committee Chair

Armir Bujari — Università degli Studi di Padova, Italy

Workshops Chair

Priscila Solis — University of Brasilia, Brazil

Publications Chair

Johann M. Marquez-Barja — CONNECT, Trinity College Dublin, Ireland

Web Chair

Carlos Calafate — Universitat Politècnica de València, Spain

Publicity and Social Media Chair

Carlos Calafate — Universitat Politècnica de València, Spain

Conference Manager

Kristina Lukáčová — European Alliance for Innovation

Program Committee

Antonella Molinari — Università Mediterranea di Reggio Calabria, Italia
Antonio Jara — HES SO University of Applied Sciences Western Switzerland

CN4IoT 2015

Organization

Steering Committee

Steering Committee Chair

Imrich Chlamtac   CREATE-NET, Italy

Steering Committee Members

Antonio Celesti	University of Messina, Italy
Burak Kantarci	Clarkson University, NY, USA
Georgiana Copil	TU Vienna, Austria
Schahram Dustdar	TU Vienna, Austria
Alex Galis	UCL, UK
Fahim Kawsar	Bell Labs, Belgium
Prem Prakash Jayaraman	CSIRO, Digital Productivity Flagship, Australia
Rajiv Ranjan	CSIRO, Digital Productivity Flagship, Australia
Massimo Villari	University of Messina, Italy
Joe Weinman	IEEE Intercloud Testbed, Telx, USA

Organizing Committee

General Chairs

Massimo Villari   University of Messina, Italy

Technical Program Committee Chair

Schahram Dustdar	TU Vienna, Austria
Alex Galis	UCL, UK
Fahim Kawsar	Bell Labs, Belgium

Publication Chair

Maria Fazio   University of Messina, Italy

Publicity Chair

Luca Foschini   University of Bologna, Italy

Conference Manager

Kristina Lukáčová   European Alliance for Innovation, Slovakia

Technical Program Committee

Dana Petcu	West University of Timisoara, Romania
Sourav Bhattacharya	Bell Labs
Kaori Fujinami	Tokyo University of Agriculture and Technology, Japan
Takuro Yonezawa	Keio University, Japan
Akhil Mathur	Bell Laboratories, Ireland
Artemis Voulkidis	Synelixis Solutions Ltd., Greece
Roberto Riggio	Create-net, Italy
Kashinath Basu	Oxford Brokes University, UK
Antonio Skarmeta	Universidad de Murcia, Spain
Flavio de Oliveira Silva	Federal University of Uberlandia, Brazil
Rajiv Ranjan	CSIRO, Australia
Antonio Manzalini	Telecom Italia, Italy
Lefteris Mamates	University of Macedonia, Macedonia
Jaime Lloret	Universidad Politecnica de Valencia, Spain
Slawomir Kuklinski	Orange Labs, Poland
Imen Grida Ban Yahia	Orange Labs, France
Stefano Giordano	Università di Pisa, Italy
Gabi Dreo Rodosek	Universität der Bundeswehr München, Germany
José de Souza	Federal University of Ceará, Brazil
Stuart Clayman	University College London, UK
Walter Cerroni	University of Bologna, Italy
David Breitgand	IBM Haifa Research Lab, Israel
Sergio Beker	DoCoMo, Germany
Rui Aguiar	University of Aveiro, Portugal
Antonio Celesti	University of Messina, Italy
Burak Kantarci	Clarkson University, NY, USA
Georgiana Copil	TU Vienna, Austria
Schahram Dustdar	TU Vienna, Austria
Alex Galis	UCL, UK
Fahim Kawsar	Bell Labs, Belgium
Prem Prakash Jayaraman	CSIRO, Digital Productivity Flagship, Australia
Rajiv Ranjan	CSIRO, Digital Productivity Flagship, Australia
Massimo Villari	University of Messina, Italy
Joe Weinman	IEEE Intercloud Testbed, Telx, USA
Maria Fazio	University of Messina, Italy
Luca Foschini	University of Bologna, Italy
Surya Nepal	CSIRO, Australia
Danilo Ardagna	Politecnico di Milano, Italy

HealthyIoT 2015

Organization

Steering Committee

Steering Committee Chair

Imrich Chlamtac — Create-Net, EAI, Italy

Steering Committee Members

Joel J.P.C. Rodrigues — Instituto de Telecomunicações, University of Beira Interior, Portugal

Antonio J. Jara — Institute of Information Systems, University of Applied Sciences Western Switzerland (HES-SO), Switzerland

Shoumen Palit Austin Datta — Massachusetts Institute of Technology; Industrial Internet Consortium, USA

Organizing Committee

General Chair

Antonio J. Jara — Institute of Information Systems, University of Applied Sciences Western Switzerland (HES-SO), Switzerland

Technical Program Chair

Diego Gachet — Universidad Europea de Madrid, Spain

Sponsorship and Exhibit Chair

Andrej Kos — University of Ljubljana, Slovenia

Publication Chair

Mohamad Badra — Zayed University, UAE

Publicity Co-chairs

Mauro Fonseca — Federal Technological University of Paraná, Brazil

Scott Fowler — Linkoping University, Sweden

Wendong Xiao — University of Science and Technology Beijing, China

Web Chair

Ramon Alcarria   Universidad Politecnica de Madrid, Spain

Local Chair

Raffaele Giaffreda   CREATE-NET, Italy

Conference Manager

Kristina Lukáčová   European Alliance for Innovation, Slovakia

Technical Program Committee

Mobyen Ahmed	Mälardalen University, Sweden
Manuel de Buenaga	Universidad Europea Madrid, Spain
Maria José Busto	Universidad Europea Madrid, Spain
Malconlm Clarke	Brunel University, UK
Ramiro Delgado	Army Forces University, Ecuador
Silvia Gabrielli	Create-net, Italy
Jesús Favela	Cicese, Mexico
Emad Felemban	Umm Al-Qura University, Saudi Arabia
Rubén García	Universidad de las Palmas de Gran Canaria, Spain
Alan Jovic	University of Zagreb, Croatia
Faisal Karim	Meharn University, Pakistan
Ahsank Khandoker	University of Melbourne, Australia
Carlos Lisboa Bento	Universidade de Coimbra, Portugal
Kunal Mankodiya	University of Rhode Island, USA
Venet Osmani	Create-Net, Italy
Enrique Puertas	Universidad Europea Madrid, Spain
Marcela Rodríguez	Universidad Autónoma de Baja California, Mexico
Liane Rockenbach Tarouco	Federal University of Rio Grande do Sul, Brazil
Emilija Stojmenova	University of Ljubljana, Slovenia
Jun Suzuki	University of Massachusetts, USA
Yunchuan Sun	Beijing Normal University, China
Christopher Thuemmler	Edinburgh Napier University, UK
Tonny Velin	AnswareTech, Spain

IoTaaS 2015

Organization

Steering Committee

General Chair

Benny Mandler   IBM Research — Haifa, Israel

Program Chair

Kostas Magoutis   University of Ioannina and ICS-FORTH, Greece

Publicity Chair

George Baryannis   ICS-FORTH, Greece

Local Chair

Raffaele Giaffreda   CREATE-NET, Italy

Conference Manager

Kristina Lukáčová   European Alliance for Innovation, Slovakia

Program Committee Members

Iacopo Carreras	U-Hopper, Italy
Eliezer Dekel	IBM, Israel
Sarunas Girdzijauskas	Royal Institute of Technology, Sweden
Vincenzo Gulisano	Chalmers University of Technology, Sweden
Kostas Magoutis	University of Ioannina and ICS-FORTH, Greece
Benny Mandler	IBM, Israel
Dana Petcu	West University of Timisoara, Romania
Joachim Posegga	University of Passau, Germany
Hong-Linh Truong	TU Vienna, Austria
Apostolos Zarras	University of Ioannina, Greece

MobilityIoT 2015

Organization

Steering Committee

Steering Committee Chairs

Imrich Chlamtac

General Chair

Dagmar Cagáňová

Organizing Committee

Dagmar Cagáňová
Paul Woolliscroft
Daynier Rolando Delgado Sobrino
Tibor Zvonár
Raffaele Giaffreda
Kristína Lukáčová

Technical Program Chairs

Milan Dado
Michal Balog
Jana Šujanová
Jaroslav Holeček
Dušan Petráš
Miloš Čambál
Daniela Špirková
Edita Hekelová
Soňa Ferenčíková
Jozef Hvorecký
Dagmar Cagáňová
Miloš Čambál
Neven Vrček
Daynier Rolando Delgado Sobrino
Paul Woolliscroft
Cristian-Gyözö Haba

Dorin Dumitru Lucache
Eduardo Tome
Florinda Matos
Predrag K. Nikolic
Krzysztof Witkowski
Peter Bindzár
Sebastian Saniuk
Tibor Zvonár
Martin Straka
Petr Štěpánek
Giovanni Del Galdo
Thomas Sporer
Konrad Osterwalder
Frank T. Anbari
Ladislav Janoušek
Michael Stankosky

Pawel Sobcyak
Marek Walancik
Joanna Kurowska Pysz
Thomas Palatin
Walter Mayrhofer
Ullas Ehrlich
Nikolay Madzharov
Ettore Bolisani
Ilpo Pohjola
Enrico Scarso
Jose Maria Viedma Marti
Malgorzata Zieba
Atul Borade

Shawn Chen
Małgorzata Zięba
Florian Marcel Nuta
Sergey Zapryagaev
Janusz K. Grabara
Giorgos Cristonakis
Emanuel-Stefan Marinescu
Yhing Sawheny
John Kelly
Abdul Dewale Mohammed
Gabriela Koľveková
Roswitha Wiedenhofer

Local Chair

Raffaele Giaffreda

S-CUBE 2015

Organization

Steering Committee

Steering Committee Chair

Imrich Chlamtac   Create-Net, Italy

Organizing Committee

General Chair

Andrey Somov   CREATE-NET, Italy

Technical Program Committee Chair

David Boyle   Imperial College London, UK

Publicity Chair

Salil Kanhere   University of New South Wales, Australia

Web Chair

Swaytha Sasidharan   CREATE-NET/University of Trento, Italy

Conference Manager

Kristina Lukáčová   European Alliance for Innovation, Slovakia

Technical Program Committee

Alexander Baranov	MATI-Russian State Technological University, Russia
Iain Bate	University of York, UK
Stefano Basagni	Northeastern University, USA
Carlo Alberto Boano	TU Graz, Austria
Matteo Ceriotti	University of Duisburg-Essen, Germany
Jason O. Hallstrom	Florida Atlantic University, USA
Salil Kanhere	University of New South Wales, Australia

InterIoT 2015

Organization

Steering Committee

Steering Committee Chair

Imrich Chlamtac   CREATE-NET, Italy

Organizing Committee

General Chairs

Nathalie Mitton   Inria, France
Thomas Noel   University of Strasbourg, France

Program Chair

Thomas Watteyne   Inria, France

Web, Publicity, and Publications Chair

Miguel Elias M. Campista   UFRJ, Brazil

Conference Manager

Kristina Lukáčová   European Alliance for Innovation, Slovakia

Technical Program Committee

Animesh Pathak   Inria, France
Antonella Molinaro   UNIRC, Italy
Antonio Puliafito   Messina University, Italy
Cedric Adjih   Inria, France
Cesar Viho   Université Rennes 1, France
Edgar Chavez   Cicese, Mexico
Emery Jou   Institute for Information Industry, Taiwan
Fumio Teraoka   Keio University, Japan
Giancarlo Fortino   University of Calabria, Italy
Gregor Schiele   Dusseldorf University, Germany
Ines Robles   Ericsson, Finland
Ivan Mezei   Novi Sad University, Serbia
John Soldatos   AIT, Greece
Konrad Wrona   NATO, The Netherlands

Malisa Vucinic   UC Berkeley, USA
Maria Rita Palattella   SnT/University of Luxembourg, Luxembourg
Ming-Whei Feng   Institute for Information Industry, Taiwan
Nicola Accettura   UC Berkeley, USA
Oliver Hahm   Inria, France
Pascal Thubert   Cisco, France/USA
Pere Tuset   UOC, Spain
Periklis Chatzimisios   Alexander Technological Educational Institute of
                            Thessaloniki, Greece
Peter Van Der Stok   Vanderstok Consultancy, The Netherlands
Pouria Zand   IMEC, Netherlands
Qin Wang   University of Science and Technology, Beijing, China
Riaan Wolhuter   Stellenbosch University, South Africa
Sebastien Ziegler   Mandat International, Switzerland
Sergio Ilarri   Universidad de Zaragoza, Spain
Simon Duquennoy   Swedish Institute of Computer Science (SICS), Sweden
Srdjan Krco   Ericsson, Serbia
Tengfei Chang   University of Science and Technology, Beijing, China
Thomas Eichinger   FU Berlin, Germany
Valérie Issarny   Inria@SiliconValley, USA
Victoria Pimentel   University of New Brunswick, Canada
Xavi Vilajosana   UOC, Spain
Zied Chtourou   Académie militaire de Sfax, Tunisie

SDWNCT 2015

Organization

Steering Committee

Steering Committee Chair

Imrich Chlamtac   CREATE-NET, Italy

Steering Committee Members

Bruno Astuto   GE Global Research Center, Brazil
Frederik Santens   Imtech ICT Belgium, Belgium
Ramanathan Subramanian   Advanced Digital Sciences Center, Singapore
Athanasios V. Vasilakos   University of Western Macedonia, Greece

Organizing Committee

General Chairs

Bruno Astuto   GE Global Research Center, Brazil
Athanasios V. Vasilakos   Lulea University of Technology, Sweden
Frederik Santens   Imtech ICT Belgium, Belgium
Radu-Laurentiu Vieriu   University of Trento, Italy

Technical Program Chair

Christian Esteve   UNICAMP, Brazil
   Rothenberg
Artur Arsenio   Universidade da Beira Interior/YDreams
                                   Robotics CEO, Portugal
Erik Mannens   MMLab/iMinds-UGent, Belgium

Web and Publicity Chair

Mateus Silva Santos   University of Campinas, Brazil
Larissa Romualdo Suzuki   UCL/Imperial College, UK
Stanislau Semeniuta   University of Trento, Italy

Workshop Chair

Amir H. Moin   Fortiss, An-Institut Technische Universität, München,
                                   Germany

Local Chair

Raffaele Giaffreda   CREATE-NET, Italy

Conference Manager

Kristina Lukáčová   European Alliance for Innovation, Slovakia

Technical Program Committee

Xiaobo Long	ONF Wireless and Mobile Working Group, USA
Hui Ni	Huawei, USA
Xin Wu	Big Switch, USA
Junaid Qadir	National University of Sciences and Technology (NUST), Pakistan
Luis Contreras	Telefónica I+D, Spain
Giancarlo Fortino	University of Calabria, Italy
Miguel Elias Campista	Federal University of Rio de Janeiro, Brazil
Jose Ferreira de Rezende	Federal University of Rio de Janeiro, Brazil
Wolfgang Kellerer	Technische Universität München (TUM), Germany
Giuseppe Carella	TU Berlin, Germany
Mateus Silva Santos	Ericsson Research, Brazil
Nuno Garcia	Beira Interior University, Portugal
Neeli R. Prasad	Aalborg University, Denmark
Nik Bessis	University of Derby, UK
Wesley De Neve	MMLab/iMinds-UGent, Belgium
Ruben Verborgh	MMLab/iMinds-UGent, Belgium
Simon Mayer	ETH Zürich - Distributed Systems Group, Switzerland
S. Shyam Sundar	The Pennsylvania State University, USA
Alice Ruggeri	University of Turin, Italy
Alessio Antonini	University of Turin, Italy
Luigi Di Caro	University of Turin, Italy

Contents – Part I

GOODTECHS

CN4IoT

HealthyIoT

Contents – Part II

S-CUBE

InterIoT

SDWNCT

SaSeIoT

Innovative TLS/DTLS Security Modules for IoT Applications: Concepts and Experiments

Pascal Urien[✉]

Telecom ParisTech, Paris Saclay University,
23 avenue d'italie, 75015 Paris, France
Pascal.Urien@Telecom-ParisTech.fr

Abstract. The Internet of Things is a new technological step in the anytime, everywhere, anything IP connectivity context. Things (sensors, wearable objects, connected cars…) are equipped with computers and various communication resources. IoT devices deal with Wireless Local Area Network, Wireless Personal Area Network, Near Field Communication, or new operated radio networks with low throughput such as SIGFOX or LoRA. In this context security and trust are very critical topics, both for users and service providers. In this paper we present new and innovative security modules based on ISO7816 chips, which have been recently introduced by an IETF draft. These low cost, low power, tamper resistant devices, run TLS and DTLS stacks. DTLS is the datagram adaptation of the well known TLS protocol, which is de facto standard for the internet security. It is the security layer of the Constrained Application Protocol (CoAP) targeting sensors networks in a context of smart energy and building automation. We shortly recall TLS and DTLS features, and introduce the flights concept. We present the TLS/DTLS security module interface, which is based on previous work dealing with the EAP-TLS protocol, widely used for authentication in wireless networks and VPNs. We describe our prototype platform based on a java framework that implement a software bridge with the TLS/DTLS security module and which is compatible with the popular Raspberry Pi board. Finally we detail the experimental performances, compatible with the constraints of IoT, observed for an implementation running in a javacard.

Keywords: IoT · Security · TLS · DTLS · Secure element

1 Introduction

The internet of things is a new technological step in the anytime, everywhere, anything IP connectivity context. Things (sensors, wearable objects, connected cars…) are equipped with computers and various communications resources. IoT devices could deal with Wireless LAN (such as legacy IPv4, 6LoWPAN), Wireless Personal Area Network (WPAN, Zigbee, Bluetooth Low Power…) Near Field Communication [3] (NFC), or new operated radio networks with low throughput such as SIGFOX [1] or LoRA [2]. Even in the case of operated networks whose access control is usually managed by symmetric credentials (for example the LoRA network security is based on device AES

© ICST Institute for Computer Sciences, Social Informatics and Telecommunications Engineering 2016
B. Mandler et al. (Eds.) IoT 360° 2015, Part I, LNICST 169, pp. 3–15, 2016.
DOI: 10.1007/978-3-319-47063-4_1

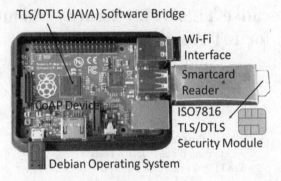

Fig. 1. Illustration of a TLS/DTLS security module in a Raspberry Pi hardware platform

keys, named Application Key - *AppKey*) there is a need to enforce a strong security for information exchange between objects and their authorized data aggregator.

As an illustration according to [4] "the Constrained Application Protocol (CoAP) is a specialized web transfer protocol for use with constrained nodes and constrained (e.g., low-power, lossy) networks. The nodes often have 8-bit microcontrollers with small amounts of ROM and RAM". CoAP messaging model provides reliable (i.e. acknowledged) and unreliable transport mechanisms.

CoAP targets sensors networks in a context of smart energy and building automation. Its security is enforced by the DTLS [7] protocol, working over the UDP datagram layer.

The DTLS protocol [7, 9] is an adaptation of the TLS [5, 6, 8] protocol, which is the de facto standard for secure information exchange over the Internet. TLS works over a reliable transport mode (TCP), while DTLS is designed in order to deal with (UDP) packets lost.

The DTLS/TLS protocols could enable identity models for IoT nodes based on *Public Keys Infrastructures* (PKI), i.e. these devices could embed X509 certificates performing strong mutual authentication with remote entities.

In this paper we define and test TLS/DTLS security modules dedicated to IoT platforms. These devices have been recently detailed by an IETF draft [10] (Fig. 1).

In this context the security module is an ISO7816 compliant and low cost chip. It fully processes the TLS and DTLS protocols, without any IP flavors (i.e. no IP resources such as TCP or UDP are available in the die), in a trustworthy computing environment.

For example the popular Raspberry Pi [11] platform based on a Debian Linux distribution, natively supports interfaces to ISO7816 chips thanks to the *pcsc-lite* library.

The basic idea behind the TLS/DTLS security module is to provide secure channels to objects, which are setup after a strong mutual authentication with remote servers. Furthermore many networks use protocols based on TLS (for example EAP-TLS [13]) for authentication and access control purposes.

This paper is constructed according to the following outline. Section 2 recalls TCP and DTLS protocols main features. Section 3 presents EAP-TLS, a standard used for authentication, based on TLS, which transports TLS without TCP/IP flavors. We introduce a similar but not standardized protocol, EAP-DTLS transporting DTLS without UDP/IP flavors. Section 4 introduces the TLS/DTLS security modules and their associated software bridges. Section 5 details the prototype platform, the basic cryptographic figures of the ISO7816 security module, and experimental performances. Finally Sect. 6 concludes this paper.

2   About TLS and DTLS

This section briefly recall TCP and DTLS protocols main features.

2.1   TLS

TLS is built over five logical blocks, the Record protocol, the Handshake protocol, the Alert protocol, the Change Cipher Spec (CCS) protocol and the Application data layer.

All TLS data are transported in Record packets, including a five bytes header in clear text, and a payload, which may be encrypted and HMACed.

The Handshake entity manages the booting of TLS sessions, it performs the key exchange operations according to anonymous, one way, or mutual authentication procedures. Ephemeral session keys are generated for record packets privacy and integrity.

The CCS entity generates a message that notifies the switching of the record protocol from clear text to encrypted and HMACed payload.

The Alert entity notifies particular events such as protocols errors or end of TLS sessions.

The application data layer, for example COAP or HTTP, delivers information transported by the record protocol.

A TLS session occurs in two logical stages, first a cryptographic context is negotiated by the handshake protocol, second encrypted data are exchanged over the record protocol.

During the setup of a session TLS messages are grouped into a series of flights, (four for the TLS full mode, and three for the TLS Session Resumption), as illustrated by Fig. 2.

TLS flights are the key concept for DTLS design; there are also the cornerstone for the definition of TLS/DTLS security modules.

2.2   DTLS

The DTLS 1.0 [7] protocol is based on TLS 1.1 [6], while DTLS 1.2 [9] is based on TLS 1.2 [8].

The DTLS protocol [12] provides three new features to TLS, in order to be compatible with a datagram and unreliable transport layer:

- A segmentation/reassembly service for the Handshake entity (see Fig. 3).
- A modified record protocol header (see Fig. 3), including a sequence number used both for clear and ciphered operations.

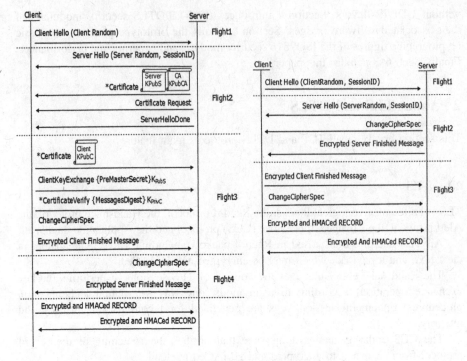

Fig. 2. TLS fights for full and abbreviated mode.

Handshake Message	
Type	1B
Length	3B
Message Sequence	2B
Fragment Offset	3B
Fragment Length	3B
Total length	12B

Record Packet	
Type	1B
Version	2B
Epoch	2B
Sequence Number	6B
Length	2B
Total Length	15B

Fig. 3. Structure of DTLS handshake messages and DTLS record packets

- Two new optional flights, DTLS-HelloVerifyRequest and DTLS-ClientHello with cookie. They manage a cookie mechanism in order to prevent some denial of service attacks. The server delivers a cookie that is thereafter included in the next ClientHello message.

Handshake cryptographic calculations are insensitive to fragmentation operations. According to [7, 12] finished messages (either client or server) have no sensitivity to fragmentation. There are computed as if each handshake message had been sent as a single fragment, i.e. with *Fragment-Length* set to Length, and *Fragment-Offset* set to zero (see Fig. 3); the *Message-Sequence* field is not used in these procedures. It also should be noticed that the DTLS-HelloVerifyRequest message and the previous

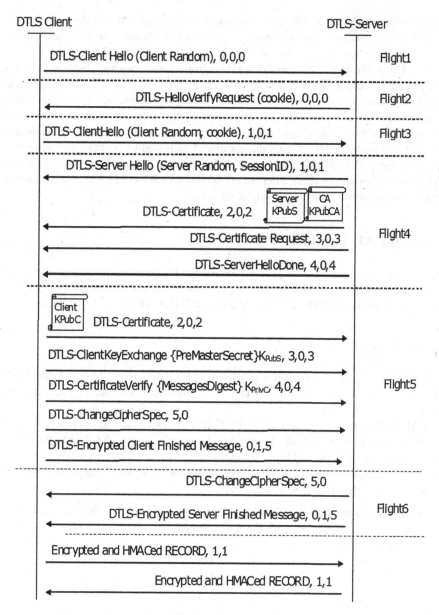

Fig. 4. DTLS flights, in the full mode

associated DTLS-ClientHello are not taken into account by the Handshake crypto-graphic calculation.

According to [7, 12] the DTLS HMAC computed by the Record protocol is the same as that of TLS 1.1. However, rather than using TLS implicit sequence number, the sequence number used to compute the MAC is the 64-bit value formed by concatenating the epoch and the sequence number in the order they appear on the wire. TLS MAC calculation is parameterized on the protocol version number, which, in the case of DTLS, is the on-the-wire version, i.e., {254, 255} for DTLS 1.0.

The Fig. 4 illustrates the setup of a DTLS full session, in which both end entities (Client and Server) are equipped with certificates and private keys. No segmentation/ reassembly operations are performed by Handshake layers. Each message is transported by a record packet. The two first number are respectively the record sequence number and the *epoch* field. The optional third number is the message sequence used by a handshake message. The *epoch* field indicates the number of delivered CCS packets. A session is started by the DTLS-ClientHello message (flight 1), it is opened after the exchange of DTLS finished messages; these latter are the first encrypted record packets, the sequence number is reset and the *epoch* attribute is set to one.

3   From EAP-TLS to EAP-DTLS

This section presents EAP-TLS [13], a standard used for authentication based on TLS, which enables the use of TLS without TCP/IP flavors. It introduces a similar but not standardized protocol, EAP-DTLS for the use of DTLS without UDP/IP flavors.

3.1   EAP-TLS

EAP-TLS [13] is an authentication protocol widely used in Wi-Fi networks (IEEE 802.11i), for VPN setup (IKEv2, PPTP) or in broadband over power line networks (such as IEEE Std 1901).

EAP-TLS packets are transported by EAP (*Extensible Authentication Protocol*) messages, according to a classical request and response scheme. EAP-TLS provides a transparent encapsulation of TLS (see Fig. 6) until the exchange of finished messages, both for server and client. It supports segmentation and reassembly operations managed via the "Flags" byte, which is detailed by Fig. 5.

- The L bit (length included) is set to indicate the presence of the four-octet TLS flight length field, and is set for the first fragment of a fragmented TLS message or set of messages.
- The M bit (more fragments) is set on all but the last fragment.
- The S bit (EAP-TLS start) is set in an EAP-TLS Start message.

b0	b1	b2	b3	b4	b5	b6	b7
L	M	S	R	R	R	R	R

Fig. 5. The EAP-TLS flags byte.

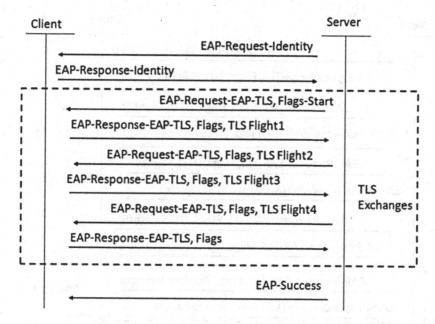

Fig. 6. EAP-TLS choreography for the transport of TLS flights

When an EAP-TLS peer receives an EAP-Request packet with the M bit set, it responds with an EAP-Response with EAP-Type = EAP-TLS and no data. This serves as a fragment acknowledgment (ACK).

Although not defined/used by the EAP-TLS protocol, decryption and encryption of record packets may be provided by dedicated EAP-Request and EAP-Response messages. This principle is used by the TLS/DTLS security module.

3.2   EAP-DTLS

The non standardized EAP-DTLS is very similar to EAP-TLS, excepted that it transports DTLS flights in spite of TLS flights.

Figure 7 illustrates the boot of a DTLS session (as described in Sect. 2.2) including six flights. The EAP-Request-Identity and EAP-Success are omitted. Two new EAP-Request and EAP-Response commands, detailed in Sect. 4 performed the following operations:

– Generation of encrypted and HMACed record packet from clear *Application Data*.
– Recovery of clear *Application Data* from encrypted and HMACed record packet.

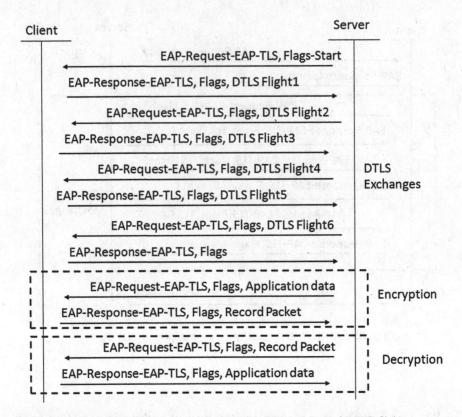

Fig. 7. EAP-DTLS: re-use of EAP-TLS for the transport of DTLS flights

4   TLS and DTLS Security Modules

TLS/DTLS security modules are secure elements that run TLS/DTLS. They are based on EAP-TLS stacks for smartcard [14, 15] designed for trustworthy computing of the EAP-TLS protocol.

4.1   About Secure Elements

Secure Elements [16, 17] are tamper resistant microcontrollers, whose security is enforced by multiple hardware and software countermeasures. Their security level is ranked by evaluations performed according to the Common Criteria standards, whose level range from one to seven. The chip area is typically 25 mm^2 (5 mm × 5 mm). The power consumption is low [18], as an illustration for SIM module 1.8 V–0,2 mA (3.6 mw) in idle state and no more than 1.8 V–60 mA (108 mW) in pike activity.

According to ISO7816 standards, secure elements exchange messages, over serial or USB IO links, whose maximum size is about 256 bytes, and which are named APDU. Request comprises a five byte header (CLA INS P1 P1 P3), the fifth byte (P3)

indicating either the length of outgoing data or the length of incoming data. Response comprises up to 256 bytes and a two byte word status (SW1, SW2).

Secure microcontrollers comprise a few hundred KB of ROM, about one hundred KB of non volatile memory (E^2PROM, Flash) and a few KB of RAM. Most of them include a Java Virtual Machine and therefore run applications written in the Javacard language, a subset of the java language.

A TLS/DTLS stack is an application, typically a javacard application, stored and executed in a secure element. Its logical interface is a set of APDUs exchanged over the IO link.

We previously designed EAP-TLS smartcards, which compute TLS flights encapsulated in EAP-TLS messages, until the generation of server and client finished messages. A full EAP-TLS exchange is detailed in [10], Sect. 17 Annex 6. EAP-TLS devices are identity oriented, i.e. they may store different PKI profiles (Certification Authority, client certificate and associated private keys…).

TLS/DTLS security modules extend from EAP-TLS smartcards [14, 15]. EAP-TLS devices support a double fragmentation mechanism, the size of an EAP fragment is about thousand bytes, which is thereafter segmented in several ISO7816 APDUs. TLS/DTLS devices only deal with small EAP fragments, whose size is about 200 bytes.

Two main ISO7816 commands are used by the security module:

- RESET (CLA = xx, INS = 19, P1 = 10, P2 = 00, P3 = 00), resets the DTLS/TLS session state machine
- Process-EAP (CLA = xx, INS = 80, P1 = 00, P2, P3 = LC) forwards an EAP-TLS packet and returns an EAP-TLS packet (either an acknowledgement or an EAP fragment)

A TLS/DTLS session always starts by the RESET request. Afterwards an EAP-TLS request, with the start indicator set, is sent whose induced response contains the TLS/DTLS ClientHello. TLS/DTLS flights exchanges are performed until the reception of TLS/DTLS client and server finished messages.

At this step the security module is ready to produce encrypted TLS/DTLS record packets or to check and decrypt ciphered record packets.

- The Process-EAP request with P2 set to (80 h or Type) is used to generate a TLS/DTLS record with a given type (see Fig. 8).
- The Process-EAP request with P2 set to zero is used for integrity checking and decryption of a ciphered record packet (see Fig. 9).

Process-EAP, type=17h, 97h= 80h or 17h, payload = 313233340D0A ("1234CrLf")
>> *A08000970C* 0111000C 0D00 313233340D0A
Encrypted TLS Record packet in EAP-Response
<< 0211002F 0D8000000025
   1703010020 1506B77D1F1F3514A8E703CAEB2EFEFD045A71E3F68
   92AF0C09C79197F7C2E6 *9000*

Fig. 8. Encryption of a clear text ("1234CrLf"), associated to a TLS protocol (type = 17 h). ISO7816 headers are in italics. EAP-TLS headers are underlined. The record packet is in bold.

Process-EAP-Decrypt
>> *A080000043* 01140043 0D00 **15FFF00010000000000020030**
   6B4A48869288953CD90D7BCD9E947B93025C75FEC1253
   E5 B0D998D1306A33D3612CDF91B230BCE6E55E1B19F39
   18FA10
   DTLS Record Clear Payload in EAP-Response= 0100h
<< 021400C 0D8000000002 0100 *9000*

Fig. 9. Decryption of a record layer packet. ISO7816 headers are in italics. EAP-TLS headers are underlined. The record packet is in bold. The return clear text is 0100 h.

4.2   TLS Security Module

TLS security modules are managed by a TLS software bridge (see Fig. 10). This entity starts TLS sessions, performs TLS flights sending and receiving operations over TCP/IP. It exchanges TLS packets with the device encapsulated in EAP-TLS messages. It also manages the interface with the application that needs a secure access to the network.

DTLS Security Module. DTLS security modules are managed by a DTLS software bridge (see Fig. 11). This entity starts DTLS sessions, performs DTLS flights sending and receiving operations over UDP/IP. It exchanges DTLS packets with the DTLS device, encapsulated in EAP-TLS messages. It performs segmentation and reassembly of handshake messages, according to network requirements. DTLS handshake messages exchanged with the device are not fragmented; the EAP layer is in charge of the fragmentation required by ISO7816 constraints. It also provides the interface with the application, such a sensor, which needs a secure access to the network.

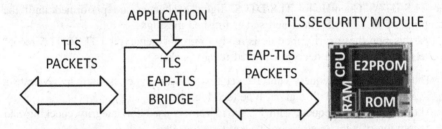

Fig. 10. A TLS security module and its associated software bridge.

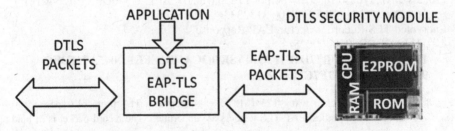

Fig. 11. A DTLS security module and its associated software bridge

5 Performances

5.1 Experimental Platform

We implemented the TLS/DTLS application on a TOP-IM_GX4 [21] javacard [20] manufactured by the GEMALTO company. The cipher suite is AES128 and SHA1. The application size is about 25 KB.

DTLS/TLS software bridges are written in Java and run in a java environment. DTLS and TLS server are based on the popular OPENSSL tool [21], which supports TLS 1.0, TLS 1.1 and DTLS 1.0.

The cryptographic module is based on the Samsung S3CC9TC chip. It includes:

- a 16 bits CPU
- 72 KB of EEPROM
- 384 KB of ROM
- 8 KB of RAM for the CPU
- 2 KB of RAM for the crypto processor

The chip manages various security sensors (glitch, temperature, voltage…) and hardware protections (bus scramble, shield, MMU) and includes a crypto processor for triple DES and PKI computing.

The DTLS/TLS application works with EAP-TLS packets whose maximum size is 128 bytes. It comprises X509 certificates dealing with 1024 bits RSA keys (both client and server and authenticated by their certificate), and uses AES and SHA1 algorithms for the ciphered and HMACed record layer.

5.2 Basic Parameters

Cryptographic performances are illustrated by Fig. 12. According to these figures the processing of encrypted record packets, with a 1024 bytes size, should require about 143 ms, according to the following relations:

- 135 ms (64 × 2,1) for the encryption/decryption of 64 blocks of data.
- 18 ms (20 × 0,9) for the HMAC (SHA1) processing of 20 (16 + 4) blocks of data

The booting of a TLS/DTLS session (until the delivering of finished messages) should cost about 878 ms consumed by the following operations:

- 556 ms for RSA procedures, one RSA private key encryption and two public key decryption (510 + 23 + 24)
- 322 ms for hash procedures, requiring the computing of 230 MD5 et 230 SHA1 blocks.

MD5 ms/block 64B	SHA1 ms/block 64B	3xDES ms/block 8B	AES ms/block 16B	RSA Pub ms 128B	RSA priv ms 128B	IO ms/B
0,50	0,90	1,8	2,1	23	510	0,1

Fig. 12. Basic performances of the TOP-IM_GX4 javacard.

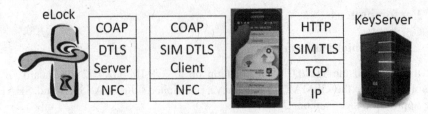

Fig. 13. COAP electronic lock prototype.

The IO attribute (0,1 ms/B) in Fig. 12 is the observed time to send/receive an ISO7816 request/response via a smartcard reader to/from an application running in the secure element. It means that 10 ms are required to transfer 100 bytes to/from the secure module. The experimental results, detailed in the next session, are in concordance with these basic cryptographic parameters.

5.3 Experimental Results

A DTLS/TLS full session is opened in 1400 ms, it is split in two parts 250 ms for information transfer (about 2500 bytes are exchanged, i.e. the throughput is around 0,1 ms/B) and 1150 ms consumed by cryptographic calculations. A DTLS/TLS resumed session is opened in 360 ms, with only 250 bytes of exchanged data. The generation of a 1024 record packet costs 400 ms, 240 ms are consumed by IO operations and 160 ms by cryptographic calculations. The checking and decryption of a 1024 record packet costs 430 ms, 240 ms are consumed by IO operations and 190 ms by cryptographic calculations.

6 Conclusion

In this paper we introduced the TLS/DTLS security module for Internet of Things applications. Future work could target the popular Raspberry Pi platforms, that are powered by an open operating system based on the Debian Linux distribution. These devices are natively compatible with secure element, thanks to the pcsc-lite library. They may interface DTLS/TLS security modules by several programming environments such as C language, Java, or Python. As illustrated by Fig. 13, we are currently working on a prototype dealing with COAP [4] electronic lock, in which two TLS/DTLS javacard applications running in a SIM card, manage secure key downloading and secure operations with an electronic lock.

References

1. LoRa Alliance: LoRaWAN™ Specification, Version: V1.0, January 2015
2. SigFox: One network A billion dreams: M2 M and IoT redefined through cost effective and energy optimized connectivity. White paper (2015)

3. ISO/IEC 18092: Near Field Communication - Interface and Protocol (NFCIP-1), April 2004
4. Shelby, Z., Hartke, K., Bormann, C.: The Constrained Application Protocol (CoAP). RFC 7252, June 2014
5. Dierks, T., Allen, C.: The TLS Protocol Version 1.0. RFC 2246, January 1999
6. Dierks, T., Rescorla, E.: The Transport Layer Security (TLS) Protocol Version 1.1. RFC 4346, April 2006
7. Rescorla, E., Modadugu, N.: Datagram Transport Layer Security. RFC 4347, April 2006
8. Dierks, T., Rescorla, E.: The Transport Layer Security (TLS) Protocol Version 1.2. RFC 5246, August 2008
9. Rescorla, E., Modadugu, N.: Datagram Transport Layer Security Version 1.2. RFC 6347, January 2012
10. TLS and DTLS Security Modules, draft-urien-uta-tls-dtls-security-module-00.txt, June 2015
11. https://www.raspberrypi.org/
12. Modadugu, N., Rescorla, E.: The design and implementation of datagram TLS. In: The 11th Annual Network and Distributed System Security Symposium, San Diego, CA, USA, February 2004
13. Simon, D., Aboba, B., Hurst, R.: The EAP-TLS Authentication Protocol. RFC 5216, March 2008
14. Urien, P.: EAP Support in Smartcard, draft-urien-eap-smartcard-29.txt, July 2015
15. Urien, P.: Collaboration of SSL smart cards within the WEB2 landscape. In: International Symposium on Collaborative Technologies and Systems, CTS 2009, 18–22 May 2009, pp. 187–194 (2009)
16. ISO 7816: Cards Identification - Integrated Circuit Cards with Contacts. The International Organization for Standardization (ISO)
17. Jurgensen, T.M., et al.: Smart Cards: The Developer's Toolkit. Prentice Hall PTR, Upper Saddle River (2002). ISBN 0-130-93730-4
18. ETSI: Specification of the 1.8 Volt Subscriber Identity Module - Mobile Equipment (SIM - ME) interface. ETSI TS 101 116 V7.0.1
19. Chen, Z.: Java Card™ Technology for Smart Cards: Architecture and Programmer's (The Java Series). Addison-Wesley, Boston (2002). ISBN 0-201-70329-7
20. GEMALTO: GemXpresso R4 E36/E72 PK - MultiApp ID 36 K/72 K - TOP IM GX4 Security Policy (2009)
21. Seggelmann, R., Tuexen, M.: DTLS Documentation, version 1.0. http://sctp.fh-muenster.de/index.html

Controlled Android Application Execution for the IoT Infrastructure

Michael N. Johnstone, Zubair Baig$^{(\boxtimes)}$, Peter Hannay, Clinton Carpene, and Malik Feroze

School of Science and Security Research Institute,
Edith Cowan University, Perth 6027, Australia
z.baig@ecu.edu.au

Abstract. Android malware has grown in exponential proportions in recent times. Smartphone operating systems such as Android are being used to interface with and manage various IoT systems, such as building management and home automation systems. In such a hostile environment the ability to test and confirm device health claims is important to preserve confidentiality of user data. This paper describes a study to determine whether an Android device could be secured to prevent malware from executing in parallel with trusted applications. The research also sought to determine whether the system image could be protected from unauthorised modifications. A prototype scheme for meeting the above requirements was developed and tested. It was observed that the prototype succeeded in preventing unauthorised modification to the system image of the test device. However, the prototype failed to prevent unauthorised IPC calls when in single process mode.

Keywords: Static malware analysis · Dynamic malware analysis · Android platform

1 Introduction

The evolution of distributed computing, most recently evinced by the Internet-of-Things (IoT) is considered to be an essential driver of contemporary information technology. The use of embedded microprocessors within a plethora of heterogeneous device types has been facilitated by substantial increases in available network bandwidth. Consequently, household devices such as televisions, refrigerators and washing machines are all embedded with computers that monitor device activity, log events, and transmit useful and pre-defined information to a centralised server for further processing and/or action. Mobile devices such as smartphones and smartbooks can serve as decentralised data collection and processing points within an IoT infrastructure. The privacy and security requirements within an IoT context will vary depending upon the IoT devices in use. For instance, a mobile phone connected through a 3G/4G communication channel to the Internet will demand a set of security controls based on large keys and

© ICST Institute for Computer Sciences, Social Informatics and Telecommunications Engineering 2016
B. Mandler et al. (Eds.) IoT 360° 2015, Part I, LNICST 169, pp. 16–26, 2016.
DOI: 10.1007/978-3-319-47063-4_2

a requirement for extensive information processing. Alternatively, a resource-constrained RFID tag may likely require a less resource demanding secret-key verifier based on smaller key lengths and efficient algorithms.

Whilst mobile devices provide an ideal central controller for household IoT devices as seen by the expansion of Home Automation Networks, the underlying operating system poses serious security concerns. The popularity of mobile devices has increased exponentially, and applications installed and executed by end-users routinely process and transmit sensitive data (e.g., banking and online shopping applications). Private user data can be compromised by an adversary through simple social engineering efforts as well as through sophisticated step-wise attacks that may involve the installation of malware onto a mobile device for subsequent invocation. The threat landscape for mobile platforms has been increased many-fold because popular end-user applications can be installed at the click of a button (thus highlighting the tension between competing non-negotiable requirements, namely security and ease of use). An example is an augmented version of the ZeuS banking Trojan [1] which appears as a legitimate application that upon execution transmits user credentials to a remote (attacker) machine. Emerging threats against mobile devices pose an even greater challenge for security architects of the IoT infrastructure. End-users do not identify the same security issues with mobile devices (compared to desktop devices) as noted in a survey by Valli et al. [2]. The need for controlled application execution on mobile devices, within a trusted context, cannot be understated. In this paper, we document and examine a prototype of a controlled mobile device trust platform for Android devices that ensures a secure application execution environment.

The remainder of the paper is organised as follows. Section 2 discusses related work done in the area of mobile device security. In Sect. 3, we present the prototype implementation of a controlled execution environment for Android applications. Section 4 discusses the tests that were performed against the Controlled Access Prototype. Section 5 describes the results of the study. Finally, in Sect. 6, we conclude and provide suggestions for further research.

2   Related Work

As pointed out by Löhr et al. [3], secure boot is a basic trusted computing concept. Löhr et al. observe that secure boot requirements for mobile devices have been collected in the Open Mobile Terminal Platform recommendations. The problem of secure boot is bound by three constraints or properties, described by Löhr et al. as: (1) The integrity of software loaded on the system must be preserved, otherwise malicious software could run without being detected; (2) The system should always boot to a defined secure state (or fail to boot at all), else attackers could violate security by forcing the system into an insecure state; and (3) Modifications of the operating system or application binaries must still be allowed, otherwise, software updates would be impossible.

Probably the first attempt at secure boot on an x86 platform was the AEGIS system [4] which used digital signatures as integrity checks and allowed recovery using a trusted repository. This concept still exists in Windows 8, which implements secure boot via a signature check for each item of boot software, although this has already been compromised (see [5]). Mobile devices, by their nature, may not have access to a trusted repository.

Kostiainen et al. [6] discuss several security issues that exist on several mobile device operating systems (including Android), but their analysis appears focussed on post-boot issues such as access control and permission granularity. Such issues would be important, however, if a secure boot failed i.e. it booted a device into an insecure state. Shabtai et al. [7] assert that Android devices are well-guarded in their normal state. Shabtai et al. conducted a risk analysis of the Android platform and concluded that corrupting or modifying private content in various forms, was a minor impact risk with an unlikely or possible likelihood of occurrence. We content that this is an optimistic analysis, especially in the context of Gostev's [8] comment that "two years of smartphone virus evolution are equivalent to twenty years of work in computer viruses".

Shabtai et al. [7] also notes that one of the security mechanisms of Android requires that "each application runs in its own virtual machine". This provides a measure of safety, but King et al. [9] evaluated virtual machine-based rootkits, the result being that they were able to subvert Linux-based systems with a proof-of-concept virtual machine-based rootkit. More specifically, Vidas et al. [10] provide a survey of current Android attacks.

Dietrich and Winter [11] highlight the need for a secure boot process on mobile devices and state that, whilst the Mobile Phones Working Group (MPWG) have outlined a secure boot process, the detail has been left to individual manufacturers to implement, thus giving manufacturers some flexibility. This flexibility, however, can lead to security issues because of the multiplicity of approaches that fit the outline provided by the MPWG.

Hendricks and van Doorn [12] contend that existing secure boot standards are not enough and that all devices should be checked, not just those attached to the CPU. Their claim was based on the assertion that modern computers consisted of semi-autonomous sub-systems containing field-upgradable firmware. Despite this assertion being over a decade old, it bears some similarity to devices that populate the Internet of Things, latterly the Internet of Everything.

3   Controlled Access Prototype Implementation

By design, the Android application framework includes various components to encourage functionality reuse. For example if an application that wishes to make a web request, it could request that another application make the request on its behalf. This reuse is achieved through application programming interfaces (APIs) such as activities, services, broadcast receivers and content providers [13]. Each of these features enable inter-process communication in various ways. Some of these are focussed on directly addressed communication and others are simply ways to request a specific item of functionality, allowing any other application to serve these requests.

A number of vulnerabilities have been identified with these APIs. These include SQL injection attacks and information theft [14]. In order to mitigate these issues it has been left to the developers of Android applications to implement defences in order to protect their application from any others that may be running. As new attacks are developed it may be that even the most carefully developed application becomes susceptible to these attacks. Of course there is still the threat posed by vulnerabilities to the Android operating system itself, which may not be able to be mitigated by the application developer. Existing approaches to address this issue have relied on implementing security layers on top of the existing Android framework, however this doesn't solve the underlying issue for the potential of interprocess communication based attacks or attacks based on other mechanisms [15]. Attacks have been implemented which do not rely on inter-process communication but instead through shared memory, showing the potential for non-inter-process communication driven attacks [16].

The proposed prototype aims to address this problem by preventing simultaneous application execution outright, via modification of the underlying Android operating system and making use of integrity checking measures to ensure that the operating system itself is not compromised.

The prototype developed aims to address two key requirements of the Android mobile platform:

- Device state at time of execution: The state of the device can always be verified to not have malicious applications running in parallel with the current application.
- Device base state: The mobile device should have protection mechanisms against unauthorised modification to the base system.

A two-part solution is proposed to meet the requirements. The first part is to limit the number of running applications to one, preventing malware from running in parallel with the application. Second, to use secure boot which prevents operating system modifications. This process results in a situation in which malware cannot be injected into the system image or cause other unauthorised changes to the platform.

Limiting the number of running applications to one, ensures that only one application is running at any point in time. As a result the operating system will force any applications other than the foreground application, to terminate (excluding core system processes).

The verified boot feature, which was introduced in Android 4.4, aims to assure the device state. This process uses an optional kernel feature called "device-mapper-verity (dm-verity)". The dm-verity feature provides a means for the device to conduct integrity checking of block devices. Consequently, dm-verity can be used to prevent rootkits, and other unauthorised modifications to the system image.

Any process on the Android platform that runs with root privileges can bypass detection by anti-malware applications or indeed the operating system itself. The software has this capability as it is running with privileges higher than

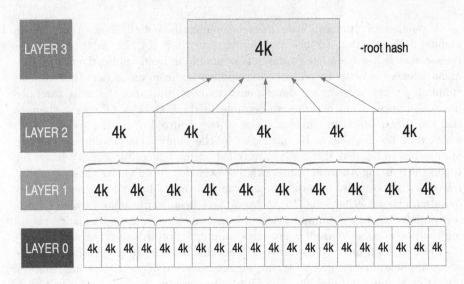

Fig. 1. Cryptographic hash tree [17].

or at the same level as the software intended to detect malware. These privileges essentially enable the software to misrepresent itself or conceal itself altogether.

Block devices form the underlying storage layer for Android systems. They can be examined using dm-verity to ensure that the device matches an expected configuration. Configuration validation is achieved through the use of a cryptographic hash tree. Every block (which is typically of 4k block size) is hashed using SHA-256 and the result stored in the hash tree. These hashes are aggregated through each layer (as depicted in Fig. 1) until Layer 3, where the root hash is computed. In practical terms this means that only the root hash needs to be verified to confirm integrity of the entire hash tree. In order to modify any of the blocks, the cryptographic hashing function (SHA-256 in this case) would need to be broken for identically sized inputs. At access time, each block is verified, which reduces overhead at boot time.

This solution ensures that a device meets the health requirements at any given time. Using Secure Boot ensures that the operating system has not been modified in any way. If the system image is changed in anyway, the device will fail to boot. If the device boots successfully, it is a guarantee that the device did not allow malware to load at boot time. Secure Boot's task is finished once the device has booted. As such, need is established for post boot mechanisms to allow execution of software without the risk of malware running in parallel, thus compromising the integrity of the whole system. For this purpose, the application limiting functionality is put in place. Limiting the number of parallel applications to one guarantees that no malware can run in the background while the target application is being executed.

To limit the number of parallel applications, we need to modify the Android source code. In order to achieve this functionality, there are two files that need to be changed, namely, `DevelopmentSettings.java` and `Activity ManagerNative.java`. `DevelopmentSettings.java` is located at: `/packages/ apps/Settings/src/com/android/settings/`. The changes required in this file are as below:

```
Line 1251: mAppProcessLimit.setValueIndex(i);
    to: mAppProcessLimit.setValueIndex(1);
Line 1251: mAppProcessLimit.setValueIndex(i);
    to: mAppProcessLimit.setValueIndex(1);
Line 1252: mAppProcessLimit.setSummary(
        mAppProcessLimit.getEntries()[i]);
    to: mAppProcessLimit.setSummary(
        mAppProcessLimit.getEntries()[1]);
Line 1256: mAppProcessLimit.setValueIndex(0);
    to: mAppProcessLimit.setValueIndex(1);
Line 1257: mAppProcessLimit.setSummary(
    mAppProcessLimit.getEntries()[0]);
    to: mAppProcessLimit.setSummary(
    mAppProcessLimit.getEntries()[1]);
Line 1264: int limit = newValue !=
        null ? Integer.parseInt(newValue.toString()) : -1;
to: int limit = newValue != null ? 0 : -1;
```

ActivityManagerNative.java is located at `/frameworks/base/core/java/ android/app/`. The changes required in this file are as below.

```
Line 1163 int max=data.readInt();
    to: int max = 0;
Line 1171 int limit = getProcessLimit();
    to: int limit = 0;
```

Once this is done, we can build a system image from this modified Android source code. This system image is then used to implement dm-verity for ensuring secure boot. The steps are as follows:

1. Create system and boot image,
2. Create hash trees for both images,
3. Generate dm-verity tables,
4. Sign generated tables,
5. Concatenate dm-verity table and signature block to generate verity metadata, and
6. Concatenate tables, signature block and metadata.

The hash tree is at the core of the security control that enables secure boot, and is implemented by the dm-verity kernel feature. Every block (in this case 4k in size) in the block device is cryptographically hashed with SHA-256. These hashes form layer 0 of the hash tree. Next, the SHA-256 hashes of layer 0 are concatenated into 4k blocks, and again each block is hashed with SHA-256. This forms layer 1 of the hash tree. This process is continued until the resulting layer n can be condensed into a single 4k block. Finally, the hashes at layer n are aggregated and hashed using SHA-256 to form a single, root hash value that serves as the integrity checker for the entire filesystem. If there is a block in a layer that is not naturally filled to the block size, the block is padded out with zeroes.

Subsequent to the creation of the root hash and salt, the dm-verity table is created and signed. The table itself is comprised of a reference to the block device, the block size, salt and root hash value. The table is signed with an RSA key of length 2048 bit ([17]). Next the verity metadata block is generated through the concatenation of the signature and the dm-verity table.

4   Controlled Access Prototype Evaluation Process

The device state and malware claims are both evaluated individually. Evaluation of the malware claim is trivial. Once the operating system has booted the settings menu can be accessed and the *Background* process limit setting examined. It should be set to "no background processes". If an attempt to change this value is made it should not take effect, on re-examining of this setting "no background processes" should again be observed. Subsequently, we can run multiple applications and to test if any of them are running in parallel, this can be accomplished through examining the running processes list under developer tools. It can be seen that only the last process launched is running, as such it can be confirmed that previous processes are killed.

To evaluate the secure boot implementation, the system image must be modified in such a way that it no longer conforms to those calculated in the initial hash tree. This task can be accomplished in various ways, from the flashing of a completely different system image, through to modification of a single byte within the system partition and/or boot partition currently located on the device. It should be noted that the entire image is not verified on boot, instead each block is verified on access. In this way boot times are reduced while the system and boot images are effectively secured. As such, if alteration of a single byte is selected it may be useful to target a byte within a particular system application, so that this application can be launched and the security feature reliably triggered.

It should be noted that if the boot image is modified the device will fail to boot and the device will be rendered near-permanently inoperable, this is by design. Recovery from this state during testing required the use of a non-public exploit. As such, it is suggested that during third party validation the system image be altered rather than the boot partition, in order to preserve device functionality.

5   Results

The Controlled Access Prototype was subjected to a number of tests to evaluate its suitability. These tests were described in Sect. 4. The results of the tests

Table 1. Details of alterations to system and boot images with details of event to trigger read and associated result

Alteration made	Triggering event	Observed result
Replace entire system image (zeros)	Power on device	Fail to boot
Replace entire system image (random)	Power on device	Fail to boot
Change single byte of system image (within application)	Launch application	Displays security warning
Change single byte of system image (at random)	Read random byte	Displays security warning
Replace entire boot image (zeros)	Power on device	Fail to boot
Replace entire boot image (random)	Power on device	Fail to boot
Change single byte of boot image (within boot code)	Power on device	Fail to boot

against the secure boot process are included in Table 1. It was observed that under almost all experimental conditions, the resulting image failed to boot once modified. This aligns with the expectations of the research. It is interesting to note that modifying a single byte of the system image, either at random, or from within an application, only caused an error to be displayed. The system otherwise functioned as normal.

The execution state testing involved using applications in the Android OS' single process mode. The outcomes of these tests are included below in Table 2. For the test to pass, any IPC calls from the malicious application could not be completed successfully (i.e. the calls were prevented).

It can be seen from the results that the IPC calls were able to successfully complete in all of the tested scenarios, indicating that the tests unanimously failed. The reason this approach does not work can be attributed to the architecture that Android uses to manage processes for applications. The application closing does not inherently mean that the process has been terminated (depicted in Fig. 2). Even in the single process mode (depicted in Fig. 2(b)), the application's memory is serialised upon termination and can be resumed by deserialisation upon relaunch. This means that although the malware may be halted temporarily during application switching, it will resume its operations when the context of execution changes back to the host application. The processing models are demonstrated in Fig. 2.

Table 2. Details of execution state testing with result, during prior to each test the evaluation application is launched

Test performed	Triggering event	Observed result
Examine process list	Launch malicious app	Evaluation app not running
Examine process list	Launch malicious service	Evaluation app not running
Attempt IPC call	Activate IPC from malicious app to evaluation app	IPC call succeeds (failed test)
Attempt activity call	Activate activity from malicious app to evaluation app	activity call succeeds (failed test)
Attempt broadcast call	Activate broadcast from malicious app to evaluation app	Broadcast received (failed test)

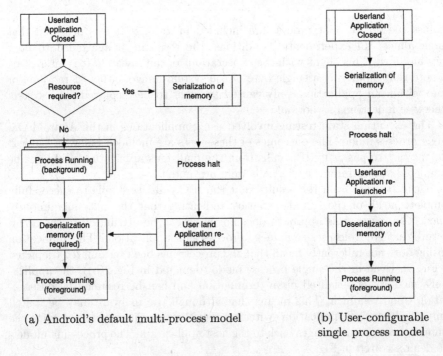

(a) Android's default multi-process model

(b) User-configurable single process model

Fig. 2. An abstract model demonstrating the differences between the operations of the Android OS' default multi-processing model, and the developer option enabled single process model.

6   Conclusions

This research set out with the aim of determining whether an Android device could be configured to prevent malware from executing in parallel with trusted applications, and whether the system image could be protected from unauthorised modifications. As Android devices are increasingly being used as controllers in IoT infrastructure, the mitigation and prevention of malware on these platforms is critical. We presented a prototype scheme for meeting the above requirements in the proposed *Controlled Access Prototype*. This prototype succeeded in preventing unauthorised modification to the system image through the implementation of the dm-verity kernel feature. However, the prototype failed to prevent unauthorised IPC calls when in single process mode. This research provides an opportunity for future work. We suggest modification of the Android sandbox to prevent IPC from running blacklisted or non-whitelisted applications. This would effectively enable an OS-level firewall for Android devices.

Acknowledgments. This work has been partially funded by the European Commission via grant agreement no. 611659 for the AU2EU FP7 project.

References

1. Barroso, D.: 21sec Security Blog: ZeuS Mitmo: Man-in-the-mobile (III) (2015). http://securityblog.s21sec.com/2010/09/zeus-mitmo-man-in-mobile-iii.html
2. Valli, C., Martinus, I., Johnstone, M.: Small to medium enterprise cyber security awareness: an initial survey of Western Australian business. In: Proceedings of the 2014 International Conference on Security and Management, pp. 71–75 (2014)
3. Lohr, H., Sadeghi, A., Winandy, M.: Patterns for secure boot and secure storage in computer systems. In: Proceedings of the 10th International Conference on Availability, Reliability, and Security, pp. 569–573 (2010)
4. Arbaugh, W.A., Farber, D.J., Smith, J.M.: A secure and reliable bootstrap architecture. In: Proceedings of the IEEE Symposium on Security and Privacy, pp. 65–71. IEEE Press, New York (1997)
5. Bulygin, Y., Furtak, A., Bazhaniuk, O.: A Tale of one software bypass of Windows 8 secure boot. In: Proceedings of Black Hat, USA (2013)
6. Kostiainen, K., Reshetova, E., Ekberg, J., Asokan, N.: Old, new, borrowed, blue: a perspective on the evolution of mobile platform security architectures. In: Proceedings of the First ACM Conference on Data and Application Security and Privacy (CODASPY 2011), pp. 13–24. ACM, New York (2011)
7. Shabtai, A., Fledel, Y., Kanonov, U., Elovici, Y., Dolev, S., Glezer, C.: Google Android: a comprehensive security assessment. In: Proceedings of the IEEE Symposium on Security and Privacy, pp. 35–44. IEEE Press, New York (2010)
8. Gostev, A.: Mobile malware evolution: an overview (2001). http://www.viruslist. com/en/analysis?pubid=200119916
9. King, S., Chen, P., Wang, Y., Verbowski, C., Wang, H., Lorch, J.: SubVirt: implementing malware with virtual machines. In: Proceedings of the IEEE Symposium on Security and Privacy, pp. 314–327. IEEE Press, New York (2006)
10. Vidas, T., Votipka, D., Christin, N.: All your droid are belong to us: a survey of current Android attacks. In: Proceedings of the 5th USENIX Conference on Offensive Technologies, p. 10. USENIX Association, Berkeley, CA, USA (2011)

11. Dietrich, K., Winter, J.: Secure boot revisited. In: Proceedings of the International Conference for Young Computer Scientists, pp. 2360–2365 (2008)
12. Hendricks, J., van Doorn, L.: Secure bootstrap is not enough: shoring up the trusted computing base. In: Proceedings of the 11th Workshop on ACM SIGOPS European Workshop. ACM, New York (2004). Article 11
13. Chin, E., Felt, A.P., Greenwood, K., Wagner, D.: Analyzing inter-application communication in Android. In: Proceedings of the 9th International Conference on Mobile Systems, Applications, and Services, Bethesda, Maryland, USA (2011)
14. Agrawal, A.: Android application security part 3-Android application fundamentals (2015). https://manifestsecurity.com/android-application-security-part-3/
15. Bugiel, S., Davi, L., Dmitrienko, A., Heuser, S., Sadeghi, A.-R., Shastry, B.: Practical and lightweight domain isolation on Android. In: Proceedings of the 1st ACM Workshop on Security and Privacy in Smartphones and Mobile Devices, Chicago, Illinois, USA (2011)
16. Chen, Q.A., Qian, Z., Mao, Z.M.: Peeking into your app without actually seeing it: UI state inference and novel Android attacks. In: Proceedings of the 23rd USENIX Conference on Security Symposium, San Diego, CA (2014)
17. Elenkov, N.: Android explorations: using KitKat verified boot (2014). http://nelenkov.blogspot.com.au/2014/05/using-kitkat-verified-boot.html. Accessed 22 Sept. 2016

Combined Danger Signal and Anomaly-Based Threat Detection in Cyber-Physical Systems

Viktoriya Degeler, Richard French, and Kevin Jones[✉]

Airbus Group Innovations, Newport, UK
{viktoriya.degeler,richard.french,kevin.jones}@airbus.com

Abstract. Increasing number of physical systems being connected to the internet raises security concerns about the possibility of cyber-attacks that can cause severe physical damage. Signature-based malware protection can detect known hazards, but cannot protect against new attacks with unknown attack signatures. Anomaly detection mechanisms are often used in combination with signature-based anti-viruses, however, they too have a weakness of triggering on any new previously unseen activity, even if the activity is legitimate. In this paper, we present a solution to the problem of protecting an industrial process from cyber attacks, having robotic manufacture facilities with automated guided vehicles (AGVs) as our use case. Our solution combines detection of danger signals with anomaly detection in order to minimize mis-labelling of legitimate new behaviour as dangerous.

Keywords: Intrusion detection · Anomaly detection · Danger Theory · Automated Guided Vehicles · Cyber-Physical Systems

1 Introduction

While increasing numbers of physical systems being connected to the internet brings enormous possibilities for technological progress, it also raises huge security concerns. Cyber-Physical Systems have already been shown to be susceptible to cyber attacks that can cause (sometimes catastrophic) physical damage. The German Federal Office for Information Security (BSI) revealed in 2014 that a steel manufacturing facility suffered massive damage after it was not able to shut-down a blast furnace in a controlled manner due to malicious code implanted into its control system [3]. Earlier, the Stuxnet virus gained fame after successfully attacking programmable logic controllers of Iran's nuclear centrifuges, changing their rotation speed, which resulted in physical damage to many of them [5].

Signature-based malware protection can detect known hazards, but cannot protect against new attacks with unknown attack signatures, which is especially important due to advances of automated malware creation [1]. Anomaly detecting intelligent mechanisms are often used in combination with signature-based anti-viruses, in order to detect and prevent anomalous activity. As an example, the *negative selection* [2] approach compares all new events with a previously

© ICST Institute for Computer Sciences, Social Informatics and Telecommunications Engineering 2016
B. Mandler et al. (Eds.) IoT 360° 2015, Part I, LNICST 169, pp. 27–39, 2016.
DOI: 10.1007/978-3-319-47063-4_3

constructed set of *non-self* entities, i.e. those that fail similarity tests with known *self* entities. Unfortunately, anomaly detection mechanisms have a known weakness of triggering on any new previously unseen activity. In some cases, such as fraud detection in banking systems, anomaly detection leads to great results, because it can be reasonably expected that "self" detector cover all types of legitimate behaviour and any anomaly ("non-self") is therefore a fraud. However, in many other types of systems, including internet of things, network-based ones, the behaviour changes over time and has legitimate anomalous events. Using anomaly-based threat detection in such systems will create huge amount of false positives, i.e. mis-detecting legitimate behaviour as an attack, thus disrupting normal course of operations, which can sometimes lead to economic and operational losses comparable to genuine attacks. Therefore it is important that the adaptive detection mechanism keeps both types of mistakes (false negative and false positive) at minimum. On the other hand, in Danger Theory [7], coming from Artificial Immune Systems research area [4], responses are triggered by *danger signals* rather than presence of *non-self* objects. Entities are allowed to exist until harmful signals are received. If a harmful activity (e.g. cell death) is detected, the immune response is triggered, attacking either all foreign entities, or all entities locally, depending on the severity of the danger.

In this paper, we present a solution to the problem of protecting an industrial process from cyber attacks, having robotic manufacture facilities with automated guided vehicles (AGVs) as our use case. Our solution combines detection of danger signals with anomaly detection to minimize mis-labelling of legitimate new behaviour as dangerous. In Sect. 2, we present our use case and system architecture. Section 3 provides detailed explanation of our danger detection module. Section 4 evaluates the solution and Sect. 5 concludes the paper.

2   Automated Guided Vehicles Protection

Factories with a complex manufacturing cycle often rely on Automated Guided Vehicles (AGVs) for moving materials across work cells. AGV control systems and equipment are usually networked and distributed to allow submitting tasks and operate AGVs remotely. This puts AGV control systems at risk of being exposed to cyber attacks, as has been shown by recent studies [8].

Our system evaluates all jobs that are performed by the AGVs, to understand the origins of danger signals and to prevent dangerous jobs from execution. Our system is also designed to minimize the amount of false danger detections, to allow legitimate jobs to be executed uninterrupted. The high-level architecture is shown in Fig. 1. Main modules include the Command and Control that issues job requests; the AGV Controller that generates low-level action plans and chooses appropriate AGVs for execution; the self-learning Danger Detection Module (DDM) that verifies jobs based on their anomaly and danger levels; and the Facility Monitor that alerts the DDM of any independently detected dangers.

The Command and Control (C&C) module oversees the whole manufacturing process. It provides dashboards and control to human operators, but is also

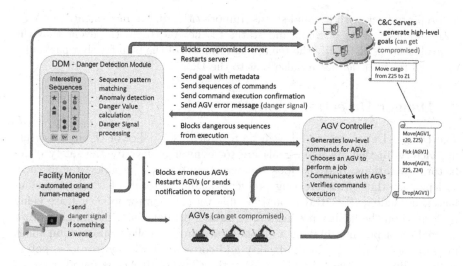

Fig. 1. System Architecture

able to automatically generate high-level requests, such as "Deliver item Omega from collection point A to delivery point B" to support a normal manufacturing process. Requests are passed to the appropriate AGV central controller (AGVC). The AGVC generates a job plan formed from a sequence of AGV atomic actions together with a choice of AGV that should satisfy the original request. This job is then sent for verification to the DDM. If the job is approved by the DDM, then the AGVC executes it by assigning the sequence to the associated AGV.

The Facility Monitor is an independent verification system that monitors the factory floor and raises an alert (called a *danger signal*) if anything goes wrong. Any event that happens unexpectedly, any discrepancy between the expected and observed states of the system causes such an alert, albeit with different severity. Examples of such events include a robot performing an action different from the one on its action queue, a robot not responding to commands, cargo being taken to the position that is not on delivery positions list, etc.

The Danger Detection Module contains a history of jobs and performs similarity detection and clustering of every new job request, to calculate its anomaly score. When a danger signal is observed, the DDM checks current and previously finished jobs to find those that are likely to be the cause of the signal. Anomalous jobs are regarded as much more likely to be the cause, but all jobs are checked. Every danger signal increases the threat level of a job. If the threat threshold is reached, the DDM terminates the job by sending the corresponding command to the AGVC, and rejects similar jobs in the future. If a subsequence of actions within a job is identified as being the cause, the DDM rejects only this subsequence, not the whole job. The AGVC takes this into consideration, and, if possible, generates and resubmits a new plan of actions in order to satisfy the C&C request. On receipt of a sequence from the AGVC, an AGV executes it and reports back with its final status. Importantly, during movement, the AGV sends updates of its position and status to the AGVC, in the event that the controller needs to modify the remaining elements of the plan for that particular task. All relevant details are also sent to the DDM.

3 Danger Detection Module

The Danger Detection Module can be regarded as a police of the manufacturing facility, in that its main goals are to monitor and verify the safety of all factory operations; find the jobs that create problems; be able to stop them and prevent them from creating problems again. In terms of a robotic manufacturing facility, the DDM should be able to: (1) monitor jobs that are being performed on the facility premises in real-time; (2) have information about how anomalous or potentially dangerous these jobs are; (3) collect information about newly detected dangers in the facility and correlate it with active jobs, potentially finding the cause of danger; (4) if the cause of danger is found, raise an alarm in order to stop the job and forbid the execution of other similar jobs.

The internal architecture of the DDM is shown in Fig. 2. Initially the DDM populates the Knowledge Base with a historical dataset of previous jobs, finding clusters of similar jobs and calculating their parameters, such as frequency rate, anomaly and danger scores. During production, the DDM monitors active jobs, keeping track of all jobs that are currently in progress, their state of execution, i.e. which actions were already performed, and which are planned, etc. The DDM also performs real-time job verification for every new job request that the AGVC creates. This includes finding similar job clusters, calculation the anomaly score of a job, checking previous danger signals of similar jobs, and deciding if a job is a normal one or a dangerous one and should be rejected. If

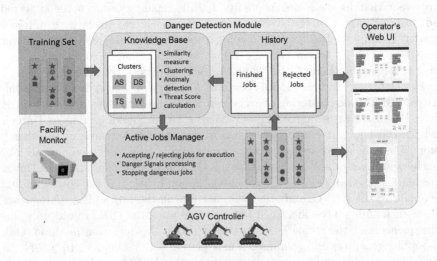

Fig. 2. Internal DDM architecture.

any danger signal arrives, the DDM correlates active jobs with danger signals, deciding on which jobs may be the cause of the signal, and if the danger is severe enough for the job to be immediately stopped. The Knowledge Base is constantly updates with recent data of executed jobs, danger signals, etc., so the algorithm keeps learning and adapting to changing conditions. Finally, the DDM has the Operator's UI that gives capability to human operators to control the system and its decisions.

3.1 Knowledge Base

The Knowledge Base contains a dataset of jobs that correspond to a normal activity of a factory, and performs clustering and anomaly detection, as well as storing the information about the danger score of clusters. Initially, a dataset of historical jobs is used to train the system, to create clusters of similar jobs, and understand their frequency rates. As soon as an active job is finished, for any reason (successful execution or stopping due to danger signals), it is also submitted to the Knowledge Base, in order to update the danger detection dataset. The job that was rejected before being started is not submitted to the dataset.

Similarity Measure. In order to perform job clustering it is necessary to have a measure of similarity between two different jobs.

There are several existing ways to calculate similarity for sequences. Among the most commonly used ones, the Levenshtein distance, the Jaccard similarity, and the longest similar subsequence can all be used in the DDM as a measure of similarity between two sequences of events. The Levenshtein distance (also called "the minimum edit distance") is calculated as the minimum number of atomic operations needed to be performed on an entity in order to transform it into the other entity. The longest similar subsequence metric can be useful in some settings, where the order of actions is very strict and limited, but is weak in the general case, because the small changes in the middle of a sequence will severely lower the total similarity score. We opted to use the Jaccard similarity because it is one of the most general similarity metrics that is applicable to sequences. The Jaccard metric allows to have variations in any part of a sequence, unlike the longest subsequence metric, but can be calculated more efficiently than the Levenshtein distance. The Jaccard similarity is usually used to define the similarity of two sets. In a general case, it is defined as the intersection of two sets divided by the union of two sets: $J(A, B) = \frac{|A \cap B|}{|A \cup B|}$. The similarity metric shows the percentage of items that are the same in two sets to all items in both sets. It returns 1, when both sets are the same, and 0, when there is not a single common item between them. When the Jaccard similarity is used to define the similarity of sequences of variable length with changing token order, the sequence should be transformed into a set [6]. This is commonly done by transforming a sequence into a set of *k-shingles* or *k-grams*. A *k-shingle* is any set of continuous tokens of a sequence. For example, for the sequence *"AirbusGroup"* and letters taken as tokens, a set of all

3-shingles is $\{$"Air","irb","rbu","bus","usG","sGr","Gro","rou","oup"$\}$. Splitting the sequence on k-shingles in order to apply set similarity measures has a number of useful properties, including the ability to cope with small insertions or changes of symbols in random places of a sequence. It is also easy to extend the notion to find a mutual similarity of more than two entities at the same time.

One more important advantage of Jaccard similarity is that it splits the sequence onto subsequences, so it is possible to re-use them to calculate the similarity and danger score of subsequences as well as full sequences. This is very helpful when trying to find the most dangerous subsequence within a sequence. With Levenshtein distance every subsequence would have to be analysed separately, therefore decreasing the total performance of the algorithm.

Clustering. The next step after the similarity between any two entities can be found, is to cluster the set of entities (jobs, or event sequences, in our case) into groups with similar objects. Ideally, each cluster should contain a single type of a job, including small variations that a job can have in its events.

In the DDM we use distance-based hierarchical clustering, with the usage of mean points as representatives of a cluster. We define *a representative sequence* of a cluster as a mean point, i.e. a point that has the maximum similarity to all other points of the cluster $argmax_{c \in C}(\sum_{i \in C} sim(c,i) * W_i)$. For distance-based clustering there is a threshold $MINSIM$, and we require the similarity of all points within a cluster with its mean point to have at least this amount of similarity: $\forall i \in C : sim(c,i) \geq MINSIM$.

Clustering happens sequentially, i.e. we regard one point at a time and add it to the closest cluster (recalculating the mean point if necessary) or create a new cluster if no sufficiently similar cluster is found. The process is the same for initial training and for the production phase, when finished jobs are added one by one. If recalculation of the mean point leads to the cluster no longer satisfying distance requirements, we split the cluster into several smaller ones.

Cluster Parameters. After we have obtained job clusters, we can calculate the parameters of any cluster or any job. For every cluster we calculate the frequency rate (or weight), the anomaly score, the danger score, and the final threat score. In order to calculate the anomaly score of a job, we find the cluster that it belongs to (or create a new one if there is no cluster that is sufficiently similar to a job), and use the anomaly score of this cluster. Conventionally, the algorithms with similar functionality are called 'anomaly detection'. However, here we talk about 'anomaly score calculation', due to the fact that we are not interested in boolean classification of job instances as anomaly vs. non-anomaly, but rather in a quantifiable score of how anomalous the job is.

Weight (W) or **Frequency Rate (FR)** values show, how common the jobs of this cluster are. The weight or the frequency rate can be used interchangeably, with only a small difference in calculation formulas. The weight shows the absolute amount of times the jobs of this cluster were seen within regarded timeframe or within a training set. Frequency rate shows the percentage of times the ·

jobs are a part of this cluster in comparison to the total number of jobs. As can be easily seen, frequency rate can be obtained by dividing the weight of the cluster by the total weight of all clusters: $FR_i = W_i/\sum_{c\in C} W_c$. Frequency rate is a slightly more adaptable value than weight, when the total amount of jobs over time can vary. However, in certain situations weight can be more preferable, for example, if the total number of jobs within our timeframe is small, and we want to limit the absolute number of jobs for a job to be regarded as non-anomalous.

Anomaly Score (AS) simply represents how anomalous is the job or the cluster. The score is always in the range between and including 0 and 1, where 1 represents that such a job is an absolute anomaly and has never before been seen in the training set, and 0 represents that a job is completely common. From a naive point of view, the AS of a cluster can be seen as being fully dependent on the frequency rate of a cluster, i.e. the higher its frequency, the lower the anomaly score. However, while the frequency rate of a cluster is indeed an important factor in determining the AS, it is not the only factor, as similarity to other clusters and their frequency rates should also be taken into account. For example, two cluster with the same frequency rate will receive different anomaly scores, if the first one has subsequences that are similar to other clusters, and the second one has completely unique sequences. It can be the case that a cluster with lower frequency rate will receive a lower anomaly score, if it has many similar neighbouring clusters that are sufficiently frequent themselves.

Another question is which clusters to regard as completely non-anomalous ($AS = 0.0$). We introduce a frequency rate threshold. It should be chosen to cover the least frequent "normal" job. E.g. if there are three clusters that represent normal activities, one with frequency rate of 0.5, another one with 0.2, and the third one with 0.3, the threshold should be chosen as 0.2. It is also wise to lower the threshold a bit more (e.g. by 10–15 %) to allow for random variations in actual real-time frequencies, therefore finally keeping it at around 0.18. We normalize the frequency rate to obtain the percentage of FR below threshold. The normalized frequency rate (NFR) can be calculated irrespectively of whether original values are represented as absolute weights (W) or as relative frequency rates (FR), however, the threshold should be given in the same units. In case the weight W_i of a cluster is given, the threshold should be given as maximum weight MW, and the normalized frequency rate is calculated as

$$NFR_i = 1 - \frac{max(MW - W_i, 0)}{MW}$$

In case the frequency rate FR_i of a cluster is given, the threshold should be given as maximum frequency MF, and the normalized frequency rate is calculated as

$$NFR_i = 1 - \frac{max(MF - FR_i, 0)}{MF}$$

NFR represents only the frequency of sequences from the cluster itself. However, when calculating the anomaly score we also want to take into account total occurrences of similar subsequences, even when these subsequences are part of sequences in other clusters. The rate we take from other clusters should be reduced proportionally to the similarity between these clusters. Therefore we introduce extended normalized frequency rate $ENFR_c(C)$ that is calculated for a cluster given a set of clusters for comparison:

$$ENFR_c(RC) = \begin{cases} (1- Sim(x,c) * NRF_x) * ENFR_c(RC \backslash x) + \\ \quad Sim(x,c) * NRF_x, & \text{for any } x \in RC \\ 0, & \text{if } RC = \emptyset \end{cases}$$

Using the ENFR, we calculate the anomaly score:

$$AS_c = 1 - ENFR_c(C)$$

Note, that it is not necessary to regard the NFR_c of a cluster c separately, if the cluster itself is included into the set C. Because $Sim(c,c) = 1$, the frequency rate of the cluster itself will be taken fully during the calculations.

In practice, the anomaly score of 1.0 cannot be obtained during training phase, because during training phase a sequence is immediately added to the set of sequences, therefore it has some non-zero weight even when seen for the first time. However, during the actual monitoring phase, when a new job is sent to the DDM for verification, it can have anomaly score equal to 1.0. This can be obtained if the new job is not only seen for the first time, but also does not contain any subsequences that were seen previously. Once the fully anomalous job is executed and completed, it will be added to the dataset, and "learned" by the DDM. Therefore the anomaly score of a similar job next time will be lower. The anomaly score of 0.0 can be obtained during training or verification phases for all clusters that have normalized frequency rate of 1.0.

Danger Score (DS) is the metric that shows, how many danger signals were detected during the execution of these jobs, how severe they were, and how likely it is that they were caused by the jobs from the cluster, and not some other jobs. A danger score of a cluster increases when active jobs from this cluster are associated with environmental danger signals. Each danger signal has a severity value. This value gets distributed among active jobs that may be responsible for the signal, depending on the type of the signal and job parameters, such as their anomaly score and previously associated danger signals. More on the distribution of the danger signal score is explained in Sect. 3.2.

A danger signal chunk ds_{t+1} that gets assigned to a cluster i during step $t+1$ is always in the range of 0.0–1.0. The increase of the total danger score happens according to the following formula:

$$DS_{t+1}^{(i)} = DS_t^{(i)} + (1 - DS_t^{(i)}) * ds_{t+1}$$

Threat Score (TS) represents the total potential perceived threat of executing a sequence of a cluster. It is a combination of how anomalous the sequence is (AS) and how often and severe danger signals related to the sequence are (DS).

In principle, threat score of a cluster can be any function of its anomaly score and danger score, $TS_c = F(AS_c, DS_c)$, as long as the following conditions hold:

1. TS_c takes values in the range of 0.0–1.0;
2. TS_c increases monotonously when AS_c increases;
3. TS_c increases monotonously when DS_c increases.

Currently we use linear formula $TS_c = \alpha * AS_c + (1 - \alpha) * DS_c$. However, other functions can be taken into consideration in the future.

3.2   Danger Signals

Danger signals can include anything that happens in the environment not accordingly to expectations or that harms the environment or the system. The origins and amount of information given by the signals can differ. Signals can be created by AGVs themselves (any error during execution can be a reason for such a signal) or the AGV controller (e.g. if an AGV stops responding). But one of the most reliable methods to obtain the information about the dangerous activity is an independent Facility Monitor. It should have the information about the goals of the jobs, their preconditions and effects, and general rules of the environment (e.g. "location Z25 is a cargo delivery point"). For some signal it is possible to pinpoint exactly the location and the cause of it, while for others such information may be unavailable, requiring the DDM to check all possible jobs in progress. When a danger signal is detected, it gets assigned to active jobs accordingly to internal calculation of probability of this particular job being the cause of the danger. This depends on a type of the danger signal and on an anomaly score of active jobs.

Danger signals have two parameters: type and severity. Severity is a numerical value that represents the expected harmful potential of the signal. For critical danger signals with high severity, a single signal is enough to cause a job to be stopped. For minor danger signals, only sustained repetition of them for the same jobs again and again will cause these jobs to be regarded as threatening. Possible danger types that we expect for the robotic manufacturing facility include: a wrong action performed by a robot, a robot stops responding, or responds erratically, goods disappearing from collection or delivery points; a foreign object is detected on one of the locations, or a general danger alarm of unknown origin.

Every danger signal gets distributed among jobs that may have caused it. The exact distribution function varies depending on the type of the signal. I.e. if a robot stops responding, the job that it was executing at the moment is regarded as the main candidate. For a general danger alarm all jobs are regarded as candidates. For a signal that is detected for a particular location, robots are regarded as likely candidates in proportion to their distance to this location. For all danger types, the distribution is further modified by the threat score of potential candidates. A job with higher anomaly score and more danger signals associated with it previously, will receive a higher chunk of the danger signal.

3.3 Active Jobs Manager

Main goals of the Active Jobs Manager (AJM) is to verify jobs, to keep the record of jobs that are currently being executed and to track their successful execution. In the presence of danger signals, the task of the AJM is to find out which active jobs may be associated with this signal, and determine if their threat level is enough to issue a command to stop them and forbid similar jobs in the future. The AJM works in real-time. When a new job is created by the AGVC, it is first sent for verification to the AJM. The AJM either approves or rejects it, based on its knowledge of previous harmful activities. If a job is rejected, the dangerous subsequence within the job is sent back as a reason for rejection. The AGVC can then try to recreate the job, to fulfill the goal using a different plan of execution that avoids this subsequence. If a job is approved, the DDM adds it to the list of active jobs. When any job event is completed by an AGV, the AGVC sends a confirmation to the DDM, so the DDM always knows at which state the job is. If a danger signal is received by the DDM, the AJM applies it to related active jobs accordingly to rules of danger score distribution. After this is done, a new verification is done to affected jobs, in order to decide if they should be stopped. If this is the case, the DDM will send a stop command to the AGV Controller.

4 Evaluation

We performed a number of experiments to assess the approach in terms of danger detection. The experiments are based on a simulated factory floor with three AGVs operating simultaneously. The factory floor has several collection and delivery points. As a first step, we create a training set by generating two thousand jobs to collect at a random collection point and deliver to a random delivery point. This dataset represents a set of "normal activities". Then we run the system in "production mode", where we generate one thousand jobs in a similar fashion, but with two additions. The first addition is the addition of new legitimate behaviors. This is done by defining a new collection point or a new delivery point. Such activities are expected to have high anomaly score, due to a robot performing previously unseen sequences of actions, but lead to intended results that can be verified by the Facility Monitor. The second addition to jobs is the addition of "bad jobs". We assume that an instance of the C&C got compromised, and sends a request to a robot to deliver goods to a wrong place that is not intended, where the goods can be collected by attackers. Due to the fact that goods disappear from the factory floor without arriving to the intended destination, the Facility Monitor raises an alarm and creates a danger signal as soon as it notices that goods have disappeared. However, since the DDM does not know which new locations are intended and which are not, it has to reason as described in Sect. 3, by distributing the Danger Signal among related jobs. If the threat score (TS) of a job reaches a predefined threshold, the job is stopped and is marked as dangerous. Further similar jobs are rejected. For every set of parameters we create one hundred randomized system runs, each consisting of 2000 jobs training set and 1000 jobs verification set, and take the average results.

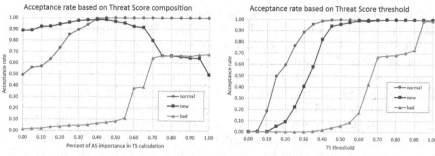

(a) Acceptance rate based on α in $TS_c =$ (b) Acceptance rate based on TS threshold
$\alpha * AS_c + (1 - \alpha) * DS_c$.   for job rejection.

Fig. 3. Acceptance rates depending on parameters

The decisions of the DDM depend on how the threat score is calculated and treated. Therefore, as the first experiment we look at the parameter α in the equation $TS_c = \alpha * AS_c + (1 - \alpha) * DS_c$. We vary α in the range of 0.0–1.0 with 0.05 step. For the purpose of this experiment we fixed the TS threshold at 0.55, i.e. any job with calculated TS higher than 0.55 is immediately stopped or is rejected from the beginning. We calculate the acceptance percentage for "normal jobs" (i.e. jobs that have collection and delivery points available in the training set), for "new jobs" (i.e. legitimate jobs, but with previously unseen collection or delivery points), and for "bad jobs" (i.e. jobs with a previously unseen and wrong delivery zone that cause disappearance of goods). Results are shown in Fig. 3a. Note that with $\alpha = 0.0$ anomaly score plays no role in the decision whatsoever, only danger signals matter. Danger signals appear closely associated with dangerous jobs, therefore most "bad" dangerous jobs are rejected, with acceptance rate staying below 0.1 up for all $\alpha < 0.55$. However, because we do not take any anomaly score into account, and only look at similarity of jobs to the ones associated with danger signals, normal jobs become associated with danger signals as often as new or bad jobs. This leads to a high rate of rejection for normal jobs ("false positives"). With increasing α, the danger signal distribution starts to take into account the anomaly value, therefore normal jobs become less and less likely to be associated with danger signals, and their acceptance rate increases rapidly, reaching values close to 1.0 at $\alpha > 0.4$. We see the best results with α in the range of 0.4–0.5, with very high acceptance of normal and new legitimate jobs, but very low acceptance of bad jobs (due to remaining importance of danger signals). However, when α increases past 0.5, we see a dramatic drop in acceptance of new jobs (due to the fact that the anomaly score is now very important, but the existence or absence of danger signals is not important). Bad jobs become more accepted as well, reaching the same percentage of acceptance as new jobs for $\alpha > 0.75$. This is due to anomaly values of new legitimate jobs and new bad jobs being on the same level, and lack of importance of danger signals to discriminate legitimate and bad behavior.

The TS threshold (TST) is also an important parameter, therefore as our second experiment we vary the TST in the range of 0.0–1.0, but now with fixed $\alpha = 0.5$. The results can be seen in Fig. 3b. We can see that with $TST = 0.0$ all jobs get rejected immediately, but with increasing TST the "normal" jobs increase their acceptance rate rapidly, with about 60 % of normal jobs being accepted with TST as low as 0.2. This is due to threat score for normal jobs being usually very low, due to low anomaly score as well as low to none relation to danger signals. However, with low TST new legitimate jobs are largely rejected, due to anomaly score alone being enough to breach the threshold. Values around 0.4–0.5 produce the best results: most normal and new jobs have the threat score lower than this threshold, and are therefore accepted, but the combination of anomaly score and related danger score leads to most bad jobs breaching the threshold and being successfully identified and rejected. With increasing the TST beyond 0.5 results worsen, as bad jobs become more and more accepted as well. It should be noted, however, that even with $TST = 0.9$ about 30 % of bad jobs are still identified and rejected.

5   Conclusions

This paper presents an approach for intelligent detection of and response to threatening activities in Cyber-Physical Systems. The system is able to recognize anomalous activities and environmental dangerous events, and relate them in order to understand, which jobs may have been the cause of the danger. Such jobs can be stopped and prevented in the future. The system, presented here, demonstrates the concept of an intelligent self-aware manufacturing facility.

It is important to mention that the Danger Detection Module is implemented in a domain-independent way. Detecting anomalies and dangerous activities in sequences of events is a general topic that can be applied to other settings as well as in safeguarding robotic manufacturing facilities. The Danger Detection Module can be applicable in such settings as incident detection in network traffic, analysis of system calls, safety of smart homes, etc.

References

1. Cani, A., Gaudesi, M., Sanchez, E., Squillero, G., Tonda, A.: Towards automated malware creation: code generation and code integration. In: Proceedings of the 29th Annual ACM Symposium on Applied Computing, pp. 157–160. ACM (2014)
2. Forrest, S., Perelson, A.S., Allen, L., Cherukuri, R.: Self-nonself discrimination in a computer. In: 2012 IEEE Symposium on Security and Privacy, p. 202. IEEE Computer Society (1994)
3. fr Sicherheit in der Informationstechnik (BSI), B.: Die lage der it-sicherheitin deutschland (2014). https://www.bsi.bund.de/SharedDocs/Downloads/DE/BSI/Publikationen/Lageberichte/Lagebericht2014.pdf?__blob=publicationFile
4. Kim, J., Bentley, P.J., Aickelin, U., Greensmith, J., Tedesco, G., Twycross, J.: Immune system approaches to intrusion detection-a review. Natural Comput. **6**(4), 413–466 (2007)

5. Langner, R.: Stuxnet: dissecting a cyberwarfare weapon. Secur. Priv. IEEE **9**(3), 49–51 (2011)
6. Manber, U., et al.: Finding similar files in a large file system. In: Usenix Winter, vol. 94, pp. 1–10 (1994)
7. Matzinger, P.: Tolerance, danger, and the extended family. Annu. Rev. Immunol. **12**(1), 991–1045 (1994)
8. Petit, J., Shladover, S.: Potential cyberattacks on automated vehicles. IEEE Trans. Intell. Transp. Syst. **16**(2), 546–556 (2015)

Performance Evaluation of Searchable Symmetric Encryption in Wireless Sensor Networks

Cristina Muñoz[✉], Lucas Rocci, Eduardo Solana, and Pierre Leone

Computer Science Department, University of Geneva, Carouge, Switzerland
{Cristina.Munoz,Eduardo.Solana,Pierre.Leone}@unige.ch,
Lucas.Rocci@etu.unige.ch

Abstract. The distributed nature of Wireless Sensor Networks leads to the use of cloud databases that need to be protected when dealing with sensitive content. In this context, Searchable Symmetric Encryption provides the appropriate framework to perform secure searches. This work proposes a combination of secure indexes with Bloom Filters to efficiently address searches in encrypted content. We evaluate the performance of two different strategies to populate Bloom Filters in XM1000, Z1 and TelosB wireless sensor devices: (1) we first consider four cryptographic hash functions using the double hashing technique and truncating message digests; (2) we then select five symmetric encryption algorithms and two fast hash functions also with double hashing. We conclude that the best strategy for securing indexes is AES plus a fast FNV hash function and double hashing.

Keywords: Searchable Symmetric Encryption · Wireless Sensor Networks · Bloom Filters · Cloud Storage

1 Introduction

The ubiquitous model of the Internet of Things (IoT) leads to manage information through secure cloud systems. In the Database as a Service (DBaaS) model data is stored and managed in the cloud. This model assumes that documents are securely stored and only accessible to authorized users. In this process the database provider is usually considered as an "honest but curious" adversary with respect to the documents stored. For example, one can imagine a DBaaS for a Wireless Sensor Network (WSN) used in a Smart City that manages sensitive citizens data such as physical characteristics, location, actions, etc. In this scenario, only public security forces should access this private information.

Searchable Symmetric Encryption (SSE) offers a solution to search for specific encrypted documents on a database. In this context, the main challenge is to prevent the database provider from extracting relevant information related to the search process.

Secure indexes based on Bloom Filters (BFs) [4,10,14,17,19,20] are generally chosen because of their efficiency. Since our architecture relies on performance constrained devices, we have considered that BFs constitute the ideal candidate.

© ICST Institute for Computer Sciences, Social Informatics and Telecommunications Engineering 2016
B. Mandler et al. (Eds.) IoT 360° 2015, Part I, LNICST 169, pp. 40–51, 2016.
DOI: 10.1007/978-3-319-47063-4_4

A BF [18] is defined as a probabilistic data structure that efficiently manages membership of a certain number of elements. Secure indexes based on BFs use cryptographic hash functions to add elements to the filter.

The aim of this research is to improve the construction of indexes in terms of security and performance. We focus on the performance evaluation of different strategies to securely populate BFs using well-known cryptographic algorithms. This means that the results of our research are valid for all methods that use secure indexes and trapdoors based on BFs in a WSN.

We compare the performance of mote devices in terms of ROM, RAM, energy and execution time using two different strategies:

- First, we evaluate four widely used cryptographic hash functions that are directly applied to keywords in order to fill in BFs in a secure way.
- The second strategy relies on encryption algorithms and fast non-cryptographic hash functions. Keywords are first encrypted and then hashed in order to populate BFs in an efficient manner.

Finally, we discuss the suitability of the aforementioned algorithms and their advantages and disadvantages in terms of security.

The rest of this paper is organized as follows: Sect. 2 points out the related work on the field. Section 3 details our methodology. Section 4 presents the results obtained. Finally, Sect. 5 summarizes our work.

2   Related Work

The first research that presents secure indexes is based on the use of BFs [4]. HMAC-SHA1 is proposed as keyed hash function but its performance is not discussed. According to [17] this scheme is still the most secure for full searches.

Secure indexes are usually based on BFs due to their efficiency [4,10,14,17, 19,20]. In [17] a strategy to support searches that allow comparisons character by character is presented. In [10], secure indexes based on BFs are introduced to secure the deduplication of data in which duplicated encrypted files are removed to improve the memory size of the cloud database. In [19] a multi-keyword fuzzy search technique is presented. It uses a locality-sensitive hashing technique to support the misspelling of keywords. Similarity searches based on a symbol-based trie-traverse technique have been proposed in [20]. Moreover, in [14] a secure anonymous database search is presented by adding a query router between data searchers and index servers. Its purpose is to enforce an authorization before accessing secure indexes based on BFs. In this process, the query router is not allowed to gain data about the queries and their results.

Furthermore, there exists some research concerning the use of secure BFs in WSNs. In [11] a technique for encrypted data aggregation is used where secure BFs reduce transmission costs. Besides this, a method to support in-network processing [22] while securing traffic has also been developed in WSNs.

Finally, it is remarkable to mention that lightweight block ciphers have been evaluated in sensor motes. In [3], AES and XTEA are highlighted due to their good performance.

3   Methodology

In this section we focus on our proposed methodology to implement SSE in WSNs. First of all, we describe the scenario and the required processes for saving and searching an encrypted document in a cloud database. Then, we detail how to fill in secure indexes based on BFs using: (1) cryptographic hash functions and (2) an encryption algorithm plus a fast hash function.

3.1   Scenario

A SSE encryption scenario requires three agents: (1) the Encrypted Database (ED), (2) the Data Owner (DO) and (3) the Data Searcher (DS). In this paper, we consider that agents are attached to a WSN composed of constrained devices. This means that efficiency is essential in the communication process. Figure 1 shows the communication process to generate and retrieve data using SSE in a WSN:

1. The first requirement is that DOs and DSs participate in a key exchange protocol to share the same symmetric key.
2. The DO generates a document to store on the ED.
3. The document is symmetrically encrypted and an index containing relevant keywords is generated to facilitate searches. In our case, the index is a BF associated to the document. To prevent information leakage, index entries should also be encrypted with a pseudo-random function as described in [4]. We then insert random 1's in order to hide the number of keywords in the index. Finally, the associated secure index and the encrypted document are stored in the ED.
4. An authorized user holding the proper symmetric key generates a trapdoor to retrieve documents associated to certain keywords. Then the secure trapdoor is sent to the ED.
5. The ED searches for indexes that match the trapdoors and sends the associated encrypted documents to the DS.
6. The search results may include false positives but this does not constitute a security breach since the DS only decrypts documents protected with his key.

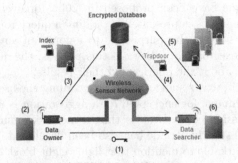

Fig. 1. SSE in Wireless Sensor Networks.

3.2 Cryptographic Hash Functions

For the evaluation of cryptographic hash functions we have chosen four widely used algorithms:

MD5 (1991). MD5 is based on a Merkle-Damgård function and produces 128 bit digests [15]. Each message block implements 4 rounds of 16 operations each one. This cryptographic hash function is highly vulnerable to collision attacks so that it was substituted by SHA1. Pre-image attacks are theoretically possible but are not practical due to their high computational cost. Nowadays, it is used as a checksum hash to verify the integrity of a file.

SHA1 (1995). SHA1 relies on a Merkle-Damgård function and produces 160 bit digests using 80 rounds [16]. It is vulnerable to collision attacks for high computational efforts. For this reason, it was decided to substitute it for SHA2 that presents no vulnerabilities.

SHA2 (2001). SHA2 is also based on a Merkle-Damgård function and produces 224, 256, 384 or 512 bit digests [16]. Digests of 224 and 256 can use 64 or 80 rounds while the rest need 80 rounds. Pre-image and collision resistance have been compromised for a limited number of rounds but it is still considered secure.

SHA3 (2012). SHA3 depends on a Sponge construction and produces 224, 256, 384 or 512 bit digests using 24 rounds [13]. SHA3 is a very recent algorithm with no significant flaws so far.

Additional Methods Used. Besides the cryptographic hash functions described above we introduce four alternative methods with the aim of improving efficiency:

- To speed up the insertion of elements in a BF the *Double Hashing technique* (DH) [9] has also been evaluated. Two initial digests h_1 and h_2 are computed. The final hash h_i is the result of an iterative linear combination of h_1 and h_2:

$$h_i = (h_1 + i \cdot h_2) mod\, n \qquad (1)$$

where n represents the hash output in $\mathbb{N}$.
- Depending on the size of the BF a different number of bits is required at the output of the hash function. To reduce the output we follow the *lazy mod mapping technique* [7]. It consists on applying a modular operation to the hash output taking the size of the filter as a parameter.
- Moreover, *truncated message digests* have been evaluated in order to use only one cryptographic hash to obtain all required hashes. This method specified in the NIST Standard FIPS 180-4 [16] proposes to take the necessary left most bits of a digest to reduce the size of the hash output. In our case, we take the necessary left most bits to compute as many positions as required for each element to insert to the filter.

– Finally, since multiple hashes are required per keyword we use the symmetric key to randomize the input of the hash function and prevent dictionary or pre-computed tables attacks. Message Authentication Code (MAC) constructions like the HMAC family of functions may also be considered for this purpose.

During this research we prioritized implementations adapted for processors with a low number of bit registers. In the case of cryptographic hash functions we did not find implementations designed for processors of 16 bits. MD5, SHA1 and SHA2 are adapted for 32 bit registers while SHA3 is adapted to 64 bit registers. Furthermore, SHA2 and SHA3 use 256 bit key lengths. It is remarkable to mention that there are a limited number of implementations of SHA3 due to its novelty.

3.3   Encryption Algorithms and Fast Hash Functions

As far as we know, no previous research based on applying SSE using BFs has proposed the use of an encryption algorithm plus a fast hash to fill in the filter. We propose to assess five widely used cryptographic algorithms with two different fast hash functions:

AES (1997). Today AES is the de facto standard [5]. It is an iterative block cipher based on a substitution-permutation network. It works with blocks of 128 bits and no major vulnerability has been unveiled so far. The number of rounds depends on the size of the key: 128/192/256 bit keys require 10/12/14 rounds respectively.

MISTY1 (1995). MISTY1 is a secure block cipher which uses a nested Feistel Network of a multiple of 4 rounds [12]. Recursively, each of these rounds uses a 3 round Feistel Network. It works with 64 bit blocks and sizes of 128 bit keys.

PRESENT (2007). PRESENT relies on a substitution-permutation network of 31 rounds for block sizes of 64 bits and key sizes of 80/128 bits [2]. PRESENT is considered secure although it has partially been broken for 26 rounds.

SKIPJACK (1998). SKIPJACK was designed to provide security on phones [6]. It is a block cipher that uses an unbalanced Feistel Network of 32 rounds and 80 bit keys. The most successful attack breaks 31 rounds but a full attack is not known to date. NIST recommends to avoid its use due to its weak key length.

XTEA (1997). XTEA is a block cipher that uses a 64 rounds Feistel Network and blocks of 64 bits with a 128 bit key [21]. Up to date, 36 rounds have been broken but is considered as secure in its full-fledge version.

FNV (1991). FNV is a non-cryptographic hash function based on an offset and a chosen prime that depends on the length of the output [8]. It is based on a Merkle-Damgård function that works byte by byte to obtain 32, 64, 128, 256, 512 or 1024 bit outputs.

Murmurhash3 (2010). This non-cryptographic hash function is based on a block inter-mixing [1]. Input bits are divided in blocks and simple operations on the block mix ensure that all blocks are affected by the precedent blocks. Bit outputs of 32 or 128 are allowed.

Additional Methods Used. For reducing the computation of encryption algorithms the *double hashing technique* has been used. In addition to this, to reduce the hash output length the *lazy mod mapping technique* has been applied. All these techniques are detailed in Sect. 3.2. Moreover, fast hash functions use different *offsets* and *seeds* to obtain different hash outputs.

In the case of AES we use a version designed for 8 bit registers in ECB mode with a 128 bit key. Besides, PRESENT uses a 80 bit key and is also adapted to 8 bits registers. SKYPJACK is adapted to 16 bit registers and the rest of algorithms to 32 bit registers. Moreover, fast hash functions used work with 32 bit lengths at the output.

4 Evaluation

A real demo using wireless sensor devices for SSE has been implemented. Secure indexes and trapdoors based on BFs have been executed on motes which use the low power consumption IEEE802.15.4 standard at 2.4 GHz. The sensors assessed are Advanticsys XM1000, Zolertia Z1 and Crossbow TelosB. The evaluated algorithms have been programmed in C using the open source OS Contiki 2.6.

In our experiments 25 secure indexes of 128 bit positions are created. 10 elements of a few tens of characters are used to fill in each filter. From these elements 7 are used as real keywords for indexing the content of the document and the rest are chosen randomly to blind the filter. With these parameters we select an optimum number of 9 different hashes per keyword.

The parameters measured correspond to ROM (kB), RAM (kB), energy consumed by the CPU (μJ) and execution time (ms). As the following results show, the energy consumed by the CPU is proportional to the execution time.

4.1 Cryptographic Hash Functions

As detailed in Sect. 3.2 four cryptographic hash functions have been evaluated. If message digests are not truncated k hash functions are needed for each element, where k is the optimum number of hashes that in our case is 9. When truncating messages only the computation of one cryptographic hash function is needed for each element. Moreover, in all cases we considered the DH to evaluate the improvement achieved.

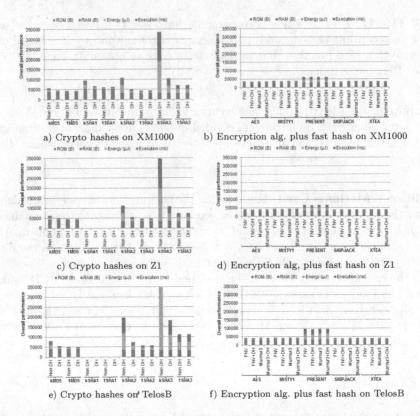

Fig. 2. Overall performance evaluation using (a, c, e) cryptographic hash functions and (b, d, f) encryption algorithms with a fast hash function.

Figure 2a shows the overall performance when using XM1000 devices. Figure 2c shows the results for Z1 motes and Fig. 2e for TelosB.

TelosB motes offer the poorest performance in all cases. XM1000 and Z1 sensors show similar performance with slightly better results in the first case.

When message digests are not truncated, the DH technique improves the performance of the system. If digests are truncated the performance is very similar but slightly better results are obtained whether the DH is not used.

In terms of overall performance we observe that truncated MD5, SHA2 and SHA1 are the best options for XM1000. Z1 and TelosB present a ROM overflow problem for SHA1, so only truncated MD5 and SHA2 functions are considered. SHA3 displays a poor performance when message digests are not truncated. In the case of TelosB we decided not to show the execution time for k SHA3 to improve the legibility of the figure. All these options are discussed in detail in Sect. 4.3.

4.2 Encryption Algorithms and Fast Hash Functions

In Sect. 3.3 we presented the five cryptographic algorithms used for the encryption of keywords and the two fast hashes required to insert them to a BF. In this section we have evaluated all these techniques plus the improvement obtained when using DH.

Figure 2b shows the overall performance when evaluating XM1000 devices. Figure 2d shows the results for Z1 motes and Fig. 2f for TelosB. At first sight, if we compare these results with the ones obtained for cryptographic hash functions we observe that the strategy of using encryption algorithms with a fast hash function improves the performance.

As in the previous section TelosB motes offer poor performance compared to the other two and XM1000 are slightly better than Z1.

In all cases the DH offers just marginally better results. Furthermore, similar overall results are obtained when using FNV and Murmurhash3. Concerning the cryptographic algorithms PRESENT offers the worst results for all devices. For this reason its evaluation is discarded in Fig. 3.

Figure 3a details the use of ROM. In all cases Murmurhash3 requires more ROM than FNV. Moreover, SKIPJACK and XTEA need less memory than the other options while MISTY1 requires more than the others. Besides, it can be observed that Z1 devices require more ROM than the other two.

The results for RAM are shown at Fig. 3b. Similar results are obtained in all cases except for AES that requires slightly more RAM. TelosB motes offer the poorest performance in this domain.

In terms of energy and execution (see Figs. 3c and d) all algorithms obtain better results when using Murmurhash3 except in the case of AES that improves

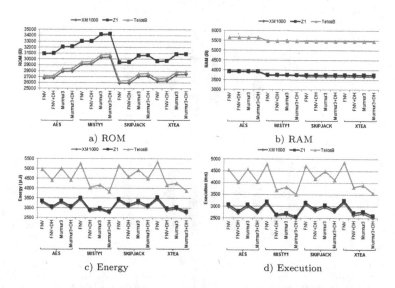

a) ROM

b) RAM

c) Energy

d) Execution

Fig. 3. Performance evaluation of the best cryptographic algorithms.

its execution when using FNV. MISTY1 and XTEA offer the best results when
used with Murmurhash3 and the DH.

Taking into account the overall performance, we state that AES, MISTY1,
SKIPJACK and XTEA with FNV and DH are the best options. As in the previous section, all these strategies are discussed in detail in Sect. 4.3.

4.3 Best Strategies

In this section we discuss the practical use of the best cryptographic hashes
and encryption algorithms plus a fast hash function. The results in terms of
overall performance for XM1000, Z1 and TelosB devices (see Figs. 4a–c) show
that encryption algorithms plus a fast hash function using the DH provide better
results.

Figure 5a shows the ROM usage for the best strategies. It is remarkable to
mention that SHA2 requires a similar memory amount than encryption algorithms. The results obtained for RAM (see Fig. 5b) indicate that all strategies
require comparable resources. Finally, it can be stated that energy and execution

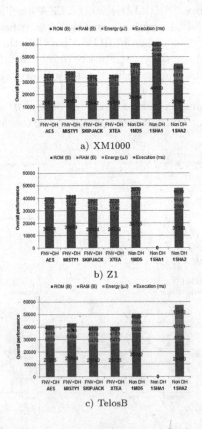

a) XM1000

b) Z1

c) TelosB

Fig. 4. Overall performance evaluation of the best strategies.

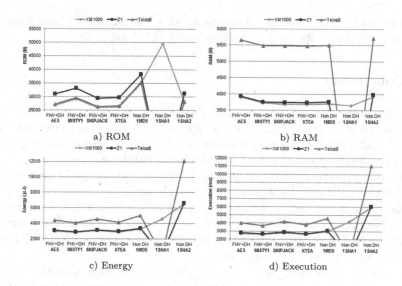

Fig. 5. Performance evaluation of the best strategies.

time (see Figs. 5c and d) required is higher for SHA2 and SHA1 while remains quite uniform in other cases.

In terms of security, we evaluate the suitability of the combination of encryption algorithms and a fast hash function. The selection of SKIPJACK is discarded due to its weak key length. MISTY1 offers poorer performance results when compared to AES and XTEA and with no security advantage, so we do not recommend its use either. The other encryption algorithms: AES and XTEA are considered secure. Nevertheless, AES is constantly subject to extensive analysis from the cryptographic community and consequently is considered as a highly resistant algorithm. For this reason, even if it displays a slightly worse behaviour than XTEA on sensors, we opt for the use of AES plus FNV and DH for constructing secure indexes and trapdoors.

If we compare the three cryptographic hash functions we observe that SHA1 offers the poorest performance. MD5 and SHA2 offer similar results but still they are paradoxically less performant than encryption algorithms. Concerning security, SHA2 is secure and MD5 is not collision resistant. This weakness does not affect security in our application due to the fact that collision attacks are typically used to impersonate someone but cannot guess the plaintext. Nevertheless, it must be taken into account that a theoretical pre-image attack has been discovered for MD5 and it is a matter of time before an attack that breaks this property in a reasonable amount of time is found. For this reason, we consider a truncated SHA2 without the DH the best option between all cryptographic hash functions.

Finally, we compare the best solution for each strategy defined: (1) AES plus FNV and DH and (2) a truncated SHA2 without the DH. We observe (see Fig. 4) that the first solution displays better results.

To summarize, we recommend the use of AES plus a fast FNV hash function using the DH due to its good performance and high level of security.

5   Conclusion

The aim of this research is to evaluate different strategies to allow the implementation of Searchable Symmetric Encryption techniques using wireless sensor devices. In this context, Bloom Filters are used to secure indexes and trapdoors related to encrypted documents saved on a cloud database.

The performance of mote devices is measured and compared in terms of ROM, RAM, CPU consumption and execution time.

Two different strategies are assessed. First of all, four well-known cryptographic hash functions are evaluated to save keywords in a filter. Furthermore, five widely used symmetric encryption algorithms combined with two different fast non-cryptographic hash functions are analyzed.

Our results show that the combination of an encryption algorithm with a fast hash function offers better results than using a cryptographic hash function. Based on our experiments, due to its higher performance on sensors and stronger level of security we recommend the use of AES plus FNV and the Double Hashing technique.

As future work we envision a strategy that allows the creation of secure indexes according to a certain entropy.

Acknowledgment. This work has been financially supported by the Swiss Hasler Foundation in the framework of the POPWiN project.

References

1. Appleby, A.: murmurhash3 (2011)
2. Bogdanov, A.: PRESENT: an ultra-lightweight block cipher. In: Paillier, P., Verbauwhede, I. (eds.) CHES 2007. LNCS, vol. 4727, pp. 450–466. Springer, Heidelberg (2007). doi:10.1007/978-3-540-74735-2_31
3. Cazorla, M., Gourgeon, S., Marquet, K., Minier, M.: Survey and benchmark of lightweight block ciphers for MSP430 16-bit microcontroller. Secur. Commun. Netw. **8**(18), 3564–3579 (2015). http://dx.doi.org/10.1002/sec.1281
4. Eu-Jin, G.: Secure indexes. Technical report (2004). http://crypto.stanford.edu/eujin/papers/secureindex/
5. FIPS PUB 197, Advanced Encryption Standard (AES), National Institute of Standards and Technology, US Department of Commerce, November 2001. http://csrc.nist.gov/publications/fips/fips197/fips-197.pdf
6. FIPS PUB 185, Escrowed Encryption Standard (EES). Federal Information Processing Standards Publication 185 (1994)
7. Fowler, G.: Fowler/Noll/Vo (FNV) hash (1991). http://isthe.com/chongo/tech/comp/fnv
8. Fowler, G., Noll, L.C., Eastlake, D.: The FNV non-cryptographic hash algorithm. Internet Draft (2015)

9. Kirsch, A., Mitzenmacher, M.: Less hashing, same performance: building a better bloom filter. In: Azar, Y., Erlebach, T. (eds.) ESA 2006. LNCS, vol. 4168, pp. 456–467. Springer, Heidelberg (2006)
10. Li, J., Chen, X., Xhafa, F., Barolli, L.: Secure deduplication storage systems with keyword search. In: 2014 IEEE 28th International Conference on Advanced Information Networking and Applications (AINA), pp. 971–977, May 2014
11. Li, T., Wu, Y., Zhu, H.: An efficient scheme for encrypted data aggregation on sensor networks. In: IEEE 63rd Vehicular Technology Conference, 2006. VTC 2006-Spring, vol. 2, pp. 831–835, May 2006
12. Ohta, H., Matsui, M.: A description of the MISTY1 encryption algorithm. RFC 2994, November 2000
13. Pub, N.: Draft FIPS pub 202: SHA-3 standard: permutation-based hash and extendable-output functions. Federal Information Processing Standards Publication (2014)
14. Raykova, M., Vo, B., Bellovin, S.M., Malkin, T.: Secure anonymous database search. In: Proceedings of the 2009 ACM Workshop on Cloud Computing Security, pp. 115–126. ACM (2009)
15. Rivest, R.: The MD5 message-digest algorithm. Internet Request For Comments 1321 (1992)
16. Standard, N.S.H.: Federal information processing standards publication fipps 180–4 (2012)
17. Suga, T., Nishide, T., Sakurai, K.: Secure keyword search using bloom filter with specified character positions. In: Takagi, T., Wang, G., Qin, Z., Jiang, S., Yu, Y. (eds.) ProvSec 2012. LNCS, vol. 7496, pp. 235–252. Springer, Heidelberg (2012). doi:10.1007/978-3-642-33272-2_15
18. Tarkoma, S., Rothenberg, C., Lagerspetz, E.: Theory and practice of bloom filters for distributed systems. Commun. Surv. Tutor. IEEE **14**(1), 131–155 (2012). First
19. Wang, B., Yu, S., Lou, W., Hou, Y.T.: Privacy-preserving multi-keyword fuzzy search over encrypted data in the cloud. In: 2014 IEEE Conference on Computer Communications, INFOCOM 2014, Toronto, 27 April–2 May 2014, pp. 2112–2120 (2014). http://dx.doi.org/10.1109/INFOCOM.2014.6848153
20. Wang, C., Ren, K., Yu, S., Urs, K.: Achieving usable and privacy-assured similarity search over outsourced cloud data. In: Proceedings of IEEE INFOCOM, 2012, pp. 451–459, March 2012
21. Wheeler, D., Needham, R.: Tea extensions, also correction to XTEA, October 1998. www.ftp.cl.cam.ac.uk/ftp/users/djw3
22. Wu, Y., Ma, D., Li, T., Deng, R.: Classify encrypted data in wireless sensor networks. In: IEEE 60th Vehicular Technology Conference, VTC-Fall, vol. 5, pp. 3236–3239, September 2004

Secure Data Exchange Based on Social Networks Public Key Distribution

Krzysztof Podlaski[✉], Artur Hłobaż, and Piotr Milczarski

Faculty of Physics and Applied Informatics, University of Lodz, Łódź, Poland
{podlaski,artur.hlobaz,piotr.milczarski}@uni.lodz.pl

Abstract. The mobile devices became the most spread tools used for everyday communication. The users of mobile applications demand high level of security. All existing encryption protocols require from the users additional knowledge and resources. On the other hand the common user does not have required knowledge and skills about security. In this paper we discuss the problem of public key distribution between interested parties. We propose to use a popular social media as a channel to publish public keys. That way of keys distribution allows the owner of the key to connect easily with the desired person or institution, that is not always easy. Recognizing that the mobile devices are the main tool of communication, we present example of a mobile application that uses the proposed security method.

Keywords: Secure communication · Data encryption · Public key distribution · Mobile applications · Social networks

1 Introduction

Nowadays, people take into account security of information exchange. There are many different methods of encryption. The most spread and probably most popular are asymmetric methods based on a pair of user keys, public and private. While private key has to be kept very secret the public should be freely distributed between all interested parties and here we arrive at the big gap in used protocols. All known methodologies are very interested in securing the keys and authorization. We can sign the public key via well-known institutions (VeriSign, Comodo SSL, GlobalSign, etc.) and prove that a defined person or a company created this key. Even having a given key of a John Smith from Milwaukee how can a person be sure that this is exactly the same John Smith he knows? For many persons (even institutions) knowing their names and addresses is not enough. On the other hand if the John Smith is somebody's friend in real life he can be a "friend" in virtual one. They usually are connected via social network (Facebook, LinkedIn, etc.). The life would be much simpler if we could obtain his public key from this social network. In this paper we introduce an architecture for applications that allows sending encrypted information between two mobile devices using public key infrastructure and social media with QRcodes as a method of seamless distribution of public key.

© ICST Institute for Computer Sciences, Social Informatics and Telecommunications Engineering 2016
B. Mandler et al. (Eds.) IoT 360° 2015, Part I, LNICST 169, pp. 52–63, 2016.
DOI: 10.1007/978-3-319-47063-4_5

The paper is organized as follows. In Sect. 2 we analyze the possibility of the storage of the public key with use of social media. The next Section contains requirements for QRcodes. Section 4 focuses on the used encryption method. Section 5 contains description of the proposed application architecture. At the end we present our final remarks and conclusions.

2 Public Key Distribution Using Social Media

There are many interesting methods of public key distribution. One of the well-known methods of public key distribution is usage of key servers. Conventional PKI and PGP are still hard to be used by average users [1,2]. The task to acquire valid public key of a friend is not an easy one. Nowadays, users are used to use the social networks as the environment for searching any personal information. The everyday social networks and mobile devices revolutionized ways of communication. The average user is used to integrate all mobile devices with some social medias and requires all important data to be synchronized with the device phone book. Unfortunately existing key servers are not ready to be used in such a way. Some important elements have to be taken into account during the process of public key distribution:

1. ownership of the stored public key,
2. correspondence between the owner and real party (person, company, foundation, etc.),
3. easy accessibility to all interested parties,
4. is the key still actual/valid or was revoked.

Even though we have the key from some public storage in order use it we have to be sure to whom it belongs. The name of the person or company and even address are not always enough. Analyzing presented requirements we can notice that usual PKI or PGP key distribution does not always fulfill point 2 and 4. We can try to use the webpage of a party or company, but there are often some additional problems:

- what the page address is,
- where the key is stored,
- how to obtain the key automatically.

On the other hand, the social media are the most spread and used mean of information distribution. Based on that experience there is an idea of using that medium for key distribution. First we have to analyze what kinds of information are already used in social medias. We can easily stress that on most of social portals users can store some data. The security measures used in such medias restrict that only the owner of the account can store and change this information. We can identify two types of information:

1. persistent data - like photos or images (usually more than one), web page address, email address,
2. transient data - like status, notes and memos.

The first type of information is usually stored in the users profile while the latter in some blog type medium. It is obvious that transient data is not a good candidate for our purpose. This means we should concentrate on elements that can be stored in users' profile. Moreover, it has to be noted that usually user is not allowed to customize what kind of information can be stored there.

It was already proposed in [3] to store link to our public key as one of user's web addresses. This is interesting idea however the user still has to have some special place for storing the key and social medium is used only as the information where to find the public key. Moreover, this method is easy accessible by machines while strange web addresses are not well perceived by humans.

The second very interesting place for the key repository is the user profile photo/image or gallery (if exists). This will give us a huge area for implementations, if we would be able to store the public key inside the photo gallery. Now, we will try to cover this case more carefully. We have to take into account that social media usually optimize images that often means resizing, increasing jpg compressions.

2.1 Storing Public Key in Photo Metadata

Almost all image formats allow storing some additional information in attached metadata (Exif [4], XMP [5], IPTC [6]). That would be a good place to store the public key inside the metadata of profile picture. Unfortunately, the most known social portals (Facebook, LinkedIn) erase all metadata after the upload. This means that if we upload a photo with some information added in its metadata the information would be lost and not available for others.

2.2 Storing Public Key in Photo File

There are many methods of steganography [7,8] that allow storing some information inside images. Unfortunately, these methods are very sensitive on operations like resizing and jpg optimization. All images uploaded to social medias are optimized and this operation would make impossible usage of steganography. Even hiding public key after the file closing marker would not work because all the information after the EOF (End Of File) marker is deleted by social media portal.

2.3 Storing Public Key Inside as a QRcode

QRcode [9,10] is an image that encodes some text. It is possible to store public key as QRcode. The idea of using QRcode as key exchange for secure mobile communication was presented in our previous paper [11]. That way of storing the key has some advantages:

1. QRcode does not lose information during usual image resizing,
2. QRcode does not lose information during changes of image format (.jpg, .png, .gif . . .).

Storing public key as QRcode inside user gallery agrees with all requirements. We should decide for some nomenclature of naming the file with public key QRcode. Unfortunately, we cannot store it as profile picture, most of the people prefer to use real photo in that place. On the other hand, QRcodes are so widespread that they should not be perceived as out of place in user's photo gallery.

2.4 Storing QRcode on a Given Picture

There are some possibilities to store QRcode and a given picture together. There are methods like colored QRcodes but they are not acceptable for profile picture. There are also approaches to include a QRcode inside a picture. This is however not possible for all images and small QRcodes can be lost during resizing and optimization procedures. It is possible that some encoding of QRcode in image using HSB color space would be resistant for resizing and optimization but the impact of such procedure on image itself has to be determined.

2.5 Conclusions

According to presented analyze the best choice is to store public key in form of QRcode inside user's profile on social portal. This solves easily the problem of propagation and accessibility, on the other hand keeping some information about authenticity - only user can store photos in his/her gallery and prevents phishing attacks [12,13]. The problem of revoking the old key is easy to organize in proposed manner also. Moreover, if somebody would like to narrow group of users that can view/use public key then access to galleries can be restricted to selected group of users (friends), this is possible in most of social portals.

3 Selection of QR Code Parameters

On the basis of [9–11] it was found that the best type of QR code to use for our purposes will be the version 17 (85×85). It will allow hiding a public key with the length of 2048 bits with the highest possible error correction feature - level H, approx. 30 %. In the Table 1 shown below there is short description of QRcodes capacity using different variants of QRcodes.

Table 1. QR code types and their capacity

Parameters	QR code type			
	QR code Model 1	QR code Model 2	Micro QR code	iQR code
Max Size [modules]	73×73	177×177	17×17	422×422
Max Capacity in numerals	1101	7089	35	40637
Max Capacity in alphanumeric	667	4296	21	24626
Max Capacity in binary [bytes]	458	2953	15	16928

4   Encryption Variants

Depending on the amount of data to be transferred between users, we can distinguish two possible encryption schemes [14,15] which have application in mobile implementation described in the next section: A. asymmetric cryptography, B. asymmetric cryptography together with symmetric.

Because the asymmetric cryptography is slower than the symmetric one, first variant should only be applied to transmit short information, such as chat or SMS. If the user wants to send information, he encrypts it by the receiver's public key, which he has collected earlier from the social networking site. The receiver decrypts the message with its private key known only to him. Similarly, this is done the other way (Fig. 1).

One of the problems is that this scheme above does not provide authentication/identification of the information about the sending user. To ensure the authentication of the sender, the sender should first encrypt the message with its private key, and after that encrypt it again by the public key of the receiver. This allows the receiver to be sure who is sending a message to him, because he

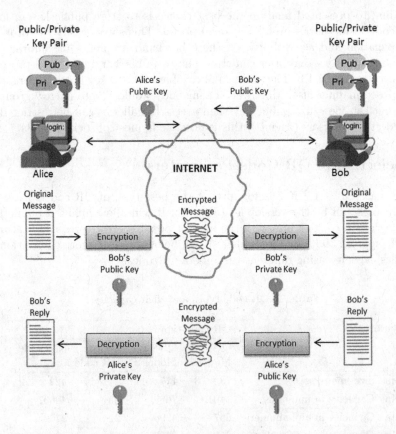

Fig. 1. Asymmetric cryptography - ensuring data integrity and confidentiality

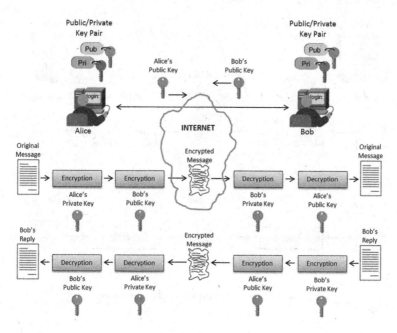

Fig. 2. Asymmetric cryptography - ensuring data integrity, confidentiality and sender authentication

will have to download the sender's public key from the social networking site in order to decrypt the information (Fig. 2).

In the case of the second encryption variant, the use of asymmetric cryptography with symmetric would allow to encrypt long information, i.e. files or stream call. In this variant, the transmission will be encrypted using symmetric cryptography. Exchange of components, which are important to establish a common one-time session key, will be done using asymmetric cryptography [16]. To establish a one-time session key, each party must first randomly generate 128 or 256-bit secret key. Secret key length depends on the used session encryption algorithm (AES-128 or AES-256). Then, the keys must be exchanged between parties using asymmetric cryptography (analogous manner as shown in Fig. 1). At this point, each party has two secret keys. To establish a common one time session key each of the sides uses XOR operation on these two secret keys (Figs. 3 and 4).

Fig. 3. The process of session key establishing

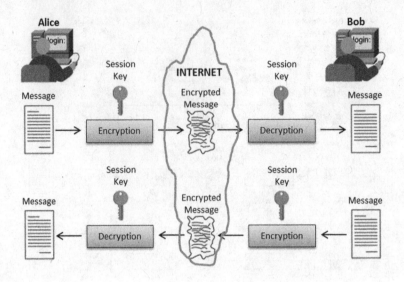

Fig. 4. Secure information exchange process

5   Analysis of Security of the Method

The proposed solution of session key establishment is different from standard methods like Diffie-Hellman algorithm. This means that no clear text information related to the key will not be possible to eavesdrop [17,18]. The attacker will be able to capture only the data already encrypted with which he will not be able to do anything.

We should analyze the impact on the presented method when somebody breaks into user's social portal account (assume it is Bob's account). Even though such possibility exists the evil party could only change the user's public key into fake one. Such action would make impossible to continue encrypted communication between Alice and Bob because Bob's original private and fake public keys would not be paired anymore. Moreover, the intruder would not be able to decrypt messages sent by Alice until the Bob's private key is compromised. In the result Bob would be informed that his social account was broken. He would probably upload original public key once again and increase security measures of his social account. This implies that the main security precautions have to be taken when implementing proposed method. This will be important to keep private key secure in mobile device application.

We can also analyse possibility of an attack of the Man in the Middle type. In order to arrange such an attack an intruder has to intercept Facebook request and supplay fake response that replace receivers public key with the public key of the attacker. This is possible with use of an appropriate fake DNS service. Next the attacker has to intercept the encrypted message before it is received by recipient, encrypt the message and resent with the appropriate public key. This means a fake BTS attack on GSM service or interception of recipients smartphone in the presented bellow SMS communication example Sect. 6.3. For example that kind of attack is possible if the attacker uses fake Facebook ssl certificate. This can be prevented by additional checking of originality of Facebook certificate before the application downloads public key.

6 Mobile Implementation

6.1 Mobile Communication

Usually encrypted communication begins with keys exchange. In proposed method of asymmetric cryptography suites perfectly for short messages and does not need any key exchange protocols at all. Interested parties can obtain appropriate receiver key from social network and stores own private one. Therefore, it can be easily deployed for smartphones to encrypt SMS communication. The latter of proposed methods need an exchange of a session encryption key and can be used on smartphones, tablets or even laptops (devices which have screen and camera) for stream communications.

6.2 Mobile Application Requirements

In order to implement mobile application that uses the presented encryption methods with usage of social network as public key store we define the application prerequisites:

- the Internet access,
- Social Medias Network access, can upload and download files/images from them,
- save data (keys),
- can generate QRcode,
- process QRcodes,
- can capture and send SMS, or capture voice telephony agent to work with the stream voice transmission,
- can encrypt and decrypt using presented methods.

The prerequisites of the application can be widened or shortened due to the application's functionality. The general communication scheme for such application is shown diagram (Fig. 5). The idea of the method and its mobile applications for SMS messages is described below (Fig. 6). The other means of mobile communication is presented in the paper [19].

6.3 Implementation Example: Encrypted SMS Messages

The proposed encrypted method can be implemented for mobile devices as an application for secure SMS exchange. The basic idea of such application is very simple and can be described in following steps:

1. associate recipient phone number with appropriate Facebook account,

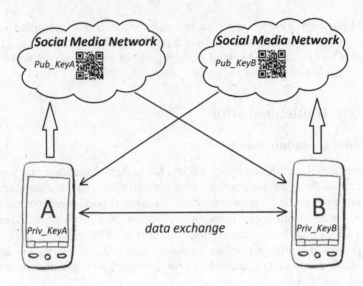

Fig. 5. General communication scheme for an application that uses proposed method

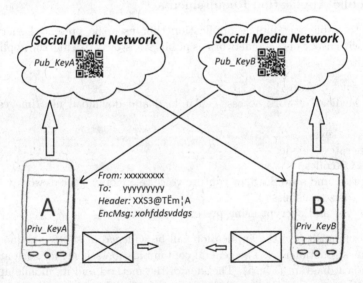

Fig. 6. Text exchange using SMS.

2. download recipient public key from Facebook gallery,
3. create and send encrypted SMS in protocol described bellow (see Fig. 6),
4. receiver's application recognizes SMS as encrypted on the base of header of the data message,
5. decrypt the received SMS.

6.4   Data Frame Format

We propose to use following Frame format to be used in different types of communication: simple data, SMS, voice calls, video, etc. In the paper we discuss the text data transmission. Below we present in Table 2 the example of the data message frame format that can be used in text messages communication, e.g. text SMS messages.

Table 2. Data message frame format.

Frame header of the message	message

In the Table 2 Frame metadata header of the message contains set number of 14 bytes:

- application ID, e.g. XXS3 – 4 bytes, where XX stands for 2 bytes special unique code,
- message type and controls, e.g. data 01000000, new key request, key received, key acknowledged, unrecognized key, etc. – 1 byte,
- timestamp of key generation of the public key (user B) in seconds – 4 bytes; we assume that users will not be able to generate keys in less than 1 s,
- version of the key used – 1 byte, e.g. RSA – 01000001 (letter A),
- message length in bytes – 4 bytes.

The proposed header can vary depending on the medium used, e.g. phone calls. In the text messaging using SMS it can be simplified by omitting the message length part of it. In the case of SMS messages the application uses simplified message header. In the header at Fig. 6 the fields stand for:

- *From: xxxxxxxxx* – source phone number - provided by smartphone of user A,
- *To: yyyyyyyyy* – destination phone number - provided by smartphone of user B; both fields From and To are not contained in the data message frame format,
- Header of the data message: **XXS3@TËm|A** – frame header of the SMS message, where:
  - **XXS3** – application ID (for SMS capturing by the application),
  - **@** - type of the message - data message, (seen as a text),
  - **TËm|** - timestamp as a string (1422618022 as an integer number),
  - **A** - type of encryption method, A stands for RSA,
- *EncMsg: xohfddsvddgs* – encrypted message.

In the SMS messaging the header field message length is not necessary.

After receiving the message the user B application captures the SMS (because of the XXS3 field). The application has to correlate the phone number of the user A with the Social Media profile. The user B application checks other metadata in the header. If the process of the header filtering is successful it proceeds with the message decryption and answering the message if needed. If the process of the header filtering fails it can send control message, e.g. unrecognized key, or user B can abort the later communication with user A. It will depends on the user application setting. The advantage of such a solution is that the users can change the communication channel during the conversation.

7   Conclusions

Nowadays, there is need for secure data exchange and the mobile devices are the most spread tools used for communication. On the other hand most of users does not have enough skills to use sophisticated encryption methods and key exchange protocols. The need for secure communication and the ease of usage are very welcome by the community. The proposal of the method of secure data exchange with everyday social network as key store solves both of the problems. We analyzed in the paper the possibility of the storage of the public key with the use of social media and QRcodes. A few ways of encryption are discussed in order to allow the authentication of the sender. In order to increase efficiency of communication we propose use of symmetric cryptography with appropriate key negotiation. On the other hand the usage of images from a social network gallery makes it easy to be accepted by an ordinary mobile user. The proposed method can be implemented on mobile smartphones. Description of an example of such application was presented. The application will be presented in more detailed manner in next articles.

References

1. Ruoti, S., Kim, N., Burgon, B., van der Horst, T., Seamons, K.: Confused Johnny: when automatic encryption leads to confusion and mistakes. In: Proceedings of the Ninth Symposium on Usable Privacy and Security, pp. 5:1–5:12 (2013)
2. Sheng, S., Broderick, L., Koranda, C.A., Hyland, J.J.: Why Johnny still can't encrypt: evaluating the usability of email encryption software. In: Symposium on Usable Privacy and Security (2006)
3. Narayanan, A., Thiagarajan, N., Lakhani, M., Hamburg, M., Boneh, D.: Location privacy via private proximity testing. In: NDSS (2011)
4. Technical Standardization Committee on AV & IT Storage Systems and Equipment: Exchangeable Image File Format for Digital Still Cameras. In: Version 2.2. Japan Electronics and Information Technology Industries Association, JEITA CP-3451 (2002)
5. ISO 16684-1:2012 Graphic technology – Extensible metadata platform (XMP) specification
6. IPTC Standard Photo Metadata IPTC Core 1.2. International Press Telecommunications Council (2015)
7. Anderson, R., Petitcolas, F.: On the limits of steganography. IEEE J. Sel. Areas Commun. 16, 474–481 (1998)
8. Kessler, G.C., Chet, H.: An overview of steganography. Adv. Comput. 83(1), 51–107 (2011)
9. BS ISO/IEC 18004:2006. Information technology. Automatic identification and data capture techniques. QR Code 2005 bar code symbology specification

10. http://www.qrcode.com/en/codes/
11. Hłobaż, A., Podlaski, K., Milczarski, P.: Applications of QR codes in secure mobile data exchange. In: Kwiecień, A., Gaj, P., Stera, P. (eds.) CN 2014. CCIS, vol. 431, pp. 277–286. Springer, Heidelberg (2014). doi:10.1007/978-3-319-07941-7_28
12. Vidas, T., Owusu, E., Wang, S., Zeng, C., Cranor, L.F., Christin, N.: QRishing: the susceptibility of smartphone users to QR code phishing attacks. In: Adams, A.A., Brenner, M., Smith, M. (eds.) FC 2013. LNCS, vol. 7862, pp. 52–69. Springer, Heidelberg (2013). doi:10.1007/978-3-642-41320-9_4
13. Tamir, C.: AVG (AU/NZ) Cautions: Beware of Malicious QR Codes. PCWorld (2011)
14. Ferguson, N., Schneier, B., Kohno, T.: Cryptography Engineering: Design Principles and Practical Applications. Wiley, New York (2010)
15. Gollmann, D.: Computer Security, 2nd edn. Wiley, New York (2006)
16. Stallings, W.: Cryptography and Network Security: Principles and Practice. Prentice Hall, Upper Saddle River (2010)
17. Nikiforakis, N., Meert, W., Younan, Y., Johns, M., Joosen, W.: Sessionshield: lightweight protection against session hijacking. In: Erlingsson, Ú., Wieringa, R., Zannone, N. (eds.) ESSoS 2011. LNCS, vol. 6542, pp. 87–100. Springer, Heidelberg (2011). doi:10.1007/978-3-642-19125-1_7
18. Adid, B.: Sessionlock: securing web sessions against eavesdropping. In: Proceedings of the 17th International Conference on World Wide Web, pp. 517–524 (2008)
19. Milczarski, P., Podlaski, K., Hłobaż, A.: Applications of Secure Data Exchange Method Using Social Media to Distribute Public Keys. In: Gaj, P., Kwiecień, A., Stera, P. (eds.) CN 2015. CCIS, vol. 522, pp. 389–399. Springer, Heidelberg (2015). doi:10.1007/978-3-319-19419-6_37

CYCLONE

An SDN and CPS Based Opportunistic Upload Splitting for Mobile Users

Maurizio Casoni, Carlo Augusto Grazia, and Martin Klapez[✉]

Department of Engineering "Enzo Ferrari", University of Modena and Reggio Emilia,
via P. Vivarelli 10, 41125 Modena, Italy
{maurizio.casoni,carloaugusto.grazia,martin.klapez}@unimore.it

Abstract. This paper proposes an hybrid approach composed by Software Defined Networking (SDN) and Cyber-Physical Systems (CPS) to boost the upload speed of mobile users in low-bandwidth environments through a next generation Mobile Collaborative Community (MCC). The core idea is to use a high-bandwidth local communication system, like IEEE 802.11 (WiFi), in order to distribute data efficiently through mobile hosts; then, the distributed data may be sent from each mobile node to the original destination through their low-bandwidth mobile interface for wide area network communication. With our solution some drawbacks of MCC are faced. With the use of SDN we defined a flexible and easy-to-configure MCC system which operates in a transparent way for the end hosts. At the same time, the use of CPS creates a feedback for the system regarding the hosts channel status; this way the system is able to fully exploit the MCC potential by increasing the upload speed for both congested and non-congested scenarios. We demonstrate the efficiency of our solution through experimental results obtained using the Mininet network emulator where POX and a Pyretic controller serve as a dynamic data repartition engine.

Keywords: Collaborative networks · CPS · MCC · SDN

1 Introduction

In the last decades, the massive introduction of mobile nodes as well as novel mobile technologies started to steer research in the networking areas. Mobile users are gaining Internet access through a widespread number of wireless technologies, and wireless networks are becoming ubiquitous. This trend has led the industry to introduce technologies for mobile wireless data communication, such as GPRS, EDGE, UMTS, HSPA and LTE. Several research activities attempted to enhance network performance, focusing on the concurrent use of multiple wireless technologies available on a host [1–4].

One possible optimization comes from users collaboration; in fact, almost all the available smartphones can benefit from a high-speed Wireless LAN (WLAN) interface and a Wireless WAN (WWAN) link which may suffer more in terms of performance and stability than the "local" links. The idea of collaboration

© ICST Institute for Computer Sciences, Social Informatics and Telecommunications Engineering 2016
B. Mandler et al. (Eds.) IoT 360° 2015, Part I, LNICST 169, pp. 67–76, 2016.
DOI: 10.1007/978-3-319-47063-4_6

is based on sharing the WWAN link bandwidths with other members of the collaborative network through the high-speed WLAN interface. This approach takes the name of Mobile Collaborative Community (MCC).

Different paradigms are also evolving so as to integrate novel technology and, following an opportunistic and collaborative approach, to provide benefits for end users. An example of this novel solutions are Cyber-Physical Systems (CPS) [5], sometimes also presented as cross-layering solutions for IoT [6]. In such systems the network nodes are exploited both as a computing terminal, as always, but also as sensors. Each node could provide information to a core system in order to maximize some functions like throughput, delay, reliability, security and so on. One of the main challenges of these systems is the complexity introduced in the network sustainability due to the presence of these sensors [7]

A different paradigm investigated in the last years is Software Define Networking (SDN), in which the network data plane is decoupled from its control plane. Following this approach the setup power of a network explodes, giving to specific nodes the possibility to filter and modify IP packet fields, to change the traffic path and to forward packets following a specific optimization function. Again, the optimization could be provided for different figures of merit like throughput, delay, load balancing [8] and so on; even business aspects have been managed through SDN solutions [9].

This two main research areas are starting to be connected to each other [10,11], and that is essentially the purpose of this paper. What we did in this work has been to merge together solutions coming from the SDN world with the CPS one, applied to the MCC problem. Throughout this solution we aim to sensibly improve the upload transfer time of a mobile user by exploiting the resources shared by the LAN neighbors.

The discussion is organized as follows: Sect. 2 summarizes related work. Section 3 describes our proposal. Section 4 introduces the test environment, while Sect. 5 shows the emulation results. In Sect. 6 the conclusions of our work are drawn.

2   Related Work

In this section we revise the literature about collaborative algorithms aimed at boosting network throughput.

Work based on MCCs have been already proposed [12–14] by several authors. In this papers, Ad-hoc MCCs have been proposed as a solution to address communication hurdles. MCC enables two or more persons to aggregate their low-bandwidth mobile network channels to achieve a virtual high-bandwidth channel for collaborative data transfer. At the same time nodes communicate with each other using their high-bandwidth local area network, as instance through IEEE 802.11 (WiFi) links. The main issue of the already proposed approaches is that they involve ISP networks and make use of algorithms that run among terrestrial infrastructures; moreover, they are not transparent for end users, needing host modification and particular scheduling algorithms as well. Last but not least, these works focus on improving downlink speeds, while the upload problem is never considered.

A different yet correlated work proposes some improvements to the MCC topic with PRISM [15], a proxy-based inverse multiplexer that enables TCP to efficiently utilize the community members. This work tries to solve the degradation performance of TCP communications that occur over MCC systems due to frequent out-of-order packet deliveries. Unfortunately, all the issues discussed before for general MCC solutions remain unsolved.

Another interesting work is a packet scheduler called DAPS [16], provided to mitigate TCP issues that incur when different interfaces are used to perform an end-to-end transfer, for example through Multipath TCP (MPTCP). DAPS introduces a smart dispatcher in charge of deciding the balance of traffic among the different interfaces, in order to maintain a linear order of arrival of packets and therefore avoiding the constriction of TCP sender window size. This idea has been revisited in our work, that instead implements an SDN controller to maintain a good balance between different interfaces, in our case represented by different nodes.

3   Solution Description

To introduce the significance of cooperative solutions we explore the context of ad-hoc networks deployed for emergency purposes [17]. We present a scenario that has been extracted from the EU FP7 project Public Protection and Disaster Relief - Transformation Center (PPDR-TC), where there are a certain number of First Responders who connect to a MEOC (Mobile Emergency Operations-Control Centre) that brings to them IEEE 802.11 coverage, thus representing a deployable (and mobile) WiFi common network for operators to exchange data. First Responders may belong to different entities, such as medical personnel, security services or firemen, and it is assumed that each one of them has at disposal a common smartphone/device connected to the respective mobile service. In unplanned disasters, however, terrestrial infrastructures are often damaged or congested, and therefore the capabilities offered by mobile networks are more often than not restricted at least. This scenario is depicted in Fig. 1. It should however be noticed that our proposal is applicable in all environments where the upload speed is constrained or should be maximized, as for example may be a domestic or office WLAN where connectivity suffers significant bandwidth drops or where it is hindered by legacy telephone lines (e.g. ADSL).

Returning to our reference scenario, suppose that a generic field operator wants to upload a file to a remote destination, an operation often needed or desired by PPDR personnel [18]; instead of using its low-bandwidth (or congested) link, this host sends first the file(s) to the MEOC using the high-quality LAN channel. The MEOC then acts as an OpenFlow switch, with an SDN Controller in charge of dynamically dispatching the incoming packets to the other field operators, which in turn *concurrently* forward the packet to the remote destination. Here is where CPS capabilities come into play; assumed that the mobile

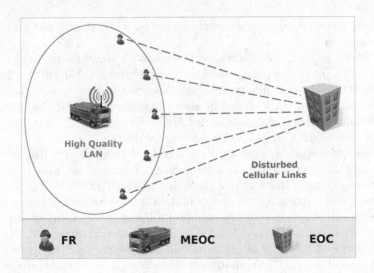

Fig. 1. Reference scenario

link type of a generic field operator is not known in advance to the MEOC, and that operators may belong to different services with different mobile contracts, field hosts may tell the MEOC the bandwidth they have available from the cellular channels with a single packet. Common smartphones have already embedded the capability of automatically detecting the signal quality of a channel; therefore, if the link degrades or, on the contrary, if the link improves (e.g. passing from 2G to 3G), field hosts may communicate the alteration to the MEOC with a simple application that runs in the smartphone user-space. CPS capabilities, however, prove even more useful in trickier cases, as when the signal coverage remains good but performance are degraded by congestion. The application can easily perform a throughput test at pre-determined intervals, and then send a packet to inform the MEOC SDN Controller of the current link capabilities.

4   Emulation Environment

To test the Cyber-Physical Mobile Collaborative Community detailed in the previous Section, we used the Mininet network emulator version 2.2.0 running on a VirtualBox Ubuntu 14.04 Virtual Machine. To manage SDN operations, we used OpenFlow 1.0 as Southbound API, while Pyretic based on POX 0.2.0 has been used to write the controller application that constitutes the Northbound API.

The architecture of the test system is depicted in Fig. 2. The MEOC is composed by a host (inserted only for consistency with the previous discussion, as the MEOC host is ignored in our tests) and an OpenFlow switch. There are five client hosts (representing field operators), each with its own LAN connection to the MEOC and with a specific mobile connection to a remote node. The latters are modeled as specified in Table 1.

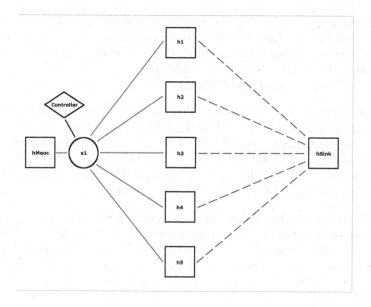

Fig. 2. Test system architecture

Table 1. Links configuration

Client host	Radio technology simulated	Max. upload speed	Latency
h1	EDGE	118 kbit/s	100 ms
h2	EDGE	118 kbit/s	100 ms
h3	UMTS	128 kbit/s	70 ms
h4	HSPA Rel.5 (HSDPA)	384 kbit/s	45 ms
h5	EDGE	118 kbit/s	100 ms

The values in the table have been extracted from [19] and from direct measures conducted by the authors. The LAN channels between client hosts and the MEOC are assumed to be high-quality, and therefore no change to the default Mininet link setup has been made. Because the clients mobile radio channels are operating at low-bandwidth, no change to the default Mininet link setup regarding queue sizes has been made either. In each client host, a Linux Bridge has been configured to forward traffic properly between its two interfaces, and the same holds for the remote node, where all its five interfaces have been bridged; both the "brctl" and "bridge" tools have been used to configure the Linux Bridges.

To measure the upload throughput we used Iperf 2.0.5, running a default Iperf server on the remote node and a default Iperf client on a specific client host (*h1* of Table 1), therefore generating regular TCP traffic. We have chosen to let a host having an EDGE link to be the one that needs uploading data because 2.5G is usually the fallback technology in rural areas or when faster solutions are not available anymore. As Table 1 attests, we chose not to artificially "pump" our results by introducing significantly faster channels in great number. The data rate is calculated on the remote host (*hSink* in Fig. 2).

All tests belong to one of the following cases:

1. *h1* sends data directly to the remote host using its EDGE channel.
2. *h1* sends data to MEOC first, then the MEOC forwards the packets coming from *h1* to hosts *h2*, *h3*, *h4*, *h5* using a Round-Robin (RR) discipline.
3. *h1* sends data to MEOC first, then the MEOC forwards the packets coming from *h1* to hosts *h2*, *h3*, *h4*, *h5* using a Weighted Round-Robin (WRR) discipline, calculated on the basis of CPS information.

Specifically, in the latter case for each packet assigned to a node with an EDGE link the Controller assigns two packets to UMTS links and three to HSDPA links, thus serving the nodes in a Weighted Round-Robin fashion thanks to the knowledge provided by the CPS engine of our proposal. In the latter two cases, the channel between *h1* and the remote host is kept free for TCP Acknowledgement packets.

Last but not least, for each of the aforementioned cases, four different tests have been carried out in order to assess the system performance under different network conditions, i.e. with no or low losses (0 % and 2 % of packet losses, respectively) and with high or very high losses (5 % and 10 % of packet losses, respectively). This brings the total tests configurations to twelve.

The complete testbed with instructions about how to perform these tests is available at [20]. The Section that follows presents tests results.

5   Performance Analysis

First of all, let us discuss about the rationale behind our results selection. Out of a total of 12 test configurations, we performed 10 runs for each of them. As representative of the results, we picked up the average value. The variance itself has not been plotted because the tests were run on a Virtual Machine (VM) (see Sect. 4); unfortunately, due to the nature of VMs, interferences from processes running on the VM host operating system cause the CPU allocation to the VM itself to drop and oscillate. Therefore, we cannot assess at this point if the registered variance is due to this reason or some other, and is thus pointless to plot the relative figures.

Figure 3 reports the results of the first test suite, when no losses occur. The upload data rate of the default configuration (i.e. without any Controller) is equal to 113 kbit/s, a little less than the maximum EDGE throughput which is of 118 kbit/s. With MCC RR, the data rate attests itself to 396 kbit/s, for a 3.5X Speedup, while with MCC WRR the same figure is equal to 424 kbit/s, for a 3.7X Speedup. Please note that a linear growth of network throughput is hindered by the out-of-order delivery of packets.

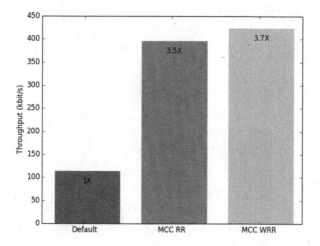

Fig. 3. Upload throughput with no losses

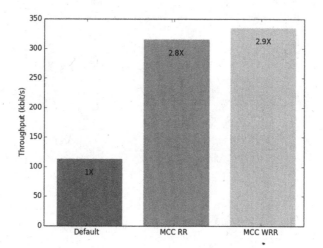

Fig. 4. Upload throughput with 2 % of packet loss

Figure 4 shows the test results with 2 % of packet losses. In this case, with MCC RR the data rate is equal to 315 kbit/s for a 2.8X Speedup, while with MCC WRR the throughput attests to 335 kbit/s, for a 2.9X Speedup.

The improvement given by our proposal starts to decrease significantly when losses are high (i.e. 5 % of packet losses), as Fig. 5 testifies. Here, with MCC RR the throughput is equal to 192 kbit/s, for a 1.7X Speedup, while with MCC WRR the data rate attests to 225 kbit/s for a 2X Speedup.

This behavior is more prominent in case of very high losses (i.e. 10 % of packet losses). Figure 6 shows how with MCC RR the upload speed reaches 140 kbit/s for a 1.2X Speedup, while MCC WRR allows 147 kbit/s for a 1.3X Speedup.

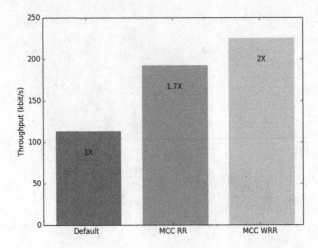

Fig. 5. Upload throughput with 5 % of packet loss

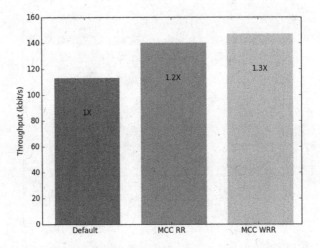

Fig. 6. Upload throughput with 10 % of packet loss

It can be therefore concluded that, even in cases of very high packet losses, our proposal can benefit the end users, although not with the same performance variance seen in more common cases.

In the case of frequent losses, it is not only the out-of-order delivery that hinders the performance growth, but also the necessary TCP retransmissions.

6   Conclusions

In this work, we proposed a Cyber-Physical Mobile Collaborative Community system to enhance upload speeds for client hosts in constrained scenarios.

The proposal is based on an SDN Controller that serves as a dynamic packet dispatcher to neighbor client nodes, that in turn are able to concurrently forward the original packets to their proper destination. This way, it is possible to realize a virtual multipath connection with a solution that is completely transparent for client hosts. Emulation results performed with Mininet confirm that the performance improvement is significant. Furthermore, they point out how the exploitation of CPS capabilities is able to further improve throughput, in a measure that varies from +5 % to +15 % with respect to the MCC system alone.

Acknowledgments. This work was also supported by the European Commission under PPDR-TC, a collaborative project part of the Seventh Framework Programme for research, technological development and demonstration. The authors would like to thank all partners within PPDR-TC for their cooperation and valuable contribution.

References

1. Han, H., Shakkottai, S., Hollot, C.V., Srikant, R., Towsley, D.: Multi-path tcp: a joint congestion control and routing scheme to exploit path diversity in the internet. IEEE/ACM Trans. Netw. **14**(6), 1260–1271 (2006). doi:10.1109/TNET. 2006.886738

2. Carter, C., Kravets, R.: User devices cooperating to support resource aggregation. In: Proceedings Fourth IEEE Workshop on Mobile Computing Systems and Applications 2002, pp. 59–69 (2002)

3. Hsieh, H.-Y., Sivakumar, R.: A transport layer approach for achieving aggregate bandwidths on multi-homed mobile hosts. In: Proceedings of the 8th Annual International Conference on Mobile Computing and Networking, ser., MobiCom 2002, pp. 83–94. ACM, New York (2002). http://doi.acm.org/10.1145/570645.570656

4. Rodriguez, P., Chakravorty, R., Chesterfield, J., Pratt, I., Banerjee, S.: Mar: a commuter router infrastructure for the mobile internet. In: Proceedings of the 2nd International Conference on Mobile Systems, Applications, and Services, ser. MobiSys 2004, pp. 217–230. ACM, New York (2004). http://doi.acm.org/10.1145/ 990064.990091

5. Park, K.-J., Zheng, R., Liu, X.: Cyber-physical systems: milestones and research challenges. Comput. Commun. **36**(1), 1–7 (2012). http://www.sciencedirect.com/ science/article/pii/S0140366412003180

6. Han, C., Jornet, J.M., Fadel, E., Akyildiz, I.F.: A cross-layer communication module for the internet of things. Comput. Netw. **57**(3), 622–633 (2013). http://www. sciencedirect.com/science/article/pii/S138912861200357X

7. Shin, D.-H., He, S., Zhang, J.: Robust and cost-effective design of cyber-physical systems: an optimal middleware deployment approach. IEEE/ACM Trans. Netw. **99**, 1–14 (2015)

8. Adami, D., Giordano, S., Pagano, M., Santinelli, N.: Class-based traffic recovery with load balancing in software-defined networks. In: Globecom Workshops (GC Wkshps), 2014, pp. 161–165 (2014)

9. Adami, D., Donatini, L., Foddis, G., Giordano, S., Roma, S., Topazzi, S.: Design and development of management functions for distributed monitoring based on sdn-based network. In: Euro Med Telco Conference (EMTC), 2014, pp. 1–5 (2014)

10. Skowyra, R.W., Lapets, A., Bestavros, A., Kfoury, A.: Verifiably-safe software-defined networks for cps. In: Proceedings of the 2nd ACM International Conference on High Confidence Networked Systems, ser. HiCoNS 2013, pp. 101–110. ACM, New York (2013). http://doi.acm.org/10.1145/2461446.2461461

11. Qin, Z., Do, N., Denker, G., Venkatasubramanian, N.: Software-defined cyber-physical multinetworks. In: 2014 International Conference on Computing, Networking and Communications (ICNC), pp. 322–326, February 2014

12. Lee, J., Choi, J.-G., Bahk, S.: Opportunistic downlink data delivery for mobile collaborative communities. Comput. Netw. 57(7), 1644–1655 (2013)

13. Jang, I., Suh, D., Pack, S.: Minimizing content download time in mobile collaborative community. In: 2014 IEEE International Conference on Communications (ICC), pp. 2490–2495, June 2014

14. Kim, K.-H., Shin, K.G.: Improving tcp performance over wireless networks with collaborative multi-homed mobile hosts. In: Proceedings of the 3rd International Conference on Mobile Systems, Applications, and Services, ser. MobiSys 2005, pp. 107–120. ACM, New York (2005). http://doi.acm.org/10.1145/1067170.1067183

15. Kim, K.-H., Shin, K.: Prism: improving the performance of inverse-multiplexed tcp in wireless networks. IEEE Trans. Mob. Comput. 6(12), 1297–1312 (2007)

16. Kuhn, N., Lochin, E., Mifdaoui, A., Sarwar, G., Mehani, O., Boreli, R.: Daps: intelligent delay-aware packet scheduling for multipath transport. In: 2014 IEEE International Conference on Communications (ICC), pp. 1222–1227, June 2014

17. Casoni, M., Grazia, C.A., Klapez, M., Patriciello, N.: Integration of satellite and LTE for disaster recovery. IEEE Commun. Mag. 53(3), 47–53 (2015). doi:10.1109/MCOM.2015.7060481

18. PPDR-TC Consortium: PPDR's Needs and Requirements. Project Deliverable D2.2, January 2014

19. Svoboda, P., Ricciato, F., Keim, W., Rupp, M.: Measured WEB performance in GPRS, EDGE, UMTS and HSDPA with and without caching. In: IEEE World of Wireless, Mobile and Multimedia Networks, 2007 (WoWMoM 2007), June 2007

20. Testbed with instructions: netlab.ing.unimo.it/sw/cpmcc.zip

A Cloud-Based Platform of the Social Internet of Things

Roberto Girau, Salvatore Martis, and Luigi Atzori[✉]

Department of Electrical and Electronic Engineering,
University of Cagliari, 09123 Cagliari, Italy
{roberto.girau,salvatore.martis,l.atzori}@diee.unica.it

Abstract. The huge numbers of objects connected to the Internet and that permeate the environment we live in are expected to grow considerably, causing the production of an enormous amount of data to be stored, processed and made available in a continuous, efficient, and easily interpretable manner. Cloud computing can provide the virtual infrastructure that meets these requirements providing the appropriate flexible and powerful tools.

This paper presents a platform that goes in this direction relying on the following features: the PaaS (Platform as a Service) model is fully exploited, for an easy management and development of applications by both users and programmers; each object is an autonomous social agent running in the cloud, according to which objects are capable of establishing social relationships in an autonomous way with respect to their owners with the benefits of improving the network scalability and information/service discovery; the data is under the control of the users, as the data generated by the objects is stored in the objects owners cloud spaces. The paper concludes presenting the implementation of the platform in the Google App Engine PaaS.

Keywords: Social network · Internet of Things · Cloud computing · IoT platform · IoT architecture

1   Introduction

Society is moving towards an always connected paradigm, where the Internet user is shifting from persons to things, leading to the so called Internet of Things (IoT) scenario. In this respect, successful solutions are expected to embody a huge number of smart objects identified by unique addressing schemes providing services to end-users through standard communication protocols. Accordingly, the huge numbers of objects connected to the Internet and that permeate the environment we live in is expected to grow considerably, causing the production of an enormous amount of data that must be stored, processed and made available in a continuous, efficient, and easily interpretable manner. Cloud computing can provide the virtual infrastructure that meets these requirements and can integrate

© ICST Institute for Computer Sciences, Social Informatics and Telecommunications Engineering 2016
B. Mandler et al. (Eds.) IoT 360° 2015, Part I, LNICST 169, pp. 77–88, 2016.
DOI: 10.1007/978-3-319-47063-4_7

sensors, data storage devices, analytic tools and artificial intelligence, management platforms providing services to end-users. Additionally, the pricing model on consumption of cloud computing, enables end-to-end services and access to on demand applications and in any place. At the same time, service oriented technologies, web services, ontologies, semantic web also allow for constructing virtual environments for industrial production and services [1]. Indeed, virtualization technologies can hide the physical characteristics of industrial equipment and devices in general implementing an effective connection, communication and control between the real world and the virtual counterpart.

In the last five years many IoT architectural proposals and implementations appeared in the literature and in the market. A great effort has been devoted in defining architectures and relevant layers functionalities around the concept of virtualizing the physical objects. This is exploited to improve resilience, service discovery and composition as well as to enhance ubiquity. Some of the implementations have been also designed to exploit the cloud computing features, often for the realization of vertical solutions addressing specific application domain requirements. As it is discussed in the following section, we still believe that to fully exploit the potentialities of the IoT paradigm, there is a need for further advancements in designing platforms that: make even easier the communications among objects; help the work of the developers in creating new applications on top of the available objects services; allow the users to have complete control of their own data and objects; are reliable and efficient to support the interaction of trillions of objects.

To further advance in this respect, this paper presents Lysis[1] a cloud-based platform that exhibits the following features: the PaaS (Platform as a Service) model is fully exploited, for an easy management and development of applications by both users and programmers; each object is an autonomous social agent running in the cloud, according to which objects are capable of establishing social relationships in an autonomous way with respect to their owners with the benefits of improving the network scalability and information/service discovery; the data is under the control of the users, as the data generated by the objects is stored in the objects owners cloud spaces. The paper also presents the implementation of the Lysis in the Google App Engine PaaS.

The paper is organized as follows. Section 2 provides some background information about the past architectural solutions and the use of cloud computing and virtualization solutions. Section 3 describes the major layers of the Lysis platform and the key functionalities. Sections 4 and 5 present some implementation details and final conclusions, respectively.

2   Background

The intention of this section is to briefly review the major works in the three major areas of interest for this work.

---

[1] Lysis is the only dialogue of Plato in which the philosopher Socrates discusses the nature of friendship with his disciples.

2.1   IoT Architectures and Objects Virtualization

The main objective of the iCore project [2,3] is to provide a framework for (almost) autonomous IoT application development and it refers to a three level architecture: in the virtual object (VO) level, virtual alter ego of any real-world object (RWO) are dynamically created and destroyed; cognitive technologies guarantee a constant link between RWO and VO and ensure self-management and self-configuration. The iCore framework, has a virtualization level which provides the following functionalities: creation process, naming, addressing, discovery, security, privacy, interfacing and communication. These functionalities are exploited by dedicated central elements like registry, repository and management servers. In the above layer, VOs are aggregated in CVOs (Composite Virtual Objects) to meet application requirements. The last layer is the service layer, which has the role to translate the application requirements into services to be fulfilled by the CVO level through the exploitation of artificial intelligence systems. The iCore team has developed a preliminary prototype, which however has not been devised for being deployed in the cloud. In a similar way, other projects such as COMPOSE [4] and IoT-A [5] exploit virtual counterparts(Service Objects and Virtual Entities respectively) to create IoT applications. The FI-WARE platform [6, 7] is based on elements (Generic Enablers) that permit re-usability and allow for sharing functions on a multiplicity of areas of use in the Internet. In the specific field of the IoT, the FI-WARE has mostly proposed GEs for handling objects communications, resource management, process automation. These are made available to be integrated in other platform but there is not a common framework for an easy deployment of these GEs.

2.2   Cloud in IoT

Many platforms exploit cloud computing features to provide IoT services in industrial environment such as smart home [8], smart cities [9], smart management of inventories [10] and production [11], iHealth [12], environmental monitoring [13], social security and surveillance [14], mine security [15], Internet of Vehicles (IoV)[16]. Although very effective for the purpose they have been proposed, these solutions are too vertical, lacking in horizontal enlarge-ability(cross-applications), de facto limiting their adoption in other IoT application domains. Indeed, in these realizations, domain-specific or project-specific requirements drove the design of all the system components and determine most technological elements ranging from sensors and smart devices to middleware components and application logic. Consequently, most of IoT applications in cloud are designed with a vertical approach as discussed in [17]. In this paper the authors highlight that isolated IoT platforms are implemented like silos and have been also named virtual verticals. Accordingly, any client of IoT solutions owns her own solution virtually isolated from the others and just share the storage and computing resources. They then propose an additional component, named domain mediator to make the different PaaS IoT platforms talk each-other. This issue is also the focus of Gubbi et al. that present a user-centric cloud based model to design new

IoT applications through the interaction of private and public cloud showing an attempt of using cloud computing to provide horizontal solutions [18].

2.3 Distributed Social Objects

There are recent studies demonstrating that the issues related to the management and effective exploitation of the huge numbers of heterogeneous devices could find a solution in the use of social networking concepts and technologies. In [19] the authors introduced the idea of objects able to participate in conversations. In [20] things are involved in social networks with humans. In [21,22], explicitly, the Social IoT (SIoT) concept is formalized, which is intended as a social network where every node is an object capable of establishing social relationships with other things in an autonomous way according to rules set by the owner. Following the specific SIoT paradigm presented in [22], an IoT platform from the open source project ThingSpeak [23] has been developed, which has been extended augmenting the objects with the social attitude. Accordingly, the objects can create the following relationships: the *Ownership Object Relationship* (OOR) is created between objects that belong to the same owner; the *Co-location Object Relationship* (CLOR) is created between stationary devices in the same place, as can be appliances of a dwelling; the *Parental Object Relationship* (POR) is created between objects of the same model, producer and production batch; the *Co-work Object Relationship* (CWOR) is created between objects that meet each others in the owners' workplace as the laptop and printer in the office; the *Social Object Relationship* (SOR) is created as a consequence of frequent encountering between objects, as can happen between smartphones of people who use the same bus every day to go to school/work, people hanging out at the same bar/restaurant/gym.

These features have however been implemented making use of a centralized approach that does not exploit the benefits of a distributed approach that can be achieved by allowing object-to-object direct and autonomous communications.

3   The overall Lysis architecture

In this paper we present an IoT platform called Lysis, which presents four basic features:

- Distributed social objects. The integration of social networking concepts into the Internet of Things has led to the Social Internet of Things paradigm, according to which objects are capable of establishing social relationships in an autonomous way with respect to their owners with the benefits of improving the network scalability in information/service discovery.
- Virtualization and PaaS model. Virtual objects implement the digital counterparts of the physical devices, speak for it and introduce some functionalities that could not be taken by the real world objects such as: supporting the discovery and mash up of services, fostering the creation of complex applications, improving the objects energy management efficiency, as well as making

the inter-objects communications possible by translating the used dissimilar languages. The cloud is the best environment where computing and storage resources can be assigned to the virtual object in a flexible way.

– Data ownership. Users are granted with the required cloud space for storing sensor data and to run simple applications such as trigger actuations, send alerts and visualize log graphs. In the near future, these services will permeate our everyday activities with all our devices connected in the cloud. This process is felt as a strong threat to the user privacy. There is the need for solutions that assure to the user the complete control of the data, which should then be stored in her reserved space.

– Re-usability. Requests for the same data from the same sensors from different IoT applications cause extreme inefficiency in accessing hardware and result in waste in terms of energy consumption and bandwidth, if not handled properly. Re-usability also refers to the code. Specifically, instantiating a new process for the communication with the physical device and processing of the data should not require rewriting code already developed but should relied on sharing of codes among the communities of users and developers. The sharing should be done at all the architectural layers, from the physical devices drivers till the upper most application layer.

Figure 1 shows the overall architecture of the Lysis platform through four functional levels: the lower level is made up of the "things" in the real world; the one above is the virtualization level, which interfaces directly with the real world and is made up of Social Virtual Objects (SVOs); the level of aggregation is responsible for composing different SVOs to set up entities with augmented functionality called Micro Engines (ME); the last level is the application level in which user-oriented macro services (APP) are deployed. In the following subsections we describe the major components, with particular attention to the major above mentioned features.

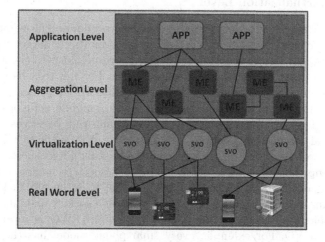

Fig. 1. The four levels of the Lysis architecture.

3.1　The Real World Level

As well-investigated in the iCore project [3], the lowest level is always made up of the Real-World Objects (RWO). Some of these are Physical Devices (PD) capable to directly communicate through the Internet, such as smartphones, laptops and TV set-top-boxes (see Fig. 2(a)). Some others cannot directly access to the internet and have to use local gateways (GW) (see Fig. 2(b)). The PDs and the GWs implement the following modules to be part of the platform:

- Hardware Abstraction Layer (HAL): it communicates with the corresponding module in the virtualization level. Its major role is to introduce a standardized communication procedure between the platform and the extremely variegate set of PDs, simplifying the platform southbound APIs. It is also in charge of creating a secure point-to-point communication (encrypted) with the SVOs.
- Data Handler: it may intervene when there is the need to process data from sensors before being sent by the PD-HAL to the virtualization level. For example, data coming from sensors could be strings of hexadecimals, which have to be processed to extract actual numerical values to encapsulate them in JSON format ready for dispatching.
- Device Management: it implements the real device logic with reference to the participation of the PD to the Lysis platform. It implements most of times simple but key operations like controlling the sensing frequency, managing local triggers, overseeing the energy consumption. It also allows for the running of code that can be updated in run-time locally in the PD.
- Environment interface / protocol adapter: in the case of the PD, it consists in the hardware drivers for all local sensors and actuators. In the case of the GW, it implements the communication with the ICT objects through the available protocol.

3.2　The Virtualization Level

The hardest challenge of the IoT is to be able to address the deployment of applications involving heterogeneous objects, often moving in large and complex environments, in a way that satisfies the quality requirements of the application itself, while not overloading the network resources. For this reasons, the virtual object has become a key component of many IoT platforms, representing the digital counterpart of any real (human or lifeless, static or mobile, solid or intangible) entity in the IoT. It supports the discovery and mash up of services, fostering the creation of complex applications, improving the objects energy management efficiency, as well as addressing heterogeneity and scalability issues.

In our implementation this entity has also a social behavior and for this reason it is named Social Virtual Object. Indeed, it is the abstraction of the RWO in terms of functionalities (i.e., the VO) with a social capability extension (Social Enabler), as shown in Fig. 3. The "Type" of RWO is represented by a *Template* of VO. For example, every smartphone model has the same VO template; however, there is a different VO instance per smartphone PD, which

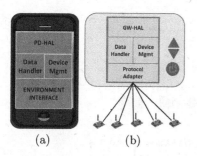
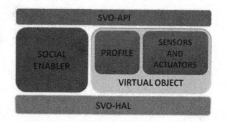

Fig. 2. (a) Physical Devices (PDs) capable to communicate with the platform and (b) objects that need a gateway to interact with the platform.

Fig. 3. The components of the Social Virtual Object

is the actual web service running in the cloud. The template consists of the VO Schema, a semantic description of the related RWO. Capabilities and resources of the real object are depicted inside the VO Schema. The second component of the template is the *Software Agent* source code, which is the computational engine of the VO to be run in the cloud.

The VO Schema can be seen as the semantic description of the class of RWOs of the same type, while the VO Profile is a precise description of the object itself. It is important for the installer to complete the semantic description of the instance of VO to allow a correct search of the resources needed for the creation of services. Data points in the VO represent sensors and actuators and are available through REST APIs, usable by the levels above.

The Social Enabler (SE) extends the functionalities of the VO and, consequently, the related Real World Object by adding social capabilities. The SE is in charge of the socialization of the SVO by allowing the establishment, management and termination of social relations. A social graph connecting each SVO with the others according to their friendships is used to find the services required at the application level. Through type and strength of relationships a trustworthiness value of an object is evaluated to provide a desired service [24].

At SVO level, three classes of permissions are foreseen: public, private and friend. In the first case accessing to the resources is allowed to anyone without the need of any API Key. If the permissions are set to "private" the Owner Key is required. Of course, in this case, applications instantiated by the Owner only are allowed to access to resources. Lastly, if the permissions are set to "friend", the access is allowed only by SVO friends which have a friend API Key.

The SVO search is the functionality the application layer is provided with when there is the need of a service and/or information that can be provided by other objects. A key role is taken by a node called SVO Root (SVOR), which is elected among all the SVOs owned by the same owner. The SVOR accepts requests from the upper levels. Once the SVOR is activated, the first action is to check if the required profile matches its own profile. In this case, the SVOR

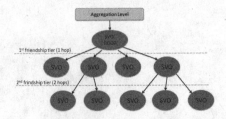

Fig. 4. Objects involved in a SVO search process

responds with its own resources. If it is not the case, it checks its local database if there are matches among its friends. In case of positive result, the SVOR returns the address of the found resource(s) (more than one node may match the profile) and the friend API Key(s) to access to it. In the case of mismatch, the query is forwarded to its friends with high potentials to know the target node or with links with strong network hubs, as shown in Fig. 4. The process is repeated until a positive result is found, which is then returned to the SVOR that sends it to the higher levels. The SVO Root is elected among the SVO in OOR (then belonging to the same user) and among these, the one with the highest value of centrality in the social graph. Since each SVO is able to respond to SVO Search queries, other SVOs in OOR provide the necessary redundancy to the SVOR in case of congestion or malfunctioning. The strength of this system is that there are no single points of failure, and in the case of failing nodes, the network adapts itself by forwarding the requests towards alternative routes of the social graph. In addition, using the SVO with greater centrality decreases the chance of forwarding the request outside the SVO Root.

To deploy SVOs in the cloud, Lysis provides the infrastructural elements shown in Fig. 5. From the Template repository the user chooses the correct Template for the installation of each SVO. The Template is then taken as input by the SVO Deployer, which is in charge of instantiating the agent and giving an initial configuration to SVO. The Deployer works only during the set up phase because once instantiated the SVO is an autonomous web service able to introduce self-updates and manage the communications with its friends as in a human Social Networks.

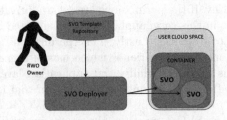

Fig. 5. The SVO deployment process

3.3   The Aggregation Level

The Micro Engine is an entity that is created to implement part of the applications running in the upper layer. It is a mash-up of one or more SVOs and other MEs. With reference to this entity there are two important components: the *Instance* and the *Schema*. The Instance is a piece of programming code running in the cloud. It must be able to reuse the output of an instance to respond to requests that present the same inputs in order to save redundant data requests that consume bandwidth and CPU unnecessarily. It must also be able to understand whether there is a malfunction of one of the input or output, and in this case, requires the reassignment of resources to the control unit. Each ME is described by a Schema that contains a semantic description of the input, the output (if any) and the activity of processing. It also contains a summary of the help that is useful as support for developers using MEs with applications.

Figure 6 shows the elements of the aggregation level. Herein, SVO resources are combined in different MEs, which are entities that inherit some or all of the functionalities of the SVOs and are augmented with more advanced features such as: statistical analysis, data forecasting, artificial intelligent cooperation etc. Associations between MEs and SVOs are managed by the ME Controller. During this phase, the controller triggers the execution of the search operation to find the right SVO and retrieve the related permissions. This SVO Search functionality is the one implemented by the root SVO of the user where the App is running. To be found by the ME Controller, each ME has to be documented in the registry. This element of the aggregation level contains a database of active MEs. Each line of the DB is related to a single ME and contains: the ME ID, the ME URLs, the access permissions, and the time-stamp of the last check.

The Micro Engine Controller is the coordination element of the entire level. When an application at the upper level sends a query for the first time, the MEC checks all the involved ME asking for the related URLs to ME Registry. It asks for SVO Search to the SVO Root of the user who started the application from which takes the owner key. Once it has the resources by the SVOs, it associates

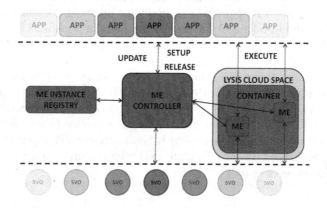

Fig. 6. The ME deployment process

them to the MEs which register the query ID and the required resources (input and output) in the local database. Finally, the MEC notifies the latest ME in the processing chain to the application. That ME will also be the one elected as responder which responds to the queries of the application. communication with its friends as in a human Social Network. Once instantiated, the SVO runs in the user cloud space.

3.4   The Application Level

At this level the applications are deployed and executed exploiting one or more Micro Engines. The interface with the user also assumes a key role; in fact, although we are in the field of the IoT solutions, which are centered around device-device communications, the center of gravity at the end is still the user. An application at this level shows a font-end interface to the user, and a back-end interface to the underlying layers. As for the deployment of SVOs, the users can choose among a list of applications in the relevant repository, and the APP deployer provides for putting the source code in the user cloud space. As discussed for the SVOs, the user is in charge of the running and storage costs.

4   Lysis Prototype Development

To implement Lysis, we chose the Google App Engine (GAE) PaaS as container at the different architectural levels. The choice was guided by the fact that any user is provided with an user-friendly environment where to instantiate 25 free web services. This fact is very important to get an initial population of SVOs allowing people to try this new IoT environment. Furthermore, GAE comes with key useful APIs [25]: Search API and Maps API. The former allowed us to implement on each SVO a template repository of friends by means of document representation enabling full-text search through the social graph; the latter allowed us to use an uniform repository of locations which are needed for the social relations CWOR and CLOR, which rely on information about objects positions. Specifically, the Search API provides a model for indexing documents that contain structured data and supports text search on string fields. The documents and indexes are stored in separate datastores optimized for search operations. It does not fit applications with large result sets; however, it is used in our social environment, where there is a separate database instance for each SVO, with a limited size given by the number of friends. The Search API are principally used during SVO search, according to which an SVO looks for friends that may provide a target service in its local database. The service is available for tests here[2]. It is still under development, but it is already capable to create relationships among registered devices, to manage device resources and to carry out a full text SVO resource search.

---

[2] http://www.lysis-iot.com.

5 Conclusions

In this paper we have presented the IoT platform called Lysis, which presents four major features: it has been designed to exploit the PaaS service model; the Social Virtual Object is a key element; user data and applications are stored and executed in the user cloud space; re-usability of templates and applications is put forward. The implementation of the platform on the Google App Engine PaaS showed that this solution was greatly facilitated by the available API for semantic search and localization. Other important aspects remain to be explored: the issue of task allocation among the real objects and the virtual counterparts through runtime code injection into the real devices; deployment of the SVO in distributed cloud (edge/fog clouds) to follow the physical device to reduce latency; large use-cases deployments.

Acknowledgment. This work has been partially supported by the project "Platform for the deployment of distributed applications in Vanets and WSNs" funded by Telit Communications SpA and by the project SocialMobility, "P.O.R. FESR 2007-2013 Regione Sardegna - Asse VI Competitività 6.2.1 a", CUP F25C10001420008

References

1. Da Xu, L., He, W., Li, S.: Internet of Things in industries: a survey. IEEE Trans. Ind. Inform. **10**(4), 2233–2243 (2014)
2. Foteinos, V., Kelaidonis, D., Poulios, G., Vlacheas, P., Stavroulaki, V., Demestichas, P.: Cognitive management for the Internet of things: a framework for enabling autonomous applications. IEEE Veh. Technol. Mag. **8**(4), 90–99 (2013)
3. ICORE Project: Deliverable 2.1 (2012). http://www.iot-icore.eu
4. COMPOSE Project: Collaborative open market to place objects at your service (2012). http://www.compose-project.eu
5. IoT-A Project. Deliverable 1.4 (2012). http://www.iot-a.eu
6. FIWARE Project (2011). http://www.fiware.org/
7. Glikson, A.: FI-WARE: core platform for future internet applications. In: Proceedings of the 4th Annual International Conference on Systems and Storage (2011)
8. Soliman, M., Abiodun, T., Hamouda, T., Zhou, J., Lung, C.H.: Smart home: integrating internet of things with web services and cloud computing. In: IEEE 5th International Conference on Cloud Computing Technology and Science (CloudCom), vol. 2, pp. 317–320. IEEE (2013)
9. Perera, C., Zaslavsky, A., Christen, P., Georgakopoulos, D.: Sensing as a service model for smart cities supported by internet of things. Trans. Emerg. Telecommun. Technol. **25**(1), 81–93 (2014)
10. Amaral, L.A., Hessel, F.P., Bezerra, E.A., Corra, J.C., Longhi, O.B., Dias, T.F.: eCloudRFIDA mobile software framework architecture for pervasive RFID-based applications. J. Netw. Comput. Appl. **34**(3), 972–979 (2011)
11. Tao, F., Cheng, Y., Da Xu, L., Zhang, L., Li, B.H.: CCIoT-CMfg: cloud computing and Internet of things-based cloud manufacturing service system. IEEE Trans. Ind. Inform. **10**(2), 1435–1442 (2014)

12. Yang, G., Xie, L., Mantysalo, M., Zhou, X., Pang, Z., Da Xu, L., Zheng, L.R.: A health-IoT platform based on the integration of intelligent packaging, unobtrusive bio-sensor, and intelligent medicine box. IEEE Trans. Ind. Inform. **10**(4), 2180–2191 (2014)

13. Fang, S., Da Xu, L., Zhu, Y., Ahati, J., Pei, H., Yan, J., Liu, Z.: An integrated system for regional environmental monitoring and management based on internet of things. IEEE Trans. Ind. Inform. **10**(2), 1596–1605 (2014)

14. Miorandi, D., Sicari, S., De Pellegrini, F., Chlamtac, I.: Internet of things: vision, applications and research challenges. Ad Hoc Netw. **10**(7), 1497–1516 (2012)

15. Sun, E., Zhang, X., Li, Z.: The internet of things (IOT) and cloud computing (CC) based tailings dam monitoring and pre-alarm system in mines. Saf. Sci. **50**(4), 811–815 (2012)

16. He, W., Yan, G., Da Xu, L.: Developing vehicular data cloud services in the IoT environment. IEEE Trans. Ind. Inform. **10**(2), 1587–1595 (2014)

17. Li, F., Vgler, M., Claeens, M., Dustdar, S.: Efficient and scalable IoT service delivery on Cloud. In: IEEE Sixth International Conference on Cloud Computing (CLOUD), pp. 740–747. IEEE (2013)

18. Gubbi, J., Buyya, R., Marusic, S., Palaniswami, M.: Internet of Things (IoT): a vision, architectural elements, and future directions. Future Gener. Comput. Syst. **29**(7), 1645–1660 (2013)

19. Mendes, P.: Social-driven internet of connected objects. In: Proceedings of the Interconn, Smart Objects with the Internet Workshop (2011)

20. Ding, L., Shi, P., Liu, B.: The clustering of internet, internet of things and social network. In: 3rd International Symposium on Knowledge Acquisition and Modeling (KAM), pp. 417–420. IEEE (2010)

21. Atzori, L., Iera, A., Morabito, G.: Siot: Giving a social structure to the internet of things. IEEE Commun. Lett. **15**(11), 1193–1195 (2011)

22. Atzori, L., Iera, A., Morabito, G., Nitti, M.: The social internet of things (siot)when social networks meet the internet of things: concept, architecture and network characterization. Comput. Netw. **56**(16), 3594–3608 (2012)

23. Girau, R., Nitti, M., Atzori, L.: Implementation of an experimental platform for the social internet of things. In: 2013 Seventh International Conference on Innovative Mobile and Internet Services in Ubiquitous Computing (IMIS), pp. 500–505. IEEE (2013)

24. Nitti, M., Girau, R., Atzori, L.: Trustworthiness management in the social internet of things. IEEE Trans. Knowl. Data Eng. **26**(5), 1253–1266 (2014)

25. Google: Google search api. https://cloud.google.com/appengine/docs/java/search/

Stand-Alone Smart Wireless Sensor Nodes Providing Dynamic Routing by Means of Adaptive Beamforming

Roberto Caso[1], Rosario Garroppo[1], Stefano Giordano[1], Giuliano Manara[1],
Andrea Michel[1(✉)], Paolo Nepa[1],
Luca Tavanti[1], Marco Magnarosa[2], and Guido Nenna[2]

[1] Department of Information Engineering, University of Pisa, Pisa, Italy
{r.caso,r.garroppo,s.giordano,g.manara,
a.michel,p.nepa,l.tavanti}@iet.unipi.it
[2] CUBIT s.c.a.r.l., Pisa, Italy
{marco.magnarosa,guido.nenna}@cubitlab.com

Abstract. In this paper, the feasibility of a single integrated autonomous device equipped with WiFI capability is analyzed, discussing its potentiality in the framework of the Internet of Things and Cyber Physical Systems. By equipping photovoltaic panels with sensors and antennas, it is possible to obtain a single stand-alone wireless network node. Specifically, integration of a number of antennas in a large solar panel is suitable to obtain an integrated antenna array. Thus, beamforming techniques can be implemented to electronically orient the array maximum gain radiation, so improving the point-to-point network link.

Keywords: Integration · Slot antennas · PV panel · Solar cells · Stand-alone systems · Wireless sensor networks

1 Introduction

The interest on connecting systems and devices to a whole and unique network is the main topic of a large number of research activities in the last decades. Wireless Sensor Networks (WSNs) have been widely studied and used to create networks of physical devices and systems equipped with sensors and electronics which are able to share data with the other nodes. That is, the Internet of Things (IoT). Such networks allow objects and devices to be remotely monitored and controlled by means of the existing network. Shared data such as temperature, real-time status of electronic devices, humidity can be collected and processed to extract information on the network status. More recently, Cyber-Physical Systems (CPS) have been created. Devices and systems are connected together creating a wide network, and feedback loops are also provided to drive the single nodes. In this way, actuators can be activated to face with environment and system issues. It is clear that these systems have a huge potential from an economic and societal point of view, and investments are being done.

Even though CPS have been largely discussed in the scientific literature, some of the desirable features of a single network node are here summarized:

© ICST Institute for Computer Sciences, Social Informatics and Telecommunications Engineering 2016
B. Mandler et al. (Eds.) IoT 360° 2015, Part I, LNICST 169, pp. 89–98, 2016.
DOI: 10.1007/978-3-319-47063-4_8

- stand-alone, equipped with green power sources such as wind turbines or solar panels;
- equipped with integrated sensors and antennas to provide wireless link in the network;
- dynamic routing capabilities to make the network flexible, reconfigurable and self-healing.

A specific attention has to be paid to the dynamic routing capabilities. Even if the static routing (Fig. 1a) is still used in networks since it is secure, easy to implement in small networks and no routing algorithms are required, dynamic routing (Fig. 1b) is preferable because it makes the network almost scalable and flexible.

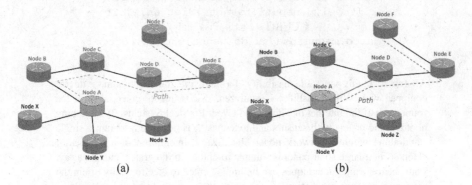

(a)   (b)

Fig. 1. Schematic wireless sensor network with (a) static and (b) dynamic routing.

However, changing the route could be demanding, especially for stand-alone wireless sensor network nodes. Indeed, in outdoor scenarios the links among network nodes are provided by antennas with a specific radiation pattern. If the position of nodes is fixed and known *a-priori*, directional antennas can be used to implement a high-quality radio link. Nevertheless, directional antennas are characterized by a narrow radiation pattern, and

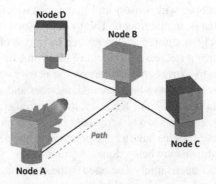

Fig. 2. In a static routing, the wireless link between two nodes can be optimized by using specific directional and high-gain antennas, since the relative position of the two nodes is a-priori known.

point-to-point links must be carefully set-up – a slight misalignment between the transmitting and receiving antennas could lead to a reduced radio link performance. Thus, static routing can be implemented by means of directional antennas. (Fig. 2).

On the other hand, if the nodes are not fixed (*e.g.* cars or drones could be nodes of a wireless sensor network), dynamic routing is preferable since the network topology changes. However, directional antennas are not suitable anymore – the position of nodes is not known *a-priori*. Thus, omnidirectional antennas are typically used, even though they are characterized by a fairly low gain. To improve the wireless link performance, directional antennas could be used and beamforming algorithms can be implemented to orient the maximum gain toward a specific direction. For example, Node A in Fig. 3 can scan the azimuthal plane and orient the radiation pattern toward Node C (Fig. 3a) or Node D (Fig. 3b), creating new paths set by dynamic routing.

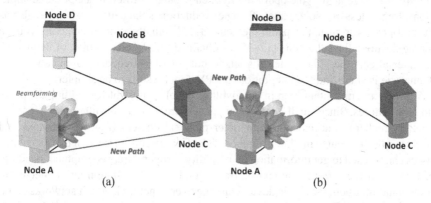

Fig. 3. In a dynamic routing, the wireless link between two nodes is not a-priori set. Therefore, beamforming capabilities can be implemented in order to orient the antenna maximum gain direction toward a diverse node.

The beamforming capability can be obtained by equipping the network node with an array of antennas and by setting a proper input current phase for each radiating element. Thus, phase shifters are needed. Microcontroller or microprocessors are also required to be remotely controlled in order to select the currents phase. Since the wireless nodes could be arranged in rural scenarios where wired feeding networks are not available, stand-alone power sources must be considered for each single node. For example, wind turbines or photovoltaic panels are effective in providing power to the network nodes.

In particular, photovoltaic (PV) energy is widely used in autonomous communication system due to its eco-friendliness and reliability. In 2009 it was estimated that at the end of this century the solar power generation will account for more than 60 % of world's totally [1]. To date, solar panels are used in some stand-alone wireless communication systems, especially in isolated environments. However, PV panel, sensors and antenna are separate elements of the same system, causing relatively great space employment, engineering and design problems. Therefore a compromise in the utilization of the limited available space is needed and sensor and antennas integration in PV panel is desirable.

Several studies have been carried out in order to assess the possibility of integrating antennas in solar cells and photovoltaic panels. For example, researchers are interested in innovative transparent antenna, made by TCOs (Transparent Conductor Oxides) [2, 3]. These antennas may represent a good integrated solution because they can be easily integrated in after-market solar cell. However these TCOs are still relatively expensive and with the existing technological capabilities is not easy to obtain a 90 % sunlight transparency, needed for the proper functioning of the solar cell [3].

Since solar cells are fabricated with conductive materials, they may be used as a radiating patch [4] or as a coupled patch [5–7]. However, in these cases the cell dimensions are strictly related to the operating frequency band, restricting the possible applications. Regardless of a solar panel efficiency reduction, solar cells may be used also as a ground plane for an upper patch element [8–11]. Finally, slot antennas have been integrated among the solar cells [12–15] or obtained by properly etching of them [16]. The latter affects the solar panel efficiency, but for high frequency applications the antenna size is small and the integration in a PV panel results to be simpler.

Anyway, antenna integration in photovoltaic panels is possible, providing the panel with new features. Since small photovoltaic panels are used in consumer products such as battery recharger, access points or other personal devices (Fig. 4), antennas and sensors can be distributed in a large number of electronic items. In some of these systems, sensors can be used to get information on humidity, temperature, geographical position, etc. Hence, all the information can be transmitted to a base station and collected to remotely monitor both the single devices and the overall network. Mesh networks could be design by using all these devices, creating a wide wireless sensor network.

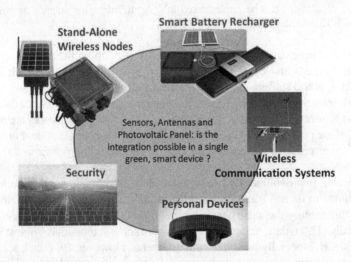

Fig. 4. Examples of applications in which sensors, antennas and photovoltaic panels could be integrated in a unique device.

In this paper, the potentiality of a Wireless Sensor Network composed by autonomous nodes equipped with integrated sensors and antennas is investigated. To improve the link quality, smart PV panels can be equipped with more than one antenna. Indeed, exploiting the available space between the solar cells, a planar array can be obtained, providing the PV panel with beamforming capabilities. As a result, the maximum gain direction can be oriented by means of phase shifters, pointing toward the network node selected by dynamic routing algorithms.

2 Preliminary Results on the Integrated Array

In the previous section, some PV panel integrated antennas are described. In order to obtain a low-cost antenna solution without affecting the PV panel solar efficiency, the integrated antennas are designed to exploit the available space among adjacent solar cells where only a cover glass layer is present above the radiating element. A typical commercial PV panel has been considered for the antenna design. It is composed by 36 156-mm-side monocrystalline silicon (m-Si) square solar cells, which are incorporated between two ethylene vinyl acetate (EVA) layers. The cells plane is covered on the top and bottom side by two glass layers, for an overall thickness of about 8 mm. The solar cells are separated from a distance of 25 mm each other. In Fig. 5a, a potential position of a slot antenna among square solar cells is shown (dark color). The top view of the proposed antenna is also shown in Fig. 5b. This antenna is characterized by low cost materials and easy-integration in a PV panel (Fig. 5c), in order to obtain a cost limitation of the manufacturing process. The radiating element has been presented in [14, 15] and here optimized for WiFi applications. The geometrical parameters of the final design are listed in Table 1.

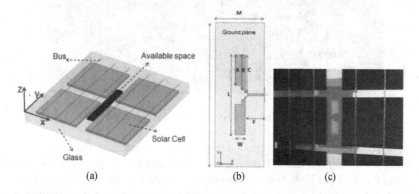

(a)   (b)   (c)

Fig. 5. The antenna presented in [14] has been here optimized for WiFi applications: (a) potential position of a slot antenna among square solar cells (b) top view of the proposed antenna and (c) antenna prototype integrated in a commercial PV panel.

Table 1.

ANTENNA DIMENSIONS, MM			
N	200	A	27.6
M	45	B	28.8
L	67.5	C	30.3
W	5.6	F	18.3

In [15], WiFi antennas have been integrated in a photovoltaic panel, and some tests have been carried out. Specifically, the slot antenna performance in terms of measured reflection coefficient, received signal power and goodput results is described and compared with that of a commercial dipole. The experimental analysis of the overall integrated system shows that the performance of the developed antenna integrated in the PV panel are no worst, or even better than the commercial antenna one.

Consequently, similar tests have been repeated by using two antennas integrated in two separate PV panels, creating a panel-to-panel WiFi link. In Fig. 6 the measurement scenario is shown.

Fig. 6. The measurement setup for the panel-to-panel tests.

The two panels are equipped with two integrated WiFi antennas. Both antennas were connected to two laptops through the TL-WN722 N modules [17]. Thus, the received power and the goodput have been measured as a function of the distance between the two panels. The results are shown in Fig. 7. With only a single radiating element and a transmission power of 20dBm, the two photovoltaic panels can communicate beyond 100 m of distance, which is suitable for a large variety of applications.

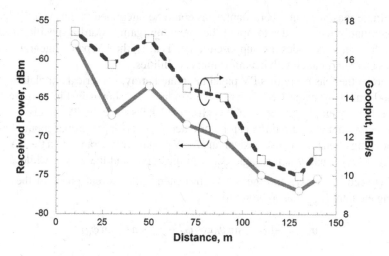

Fig. 7. Panel-to-panel WiFi link performance in terms of received power and goodput, as a function of the distance between the two PV panels.

The measured performance on the WiFi integrated antenna demonstrated that a single, integrated, photovoltaic panel can be fabricated and used as an autonomous node of a Wireless Sensor Network. However, a specific attention has to be paid on the photovoltaic panel orientation. It is clear that the solar cells must be oriented toward the sun in order to maximize the power generation. On the other hand, two communicating network nodes can be arbitrarily positioned in the open space. Moreover, if a dynamic routing is implemented or the network nodes position changes (*i.e.* mobile nodes), the smart panel has to be "smart" and able to orient the maximum gain direction toward the node position.

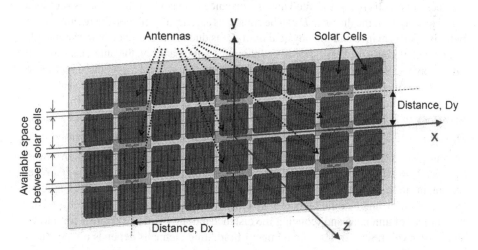

Fig. 8. WiFi antennas have been integrated in a photovoltaic panel to obtain a 3 × 3 array.

For these reasons, a number of antennas could be integrated in the same PV panel, and opportunely fed in order to orient the maximum gain toward a specific direction where other network nodes are supposed to be. That is, the PV panel integrated array provides the smart panel with beamforming capabilities.

To prove the feasibility of a PV panel integrated array, numerical simulations have been performed by using CST Microwave Studio®. As shown in Fig. 8, nine WiFi antennas have been placed between the cells of a 4×9 solar cells PV panels.

The maximum gain direction can be oriented by choosing a proper input phase of each radiating element. Let us consider an $M \times N$ planar array arranged on the XY plane as in Fig. 8. As usual, θ is the angle between the z-axis and the x-axis, while ϕ is the angle between the x-axis and the y-axis. In general, the current phase of the $(m,n)^{th}$ radiating element $(\alpha_{m,n})$ has to be set to

$$\alpha_{mn} = -\beta \left(x_{mn} \sin \theta_0 \cos \phi_0 + y_{mn} \sin \theta_0 \sin \phi_0 \right)$$

where

- β is the wavenumber in free space, and it is directly proportional to the operating frequency;
- $(x_{m,n}, y_{m,n})$ represents the position of the $(m,n)^{th}$ element in the XY plane;
- (θ_0, ϕ_0) represents the direction where the gain has to be maximized.

The distance D between two adjacent radiating elements plays an important role in the array radiative performance. In particular, the higher the distance between the antennas (but lower than λ which represents the free-space wavelength), the higher is the gain. However, the distance D is also strictly related to the radiation pattern characteristics in case of beamforming (for example, for large distances D the grating lobes phenomenon could appear). Nevertheless, the distance between the radiating elements, is highly affected by the presence of the radiating cells. Indeed, the available space between solar cells rows is limited and the distance between two free slots is set by the cell size. Anyway, the distance D can be chosen as a trade-off between the required array radiative performance and the physical limitations due to the presence of the solar cells.

To better assess the feasibility of an integrated antenna array, the antennas shown in Fig. 8 have been properly fed to maximize the radiation toward a specific direction. In Fig. 9 the normalized radiation patterns of the 3×3 array of PV panel integrated antennas for WiFi applications are shown for the XZ plane (Fig. 8), by considering a fixed frequency of 2445 MHz. In particular, the distance D_X is set to 85 mm and the distance D_Y is set to 125 mm which corresponds to the typical solar cells size. Therefore, input current phases have been computed in order to orient the main lobe direction toward $\theta_0 = 0°$, $\theta_0 = 10°$ and $\theta_0 = 30°$ - for the sake of simplicity we assumed $\varphi_0 = 0°$. When the main lobe is tilted toward $\theta_0 = 30°$, the side lobe level is not negligible (SLL = -4 dB), and it could be not satisfactory for communication systems. Increasing the number of antennas and reducing the distance among them could allow for a lower side lobe level; however, also the number of radiating elements depends on the photovoltaic panel size.

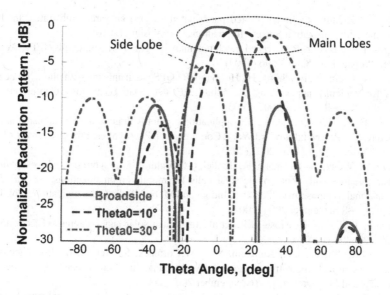

Fig. 9. Normalized radiation pattern of the 3 × 3 array of PV panel integrated antennas for WiFi applications.

3   Conclusion

Solar panels allow communication systems to be stand-alone, without the need of wired-feeding networks. That is, they can be installed and used in wild and rural environments. Arranging small devices equipped with green power sources (*e.g.* PV panels or wind turbine) in outdoor scenarios could represent a valuable solution for remote control and management of isolated areas. Moreover, wireless sensor and mesh networks can be constructed to collect and share data. Integrated sensors and antennas in the same autonomous device represent a challenge for the future Internet of Things. In this paper, the feasibility of an array of antennas integrated in a single photovoltaic panel has been investigated. Preliminary numerical results have been also presented, confirming that beamforming techniques can be implemented to orient the integrated array maximum gain direction toward a wireless network node, improving the overall network performance. This opens also to the possibility of performing dynamic routing with high directional antennas. By steering the beam in accordance with the routing decision, the maximum gain can be aligned towards the node the traffic is destined to.

References

1. Yan, H., Zhou, Z., Lu, H.: Photovoltaic industry and market investigation. In: International Conference on Sustainable Power Generation and Supply, (SUPERGEN 2009), pp. 1–4, 6–7 April 2009 (2009)
2. Roo-Ons, M.J., Shynu, S.V., Ammann, M.J., McCormack, S.J., Norton, B.: Transparent patch antenna on a-Si thin-film glass solar module. Electron. Lett. **47**(2), 85–86 (2011)

3. Yasin, T., Baktur, R.: Inkjet printed patch antennas on transparent substrates. In: IEEE Antennas and Propagation Society International Symposium (2010)
4. Turpin, T.W., Baktur, R.: Meshed patch antennas integrated on solar cells. IEEE Antenna Wirel. Propag. Lett. **8**, 693–696 (2009)
5. Henze, N., Giere, A., Friichting, H., Hofmann, P.: GPS patch antenna with photovoltaic solar cells for vehicular applications. In: 58th IEEE Vehicular Technology Conference Fall, Orlando, US, 6–9 October 2003 (2003)
6. Bendel, C., Kirchhof, J., Henze, N.: Application of photovoltaic solar cells in planar antenna structures. In: Proceedings of 3rd World Conference on Photovoltaic Energy Conversion, vol. 1, pp. 220–223, 11–18 May 2003 (2003)
7. Henze, N., Weitz, M., Hofmann, P., Bendel, C., Kirchhof, J., Fruchting, H.: Investigation of planar antennas with photovoltaic solar cells for mobile communications. In: 15th IEEE International Symposium on Personal, Indoor and Mobile Radio Communications, vol. 1, pp. 622–626, 5–8 September 2004 (2004)
8. Vaccaro, S., Torres, P., Mosig, J.R., et al.: Integrated solar panel antennas. Electron. Lett. **36**(5), 390–391 (2000)
9. Ons, M.J.R., Shynu, S.V., Ammann, M.J., McCormack, S., Norton, B.: Investigation on proximity-coupled microstrip integrated PV Antenna. In: 2nd European Conference on Antennas and Propagation, 11–16 November 2007 (2007)
10. Shynu, S.V., Ammann, M.J., Norton, B.: Quarter-wave metal plate solar antenna. Electron. Lett. **44**(9), 570–571 (2008)
11. Shynu, S.V., Ons, M.J.R., McEvoy, P., Ammann, M.J., McCormack, S.J., Norton, B.: Integration of microstrip patch antenna with polycrystalline silicon solar cell. IEEE Trans. Antenna and Propag. **57**(12), 3969–3972 (2009)
12. Danesh, M., Long, J.R.: Compact solar cell ultra-wideband dipole antenna. In: IEEE Antennas and Propagation Society International Symposium (2010)
13. Wu, T., Li, R.L., Tentzeris, M.M.: A mechanically stable, low profile, omni-directional solar cell integrated antenna for outdoor wireless sensor nodes. In: IEEE Antennas and Propagation Society International Symposium (2009)
14. Caso, R., D'Alessandro, A., Michel, A., Nepa, P.: Integration of slot antennas in commercial photovoltaic panels for stand-alone communication systems. IEEE Trans. Antenna Propag. **61**(1), 62–69 (2013)
15. Michel, A., Caso, R., Tavanti, L., Gazzarrini, L., Garroppo, R., Nepa, P.: Design and performance analysis of a slot antenna integrated in a photovoltaic panel. In: IEEE Antennas Propagation Society International Symposium (APSURSI), pp. 1–2, 8–14 July 2012 (2012)
16. Shynu, S.V., Ons, M.J.R., Ammann, M.J., Norton, B., McCormack, S.: Dual band a-Si:H solar-slot antenna for 2.4/5.2 GHz WLAN applications. In: 3rd European Conference on Antennas and Propagation, pp. 408–410, 23–27 March 2009 (2009)
17. http://www.tp-link.com/en/support/download/?model=TL-WN722N

A Centrality-Based ACK Forwarding Mechanism for Efficient Routing in Infrastructureless Opportunistic Networks

Sanjay K. Dhurandher[1], Isaac Woungang[2](✉), Anshu Rajendra[1],
Piyush Ghai[1], and Periklis Chatzimisios[3]

[1] CAITFS, Netaji Subhas Institute of Technology,
University of Delhi, New Delhi, India
dhurandher@gmail.com, {anshurajendra,piyushghai}@nsitonline.in
[2] Department of Computer Science, Ryerson University, Toronto, Canada
iwoungan@scs.ryerson.ca
[3] Department of Informatics, ATEITHE, Thessaloniki, Greece
peris@it.teithe.gr

Abstract. In the next generation Internet, it is expected that human, smart devices, and "things" will be able to communicate and interact with each other opportunistically in order to share their data. An analysis of this type of relationship is made possible due to the advent of the Opportunistic Internet of Things (OppIoT), a new paradigm that enable information sharing and dissemination among opportunistic communities formed based on human mobility and opportunistic contacts. Designing data dissemination and routing protocols for opportunistic IoT is a challenge since contacts between nodes and users' social behaviors are to be tighten together as design constraints. Nonetheless, as opportunistic networking rely on spontaneous connectivity between the users and wireless devices, it can be argued that OppIoT is a form of opportunistic social networks (OppNets) extension, with focus on the relationship between human and opportunistic connection of smart things. As such, some routing protocols that have been designed to work for infrastructureless OppNets can also be applied in OppIoT systems. In this context, the History Based Routing Protocol for Opportunistic Networks (HiBOp) is an appealing choice. In this paper, an acknowledgement (ACK) forwarding mechanism to boost the performance of HiBOp is proposed based on the concept of centrality. Simulation results are provided, showing that HiBOp with centrality outperforms HiBOp in terms of predefined performance metrics.

Keywords: Opportunistic networks (OppNets) · Centrality · ACK · Routing protocol · HiBOp

1 Introduction

The next generation Internet is expected to provide facilities for human and smart things to connect and interact with each other. Examining the social

© ICST Institute for Computer Sciences, Social Informatics and Telecommunications Engineering 2016
B. Mandler et al. (Eds.) IoT 360° 2015, Part I, LNICST 169, pp. 99–108, 2016.
DOI: 10.1007/978-3-319-47063-4_9

side of Internet of Things (IoT) from a human-centric perspective is the goal of OppIoT [1], a novel computing paradigm and technology that promotes the idea that smart 'things' can be opportunistically connected with human user by means of short-range communication and sensing technologies. Typically, an OppIoT system can be viewed as an ad hoc infrastructureless OppNet architecture of devices that can enable data sharing and dissemination within opportunistic communities formed based on human mobility and opportunistic contacts. In [1], a reference architecture for the development of an OppIoT system is proposed. In contrast, in infrastructureless oppNets [2,3], an instantaneous connectivity is established among the users equipped with wireless devices, forming a kind of decentralized ad hoc network that allows inter-device data routing and forwarding. The sender of a message has no proof of knowledge about its delivery and node mobility is exploited to send the messages in a disconnected environment based on opportunistic communication. In such environment, the transmission and reception of ACK messages remains an issue that has not been addressed by existing routing schemes. Indeed, OppNets make no prior assumption about the network topology and evaluate the delivery probability of a node based on a forwarding strategy, taking into account the limited time in which nodes are in the radio range of each other. Typically, each node has a limited buffer storage; hence, messages drop, node failure, or incomplete transmission may occur, if this buffer is not properly managed.

Unlike conventional flooding techniques, HiBOp [3] makes use of a context-based knowledge to calculate the delivery probability from a sender to a receiver, but the ACK management and buffer saturation are not considered in its design. In this paper, a centrality-based mechanism for the delivery of ACKs from destination to source is implemented on top of HiBOp to help clearing the buffers of residual messages, leading to an enhancement in message delivery.

The rest of the paper is organized as follows. In Sect. 2, some routing protocols for OppNets are discussed. Section 3 describes our proposed ACK forwarding mechanism. Section 4 presents some simulation results. In Sect. 5, we conclude the paper.

2   Related Work

Several routing protocols have been proposed for OppNets [4–8], most of which are based on the principle of deciding which messages are to be forwarded or dropped when a peer comes in contact with another as the buffer reaches its maximum capacity. The Epidemic protocol [4] uses a flooding technique with no limit on the buffer capacity. The Spray and Focus protocol [5] utilizes a form of controlled flooding technique to send the messages. The Prophet+ [6], MaxProp [7], HBPR [8] and HiBOp [3] protocols all exploit some form of context-based information to calculate the node's delivery probability. The data processing overhead in these protocols calls for an efficient ACK mechanism to prevent buffer saturation. The HiBOp protocol [3] relies on the following data structures: Identity Table - used by nodes to learn about the context in which they are currently immersed in (e.g. home and work locations, name, etc.); Current Context Table - this stores all Identity Tables of neighbors of a node; History Table - this keeps track of the past information seen by the current node; and Repository Table - used for updating the History Table. Based on these data structures, the delivery probability of a node is estimated. Accordingly, a limited number of neighbors of a node are retained as best candidates for message forwarding purpose.

3 Proposed Centrality-Based ACK Forwarding Mechanism

In HiBOp [3], no ACK mechanism is provided to confirm to the source that a message has been successful delivered. This has motivated the following changes to the design of HiBOp: a list of ACK message IDs is maintained at each node. Whenever two nodes meet each other, the Current Context is updated, and the exchange of ACKs takes place as described in Algorithm 2. Nodes whose ACKs have been received by the source thus relieve their respective buffers. On the other hand, those ACKs which have not yet reached their respective senders (after a timeout period) are forwarded to the best nodes filtered according to the centrality parameter. This parameter exploits the fact that central nodes in the network have the maximum connectivity and will more likely be part of the routing path that is being build on the fly. The home and work locations are used to calculate the centrality of a node as described in Algorithm 1. This algorithm checks whether the node's location has changed or not. If the node is mobile, the previous value of the centrality is retained. Else, the centrality values at home and at work are calculated.

Algorithm 1. Calculation of the centrality of a node.

Fetch the location of the node
if Location = Old Location **then**
    $Centrality \leftarrow OldCentrality$
else if Location = Home Location **then**
    Calculate centrality C_h at home
    $Centrality \leftarrow C_h$
else if Location = Work Location **then**
    Calculate centrality C_w at work
    $Centrality \leftarrow C_w$
end if
$Centrality \leftarrow Max(C_h, C_w)$
return

Forwarding the ACK message takes into account the centrality with respect to the message. Using Algorithm 1, the most central node on the path followed by the message being transmitted from source to destination is identified and appended to the message. Its *centrality value* is updated on each successive hop of the message subject to some conditions. While sending an ACK, the destination first sends it to the node with maximum centrality on the path taken by the message (as per Algorithm 2). If the destination is not in direct contact with this central node, it forwards the ACK to its most central neighbor (i.e. node with the highest centrality value) for further forwarding. This process continues recursively until the ACK reaches within one-hop distance of the source. Upon receipt of this ACK, the source then clears its buffers of residual messages. Note that during this process, no copy of the ACK is kept within the current node.

Algorithm 2. Forwarding and Exchange of ACK Messages

---

for all message m in Buffer do
   $CentralNode \leftarrow CentralNode$ of m
   if CurrentNode $= CentralNode$ then
      Determine the next Central Node id and append it to m
      if OtherNode $= CentralNode$ then
         Forward the ACK and clear the buffer
         if $OtherCentrality \geq CurrentNodeCentrality$ then
            Forward the ACK and clear the buffer
         end if
      end if
   end if
end for
return

---

4   Simulation Results

The ONE simulator [9] is used, along with the Working Day movement model and a network consisting of 8 groups of 50 nodes each. Each node is initially at its home (or work) location, then travels towards its work (or home) location at a random speed chosen in the range 7–10 m/s after an initial rest period. For generating some randomness in the movement of the nodes, a shopping probability of 0.5 is assumed. This process continues throughout the simulations, causing some dynamic changes in the network topology. It is also assumed that the interpersonal communication between mobile users holds using mobile phones or Bluetooth devices at 2 Mbits/s data rate, with 10 m radio range. Messages are generated randomly by the nodes every 25–35 s. Other main simulation are captured in Tables 1 and 2.

The studied protocols are compared in terms of message throughput over different simulation time intervals. The results are captured in Fig. 1. It is observed that HiBOp with centrality outperforms HiBOp with respect to that metric. This is attributed to the efficient routing of the ACKs that occurs when HiBOp with centrality is used, leading to a reduced buffer occupancy by messages.

Next, HiBOp with centrality is compared against HiBOp in terms of Message Loss when the TTL, buffer size, and Working Day Length are varied respectively.

Table 1. Simulation parameters

Parameter	Value
Signaling interval	5 s
Death interval	10 s
Repository flushing interval	1800 s
Flushing Interval	10 s
Default message size	500 KB–1 MB
Default buffer size	50 M

Table 2. Mobility parameters

Parameter	Value
Message TTL	300 min
Number of offices	50
Default work day length	15 h
Repository flushing interval	1800 s
Shopping probability	0.5
Office size	10
Minimum office wait time	10 s
Maximum office wait time	10000 s

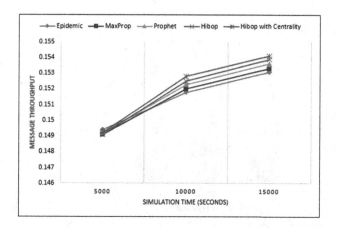

Fig. 1. Message throughput under varying simulation times

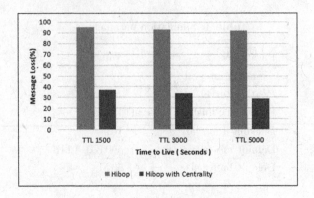

Fig. 2. Message loss under varying TTL

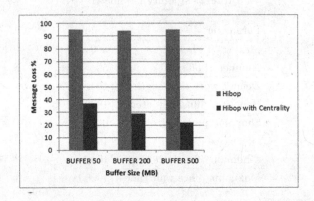

Fig. 3. Message loss under varying buffer size

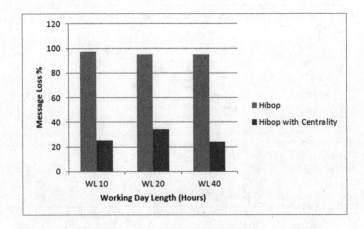

Fig. 4. Message loss under varying Working Day Length

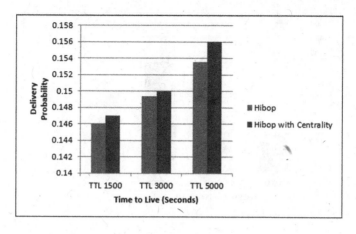

Fig. 5. Delivery probability over varying TTL

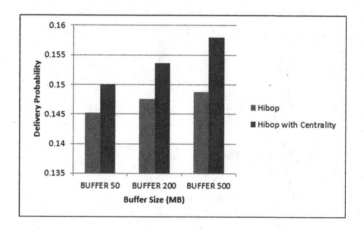

Fig. 6. Delivery probability over varying buffer size

The results are captured in Figs. 2, 3, and 4 respectively, where the Message Loss is obtained:

$$MessageLoss = \frac{Number\ of\ messages\ dropped}{Number\ of\ messages\ generated}$$

In Fig. 2, it is observed that under varying TTL, there is a significant reduction in the Message Loss (about 75–80 %) when HiBOp with centrality is used. Similar results prevail when the buffer size and Working Day Length are varied respectively (as shown in Figs. 3 and 4). When the buffer size and TTL increases respectively, it is observed that the number of Message Loss decreases.

Next, HiBOp with centrality is compared against HiBOp in terms of delivery probability when the TTL and buffer size are varied respectively. The results are

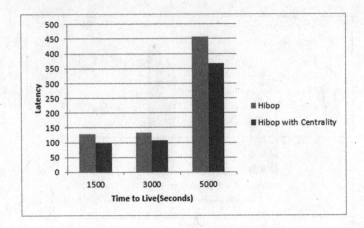

Fig. 7. Latency over varying TTL

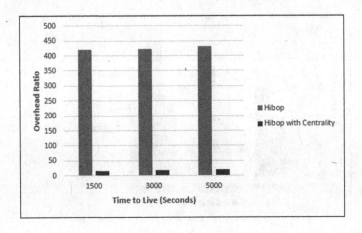

Fig. 8. Overhead ratio over varying TTL

captured in Figs. 5 and 6. In Fig. 5, it is observed that HiBOp with centrality performs better than HiBOp, even with the space constraints introduced by the buffer size. The improvement is in the order of about 5–10 %. This is attributed to the low message loss generated by HiBOp with centrality (compared to that obtained from HiBOp). In Fig. 7, it is observed that HiBOp with centrality yields an improved latency compared to HiBOp (about 30 % improvement). In Fig. 8, it is observed that there is a significant improvement in the buffer overhead generated by HiBOp with centrality compared to that generated by HiBOp (about 90–95 % improvement).

Finally, MaxProp is compared against HiBOp with centrality in terms of buffer occupancy, traffic overhead, and latency. The results are captured in Fig. 9. In Fig. 9, it can be observed that HiBOp with centrality yields an improvement

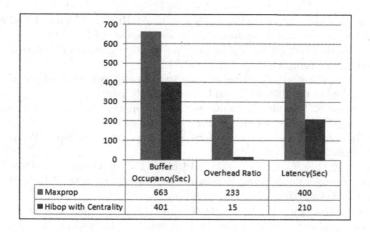

	Buffer Occupancy(Sec)	Overhead Ratio	Latency(Sec)
■ Maxprop	663	233	400
■ Hibop with Centrality	401	15	210

Fig. 9. HiBOp with centrality vs. MaxProp

over HiBOp of about 40 % in terms of buffer occupancy, 50 % in terms of latency, and 90 % in terms of traffic overhead. The above results illustrate the advantages of using our proposed ACK mechanism as a way to reinforce the routing in OppNets.

5   Conclusion

In this paper, a novel approach for the routing of ACKs based on the concept of centrality has been proposed, leading to an enhancement of the HiBOp routing protocol for OppNets. Due to its generic nature, the proposed centrality-based ACK mechanism can be implemented on top of any known routing protocols for OppNets. Simulation results have shown that: (1) this mechanism can significantly reduce the message loss rate while preserving the performance of HiBOp; (2) HiBOp with centrality outperforms the MaxProp protocol in terms of buffer occupancy, traffic overhead, and latency. As future work, the proposed centrality-based ACK mechanism can further be assessed by considering other realistic movement models. In addition, the calculation of the centrality of a node assumes a direct relation to the number of active connections of a node. Other factors such as the duration of active connections can be considered in this calculation.

References

1. Guo, B., Zhang, D., Wang, Z., Yu, Z., Zhou, X.: Opportunistic IoT: exploring the harmonious interaction between human and the Internet of Things. J. Netw. Comput. Appl. **36**(6), 1531–1539 (2013)
2. Boldrini, C., Conti, M., Delmastro, F., Passarella, A.: Context and social-aware middleware for opportunistic networks. J. Netw. Comput. Appl. **33**(5), 525541 (2010)

3. Boldrini, C., Conti, M., Jacopini, J., Passarella, A.: HiBOp: a history based routing protocol for opportunistic networks. In: Proceedings of IEEE International Symposium on World of Wireless, Mobile and Multimedia Networks (WoWMoM 2007), Helsinki, 18–21 June 2007, pp. 1–12 (2007)

4. Vahdat, A., Becker, D.: Epidemic routing for partially-connected ad hoc networks, Technical report CS-2000-06. Duke University, July 2000

5. Thrasyvoulos, S., Psounis, K., Raghavendra, C.S.: Spray and focus: efficient mobility-assisted routing for heterogeneous and correlated mobility. In: Proceedings of Pervasive Computing and Communications Workshops (PerCom 2007), White Plains, 19–23 March 2007, pp. 79–85 (2007)

6. Huang, T.-K., Lee, C.-K., Chen, L.-J.: PRoPHET+: an adaptive PRoPHET-based routing protocol for opportunistic network. In: Proceedings of the 24th IEEE AINA, Perth, 20–23 April 2010, pp. 112–119 (2010)

7. Burgess, J., Gallagher, B., Jensen, D., Levine, B.N.: MaxProp: routing for vehicle-based disruption-tolerant networks. In: Proceedings of INFOCOM 2006, Barcelona, 23–29 April 2006, pp. 1–11 (2006)

8. Dhurandher, S.K., Sharma, D.K., Woungang, I., Bhat, S: HBPR: history based prediction for routing in infrastructure-less opportunistic networks. In: Proceedings of the AINA 2013, Barcelona, pp. 931–936 (2013)

9. Keränen A., Ott J., Kärkkäinen T.: The ONE simulator for DTN protocol evaluation. In: Proceedings of the 2nd International Conference on Simulation Tools and Techniques (SIMUTools 2009), Rome, 2–6 March 2009

Zone-Based Living Activity Recognition Scheme Using Markov Logic Networks

Asaad Ahmed[1(✉)], Hirohiko Suwa[2], and Keiichi Yasumoto[2]

[1] Faculty of Science, Mathematics and Computer Science Department,
Al-Azhar University, Nasr City 11884, Cairo, Egypt
asaadgad@azhar.edu.eg
[2] Nara Institute of Science and Technology 8916-5,
Ikoma, Nara, Takayama 630-0192, Japan
{h-suwa,yasumoto}@is.naist.jp

Abstract. In this paper, we propose a zone-based living activity recognition method. The proposed method introduces a new concept called activity zone which represents the location and the area of an activity that can be done by a user. By using this activity zone concept, the proposed scheme uses Markov Logic Network (MLN) which integrates a common sense knowledge (i.e. area of each activity) with a probabilistic model. The proposed scheme can utilize only a positioning sensor attached to a resident with/without power meters attached to appliances of a smart environment. We target 10 different living activities which cover most of our daily lives at a smart environment and construct activity recognition models. Through experiments using sensor data collected by four participants in our smart home, the proposed scheme achieved average F-measure of recognizing 10 target activities starting from 84.14 % to 94.53 % by using only positioning sensor data.

Keywords: Daily living activity recognition · Markov Logic Networks · Smart home · Activity zone

1   Introduction

Recently, sensing various contexts in households as human activities and device usage conditions became available in addition to the existing environmental information such as temperature and humidity. Therefore, various daily living support context-aware services including energy-saving appliance control in homes [1], elderly monitoring systems [2], and context-aware appliance setting recommendations can be provided. Due to the presence of such services, which require highly accurate living activity recognition rate, the needs of new daily living activity recognition systems have become one of the greatest concerns in building a smart environment.

Many studies have been proposed for activity recognition [3–8]. Most of existing works suffer from the following problems: (1) high deployment and maintenance costs due to many sensors used [4]; (2) privacy intrusion due to utilization

© ICST Institute for Computer Sciences, Social Informatics and Telecommunications Engineering 2016
B. Mandler et al. (Eds.) IoT 360° 2015, Part I, LNICST 169, pp. 109–117, 2016.
DOI: 10.1007/978-3-319-47063-4_10

of cameras and microphones [3]; (3) few recognizable activities or low recognition accuracy; and (4) using Support Vector Machines which can not represent temporal and uncertain information in an efficient way [6]. So, we propose a new zone-based living activity recognition method for solving the aforementioned problems. The proposed method uses Markov Logic Network (MLN) [9] for handling uncertainty information in living activities and enhancing the recognition capability of the system through its rules by representing common sense knowledge (i.e. area of each activity).

2   Proposed Activity Recognition Scheme

In this section, we will introduce our proposed living activity recognition scheme called *Zone-Based Living Activity Recognition Method* (ZLAR) that constructs a reusable and efficient contextual activity model. Here, we assume that only one object is involved in each activity, so a complex activity taking place over multiple objects is out of scope of this paper and it will be part of our future work.

Basic Idea: The basic idea of ZLAR is based on two aspects: (1) representing all available knowledge which are related to a habitant behavior as relationship with objects, position, time, duration, area for each activity, and consumed power and (2) representing uncertainty information by using MLNs rules [9]. To represent all available knowledge as the area for each activity, the temporal information as a time and duration for doing a certain activity by a habitant, and the total amount of consumed power by an object to do its related activity, ZLAR proposed a new concept called activity zone which defines the location and the area of a certain activity that can be done by a habitant inside the smart environment. For example, activity "dining" happens in a zone near "dining table". This activity zone has a geometric shape which depends on the properties of its related activity object (ao) as object location and object mobility. For example, the zone of watching TV activity is related to the location of TV object inside a home and it may have a fixed shape and location; if the location of TV object is not changed. While, the zone of listening music activity is related to the location of an audio device (e.g. Stereo or iPod) inside a home and it may have a variable shape and location based on the mobility of this audio device. By using this activity zone, ZLAR builds a new data and knowledge-driven system by using MLN rules to represent uncertainty information in a system. So, ZLAR defines two features for each activity as follows.

(1) *Time interval*, $TI(u, Z_{ao}, t_{in}, t_{out})$, which represents the time duration value taken by a habitant u inside an activity object zone Z_{ao} for doing its related activity, where a habitant enters a zone at time t_{in} and he leaves a zone at time t_{out}.

(2) *Consumed power*, $PW(ao, t_{in}, t_{out})$, which represents the consumed power value by an activity object ao during the interval $(t_{out} - t_{in})$ to execute its related activity.

2.1   Proposed Activity Zone Concept

ZLAR uses activity zone concept to determine all possible positions of a habitant that he can do a certain activity inside a smart environment. This activity zone is defined by the location of activity object ao and the area that exists around ao which covers all possible positions of a habitant for this activity. As a result, this area has a plane geometric shape as a circle, rectangle, square, triangle, polygon, ellipse, or others. In this paper, for the sake of simplicity, we represent each activity zone as a circle with a certain radius value, ZR_{ac}. However, it is important to find the most suitable zone shape for each activity. This will be part of our future work. We assume that the locations of activity objects inside a smart environment are given by a user in advance. By knowing the locations of these objects, ZLAR can determine the center of each activity zone. As shown in Fig. 1, the location of activity object ao inside a zone has a two cases: (1) the location of ao exists on the circumference of activity zone which is called *edge activity zone* as the zone of watching TV activity with TV object (Fig. 1(a)). This case means that the activity can be done only if a user exists at a location in front of its object inside the activity zone. (2) the location of ao exists at the center of its activity zone which is called *centroid activity zone* as the zone of taking a meal activity with a dining table object (Fig. 1(b)). This case means that the activity can be done if a habitant exists at any position inside the activity zone relative to its center. So, one of ZLAR advantages that it uses a relative user position instead of his/her absolute position. Here, the problem is how to get the most suitable radius of each activity zone, ZR_{ac}. To solve this problem, ZLAR proposes a new optimization process by using a set of training datasets. This process will be explained in Sect. 2.3.

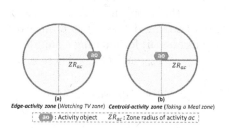

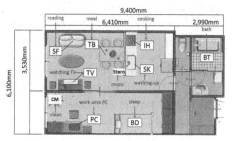

Fig. 1. Two cases of activity zone in ZLAR

Fig. 2. A used smart home

2.2   Proposed Markov Logic Network Rules

ZLAR constructs two MLN rules which are based on activity zone, Z_{ao}, time duration feature, $TI(u, Z_{ao}, t_{in}, t_{out})$, and consumed power feature, $PW(ao, t_{in}, t_{out})$. These two rules are defined as follows.

(•) **Rule 1:** The first MLN rule of ZLAR deals with objects that must consume power to execute their related activities as watching TV or listening music. This consumed power by objects is associated with the time duration of a user existence inside their activity zones. This rule is defined as follows.

R1: $TI(u, Z_{ao}, t_{in}, t_{out}) \geq OT_{ac} \land PW(ao, t_{in}, t_{out}) \geq OP_{ac} \Rightarrow DoActivity$
(u, ac_{ao})

(•) **Rule 2:** The second MLN rule of ZLAR deals with objects that do not need to consume any power to execute their related activities as taking a meal or reading a book. So, this rule depends only on the time duration of a user existence inside their activity zones. This rule is defined as follows.

R2: $TI(u, Z_{ao}, t_{in}, t_{out}) \geq OT_{ac} \Rightarrow DoActivity(u, ac_{ao})$

Here, OT_{ac} and OP_{ac} are the values of time duration and consumed power thresholds for each activity which will be determined by using our proposed optimization process in Sect. 2.3. $DoActivity(u, ac_{ao})$ represents the doing activity ac_{ao} of an object ao by a user u if the rule features are met.

2.3   Proposed ZLAR Architecture

ZLAR designs a new living activity recognition architecture which consists of the following three processes:

(1) **Optimization Process:** In ZLAR, the activity zone of a certain object has a circle shape with a specific radius value, ZR_{ac}, as described in Sect. 2.1. Also, the two MLN rules of ZLAR contain time duration OT_{ac} and consumed power OP_{ac} thresholds as described in Sect. 2.2. Here, the main problem is how to find the most suitable values of zone radius ZR_{ac}, time duration OT_{ac}, and consumed power OP_{ac} thresholds. To solve this problem, ZLAR proposes a new optimization process by using a set of training datasets based on two issues: (i) using one of optimization algorithms and (ii) formulating a suitable fitness function to find optimal values of ZR_{ac}, OT_{ac}, and OP_{ac}. These two issues are described as follows.

   (a) *Optimization algorithm:* Here, ZLAR uses evolution algorithm called *Differential Evolution* algorithm (DE) [10] which is one of the most efficient algorithms for optimization problems. DE is a genetic method that optimizes a problem by iteratively trying to improve a candidate solution with regard to a given measure of quality and is used for multidimensional real-valued functions.

   (b) *Optimization Fitness function:* Based on the set of training datasets, ZLAR formulates its fitness function, which will be used by DE algorithm, for each activity ac in the system. We assume that the following: (1) there is a training dataset $TData_u$ for a user u; (2) the real time durations for every activity ac in $TData_u$ are $<1, 2, ..., h, ..., H>$; (3) a set of real location instances of a user u at interval h for activity ac is $RL^u_{ac}(h)$; (4) a set of real time instances of a user u at interval h for activity ac is

$RI_{ac}^u(h)$; and (5) a set of real power instances for using an activity object ao by a user u at interval h for activity ac is $RP_{ac}^u(h)$. The proposed fitness function, $F_{ac}^u(ZR_{ac}, OT_{ac}, OP_{ac})$ is defined as follows.

$$F_{ac}^u(ZR_{ac}, OT_{ac}, OP_{ac}) = \frac{\sum_{h=1}^{H} V_{ac}^u(ZR_{ac}, OT_{ac}, OP_{ac}, h)}{H} \quad (1)$$

and

$$V_{ac}^u(ZR_{ac}, OT_{ac}, OP_{ac}, h) = \frac{1}{R}\left(\frac{|L_{ac}^u(ZR_{ac}, h)|}{N_h} + \frac{|I_{ac}^u(OT_{ac}, h)|}{M_h} + \frac{|P_{ac}^u(OP_{ac}, h)|}{K_h}\right) \quad (2)$$

where $L_{ac}^u(ZR_{ac}, h) \subseteq RL_{ac}^u(h)$ is a set of real location instances that are covered by optimized radius ZR_{ac}, $I_{ac}^u(OT_{ac}, h) \subseteq RI_{ac}^u(h)$ is a set of real time instances that are covered by optimized time duration threshold OT_{ac}, $P_{ac}^u(OP_{ac}, h) \subseteq RP_{ac}^u(h)$ is a set of real consumed power instances that are covered by optimized consumed power threshold OP_{ac}, and R represents the number of optimized parameters. The value of R equals 3 (radius, time duration, consumed power), if the activity object uses a power threshold. If the activity object does not use a power threshold, the value of R equals 2 (radius, time duration) and $\frac{|P_{ac}^u(OP_{ac}, h)|}{K_h} = 0$ in Eq. 2. Also, N_h, M_h, and K_h represent the number of real instances that exists in $RL_{ac}^u(h)$, $RI_{ac}^u(h)$, and $RP_{ac}^u(h)$, respectively.

The fitness function F_{ac}^u, in Eq. 1, determines the total number of accumulated real instances of user location, activity time, and consumed power that are covered by the optimized values of ZR_{ac}, OT_{ac}, and OP_{ac}. Here, our goal is maximizing the value of F_{ac}^u. Note that, the value of F_{ac}^u is a ratio $\in [0, 1]$. Finally, the optimization process of ZLAR uses F_{ac}^u as a fitness function in DE algorithm to find the most suitable values of ZR_{ac}, OT_{ac}, and OP_{ac} for each activity and its related proposed MLN rules.

(2) **Weight Learning Process:** In this process, ZLAR executes a specific weight learning algorithm to find a value of the associated weight with each proposed MLNs rule based on a set of training datasets. There are a lot of weight learning algorithms for MLNs rules. In ZLAR, the Diagonal Newton discriminative learner as described in Lowd and Domingos [11] is used to get a suitable weights for the proposed rules.

(3) **Recognition Process:** In this process, ZLAR executes a specific inference algorithm based on a set of testing datasets by using proposed MLN rules with their optimization values of time duration threshold with/without consumed power threshold to recognize a habitant's activities. There are a lot of inference algorithms that can be used for MLNs inference process. In ZLAR, the Maximum a Posteriori Estimation (MAP) inference algorithm called WalkSAT [12] is used in its recognition process.

3   Experimental and Qualitative Evaluations

3.1   Experimental Outline and Results

The experiment targeted to recognize 10 types of activities which classified into two groups: (1) *Powered group: {Cooking, WatchingTV, WashUp, Bath, Clean-*

ing, *PC*, *Music*} which uses time duration and consumed power features and (2) *Nonpowered group*: {*Meal*, *Reading*, *Sleeping*} which uses only a time duration feature. Four participants *U1*, *U2*, *U3*, and *U4* (three males and a female in twenties) lived for three days each in our smart home which was built in Nara Institute of Science and Technology, Japan. Each of the participants wore an ultrasonic position transmitter and they performed normal daily activities at home as usual. Data were collected for a total of twelve days. After collecting the data, we labeled the sensor data according to activity type using the living activity labeling tool which was proposed in [6]. All labeled sensor data were divided into 30 s intervals (time window) and manually labeled each interval with an appropriate activity using this labeling support tool. Figure 2 shows the location of appliances and furniture used for the activities in the smart home. To validate the proposed ZLAR method, we designed our own GUI application based on *Tuffy* which is an open-source Markov Logic Network inference engine [13]. We evaluated four scenarios **S1**, **S2**, **S3**, and **S4** as cross validation experiment. In each evaluated scenario, we used all data for three participants (total of nine days) in optimization and weight learning (WL) processes of ZLAR. For testing phase, we used the forth user data(total of three days) in recognition process of ZLAR. Finally, the evaluation results were measured by *Precision*, *Recall* and *F-measure* as defined in [6]. The results based on this scenario as follows.

(1) **Optimization results:** The optimization results for ZR_{ac} (millimeter), OT_{ac} (seconds), and OP_{ac} (power unit) of 10 activities were {[1220, 4700], [128, 488], [1.3, 4]}, {[1000, 4500], [168, 488], [1, 10]}, {[1700, 4000], [125, 488], [1, 8]}, and {[1000, 4940], [110, 488], [1.3, 9]} by using **S1**, **S2**, **S3**, and **S4**, respectively. As a result, the optimized values of $ZR_{ac}, OT_{ac}, OP_{ac}$ for different scenarios are different, this is because ZLAR uses different training datasets in its optimization process.

(2) **Weight learning results:** By using the training datasets, the weight learning results of **R1** and **R2** were [10.7282,11.4248] and [10.7282,11.7654] by using **S1**, [10.8617,11.2491] and [10.2502,11.8668] by using **S2**, [11.0477,11.3491] and [11.0656,12.1762] by using **S3**, and [11.0779,11.3378] and [11.0477,11.8792] by using **S4** for the 10 activities. As shown from these results, the weight of each MLN rule depends on the training datasets of each scenario.

(3) **Recognition results:** Table 1 shows the results of Precision, Recall, and F-measure by using time duration and consumed power thresholds (**R1**) for bath, cleaning, cooking, watching TV, PC, music, and Washing up activities and using time duration threshold (**R2**) for sleeping, meal, and reading activities. In Table 1, we set *None* for the activity, if the testing user did not do this activity during his stay inside the smart home. As shown in Table 1, the values of Precision, Recall, and F-measure were between [92.02 %, 97.41 %], [76.56 %, 82.4 %], and [83.74 %, 88.78 %] on average, respectively. As a result, ZLAR can recognize living activities with high F-measure accuracy by using only two types of sensors. This is because, ZLAR can efficiently represent all available knowledge in smart environments as area of activity, consumed

Table 1. Precision (P), Recall (R), and F-measure (F) results for **S1**, **S2**, **S3**, and **S4** by using **R1** and **R2**

Activity (Rule)	Using S1			Using S2			Using S3			Using S4		
	P	R	F	P	R	F	P	R	F	P	R	F
Bath (R1)	100	62.07	76.6	100	67.78	80.79	100	70.83	82.94	100	94.87	97.37
Cleaning (R1)	91.67	100	95.65	None	None	None	100	79.52	88.59	97.5	100	98.73
Cooking (R1)	100	75.9	86.3	94.74	61.29	74.43	96.23	73.1	83.09	95.56	61.22	74.63
WatchTV (R1)	99.5	71.17	83.98	98.55	81.18	89.02	98.61	91.43	94.88	96.52	78.9	86.83
PC (R1)	99.06	71.62	83.13	100	92.98	96.36	100	87.36	93.25	98.85	75.94	85.9
Music (R1)	99.03	65.61	78.92	97.89	79.17	87.54	99.62	88.63	93.8	94.81	59.08	72.8
WashUp (R1)	100	68.52	81.32	95.45	84.62	89.71	93.75	76.19	84.06	88.1	77.78	82.62
Sleeping (R2)	99.84	68.49	81.25	None	None	None	None	None	None	None	None	None
Meal (R2)	93.84	80.66	86.75	97.18	97.93	97.56	83.33	66.67	74.07	66.4	56.31	60.94
Reading (R2)	90.7	93.48	92.07	95.45	94.29	94.87	99.66	100	99.83	90.42	97.56	93.85
Average	97.09	76.56	84.86	97.41	82.4	88.78	96.8	81.53	88.28	92.02	77.96	83.74

power by activity object, and time duration of using activity object for doing its related activity. In addition, using MLN rules in ZLAR gives a good representation ability of uncertainty information for each living activity. Also, F-measure precision of all activities was not 100 %, this is because some activities were mistakenly classified to another activity due to overlapped zones of those activities. So, ZLAR misrecognized the current activity. Solving this overlapped zones problem will be part of our future work. In addition, we conducted another experiment by using time duration threshold only (**R2**) for all activities and the values of Precision, Recall, and F-measure were between [87.23 %, 97.19 %], [81.55 %, 92.73 %], and [84.14 %, 94.53 %] on average, respectively. As a result, the Recall value increased for all activities in case of using time duration threshold only for MLN rule (**R2**). Therefore, the value of F-measure increased. This is because, some of real activity instances, which do not meet the consumed power threshold in MLN rule (**R1**), were added to the recognized instances when the consumed power threshold did not be considered.

3.2   Qualitative Evaluation

Here, the evaluation results based on qualitative metrics is presented to show the efficiency of ZLAR compared to some of existing simple activity recognition schemes. The evaluation process requires studying the schemes and finding their attributes that satisfy a certain evaluation criteria. We assume that the best evaluation criteria must take into account accuracy, number of recognized activities, deployment and maintenance (D&M) costs, privacy intrusion, representing uncertainty, and reusability as qualitative metrics. The optimal values for this evaluation criteria are *High* accuracy, *Many* recognized activities, *Low*

Table 2. Qualitative performance comparison

Qualitative metric	Accuracy	# recognized activities	D&M costs	Privacy intrusion	Representing uncertainty	Reusability
[3]	Approx. High	Few	Average	Yes	No	No
[4]	Low/High	Many	High	No	No	No
[5]	High	Few	Average	No	No	No
[6]	Approx. High	Median	Low	No	No	No
[7]	Approx. High	Many	Average	Yes	Satisfies	No
[8]	Medium	Median	Average	No	No	No
ZLAR	High	Many	Low	No	Satisfies	Satisfies

deployment and maintenance costs, *No* privacy intrusion, *Satisfies* representing uncertainty, and *Satisfies* reusability. Table 2 shows the qualitative performance comparison based on these qualitative metrics. As shown in Table 2, none of existing schemes can meet all qualitative metrics of the required criteria. While, ZLAR meets all the required qualitative metrics. As a result, ZLAR has a high qualitative performance compared to existing schemes.

4   Conclusion

In this paper, we proposed a zone-based living activity recognition method called ZLAR. ZLAR outperforms most of existing schemes by achieving the following issues: (1) using a relative position of a user position instead of his/her absolute position, (2) minimizing the cost of deployment and maintenance costs, (3) achieving a high recognition accuracy, and (4) representing the temporal information of activities and the habitant efficiently by using MLN. In addition, the best benefit of ZLAR is the possibility used for different users, places and environments without having to repeat the learning process of ZLAR. So, the overhead cost due to collection of sensor data is limited. In our future works, we will study the effect of changing the locations of objects inside the smart environment on the performance of ZLAR method.

References

1. Sean, B., Aditya, M., David, I., Prashant, S.: SmartCap: flattening peak electricity demand in smart homes. In: Proceedings of 13th International Conference on Pervasive Computing (PerCom 2012), Lugano, pp. 67–75 (2012)
2. Rashidi, P., Mihailidis, A.: A survey on ambient assisted living tools for older adults. IEEE J. Biomed. Health Inf. **17**, 579–590 (2013)
3. Brdiczka, O., Langet, M., Maisonnasse, J., Crowley, J.: Detecting human behavior models from multimodal observation in a smart home. IEEE Trans. Autom. Sci. Eng. **6**, 588–597 (2009)

4. van Kasteren, T.L.M., Krose, B.J.A.: An activity monitoring system for elderly care using generative and discriminative models. J. Pers. Ubiquit. Comput. **14**, 489–498 (2010)
5. Lara, O.D.: A survey on human activity recognition using wearable sensors. IEEE Commun. Surv. Tutor. **15**, 1192–1209 (2013)
6. Ueda, K., Tamai, M., Yasumoto, K.: A method for recognizing living activities in homes using positioning sensor and power meters. In: Proceedings of 2nd IEEE PerCom Workshop on Smart Environmentss: Closing the Loop (SmartE 2015), Missouri (2015)
7. Helaoui, R., Niepert, M., Stuckenschmidt, H.: Recognizing interleaved and concurrent activities. In: Proceedings of IEEE Pervasive Computing and Communications (PerCom 2011), Seattle, pp. 1–9 (2011)
8. Maekawa, T., Kishino, Y., Sakurai, Y., Suyama, T.: Recognizing the use of portable electrical devices with hand-worn magnetic sensors. In: Lyons, K., Hightower, J., Huang, E.M. (eds.) Pervasive 2011. LNCS, vol. 6696, pp. 276–293. Springer, Heidelberg (2011). doi:10.1007/978-3-642-21726-5_18
9. Richardson, M., Domingos, P.: Markov logic networks. J. Mach. Learn. **62**, 107–136 (2006)
10. Feoktistov, V.: Differential Evolution: Search of Solutions. Springer, US (2006)
11. Lowd, D., Domingos, P.: Efficient weight learning for Markov logic networks. In: Kok, J.N., Koronacki, J., Lopez de Mantaras, R., Matwin, S., Mladenič, D., Skowron, A. (eds.) PKDD 2007. LNCS (LNAI), vol. 4702, pp. 200–211. Springer, Heidelberg (2007). doi:10.1007/978-3-540-74976-9_21
12. Kautz, H., Selman, B., Jiang, Y.: A general stochastic approach to solving problems with hard and soft constraints. In: DIMACS Series, the Satisfiability Problem: Theory and Applications, vol. 35, pp. 573–586 (1997)
13. Niu, F.R.C., Doan, A., Shavlik, J.: Tuffy: scaling up statistical inference in Markov logic networks using an RDBMS. In: The VLDB Endowment, vol. 4, pp. 373–384 (2011)

Acumen: An Open-Source Testbed for Cyber-Physical Systems Research

Walid Taha[1]([✉]), Adam Duracz[1]([✉]), Yingfu Zeng[2], Kevin Atkinson[2],
Ferenc A. Bartha[2], Paul Brauner[2], Jan Duracz[1], Fei Xu[1], Robert Cartwright[2],
Michal Konečný[3], Eugenio Moggi[4], Jawad Masood[2], Pererik Andreasson[1],
Jun Inoue[2], Anita Sant'Anna[1], Roland Philippsen[1], Alexandre Chapoutot[5],
Marcia O'Malley[6], Aaron Ames[7], Veronica Gaspes[1], Lise Hvatum[8],
Shyam Mehta[8], Henrik Eriksson[9], and Christian Grante[10]

[1] School of Information Technology, Halmstad University, Halmstad, Sweden
{walid.taha,adam.duracz,jan.duracz,fei.xu,pererik.andreasson,
anita.santAnna,roland.philippsen,veronica.gaspes}@hh.se
[2] Department of Computer Science, Rice University, Houston, TX, USA
{yingfu.zeng,kevin.atkinson,ferenc.bartha,paul.brauner,
robert.cartwright,jawad.masood,jun.inoue}@rice.edu
[3] Computer Science Group, Aston University, Birmingham, UK
m.konecny@aston.ac.uk
[4] DIBRIS, University of Genova, Genoa, Italy
moggi@unige.it
[5] ENSTA ParisTech - U2IS, Paris, France
alexandre.chapoutot@ensta.fr
[6] Department of Mechanical Engineering, Rice University, Houston, TX, USA
omalleym@rice.edu
[7] School of Mechanical Engineering, Georgia Institute of Technology,
Atlanta, GA, USA
ames@gatech.edu
[8] Schlumberger, Houston, TX, USA
{lise.hvatum,shyam.mehta}@slb.com
[9] Dependable Systems, SP Technical Research Institute of Sweden, Borås, Sweden
henrik.eriksson@sp.se
[10] AB Volvo, Gothenburg, Sweden
christian.grante@volvo.com

Abstract. Developing Cyber-Physical Systems requires methods and tools to support simulation and verification of hybrid (both continuous and discrete) models. The Acumen modeling and simulation language is an open source testbed for exploring the design space of what rigorous-but-practical next-generation tools can deliver to developers of Cyber-Physical Systems. Like verification tools, a design goal for Acumen is to provide rigorous results. Like simulation tools, it aims to be intuitive, practical, and scalable. However, it is far from evident whether these two goals can be achieved simultaneously. This paper explains the primary design goals for Acumen, the core challenges that must be addressed in order to achieve these goals, the "agile research method" taken by the project, the steps taken to realize these goals, the key lessons learned, and the emerging language design.

© ICST Institute for Computer Sciences, Social Informatics and Telecommunications Engineering 2016
B. Mandler et al. (Eds.) IoT 360° 2015, Part I, LNICST 169, pp. 118–130, 2016.
DOI: 10.1007/978-3-319-47063-4_11

Keywords: Testbed · Cyber-Physical Systems (CPS) · Modeling ·
Simulation · Hybrid systems · Open source software

1 Introduction

Developing novel Cyber-Physical and IoT Systems requires methods and tools
to support simulation and verification of hybrid systems models. Hybrid systems
modeling languages are mathematical formalism that support the descriptions of
dynamics that can be continuous in some parts and discontinuous or discrete in
others. Acumen is an open source testbed for exploring the design space of what
rigorous-but-practical next-generation tools can deliver to developers of Cyber-
Physical Systems. Like verification tools, a design goal for Acumen is to provide
correct and mathematically rigorous results. Like simulation tools, it aims to be
intuitive, practical, and scalable. However, it is far from evident whether these
two goals can be achieved simultaneously.

Contributions: The key contributions of this paper are to articulate and report
on the results of a method for addressing a complex set of goals such as those
put for the design of Acumen. We begin by presenting the goals set for Acumen
(Sect. 2). Next, we analyze the challenges that face an undertaking of this scope
(Sect. 3). We then describe the key features of the "agile research method" to
advance towards these goals, the main milestones in applying this method to
date, and some key lessons in the last five years of the project (Sect. 4). We
briefly describe the emerging language design (Sect. 5), and conclude with a
summary and an overview of current priorities for the development of Acumen.

We posit that the ambitious goals of the project as well as the challenges
that face it are representative of the goals and challenges of interdisciplinary
paradigms such as CPS and IoT, and see the gradual progress made by the
project as giving assurance about the deep advances that can be expected from
those disciplines. Through this exposition, we hope to interest other academic
and industrial partners to become involved in developing of Acumen.

Related Work: In terms of "final product", the most closely related tools to our
work are hybrid systems verification tools, such as CHARON [2], KeyMaera [18],
and SpaceEx [10], as well as equational modeling languages such as Modelica [4].
At the highest level, the work described here can be viewed as an effort to
bridge the gap between the first class of (rigorous) tools and the second class
of widely popular tools that are generally viewed as being much more accessible and broadly applicable (but provide no guarantees of correctness). Technical
comparisons between the tools and Acumen on technical grounds can be found
in the papers on Acumen cited in this paper. The focus of this paper is the

This work was supported by US NSF award CPS-1136099, the Swedish Knowledge
Foundation (KK), The CERES Center, and VINNOVA (Dnr. 2011-01819).

process through which a rigorous modeling language aimed specifically at the CPS domain is being developed. Unfortunately, the literature on the development process for such tools in particular, or domain-specific languages in general, is relatively sparse. Related work includes commonality and variability analysis [7], but the CPS domain is much broader than the intended types of problems for this analysis. The survey by Mernik et al. [17] suggests that existing methods require that the domain is much more clearly defined than is possible for a large and evolving area such as CPS.

2   Inception and Design Goals

The primary goal for Acumen is to serve as a testbed that facilitates research into rigorous-but-practical tools for CPS. A secondary goal, which stems from a necessity for achieving the primary goal in the absence of standard methods for studying such tools, is to serve as a testbed for programming languages and software engineering research. A tertiary goal, which stems in part from the need for developing evaluation methods for the primary goal, is accessibility to users. This goal entails that Acumen had to prove to be an effective device for teaching. The rest of this section elaborates these three goals.

Testbed for CPS Research: At the very outset of the project the motivation was simply to develop controllers for horizontal drilling tractors (robots) for oil wells. Quickly, this concrete problem pointed to a much broader problem of the need for coherent toolchains for CPS design. Discussions with domain experts suggested and eventually confirmed that a wide range of different tools are used to design and analyze different components of products such as horizontal drilling tractors, or any of a wide range of non-trivial robotic systems. The problem of "coherence" of the existing toolchains is largely due to:

- The need to use different formalisms and tools for different subsystems,
- The absence of mechanized methods for checking consistency between the results of these tools, and
- The absence of methods that ensure the correctness of the results of individual tools, even for the smallest problems.

Overcoming the "coherence" problem is a central goal for Acumen [24].

Toolchains consist of software applications that support modeling, simulation, and verification of various subsystems. Such tools constitute infrastructure for supporting virtual prototyping and testing of these subsystems, as well as tools for visualizations. We were inspired by the power of specialized tools such as CarSim [3] (for vehicles) or Gazebo [11] (for robotics), but also surprised by the lack of transparency and user control over underlying dynamical models, as well as the need for such radically different tools to support these closely related domains. Access to such models is essential for allowing users to control the computational cost (and accuracy) of the models being used for virtual testing, and to interpret the results of such tests. Out of these observations emerged the goal of transparency with respect to models, and ensuring that the user has full access to (and control over) such models, as well as the goal of being a unifying language that can be used across a wide range of CPS domains.

A practical criterion for an effective testbed is accessibility. We define accessibility as the ease with which new users from a wide range of backgrounds can acquire the software and use it to solve a problem that interests them, or use it to learn something of value to them. First, it should be self-evident that convenience to users is an integral part of testbeds success, and that this has a direct impact on the size of audience the tool can reach. But it is also the kind of goal that is essential to spell out and stress throughout the process of developing it. As we will see in the rest of this paper, accessibility is both a source of stringent requirement ón design choices and an easy criteria for members of the research team to forget as they become engaged in solving much more specific technical problems. Second, our emphasis on accessibility was driven in part out of the idea that the ability to model and simulate the world around us is important to individual and societal well-being. This partly came from Lessigs "Code is Law" [13] and, in particular, the idea that our society is increasingly being shaped by codes that only few of us understand and that even fewer truly consent to incorporating the socially-significant values induced by these codes.

Testbed for Language and Software Engineering Research: At the time of starting the development of Acumen, in the mainstream programming languages community, the formalism that came closest to providing a modeling language for Cyber-Physical Systems was Functional Reactive Programming [23] (FRP). It had been used successfully in a wide range of domains, including robotics and computer animation. However, its denotational semantics was presented in complete partial orders (CPOs) without giving real numbers detailed treatment. It therefore remained an open question whether this language could be extended to incorporate such treatment. Ideas presented in work by Edalat and Pattinson on the semantics of hybrid systems [9] appeared to provide some or all of the necessary foundations, but the connection between these two lines of work was not obvious. Developing a semantic foundation that unified these lines of work is a key goal of the Acumen project. Once such a unifying foundation is established, it can be used to elaborate various notions of computation for Cyber-Physical Systems as well as their inter-relations.

There are also more practical goals relating to investigating better methods for the design and implementation of domain-specific languages. These include the use of staging [19] (both for implementing the language and as a mechanism supported by the language) and property-based testing [22] for ensuring the quality of the code base. A related goal is the use of Acumen to investigate the possibility of exploiting parallel resources without introducing concurrency problems [6].

Tool for Teaching CPS: Tools that can be used in practice must be accessible to their users, and waiting to evaluate accessibility at the end of the project entails unreasonably high risk of failure. There are two natural proxies to evaluating such accessibility. The first is usability by domain-experts, which we have already addressed in the discussion of the primary goal of serving as a testbed for CPS. The second is usability by novice users. Fortunately, this goal is highly synergistic with well-recognized need for better content, methods, and tools for teaching the emerging topic of CPS.

Because it is a new and high interdisciplinary area, CPS students come from a highly diverse set of backgrounds, and with different goals. We identified from the outset three different groups of students: The first group is college-level CPS students. It includes embedded systems and mechatronics students, who expect to have a career developing CPSs. The second group is college-level students specializing in related areas, which could be computer-related, engineering-related, science-related, or arts and humanities. Clearly, students in each of these sub-areas have different interests. They are seeking a professional degree and will spend their careers in the context of a world populated by Cyber-Physical Systems, and may well contribute to solving problems relating to such systems. The third group is high-school students that have a general interest in science, technology, engineering, and math (STEM) disciplines. A tool that can address the toolchain coherence problem should make a positive contribution to the education of these three categories of students, but it is far from obvious that one tool can cater to such different audiences.

In the next section we discuss the issues that make these goals challenging.

3   Challenges

In this section we describe some of the key challenges, especially in relation to the CPS testbed goal (and in tool chain coherence in particular). For reasons of space, we address the programming languages and teaching goals only briefly.

To address the question of how to best support the engineering process we must understand how engineers carry out their work in practice. This includes both how engineers go about designing a new product, and the more specialized skills of how they think about models of the systems they design. Even the latter is challenging for someone interested in its computational mechanization. For example, research papers are a natural source for understanding the notation and calculations used to reason about models of Cyber-Physical Systems. However, such papers rarely focus on the mechanics of derivation, and assume significant knowledge about mathematics, control, and the domain. Developing a formalism for modeling such systems entails acquiring a deep understanding of such domains. A somewhat more practical challenge is that research papers are often incomplete in their specification of concrete examples and rely instead on the intuition of experts. This complication means that even testing theories about correctly understanding the mechanics of the computations used in these papers can be challenging.

In terms of specific simulation tools, it is clear that MATLAB/Simulink is one of the main tools used in industrial practice. If MATLAB/Simulink was not just the most popular tool but the only tool, the research question would be simpler: "How do we improve MATLAB/Simulink?" For better or for worse, there is a myriad of other specialized tools also used by practitioners. The upside of this multiplicity is that it can be a source of inspiration. The downside is that it makes the search space of prior work vast and highly fragmented. If we are interested only in discrete-time simulation we may be able to focus on computer science and operations research venues. For continuous time simulation, almost every discipline of science has its own literature. For hybrid continuous/discrete systems, the literature becomes somewhat sparse, but locating related work remains challenging.

For the goals of transparency of models and user control it is natural to focus on mathematical notation as the syntax for models. After all, mathematics is the de facto lingua franca across many technical disciplines. But to make a lingua franca of human discourse into a mechanical formalism is a significant challenge. It helps, of course, that mathematics is a rigorous domain, but mechanical formalization rests not just on meaning but also on syntax. Mathematical notation includes multiple syntactic notations for the same concept, as well assignments of multiple different meanings to the same notation. Navigating the space of possibilities to identify what is intuitive for novices and acceptable across domains is a key language design challenge for this project. Another is defining mechanical interpretations (semantics) for such notations. Often, especially at the boundary of integrating continuous and discrete mathematics, we are able to define an interpretation for two constructs independently, but it is not obvious how to define an interpretation that allows both to be used together. One of the most profound challenges is to understand the mathematical space of meanings (or solutions) for mathematical expressions (problems).

With respect to the correctness of simulation tools (part of the toolchain coherence problem), a fundamental question is whether it is at all possible to find or develop rigorous methods for all aspects of simulation. In particular, working rigorously with just real numbers (not to mention functions over reals) introduces known computability and decidability issues [20]. This means that even computability is a fundamental challenge for the development of Acumen. A more nuanced (but equally important) question is whether, when such methods exist, they are precise enough, fast enough, and have all the computational properties that are needed to make for practical tools.

From the point of view of programming languages research, a core challenge is how to manage the high-dimensional problem of language design. In particular, a DSL that has not yet been fully specified has a large number of degrees of freedom. Basic examples include: syntax, semantics, user interface, documentation and tutorial materials, intended user base, language design and development team, and intellectual property and licensing issues. While there is significant literature, tools, and advice on many of these aspects individually or in combination with some others, literature addressing all these aspects simultaneously is sparse. Programming languages methods are readily available to identify which part of a language is broken and how to fix that part; but the more profound question of what language should exist and how to create it does not seem to have been sufficiently investigated.

In terms of teaching, the practical challenge is that, as programming languages researchers, we have limited contact and direct and regular access to students in CPS-related domains. Of course, at the time the project started, there were no CPS programs as such. Practical methods need to be found to address this challenge, so that it is possible to develop a concrete understanding of the needs of different types of students and potential users, as well as to have a basis for evaluating and quantifying the success of Acumen.

4   Approach and Implementation

In this section we summarize the approach, milestones in the effort to implement it, and key lessons learned in the process.

An Agile Research Method: Given the complexity of the task of realizing the goals of Acumen, it was accepted from the outset that decomposing the process into clearly isolated technical problems may not be effective. For example, separating the process into selecting a semantics, a type system, and a syntax or even the reverse order would not be practical, and may not even be possible. There is a strong interdependence between these choices, as well as in other aspects of the design goals. It was therefore accepted that the development of Acumen would be a highly iterative and adaptive process that involves creating prototypes that would allow us as designers to gradually understand the space of technical design choices as well as to gain a better understanding of user needs and abilities.

Key features of the approach include frequent interaction between design (or design-critique) and implementation and close collaboration with potential users, especially domain-experts in domains that intersect with an evolving notion of the user base and novice users (often students). These continual activities allow us as the designers to gradually develop:

A clear understanding of the CPS domain in terms of technical needs from modeling and simulation tools, A portfolio of concrete example models for evaluation of the language and validation of hypotheses about actual engineering processes, A clear notion of a user base including size, interests, and expertise, A clear understanding of the semantic foundations and technically feasible functions that modeling and simulation tools can provide, A model of how to plan and manage a research-oriented, open-source effort that is manned primarily by researchers, students, and volunteers.

For lack of a better term, this approach can be described as an "agile research method", borrowing from the "agile" software development [5] literature. There is a similar emphasis on maintaining enough structure or "scaffolding" to enable reasonable testing of new ideas at all times, as well as on understanding the "customer" of the software application and engaging continually in the gradual development of the technical requirements for the final product.

Given the complexity in simultaneously developing these expertise, an obvious risk is spreading resources too thin. The key mechanisms for mitigating this risk have been careful consideration of all the possible language development initiatives (exploration or even addition of seemingly trivial but attractive features), and keeping the language and its implementations as small and simple as possible to reduce the effort of maintaining it.

Milestones and Lessons: We followed the above method from the beginning of work on Acumen (in 2007) to the present. For reasons of space, we focus here on the second and current prototype of Acumen.

In 2010, and within three to six months, the first version of the current, Scala-based, implementation was created. It included a GUI, a simple editor, a reference interpreter and an optimized interpreter, and support for automatic plotting. Work on Acumen then took a brief break due to a gap between the end of one research project and the start of a new one. In 2011, work by a masters student introduced support for 3D visualization [24]. Students taking the first instance of our CPS course [21], which used Acumen, showed a strong preference to using the implementation that supported 3D visualization, as it made working with virtual CPS design problems noticeable easier than looking only at plots of individual signals.

In 2012, work began on one of the most significant technical results of the effort to date: developing a method for the correct simulation of Zeno systems [12]. This included the implementation of the first rigorous, enclosure-based simulator for a subset of Acumen. A problem that faced the implementation, and which was addressed around the same time, was the responsiveness and intermittent crashing issues with the GUI. Although the fix was seemingly minor, substantial effort went into understanding, diagnosing, and designing the fix. As programming languages researchers from a more "theoretical" background, it was startling to realize that concurrency problems in GUIs are not a solved problem, even in Javas SWING library. Difficulties in maintaining the integration between the core language interpreters and the interactive GUI proved to be a constant sink of engineering effort throughout the project.

As the activity under new funding was ramping up, there was a concerted effort to find ways to support more concurrent development on the code base. To avoid dependency on network connectivity and a centralized repository, a decision was made to move from svn to git. After some initial experience with github, we found that it had only limited support for external/internal visibility and "issue management", a decision was made to move to paid services by Atlassian (bitbucket and JIRA). These tools have played an essential role in facilitating development by a growing team, and in documenting key open challenges and the rationale for resolutions made.

In 2013 there was a concerted effort to expand the portfolio of case studies. This included developing low-order models of vehicle dynamics [16] by a domain-expert (with a recent PhD in mechanical engineering, specializing in robotics). Improvements visible to the user were made in the GUI and included syntax highlighting and code completion. Internally, with the version management and issue management systems in place, regression testing and continuous integration were introduced. This paved the way to exploring the use of property-based testing. In particular, a generator for random Acumen programs was built. It was not based solely on syntax, but on trying to exhibit interesting behaviour in order to catch problems when using the generated program to compare two semantics. Due to performance issues, it has so far only been used on a small scale. Building this infrastructure did draw our attention to the importance of carefully planning property-based testing in the context of computationally intensive codes.

There were also early efforts to explore the development of a compiled implementation; to study the mapping of Acumen to hybrid automata; and to allow the user to manipulate the textual models indirectly by manipulating the 3D rendering of objects. Such explorations were seen as premature by the project leadership, but it was nevertheless approved as it was in strong alignment with the interests of the researcher who wished to pursue it. It remains in the code base but is not actively supported. For a variety of reasons, such investment in activities with uncertain outcomes are a necessary part of any team effort, and we hope that there will be opportunities for capitalizing on the experience gained from these efforts at a later time.

A significant effort was made in 2014 to research licensing options, and the feasibility of shifting from GPL to BSD. The Acumen development team was fortunate to have a researcher with expertise in open source licensing. The effort included understanding both the needs/expectations of different contributing institutions, as well as the libraries available to enable such a migration. Activities directly visible to users included developing a new optimized implementation, more accurate integrators, including line numbers in error messages, and completing support for vectors and matrices. Development of the second-generation enclosure-based interpreter also began the same year. A practical problem with ease of installation was solved, namely, the migration from Java3D/OpenGL to jPCT [1]. In particular, the former requires the separate installation of a nonstandard library - an additional step that was not easy for novice users, and can be seen as time consuming by potential expert users. The quality of 3D rendering was affected, but some interesting new possibilities were introduced. On the administrative front, a command line interface was introduced to provide researchers with the ability to access/configure most of Acumens features through command line, making Acumen scriptable.

In 2015, the development of two generations of enclosure interpreters had enabled the formalization of the enclosure semantics. This was done using the techniques of both denotational semantics (which formalized the notion of a solution to a hybrid systems model in the first place) and operational semantics (which provided a concrete way to compute rigorous over-approximations for these solutions). Contemporaneously, the methods for processing partial derivatives and bounded quantification (needed for the Euler-Lagrange equation) were formalized. There were also two key engineering efforts, namely, support for real-time 3D animation and for real-time input from external devices such as smart phones.

5   Emerging Design

As noted earlier, the purpose of the iterative/agile approach taken is to accumulate knowledge relating to multiple complex questions. For reasons of space it is not possible to cover all that has been learned about these different questions. However, we can briefly describe the central concrete artifact of the project, which is the language design emerging from this process.

Syntax: As noted earlier, the emerging core syntax includes guarded equations, where equations can specify either behaviors continuous over time or discrete (discontinuous) transitions over time. Expressions in equations can include arithmetic operations and derivatives. This way, the language can express ordinary differential equations with discontinuities. Partial derivatives are allowed, but only if they can be eliminated through symbolic differentiation at compile time. Until recently, equations had to be directed. Recently, through the introduction of symbolic Gaussian elimination, it is possible to relax this requirement and allow users to express models as undirected equations as long as the system can automatically direct them through Gaussian elimination at compile time.

Semantics: Values in Acumen are all functions of real-valued time, and their co-domain can be atomic constants (strings), reals, vectors, and matrices. In addition, the language supports an object-like notion of a sub-model [6], which can be instantiated to model the creation of an object dynamically at a certain point in simulation (logical) time, and which can also be terminated. Models are hierarchical in that any sub-model instantiated dynamically by a particular model is considered a "child" model. Communication only occurs between "parent" and "child" models. Models can, however, be moved from one parent model to another. These choices where made in part to facilitate the automatic parallelization of models.

Support for 3D visualization is provided by allowing any model to contain a special variable _3D, which can be equated to special constructors that result in the display of 3D objects in a particular pane in the GUI.

The implementation supports a "traditional" semantics which uses traditional (non-validated) numerical methods. This is the most complete and most widely used semantics, and suffices for basic educational uses. This implementation has played a crucial role in allowing us to explore the design space and to converge on an expressive, minimal syntax for modeling hybrid systems, as well as semantics for solutions. For example, it allowed us to make an early decision to support the notion of "super-dense" time, first introduced in the verification literature [15], and later advocated by Lee [14].

The implementation also supports an "enclosure" semantics, which is intended to produce rigorous over-approximations (guaranteed upper and lower bounds) for all simulations [12]. This is the semantics that we would like Acumen, ultimately, to provide. While the current implementation of this semantics is not perfect, our recent work on the theoretical foundations for this semantics provides evidence that it is, at least in principle, feasible. The enclosure interpreter supports the use of intervals (closed, compact, connected sets on the reals) in source programs. As representations of sets (or, in computer science terminology, nondeterminism), enclosures and intervals enabled rigorous analysis of systems with uncertain parameters. This was particularly important for the collaboration with partners from the automotive industry [8,16].

So far, the introduction of a static type system in the implementation has been actively avoided. This choice is only a temporary one, to facilitate results on implementation techniques and semantic foundations, and to maintain a low entry barrier to the language. The language is seen as being in a phase where requirements for the type system are still being gathered.

6   Conclusions

This paper presented the design goals for the Acumen, explained the intrinsic challenges in achieving such ambitious goals, and articulated the research method taken to advance towards these goals. The complex interdependence between the individual goals is representative of the challenges that face the ambitious efforts to advance the state of the art by both the CPS and IoT communities. At the same time, the progress made to date gives us hope that this approach, which is characteristic of the philosophy of both communities, can be effective at enabling advances that would not possible through more narrowly focused efforts. The paper also presented several lessons learned in the context of specific activities in the development of Acumen.

One insight that cannot be placed in the context of a particular milestone relates to the gap between CPS and IoT. It appears that there is a gap in foundations between CPS (especially based on computer science) and IoT (especially based on information and communication theory) that is echoed in a disconnect in tools that support non-deterministic uncertainty and stochastic uncertainty, respectively. Our awareness of this gap developed gradually as we made several efforts to model networking system and found non-deterministic modeling of uncertainty insufficient for typical problems in this domain. Stochastic methods seem necessary for many of those problems. At the tool level, stochastic models (such as Markov chains or queueing systems) can seem simpler or independent from non-deterministic methods. Semantically, however, stochastic models are more naturally built after non-determinism has been fully treated and notions of distributions can be overlayed on notions of sets. With this insight in mind, we anticipate that when distributions can be introduced into Acumen that this will help bring closer the disciplines of CPS and IoT.

At a more practical level, Acumen is at a stage where performance issues should be given priority. There are two distinct concerns relating to performance. The first is with enabling casual users to experiment with larger models that can be simulated easily (and for many applications, usefully) using the traditional (non-validated) semantics. The second is with enabling rigorous simulation in reasonable time. We expect that the latter will be essential for user acceptability of the ultimate results of the Acumen development effort. A particular problem for the enclosure semantics that will also need to be addressed is to improve error messages. They are currently less intuitive compared to the traditional semantics, mainly because of the less familiar (and maybe less intuitive) process used for computing enclosures. Finally, we are also working on applying well-understood mathematical techniques for producing more precise over-approximations.

Acknowledgement. Numerous colleagues have contributed to the development of Acumen. We thank in particular the students of the CPS course at Halmstad University.

References

1. The jPCT web page. http://www.jpct.net. Accessed 10 Aug 2015
2. Alur, R., Grosu, R., Hur, Y., Kumar, V., Lee, I.: Modular specification of hybrid systems in charon. In: Lynch, N., Krogh, B.H. (eds.) HSCC 2000. LNCS, vol. 1790, pp. 6–19. Springer, Heidelberg (2000). doi:10.1007/3-540-46430-1_5
3. Arbor, A.: CarSim reference manual, ver. 6.03 (2005)
4. Modelica Association et al.: Modelica-a unified object-oriented language for physical systems modeling. Language Specification, Version, 2 (2005)
5. Beck, K., Beedle, M., Van Bennekum, A., Cockburn, A., Cunningham, W., Fowler, M., Grenning, J., Highsmith, J., Hunt, A., Jeffries, R., et al.: Manifesto for agile software development (2001)
6. Brauner, P., Taha, W.M.: Globally parallel, locally sequential: a preliminary proposal for acumen objects. In: Proceedings of the 9th Workshop on Parallel/High-Perf. Object-Oriented Scientific Computing, p. 2. ACM (2010)
7. Coplien, J., Hoffman, D., Weiss, D.: Commonality and variability in software engineering. IEEE Softw. **15**(6), 37–45 (1998)
8. Duracz, A., Eriksson, H., Bartha, F.Á., Zeng, Y., Xu, F., Taha, W.: Using rigorous simulation to support ISO 26262 hazard analysis and risk assessment. In: 12th IEEE International Conference on Embedded Software and System (2015)
9. Edalat, A., Pattinson, D.: Denotational semantics of hybrid automata. J. Log. Algebraic Program. **73**(1), 3–21 (2007)
10. Frehse, G., Le Guernic, C., Donzé, A., Cotton, S., Ray, R., Lebeltel, O., Ripado, R., Girard, A., Dang, T., Maler, O.: SpaceEx: scalable verification of hybrid systems. In: Computer Aided Verification
11. Koenig, N., Howard, A.: Design and use paradigms for Gazebo, an open-source multi-robot simulator. In: IEEE/RSJ International Conference on Intelligent Robots and Systems, Proceedings, vol. 3, pp. 2149–2154. IEEE (2004)
12. Konečný, M., Taha, W., Duracz, J., Duracz, A., Ames, A.: Enclosing the behavior of a hybrid system up to and beyond a zeno point. In: IEEE 1st International Conference on Cyber-Physical Systems, Networks, and Applications (2013)
13. Lessig, L.: Code is Law: On Liberty in Cyberspace. Harvard Magazine, Cambridge (2000)
14. Liu, X., Matsikoudis, E., Lee, E.A.: Modeling timed concurrent systems. In: Baier, C., Hermanns, H. (eds.) CONCUR 2006. LNCS, vol. 4137, pp. 1–15. Springer, Heidelberg (2006). doi:10.1007/11817949_1
15. Maler, O., Manna, Z., Pnueli, A.: Prom timed to hybrid systems. In: Bakker, J.W., Huizing, C., Roever, W.P., Rozenberg, G. (eds.) REX 1991. LNCS, vol. 600, pp. 447–484. Springer, Heidelberg (1992). doi:10.1007/BFb0032003

16. Masood, J., Philippsen, R., Duracz, J., Taha, W., Eriksson, H., Grante, C.: Domain analysis for standardised functional safety: a case study on design-time verification of automatic emergency braking
17. Mernik, M., Heering, J., Sloane, A.M.: When, how to develop domain-specific languages. ACM Comput. Surv. (CSUR) **37**(4), 316–344 (2005)
18. Platzer, A., Quesel, J.-D.: KeYmaera: a hybrid theorem prover for hybrid systems (System Description). In: Armando, A., Baumgartner, P., Dowek, G. (eds.) IJCAR 2008. LNCS (LNAI), vol. 5195, pp. 171–178. Springer, Heidelberg (2008). doi:10.1007/978-3-540-71070-7_15
19. Taha, W.: A gentle introduction to multi-stage programming. In: Lengauer, C., Batory, D., Blum, A., Odersky, M. (eds.) Domain-Specific Program Generation. LNCS, vol. 3016, pp. 30–50. Springer, Heidelberg (2004)
20. Taha, W., Cartwright, R.: The trouble with real numbers. In: Informatik 2011, p. 325. Bonner Köllen Verlag (2011)
21. Taha, W., Cartwright, R., Philippsen, R., Zeng, Y.: A first course on cyber physical systems. In: Workshop on Cyber-Physical Systems Education (2013)
22. Taha, W., Gaspes, V., Page, R.: Accurate programming: thinking about programs in terms of properties. arXiv preprint arXiv:1109.0786 (2011)
23. Wan, Z., Hudak, P.: Functional reactive programming from first principles.In: ACM SIGPLAN Notices, vol. 35, pp. 242–252. ACM (2000)
24. Zeng, Y., Rose, C., Brauner, P., Taha, W., Masood, J., Philippsen, R., O'Malley, M., Cartwright, R.: Modeling basic aspects of cyber-physical systems, part ii. In: IEEE 11th International Conference on Embedded Software and System (2014)

Spatial Reuse Based Resource Allocation in Device-to-Device Communications

Tiansheng Sun[1], Li Wang[1,2]($\boxtimes$), Zilong Wu[1], and Tommy Svensson[3]

[1] Beijing University of Posts and Telecommunications, Beijing 100876, China
liwang@bupt.edu.cn
[2] National Mobile Communications Research Laboratory, Southeast University,
Nanjing, People's Republic of China
[3] Chalmers University of Technology, Gothenburg, Sweden
tommy.svensson@chalmers.se

Abstract. Device-to-Device (D2D) communications have attracted more concern recently, since it provides a supplemental paradigm of short range communications for the current cellular networks. In D2D communications information bits are directly transmitted between devices without traversing base station (BS). As a result, D2D communications can potentially facilitate the improvement of the network capacity, extension of the network coverage, enhancement of the spectrum efficiency, and the energy efficiency as well. It also works well for couple of new applications, such as information exchange between devices in Internet of Things (IoT) and low delay video content sharing. From the perspective of resource allocation in D2D communications, multiple D2D users (DUs) may reuse the same resource of cellular users (CUs). Thus, we put our focus on the spatial reuse resource allocation in this paper. We formulate the spatial reuse problem which aims to maximize the system throughput while maintaining the desirable signal-noise-interference-ratio (SINR) at receivers. Accordingly, a greedy based user set selection algorithm is proposed to filter the candidate DU set to further reduce the computation complexity. Simulation results show that the cellular network can achieve a higher throughput by using our proposed scheme.

Keywords: Device-to-device communications · Resource allocation · Spatial reuse

1 Introduction

With the development of mobile Internet and the continuous improvement of terminal functions, many new technologies have emerged with demanding, such as the Internet of things, IoT. These service providers are offering a variety of applications, and thus frequently changing users' demands, which has been challenging the current wireless communications technologies. In the previous cellular network, communications between the users have to go through the BS. However, nowadays the communications between the equipments are frequently

© ICST Institute for Computer Sciences, Social Informatics and Telecommunications Engineering 2016
B. Mandler et al. (Eds.) IoT 360° 2015, Part I, LNICST 169, pp. 131–143, 2016.
DOI: 10.1007/978-3-319-47063-4_12

carried out in a relatively close range in many scenes, for example, in the Internet of things, many adjacent devices need to connect with others to share information. Device-to-Device communications, as a supplement to cellular networks, which can meet user communications needs, reduce the burden of the network, and improve the overall throughput of the network at the same time [1].

D2D communications enable the users in the cellular network to communicate with the users in his neighborhood through direct link rather than circumvent the BS as the traffic relay. D2D communications can share the wireless resource of cellular networks unlike Bluetooth and WiFi technologies. D2D communications can be easily implemented without making too much changes to the infrastructure of the cellular network while improving the system capacity, lowering the energy consumption of users' handhold devices, enhancing the spectral efficiency, reducing communications delay, and reducing the load of the BS. Owing to the above advantages, D2D communications have attracted a lot of attention.

There are many research topics in the D2D communications technology, such as proximity discovery, connection establishment, access control, mode selection, resource allocation, e.g. [2–4]. The Social-Dependent Chinese Restaurant Process D2D user clustering scheme in [5] used both social information and physical distance information to cluster. Aiming at the problem of resource matching, [6] proposed a fast pairing strategy which can improve the matching speed compared with the previous scheme. [7] provided the clustering scheme based on access strategy after analyzing the important factors like interests, hobbies, location and equipment abilities which affected the behavior of users. Authors discussed applications of D2D communications in heterogeneous networks [8]. In addition, D2D communications were also applied to enhance the conventional multicast scheme for delivering video content in 4G networks [9–11].

A lot researchers have already done some work about spatial reuse in ad-hoc networks and wireless mesh networks, e.g. [12,13]. As the network structure and the attribute of nodes in the ad-hoc networks are different from those in the cellular network, those research findings cannot be used directly to analyze the spatial reuse in cellular networks. However, there are also researches on spatial reuse in D2D communications in cellular networks recently from different perspectives. Authors in [14] proposed the semi-distributed resource allocation scheme to maximize the spatial reuse of radio resource in the D2D communications which is in the overlay mode. To exploit spatial reuse and maintain fairness among D2D pairs, a resource scheduling algorithm was also studied in [15]. A two-stage resource management scheme was proposed in [16], which aims to maximize the resource efficiency in a hybrid mode of underlay and overlay. Researchers in [17] demonstrated the spatial reuse gain through joint mode selection and resource allocation. Graph coloring theory was applied to analyze the spatial reuse cellular resource in [18,19]. A location dependent resource allocation scheme in [20] considered the mobility of D2D communications. Although the spatial reuse in D2D communications has been studied from different perspectives, few people study the problem that how to choose appropriate D2D pairs when one CU's resource can be reused by multiple D2D pairs. We study the problem and give the solution.

In this paper, we first formulate the problem of resource allocation based on spatial reuse with the objective of maximizing the throughput of cellular network by allowing the simultaneous transmission of D2D users (DUs) on the same resource while ensuring the SINR demand at receivers. Then the problem becomes to select a group of appropriate DUs to reuse the resource of each CU and guarantee the communications quality of each DU and CU at the same time. A greedy algorithm is proposed to solve the problem, based on which we can obtain the results of resource allocation for D2D communications. Simulation results confirm that a higher system throughput can be obtained by using the proposed spatial reuse based scheme compared to the benchmark.

The remaining part of this paper is organized as follows: we describe the system model and analyze the interference at D2D receivers and the BS in Sect. 2. In Sect. 3, we formulate the resource allocation problem and Sect. 4 propose a greedy based user set selection algorithm to solve it. Section 5 present the simulation result and Sect. 6 gives the conclusion of this paper.

2   System Model

In this section, we describe the system model and analyze the interference between CU and D2D pair, D2D pair and D2D pair using the same resource in the scenario.

We investigate spectrum sharing for D2D communications underlay in cellular networks as depicted in Fig. 1. Assume the eNB is in the center of the cell, the users are divided into two types, CUs and DUs. CUs and DUs are randomly located

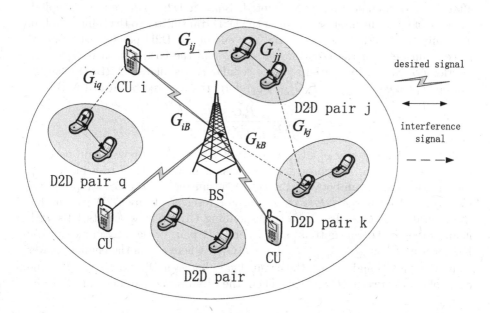

Fig. 1. System model.

around the center. There are M CUs represented by $C = \{1, 2, ..., i, ..., M\}$, and J D2D pairs denoted by $D = \{1, 2, ..., j, ...J\}$. Every D2D pair consists of a transmitter D^t and a receiver D^r. The distance between the D2D transmitter and the D2D terminal of the same D2D pair should be less than the maximum distance constraint of D2D communications, thus ensuring the QoS for D2D communications.

In particular, uplink resource reusing is adopted in this paper, since uplink spectrum is under-utilized compared to that of the downlink in the frequency division duplexing (FDD) based cellular systems [21]. A resource block (RB) is the basic unit for the radio resource allocation which represents one subchannel of the uplink band. The BS is responsible for allocating RBs for CUs based on their requests. DUs then can reuse the uplink resource of these CUs. Different from previous studies where each DU can only reuse the resource of one CU, we assume that each DU can reuse the uplink resource of a plurality of CUs and the uplink resource of each CU can be multiplexed by multiple DUs as well in this model.

We assume a fully loaded cellular network scenario like [22,23]. For the CUs, the system assign them the same number of RBs, that is the orthogonal frequency bands. CU i uses the assigned RBs to communicate with the BS. And then in order to benefit from spatial reuse, we define a set of D2D pairs K_i $(K_i \subset D)$, which means that only the D2D pairs in K_i can reuse the RBs of CU i for D2D communications.

We assume that the BS can obtain accurate channel state information of all the links in the network by nodes reporting. The large scale path loss model based on physical distance is considered for the channel fading.

Next, we analyze the only problem of the interference in cellular networks after D2D communications are adopted. Since a D2D pair reuse the uplink resource of CUs, the interference from the D2D transmitter to the cellular uplink is mainly the interference to the BS. For one of the D2D pairs j, the channel power gain between the DU transmitter D_j^t and the base station is G_{jB}. The interference caused by spatial reuse of cellular user's allocated RBs, to the BS can be expressed as $\sum_{j \in K_i} P_d G_{jB}$. Therefore, the received SINR at the BS is:

$$\gamma_i^c = \frac{P_c G_{iB}}{\sum_{j \in K_i} P_d G_{jB} + \sigma^2}. \tag{1}$$

P_c is the transmit power of CU i, G_{iB} denotes the channel power gain between the CU and the BS, P_d represents the transmit power of D2D transmitter D_j^t, the channel power gain between the D2D transmitter and the BS is represented by G_{jB}, and σ^2 is the power of noises. For receiver of any D2D pair in K_i, the interference comes from the corresponding CU i who share its RBs with it and other D2D transmitters in K_i. For D2D pair j, the interference to the DU receiver D_j^r is $\sum_{k \neq j, k \in K_i} (P_d G_{kj} + P_c G_{ij})$, where G_{ij} is the channel power gain between CU and D_j^r, G_j the channel gain between D_j^t and D_j^r and G_{kj} the channel gain between D_k^t and D_j^r. Then, the SINR at D_j^r can be expressed as:

$$\gamma_{ji}^d = \frac{P_d G_j}{\sum_{k \neq j, k \in K_i} (P_d G_{kj} + P_c G_{ij} + \sigma^2)}. \tag{2}$$

In order to guarantee the communications quality, the SINR at BS and D2D receivers are required to satisfy the desired SINR demand when they reuse the same RBs which can be constrained by $\gamma_i^c \geq \gamma_{min}^c$ and $\gamma_j^d \geq \gamma_{min}^d$, respectively. γ_{min}^c is the desired SINR demand for cellular and γ_{min}^d for D2D.

3   Resource Sharing Between CUs and D2D Pairs

Based on the above mathematical model, this paper presents a resource allocation scheme. Next, we describe the scheme in detail.

3.1   Problem Formulation

Recall the description above, since each CU uses orthogonal frequency band resource that has been assigned by the system, there is no interference between users when they communicate in different frequency bands, and D2D pairs can use different resource to communicate, i.e., one D2D pair can be assigned the resource of multiple CUs in the resource allocation for D2D communications. Therefore, the problem above can be divided into M subproblems, namely, finding out the set of D2D pairs which can reuse resource of each CU to maximize the sum rate of the combination R_i. This can make the network system throughput to reach the maximum. CU i and D2D pair set K_i share the same frequency band resource, which causes interference with each other in the communications as analyzed before. The co-channel interference are different to the set of D2D pair set K_i and CU i as a whole when different D2D pair is added to K_i. We need to consider the D2D pair selection process in this case: which D2D pair group can reuse the resource of CU i that can maximize the sum rate of the CU i and D2D pairs while guaranteeing the communications quality of both CU and D2D pairs, that is $\gamma_i^c \geq \gamma_{min}^c$ for CU i and $\gamma_j^d \geq \gamma_{min}^d$ for any D2D pairs in K_i. Therefore, the problem is converted to the problem of selecting appropriate D2D pairs to obtain the maximum sum rate of CUs and D2D pairs.

3.2   Problem Derivation

Resource of every CU can be reused by multiple D2D pairs, while each D2D pair can also reuse resource of multiple CUs. We have assume that all the DUs are capable of reusing the resource of CU i as a set K_i $(K_i \subset D)$. The transmission rate of each uplink cellular link can be represented as:

$$R_i^c = \log_2 \left(1 + \frac{P_c G_{iB}}{\sum\limits_{j=1}^{J} l_{ji} P_d G_{jB} + \sigma^2} \right), \tag{3}$$

where $l_{ji} \in \{0,1\}$ with $l_{ji} = 1$ means that the D2D pair j is in set K_i, and $l_{ji} = 0$ the opposite. On the other hand, the transmission rate of each D2D pair obtained by reusing resource of CU i is:

$$R_{ji}^d = l_{ji} \log_2 \left(1 + \frac{P_d G_j}{\sum\limits_{\substack{k=1 \\ k \neq j}}^{J} l_{ki} P_d G_{jk} + P_c G_{ij} + \sigma^2} \right). \tag{4}$$

The sum rate of CU i and D2D pairs which reuse its resource is:

$$R_i = R_i^c + \sum_{j=1}^{J} R_{ji}^d. \tag{5}$$

We have assumed that each CU will be assigned resource by the system, as mentioned before, and DUs can reuse resource of more than one CU. The total system throughput can be expressed as:

$$R = \sum_{i=1}^{M} R_i = \sum_{i=1}^{M} R_i^c + \sum_{i=1}^{M} \sum_{j=1}^{J} R_{ji}^d. \tag{6}$$

Note that, although we have assumed a fully loaded cellular network scenario before, the scheme can also be used for other scenarios. We can formulate the resource allocation problem as below:

$$(l_{11}, l_{12}...l_{ji}...l_{JM}) = \ \text{argmax} \ R \tag{7}$$

Subject to

$$\gamma_i^c \geq \gamma_{\min}^c \qquad \forall i \in C, \tag{8}$$

$$\gamma_j^d \geq \gamma_{\min}^d \qquad \forall j \in K_i, \tag{9}$$

$$l_{ji} \in \{0,1\} \qquad \forall j \in D. \tag{10}$$

Our goal is to calculate appropriate l_{ij} values to leverage the system throughput. The expression $\gamma_i^c \geq \gamma_{\min}^c$ means that when the CU communicates with the BS, the received SINR need to be greater than $\gamma_{\min}^d$. Similarly, $\gamma_j^d \geq \gamma_{\min}^d$ indicates that when the D2D pairs communicate with each other, the SINR at the receiver should be greater than $\gamma_{\min}^d$, otherwise the D2D pair cannot reuse the resource.

4   The Matching Problem Between CU and D2D Pairs

In this section, we describe the problem and introduce the greedy based user set selection algorithm and give an example to illustrate it.

4.1   Problem Description

According to the description of the previous paragraph. The problems we are facing can be described in this way. Resource of CU can be reused by multiple D2D pairs, the reuse of resource improves the system throughput. But, Due to the use of same channel, users interfere with each other. The more D2D pairs join to reuse, the more serious the interference will be. In order to ensure the quality of communications, only part of the D2D pairs can be able to reuse resource. Therefore, in order to improve the throughput of the system and guarantee the user's communications quality, appropriate D2D pairs which can reuse resource need to be choosen by calculation.

4.2   Greedy Based User Set Selection Algorithm

It is very difficult to find the optimal solution of the problem above directly. Now, we present a greedy algorithm for solving the proposed problem. A greedy based user set selection algorithm (GUS-algorithm) is an algorithm that follows the problem solving heuristic of making the locally optimal choice at each stage with the hope of finding a global optimum. In many problems, the greedy strategy can not produce an optimal solution in general, but it is still a greedy heuristic that may produce a locally optimal solution in a reasonable time to approximate the global optimal solution. As presented in Algorithm 1, this algorithm starts with setting up an empty set K_i, which represents the set of D2D pairs who will reuse the resource of CU i, and then set a set $D = \{1, 2...j...J\}$ which is the candidate D2D pair set. At first step, the D2D pairs in D will be sorted according to the channel gain information G_{jB} on the basis of descending order. Then the D2D pairs with smaller G_{jB} values will be in the front, and each step will be carried out in accordance with this order in the next calculation process. Calculate the sum rate of CU i and all the D2D pairs in K_i in case of one D2D pair j joins K_i for every D2D pair j in D. Then we have the results of every D2D pairs in D. Since our goal is to leverage the sum rate of the CUs and D2D pairs, we choose the only one DU j^* which can maximize the sum rate at each step. On the other hand, we still need to verify that the DU j^* we have chosen can meet the needs of communications quality for CU i, D2D pairs in set K_i and itself. If the SINR value of anyone mentioned above is below the desire SINR demand, the chosen D2D pair j^* cannot join K_i, and it will be removed from D, and otherwise it can stay in K_i and we still remove it from D. After the set K_i and D are updated, and the same process will continue until the set D is empty. Then set $l_{ji} = 1$ for the D2D pair j^* successfully joining in K_i, and otherwise $l_{ji} = 0$.

4.3   Algorithm Example

In order to illustrate this scheme more clearly, let us give a simple example to illustrate the algorithm. Assume that there are 10 CUs and 10 D2D pairs in a cellular network cell, the CUs are assigned the same amount of the resource. CUs uses the orthogonal frequency band, and each D2D pair can reuse resource

---

Algorithm 1. Greedy based user set selection algorithm

1: $K_i \Leftarrow \emptyset$
2: $D \Leftarrow \{1, 2...j \cdots J\}$
3: **for all** $j \in D$ **do**
4:    sort D2D pair in D according to G_{jB}
5: **end for**
6: **return** *sorted* D
7: **while** $D \neq \emptyset$ **do**
8:    $j^* \Leftarrow \arg\max_{j \in D} R_i$
9:    $K_i \Leftarrow K_i \cup \{j^*\}$
10:    **if** $\gamma_i^c \geq \gamma_{\min}^c$ **then**
11:      **if** $\gamma_j^d \geq \gamma_{\min}^d$ for all $j \in K_i$ **then**
12:        $l_{j^*i} = 1$
13:      **else**
14:        $l_{j^*i} = 0$, $K_i \Leftarrow K_i - \{j^*\}$
15:      **end if**
16:    **else**
17:      $l_{j^*i} = 0$
18:      $K_i \Leftarrow K_i - \{j^*\}$
19:    **end if**
20:    $D \Leftarrow D - \{j^*\}$
21: **end while**
22: **return** $l_{1i}, l_{2i}...l_{Ji}$

---

of multiple CUs. So, the resource allocation for D2D can be converted to choose the optimal D2D pairs to reuse resource of each CU. That is to say, the same selection process is needed to be carried out for each CU. For CU 1, there are 10 D2D pairs who may reuse the resource. So we set up a set $D = \{1, 2...j...10\}$ which means the candidate D2D pairs, and set an empty set $K_1 = \{\}$ which will be added the feasible D2D pairs. First, we sort the 10 D2D pairs in D according to the channel gain G_{jB} in descending order, then we get an ordered list of D2D pairs, for example, $D = \{2, 4, 1, 5, 3, 6, 7, 9, 8, 10\}$. The next calculation carried out in this order. We assume that D2D pair 2 in the set D is reusing the resource of the CU 1, and use the formula (5) mentioned above to calculate the sum rate of CU and DUs. In the same way, we assume other D2D pairs 4,1...10 to reuse the resource of CU 1 respectively. By comparing these ten rate results, we choose the D2D pair which has the maximum value. Next, suppose D2D pair 2 is selected, it needs to verify that the SINR of CU 1 and D2D pair 2 satisfy the conditions. If the conditions are fulfilled, then D2D pair 2 is added to set K_1, else, it is ruled out to reuse the resource.

After several calculations, assume that there has been three D2D pairs in K_1, as $K_1 = \{2, 4, 5\}$ and $D = \{6, 7, 9\}$. To continue to execute the algorithm, we calculate the sum rate of CU 1 and D2D pair 2, 4, 5, 6 supposing D2D pair 6 to join to reuse the resource. Similarly, we also do this for D2D pair 7 and 9. Then choose D2D pair 6 which has the max sum rate and verify the SINR demands of CU 1 and D2D pair 6, 2, 4, 5 are met. If the conditions are satisfied, 6 joins K_1, else it should be removed. Continue to repeat the calculation process mentioned above until the set D is empty.

Iterate the algorithm for each CU in C, and the D2D pair set which can reuse its resource is determined, and thus we complete resource allocation for D2D users.

5   Numerical Simulation and Performance Analysis

In this part we set up the simulation to verify the performance of the proposed scheme. The simulation scenario is set up in a cellular network whose radius is 500 m, where users are randomly distributed within this range. The BS is located in the center of the circle. The spectral density of the noise is set to $-174\,\mathrm{dBm/Hz}$. At simulation initialization, D2D links are randomly generated with the constraint that the distance between the transmitter and the receiver of each D2D pair is less than 40 m. According to the large scale path-loss model, all link channel gains are related to the distance. Assume the large scale path-loss exponent between the BS and CU to be $\alpha = 3.5$ and that of D2D pair is $\alpha = 4$. The channel power gain between the cellular users and the BS is $G_{cB} = d_{cB}^{-\alpha}$, where d_{cB} is the distance between them. Similarly, $G_{cd} = d_{cd}^{-\alpha}$ stands for the channel power gain between CUs and the D2D receiver, where the distance between them is d_{cd}. The channel power gain between D2D pairs is denoted as $G_{dd} = d_{dd}^{-\alpha}$, where d_{dd} represents the distance between them. The uplink resource are assigned to CUs for cellular network communications according to the round robin scheduling, and based on the proposed scheme, these resource are reused by D2D pairs. We assume that the transmit power of CUs and D2D transmitters are, respectively, 200 mw and 10 mw. The desired SINR demand of cellular link and D2D links are 10 dB and 5 dB, respectively. The benchmark scheme is a simple resource allocation scheme without considering the optimization of spatial reuse. In this scheme, the system chooses the D2D pairs to reuse the resource of CUs randomly, which also need to ensure the communications quality requirements of the CUs and the D2D pairs at the same time. Our simulation is averaged over 1000 random trials.

Figure 2 shows the system throughput performance varying with different number of CUs. With the increase of the number of CUs, the overall throughput gradually increases, because the available wireless resource for D2D communications are increasing. As shown in the figure, the blue line with triangular pattern is the spatial reuse resource allocation scheme which uses the GUS-algorithm and the red line with square pattern is the benchmark scheme which choose the D2D pair to reuse in a random fashion. With the increase of M, the growth rate of the two schemes is similar, which is mainly because the number of D2D pairs remains unchanged, and thus the interference level between the two scheme is the same, and the number of reusable resource is increasing. The number of D2D pairs which can reuse the resource is subject to the desired SINR demand of CUs and D2D pairs, so the composition of set K_i is important to the system throughput. In the proposed scheme, the D2D pairs which can reuse the resource

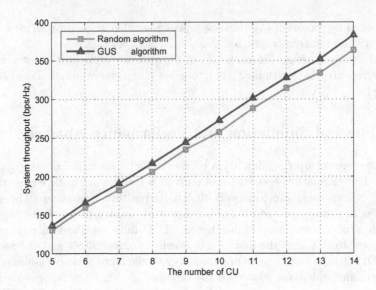

Fig. 2. System throughput versus number of CUs. (Color figure online)

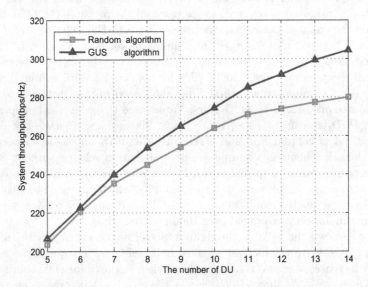

Fig. 3. System throughput versus number of DUs.

of CU are selected by the algorithm which aims to maximize the sum rate. We can see that the overall performance of the proposed scheme is better than the benchmark one.

Figure 3 indicates the relationship between the system throughput and the number of D2D pairs when the number of CUs is fixed at $M = 10$. As can be seen from the graph, the overall throughput of the network is increasing when the number of D2D pairs increases. This is because the increase in the overall number of D2D pairs lead to an increase number of D2D pairs that can reuse the RBs of CUs. However, with the growth of D2D pairs, the interference the CUs also increase. The system throughput may not grow rapidly considering the SINR demand of the CUs and D2D pairs. In the proposed scheme, D2D pairs are selected to reuse the RBs of CUs which can make the sum rate to reach the maximum at each iteration of D2D resource allocation algorithm. On the other hand, the benchmark scheme did not consider choosing the best D2D pair to reuse resource. The performance of the proposed scheme is better than the benchmark one, especially with the increasing number of D2D pairs.

6   Conclusions

In this paper, we proposed a spatial reuse resource allocation scheme for D2D communications in cellular networks. We presented a greedy based user set selection algorithm to select appropriate D2D pairs to reuse the resource of CUs so as to maximize the throughput. More specifically, the basic communications quality is also guaranteed to satisfy the minimum required SINR for both CUs and D2D pairs. The results of the simulation show that the cellular network can obtain a better network throughput by using the proposed scheme.

Acknowledgements. This work was supported in part by the Natural Science Foundations of China under Grants 61571056 and 61201150, the open research fund of National Mobile Communications Research Laboratory of Southeast University under Grants 2016D04, and the Beijing Higher Education Young Elite Faculty Grant No. YETP0442.

References

1. Doppler, K., Rinne, M., Wijting, C., Ribeiro, C., Hugl, K.: Device-to-device communication as an underlay to lte-advanced networks. IEEE Commun. Mag. **47**(12), 42–49 (2009)
2. Fodor, G., Dahlman, E., Mildh, G., Parkvall, S., Reider, N., Miklos, G., Turanyi, Z.: Design aspects of network assisted device-to-device communications. IEEE Commun. Mag. **50**(3), 170–177 (2012)
3. Xu, Y., Yin, R., Han, T., Yu, G.: Interference-aware channel allocation for device-to-device communication underlaying cellular networks. In: 2012 1st IEEE International Conference on Proceedings of the Communications in China (ICCC), Beijing, China, August 15–17, 2012, pp. 422–427
4. Wang, L., Tang, H., Cierny, M.: Device-to-device link admission policy based on social interaction information. IEEE Trans. Veh. Technol. **64**(9), 4180–4186 (2015)
5. Wang, L., Araniti, G., Cao, C., Wang, W., Liu, Y.: Device-to-device users clustering based on physical and social characteristics. Int. J. Distrib. Sens. Netw. **501**, 165608 (2015)
6. Wang, L., Wu, H.: Fast pairing of device-to-device link underlay for spectrum sharing with cellular users. IEEE Commun. Lett. **18**(10), 1803–1806 (2014)

7. Cao, C., Wang, L., Song, M., Zhang, Y.: Admission policy based clustering scheme for d2d underlay communications. In: 2014 IEEE 25th Annual International Symposium on Proceedings of the Personal, Indoor, and Mobile Radio Communication (PIMRC), Washington DC, September 2–5, 2014, pp. 1937–1942
8. Wang, L., Tian, F., Svensson, T., Feng, D., Song, M., Li, S.: Exploiting full duplex for device-to-device communications in heterogeneous networks. IEEE Commun. Mag. **53**(5), 146–152 (2015)
9. Militano, L., Condoluci, M., Araniti, G., Molinaro, A., Iera, A., Muntean, G.-M.: Single frequency-based device-to-device-enhanced video delivery for evolved multimedia broadcast and multicast services. IEEE Trans. Broadcast. **61**(2), 263–278 (2015)
10. Militano, L., Condoluci, M., Araniti, G., Molinaro, A., Iera, A.: When d2d communication improves group oriented services in beyond 4g networks. Wirel. Netw. **21**(4), 1363–1377 (2014)
11. Orsino, A., Militano, L., Araniti, G., Molinaro, A., Iera, A.: Efficient data uploading supported by d2d communications in lte-a systems. In: Proceedings of European Wireless 2015, 21st European Wireless Conference, Budapest Hungary, May 20–22, 2015, pp. 1–6
12. Ning, Z., Song, Q., Guo, L., Jamalipour, A.: Throughput improvement by network coding and spatial reuse in wireless mesh networks. In: Proceedings of the Global Communications Conference (GLOBECOM), 2013 IEEE, Atlanta, GA, USA, December 9–13, 2013, pp. 4572–4577
13. Guo, X., Roy, S., Conner, W.: Spatial reuse in wireless ad-hoc networks. In: 2003 IEEE 58th Proceedings Vehicular Technology Conference, VTC 2003-Fall, Orlando, FL, USA, October 6–9, 2003, vol. 3, pp. 1437–1442
14. Lee, D.H., Choi, K.W., Jeon, W.S., Jeong, D.G.: Resource allocation scheme for device-to-device communication for maximizing spatial reuse. In: Proceedings of the 2013 IEEE Wireless Communications and Networking Conference (WCNC), Shanghai, China, April 7–10, 2013, pp. 112–117
15. Wang, H.-H., Chen, J.-C., Liu, Z.-N.: Resource allocation in central-controlled device-to-device communications networks. In: Proceedings of the Global Communications Conference (GLOBECOM), 2013 IEEE, Atlanta, GA, USA, December 9–13, 2013, pp. 4871–4876
16. Lee, D.H., Choi, K.W., Jeon, W.S., Jeong, D.G.: Two-stage semi-distributed resource management for device-to-device communication in cellular networks. IEEE Trans. Wirel. Commun. **13**(4), 1908–1920 (2014)
17. Chien, C.-P., Chen, Y.-C., Hsieh, H.-Y.: Exploiting spatial reuse gain through joint mode selection and resource allocation for underlay device-to-device communications. In: Proceedings of the 2012 15th International Symposium on Wireless Personal Multimedia Communications (WPMC), Taipei, September 24–27, 2012, pp. 80–84
18. Tsolkas, D., Liotou, E., Passas, N., Merakos, L.: A graph-coloring secondary resource allocation for d2d communications in lte networks. In: Proceedings of the 2012 IEEE 17th International Workshop on Computer Aided Modeling and Design of Communication Links and Networks (CAMAD), Barcelona, September 17–19, 2012, pp. 56–60
19. Zhang, R., Cheng, X., Yang, L., Jiao, B.: Interference-aware graph based resource sharing for device-to-device communications underlaying cellular networks. In: Proceedings of the Wireless Communications and Networking Conference (WCNC), 2013 IEEE, Shanghai, China, April 7–10, 2013, pp. 140–145

20. Botsov, M., Klugel, M., Kellerer, W., Fertl, P.: Location dependent resource allocation for mobile device-to-device communications. In: Proceedings of the Wireless Communications and Networking Conference (WCNC), 2014 IEEE, Istanbul, April 6–9, 2014, pp. 1679–1684

21. Zulhasnine, M., Huang, C., Srinivasan, A.: Efficient resource allocation for device-to-device communication underlaying lte network. In: Proceedings of the 2014 IEEE 6th InternationalConference on Wireless and Mobile Computing, Networking and Communications (WiMob), Niagara Falls, ON, October 11–13, pp. 368–375 (2010)

22. Kaufman, B., Aazhang, B.: Cellular networks with an overlaid device to device network. In: 2008 42nd Asilomar Conference on Proceedings Signals, Systems and Computers, Pacific Grove, CA, USA, October 26–29, 2008, pp. 1537–1541

23. Janis, P., Koivunen, V., Ribeiro, C., Korhonen, J., Doppler, K., Hugl, K.: Interference-aware resource allocation for device-to-device radio underlaying cellular networks. In: Proceedings of the IEEE 69th Vehicular Technology Conference, 2009, VTC Spring 2009, Barcelona, April 26–29, 2009, pp. 1–5

Wireless M-BUS: An Attractive M2M Technology for 5G-Grade Home Automation

Pavel Masek[1], Krystof Zeman[1], Zenon Kuder[1], Jiri Hosek[1(✉)],
Sergey Andreev[2], Radek Fujdiak[1], and Franz Kropfl[3]

[1] Brno University of Technology, Technicka 3082/12, 61600 Brno, Czech Republic
xmasek12@phd.feec.vutbr.cz, hosek@feec.vutbr.cz
[2] Tampere University of Technology, 33720 Tampere, Finland
sergey.andreev@tut.fi
[3] Telekom Austria Group, Lassallestraße 9, 1020 Wien, Austria
franz.kroepfl@telekomaustria.com

Abstract. The aggressive introduction of new smart devices for households is considered today as one of the most challenging issues in the Internet of Things (IoT) world. According to the wide variety of radio technologies used for communication between smart devices, there is a growing need to answer the question of which communication standard can be used to drive communication in smart homes and intelligent buildings as part of the emerging 5G ecosystem. To this end, we provide in this paper a performance analysis of Wireless M-BUS communication protocol which has recently increased its popularity especially in smart-metering domain in Western Europe. First, the developed WM-BUS module in Network Simulator 3 (NS-3) is described. Further, we investigate in detail the obtained simulation results which are compared with the real data from Kamstrup smart metering devices. Especially, the attention is focused on the packet delivery ratio and interference between smart devices. In particular, we demonstrate that our constructed module provides adequate correlation between the results obtained from the simulation and those from real-world measurements.

Keywords: Home automation · 5G-grade · IoT · NS-3 · Packet delivery estimation · Smart metering · Wireless M-BUS (WM-BUS)

1 Introduction and Motivation

During the last few years, the Internet of Things (IoT) attracted an enormous interest practically from all sectors of industry. According to Cisco forecast, the Machine-to-Machine (M2M) connections will grow from 495 million in 2014 to more than 3 billion in 2019 [1]. Today, we can see the wide variety of smart devices (e.g., smart meters, sensors, actuators) coming on the market in waves and trying to bring intelligent behavior into today's households. The initial idea of smart homes was built on collecting information from small groups of devices (very likely only from one device) and providing this information to the end user.

© ICST Institute for Computer Sciences, Social Informatics and Telecommunications Engineering 2016
B. Mandler et al. (Eds.) IoT 360° 2015, Part I, LNICST 169, pp. 144–156, 2016.
DOI: 10.1007/978-3-319-47063-4_13

Today, the smart devices become more intelligent and provide new functions for measuring (e.g., energy consumption and production measured by one device), reporting (sending data to energy provider) and creating statistics for end users. To fully meet the described vision, the communication networks need to be ready for this. Today, the 4G and beyond networks (Long Term Evolution, LTE) increasingly introduce Device-to-Device (D2D) communication capabilities. Nevertheless, the 4G was build with the goal to provide higher capacity, user data rates, improve spectrum usage and latency with respect to previous generations of cellular networks. However, in today's world, the IoT brings new challenges which cannot be solved solely by a single technology, but rather by the harmonized set of communication platforms, protocols and applications which all create the 5G vision [2]. The emerging 5G ecosystem as a bridge between a massive number of energy- and power-constrained smart objects deployed e.g. within a connected home and remote cloud-based applications will act as a key enabler for the IoT domain. Whereas, there is an undivided attention given by industry and academia to the 5G communication technologies, the deployment of home automation scenarios is somewhat lagging behind. Therefore, we target to bridge this gap by investigating of the promising communication candidates for connected home.

In the light of the above, there are currently multiple devices providing similar functionality independently from the communication technologies (IEEE 802.15.1, IEEE 802.15.4 (6LoWPAN, ZigBee), KNX, Wired/Wireless M-BUS) [3]. Therefore the question of aggregation the inputs from smart devices on their way to the remote servers is considered as highly demanded issue together with providing the unified approach for end users to manage data from different types of smart devices [4,5][1]. Currently, the effort to standardize the IoT frameworks, message structures and communication procedures is growing strong world-wide [6,7].

In this paper we propose a scenario where smart devices perform data in a house together, see Fig. 1. The collected values of electricity (orange), water (blue), temperature and humidity (green), motion sensor (violet) are sent towards an aggregation point (purple) where the data is transmitted via the 5G-ready infrastructure to the remote cloud application, see Fig. 1. The wireless communication technologies for smart metering provide high installation flexibility and therefore can be easily retrofitted in today's households.

This leads us to the question on the choice of the suitable communication technology/standard providing the energy efficiency, short message format and support from the industry companies [8]. Following our previous works within this field [12] where we paid our attention especially to the development of universal smart home gateway [4,10,11], we selected the Wireless M-BUS [9] as a promising driver for communication between devices (direct communication (MTCD - MTCD) and communication from smart device to remote server (MTCD - MTCG)).

---

[1] The aggregation point for smart devices based on different communication technologies is often called Machine Type Communication Gateway (MTCG). The smart devices are then described as Machine Type Communication Devices (MTCDs).

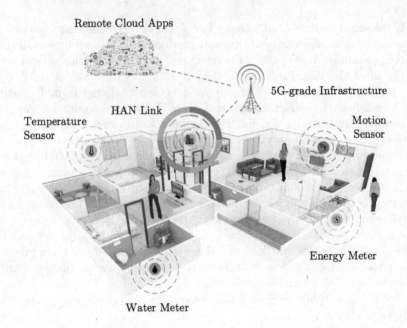

Fig. 1. In-house deployment of smart meters/sensors. (Color figure online)

Addressing the scenario where the key information about the electricity/water consumption is collected by the aggregation node, we provide the possibility for industry to assess behavior of WM-BUS devices and plan their deployment in dense urban areas with respect to the key metrics such as interference between installed devices, energy efficiency (battery life), active/idle time, transmission range and probability of successful data delivery. All these requirements were taken into account during the implementation of Wireless M-BUS into our simulation environment based on Network Simulator 3 (NS-3). We paid specific attention to utilization of the latest version of WM-BUS standard (following the requirements given in EN 13757-4:2005) and therefore our created module is able to deliver results where the data message follows the structure used in today's devices. As a verification of the obtained data from our module, we used the data set provided for us by Kamstrup [13] – one of the leading European companies in the smart grid communication domain.

2 Related Works

Most of the research activities during the recent several years were focused on the architecture and the key features/characteristics of selected wireless technologies considered for home automation and, more specifically, for smart metering [14,15]. We studied in detail published works which address the prominent wireless technologies in smart grids/smart homes with the aim to provide their performance evaluation.

Authors of [16] describe how to evaluate the wireless technologies for smart grid networks. However, recommendations from [16] cannot be used for evaluation in indoor environments due to the fact that authors paid attention to wide area networks in their research; further the effects of multipath propagation are not taken into account by this publication.

In [17], the unified metrics (PHY layer metric and MAC layer metric) of Home Automation Networks (HANs) are given. Especially, authors focused on IEEE 802.15.4, IEEE 802.11 and P1901 communication technologies and their functionality for smart grid applications.

Another solution for smart homes and Energy Management System (EMS) is presented in [18,19]. Authors offer design and implementation instructions for an EMS based on ZigBee, but not covering the performance of the ZigBee network within the indoor environment.

Evaluation of the performance of wireless sensor networks in different electric power system environments is provided in [20]. Authors perform measurements in order to determine the link quality; the measurements consider to an exemplary chipset implementing the 2.4 GHz physical layer of IEEE 802.15.4. Obtained results show degradation of the link quality and the number of successfully transmitted packets.

In addition to previous research work, authors of [21,22] focus on the IEEE 802.15.4 data transmission in different channels. However, presented model is very simple and authors do not provide comparison between performance of different technologies. Regarding the interference within the 2.4 GHz ISM band, authors of [23] provide the performance evaluation of IEEE 802.15.4 under the IEEE 802.11 interference. Obtained results indicate the significant impact on the reliability of a ZigBee network from the side of IEEE 802.11, which is in line with the results published in [24,25]. Based on that, authors propose guidelines on how to deploy the ZigBee network in order to minimize the impact of harmful

Table 1. Comparison of the key parameters of WM-BUS and IEEE 802.15.4. As the main findings, two parameters can be highlighted – in case of WM-BUS, the transmission frequency 868 MHz offers large area coverage and together with using the n/a channel access (data is sent as broadcast; especially in T mode), WM-BUS represents possible candidate for transmitting measurement data from sensors/meters.

Standard	Data rate	Transmission frequency	Effective bandwidth	Transmission power	Channel access
Bluetooth LE	1024 kb/s	2,4 GHz	1 MHz	10 mW	n/a
IEEE 802.15.4 (Worldwide)	250 kb/s	2,4 GHz	2 MHz	20 mW	CSMA/CA
IEEE 802.15.4 (Europe)	20 kb/s	868 MHz	600 kHz	25 mW	CSMA/CA
WM-BUS S mode	16,384 kb/s	868 MHz	200 kHz	25 mW	LBT/n/a
WM-BUS T mode	66,67 kb/s	868 MHz	300 kHz	25 mW	n/a

interference. Additionally, authors performed simulations in order to analyze the impact of PHY parameters (simulations were restricted to AWGN channel only).

In the light of the above, we recognized that almost all relevant publications focus on the IEEE 802.15.4 (ZigBee, 6LoWPAN) radio technology. However, following the information in [4,11], we identified Wireless M-BUS as a preferred communication protocol used widely in today's smart meters and sensors, see Table 1 for comparison between WM-BUS and IEEE 802.15.4. Owning to the tight cooperation with the Kamstrup [13] we had a clear idea on the issues with deploying new smart devices in dense populated areas faced by industry companies. Therefore we believe that our work brings valuable insights on how to evaluate communication between unattended devices based on the Wireless M-BUS and helps to resolve possible issues during deployment of smart devices in real use cases.

3   WM-BUS Module in NS-3

In this work, we describe the extended WM-BUS module for simulation environment NS-3. In the first version of our module for NS-3, described in [26], we only paid our attention to implementation of the core/main principles of WM-BUS communication.

Following the fact that our first implementation did not cover the frame structures of WM-BUS data, we extended our cooperation with the industry companies offering metering devices with the aim to come up with the improved implementation suitable for comprehensive testing of real data frame exchange between WM-BUS devices in practical environment. Therefore in this section the most important features and functions, beyond the scope of the first implemented version, will be described together with the developed frame dropping algorithm.

3.1   WM-BUS Protocol and Network

The general idea of created module is to provide the tool for evaluation of WM-BUS communication between metering devices. To be able to cover all scenarios where WM-BUS can be deployed, we implemented all supported operation modes of WM-BUS communication protocols; the description of network structure is given in what follows.

The topology of Wireless M-BUS [9] network can differ depending on the level of automation required for the application. Today, in static configuration, a network can consist of three types of nodes: meters (transmission mode T or S), repeaters (mode R) and concentrators (mode C). Meters periodically send broadcast messages containing the current information about the measured values. These signals are received by the concentrator(s) where the data can be processed. Then, repeaters are used in situations where the signals from the meters are not successfully received on the side of concentrator. They can be configured to re-broadcast received signals from meters and thus extend the effective range of the concentrators with respect to those meters.

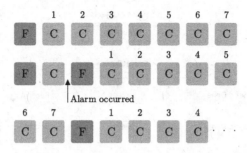

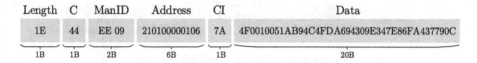

Fig. 2. Diagram of full (F)/compact (C) frame sequence with the alarm event.

Length	C	ManID	Address	CI	Data
1E	44	EE 09	210100000106	7A	4F0010051AB94C4FDA694309E347E86FA437790C
1B	1B	2B	6B	1B	20B

Fig. 3. Implemented WM-BUS frame structure for water meter.

To decrease the amount of redundant data sent after the connection between meters and concentrator(s) is established, real meters (e.g. Kamstrup Multical 21, Multical 402 and Multical 602) [27] implement two types of frames: full and compact. Data in the compact frames cannot be decoded in case that the full frame has not been previously received from a meter. Under normal conditions, a meter sends full frame followed by 7 compact frames and the cycle is repeated. Otherwise, in case that alarm occurs at the meter, the cycle is restarted immediately and a full frame is sent followed by 7 compact frames, see Fig. 2.

Frame Structure was implemented following our cooperation with the Czech and Austrian telecom and smart metering companies offering their temperature/water/electricity meters. Therefore we are able to simulate data traffic with the real frame structures (with and without the AES 128 encryption). The example of implemented frame structure (31B) for water meter is shown in Fig. 3.

All described features, defined in [9], were taken into account and implemented, see Sect. 3.2.

3.2 Implementation

The implementation of Wireless M-BUS communication protocol is based on simple Carrier Sense Multiple Access / Collision Avoidance (CSMA/CA) protocol for NS-3 introduced in [28]. This module (initially provided for NS-3.13) was modified in order to adhere to the requirements for WM-BUS given in [9]; the channel access method Listen-Before-Talk (LBT) is used in special cases in mode S. In most cases data is send via broadcast (mode T and S). A summary of constructed classes used in our module is depicted in Fig. 4; we introduce here

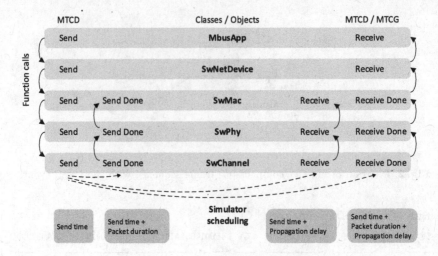

Fig. 4. Created classes for WM-BUS module.

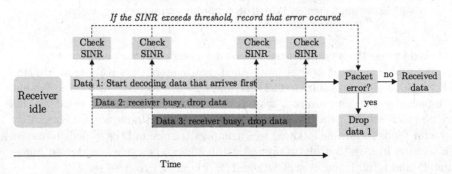

Fig. 5. Implemented frame dropping algorithm.

the completely new internal logic for communication inside the module allowing to implement all features given in [9][2].

When a frame is acquired during the simulation, its received signal strength is compared with the sensitivity of the receiver/concentrator. If this value is above the set threshold[3], the frame is recorded and the state of the receiver is set to busy. Whenever any other message arrives, the Signal-to-Interference-plus-Noise Ratio (SINR) is calculated at the beginning and at the end of the reception; to check if the SINR of the frame being decoded remained higher than the required value. In case the SINR becomes too low at any point, an internal variable is set to indicate a packet error. The state of the variable is read after the reception of the desired packet and the packet is dropped in case there was an error; this behavior is illustrated in Fig. 5.

---

[2] Description of proposed module structure is given in our previous work [26].

[3] For the purpose of our work, the threshold was set to −100 dBm.

The SINR is calculated in Eq. 1 as a ratio of the received desired signal power $P_{rx,desired}$ and the sum of all other signals $P_{rx,other}$ at the given receiver/concentrator and configurable noise floor, in linear values.

$$SINR_{db} = 10\log_{10}\left(\frac{P_{rx,desired}}{N + \sum P_{rx,other}}\right). \tag{1}$$

4   Performance Evaluation of Characteristic Scenarios

To increase the importance of the considered simulation scenarios and also to assess their performance, a set of measured data from real smart meters deployed by Kamstrup [13] was used[4]. In this section we paid our attention to two simulation scenarios. First, the results for the average number of delivered packets between concentrator-meter is given; this scenario contains the generic data structure and only the length defined in [9] is accounted for. Second, the probability of successfully received data frames has been recorded where the real data structure for water, electricity, humidity and temperature meters/sensors is considered.

The purpose of dividing the results into two sections follows from the need to have successfully calibrated module which can be used further for industry-grade simulation.

4.1   Model Calibration

All performed simulations were completed with the aim of the proper calibration of our created module in NS-3 in relation to the real-world measurements. The created scenario, potentially interesting for industry, is discussed later in this Sect. 4.2.

We performed two sets of simulation experiments as shown in Fig. 6. In the first experiment, the measured signal levels were used as the input data for simulation. In the second experiment, the signal levels were estimated by a log-distance propagation model [29] in 2 which was configured to match with common indoor environment in residential buildings:

$$PL(d) = PL\left(d_0 + 10n\log(\frac{d}{d_0})\right) + X_\sigma. \tag{2}$$

The $PL(d)$ represents the path loss at the distance d, $PL(d_0) = 31.22$ dB and represents the theoretical free-space path loss at the reference distance $d_0 = 1$ m. Path loss exponent is taken as $n = 2.97$ [29]. Further, σ [dB] is a zero mean Gaussian random variable which represents the local shadowing that is assumed to be log-normally distributed; the standard deviation is set as $\sigma = 3$ dB and was added to the measured values in the first experiment to model random fluctuations of the signal strength.

---

[4] The tool for downloading the real data from meters was developed in parallel with this research work; the geographical positions of meters, repeaters and concentrators, as well as signal levels and packet delivery (data hit) rates for each pair (concentrator-meter) were obtained and processed.

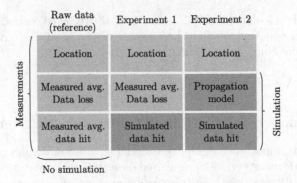

Fig. 6. Overview of the performed simulations in first scenario.

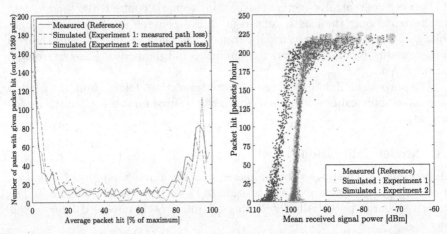

(a) Number of concentrator-meter pairs being in a given hit rate range.

(b) Data hit vs. path loss from all measurements.

Fig. 7. Model calibration.

The measured values of data hit (packet delivery rates for each pair (meter-concentrator)) were used as a reference (test data set) for the simulated values in both experiments. Figure 7(a) illustrates the number of concentrator-meter pairs which reached a given packet delivery ratio.

Figure 7(b) represents the dependence between the average number of data hits and the average received signal strength. Each point in the graph corresponds to one concentrator-meter pair. Further, the dispersion of measured data can be observed; based on these results the created module provides excellent correlation in range −100 dBm to −70 dBm. On the other hand, the discrepancy at the lower values can be seen. This behavior is caused by the frame dropping algorithm; the logic will be modified in our future works to better recognize the signals in range −100 dBm to −110 dBm.

4.2   Calibrated Simulation Scenario

Based on the results obtained in Sect. 4.1, we created an optimized scenario in Network Simulator 3 (NS-3) [30], where dozens of different smart devices (water meters, electricity meters, temperature sensors) communicate with the concentrator. Devices are distinguished by using different formats of WM-BUS message (length and structure) which was implemented exactly as in real devices, see Sect. 3.2.

Owning to good correlation of the constructed module, see Sect. 4.1, the presented simulation results provide an appropriate first-order picture for deployment of smart devices in real environment. In Fig. 8, the probability of successful reception (on the side of concentrator device) of data sent by meters is shown (blue line).

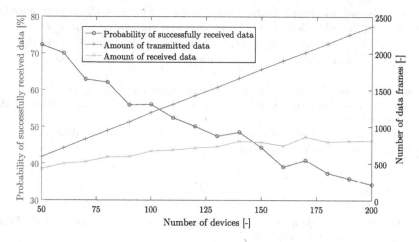

Fig. 8. Probability of successfully received data on the side of concentrator. Following the fact that nature of data transmission is based on broadcast, it could be expected that the collision rate will increase with the higher number of metering devices. (Color figure online)

The number of metering devices was gradually increasing during the simulation from 50 to 200 nodes with the step of 10 devices. All nodes were deployed within the area of 100 × 100 m following random distribution pattern with the minimal inter-distance 1.5 m (internal Kamstrup logic). Devices were sending measured data periodically; in practice, the transmission interval is defined by each vendor independently, but for our research we set transmission intervals as follows: water (30 s), electricity (60 s), temperature (300 s); all intervals were set exactly as in real scenarios for employed devices.

5   Summary and Conclusions

In this work, we analyzed the emerging concept of smart devices providing the information on utility consumption and production in urban locations with particular focus on indoor environment. Our constructed simulation module developed in NS-3 tool is open source and available for download on GitHub [31]. We believe that it might be considered as a powerful tool to estimate the ratio of successfully received data in case of using Wireless M-BUS communication protocol between meters and concentrator(s) which can serve as an initial evaluation (e.g. number of repeaters; devices in mode R) of planned deployments of metering devices.

To achieve this functionality, the calibration data provided by the Kamstrup company served as a test data set. As a consequence, the proposed module is able to predict the general trend of hit rate (successfully received data from meter on the concentrator side) in the real deployment. After the calibration of the created module has been completed, we also constructed optimized scenario which gives answer to the question on the probability of successfully received data from meters at the side of central point (concentrator). This scenario is very popular today e.g., in households and neighborhoods and therefore we believe that our proposed solution can serve as a valuable simulation tool for planning the real deployment of smart meters/sensors within the maturing 5G ecosystem.

Acknowledgment. Research described in this paper was financed by the National Sustainability Program under grant LO1401. For the research, infrastructure of the SIX Center was used.

We would like to thank to Kamstrup [13] for access to measured data and insight into the protocol and its real-life usage.

References

1. Cisco Visual Networking Index, Global mobile data traffic forecast update, 2014–2019, White Paper, February 2015
2. Condoluci, M., Dohler, M., Araniti, G., Molinaro, A., Zheng, K.: Toward 5G densenets: architectural advances for effective machine-type communications over femtocells. IEEE Commun. Mag. **53**(1), 134–141 (2015). doi:10.1109/MCOM.2015.7010526
3. Niyato, D., Xiao, L., Wang, P.: Machine-to-machine communications for home energy management system in smart grid. IEEE Commun. Mag. **49**(4), 53–59 (2011)
4. Masek, P., Hosek, J., Kovac, D., Kropfl, F.: M2M gateway: the centerpiece of future home. In: 2014 6th International Congress on Ultra Modern Telecommunications and Control Systems and Workshops (ICUMT). St. Petersburg, Russia, pp. 286–293 (2014). ISBN: 978-1-4799-5290-8
5. Di Fazio, A.R., Erseghe, T., Ghiani, E., Murroni, M., Siano, P., Silvestro, F.: Integration of renewable energy sources, energy storage systems, and electrical vehicles with smart power distribution networks. J. Ambient Intell. Hum. Comput. **4**(6), 663–671 (2013)
6. AllSeen Alliance. https://allseenalliance.org/
7. Home Gateway initiative (HGi). http://www.homegatewayinitiative.org/
8. Home Gateway initiative (HGi), Requirements for wireless home area networks(WHANS) supporting smart home services. http://bit.ly/1JlAFIC

9. EN 13757-4:2005: Communication systems for meters and remote reading of meters- Part 4: Wireless meter readout (Radio meter reading for operation in the 868 MHz to 870 MHz SRD band)
10. Hosek, J., Masek, P., Ries, M., Kovac, D., Bartl, M., Kropfl, F.: Use case study on embedded systems serving as smart home gateways. In: Recent Advances in Circuits, Systems, Automatic Control. Budapest: EUROPMENT, pp. 310–315 (2013). ISBN: 978-960-474-349-0
11. Hosek, J., Masek, P., Kovac, D., Ries, M., Kropfl, F.: Universal smart energy communication platform. In: 2014 International Conference on Intelligent Green Building, Smart Grid (IGBSG), pp. 1–4. IEEE, Taipei (2014). ISBN: 9781467361217
12. Austria Telekom Group. http://www.telekomaustria.com/
13. Kamstrup. https://www.kamstrup.com/en-uk/
14. Gomez, C., Paradells, J.: Wireless home automation networks: a survey of architectures and technologies. IEEE Commun. Mag. **48**(6), 92–101 (2010). IEEE
15. Ferrari, G., Medagliani, P., Di Piazza, S., Martalo, M.: Wireless sensor networks: performance analysis in indoor scenarios. EURASIP J. Wirel. Commun. Netw. **2007**, 41–55 (2007)
16. Souryal, M., Gentile, C., Griffith, D., Cypher, D., Golmie, N.: A methodology to evaluate wireless technologies for the smart grid. In: Proceedings of the 1st IEEE International Conference on Smart Grid Communications (SmartGridComm), October 2010
17. Godfrey, T., Rodine, C.: Unified metrics for management of smart grid home area networks. In: Proceedings of the IEEE International Conference on Communications (ICC), May 2010
18. Han, D.-M., Lim, J.-H.: Design and implementation of smart home energy management systems based on ZigBee. IEEE Trans. Consum. Electron. **56**(3), 1417–1425 (2010)
19. Gill, K., Yang, S.-H., Yao, F., Lu, X.: A ZigBee-based home automation system. IEEE Trans. Consum. Electron. **55**(2), 422–430 (2009)
20. Gungor, V.C., Lu, B., Hancke, G.P.: Opportunities and challenges of wireless sensor networks in smart grid. IEEE Trans. Ind. Electron. **57**(10), 3557–3564 (2010)
21. Fang, S., Berber, S., Swain, A., Rehman, S.U.: A study on DSSS transceivers using OQPSK modulation by IEEE 802.15.4 in AWGN and flat Rayleigh fading channels. In: Proceedings of the TENCON 2010–2010 IEEE Region 10 Conference
22. Fang, S., Berber, S., Swain, A.K.: Energy consumption evaluations of cluster-based sensor nodes with IEEE 802.15.4 transceiver in flat Rayleigh fading channel. In: Proceedings of the Wireless Communications & Signal Process (2009)
23. Yi, P., Iwayemi, A., Zhou, C.: Developing ZigBee deployment guideline under WiFi interference for smart grid applications. IEEE Trans. Smart Grid **2**(1), 110–120 (2011)
24. Shuaib, K., Alsnuaimi, M., Boulmalf, M., Jawhar, I., Sallabi, F., Lakas, A.: Performance evaluation of IEEE 802.15.4: experimental and simulation results. J. Commun. **2**(4), 29–37 (2007)
25. Chowdhury, K.R., Akyildiz, I.F.: Interferer classification, channel selection and transmission adaptation for wireless sensor networks. In: Proceedings of the IEEE International Conference on Communications (ICC), June 2009
26. Kuder, Z., Jacobsen, R.-M.: Feasibility of wireless M-Bus protocol simulation. Elektrorevue **3**(3), 57–63 (2012)
27. Kamstrup, Mulical 21 Data Sheet. http://kamstrup.com/media/16541/file.pdf
28. Junseok, K.: Simple CSMA/CA Protocol for NS-3, 17 Oct 2011. http://www2.engr.arizona.edu/junseok/simple_wireless.html

29. Andersen, J.-B., Rappaport, T.-S., Yoshida, S.: Propagation measurements and models for wireless communications channels. IEEE Commun. Mag. **33**(1), 42–49 (1995)
30. Network Simulator 3: Discrete-event network simulator. http://www.nsnam.org
31. GitHub, Wireless M-BUS module for NS-3. https://github.com/xmasek12/WM-BUS-module-NS-3

Carpooling in Urban Areas: A Real-Time Service Case-Study

Matteo Mallus[1,2](✉), Giuseppe Colistra[1,2], Luigi Atzori[1],
and Maurizio Murroni[1]

[1] DIEE, University of Cagliari, Cagliari, Italy
{matteo.mallus,giuseppe.colistra,l.atzori,murroni}@diee.unica.it
[2] GreenShare SRL, Cagliari, Italy

Abstract. The realization of the smart city paradigm relies on the implementation of various innovative systems. Among the sectors of interest for a smart city, the sustainable transport is a key service where carpooling solutions are gaining more and more popularity in the last years. The most widespread use of the carpooling relies on a bakeca approach (i.e., the trips are planned well in advance), which is however not suitable in urban areas where the users are looking for an immediate companion. In this paper, we focus on the challenge of a real-time carpooling service and provide the following contribution: the Clacsoon platform is described, which is intended to make easy for the clacsooners to find the companion of the trip; an emulation system is implemented, which is used to generate increasing numbers of users that interact with the Clacsoon platform to evaluate the performance; based on the emulator, extensive trials are implemented to analyse the quality of experience provided to the users varying the characteristics of the population; from the results we extract important information about the challenges to be addressed for successful deployments of a real-time carpooling service.

Keywords: Real-time carpooling · Smart city · Internet of Things · Smart transport

1 Introduction

Sustainable transport is a key service of smartcities. It is expected to be friendly in the sense of social, environmental and climate impacts and the ability to, in the global scope, supply the source energy indefinitely. For the evaluation of the impact it has to be taken into account the particular vehicles used for the transport, the source of energy and the infrastructure used to implement the transport (Mihyeon Jeon and Amekudzi 2005). For sure public transport

This work has been partially funded by GreenShare SRL during the development of CLACSOON project (www.clacsoon.com) and Carpooling for Green Communities (COOG-IT) project (P.O.R. Sardegna F.S.E. Operational Programme of the Autonomous Region of Sardinia).

© ICST Institute for Computer Sciences, Social Informatics and Telecommunications Engineering 2016
B. Mandler et al. (Eds.) IoT 360° 2015, Part I, LNICST 169, pp. 157–166, 2016.
DOI: 10.1007/978-3-319-47063-4_14

services are those that have received a great attention in this respect, with several solutions that have been proposed and deployed according to the specific city configurations (city buses, trolleybuses, trams (or light rail) and passenger trains, rapid transit (metro/subways/undergrounds etc.) and ferries).

An alternative solution that is receiving a lot of attention in the last years is carpooling. It is the sharing of the private car journeys so that more than one person travels in a car. By having more people using one vehicle, carpooling reduces each person's travel costs such as fuel costs, tolls, and the stress of driving. Carpooling is seen as a more environmentally friendly and sustainable way to travel than the classical use of private cars. Indeed, sharing journeys reduces carbon emissions, traffic congestion on the roads, and the need for parking spaces. Authorities often encourage carpooling, as it is the case of the highways lanes that in the USA are reserved to cars with more than one person inside. Other than the above mentioned advantages, carpooling service presents the important features of giving people the possibility to interact during the setting of the sharing ride but especially during the ride, which represent a particular moment for the commuters that are typically keen on sharing thought and experience as well (Dakroub et al. 2013).

It is a matter of fact that this service is having a bootstrap thanks to the advancements in the ICT sector and wide diffusion of Internet connection that allow for the deployment of powerful tools for both the carpoolers to meet potential companions and reach an agreement on the shared trips (Blablacar 2015; CUTR 2015). These tools also help in evaluating the trustworthiness of the companions and the use of the social networks to share feedback about the members. However, the most widespread use of the carpooling solutions rely on a bakeca approach, i.e. the carpoolers post the request and the offers for a future transportation need. They have then the time to think about the posts and find an agreement on the remunerations. Indeed, a real-time approach has some difficulties in finding real exploitations. In this case, the users are looking for an immediate companion because the need for mobility is now (or up to 10 min). This scenario is typical of urban or suburban mobility where the flexibility is a key requirement as so the mobility needs cannot be scheduled one day before.

In this paper, we focus on the challenge of a real-time carpooling service and provide the following contribution: the Clacsoon platform (CLACSOON 2015) is described, which is intended to make easy for the clacsooners to find the companion of the trip; an emulation system is implemented, which is used to generate increasing numbers of users that interact with the Clacsoon platform to evaluate the performance; based on the emulator, extensive trials are implemented to analyse the quality of experience provided to the users varying the characteristics of the population; from the results we extract important information about the challenges to be addressed for successful deployments of a real-time carpooling service. The paper is organized as follows. Section 2 presents past works of relevance. Section 3 describes the implemented platform. Section 4 presents the experimental results. Conclusions are drawn in last section.

2 Past Works

The concept of Smart City has been commonly defined as the use of Information and Communication Technology (ICT) to sense, analyse and integrate the key information of core systems in running cities. In a more social way Smart City is an innovative city that uses ICTs and other means to improve quality of life, efficiency of urban operation and services, and competitiveness, while ensuring that it meets the needs of present and future generations with respect to economic, social and environmental aspects (ITU 2010). On the technical side, telecommunication infrastructures play a vital role in enhancing the connectivity and sustainability of the cities and, more specifically, Machine to Machine (M2M) communications play an important role within ICT for enabling Smart Cities. M2M communications for Smart Cities refers to the exchange of information between autonomous devices in control and monitoring applications without human intervention (Wu et al. 2011). The decline in communication fees, altogether with the massive adoption of real-time access of information is expanding the consideration of new services and applications and solutions based on this type of communication. Internet of Things (IoT) (Atzori et al. 2010) services are candidate to enable M2M communications and in general to support the development of smart applications, such as smart transportation (Nitti et al. 2014), smart buildings (Cherchi et al. 2014), etc. Carpooling on the strength of ICT has been a widely accepted concept to implement better transportation systems in Smart Cities. However in reality, most of current carpooling systems or applications are not functioned well as the expected. Carpooling system aims at raising vehicle occupancy based on a user collaborative environment motivated on a credits mechanism that can be converted into parking licenses in facilities of big cities. The carpooling happens whenever at least two people ride the same car. Each person would have made the trip independently if the carpool had not been there. Driver and passengers know beforehand the trips that they will be sharing the ride. This idea is not new and several initiatives have been tried in the past in the field of business, but also like a research topic (Agatz et al. 2012; Arnould et al. 2011; Blablacar 2015; CUTR 2015; Teal 1987). Most of these systems allow convenient trip arrangements over the internet, support trust building between registered users, and they implement billing systems to charge passengers and compensate drivers. The main technical drawback of existing ride sharing services is that do not allow truly ad-hoc real-time trip arrangements. Today's mobile computing with current advances on geographic location systems (e.g.,GPS, WiFi) (Araniti et al. 2010), mobile communications (e.g., 4-5 G) (Araniti et al. 2012) and new mobile devices (e.g., smart-phones, tablet) and navigations platforms overcame this limitation and enable for the first time truly ad-hoc real-time ride sharing services.

3   Reference System Architecture

In this work we consider a urban scenario where the aim is to offer a real-time carpooling service. The main functional requirements to develop this service can be described as follows:

- *Accounting*: to allow the user to access the service. Each user has a profile various information is stored, such as name, age, type of car, received feedback, etc.
- *Request and offer insertion*: through this feature each user can insert an offer or request of a ride. Each ride is identified by a start point, arrival point and a researc radius representing the maxim deviation from the scheduled trip.
- *Automatic matching*: the server calculates if there is a matching between an offer and a request of a ride. Matching is evaluated in real-time considering: the starting and arrival points of passenger, passenger's research radius, route travelled by the driver and driver's research radius.
- *Matching notification*: if there is a matching the system notifies the user. This notification contains the pick-up point (where the ride can start), the drop-off point (where the ride can finish) and the expected driver arrival time. Each user can accept o refuse the notification.

The system has to be used by users in mobility, so the access of the system has to be guaranteed by mobile devices. Accordingly, the design of the system architecture considers this facility and the front-end layer is projected for a mobile devices. As to the back-end, the system is developed completely in the cloud to offer good reliability for a lot of connections and to offer a better flexibility in terms of resources scaling. In the implementation of this case study the technology chosen is GoogleAppEngine and its tools for cloud solution.

As already mentioned, the system follows the paradigm mobile-cloud. Figure 1 shows the major components:

- *Mobile client* allows the user to access the carpooling service in mobility. Its sensors (e.g. GPS) are used to simplify the access of the service and to enhance the user experience. For all communications toward the server JSON format is used.
- *Cloud application server* is the core of the system. It enables the access of users, processes all requests and offers of rides and calculates the matching between requests and offers.
- *MySQL cloud database* has the task to store all data useful for the service: user profile, ride offers, ride requests, etc.
- *Facebook APIs* are used to simplify the process of registration by offering a quick and easy service to access on the system. Using the facebook social graph the aim is to increase the social participation of users.
- *Direction and location services* are used to evaluate the route between the two points (start point and arrival point) chosen by the user for its ride. These services are used also for the geocoding of address, that is the conversion of text in coordinates.
- *Push notification services* are used to enable the push notification toward smartphones. This feature is a milestone to obtain the real-time requirement.

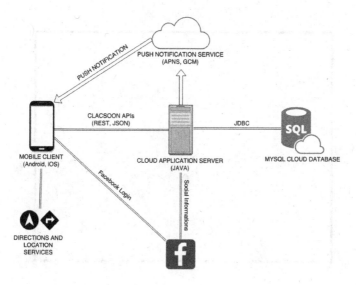

Fig. 1. Functional blocks description

4 Cagliari Case Study

This section describes the case study simulated. A large scale deployment of the system, to a real experiments, it's not easy because we need a lot of volunteers. Therefore the first experiment is an emulation of the carpooling service in a real area using simulated users. The place selected for the experiment is a real city: the metropolitan area of Cagliari. It is an Italian municipality. It has nearly 150.000 inhabitants, while its metropolitan area (including Cagliari and 15 other municipalities) has more than 422,000 inhabitants (Wikipedia 2015). Using a real area we can emulate the service in real urban conditions, considering real roads in the city and real paths between two points (e.g. pedestrian zone, one-way roads, limited traffic zones). A real-time carpooling service in Cagliari is simulated to evaluate two KPIs: the number of ride concluded and the waiting time to find a ride. The simulation achievement is to study the service performance in a typical urban scenario, analysing the contribution of spatial and time distributions.

4.1 Simulation Setup

At the first the area of interest is delimited by a box centered in point (39.23,9.14), which has a surface (A) of about 64 kmq, so the user can operate only inside this zone. Figure 2 shows the place selected for this case study, the area of interest is delimited by a black line.

The effectiveness of the carpooling service has been simulated considering the evaluation of two key performance indicators (KPIs): the first is the number of rides concluded and the second is the waiting time to find a ride (i.e., passenger

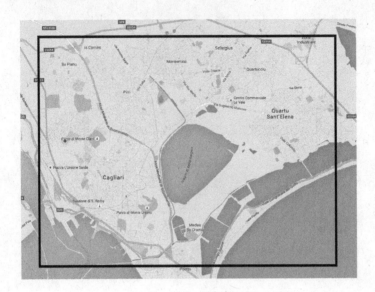

Fig. 2. The area for the case study

waiting time). Both these indicators are computed from the passenger perspective. A timeout (T) has been set, which is the limit within which a ride has to be found for the passenger before retiring her request (it has been set to 10 min in the experiments). During the experiments we have changed some parameters to evaluate the effects on the KPIs. The list of parameters that we have changed during the simulation is described in Table 1.

The emulator, according to the rate of ride creation, creates a request or an offers of ride between a starting point and arrival point. These two points are chosen randomly uniformly inside the area delimited during the setup. If the user is a driver (i.e. ride offer), the system calculates the route between the two points, moreover it evaluates the travel time, using Google services, to simulate the mobility pattern inside the route. The back-end receives all the offers and the requests to evaluate the matching according to the research radius of each user. The research radius of passenger (Rp) is 100 m and for driver (Rd) is 1000 m. If there is a matching, before the timeout, the system simulates the notification to appropriates users. In this first case study, if there is a matching the ride is considered agreed.

4.2   Simulation Results

To evaluate the performance in relation with the spatial distribution, the percentage of population who uses the service is changed. The number of users per kmq is changed to evaluate the dependence in relation of the service penetration among citizens. Instead to evaluate the dependence with the number of passengers and drivers, also the ratio between number of drivers (nd) and number of

Table 1. Values of parameters varied during experiment

System parameters		
Total users	N	from 600 to 2500
Overall area	A	64 kmq
Requests timeout	T	10 min
Users/kmq	Nk	from 9 to 39
Research radius of passengers	Rp	100 m
Research radius of drivers	Rd	1000 m
Percentage of drivers	nd	nd/np in the range from 0.25 to 4
Percentage of passengers	np	
Temporal rate of ride offers	Ld	Ld/Lp in the range from 0.2 to 5
Temporal rate of ride requests	Lp	

passengers (np) is changed. The performance, in relation with the time distribution of the service utilization, are evaluated varying the rate of ride offers and the rate of ride requests. The creation of ride events is modeled using an exponential distribution. To evaluate the dependence, during the simulation has been varied the ratio between the average ride inter-offer time (named Ld) and the average ride inter-request time (named Lp). Both distributions are exponential functions. Figures 3 and 4 show the KPIs analysed during this study. In each graph the KPIs are evaluated varying the parameters with the values indicated in Table 1.

Figure 3 shows the request success rate in the discussed case study. The first trend highlighted is that the success rate decreases if the population of user decreases. This trend is clear because if the spatial distribution of users is low, the probability to have a matching is small. Another important trend is that if there are more drivers, the passenger success rate is high. Also this trend is obvious, if there are more offers of service, the probability to satisfy a generic request is higher than a case with few offers. The last trend is the dependence of the temporal distribution. The success rate is plotted varying the ratio between the mean of temporal ride distribution. Analysing the figure, the trend of the success rate is concave. The maximum is near the centre, where the ratio is one, so the temporal distribution of requests and offers is the same. If the temporal distribution of requests and offers is the same, the system is balanced and the probability to find a matching is higher than an unbalanced system.

Figure 4 shows the passenger waiting time in the discussed case study. The first trend highlighted is the dependence between the waiting time and the temporal rate of requests and offers. In all cases simulated the waiting time increases if the ratio Ld/Lp increases, so the mean of temporal distribution of ride requests is smaller than ride offers. In this case the requests of passengers are distributed in an interval more tight than the drivers, so the probability to find for all requests a ride quickly is low. Instead if the situation is overturned, the probability to find a

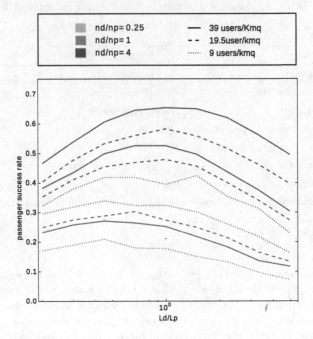

Fig. 3. Passenger success rate

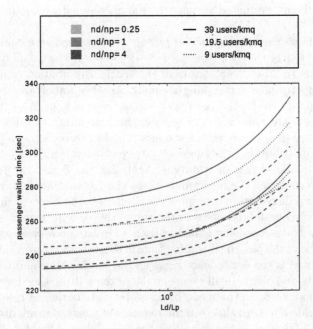

Fig. 4. Passenger waiting time

ride quickly is substantial so the average of waiting time decreases. Another trend very clear is the dependence of percentage of passengers. If the ratio nd/np is high (i.e. more drivers) the waiting time is low and vice versa. In the case with more drivers, there are more offers, so the probability to find a ride quickly is higher than the case where there are few drivers.

5   Conclusion and Future Works

In this work, a case study of urban real-time carpooling service has been studied. The results presented in this paper can be used to evaluate the requirements to build a urban carpooling with good performance. The city of Cagliari has been the real scenario to simulate the service. In this context has been simulated the presence of users who offer or require a ride between two point in the city.

Proposed case study is intended to evaluate the performance of service in relation with the spatial distribution of users, the population of drivers and passengers and the temporal distribution of ride offers and requests. The performance of the service has been evaluated considering two KPIs: rate of ride concluded and waiting time to find a travel companion. For both KPIs are identified the dependence between them and other important factors like: spatial distribution of users, percentage of drivers and passengers, temporal distribution of requests and offers.

Future works will be focused on the use of even more real scenario. During the design of the model can be identified the main start and end points in the uptown and the commercial areas. This model permits to simulate the main pattern of the urban travel between home and work. Furthermore, the proposed real-time carpooling service can be tested in real situation involving a community of volunteers to validate the simulation results.

References

Agatz, N., Erera, A., Savelsbergh, M., Wang, X.: Optimization for dynamic ridesharing: a review. Eur. J. Oper. Res. **223**(2), 295–303 (2012)

Araniti, G., Sanctis, M., Spinella, S.C., Monti, M., Cianca, E., Molinaro, A., Iera, A., Ruggieri, M.: Hybrid system HAP-WiFi for incident area network. In: Sithamparanathan, K., Marchese, M., Ruggieri, M., Bisio, I. (eds.) PSATS 2010. LNICSSITE, vol. 43, pp. 436–450. Springer, Heidelberg (2010). doi:10.1007/978-3-642-13618-4_33

Araniti, G., Scordamaglia, V., Condoluci, M., Molinaro, A., Iera, A.: Efficient frequency domain packet scheduler for point-to-multipoint transmissions in LTE networks. In: 2012 IEEE International Conference on Communications (ICC), pp. 4405–4409. IEEE (2012)

Arnould, G., Khadraoui, D., Armendáriz, M., Burguillo, J.C., Peleteiro, A.: A transport based clearing system for dynamic carpooling business services. In: 2011 11th International Conference on ITS Telecommunications (ITST), IEEE, pp. 527–533. IEEE (2011)

Atzori, L., Iera, A., Morabito, G.: The internet of things: a survey. Comput. Netw. **54**(15), 2787–2805 (2010)

Blablacar, Blablacar ridesharing (2015). https://www.blablacar.it/. Accessed 30 July 2015

Cherchi, R., Colistra, G., Pilloni, V., Atzori, L.: Energy consumption management in Smart Homes: an M-Bus communication system. In: 2014 International Conference on Telecommunications and Multimedia (TEMU), IEEE, pp. 80–85. IEEE (2014)

CLACSOON, CLACSOON urban real-time carpooling (2015). https://www.clacsoon.com/. Accessed 30 July 2015

CUTR, Ridematching software – CUTR Center for Urban Transportation Research (2015). http://www.nctr.usf.edu/programs/clearinghouse/ridematching-software/. Accessed 30 July 2015

Dakroub, O., Boukhater, C.M., Lahoud, F., Awad, M., Artail, H.: An intelligent carpooling app. for a green social solution to traffic and parking congestions. In: 2013 16th International IEEE Conference on Intelligent Transportation Systems-(ITSC), IEEE, pp. 2401–2408. IEEE (2013)

ITU, Smart sustainable cities: An analysis of definitions. Focus Group of Telecommunication Standardization Sector of ITU (2010)

Mihyeon Jeon, C., Amekudzi, A.: Addressing sustainability in transportation systems: definitions, indicators, and metrics. J. Infrastruct. Syst. 11(1), 31–50 (2005)

Nitti, M., Girau, R., Floris, A., Atzori, L.: On adding the social dimension to the internet of vehicles: friendship and middleware. In: 2014 IEEE International Black Sea Conference on Communications and Networking (BlackSeaCom), IEEE, pp. 134–138. IEEE (2014)

Teal, R.F.: Carpooling: who, how and why. Transp. Res. Part A Gen. 21(3), 203–214 (1987)

Wikipedia, Cagliari – Wikipedia, The Free Encyclopedia (2015). https://en.wikipedia.org/w/index.php?title=Cagliari&oldid=671950070. Accessed 30 July 2015

Wu, G., Talwar, S., Johnsson, K., Himayat, N., Johnson, K.D.: M2m: from mobile to embedded internet. IEEE Commun. Mag. 49(4), 36–43 (2011)

Spectrum Sharing Approaches for Machine-Type Communications over LTE Heterogeneous Networks

Antonino Orsino, Massimo Condoluci$^{(\boxtimes)}$, and Giuseppe Araniti

ARTS Laboratory, DIIES Department, University Mediterranea of Reggio Calabria,
Reggio Calabria, Italy
{antonino.orsino,massimo.condoluci,araniti}@unirc.it

Abstract. Machine-type communications (MTC) are expected to be a key enablers in the Internet of Things (IoT) ecosystem by providing ubiquitous connectivity among a new type of small devices (e.g., sensors, wearable devices, smartphone) without (or with minimal) the need of human intervention. In such a scenario, the architecture as well as the radio resource management (RRM) of next-to-come 5G systems needs to be enhanced in order to cope with the exponential growth of low-latency and low-energy MTC traffic. To this end, we propose a dynamic RRM policy which *(i)* exploits an heterogeneous networks (HetNets) deployment aiming to handle massive huge load of MTC devices and *(ii)* adopts a spectrum sharing approach tailored to improve the spectrum utilization in MTC environments. By comparing our proposal with current policies in literature, simulations conducted through the open-source Network Simulator 3 (NS-3) shown that our proposed use of spectrum sharing technique can efficiently improve the performance of MTC traffic in terms of spectral efficiency, power consumption, and fairness.

Keywords: M2M · HetNets · LTE · IoT · Spectrum sharing

1 Introduction

Machine-type communications (MTC) over Long Term Evolution (LTE) and beyond networks represents one on the killer communication paradigms to be exploited by network providers in order to fulfill the requirement of the future fifth generation (5G) wireless networks [1]. In fact, MTC promise to be a value-adds in the exponential growth of the data traffic generated by a new type of devices (e.g., traffic cameras, sensors, wearable devices) in either large- and small-scale environments. MTC open novel scenarios ranging from outdoor to indoor applications, such as smart city solution, for e.g. with intelligent metering, city automation, traffic control, house management, and remote clinical health care (e.g., see Fig. 1) [2]. This allows unprecedented opportunities in different fields (e.g., transport and logistics, smart power grids) belonging to the Internet of Things (IoT) ecosystem [3]. Nevertheless, the huge deployment of MTC devices

© ICST Institute for Computer Sciences, Social Informatics and Telecommunications Engineering 2016
B. Mandler et al. (Eds.) IoT 360° 2015, Part I, LNICST 169, pp. 167–178, 2016.
DOI: 10.1007/978-3-319-47063-4_15

Fig. 1. Smart city scenario

expected in the next years dictates for a more effective network architecture in order to meet the low-latency and low-energy MTC requirements and to mitigate as much as possible the impact of MTC traffic on traditional human-type communications (HTC).

To overcome the above considered issues, a possible solution is given by an enhanced LTE architecture where the extremely dense MTC deployment is supported by the usage of *small-cells*. Indeed, the exploitation of *heterogeneous networks (HetNets)* guarantees low-latency MTC without meaningful additional costs compared to non-3GPP wireless networks and without affecting the performance of HTC traffic.

The concept of HetNets has recently attracted considerable attention in the research community. In contrast to homogeneous networks, designed through a careful planning of the high-power base stations (eNodeBs) guaranteeing wide-area coverage, HetNets are deployed in an uncoordinated manner. The high power nodes (i.e., macro-cells) are jointly integrated with low power small-cells (i.e., pico and femto-cells, relay nodes) that are dynamically arranged and turned on/off directly by the end users according to their own needs [4]. In addition, small-cells, like home-eNodeBs (HeNBs), are *(i)* cheaper compared to macro-cell, *(ii)* plug and play (i.e., they do not need planning by network providers), *(iii)* generally positioned closed to the end user in indoor environment (and this guarantee, in general, improved quality of services to served devices) [5].

Nevertheless, even if MTC devices are managed through the usage of femto-cells, i.e., HeNBs, these exploit the same spectrum bandwidth assigned to the macro-cells eNBs. In such a case, the inter-cell interference can increase significantly thereby degrading the performance in both macro- and small-cells. Therefore, radio resource management (RRM) and scheduling procedures play an key role to efficiently manage the spectrum allocation among macro- and femto-cells with the aim to reduce the *inter-cell interference* and to increase the *spectral efficiency* [6, 7].

An emerging approach able to meet such requirements is characterized by the exploitation of *spectrum sharing* policies over HetNets, as reported in [8–10]. Actually, spectrum sharing may be orthogonal, i.e., when an operator exploits a shared resource, this cannot be simultaneously used by other operators. However, this kind of spectrum sharing just achieves marginal gains due to a slight increase in frequency diversity of the system. In this paper we consider a more advanced cooperation representing by the *non-orthogonal spectrum sharing*, where the operators are allowed to simultaneously use the same frequency resources. In this way, we are able to achieve higher efficiency in the spectrum usage and to consequently improve the performance in terms of *capacity* and *throughput* by means of increased *spatial and frequency diversity*.

By considering our HetNets environment, three different spectrum sharing techniques have been investigated in literature [11]:

- *Frequencies separation*: Radio spectrum is divided between the macro-cell and femto-cell in an adjacent manner. In this way, due to the Orthogonal Frequency Division Multiple Access (OFDMA) technique, the inter-cell interference can be neglected.
- *Partial sharing*: macro-cell and femto-cell share only a portion of the spectrum. The non-shared spectrum is exclusively assigned only to macro- or small-cells. Obviously, only the shared spectrum is affected by inter-cell interference.
- *Total sharing*: macro-cell and femto-cell share the overall assigned spectrum. Inter-cell interference needs to be taken into account on the overall spectrum and an efficient RRM policy has to be implemented in order to mitigate this phenomena.

In partial and total sharing, there are two further approaches that allow to share a single radio Resource Block (RB), i.e., the time-frequency unit to be scheduled during the RRM procedure, between the macro-cell and femto-cell [11]: *(i)* orthogonal spectrum sharing policy, where a shared RB is assigned to a given User Equipment (UE) in a mutually exclusive manner; *(ii)* non orthogonal spectrum sharing policy, where two UEs exploit the same RB in the same time.

The aim of the paper is to propose an orthogonal spectrum sharing approach between macro-cell and femto-cell with the aim to improve the overall spectral efficiency and reduce the latency and energy consumption of the MTC devices. Differently from what reported in literature [8], where the shared spectrum is dynamically assigned on portion of bandwidth, in the proposed policy the spectrum is shared on the RB-basis taking into account the channel state variations for each MTC device. Furthermore, two different per-user scheduling algorithms have been proposed and compared with [8] through an exhaustive simulation campaign by using the Network Simulator 3 (NS-3) [12].

The remainder of the paper is organized as follows. In Sect. 2 we briefly discuss the main related work, whereas in Sect. 3 we introduce the proposed resource allocation process. Simulation setting and results are given in Sect. 4, while conclusive remarks and future works can be found in Sect. 5.

2   Related Work

In the last years, several research activities have been conducted with the purpose of addressing the main challenges inherent to the HetNets architecture [5]. In particular, with the aim of improving HetNets performance in terms of efficient radio resources allocation, different RRM techniques have been investigated. Nevertheless, further enhancements could be obtained by introducing the concept of spectrum sharing based on the idea that sharing the same frequency among more eNodeBs can improve the system performance. References [13,14], are two of the earliest works that introduce this concept in wireless networks. In such works shared resources are used as a last resort when private frequencies[1] are not sufficient to handle the normal traffic. While, in [11] spectrum sharing is considered as the main technique for improving spectral efficiency. However, in [11] the spectrum sharing is applied only over a multi-operator scenario, without considering the introduction of low power eNodeBs (i.e., femto-cell) and, hence, of HetNets. In addition, Andrews et al. in [8] efficiently implements spectrum sharing among femto-cell and macro-cell in the HetNets environment. It focuses on the dynamic allocation of portions of bandwidth at the top level of the scheduling users process, selecting the shared bandwidth size, between macro and femto-cells, according to a periodically evaluation of the average inter-cell interference.

The role of small-cells technology and spectrum sharing policies for MTC applications is addressed in [15]. The authors analyze the role of small-range cells and novel technology developed for the current cellular system (e.g., spectrum sharing) in order to provide a comprehensive understanding about the most critical issues and challenges. Dynamic spectrum allocation for Machine-to-Machine (M2M) application is also proposed in [16]. In such a paper, an opportunity access method is utilized to share the spectrum among different newly deployed broadband system and MTC devices for Smart Grid applications. In particular, two novel dynamic spectrum planing algorithms, cognitive single channel assignment(CSCA) and cognitive single channel assignment with look-ahead (CSCA LA) are proposed. Finally, authors in [17] proposed a framework in order to analyze signal-to-interference-ratio distributions and derive efficient resource allocation schemes for spatial multi-group random access in multicell systems, using the Poisson point process model. Using this tool, the

---

[1] *Private frequencies* are the portion of bandwidth assigned exclusively to a base station.

spectrum-sharing performance of multiple systems are evaluated by considering simultaneous transmissions of MTC devices deployed within the same cell.

3   Resource Allocation Process

We focus on the downlink direction of the Long Term Evolution (LTE) technology [18], where user multiplexing is based on OFDMA. The RB corresponds to the smallest time-frequency resource that can be allocated to a user (12 subcarriers, 0.5 ms) in an Long Term Evolution (LTE) system. For example, a channel bandwidth of 20 MHz corresponds to 100 RB. For the cellular link between the MTC device/cellular user and the eNodeB, a UE in an LTE-A network typically communicates through a macro-cellular link by sending its own data to the eNodeB. In addition, the eNodeB executes the resource allocation every Transmission Time Interval (TTI, lasting 1 ms) by assigning the adequate number of RB pairs to each scheduled UE and by selecting the related Modulation and Coding Scheme (MCS). Scheduling decisions are based on the Channel Quality Indicator (CQI) that is associated to a maximum supported MCS (please, refer to Table 1).

In this paper the scenario illustrated in Fig. 2 is adopted, where a macro and a femto-cell exploit the same radio spectrum. In particular, the macro can totally or partially shares its spectrum with the femto-cell in an orthogonal manner.

Table 1. CQI-MCS mapping [19]

CQI index	Modulation scheme	Code rate x 1024	Efficiency [bit/s/Hz]	Minimum rate [kbps]
1	QPSK	78	0.1523	25.59
2	QPSK	120	0.2344	39.38
3	QPSK	193	0.3770	63.34
4	QPSK	308	0.6016	101.07
5	QPSK	449·	0.8770	147.34
6	QPSK	602	1.1758	197.53
7	16-QAM	378	1.4766	248.07
8	16-QAM	490	1.9141	321.57
9	16-QAM	616	2.4063	404.26
10	64-QAM	466	2.7305	458.72
11	64-QAM	567	3.3223	558.72
12	64-QAM	677	3.9023	655.59
13	64-QAM	772	4.5234	759.93
14	64-QAM	873	5.1152	859.35
15	64-QAM	948	5.5547	933.19

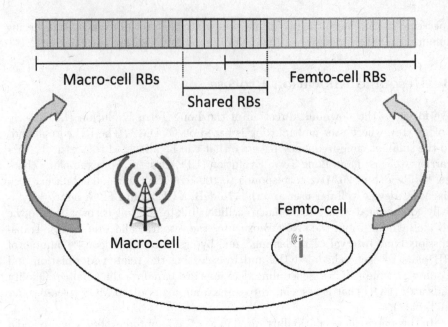

Fig. 2. Adopted scenario

We remark that only the radio spectrum is shared, while users are connected exclusively to their own base station (no infrastructure sharing).

Let Q be the number of all RBs in downlink direction and $s \in (0,1)$ the percentage of RBs orthogonally shared between macro and femtocell. We assumed the non shared RBs are equally split between the two eNodeBs. As a consequence, $Q \cdot s = Q\_s$ and $Q\_p = Q - Q\_s$ are the number of shared and private RBs, respectively. It is worth noting that a BS can assigns a private RB only to their own UEs, vice versa a shared RB can be utilized by UEs belonging to both macro and femto-cell. The resource allocation process consists of two phases. During the first one, named *CQI Acquisition*, macro and femto-cells receive the CQI feedbacks from each own UE and sorted in increasing CQI order (highest CQI).

After all CQIs have been collected and properly sorted, the scheduling algorithm is carried out in order to assign efficiently the RBs (shared and not-shared) to all the users belonging to both macro and femto-cell. Two different scheduling algorithms have been proposed in this paper:

– The Fixed Spectrum Sharing (FSS)
– The Dynamic Spectrum Sharing (DSS)

In the FSS policy, the number of the shared RBs Q_s is fixed and does not vary in the time. Each RB is assigned in a mutually exclusive manner to users belonging to both macro and femto-cell according to the sorted list created during the

CQI acquisition phase. The intra-cell interference due to the OFDMA modulation is not taken into account. Differently to FSS, the in the DSS policy the number of the shared RBs Q_s can dynamically vary every TTI. Moreover, each RB is shared between the macro and the femto-cell only if the inter-cell interference achieved is lowest to a given threshold. Otherwise, the RB is privately given to the BS of the user with the highest CQI. In both scheduler policies, in case of collision of two users in the same RB at the same time, the conflict is solved by assigning the RB to the user with the highest CQI. Furthermore, in both FSS and DSS scheduler the private RBs Q_p are assigned following a Max Throughput policy in order to achieve the highest performance. We remark that Max Throughput policy assigns each resource block to the user that achieves the best channel conditions. We compared the proposed algorithms with the dynamic spectrum allocation approach proposed in [8], hereinafter named Dynamic Spectrum Allocation (DSA). The DSA scheduler assigns a priori the shared bandwidth among the macro and the femto-cell based on the average interference achieved by all the system user. Differently, our proposed scheduling algorithms (FSS, DSS) works on the single resource block and not on portion of bandwidth.

4   Simulation Results

Performance evaluation of the proposed algorithms have been conducted through the well-know Network Simulator 3 (NS-3) [12]. We started from an existing NS-3 module thought for implementing the LTE multi-operator spectrum sharing, and we added new functionalities (i.e., new suitable path loss models, low-power nodes, femto-cells, MTC devices, and so on) in order to define a MTC system within an HetNets scenario. The new module allow us to simulate different network behaviors and to set up several system parameters, such as cell coverage, transmitted power, number of MTC devices, number of femto-cells and their position within the macro-cell.

In details, the proposed scenario is characterized by a macro-cell and a femto-cell with different transmitted powers and coverage areas. Different MTC devices are uniformly distributed within the coverage of the macro-cell and femto-cell and a number of cellular users (i.e., HTC traffic) equal to 50 is deployed within the macro-cell. The number of MTC devices varies in the range [2, 500] and the network traffic is modeled through packets with size equal to 100 byte with a time interval of 10s. In addition, each cellular users download through the eNodeB multimedia content with size equal to 500 bytes (constant bit rate, CBR, traffic). The shared spectrum is fixed to a percentage of 100 %, therefore all resource blocks are totally shared between the macro and the femto-cell.

Simulations have been conducted by varying the number of users belonging to both the macro-cell and the femto-cell. Outputs have been achieved by averaging a sufficient number of simulation results in order to guarantee a 95 % confidence interval (Table 2).

In order to evaluate the system performance, we take into account three system parameters: *(i)* average throughput achieved by the MTC devices, *(ii)* average energy consumption, and *(ii)* the well-known Jain's fairness index [20].

Table 2. Main system parameters

Parameters	Value	
Downlink Bandwidth	10 MHz	
Frame duration	10 ms	
TTI duration	1 ms	
TX power	**Macro-cell**	**Femto-cell**
	30 dBm	8 dBm
User TX power	23 dBm	
MTC device TX power	0 dBm	
Pathloss (dB)	**Macro-cell**	**Femto-cell**
	15.6 + (35 * log(R))	38.46 + (20 * log(R))
Wall penetration	7,10,15 dB	
# HTC users	50	
Radius	**Macro-cell**	**Femto-cell**
	500 m	50 m
Interdistance	400 m	

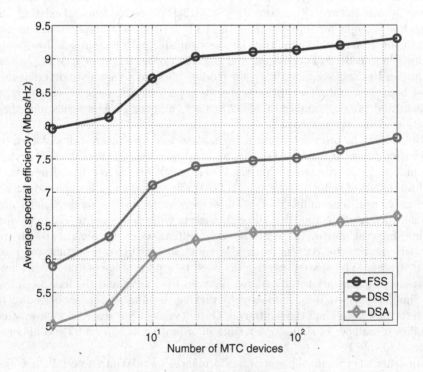

Fig. 3. Average spectral efficiency

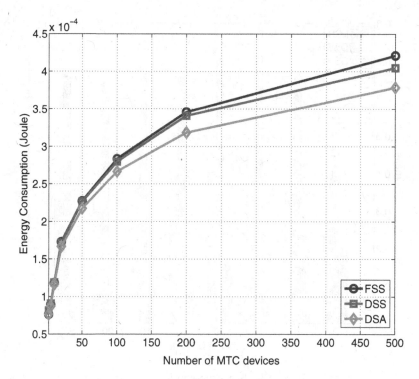

Fig. 4. Average energy consumption

Figure 3 shows the system spectral efficiency by varying the number of MTC devices. DSS scheduler is more performing than DSA. Indeed, in DSA the amount of shared spectrum varies frame-by-frame (i.e., every 10 TTI) depending on the inter-cell interference, whereas in DSS the amount of shared RBs are evaluated on TTI basis taking into account for each RB both the load traffic and the inter-cell interference. It worth noting that FSS is the most performing policy in terms of spectral efficiency. This behavior is due to the fact that in FSS the fixed amount of shared RBs is evaluated assuming negligible the inter-cell interference. Therefore, it represents an ideal case and the obtained result can be considered as an upper bound. In addition, the average percentage gain introduced by the DSS algorithm varies in a range of 20–30%, especially when the traffic load is high. It is due to the increase of the multi-user diversity and the more degrees of freedom in choosing the best users.

The average energy consumption per MTC device is shown in Fig. 4. The energy consumption increases with the traffic load. As we can observe, the DSS policy always performs better compared to the DSA. The slight improvement shown in Fig. 4 is due to the typically low packet size that MTC device has to deliver.

Finally, the fairness achieved using the three different scheduler policies, by varying the number of MTC devices is shown in Fig. 5. We use the *max-min*

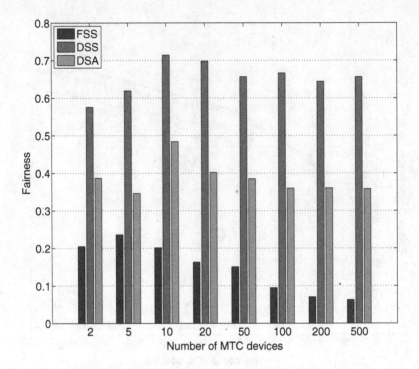

Fig. 5. Fairness index

fairness approach where a feasible allocation of rates is max-min fairness if and only if an increase of any rate within the domain of feasible allocations must be at the cost of a decrease of some already smaller rate. It is worth noting that the RBs are allocated more fairly by considering both the two dynamic allocation of the radio spectrum because only the resources with a lower level of interference are shared among the macro and femto-cell. In particular, the DSS scheduler, respect the DSA scheduler, assigns more fairly the RBs due to the timely response to the traffic load of the base stations. Even though the FSS scheduler achieves the better performance in terms of spectral efficiency and power consumption, it does not provide a good fairness as the RBs are not equally assigned to the macro and femto-cell. As a conclusion, the preliminary results shown in this paper demonstrate that the spectrum sharing techniques are a possible solution to efficiently manage the growing demand of multimedia traffic given by the MTC systems, and that the scheduling algorithms play an important role in the allocation of the shared resource blocks in order to improve the system performance.

5   Conclusion and Future Works

We investigated the spectrum sharing technique for MTC systems over Heterogeneous Networks through simulations by considering spectral efficiency, power consumption and fairness. We integrated our scenario within an existing NS-3 module for LTE spectrum sharing and a simulation campaign varying some the number of MTC devices has been performed. Obtained results show that the dynamic allocation of the radio spectrum (TTI-by-TTI) according to an efficient per-user scheduling process increases the performance of the MTC device with respect to a resource allocation process at top levels (frame-by-frame). Sharing the radio resources on a RB-basis when the the deployment of MTC devices relatively huge allows to achieved high-levels of gain due to the timely response of the proposed algorithms. Therefore, the correct allocation of the shared resource blocks considering the evolution on the system parameter user-by-user plays an important role. As a future work, the same approach can be extended to a scenario with a large number of femto-cells, where an efficient distribution of the radio resources and spectrum sharing techniques is recommended. In fact, efficient approaches in order to manage the spectrum (shared or private) assigned to the femto-cells and macro base stations have to be investigated.

References

1. Zheng, K., Ou, S., Alonso-Zarate, J., Dohler, M., Liu, F., Zhu, H.: Challenges of massive access in highly dense lte-advanced networks with machine-to-machine communications. IEEE Wirel. Commun. **21**(3), 12–18 (2014)
2. Bisio, I., Lavagetto, F., Marchese, M., Sciarrone, A.: Smartphone-centric ambient assisted living platform for patients suffering from co-morbidities monitoring. IEEE Commun. Mag. **53**(1), 34–41 (2015)
3. Nitti, M., Girau, R., Floris, A., Atzori, L.: On adding the social dimension to the internet of vehicles: friendship and middleware. In: IEEE International Black Sea Conference on Communications and Networking (BlackSeaCom), pp. 134–138. IEEE (2014)
4. Andreev, S., Gerasimenko, M., Galinina, O., Koucheryavy, Y., Himayat, N., Yeh, S.-P., Talwar, S.: Intelligent access network selection in converged multiradio heterogeneous networks. IEEE Wirel. Commun. **21**(6), 86–96 (2014)
5. Damnjanovic, A., Montojo, J., Wei, Y., Ji, T., Lou, T., Vajapeyam, M., Yoo, T., Song, O., Malladi, D.: A survey on 3GPP heterogeneous networks. IEEE Wirel. Commun. **18**(3), 10–21 (2011)
6. Murroni, M.: A power-based unequal error protection system for digital cinema broadcasting over wireless channels. Sig. Process. Image Commun. **22**(3), 331–339 (2007)
7. Di Fazio, A.R., Erseghe, T., Ghiani, E., Murroni, M., Siano, P., Silvestro, F.: Integration of renewable energy sources, energy storage systems, and electrical vehicles with smart power distribution networks. J. Ambient Intell. Human. Comput. **4**(6), 663–671 (2013)
8. Andrews, M., Capdevielle, V., Feki, A., Gupta, P.: Autonomous spectrum sharing for mixed lte femto and macro cells deployments. In: Proceedings of IEEE Conference on Computer Communications, pp. 1–5, March 2010
9. Badia, L., Del Re, R., Guidolin, F., Orsino, A., Zorzi, M.: A tunable framework for performance evaluation of spectrum sharing in LTE networks. In: 2013 IEEE 14th International Symposium and Workshops on a World of Wireless, Mobile and Multimedia Networks (WoWMoM), vol. **4**(7), pp. 1–3, June 2013

10. Guidolin, F., Orsino, A., Badia, L., Zorzi, M.: Statistical analysis of non orthogonal spectrum sharing and scheduling strategies in next generation mobile networks. In: 2013 9th International Wireless Communications and Mobile Computing Conference (IWCMC), vol. 1(5), pp. 680–685, July 2013

11. Jorswieck, E.A., Badia, L., Fahldieck, T., Karipidis, E., Luo, J.: Spectrum sharing improves the network efficiency for cellular operators. IEEE Commun. Mag. **52**(3), 129–136 (2013)

12. The ns3 simulator. http://www.nsnam.org/

13. Bennis, M., Lilleberg, J.: Inter base station resource sharing and improving the overall efficiency of B3G systems. In: IEEE 66th Vehicular Technology Conference, VTC- Fall, pp. 1494–1498, 30 September–3 October 2007

14. Middleton, G., Hooli, K., Tolli, A., Lilleberg, J.: Inter-operator spectrum sharing in a broadband cellular network. In: 2006 IEEE Ninth International Symposium on Spread Spectrum Techniques and Applications, vol. 28(31), pp. 376–380, August 2006

15. Cimmino, A., Pecorella, T., Fantacci, R., Granelli, F., Rahman, T.F., Sacchi, C., Carlini, C., Harsh, P.: The role of small cell technology in future smart city applications. Trans. Emerg. Telecommun. Technol. **25**(1), 11–20 (2014)

16. Wang, Q., He, T., Chen, K.-C., Wang, J., Ko, B., Lin, Y., Lee, K.-W.: Dynamic spectrum allocation under cognitive cell network for M2M applications. In: 2012 Conference Record of the Forty Sixth Asilomar Conference on Signals, Systems and Computers (ASILOMAR), vol. 4(7), pp. 596–600, November 2012

17. Kwon, T., Choi, J.-W.: Multi-group random access resource allocation for M2M devices in multicell systems. IEEE Commun. Lett. **16**(6), 834–837 (2012)

18. LTE physical layer - general description, TS 36.201 (V9.1.0), 3GPP, March 2010

19. Lopez-Perez, D., Ladanyi, A., Juttner, A., Rivano, H., Zhang, J.: Optimization method for the joint allocation of modulation schemes, coding rates, resource blocks and power in self-organizing LTE networks. In: 2011 Proceedings IEEE INFOCOM, vol. 10(15), pp. 111–115, April 2011

20. Ometov, A.: Fairness characterization in contemporary IEEE 802.11 deployments with saturated traffic load. In: Proceedings of 15th Conference of Open Innovations Association FRUCT, vol. 21(25), pp. 99–104, April 2014

Softwarization and Virtualization in 5G Networks for Smart Cities

Massimo Condoluci[1(✉)], Fragkiskos Sardis[2], and Toktam Mahmoodi[2]

[1] Mediterranean University of Reggio Calabria, Reggio Calabria, Italy
massimo.condoluci@unirc.it
[2] Department of Informatics, King's College London, London, UK
{fragkiskos.sardis,toktam.mahmoodi}@kcl.ac.uk

Abstract. Smart cities are one of the foreseeable mission-critical hybrid networks connecting machines and humans to provide various public services through highly reliable, ultra-low latency and broadband communications. It is known that the next generation mobile networks, a.k.a 5G networks, should address requirements of such hybrid network inherently. Among the main features of 5G networks, therefore, are cognition and programmability that allow for addressing different needs. These features are so far discussed with the introduction of softwarization and virtualization technologies. In this paper, we briefly discuss how the two technologies enable use of 5G in the smart cities and allow for multiple tenants to share a common physical infrastructure. We further describe an example use case through which such multiple tenant environment can be designed.

Keywords: 5G · SDN · NFV · Smart cities · Multi-tenancy

1 5G in Smart Cities

Faced with an ever larger portfolio of applications to serve, it is now commonly recognized that future networks will have to consider requirements by different vertical sectors. Despite earlier network generations that have been designed as general purpose connectivity platforms with limited differentiation capabilities across use cases and application environments [1], 5G needs to consider different sectors inherently in its design. Such design requirement is not only to consider very high bandwidth usage, but also for range of targeted applications such as mission-critical applications. The 5G mission-critical networks are hybrid networks that connect machines and humans to provide future services through highly reliable, ultra-low latency and broadband services. A good example of such hybrid network are the smart cities. Smart cities bring together mix traffic of machines and humans generated by various city-wide infrastructures and introduce plethora of opportunities as well as challenges.

Two of the main features of 5G design are cognition and programmability through softwarization and virtualization of the end-to-end chain of the radio,

© ICST Institute for Computer Sciences, Social Informatics and Telecommunications Engineering 2016
B. Mandler et al. (Eds.) IoT 360° 2015, Part I, LNICST 169, pp. 179–186, 2016.
DOI: 10.1007/978-3-319-47063-4_16

networks, applications and services. The two promising and well-developed technologies in this path are Software-defined networking (SDN) and Network Function Virtualization (NFV). Among other functionalities, SDN & NFV enable multiple tenants to share a common physical infrastructure. Comprising of various inter-related infrastructure, smart cities scenarios can benefit significantly from multi-tenant design.

To this end, we depict the vision of 5G in smart cities and briefly discuss role of SDN and NFV technologies in developing smart city networks in Sects. 2 and 3. Afterwards, through a specific use case instance of emergency and transport services, we demonstrate how different actors can interconnect and how a multiple tenants can co-exist and co-operate (in Sect. 4). Finally, some concluding remarks are summarized in Sect. 5.

2   Softwarization and Virtualization in 5G

The introduction of cognition and programmability is considered as one of the main challenges to be handled in the mobile 5G with the aim to manage the increasing volume of traffic with different Quality of Service (QoS) requirements generated by huge load of heterogeneous devices. Both cognition and programmability are needed to guarantee flexibility, reliability and auto-reconfiguration to 5G systems to always exploit the optimal network configuration according to the current state of the network. Different paradigms are currently investigated as enablers of such cognition and programmability in 5G. Among those, as for instance stated by [2], *softwarization* and *virtualization* are expected to have a significant impact on forthcoming 5G deployment trends as they guarantee to speed up the innovation of network architectures. Furthermore, softwarization and virtualization play a key role in *multi-tenancy* environments, where a single instance of a software application may serve multiple network operators. Furthermore, multi-tenancy allows for multiple users and organizations to share a common infrastructure by virtualizing hardware and sharing resources without private data and network traffic being exposed outside of their virtual boundaries. In the following, we will consider in detail these two enablers paradigms.

2.1   Software Defined Networking (SDN)

Softwarization is considered a key enhancement in the network design of next-to-come 5G systems, as for instance stated by [2,3]. In this direction, software-defined networking (SDN) is a promising architecture which aims to introduce meaningful benefits through *isolation of control plane* and the use of a *centralized network controller* handling control plane functionalities, such as the allocation of traffic to network elements. Network intelligence is centrally managed by the network controller and, thus, the network controller can output the best fine granular flow routing control rules to the heterogeneous network devices.

The network controller interacts with other network entities/layers through two interfaces, as considered in detail by [3] and depicted in Fig. 1(a). The controller exploits the *northbound interface* with the aim to be as a single, logical

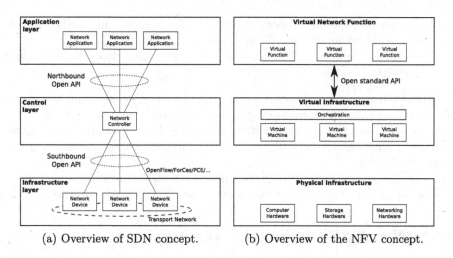

(a) Overview of SDN concept.   (b) Overview of the NFV concept.

Fig. 1. SDN & NFV Illustration.

switch to the upper layer network applications: this provides an overall overview of the whole network status (overloading, congestion, and so on) to network applications. The main benefit is in the deployment time of novel network functions/applications. The *southbound interface* is defined between the network controller and the network devices. Being widely supported by various device manufacturers, service providers, and operators, *OpenFlow* (defined by the Open Networking Foundation, ONF) is broadly considered as the dominating solution for implementing the southbound interface; more details on OpenFlow are given by [4]. Further solutions, such as ForCES and PCE, defined by the Internet Engineering Task Force (IETF) [5,6], are available as southbound interfaces.

2.2 Network Function Virtualization (NFV)

The Network Function Virtualization (NFV) can provide the infrastructure on which SDN can run. Indeed, as discussed by [2,7], NFV is a complementary technology of SDN which allows *(i)* to build a virtual-based end-to-end network infrastructure and *(ii)* to enable the consolidation of many heterogeneous network devices onto industry standard high-volume servers, switches, and storage.

The key characteristic of NFV paradigm is that network functions of a network device are implemented in a *software package(s)* and *virtual machine(s)* are used to run such packages. Therefore, NFV introduces flexibility in the network deployment as it the introduction/test of novel network functionalities becomes easier: only installation/upgrading of software package(s) is needed, without the need of hardware upgrade to network entities which obviously introduces higher delays. As a consequence, NFV reduces the time to market of novel network functionalities with thus money saving. In addition, NFV allows network operators to build and operate a network with reduced equipment costs, as generic hardware can be used and properly tuned via software according to the need of the operator. More details on NFV technology are given by [8].

The architecture of NFV, described in Fig. 1(b), has the following characteristics:

- *Virtual infrastructure*: virtual machines run on generic high-volume hardware servers, equipped by storage devices and connected by network switches.
- *Software separation*: generic hardware is used by the software that defines the network functions for network devices, i.e., the hardware is not designed for specific task(s).
- *Automated orchestration*: the orchestration automates installation and management of the virtualized network functions on the generic hardware.

3   SDN and NFV in Smart Cities

The smart city scenario poses several challenges in the management of network resources. Indeed, a smart city environment is expected to be a heterogeneous scenario where different types of devices (e.g., smartphones, sensors, actuators) co-exist in heterogeneous deployments (e.g., macro, pico, femto-cells) and have heterogeneous traffic patterns (e.g., machine-type communications require high-reliability and low-latency to reduce the energy consumption while human-oriented traffic has less stringent requirements in terms of energy consumption).

This intrinsic heterogeneity in smart city environments requires quick reconfiguration of network parameters/deployment according to the current state of the network: this clearly shows the inefficiency in the current deployment strategies adopted by network operators, mainly based on pre-configured network parametrization and ad-hoc network devices with pre-defined tasks. In 5G systems, network has to be configured according to the use case but also the information such as traffic, mobility levels, interference levels, QoS requirements, overloading of radio/core segments and so on. Such information is obviously time-varying, and this consequently dictates for novel solutions allowing low-latency network reconfiguration. The above discussed softwarization and virtualization paradigms are useful to achieve the flexibility that smart city environments pose on 5G systems. Examples of the enhancements introduced by the exploitation of SDN/NFV are provided by [2] and are summarized here:

- dynamic cell configuration, traffic balance and resource management;
- spectrum and transmission powers to be assigned to involved cells;
- best interconnections between network devices;
- best connections between transceivers and physical elements;
- activation of the appropriate transceivers that will be involved in the handling of a particular situation.

Nevertheless, to reach these goals, several issues are to be taken into account. A first aspect is the need of dynamically redirecting user traffic when scaling offered services: this becomes challenging as is still not clear how existing SDN controllers perform in the wide area of 5G cellular systems. When considering the huge load relevant to smart cities, where enormous and unpredictable number of devices are expected to be simultaneously connected in a limited coverage area, *scalability* becomes the major concern to avoid network overloading and congestion. In addition, when focusing on applications where sensors and actuators need to communicate under strict latency requirements, overloading may involve unacceptable delays which may cause instabilities in some segments of the smart city.

Another interesting challenge is in the overhead reduction in applications like machine-type and the IoT, which are considered as primary services for smart cities. Communications inherent to such applications deal with the transmission of very limited traffic (few bytes) whose management in the current 3GPP standard involve high consuming of bearer resources in the core network. The overhead reduction needs a novel design for the protocol interfaces in the SDN/NFV 5G architecture to guarantee benefits for low-cost sensor devices (i.e., energy savings as lower number of control bits are needed for each data bit to be transmitted) and in the radio/core networks (i.e., lower amount of data/control resources are needed for data/control bearers).

Finally, a concern of notable importance is in terms of *security*. Indeed, in a NFV network, virtual applications run in data centers which may not be owned by network operators directly, i.e., virtualization may even be outsourced to third parties as considered by [9]. In addition, the introduction of orchestrators may generate additional security vulnerabilities with thus higher loads (and consequent higher delays) to the systems/functionalities of intrusion detection. Finally, security threats are also due to the use of shared networking and storage, i.e., when virtual machines share the physical resources with other network appliances or when software-based components are offered by different vendors; these scenarios may potentially create security holes due to integration complexity. As a consequence, operators need to make sure that the security features of their network will not be affected by above considered issues and this dictates to rethink security issues when designing/building 5G NFV systems.

4   Case of Multi-tenancy in Smart City

This section illustrates an example use case in smart cities that is built on SDN & NFV-based 5G network, and explains a multi-tenancy design. We investigates how transport and emergency services in smart cities can make use of a shared network infrastructure to drive down their running costs, integrate more efficiently and automate certain aspects of their operations. According to a recent report by the UK metropolitan police, they receive more than five million calls per year on their emergency numbers and public increasingly want more flexible ways on interacting with the police [10]. Hence, automation in emergency services can potentially have significant social impact. To study the interaction between emergency and transport services, we consider the use-case of an emergency incident occurring on the transport network and explore how the two services may communicate between them and with external actors in order to respond to the event.

4.1   Modelling Transport and Emergency Services

Transport and emergency services are composed of actors that report information, process data, make decisions and execute operations. The first actor involved in the use-case is the *emergency services* that receive incident reports from patrol units, civilians or roadside devices. The main task of this actor is to process such reports and determine how emergency services should respond in terms of units needed (police, ambulance, fire brigade), and what is the urgency level. It is therefore an actor focused on processing information and issuing instructions. Location of the incident, availability of emergency teams nearby and the traffic conditions on the roads are among the information that should be known to the actor. The second actor is the *transport services* with its main role in this use-case being, keeping track of the transport network's condition, the locations of emergency units, issuing traffic updates to the public and making traffic control adjustments when necessary. The third actor is the *roadside equipments and the officers*, that are the patrol units, roadside sensors, smart cars and civilians. This set of actors gives input to the emergency service by reporting incidents.

Finally, the fourth actor is the *traffic control* such as traffic lights, traffic sensors, electronic road signs and transport service officers. They are primarily tasked with informing civilians (or smart devices) of incidents and shaping the traffic in the transport network. Actors in this group also send periodic traffic updates to the transport services in order to maintain an overview of the congestion in the transport network. Figure 2 presents the main components of the framework and the flow of information between them. It also includes input from policies that affect the behaviour of the system in terms of responding to events and handling traffic. The components of the framework are as follows:

- Emergency Service Policy: is responsible for controlling how the emergency systems respond to events.
- Event Response: receives information from *incident reporting actors* and the *location tracking*, utilizes the *emergency service policy*, and issues instructions to response units that can reach the location of the incident in the most optimal form.
- Location Tracking: tracks the location of incidents via input from the *incident reporting actors* via periodic updates from the units.
- Traffic Monitoring & Control: that is the main part of the transport network and receives input from the *transport service policy* and *roadside equipment and officers*.
- Roadside Equipment & Officers: includes devices such as traffic lights and electronic road signs that may be remotely programmed, sensors for traffic measurements, and human officers.
- Incident Reporting Actors: include roadside sensors, embedded devices in smart cars, officers on patrol and civilians. When an incident is reported, the location of the incident is also submitted to the *location tracking*.

Fig. 2. Actors' communication in Transport & Emergency service model.

– Response Units: are the officers and fleet of vehicles of emergency services. They receive dispatch instructions from the *event response*. They also report periodically their status and location to the *location tracking*.

4.2   Illustration of the Example Use Case

Using the above framework and actors, we can now envision a scenario where an emergency event has occurred in the city. Let's assume that the incident is reported by a smart car via the Internet. The *event response* will process the location of the incident as well as the vehicle involved and request the location of Response Units nearby. Upon determining the severity of the incident, it will dispatch the required units to the location. At the same time, it will send a request to the *traffic monitoring & control*, to prioritize traffic on the route of the emergency services; for example to update the timing on traffic lights.

4.3   Multi-tenancy Network Considerations Using SDN

After considering the example above, we can begin to examine the various communication methods and networking technologies required for this system to operate. We can identify four distinct infrastructures that are involved in achieving communication between the actors. The first one is the public network where all information gathering points, either machines or humans, are connected to. The second and third are the emergency services and the transport networks virtual infrastructure which are also connected to the public networks for data communications. Finally, the fourth infrastructure is the shared physical infrastructure that hosts the virtual infrastructures for emergency and transport services. This infrastructure physically peers with other public or private networks.

Communication between these infrastructure entities needs to adhere to QoS parameters in order to facilitate the communication between components in a reliable and timely fashion. Because the physical infrastructure is shared between the two services, multi-tenancy and scalability issues have to be addressed in order to guarantee an optimal distribution of resources. Furthermore, depending on the type of communication and the volume of information, additional communication channels between the two virtual infrastructures may be created or removed. This will allow the physical infrastructure to provide additional resources when required or switch off physical interfaces to reduce power consumption when they are not needed.

5   Concluding Remarks

In this paper, we depict the vision of 5G in smart cities and briefly discuss role of SDN and NFV technologies in developing smart city networks. Through a specific use case instance of emergency and transport services, we demonstrate how multiple tenants can co-exist and co-operate. While complying with the traditional definition of multi-tenancy requires tenants to be restricted to control only their virtual space and not the physical infrastructure, our detailed use case here needs more stringent control. In this case, either of the emergency and transport services should have some control over the physical infrastructure so that they can program the SDN controller according to their needs. This requirement is mainly due to the sensitivity and critically of the emergency and transport services, and the fact that functionality of the physical layer plays an important role in the response time and the reliable operation of these services.

Acknowledgement. This work has been supported in part by the 5GPP VirtuWind (Virtual and programmable industrial network prototype deployed in operational Wind park) Project.

References

1. Araniti, G., De Sanctis, M., Spinella, S.C., Monti, M., Cianca, E., Molinaro, A., Iera, A., Ruggieri, M.: Hybrid system HAP-WiFi for incident area network. In: Sithamparanathan, K., Marchese, M., Ruggieri, M., Bisio, I. (eds.) PSATS 2010. LNICST, vol. 43, pp. 436–450. Springer, Heidelberg (2010). doi:10.1007/978-3-642-13618-4_33
2. Demestichas, P., Georgakopoulos, A., Karvounas, D., Tsagkaris, K., Stavroulaki, V., Lu, J., Xiong, C., Yao, J.: 5G on the horizon: key challenges for the radio-access network. IEEE VT Magz. **8**, 47–53 (2013)
3. Kreutz, D., Ramos, F., Verissimo, P.E., Rothenberg, C.E., Azodolmolky, S., Uhlig, S.: Software-defined networking: a comprehensive survey. Proc. IEEE **103**, 14–76 (2015)
4. Lara, A., Kolasani, A., Ramamurthy, B.: Network innovation using openflow: a survey. IEEE Commun. Surv. Tutorials **16**, 493–512 (2014). First
5. Forwarding and Control Element Separation (ForCES). IETF RFC 5810 (2009)
6. Path Computation Element (PCE) Communication Protocol (PCEP). IETF RFC 5440 (2009)
7. Wood, T., Ramakrishnan, K., Hwang, J., Liu, G., Zhang, W.: Toward a software-based network: integrating software-defined networking and network function virtualization. IEEE Netw. **29**, 36–41 (2015)
8. Han, B., Gopalakrishnan, V., Ji, L., Lee, S.: Network function virtualization: challenges and opportunities for innovations. IEEE Commun. Magz. **53**, 90–97 (2015)
9. Sherry, J., Hasan, S., Scott, C., Krishnamurthy, A., Ratnasamy, S., Sekar, V.: Making middleboxes someone else's problem: network processing as a cloud service. In: ACM SIGCOMM CCR, pp. 13–24 (2012)
10. One Met Total Technology 2014–2017. Metropolitan Police (2014)

Feasibility of Signaling Storms in 3G/UMTS Operational Networks

Frederic Francois$^{(\boxtimes)}$, Omer H. Abdelrahman, and Erol Gelenbe

Intelligent Systems and Networks Group, Department of Electrical and Electronic Engineering, Imperial College, London SW7 2BT, UK
{f.francois,o.abd06,e.gelenbe}@imperial.ac.uk

Abstract. Signaling storms are becoming prevalent in mobile networks due to the proliferation of smartphone applications and new network uses, such as machine-to-machine communication, which are designed without due consideration to the signaling overheads associated with the de/allocation of radio resources to User Equipment (UE). In this work, we conduct a set of experiments on a 3G operational mobile network to validate previous claims in literature that it is possible to significantly change the signaling behavior of a normal UE so that the UE has an adverse impact on the mobile network. Our early results show that it is possible to increase by 0.330 *signaling messages/s* the signaling rate of a normal 3G UE loaded with popular applications when it is not in active use by the owner. In addition, we explore the different factors which can either increase or decrease the effectiveness of signaling attacks on mobile networks.

Keywords: Signaling storms · Radio resource control · 3G/UMTS · Malicious mobile applications · 4G/LTE · M2M

1 Introduction

Mobile networks are increasingly susceptible to Radio Resource Control (RRC) based signaling storms because of the proliferation of smartphone applications [5, 8,16] and new network uses such as machine-to-machine and Internet of Things communication [22] which are not optimized in terms of signaling load and are not tested by mobile operators. In this paper, we present experiments to verify the feasibility of RRC-based signaling storms in operational 3G networks by measuring the number of successful RRC transitions that an attacker can trigger on a targeted User Equipment (UE). The attack is performed over the public Internet where a computer, acting as the attacker, is used to ping the targeted UEs at a variable interval to observe the relationship between the ping frequency and number of successfully triggered RRC transitions. This setup emulates both deliberate RRC-based signaling attacks as well as signaling storms caused by either misbehaving or malicious applications that frequently establish and tear-down data connections in order to transfer small amounts of data.

© ICST Institute for Computer Sciences, Social Informatics and Telecommunications Engineering 2016
B. Mandler et al. (Eds.) IoT 360° 2015, Part I, LNICST 169, pp. 187–198, 2016.
DOI: 10.1007/978-3-319-47063-4_17

In 3G/UMTS networks, each UE has a RRC state machine which controls the amount of bandwidth resources that it is currently allocated [6]. The RRC state machine has 4 states ordered in terms of increasing energy consumption and bandwidth allocation: *IDLE, PCH, FACH* and *DCH*. The RRC state of a UE in a 3G network is controlled by a mobile network element called *Radio Network Controller* (RNC) where the transition between the different RRC states requires different number of signaling messages [13] to be exchanged between the UE and the RNC. A UE can move from a higher-bandwidth RRC state to a lower one after a network operator specified timeout if no data traffic is communicated between the UE and the mobile network during this timeout.

In current literature, there are numerous prior experimental work [3,14,15, 18,19,23] which looks mainly at how to infer the RRC timeouts and the impact of applications on RRC signaling load. In [19], the authors infer the type and parameters of the RRC state machine of 2 operational 3G networks by probing the network through the transmission of different amount of data between a UE and a server on the public Internet. In contrast, [3] assumes only one type of RRC state machine and infer its parameters by using ICMP packets as probe packets. The main author of [19] developed a new RRC state inference algorithm in [18] which provides better accuracy and then uses the algorithm to characterize the signaling, energy and bandwidth utilization of mobile applications by analysing their packet traffic traces only. The authors of [23] carried experiments to measure the impact of RRC timeouts on the power consumption, signaling load and web quality of experience. [15] analyzes the impact of the frequency of keep-alive messages on the energy consumption of the UE in 3G networks while we concentrate on the signaling load and use a UE which is a modern smartphone loaded with popular applications that most users have installed on their phone nowadays. In [14], the authors develop an android application which can measure the RRC signaling, radio resources and energy efficiency of background applications by logging the data packets and corresponding RRC state on a targeted UE.

Our previous work on signaling storms in the context of the NEMESYS project [2,10] has involved the mathematical modeling, simulation and analysis of the impact of different RRC-based signaling storms in 3G/UMTS networks [1,11,12] and 4G/LTE networks [7]. In our recent work, we also investigated methods for the detection and mitigation of signaling storms through the use of RRC timeout adjustment [17] and counters [9].

1.1 Motivation

Nowadays, smartphones often run many applications that communicate over the Internet even when users are inactive in order to enable always-on connectivity which allows users to receive promptly new data such as social media updates, VoIP calls and messages and location-based services. This mix of applications may hinder the ability of either a deliberate RRC-based signaling attacker or a malfunctioning application to cause high signaling load since some of the attacking traffic will not trigger changes in the RRC state because other normal appli-

cations have already performed unknowingly the required changes in RRC state
to carry the attacking traffic.

Although the impact of RRC-based signaling overload on mobile networks has
been evaluated extensively in [1,7,12] using mathematical and simulation models, the assumption therein is that the attacker is able to control to a great extent
the severity of the attack so that the resulting load in the network is proportional to the rate at which either attacking or misbehaving traffic is generated.
The set of experiments designed in this paper aims to validate this assumption in a realistic setting by carrying out RRC-based signaling attacks on an
operational mobile network. Furthermore, an additional objective of this set of
experiments is to evaluate whether attacks can be optimized in the presence of
active mobile applications by modifying the frequency of either malicious or misbehaving transmissions. The results of such experiments will help in the design
of more accurate normal UE and attack models which will lead to the ability of
running more realistic simulation experiments.

2   Description of the Experiments

2.1   Equipment Used

The experiments were conducted on the 3G network of a large operator in the
UK, and included the following components which are connected as shown in
Fig. 1:

- **Samsung Galaxy SII (GT-I9100):** A 3G phone which acts as the targeted
  UE. The phone runs stock Android 4.1.2 (carrier branded) and has been rooted
  to allow applications to run with root privileges. In addition, the phone has the
  popular packet capture utility *tcpdump* installed on it. Several popular mobile
  applications, which communicate over the Internet even when the user is not
  interacting with the device, have been installed on the UE to emulate normal
  UEs in existing mobile networks. It is expected that the overall communication
  pattern of these installed applications will reduce the number of successful
  RRC transitions that can be triggered by the attacker.
- **3G SIM:** To allow the UE to connect to the 3G network of the selected
  operational mobile operator. The Access Point Name (APN) used by the SIM
  card was modified so that the phone appears to the network as a cellular WiFi
  router (known as MiFi) and is allocated a public IP address, rather than a
  private one, by this particular network operator. Having a public IP allowed us
  to ping the smartphone from the public Internet to conduct our experiments,
  which would not have been possible otherwise since direct mobile-to-mobile
  communication over the cellular network is blocked on this particular network.
  It should be noted that many mobile operators across the world provide public
  IP address by default to their customers [20] and therefore, signaling attacks
  based on pinging the public IP address of UEs can occur on these mobile
  networks without any APN change. In addition, signaling attacks can still
  occur when UEs are allocated private IP addresses only if the UEs have either

malicious or misbehaving applications which regularly send user traffic to the mobile network.

- **Linux-based computer:** To act as attacker and to record the changing RRC state and packets communicated over time by the targeted UE. The RRC attacks are carried by a ping generator which pings the public IP of the targeted UE at regular interval. In addition, the targeted UE is connected via a USB cable to the computer and the Android Debug Bridge (ADB) command line tool is used to connect to the targeted UE to retrieve logged information about the changes in RRC state and the packets that are communicated by the UE over the mobile network during the duration of the experiments.

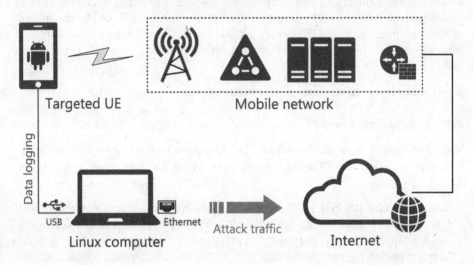

Fig. 1. RRC experiment setup in an operational 3G network.

2.2 Methodology

The RRC experiments are carried by following the following steps: in the first step, Wi-Fi is first deactivated on the targeted UE and then 3G is activated on it so that the UE connects via cellular connection to the Internet and RRC-based attacks can be carried out. The public IP address of the UE is noted so that the ping generator can be configured to attack the UE.

In the second step, two ADB terminals are open on the computer attached to the targeted UE. The first terminal is used to issue commands to the *tcpdump* utility on the targeted UE to start capturing all packets that the UE is receiving through the radio interface; *tcpdump* also records the time when its filters capture the packets. The second terminal is used to record the RRC state of the UE at regular interval. For the UE to start logging the RRC state, it must be put into *ServiceMode* by dialling **#0011#* on the Samsung Galaxy SII phone (this

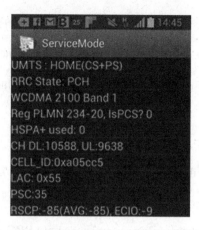

Fig. 2. Screenshot showing the RRC state on the UE after it enters the *ServiceMode* state.

number is known to work only on Samsung Galaxy phones, and other manufacturers may use other codes). When the phone is in *ServiceMode*, it will show the current RRC state as shown in Fig. 2. The second ADB terminal is used to record the RRC state displayed on the UE through the filtering of the system log of the UE for *ServiceMode* information only.

In the third step, the targeted UE is pinged from the attacking computer for the duration of T seconds with a time interval of P seconds between successive pings. The duration of each experiment run T is chosen according to the inter-ping time P such that the total number of attack pings T/P is sufficiently large to provide statistically significant results. In this set of experiments, the default size of the *ICMP Echo Request* packets of the *ping* utility is not changed and was measured to be 100 bytes in the *tcpdump* capture. The impact of the payload size of the *ICMP Echo Request* packets on the type and frequency of RRC transitions triggered is left for future work.

In the final step, the packet and RRC records are then analyzed to obtain the number of successful transitions due to the attack: an attacking ping is deemed to have triggered a successful RRC attack if there is a RRC promotion within $\pm\epsilon$ seconds from the time the attacking ping is recorded by *tcpdump* and there is a RRC demotion within D seconds from the time a successful promotion has been triggered and completed.

2.3 Metrics of Interest

We use two performance measures in order to quantify the effectiveness of the attack. The first metric S captures the proportion of ping messages that successfully trigger a RRC attack:

$$S = \frac{\#\text{successfully triggered RRC attacks}}{\#\text{ping messages captured at the UE}} \times 100\,\% \tag{1}$$

Clearly, higher values of S reflect higher attack success probability. However, each type of RRC state transition causes a certain number of signaling messages to be exchanged in the network as shown in Table 1. Therefore, the impact of the attack is better characterized by taking into consideration the number of successful transitions of each type $r_{x \to y}$ and using the values $n_{x \to y}$ in Table 1 to compute the effective attack rate A as follows:

$$A = \frac{\sum_{\forall x \to y} r_{x \to y} \times n_{x \to y}}{T} \qquad (2)$$

Note that not all possible RRC transitions are shown in Table 1, since only certain transitions were observed in the experiment.

Table 1. No. of signaling messages exchanged per RRC transition type [1]

Start state, x	End state, y	No. of messages, $n_{x \to y}$
PCH	FACH	3
FACH	DCH	7
PCH	DCH	10
DCH	PCH	5
FACH	PCH	2
DCH	FACH	5

3   Results

The parameter D in our set of experiments controls the maximum time limit that a demotion must happen after a promotion occurred near an attacking ping for the transitions to be considered as an attack. During a successful attack, the time that it takes for the UE to demote back to a lower RRC state depends on many factors, the first one being the time it takes to finish communicating all the packets related to the attack, this includes the varying end-to-end delay between the UE and the attacking computer. The second factor is the timeout that the network operator has set for RRC demotion to occur if no data traffic is being transmitted between the UE and the mobile network. It should be noted that normal UE data traffic can cause the UE to either stay in the higher RRC state that the attacking ping caused it to promote to or promote to an even higher RRC state. When normal traffic happens after an attacking promotion but before its associated demotion, the attack is deemed to have failed. Hence, the value of D helps to identify RRC promotion and demotion transition pairs that are affected by normal traffic and should not be counted as attacks. In order to help us identify the appropriate value of D, we compare in Fig. 3 the histogram of the time between promotion and demotion when there are ping attacks occurring and not. It can be observed that most of the change in the

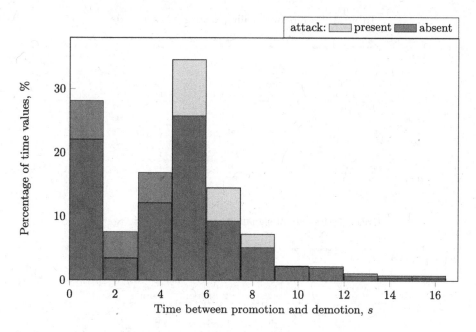

Fig. 3. Bar chart showing the percentage of "time spent in promoted RRC state before demotion" values falling within a specified time interval when RRC-based signaling attack is present and absent. The bin size is set to $1.5\,s$.

distribution of the time spent in promoted RRC state happens before $9\,s$ and hence, in this work we choose D to be 9. We also set D to ∞ to have a measure of RRC transitions that were not counted.

Tables 2 and 3 show the results of the RRC experiment for different ping intervals P and maximum time between an attacking promotion and demotion for an attack to be considered successful D, with the parameter ϵ set to $2\,s$ to match the longest sampling interval (which is not under our control) of the RRC state of the targeted UE during the whole set of experiments. The results show that the effective attack rate A is highest when the ping interval $P = 10\,s$ for all considered values of D. In all the experiments, it can be observed that most of the attacking transitions are of type $PCH \rightarrow FACH$ and vice versa because ping attacks are low traffic volume attacks and therefore, the $FACH$ RRC state is enough in most cases for the targeted UE to handle the traffic linked with the ping attacks. The targeted UE can move to the highest RRC state DCH when the ping attacks happen at the same time as when legitimate user traffic is being communicated by the targeted UE and therefore, a transition to DCH state is required in order to carry the additional attack traffic.

Figure 4 shows that the success rate of the attack S increases with the time interval between two consecutive pings P up to a level ($P = 10s$) after which S stays almost constant. When carrying out a RRC-based signaling attack, attackers may be tempted to set the ping frequency interval P to be slightly larger

Table 2. Results of signaling attacks when $D = 9s$

Ping interval $P s$	Exp. Duration $T s$	# successful transitions							# Attack pings logged	Attack success rate, $S\%$	Effective attack rate, A msg/s
		Total	PCH → FACH	PCH → DCH	FACH → DCH	FACH → PCH	DCH → PCH	DCH → FACH			
2	1080	0	0	0	0	0	0	0	487	0	0
3	1620	36	0	0	18	0	15	3	445	4.04	0.133
5	2700	194	81	1	15	81	14	2	376	25.8	0.222
10	5400	620	278	2	30	278	31	1	464	66.8	0.330
20	10800	608	266	2	36	266	37	1	491	61.9	0.166
30	16200	698	307	3	39	307	40	2	509	68.6	0.126
40	21600	696	311	1	36	311	35	2	522	66.7	0.093

Table 3. Results of signaling attacks when $D = \infty s$

Ping interval $D s$	Exp. Duration $T s$	# successful transitions							# Attack pings logged	Attack success rate, $S\%$	Effective attack rate, A msg/s
		Total	PCH → FACH	PCH → DCH	FACH → DCH	FACH → PCH	DCH → PCH	DCH → FACH			
2	1080	0	0	0	0	0	0	0	487	0	0
3	1620	48	1	0	23	1	19	4	445	5.39	0.173
5	2700	332	146	1	19	146	18	2	376	44.1	0.360
10	5400	736	333	2	33	333	34	1	464	79.3	0.387
20	10800	736	326	2	40	326	40	2	491	74.9	0.198
30	16200	784	346	3	43	346	43	3	509	77.0	0.141
40	21600	786	355	1	37	355	36	2	522	75.3	0.103

than the timeouts for demotion in order to maximize the severity of the attacks. Unfortunately, this way of carrying out attacks is not the most efficient one since only a fraction of the attack pings can trigger RRC transitions due to variations in the end-to-end delay between the attacker and the targeted UE, which can decrease the inter-arrival times of ping messages at the UE and do not allow the targeted UE to have enough time to undergo RRC demotions so that the attack pings can trigger malicious RRC promotions again. Therefore, the attacker should add additional time between his attacks to take into consideration the variation in end-to-end delay.

When P is very small, the majority of the attack pings fails to trigger RRC transitions because the targeted UE does not have enough time to undergo the RRC timeout(s) and demote to lower RRC states before the next attack ping arrives. The targeted UE stays most of the time in the higher RRC states where it is able to handle the additional traffic associated with the attack pings without further promotions. Indeed, a large scale attack with very small P can potentially cause bandwidth starvation in the network, which is a data plane type of attack, since the UE remains active throughout the duration of the attack, effectively reducing the available bandwidth in the affected base stations and depleting the battery of the targeted UEs.

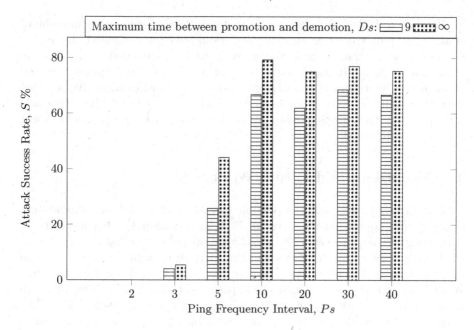

Fig. 4. Change in the attack success rate S when the ping interval P is increased and the maximum time between a successful attacking promotion and demotion is changed D.

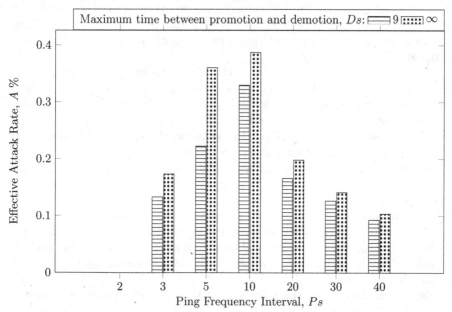

Fig. 5. Change in the effective attack rate A when the ping interval P is increased and the maximum time between a successful attacking promotion and demotion is changed D.

Note again that the success rate of the attack S only measures the probability of an attack ping triggering an RRC transition, but does not reflect the impact of these triggered transitions in the network, which is captured by the effective attack rate A shown in Fig. 5 where the number of signaling messages required for each type of triggered transitions is taken into consideration. We see that A increases with P up to a maximum value when $P = 10\,s$ (or the attack rate $= 0.1\ pings/s$), then drops monotonically as P is increased as one would expect from a low rate attack.

4   Conclusions and Future Work

This paper has shown that it is possible to carry RRC-based signaling attacks at a very high success rate, i.e. around 70 %, in operational mobile networks by optimizing the frequency at which attacks are carried out so that the attacks are not heavily reduced by the communication pattern of normal applications and by variations in the end-to-end delay between the attacker and targeted UEs. While it was possible to maximize the impact of the attack for a single UE, with a high effective attack rate of $0.330\ signaling\ messages/s$ at a ping rate of 0.1 $pings/s$, it may be difficult to optimize the attack for all UEs using the same attack interval because different users have different communication pattern.

An important finding in this paper is that, in contrast to previous belief, RRC-based signaling attacks cannot be optimized based only on the configurations of the networks (i.e. timeout values) since variations in the end-to-end delay between the attacker and targeted UEs and the communication patterns of normal applications on the targeted UEs can significantly reduced the effectiveness of the attacks.

Finally, the experiment has shown that mobile network operators are now following best practices by setting the timeout in state PCH to be very large and the buffer threshold at the RNC for transitioning from $FACH$ to DCH to be also large, thus significantly reducing the effect of chatty mobile applications on the control plane of the network but this comes at the expense of higher energy consumption for the radio subsystem of the UEs.

In future work, there are a number of limitations to the current setup of the experiments which can be improved. First, the RRC state can only be logged when the targeted UE is in *ServiceMode*, i.e. when the RRC state is displayed on the UE screen. This limits the ability to carry out the experiment when the user is actively using the UE. Thus, we expect that the values of A, shown in Fig. 5, represent an upper bound for the load on the network. In practice, this load will be reduced by the activities of the user which will generate normal traffic more frequently.

Second, we found that the most reliable way to capture packets, with ping still working, was through *tcpdump* which is controlled by an ADB terminal. Future work will involve using a terminal directly on the phone, which will be running in the background, to run *tcpdump* so that together with the logging of RRC states in the background, the collection of both packets and RRC data can be done without preventing users from actively using the phone and also be mobile. This will provide more realistic data about when and at what frequency the attacks can be performed against the phone.

In our current work, the attacking ping messages cause the RRC transitions to be mostly of type $PCH \rightarrow FACH$ and vice versa because ping packets are small and can be handled with the $FACH$ RRC state. If the UE is already in $FACH$, the UE has in most cases enough capacity to handle the ping packets without transitioning to the DCH state. In future work, it might be useful to perform more volumetric attacks, by for e.g. increasing the payload of the $ICMP$ $Echo\ Request$ packets to the maximum, to try to trigger more $PCH \rightarrow FACH$ $\rightarrow DCH$, $FACH \rightarrow DCH$ and vice versa transitions which may lead to higher attack success ratio and also higher induced signaling in the mobile network.

Finally, we aim to repeat the RRC-based signaling attack experiments carried in this paper in the context of an operational 4G/LTE network where a simplified RRC state machine is used and new enhancements such as Machine Technology Communication (MTC) are being introduced to alleviate the impact of machine-to-machine communications on 4G/LTE networks [4,21].

Acknowledgments. The work presented in this paper was supported by the EU FP7 research project NEMESYS (Enhanced Network Security for Seamless Service Provisioning in the Smart Mobile Ecosystem), under grant agreement no. 317888 within the FP7-ICT-2011.1.3 Trustworthy ICT domain.

References

1. Abdelrahman, O.H., Gelenbe, E.: Signalling storms in 3G mobile networks. In: Proceedings of IEEE International Conference on Communications (ICC), pp. 1017–1022 (2014)
2. Abdelrahman, O.H., Gelenbe, E., Gorbil, G., Oklander, B.: Mobile network anomaly detection and mitigation: the NEMESYS approach. In: Gelenbe, E., Lent, R. (eds.) ISCIS 2013. LNEE, vol. 264, pp. 429–438. Springer, New York (2013)
3. Barbuzzi, A., Ricciato, F., Boggia, G.: Discovering parameter setting in 3g networks via active measurements. IEEE Commun. Lett. **12**(10), 730–732 (2008)
4. Cheng, M.Y., Lin, G.Y., Wei, H.Y., Hsu, A.C.C.: Overload control for machine-type-communications in lte-advanced system. IEEE Commun. Mag. **50**(6), 38–45 (2012)
5. Corner, S.: Angry Birds + Android + ads = network overload. IT Wire (2011). http://www.itwire.com/business-it-news/networking/47823
6. ETSI 3GPP: 3Gpp. TS 25.331: Universal mobile telecommunications system (UMTS) radio resource control (RRC) protocol specification (2015)
7. Francois, F., Abdelrahman, O.H., Gelenbe, E.: Impact of signaling storms on energy consumption and latency of LTE user equipment. In: Proceedings of the 7th IEEE International Symposium on Cyberspace safety and security (CSS 2015), New York (2015)
8. Gabriel, C.: DoCoMo demands Google's help with signalling storm. Rethink Wireless (2012). http://www.rethink-wireless.com/2012/01/30/docomo-demands-googles-signalling-storm.htm

9. Gelenbe, E., Abdelrahman, O.H.: Time-outs and counters against storms (2014)
10. Gelenbe, E., Gorbil, G., Tzovaras, D., Liebergeld, S., Garcia, D., Baltatu, M., Lyberopoulos, G.: Security for smart mobile networks: the NEMESYS approach. In: Proceedings of IEEE Global High Tech Congress on Electronics (GHTCE), pp. 63–69, Shenzhen (2013)
11. Gorbil, G., Abdelrahman, O.H., Gelenbe, E.: Storms in mobile networks. In: Proceedings of 10th ACM Symposium on QoS and Security for Wireless and Mobile Networks (Q2SWinet), pp. 119–126, Montreal, Canada (2014)
12. Gorbil, G., Abdelrahman, O.H., Pavloski, M., Gelenbe, E.: Modeling and analysis of RRC-based signalling storms in 3G networks. IEEE Trans. Emerg. Topics Comput. 4(1), 113–127 (2015)
13. GSMA: Fast dormancy best practises. White paper (2011). http://www.gsma.com/newsroom/ts18-v10-tsg-prd-fast-dormancy-best-practices
14. Gupta, S., Garg, R., Jain, N., Naik, V., Kaul, S.: Android phone based appraisal of app. behavior on cell networks. In: Proceedings of the 1st International Conference on Mobile Software Engineering and Systems, MOBILESoft 2014, pp. 54–57 (2014)
15. Haverinen, H., Siren, J., Eronen, P.: Energy consumption of always-on applications in wcdma networks. In: IEEE 65th Vehicular Technology Conference, 2007, VTC2007-Spring, pp. 964–968 (2007)
16. Jiantao, S.: Analyzing the network friendliness of mobile applications. Technical report (2012)
17. Pavloski, M., Gelenbe, E.: Signaling attacks in mobile telephony. In: Proceedings of the 11th International Conference on Security and Cryptography (SECRYPT 2014), pp. 206–212 (2014)
18. Qian, F., Wang, Z., Gerber, A., Mao, Z., Sen, S., Spatscheck, O.: Profiling resource usage for mobile applications: a cross-layer approach. In: Proceedings of the 9th International Conference on Mobile Systems, Applications, and Services, MobiSys 2011, pp. 321–334 (2011)
19. Qian, F., Wang, Z., Gerber, A., Mao, Z.M., Sen, S., Spatscheck, O.: Characterizing radio resource allocation for 3g networks. In: Proceedings of the 10th ACM SIGCOMM Conference on Internet Measurement, IMC 2010, pp. 137–150 (2010)
20. Qian, Z., Wang, Z., Xu, Q., Mao, Z.M., Zhang, M., Wang, Y.M.: You can run, but you can't hide: exposing network location for targeted DoS attacks in cellular networks. In: Proceedings of 19th Annual Network and Distributed System Security Symposium (NDSS), San Diego, CA (2012)
21. Qualcomm: LTE MTC: optimizing LTE advanced for machine-type communications (2014). https://www.qualcomm.com/media/documents/files/lte-mtc-optimizing-lte-advanced-for-machine-type-communications.pdf
22. Research, R.: Gsma seeks to avert chaos on mobile iot networks (2014). http://www.rethinkresearch.biz/articles/gsma-seeks-avert-chaos-mobile-iot-networks/
23. Schwartz, C., Hoßfeld, T., Lehrieder, F., Tran-Gia, P.: Angry apps: the impact of network timer selection on power consumption, signalling load, and web QoE. J. Comput. Netw. Commun. 2013, 13 (2013). Article ID 176217

Countering Mobile Signaling Storms with Counters

Erol Gelenbe$^{(\boxtimes)}$ and Omer H. Abdelrahman

Department of Electrical and Electronic Engineering,
Imperial College, London SW7 2BT, UK
{e.gelenbe,o.abd06}@imperial.ac.uk

Abstract. Mobile Networks are subject to signaling storms launched by misbehaving applications or malware, which result in bandwidth overload at the cell level and excessive signaling within the mobile operator, and may also deplete the battery power of mobile devices. This paper reviews the causes of signaling storms and proposes a novel technique for storm detection and mitigation. The approach is based on counting the number of successive signaling transitions that do not utilize allocated bandwidth, and temporarily blocking mobile devices that exceed a certain threshold to avoid overloading the network. Through a mathematical analysis, we derive the optimum value of the counter's threshold, which minimizes both the number of misbehaving mobiles and the signaling overload in the network. Simulation results are provided to illustrate the effectiveness of the proposed scheme.

Keywords: Signaling overload · Radio resource control · M2M · IoT · Application malfunctions · Malware · QoS

1   Introduction

There has been significant industry interest worldwide regarding mobile signaling overload or "signaling storms" which have been publicly documented in the real world numerous times [6,10,11,15,31]. Signaling storms can be triggered by various factors, which all lead to a large number of mobile devices making successive connection requests that then time-out because of inactivity, triggering repeated signaling to allocate and de-allocate radio channels and other resources in the network.

This type of behavior on wireless networks can result in abusive bandwidth occupancy, excessive signaling at the mobile operator [2,22], battery dissipation at mobile devices [14], and extra energy consumption in base stations and backbone networks [17,18,34]. If mobile technology is exploited in cyber-physical infrastructures such as the smart grid, or for the Internet of Things (IoT) including vehicular technologies, smart homes, and emergency management systems [20], such signaling storm effects can delay or impair communications which are of vital importance. In IoT and machine to machine (M2M) applications, the

© ICST Institute for Computer Sciences, Social Informatics and Telecommunications Engineering 2016
B. Mandler et al. (Eds.) IoT 360° 2015, Part I, LNICST 169, pp. 199–209, 2016.
DOI: 10.1007/978-3-319-47063-4_18

massive number of devices to be supported and actions which may be synchronized, require new efforts to make such networks resilient and reliable [4]. Thus in this paper, we propose and analyze a novel approach that aims to protect cellular networks against signaling storms that can be caused by mobile malware or misbehaving applications.

1.1 Signaling Storms

The vulnerability of mobile networks to signaling denial of service (DoS) attacks is not new. Indeed, early work has identified different ways to attack the control plane of mobile networks, e.g. through paging [35], service requests [37] and radio resource control (RRC) [26,33]. Poorly designed mobile applications are perhaps one of the most common triggers of signaling overloads [6] that lead to performance degradation and even network outages [11,15]. Such "chatty" applications constantly poll the network, even when users are inactive, in order to provide always-on connectivity, background updates [29] and in-application advertisements [10]. Similar problems have been reported with M2M systems that transmit small amounts of data with deterministic intervals [1,25,36]. A common issue with those applications is that developers are not familiar with the control plane of mobile networks, so they build applications without considering their adverse effect on the networks. This has prompted the mobile industry to promote best practices for developing network-friendly applications [7,13,23,24].

Industry guidelines, however, do not provide adequate protection against signaling storms which can be triggered by well-designed applications, when an unexpected event occurs in the Internet. Examples of such events include outages in mobile cloud services [8,31] and in VoIP peer-to-peer networks [9]. During those incidents, a large number of mobile devices attempt to recover connectivity to the application servers, generating significantly more keep-alive messages [5] and an unexpectedly high signaling load in the process.

In addition, signaling storms may occur as a by-product of malicious activity that is not intended to cause a signaling DoS attack. The perpetrators in many of those incidents rely on the Internet to carry out profitable attacks, and therefore it is against their interest to cause disruption in the access to the infrastructure. Examples of such scenarios include: (i) Large-scale malware infections with frequent communications, such as premium SMS dialers, spammers, adware and bot-clients, which are among the top encountered threats on smartphones [28] and have been shown [27] to exhibit resource-inefficient communication patterns. (ii) Unwanted traffic in the Internet [32], including backscatter noise from remote DoS attacks, scanning worms, and spam campaigns, which pose a risk to mobile networks that can be eliminated using middleboxes, but is often not due to carriers' policies [30,38]. (iii) Network outages due to cyber-attacks which could be followed (and hence prolonged) by a signaling storm, due to the large number of user devices that will attempt to reconnect after the service is restored [12].

2   The Model

We represent the set of normal and malicious mobile calls in the system at time t by a state $s(t) = (b, B, C, A_1, a_1, ..., A_i, a_i, ...; t)$ where:

- b is the number of mobiles which are in low bandwidth mode,
- B is the number of normal mobiles which are in high bandwidth mode,
- C is the number of normal mobiles that have started to transfer or receive data or voice in high bandwidth mode,
- A_i is the number of attacking mobiles which are in high bandwidth mode and have undergone a time-out for $i - 1$ times,
- a_i is the number of attacking mobiles which have entered low bandwidth mode from high bandwidth mode after i time-outs.

We assume a Poisson arrival process of rate λ of new mobile activations or calls, and a call that is first admitted in state b then requests high bandwidth at rate r. Note that r^{-1} can be viewed as the average time it takes a call to make its first high bandwidth request to the network. With probability $\bar{\alpha} = 1 - \alpha$ such a call will be of normal type and will enter state B, while with probability α it will be an attacking call and will request high bandwidth and hence enter state A_1 indicating the first request for bandwidth that is made by a defectively operating application or malware that can contribute to a storm. Thus, α is a metric that represents the fraction of all activations that are attacking or mobiles which contain malware or a deficient application.

Once a call enters state A_1, since it is misbehaving, it will not start a communication and will time-out after some time of average value τ^{-1}. Note that the time-out is a parameter that is set by the operator for all the mobile devices so that they will not occupy the high bandwidth mode if they are actually not making use of it, and in practice it is of the order of a few seconds. After entering state a_1, the call may be detected as being anomalous, and will be removed or blocked from the system at rate β_1, where β_1^{-1} is the average time it takes the detector to identify that this call has the potential to contribute to a storm, and to block the device from making further connections. However, it is very unlikely that the system is so smart that it can make this decision correctly regarding the call so early in the game, so typically $\beta_1 \simeq 0$ and the call will manage to request high bandwidth and then enter state A_2 at rate r. Proceeding in the same manner, in state A_i the anomalous call will again not start a normal communication, so it will eventually time-out after an average time τ and enter state a_i, and so on.

Now with regard to normal calls, a normally operating mobile in high bandwidth mode B may transition to the communicating mode C at rate κ, signifying that transmission or reception has started, or it will transition back to the low bandwidth mode at a rate τ that signifies a time-out. From state C the call's activity may be interrupted, as when a mobile device stops sending or receiving data to/from a web site, in which case the call will return to state B at rate μ. Similarly, the call may end at rate δ, leaving the system. The parameters κ, μ and δ can represent a wide range of normal mobile usage patterns. For example,

Table 1. State transitions in the model.

Transition	Rate	Cause
$b \to b + 1$	λ	network activation (attach)
$(b, B) \to (b - 1, B + 1)$	$br\bar{\alpha}$	new normal call
$(B, C) \to (B - 1, C + 1)$	$B\kappa$	start sending or receiving traffic
$(b, B) \to (b + 1, B - 1)$	$B\tau$	time-out for a normal call
$C \to C - 1$	$C\delta$	end of a normal call
$(B, C) \to (B + 1, C - 1)$	$C\mu$	stop sending or receiving traffic
$(b, A_1) \to (b - 1, A_1 + 1)$	$br\alpha$	new attack call
$(a_{i-1}, A_i) \to (a_{i-1} - 1, A_i + 1)$	$a_{i-1}r$	i-th superfluous transition of an attack call, $i > 1$
$(a_i, A_i) \to (a_i + 1, A_i - 1)$	$A_i\tau$	i-th time-out of an attack call, $i \geq 1$
$a_i \to a_i - 1$	$a_i\beta_i$	attack call blocked after i time-outs, $i \geq 1$

a web browsing session or call normally lasts for several minutes or even hours (thus δ is typically very small), but may include several downloading and reading times, with mean of μ^{-1} and κ^{-1}, respectively; in this case, the time-out operates only while the user is reading, taking the state from B to b.

With the above assumptions, Table 1 shows the possible transitions from the state $s(t)$. Note that all of the state transitions which are not indicated in the table are simply the ones where the state is unchanged, and furthermore note that apart from the first case, the state transition rates are population dependent.

Assuming that all the rates that are indicated are the parameters of independent and identically distributed exponential random variables, and that the probability α corresponds to successively independent and identically distributed events, the above model has an exact equilibrium solution [16,19] that can be easily calculated, and thus can provide the joint probability distribution of the state $s(t)$. However the rate parameters r and μ are actually congestion dependent. This means that they will essentially dependent on the number of calls in each of the states because for a total amount of bandwidth in the system at a base station level of say W, the total amount of bandwidth available may be expressed as some value $W^* = W - w_1(b + \sum_i a_i) - w_2(B + \sum_i A_i) - w_3 C$ where w_1, w_2 and w_3 denote the bandwidth allocated per low bandwidth, inactive high bandwidth and active high bandwidth requests, respectively. Thus in reality the rate r will be "slowed down" as W^* becomes smaller since requests will be delayed or will even remain unsatisfied. The matter is of course more complex, because not only the bandwidth allocation itself but the error probabilities in the channel will be affected by the amount of bandwidth that is already allocated and thus the channel holding time μ^{-1} will also depend on W^*.

A schematic diagram of the model is presented in Fig. 1(a), showing the states $s(t) \in \{b, B, C, a_1, A_1, \ldots, a_i, A_i, \ldots\}$, possible transitions, and rates at which *each* of the calls in one state will transition to another state. Assuming that the transition rates r and μ do *not* depend on the number of mobiles that are

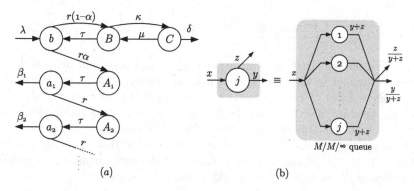

Fig. 1. (a) A schematic diagram of the state transition model for the number of normal and attacking calls in the network. (b) An $M/M/\infty$ queueing representation of a node j with arrival rate x and transition rates (for each of the calls in j) y and z; the ratios $y/(y+z)$ and $z/(y+z)$ denote the transition probabilities from state j

using the bandwidth, calls act independently of each other so that the evolution of the number of calls in any of the states can be represented by an equivalent $M/M/\infty$ queueing model as shown in Fig. 1(b).

2.1 Traffic Equations and Equilibrium Probability Distribution

The arrival rate of calls into each of the possible states may be written as Λ_j where $j \in \{b, B, C, A_1, a_1, ..., A_i, a_i, ...\}$ which satisfy a system of linear equations. Specifically, the rates at which calls enter the attack states are simply:

$$\Lambda_{a_i} = \Lambda_{A_i},$$
$$\Lambda_{A_1} = \alpha \Lambda_b,$$
$$\Lambda_{A_i} = \Lambda_{a_{i-1}} \frac{r}{r + \beta_{i-1}} = \alpha \Lambda_b \prod_{l=1}^{i-1} \frac{r}{r + \beta_l}, \quad i > 1 \qquad (1)$$

where Λ_b is the rate at which calls enter state b which is calculated as follows. The rates at which calls enter the normal operating states are described by the linear equations:

$$\Lambda_b = \lambda + \frac{\tau}{\tau + \kappa}\Lambda_B,$$
$$\Lambda_B = (1 - \alpha)\Lambda_b + \frac{\mu}{\mu + \delta}\Lambda_C,$$
$$\Lambda_C = \frac{\kappa}{\kappa + \tau}\Lambda_B, \qquad (2)$$

so that $\Lambda_B = \gamma \Lambda_b$, where $\gamma = \frac{1-\alpha}{1 - \frac{\mu\kappa}{(\mu+\delta)(\kappa+\tau)}}$, and:

$$\Lambda_b = \frac{\lambda}{1 - \frac{\tau}{\tau+\kappa}\gamma} = \frac{\lambda}{1 - \frac{\tau(1-\alpha)}{\tau+\kappa-\frac{\mu\kappa}{\mu+\delta}}}, \quad \Lambda_B = \frac{\lambda\gamma}{1 - \frac{\tau}{\tau+\kappa}\gamma}, \quad \Lambda_C = \frac{\kappa\lambda\gamma}{\kappa + \tau(1-\gamma)}. \quad (3)$$

Since we assume that the transition rates r and μ do *not* depend on the number of mobiles in the system, calls act independently of each other so that the *average number* of calls in each of the states is the *average arrival rate* of calls into the state, multiplied by the *average time* spent by a call in that state. We will present here only results for the attacking states, since we are interested in mitigating the storm. We first note that the average time spent by a mobile in state a_i is $(r + \beta_i)^{-1}$ and in A_i is τ^{-1}, so that the average number of mobiles in equilibrium N_j in each of the attacking states becomes:

$$N_{A_1} = \frac{\alpha\Lambda_b}{\tau},$$

$$N_{A_i} = \frac{\alpha\Lambda_b}{\tau} \prod_{l=1}^{i-1} \frac{r}{r + \beta_l}, \quad i > 1,$$

$$N_{a_i} = \frac{\alpha\Lambda_b}{r + \beta_i} \prod_{l=1}^{i-1} \frac{r}{r + \beta_l}, \quad i \geq 1. \quad (4)$$

As a consequence, the total average number of malicious calls becomes:

$$N_\alpha = \sum_{i=1}^{\infty}[N_{a_i} + N_{A_i}] = \alpha\Lambda_b \sum_{i=1}^{\infty} \left[(\frac{1}{\tau} + \frac{1}{r + \beta_i}) \prod_{l=1}^{i-1} \frac{r}{r + \beta_l} \right]. \quad (5)$$

2.2   Optimum Counter for Mitigation

Although choosing a relatively small value of the time-out of the order of a few seconds can be useful, we see that some additional mechanism needs to be inserted to mitigate the effect of signaling storms. Therefore we suggest that a counter value n be selected so that as long as the number of successive times that the mobile uses the time-out is less than n, then the mobile remains attached to the network. However as soon as this number reaches n, then the mobile is detached after a time of average value β^{-1}. Thus β^{-1} can be viewed as the decision time plus the physical detachment time that is needed.

A large value of n will improve the chances of *correctly* detecting a misbehaving mobile user, providing the system with full confidence to activate the mitigation policy. If n is small we may have false positives, requiring analysis of the users behavior with other ongoing connections, or checking some data plane attributes such as destination IP addresses or port numbers that may be associated with malicious activities. Thus the higher the n, the faster the decision can be to disconnect the mobile, i.e. β increases with the threshold n, with a slope or derivative with respect to n expressed as β'.

Based on this principle, and with reference to our earlier definition of β_i, we have:

$$\beta_i = \begin{cases} 0, & 1 \leq i < n, \\ \beta(n), & i \geq n \end{cases} \quad (6)$$

so that storm mitigation is activated when high bandwidth is requested n successive times, each followed by a time-out. Using the previous analysis, the average number of malicious calls becomes:

$$N_\alpha = \alpha \Lambda_b [(n - 1 + \frac{r}{\beta})(\frac{1}{\tau} + \frac{1}{r}) + \frac{1}{\tau}] \tag{7}$$

while the resulting signaling load from the attack is given by the total rate of malicious transitions between low and high bandwidth states:

$$\Lambda_\alpha = \alpha \Lambda_b + \sum_{i=1}^{\infty} [\Lambda_{a_i} + \Lambda_{A_i}] = \alpha \Lambda_b [2n + 1 + \frac{2r}{\beta}] \tag{8}$$

With some further simple analysis we can show that the value n^* that minimizes *both* N_α and Λ_α, is the value that satisfies:

$$\beta(n^*)^2 \approx r.\beta'(n^*). \tag{9}$$

As an example, consider a detection rate that increases linearly with the threshold according to $\beta(n) = mn$, $m > 0$. In this case, the optimum value of the counter's threshold is obtained by solving the quadratic equation $m^2 n^2 = rm$ which yields:

$$n^* = \sqrt{r/m}.$$

We see that n^* decreases with m, which means that the optimum threshold becomes smaller when the network is more able (i.e. larger m) to detect malicious connections using data plane attributes. This simple example illustrates how the proposed counter-based approach can be optimized when deployed in conjunction with detection systems [3] that analyze IP packets to identify attacks.

3   Simulation Experiments

In this section we evaluate the performance of the joint detection and mitigation approach that we have proposed using the mobile network simulator described in [21,22]. We illustrate how the proposed scheme allows quick reaction to malicious signaling behaviors or to malfunctioning applications, by showing the temporal behavior of network signaling load and delay during normal operation and then during an attack which is being detected and mitigated with our approach. However, we have not addressed the problem of how to set the parameters of the mathematical model based on the average mobile user profile and network configurations, so as to optimize the counter's threshold using Eq. (9); we leave this issue for future work.

The results that we present were obtained by simulating 500 mobile devices, each running the detection and mitigation mechanism, in an area of $2 \times 2\,\mathrm{km}^2$ which is covered by 7 UMTS base stations connected to a single radio network controller (RNC). All mobiles join the network at the beginning of the simulation, and generate web browsing traffic following a model based on industry recommendations and web metrics released by Google. We assume 20 % of the mobiles are malicious or compromised, which overload the RNC by causing superfluous promotions to the high bandwidth DCH state. The service times in the RNC have been artificially increased in order to simulate overload conditions with a small number of mobiles.

In Fig. 2, the signaling misbehavior starts gradually between 2800 and 4000 s from the beginning of the simulation, rather than suddenly, in order to prevent artifacts such as a huge spike of signaling load due to many devices attacking at the same time. Also, for the purpose of showing the effect of the storm and the proposed countermeasure, we activate the mitigation mechanism at 7000 s.

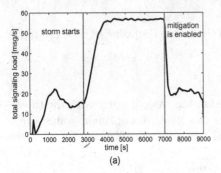 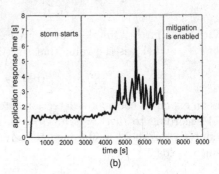

(a)   (b)

Fig. 2. Simulation results: (a) total signaling load at the RNC, and (b) application response time. The mitigation mechanism is activated at 7000 s to allow the storm to develop and to show the effectiveness of the approach. The counter's threshold was set experimentally to $n = 3$ based on performance.

Figure 2(a) shows the number of signaling messages sent and received per second by the RNC as captured during a simulation run. The application response time at a normal mobile is shown in Fig. 2(b), which is the duration between when the user requests a web page and when all of the web page is received. The results are obtained by using an averaging window of size 50 s. It can be observed that the signaling load increases significantly as a result of the attack, which in turn increases the time it takes for a mobile to acquire a radio channel to send and receive data, leading to higher latency and jitter. However, the proposed detection and mitigation scheme is able to quickly identify and mitigate the attack, effectively recovering the average response time for the normal users to the level they had before the storm.

4   Conclusions

Mobile operators have recently experienced an exponential growth in mobile data traffic, coupled with a greater surge in signaling loads which degrade the quality of service for users. These signaling storms will continue to pose challenges to operators, especially with the expected wide deployment of M2M and

IoT applications over cellular networks, due to the massive number of devices to be supported, the fact that those devices may act in a synchronized manner, and the absence of the human-in-the-loop in most applications. As the demand for always-on connectivity increases from mobile and M2M applications, signaling storms can become a significant show stopper, particularly from the perspective of the response time requirements of applications, hence underscoring the need for new approaches to make networks more resilient and reliable.

Thus we have suggested a novel mitigation approach for signaling storms, that maintains a counter for each active mobile device, either within the device or at the network signaling server. If the counter exceeds a certain threshold, indicating excessive radio resource control requests, the mobile device is temporarily blocked to avoid overloading the signaling plane. We developed a mathematical model which examines the role of the time-out and computes the counter's threshold that minimizes both signaling load and number of misbehaving devices. Simulation results illustrate these behaviors, showing that the counter-based technique restores the signaling load and application response times to their values before the storm began.

Acknowledgments. We thank Mihajlo Pavloski and Gokce Gorbil for the simulation results, and the EU FP7 project NEMESYS (Enhanced Network Security for Seamless Service Provisioning in the Smart Mobile Ecosystem), grant agreement no. 317888, for financial support.

References

1. 3GPP: Study on machine-type communications (MTC) and other mobile data applications communications enhancements (release 12) (2013). 3GPP TR 23.887. http://www.3gpp.org/DynaReport/23887.htm
2. Abdelrahman, O.H., Gelenbe, E.: Signalling storms in 3G mobile networks. In: Proceedings of IEEE International Conference on Communications (ICC), pp. 1017–1022, Sydney (2014). doi:10.1109/ICC.2014.6883453
3. Abdelrahman, O.H., Gelenbe, E.: A data plane approach for detecting control plane anomalies in mobile networks. In: Proceedings of International Conference on Cyber Physical Systems, IoT and Sensors Networks (Cyclone), Rome (2015)
4. Abdelrahman, O.H., Gelenbe, E., Gorbil, G., Oklander, B.: Mobile network anomaly detection and mitigation: the NEMESYS approach. In: Gelenbe, E., Lent, R. (eds.) Information Sciences and Systems 2013. Lecture Notes in Electrical Engineering, vol. 264, pp. 429–438. Springer, Switzerland (2013). doi:10.1007/978-3-319-01604-7_42
5. Amrutkar, C., Hiltunen, M., Jim, T., Joshi, K., Spatscheck, O., Traynor, P., Venkataraman, S.: Why is my smartphone slow? on the fly diagnosis of underperformance on the mobile internet. In: Proceedings of 43rd Annual IEEE/IFIP International Conference on Dependable Systems and Networks (DSN), pp. 1–8. IEEE Computer Society, Budapest (2013). doi:10.1109/DSN.2013.6575301
6. Arbor Networks: Worldwide infrastructure security report (2014). http://pages.arbornetworks.com/rs/arbor/images/WISR2014.pdf
7. AT&T: Best practices for 3G and 4G app development. Whitepaper (2012). http://developer.att.com/static-assets/documents/library/best-practices-3g-4g-app-development.pdf

8. Choi, Y., Yoon, C.H., Kim, Y.S., Heo, S.W., Silvester, J.: The impact of application signaling traffic on public land mobile networks. IEEE Commun. Mag. **52**(1), 166–172 (2014). doi:10.1109/MCOM.2014.6710079

9. Coluccia, A., D'alconzo, A., Ricciato, F.: Distribution-based anomaly detection via generalized likelihood ratio test: a general maximum entropy approach. Comput. Netw. **57**(17), 3446–3462 (2013). doi:10.1016/j.comnet.2013.07.028

10. Corner, S.: Angry birds + android + ads = network overload (2011). http://www.itwire.com/business-it-news/networking/47823

11. Donegan, M.: Operators urge action against chatty apps. Light Reading Report (2011). http://www.lightreading.com/operators-urge-action-against-chatty-apps/d/d-id/687399

12. Ericsson: High availability is more than five nines (2014). http://www.ericsson.com/real-performance/wp-content/uploads/sites/3/2014/07/high-avaialbility.pdf

13. Ericsson: A smartphone app developers guide: Optimizing for mobile networks. Whitepaper (2014). http://www.ericsson.com/res/docs/2014/smartphone-app-dev-guide.pdf

14. Francois, F., Abdelrahman, O.H., Gelenbe, E.: Impact of signaling storms on energy consumption and latency of LTE user equipment. In: Proceedings of 7th IEEE International Symposium on Cyberspace safety and security (CSS), New York (2015)

15. Gabriel, C.: DoCoMo demands Google's help with signalling storm (2012). http://www.rethink-wireless.com/2012/01/30/docomo-demands-googles-signalling-storm.htm

16. Gelenbe, E.: The first decade of G-networks. Eur. J. Oper. Res. **126**(2), 231–232 (2000)

17. Gelenbe, E., Mahmoodi, T.: Energy-aware routing in the cognitive packet network. In: ENERGY, Venice (2011)

18. Gelenbe, E., Morfopoulou, C.: A framework for energy-aware routing in packet networks. Comput. J. **54**(6), 850–859 (2011)

19. Gelenbe, E., Timotheou, S.: Random neural networks with synchronized interactions. Neural Comput. **20**(9), 2308–2324 (2008)

20. Gelenbe, E., Wu, F.J.: Large scale simulation for human evacuation and rescue. Comput. Math. Appl. **64**(12), 3869–3880 (2012)

21. Gorbil, G., Abdelrahman, O.H., Gelenbe, E.: Storms in mobile networks. In: Proceedings of 10th ACM Symposium on QoS and Security for Wireless and Mobile Networks (Q2SWinet), Montreal, pp. 119–126 (2014). doi:10.1145/2642687.2642688

22. Gorbil, G., Abdelrahman, O.H., Pavloski, M., Gelenbe, E.: Modeling and analysis of RRC-based signalling storms in 3G networks. IEEE Trans. Emerg. Topics Comput. **4**(1), 113–127 (2016). doi:10.1109/TETC.2015.2389662

23. GSMA: Smarter apps for smarter phones, version 4.0 (2014). http://www.gsma.com/newsroom/wp-content/uploads//TS-20-v4-0.pdf

24. Jiantao, S.: Analyzing the network friendliness of mobile applications. Technical report, Huawei (2012). http://www.huawei.com/ilink/en/download/HW_146595

25. Ksentini, A., Hadjadj-Aoul, Y., Taleb, T.: Cellular-based machine-to-machine: overload control. IEEE Netw. **26**(6), 54–60 (2012). doi:10.1109/MNET.2012.6375894

26. Lee, P.P., Bu, T., Woo, T.: On the detection of signaling DoS attacks on 3G wireless networks. In: Proceedings of 26th IEEE Internatioanl Conference on Computer Communications (INFOCOM), pp. 1289–1297 (2007). doi:10.1109/INFCOM.2007.153

27. Li, J., Pei, W., Cao, Z.: Characterizing high-frequency subscriber sessions in cellular data networks. In: Proceedings of IFIP Networking Conference, Brooklyn, pp. 1–9 (2013)

28. Maslennikov, D.: Mobile malware evolution: Part 6. Technical report, Kaspersky Lab (2013). https://securelist.com/analysis/publications/36996/mobile-malware-evolution-part-6/

29. NSN Smart Labs: Understanding smartphone behavior in the network. White paper (2011). http://networks.nokia.com/system/files/document/nsn_smart_labs_white_paper.pdf

30. Qian, Z., Wang, Z., Xu, Q., Mao, Z.M., Zhang, M., Wang, Y.M.: You can run, but you can't hide: exposing network location for targeted DoS attacks in cellular networks. In: Proceedings of Network and Distributed System Security Symposium (NDSS), San Diego, pp. 1–16 (2012)

31. Redding, G.: OTT service blackouts trigger signaling overload in mobile networks (2013). https://blog.networks.nokia.com/mobile-networks/2013/09/16/ott-service-blackouts-trigger-signaling-overload-in-mobile-networks/

32. Ricciato, F.: Unwanted traffic in 3G networks. ACM SIGCOMM Comput. Commun. Rev. **36**(2), 53–56 (2006). doi:10.1145/1129582.1129596

33. Ricciato, F., Coluccia, A., D'Alconzo, A.: A review of DoS attack models for 3G cellular networks from a system-design perspective. Comput. Commun. **33**(5), 551–558 (2010). doi:10.1016/j.comcom.2009.11.015

34. Sakellari, G., Morfopoulou, C., Mahmoodi, T., Gelenbe, E.: Using energy criteria to admit flows in a wired network. In: Gelenbe, E., Lent, R. (eds.) Computer and Information Sciences III, pp. 63–72. Springer, London (2013). doi:10.1007/978-1-4471-4594-3_7

35. Serror, J., Zang, H., Bolot, J.C.: Impact of paging channel overloads or attacks on a cellular network. In: Proceedings of 5th ACM Workshop Wireless Security (WiSe 2006), New York, pp. 75–84 (2006). doi:10.1145/1161289.1161304

36. Shafiq, M.Z., Ji, L., Liu, A.X., Pang, J., Wang, J.: A first look at cellular machine-to-machine traffic: large scale measurement and characterization. SIGMETRICS Perf. Eval. Rev. **40**(1), 65–76 (2012). doi:10.1145/2318857.2254767

37. Traynor, P., Lin, M., Ongtang, M., Rao, V., Jaeger, T., McDaniel, P., La Porta, T.: On cellular botnets: measuring the impact of malicious devices on a cellular network core. In: Proceedings of 16th ACM conference on Computer and Communications Security (CCS), Chicago, pp. 223–234 (2009). doi:10.1145/1653662.1653690

38. Wang, Z., Qian, Z., Xu, Q., Mao, Z., Zhang, M.: An untold story of middleboxes in cellular networks. In: Proceedings of ACM SIGCOMM, Toronto, pp. 374–385 (2011). doi:10.1145/2018436.2018479

A Data Plane Approach for Detecting Control Plane Anomalies in Mobile Networks

Omer H. Abdelrahman$^{(\boxtimes)}$ and Erol Gelenbe

Department of Electrical and Electronic Engineering,
Imperial College, London SW7 2BT, UK
{o.abd06,e.gelenbe}@imperial.ac.uk

Abstract. This paper proposes an anomaly detection framework that utilizes key performance indicators (KPIs) and traffic measurements to identify in real-time misbehaving mobile devices that contribute to signaling overloads in cellular networks. The detection algorithm selects the devices to monitor and adjusts its own parameters based on KPIs, then computes various features from Internet traffic that capture both sudden and long term changes in behavior, and finally combines the information gathered from the individual features using a random neural network in order to detect anomalous users. The approach is validated using data generated by a detailed mobile network simulator.

Keywords: Mobile security · Random neural network · M2M · IoT · Signaling overload · Radio resource control · Key performance indicators

1 Introduction

The number of smart mobile devices which require constant access to the Internet has grown exponentially in recent years, placing significant pressure on the data and signaling infrastructures of service providers. While mobile network operators are able to cope with the growth in user traffic by increasing capacity, overloads in the signaling plane are often unpredictable and lead to performance degradation and even outages. Thus, there has been considerable interest from standardization bodies, operators and equipment vendors in addressing mobile *signaling storms*, particularly with the advent of machine to machine (M2M) and Internet of Things (IoT) whose traffic profiles can be resource-inefficient. Initial attempts have focused on developing new standards for M2M communications [1], and promoting best practices for developing network-friendly applications or optimizing network configurations [5,8,16,18].

This paper presents a random neural network (RNN) [11,12] based approach for detecting mobile devices that generate excessive radio resource control (RRC) signaling, without directly monitoring the control plane itself. In contrast to signaling based techniques [7,13], which can be more effective but require modification to cellular network equipment and/or protocols, the present approach captures packets at the edge of the mobile core network using standard switch

© ICST Institute for Computer Sciences, Social Informatics and Telecommunications Engineering 2016
B. Mandler et al. (Eds.) IoT 360° 2015, Part I, LNICST 169, pp. 210–221, 2016.
DOI: 10.1007/978-3-319-47063-4_19

technologies (e.g. port mirroring, fibre taps, etc.). This offers the advantages of not requiring to decode lower radio related layers, lack of network encryption, and fewer number of nodes to monitor [23]. Moreover, the detector relies mainly on timestamps and packet header information to classify users, and does not require knowledge of the application generating a packet nor its service type, eliminating the need to use a commercial deep packet inspection tool which results in considerable overhead for real-time detection. It also interacts with existing network management and monitoring systems to reduce computational overhead, storage requirements and false alarm rate. We use supervised learning to distinguish between normal and anomalous signaling behaviors, which is well suited for classifying known patterns such as signaling storms whose characteristics and root causes are well understood [3,4,9,15].

The rest of the paper is structured as follows. Sections 1.1 and 1.2 discuss related work and the RNN as applied to our problem. Section 2 presents the detection system, along with a description of its input features and the parameters that can influence its performance. In Sect. 3, we evaluate our detection mechanism using simulations. Finally, we summarize our findings in Sect. 4.

1.1 Related Work

Mobile networks are subject to RRC-based signaling storms, which occur when a large number of mobiles make successive connection requests that time-out because of inactivity, overloading the control plane of the network [3,15] and draining the mobile devices' batteries [9]. This type of misbehavior can be triggered by poorly designed applications and M2M systems, outages in mobile cloud services or malicious activities, and it is difficult to recognize using traditional DDoS detection systems because of the low traffic volume nature of the attack.

Online detection of deliberate signaling attacks was first considered in [19], where connection inter-setup times for each mobile are estimated from IP metrics in order to detect the intention of a remote host to launch an attack. A general framework for anomaly detection was proposed in [6] based on time-series analysis of one dimensional feature distributions. While [19] and [6] aim to identify large scale events by aggregating and analyzing statistics from all hosts and mobile users, respectively, we aim to identify in real-time users that are contributing to a problem (i.e. signaling overload) rather than detect the problem itself. A supervised learning approach was used in [17] to detect mobile-initiated signaling attacks, by monitoring transmissions that trigger a radio access bearer setup procedure, and extracting various features from the corresponding packets relating to destination IP and port numbers, packet size, and response-request ratio. Although we utilize similar attributes in our approach, we do not assume knowledge of the effect that a packet has on the control plane (i.e. whether it has triggered a connection setup procedure), thus simplifying the deployment of our solution in operational networks.

A number of commercial solutions also started to appear in response to recent incidents of signaling storms, and can be classified into three groups:

(i) Anomaly detection and mitigation tools [7] similar to the approach we suggested in [13]. (ii) Air interface optimization which aims to increase the number of simultaneously connected devices in the access network; such technologies are constantly evolving with new standards, specifications and proprietary admission/congestion control and scheduling algorithms added all the time, and our solution operates on top of and is complimentary to them. (iii) Dedicated signaling infrastructure solutions to handle the expected growth in core network signaling pertaining to policies, charging, mobility management and other new services offered for the first time in LTE networks; however, it is expected that congestion management and load balancing in the core network will be less of an issue, with the trend towards network functions virtualization that will enable dynamic resource scaling as required by network load.

1.2 The Random Neural Network

The RNN is a biologically inspired computational model, introduced by Gelenbe [11], in which neurons exchange signals in the form of spikes of unit amplitude. In RNN, positive and negative signals represent excitation and inhibition respectively, and are accumulated in neurons. Positive signals are canceled by negative signals, and neurons may fire if their potential is positive. A signal may leave neuron i for neuron j as a positive signal with probability p_{ij}^+, as a negative signal with probability p_{ij}^-, or may depart from the network with probability d_i, where $\sum_j [p_{ij}^+ + p_{ij}^-] + d_i = 1$. Thus, when neuron i is excited, it fires excitatory and inhibitory signals to neuron j with rates:

$$w_{ij}^+ = r_i p_{ij}^+ \geq 0, \quad w_{ij}^- = r_i p_{ij}^- \geq 0,$$

where $r_i = (1 - d_i)^{-1} \sum_j [w_{ij}^+ + w_{ij}^-]$. The steady-state probability that neuron i is excited is given by:

$$q_i = \frac{\Lambda_i + \sum_j q_j w_{ji}^+}{\lambda_i + r_i + \sum_j q_j w_{ji}^-},$$

where Λ_i and λ_i denote the rates of exogenous excitatory and inhibitory signal inputs into neuron i, respectively.

A gradient descent supervised learning algorithm for the recurrent RNN has been developed in [12]. For a RNN with n neurons, the learning algorithm estimates the $n \times n$ weight matrices $\mathbf{W}^+ = \{w_{ij}^+\}$ and $\mathbf{W}^= \{w_{ij}^-\}$ from a training set comprising K input-output pairs $(\mathbf{X}, \mathbf{Y})$. The set of successive inputs to the algorithm is $\mathbf{X} = (\mathbf{x}^{(1)}, \cdots, \mathbf{x}^{(K)})$, where $\mathbf{x}^{(k)} = (\mathbf{\Lambda}^{(k)}, \boldsymbol{\lambda}^{(k)})$ are the pairs of exogenous excitatory and inhibitory signals entering each neuron from outside the network:

$$\mathbf{\Lambda}^{(k)} = (\Lambda_1^{(k)}, \cdots, \Lambda_n^{(k)}), \quad \boldsymbol{\lambda}^{(k)} = (\lambda_1^{(k)}, \cdots, \lambda_n^{(k)}).$$

The successive desired outputs are $\mathbf{Y} = (\mathbf{y}^{(1)}, \cdots, \mathbf{y}^{(K)})$, with the k-th vector $\mathbf{y}^{(k)} = (y_1^{(k)}, \cdots, y_n^{(k)})$ whose elements $y_i^{(k)} \in [0, 1]$ correspond to the desired output values for each neuron. The training examples are presented to the network sequentially, and the weights are updated according to the gradient descent rule to minimize an error function:

$$E^{(k)} = \frac{1}{2} \sum_{i=1}^{n} a_i [q_i^{(k)} - y_i^{(k)}]^2, a_i \geq 0.$$

The update procedure requires a matrix inversion operation for each neuron pairs (i, j) and input k which can be done in time complexity $O(n^3)$, or $O(mn^2)$ if m-step relaxation method is used, and $O(n^2)$ for feed-forward networks. We use the RNN because it has been successfully applied to several engineering problems [24] including pattern recognition, classification and DoS attack detection [14,20], but our detection system can work with other machine learning algorithms.

2 The Detection System

Figure 1 shows the basic architecture of the packet-switched domain of a mobile network, along with the detection system which intercepts packets directed to/from the gateway (i.e. Gn/S5 interface in UMTS/LTE). The user data transported over this interface are encapsulated in GTP-U (a simple IP based tunneling protocol) packets. The detector utilizes also information from the operation support system to reduce search space and optimize performance, and produces in real-time a list of anomalous mobiles for root cause analysis and mitigation. The three data processing stages of the algorithm are: (i) user filtering and parameter selection based on network configuration settings and KPIs related to signaling load on various network components, (ii) feature generation, and (iii) user classification with a trained RNN model. For reasons that should become apparent, we describe these processing steps in a logical order rather than the order in which they happen during run time.

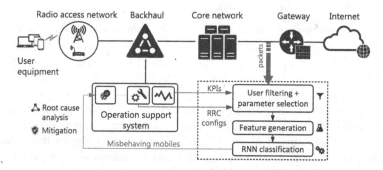

Fig. 1. The detection system and its interactions with the elements of a mobile network.

2.1   Online RNN Classification

The RNN-based algorithm monitors the activity of a set of mobile devices, specified by the data filter, and calculates expressive features that describe various characteristics of the users' behavior. Time is divided into slots, each of duration Δ seconds, in which summary statistics of several quantities related to IP traffic of each user are collected. The algorithm stores the most recent w set of measurements, and uses them to compute the current values of the input features, i.e. the features for time slot τ are computed from measurements obtained for time slots $\tau, \tau - 1, \cdots, \tau - (w - 1)$ so that the observation window of the algorithm is $W = w\Delta$. Let $z^{(\tau)}$ denote a measured or calculated quantity for time slot τ, then the i-th input feature $x_i^{(\tau)}$ is obtained by applying a statistical function ϕ_i of the following form:

$$x_i^{(\tau)} = \phi_i\big(z^{(\tau)}, z^{(\tau-1)}, \cdots, z^{(\tau-w-1)}\big).$$

Hence, by employing different operators ϕ_i on different statistics z stored for the observation window of w slots, it is possible to capture both instantaneous and long-term changes in the traffic profile of a user. In our experiments, we have applied a number of simple statistical functions including:

- The mean and standard deviation of z across the entire window.
- An exponential moving average filter in which the current feature is computed as $x_i^{(\tau)} = \alpha x_i^{(\tau-1)} + (1 - \alpha)z^{(\tau)}$, where α is some constant $0 < \alpha < 1$ typically close to 1, with higher values discounting older observations faster.
- Shannon entropy which measures the uncertainty or unpredictability in the data, and is defined as $x_i^{(\tau)} = -\sum_{t=\tau-w-1}^{\tau} p_{z^{(t)}} \log p_{z^{(t)}}$, where $p_{z^{(t)}}$ is the probability of observing data item $z^{(t)}$ within the window, which can be estimated from the histogram of the data. A small entropy indicates deterministic behavior which is often associated with signaling anomalies [10,21].
- Anomaly score based on how close the measured quantities are to a range of values considered to be suspicious.

Once the input features for a slot have been computed, they are fused using a trained feed-forward RNN architecture such as the one presented in Fig. 2 to yield the final decision; the input neurons receive the features computed for the current time slot as exogenous excitatory signals, while all exogenous inhibitory signals are set to zero, and the output nodes correspond to the probabilities of the input pattern belonging to any of two traffic classes (i.e. attack or normal). The final decision about the traffic observed in the time slot is determined by the ratio of the two output nodes, which is q_{14}/q_{15} in the figure: it is classified as attack if the ratio is greater than 1 and normal otherwise. We have used an implementation of the RNN provided in [2].

2.2   Feature Selection

Selecting highly informative features for any classification problem is one of the most important parts of the solution. The features that we wish to use should

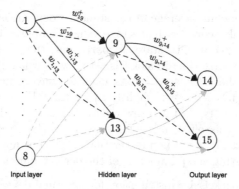

Fig. 2. The feed-forward RNN structure used for detection, with 8 input nodes, 5 hidden neurons and 2 output nodes corresponding to attack and normal traffic. The learning algorithm processes the input training patterns in sequence and updates the weights. The k-th training set consists of a feature vector $\mathbf{x}^{(k)} = (\Lambda_1^{(k)}, \cdots, \Lambda_8^{(k)})$ and its classification $\mathbf{y}^{(k)} = (y_{14}^{(k)}, y_{15}^{(k)})$ which is set to $(1, \epsilon)$ for attack and $(\epsilon, 1)$ for normal samples, where $\epsilon \simeq 0$. All other exogenous signals are set to zero.

capture the RRC signaling dynamics of users, be easy to measure or calculate without high computational or storage cost, and reflect both the instantaneous and long term trends of the traffic. We extract for each mobile under observation information related to inter-arrival times, lengths and destination IP addresses of packets, which have been suggested previously [6, 17, 22] as good indicators of signaling misbehavior:

Inter-arrival Times: RRC signaling occurs whenever the user equipment (UE) sends or receives packets following an inactivity period that exceeds an RRC timer. Thus, the volume of traffic exchanged by a UE does not map directly into signaling load which is more influenced by the frequency of intermittent transmissions. To capture this coupling between the data and RRC signaling planes, we define a *burst* as a collection of packets whose inter-arrival times are less than δ seconds, where δ is smaller than the RRC timers, typically in the order of few seconds. Thus, for a sequence of packets whose arrival instants are $\{t_1, t_2, \cdots\}$, we group all packets up to the n-th arrival into a single burst, where $n = \inf\{i : t_i - t_{i-1} > \delta\}$, and then proceed in a similar manner starting from the $(n + 1)$-th packet arrival. Note that a burst may not necessarily generate signaling, even if it arrives after the time-out, due to possible network delays that may modify inter-arrival times of packets. However, packets within a single burst are likely not to trigger any signaling, while inter-arrival times of bursts will be correlated with the actual signaling load generated by the UE. In this manner, we remove any bias regarding the volume of traffic and focus on the frequency of potentially signaling-intensive communications.

The features based on the times between bursts are then calculated as follows. The algorithm stores the mean and standard deviation of the inter-burst times in each slot then, using the most recent w values, it computes (i) entropy of these average values, (ii) moving average of the standard deviations, and (iii) moving average of an anomaly score for the average values computed based on the RRC timer T in the high bandwidth state. In particular, the anomaly score $a(z^{(t)})$ of the average inter-burst time in slot t is set to zero when $z^{(t)} < T$, reflecting the fact that such shortly spaced bursts may not have generated many RRC transitions; it is high when $z^{(t)}$ is slightly larger than T, indicating potentially resource-inefficient bursts; and it drops quickly when $z^{(t)}$ is few seconds larger than T. We obtain this effect using for example a Pareto or gamma density functions that assert $z^{(t)}$ must be greater than $T - \epsilon$ but not too much greater (controlled by adjusting the parameters of the density function).

Packet Size: The packet size distribution for a normal device can be markedly different from that of a device that runs a misbehaving application. For example, it is well-known that signaling storms can be triggered by failures in mobile cloud services [21] or peer-to-peer networks used by VoIP applications [6]. In such cases, the client application attempts to reconnect to its servers more frequently, causing significant increase in the number of TCP SYN packets sent by the user. This in turn changes the randomness associated with the size of packets, and can be used to identify misbehaving mobiles in the event of a signaling storm. Our algorithm computes the average size of packets sent by a UE within each slot, and evaluates a feature based on the entropy of the most recent w measurements.

Burst Rate: Another obvious characteristic of signaling storms is the sudden sustained rate acceleration of potentially harmful bursts generated by a misbehaving user. Moving average of the burst rate per slot and entropy of the rates across the observation window are used as features in order to capture, respectively, the frequent and repetitive nature of nuisance transmissions. Furthermore, a misbehaving application may change the traffic profile of a user in terms of the ratio of received and sent bursts (known as response ratio), as in the case of the outage induced storm described above where many SYN packets will not generate acknowledgments. Hence, we also use as a feature the mean of the response ratios within the window of w slots.

Destination Address: The number of destination IP addresses for a normally functioning mobile device can be very different from that of an attacker [17], whether the attack originates from the mobile network due to a misbehaving application, or from the Internet as in the case of unwanted traffic (e.g. scanning probes, spam, etc.) reaching the mobile network [22]. In the former, the number of destination IP addresses will be very small *compared to* the frequency of bursts, while in the latter this number is high. Thus we calculate the percentage of *unique* destination IP addresses contacted within each time slot, and use the average of the most recent w values as a feature.

2.3   User Filtering and Parameter Selection

Information about the "health" of network servers is typically available to mobile carriers in the form of KPIs, which can be fed to the algorithm to determine the users that should be monitored (e.g. those attached to overloaded parts of a network). Also, using KPIs the detector can be switched off when signaling loads are below a certain threshold, effectively eliminating the need to continuously analyze users' traffic. Next we summarize the parameters of the RNN algorithm and discuss how they should be selected adaptively, based on both KPIs and RRC settings, and how the choice of each parameter influences the performance of the detector:

- Slot size Δ: This defines the resolution of the algorithm and the frequency at which classification decisions are made. It should be long enough for the measured statistical information to be significant, but not too long to make the algorithm react slowly to attacks. In our experiments we set $\Delta = 1$ min.
- Window size $W = w\Delta$: This determines the amount of historical information to be included in a classification decision. The choice of the window size presents a trade-off between speed of detection and false alarm rate, since a small window makes the algorithm more sensitive to sudden changes in the traffic profile of a user, which in turn increases both detection and false alarm rates. This trade-off can be optimized by adjusting W according to the level of congestion in the control plane, with shorter windows for higher signaling loads to enable the algorithm to quickly identify misbehaving UEs. The value of w used in our experimental results is 5, but we also experimented with other values which confirmed the aforementioned observations.
- Maximum packet inter-arrival time within a burst δ: This should be selected based on the RRC timers, so that potentially resource-inefficient transmissions can be tracked. In our simulations of a UMTS network, the timers in DCH and FACH states are set to $T_1 = 6$ s and $T_2 = 12$ s, respectively. We have evaluated different values of δ in $\frac{1}{2}\min(T_1, T_2) < \delta < \min(T_1, T_2)$, which all led to similar detection performance, but training time drops as δ is increased within this range.

3   Simulation Experiments

In this section, we evaluate the *detection performance* of our algorithm using the mobile network simulator described in [15]. Since the impact of signaling storms on mobile networks has been studied extensively in [3,9,15], we consider here a small scenario with 200 UMTS UEs in an area of $2 \times 2\,\text{km}^2$ which is covered by 7 Node Bs connected to a single radio network controller (RNC). The core network consists of the SGSN and the GGSN which is connected to 37 Internet hosts acting as application servers, including 5 for instant messaging, 30 web servers and 2 are contacted by 100 misbehaving UEs. Half of these 100 UEs are deliberate signaling attackers that know when RRC transitions occur, and they are used for training the RNN; the second half, used for testing, run a malfunctioning application or operating system that sends periodic messages whenever the user is inactive, with the transmission period set to be slightly larger than the DCH timer in order to increase the chances of triggering state transitions.

The RNN provides at the end of a time slot the odds of the input features belonging to attack behavior. Figure 3 shows the classifier output (top) and the actual RRC state transitions (bottom) of a *misbehaving* UE as captured during a simulation run. It can be observed that when the malfunctioning application is active, the number of state transitions significantly increases, with most transitions occurring between the FACH and DCH states. This alternating behavior causes excessive signaling load in the network, while predominantly generating normal traffic volume, rendering traditional DoS defense techniques ineffective. However, our detection mechanism is able to track very accurately the RRC state transitions of the UE, and to quickly identify when excessive signaling is being generated, although it does not directly monitor these transitions but rather infers them from the features that we have described. One can also see that the classifier's output sometimes drops close to 1 during an attack epoch, which is attributed to other normal applications generating traffic in those time instants, thus reducing the severity of the attack. As mentioned earlier, the detection speed and tolerance to signaling misbehavior can be adjusted by modifying the size of the observation window.

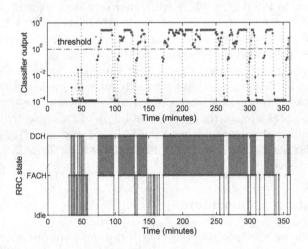

Fig. 3. Classifier output (top) and state transitions (bottom) for a misbehaving UE.

Next we examine in Fig. 4 how our algorithm performs when presented with a normal user that generates moderately more state transitions than the average normal user in our simulations. Interestingly enough, the classifier outputs a single alarm (out of 360 samples) when the corresponding state transitions are indeed excessive. Since the anomaly detection algorithm is supposed to be activate only when there is a signaling overload condition, such classification decisions may not always be considered as false alarms, as the goal would be to identify users that are causing congestion, regardless of whether they are attacking deliberately or not.

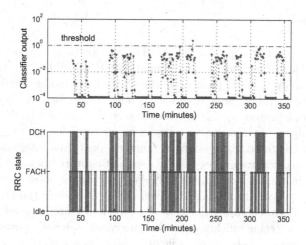

Fig. 4. Classifier output (top) and state transitions (bottom) for a heavy normal UE.

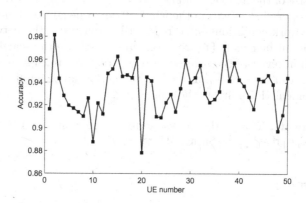

Fig. 5. The accuracy of the RNN algorithm, measured as the fraction of correct decisions over the activity period of 6 hours, for 50 misbehaving UEs.

Finally, Fig. 5 illustrates the accuracy of our classifier, namely the proportion of correct decisions (both true positives and true negatives) out of all test samples. The figure shows results for 50 UEs, where each data point represents the average of 360 classification decisions taken during the simulation experiment. For each UE, we assume that if it generates at least 1 attack packet within a time slot, then the corresponding output of the classifier should be larger than 1, otherwise a false decision is declared. The results indicate an accuracy between 88 % and 98 % with an average of 93 % over the 50 test cases. This fluctuation can be attributed to the fact that our algorithm does not classify an attack as such until few time slots have passed, and therefore misbehaving UEs with many silent periods will produce higher false positives; fortunately, these less aggressive UEs will generate lower signaling load.

4   Conclusions

This paper proposed an approach for real-time detection of signaling-intensive mobiles based on the random neural network (RNN) [11,12]. The algorithm relies on the analysis of IP packets at the edge of the mobile network to infer the signaling behavior of users; therefore, it does not require changes to network components and protocols, and can be used with standard traffic monitoring tools. In the algorithm, summary statistics about the behavior of a mobile user are collected and stored in a moving window at fixed time intervals (slots) and used in order to calculate expressive features that capture both sudden and long term changes in the user's behavior. The features for the most recent time slot are subsequently combined using a trained RNN to produce the final classification decision. Through simulations, we have demonstrated the effectiveness of the method in detecting quickly users that are causing signaling overloads in the network. The proposed approach is flexible, providing a number of parameters to optimize the trade-off between detection speed, accuracy and overhead. For instance, the size of the moving window and the frequency of statistical measurements (i.e. number of slots within the window) could be adjusted in real-time to respond to network conditions or to reflect the capacity of the network to tolerate a specific misbehavior. Future work will investigate the scalability of the approach both in terms of the processing power required to capture and process packets from a central location as well as the performance implications on the network equipment that mirrors the traffic.

Acknowledgments. This work was supported in part by the EU FP7 project NEMESYS under grant agreement no. 317888.

References

1. 3GPP TR 23.887: Machine-type and other mobile data applications communications enhancements (release 12) Technical report (2013). http://www.3gpp.org/DynaReport/23887.htm
2. Abdelbaki, H.: Random neural network simulator (RNNSIM v.2). Technical report,University of Central Florida (1999). http://www.cs.ucf.edu/~ahossam/rnnsimv2/rnnsimv2.pdf
3. Abdelrahman, O.H., Gelenbe, E.: Signalling storms in 3G mobile networks. In: Proceedings of IEEE International Conference on Communications (ICC), Sydney, pp. 1017–1022 (2014). doi:10.1109/ICC.2014.6883453
4. Abdelrahman, O.H., Gelenbe, E., Gorbil, G., Oklander, B.: Mobile network anomaly detection and mitigation: the NEMESYS approach. In: Gelenbe, E., Lent, R. (eds.) Information Sciences and Systems 2013. Lecture Notes in Electrical Engineering, vol. 264, pp. 429–438. Springer, Switzerland (2013). doi:10.1007/978-3-319-01604-7_42
5. AT&T: Best practices for 3G and 4G app development. Whitepaper (2012). http://developer.att.com/static-assets/documents/library/best-practices-3g-4g-app-development.pdf

6. Coluccia, A., D'Alconzo, A., Ricciato, F.: Distribution-based anomaly detection via generalized likelihood ratio test: a general maximum entropy approach. Comput. Netw. **57**(17), 3446–3462 (2013). doi:10.1016/j.comnet.2013.07.028

7. Ericsson: High availability is more than five nines (2014). http://www.ericsson.com/real-performance/wp-content/uploads/sites/3/2014/07/high-avaialbility.pdf

8. Ericsson: A smartphone app developers guide: Optimizing for mobile networks. Whitepaper (2014). http://www.ericsson.com/res/docs/2014/smartphone-app-dev-guide.pdf

9. Francois, F., Abdelrahman, O.H., Gelenbe, E.: Impact of signaling storms on energy consumption and latency of LTE user equipment. In: Proceedings of 7th IEEE International Symposium on Cyberspace safety and security (CSS), New York, 1248–1255 (2015). doi:10.1109/HPCC-CSS-ICESS.2015.84

10. Gabriel, C.: DoCoMo demands Google's help with signalling storm (2012). http://www.rethink-wireless.com/2012/01/30/docomo-demands-googles-signalling-storm.htm

11. Gelenbe, E.: Random neural networks with negative and positive signals and product form solution. Neural Comput. **1**(4), 502–510 (1989)

12. Gelenbe, E.: Learning in the recurrent random neural network. Neural Comput. **5**(1), 154–164 (1993)

13. Gelenbe, E., Abdelrahman, O.H.: Countering mobile signaling storms with counters. In: Mandler, B., et al. (eds.) IoT 360° 2015, Part I. LNICST, vol. 169, pp. 199–209. Springer, Heidelberg (2016)

14. Gelenbe, E., Loukas, G.: A self-aware approach to denial of service defence. Comput. Netw. **51**(5), 1299–1314 (2007)

15. Gorbil, G., Abdelrahman, O.H., Pavloski, M., Gelenbe, E.: Modeling and analysis of RRC-based signalling storms in 3G networks. IEEE Trans. Emerg. Topics Comput. **4**(1), 113–127 (2016). doi:10.1109/TETC.2015.2389662

16. GSMA: Smarter apps for smarter phones, version 4.0 (2014). http://www.gsma.com/newsroom/wp-content/uploads//TS-20-v4-0.pdf

17. Gupta, A., Verma, T., Bali, S., Kaul, S.: Detecting MS initiated signaling DDoS attacks in 3G/4G wireless networks. In: Proceeedings of 5th International Conference on Communication Systems and Networks (COMSNETS), Bangalore, pp. 1–6 (2013). doi:10.1109/COMSNETS.2013.6465568

18. Jiantao, S.: Analyzing the network friendliness of mobile applications. Technical report, Huawei (2012). http://www.huawei.com/ilink/en/download/HW_146595

19. Lee, P.P., Bu, T., Woo, T.: On the detection of signaling DoS attacks on 3G wireless networks. In: Proceedings of 26th IEEE International Conference on Computer Communications (INFOCOM), pp. 1289–1297 (2007). doi:10.1109/INFCOM.2007.153

20. Oke, G., Loukas, G., Gelenbe, E.: Detecting denial of service attacks with Bayesian classifiers and the random neural network. In: Proceedings of Fuzzy Systems Conference (Fuzz-IEEE), London, pp. 1964–1969 (2007)

21. Redding, G.: OTT service blackouts trigger signaling overload in mobile networks (2013). https://blog.networks.nokia.com/mobile-networks/2013/09/16/ott-service-blackouts-trigger-signaling-overload-in-mobile-networks/

22. Ricciato, F.: Unwanted traffic in 3G networks. ACM SIGCOMM Comput. Commun. Rev. **36**(2), 53–56 (2006). doi:10.1145/1129582.1129596

23. Telesoft Technologies: Mobile data monitoring. White paper (2012)

24. Timotheou, S.: The random neural network: a survey. Comput. J. **53**(3), 251–267 (2010). doi:10.1093/comjnl/bxp032

Demonstrating the Versatility of a Low Cost Measurement Testbed for Wireless Sensor Networks with a Case Study on Radio Duty Cycling Protocols

Maite Bezunartea[1]([✉]), Marie-Paule Uwase[1,2,3], Jacques Tiberghien[1,2],
Jean-Michel Dricot[2], and Kris Steenhaut[1]

[1] Vrije Universiteit Brussel, ETRO, Ixelles, Belgium
{mbezunar,ksteenha}@etro.vub.ac.be
[2] Université Libre de Bruxelles, OPERA, Brussels, Belgium
Jean-Michel.Dricot@ulb.ac.be, muwase@etro.vub.ac.be,
jacques.tiberghien@vub.ac.be
[3] National University of Rwanda, Butare, Rwanda

Abstract. Today, Wireless Sensor Networks (WSNs) with open source operating systems still need many efforts to guarantee that the protocol stack succeeds in delivering its expected performance. This is due to subtle implementation problems and unexpected interactions between protocol layers. The subtleties are often related to the judicious choice of parameters, in particular those related to timing issues. As these issues are often not visible in simulation studies, this paper proposes a low-cost versatile measurement testbed and demonstrates its usefulness in measuring the performance of RDC protocols. We demonstrate how the testbed helped to identify bugs in the implementation of an RDC protocol.

Keywords: Wireless Sensor Networks · Testbed · Field deployment · Measurements · Radio Duty Cycling · Contiki

1 Introduction

For studying the interactions between RDC and Routing over Low power and Lossy Networks (RPL) protocols for WSNs, Packet Delivery Ratio (PDR), packet latency and power consumption for the different RDC protocols available under Contiki on the Zolertia Z1 motes were measured, using the simple setup described in [1]. Unfortunately, this setup proved inadequate for accurately measuring packet latencies exceeding the inter-packet interval.

This was the motivation for designing a new, affordable, easily configurable testbed for exploring simple, point to point links as well as complex multi-hop networks. It is composed of two WSNs. One, called the *black* network runs the applications and protocols under study, the other called the *white* network observes the first one and transmits these observations to a sink node in which they are recorded (see Fig. 1). The *black* motes contain Z1 motes that belong to the observed network. Their built-in ceramic antenna limits its radio range to a few meters. The *white* motes are Z1 motes that belong

B. Mandler et al. (Eds.) IoT 360° 2015, Part I, LNICST 169, pp. 222–230, 2016.
DOI: 10.1007/978-3-319-47063-4_20

to the observer network. They use external antennas, allowing single hop communications with the sink. Both networks use different frequency bands, typically channel 26 for the *black* network and channel 16 for the *white* network.

Fig. 1. A dual mote from the testbed.

2   Measurement Techniques

The *black* nodes run application programs that send short messages to each other. These messages are uniquely identified by the address of the node in which they were created and a local sequence number generated by the node. Whenever a *black* application program sends or receives a packet, it communicates the sequence number to the associated *white* node, which sends to the *white* sink a packet containing the sequence number as well as the power used by the *black* node since the last packet was transmitted or received. A computer connected to the *white* sink stores the received packets, together with the address of the sender and a timestamp that gives, according to the clock of the *white* sink, the moment the start of frame bit of the message arrives.

The recorded data allows a full inventory of the data packets transmitted and received by applications running on the *black* nodes, from which it is easy to compute the PDR, the per packet latency and the average power used in the initial sender and the final receiver.

2.1   The Link Between the *Black* and *White* Motes

Transferring data between two motes can be done via the serial USB port or via some of the parallel GPIO pins of the Z1. As transferring data through the serial port requires approximately 80 μs per character, which would disturb beyond reasonable limits the normal operation of the *black* network and might affect its power requirements, the parallel pins were chosen. A Z1 designer recommends to use GPIO pins 1.0, 1.6, 1.7, 2.3, 4.0, 4.2 and 4.3 as those are not used by the built-in features of the Z1s. Those pins of the *black* and *white* motes were directly connected with each other. Setting them requires ±25 instructions in the *black* mote, which is negligible from a delay and power point of view. Six of those pins will transfer the least significant bits of the sequence number of a packet sent by a *black* mote. Pin 1.0 is a trigger for the *white* mote. At the very moment the toggling of pin 1.0 by the *black* mote gets detected by the *white* mote, this last one records this moment and sends a message to the *white* sink.

2.2 Measuring Technique for Packet Delivery Ratio, Latency and Power Usage

As discussed in Sect. 2.1, GPIOs carry the 6 least significant bits of the *black* packet sequence number. Matching the sequence numbers of transmitted and received packet descriptors received by the *white* sink allows to determine the PDR for each *black* end to end link.

We define the latency for a packet travelling from node A to B in the *black* network as the difference between the moment (denoted $m1$) at which the application in A offers the packet to the lower layer and the moment (denoted $m2$) at which the application in B has received the full packet. Calculating packet latency by including in the packet $m1$ and subtracting it from $m2$ is only correct when $m1$ and $m2$ are measured with synchronized clocks. Motes in the *black* network are seldom synchronized. As explained in Sect. 2.1, $m1$ and $m2$ are also recorded in the *white* motes, through the toggle pins. Simply deducing $m1$ from $m2$ is not appropriate as the clocks of the motes in the *white* network are not synchronized either, since synchronization overhead [5] would jeopardize its intended functioning. Fortunately, the sink will record the messages triggered by the toggles and timestamp their arrival. The difference between the two timestamps (denoted $m3$ and $m4$) is a good estimation of the latency, on condition that both messages generated by the toggles undergo the same latency to reach the sink. This is realistic when no MAC nor RDC protocols are used in the *white* network. RDC protocols are not needed in the *white* network, as its power usage is of no importance, but a MAC protocol is needed to avoid loss of messages in the *white* network.

Therefore, a second, more accurate technique consists in measuring the latencies of the *white* messages and correcting the difference between the timestamps $m3$ and $m4$ by subtracting these latency measurements.

Figure 2 shows packet latency for a single hop transmission, composed of:

- The time interval between the moment the application offers the packet to the lower layer and the moment that the last bit of the start of frame is clocked out of that packet (re)transmission that will be acknowledged in the future. We call this interval the "sender latency", calculated as *tsr-tsa*. During this interval, several unsuccessful attempts to transmit can have been made.
- The time required for the physical propagation from sender to receiver. Considering the typical distances between motes in WSNs, this time can always be neglected (<100 ns).
- The time interval between detecting the start of frame byte and the arrival of the packet at the application layer in the receiver after verification of the destination address and the frame control sequence. We call this delay the "receiver latency", calculated as *tra-trr*. This delay results mostly from clocking in the packet and is almost constant for white messages.

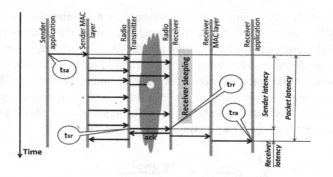

Fig. 2. Packet latency.

The sender latency can be measured by instrumenting the driver of the cc2420 radio in the white motes. It is possible to modify the contents of the last bytes of the transmitter FIFO while the first bytes are already being transmitted [2]. The modified driver polls the "start of frame detected" bit provided by the radio while the packet is being transmitted. When it goes high, the local real time clock *tsr* is read and its value is copied in the transmitter FIFO in the two last data bytes of the packet. The application program, just before passing the packet to the MAC layer has already read the local real time clock and inserted its value in another reserved location in the packet (*tsa*). When receiving a successfully transmitted packet, the *white* sink can compute the sender latency by subtracting from the time the successful packet was actually transmitted (*tsr*) the time it was passed to the sender's MAC layer (*tsa*), since these two times are both readings of the same real time clock in the *white* sender. Only when latencies exceed a full cycle of the mote's real time clock (2 s in our case), we use the Linux timestamps from the computer recording the *white* messages, to evaluate the number of clock cycles that need to be added to the computed packet latency.

For comparing the power requirements of different protocols, Contiki has four "energest" variables that are used to totalize the time during which the CPU, the sender and the receiver were active and the time during which the mote was "sleeping" [3]. By multiplying each of these times by the power required by the different components of a mote, one could compute the energy required for a given task. Hurni et al. [4] showed that this technique can result in high precision (1 %) power measurements, provided that the power requirements of the components of each mote are accurately known. They suggest to individually characterize each mote by means of current drain measurements with enough temporal resolution to distinguish the different states of the mote. A sensor node management device [5] sampling the current at 1000 Hz was used for that purpose. Another device, with even better resolution, was presented at the Como RealWSN workshop [6] in 2013.

However, many monolithic radios, and particularly the cc2420 [2] which is present in the Zolertia Z1 motes, are powered through a built-in DC to DC converter that keeps the voltage in the radio constant, regardless of the battery state. Observations by means of an oscilloscope showed that the activity type of the radio could not accurately be deduced from the instantaneous power drawn by the mote. Therefore, our performance studies exclusively rely on power figures obtained by measuring the average current absorbed by the motes. The *black* motes are powered from the batteries of the *white* motes via a 1Ω series resistor between the ground lines, and decoupled by a 4700 µF capacitor, ensuring that no significant aliasing error will occur if the voltage across the resistor is sampled 100 times per second to record the current drawn by the *black* mote. Figure 3 shows how the *black* mote is powered and its current measurement amplified by a differential instrumentation amplifier before being sampled at 100 Hz and digitized by the built-in AtoD converter with sample and hold of the *white* mote.

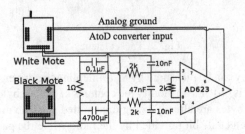

Fig. 3. Measuring black mote's power consumption.

3   Experimental Validation

As many hard to explain incidents were observed when RDC protocols on unicast single hop links were evaluated [1], a reevaluation of these protocols with better observation techniques was considered a good way to validate the new testbed and to get familiar with its possibilities and limitations.

The experimental set-up, shown in Fig. 4 consists in four dual motes and one *white* sink connected to a portable computer running the Linux Operating System (OS). A second PC with Windows is used to monitor the radio traffic by means of a Texas Instruments sniffer cc2531 and the associated free sniffer software SmartRF. This monitoring proves very helpful to quickly detect errors in the choice of communication parameters and/or detect mote malfunctioning.

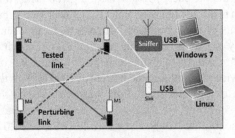

Fig. 4. Set-up for unicast tests.

The unicast link under study goes from the *black* mote M2 to the *black* mote M1. The behaviour of this link is obviously influenced by radio transmissions in the neighbourhood. For studying unicast links, such unrelated radio-traffic is created by two communicating *black* motes M4 and M3. Sending and receiving of packets by the *black* motes is reported by the corresponding *white* motes to the *white* sink and recorded on the Linux PC. All dual motes are powered by AA alkaline batteries in the *white* motes.

3.1 The Radio Traffic on the *Black* Network

The traffic generated by the sending mote M2 consists in 59 bytes unicast messages transmitted at an average rate of 1 message per second (the inter-message interval is uniformly distributed between 10 and 1990 ms to prevent any correlation between the transmit cycle and the wake-up cycle of RDC protocols). In order to obtain statistically valid measurements, at least 1200 messages are observed per experiment. This results in 34 sets of 34 messages. Latency, PDR and power usage is computed for each set of messages allowing to calculate the 95 % confidence intervals. Perturbing traffic can be generated by M4 sending unicast messages to M3. To simulate the perturbing effect of a network where each mote has three reachable neighbors, M4, when active, sends 2 times more messages than M2. Lightly interfering traffic is generated when both M3 and M4 are active. Heavier traffic results from switching off M3 as then M4 will repeatedly try to transmit its packets to the non-responding M3. We name these three traffic classes NP for "No Perturbation", PR for "Perturbed with Receiver" and PNR for "Perturbed with No Receiver". The Contiki Rime software is used for managing the unicast transmissions and CSMA is used as MAC protocol. Four different RDC protocols, readily available on Contiki, have been tested. They are ContikiMAC [7], CXMAC (a version optimized for Contiki of XMAC [8]), Low Power Probing (LPP) [9] and, as a reference, NullRDC (this protocol leaves the radio always on). In case of LPP, tests with a perturbing sender and no receiver (PNR) should not differ from those with no external perturbation (NP), because a sender does not send unless invited by the target receiver; for that reason no "PNR" results are given for LPP tests. To the best of our knowledge, no extensive comparison of these protocols has been published. Only XMAC has recently been studied in depth [10].

3.2 The Protocols Used in the *White* Network

As in the *white* network power is not an issue while latency should be kept small, the choice of NullRDC is obvious. In Contiki, NullRDC is available with or without acknowledgements. Up to two retransmissions of unacknowledged packets by the MAC layer can reduce the risk of lost *white* messages, but at the price of a more variable latency. As differences in *white* latency can be compensated as described in Paragraph 2.2, NullRDC with acknowledgements has been chosen. Experimentally, we found that up to 10 % of the *white* messages got lost when acknowledgments were disabled, while no lost messages were observed when acknowledgments were enabled.

3.3   Packet Delivery Ratio, Latency and Power Measurements

After a series of tests (as described in Sect. 3.1) involving the four different Contiki RDC protocols the PDRs were computed and gave results above 98 %. These results confirm our previous experiments, reported in [1].

Extensive latency and power measurements had been done with much more limited technical means [1]. Repeating these measurements with the new testbed was a straight-forward validation technique. Figure 5 shows some results of the latency measurements, together with the corresponding results obtained previously. These measurements were made with no perturbing traffic. The solid bars represent average values of all the meas-ured latencies. One can observe that for ContikiMAC, CXMAC and LPP old and new measurements match very well. Only for NullRDC significant differences are visible, but, this is due to the use of Acks in NullRDC, while in the past acknowledging was deactivated as this was the default setting. The Ack activation was necessary for the fairness of the comparisons, as all other RDC protocols use Acks.

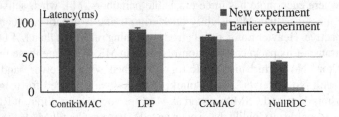

Fig. 5. Old and new measurement tool give the same results, except for NullRDC.

The next step in our validation experiments consisted in showing how RDC protocols trade latency for power under the three different traffic conditions. Figure 6(a) and (b) show respectively the latency and the power usage for ContikiMAC waking up 4, 8 and 16 times per second.

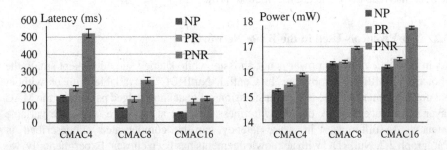

Fig. 6. Increasing the traffic density increases the (a) packet latency (b) power consumption.

For unperturbed traffic (NP) the average latency should be half the wake-up interval, augmented by the receiver delay and the occasional delays caused by transmission errors, as no collisions should occur. The observed latencies exceed on average the half wake-up interval by some 20 ms which seems normal. Perturbing traffic should increase the sender delay through collisions. This effect is clearly visible and is very important when the wake-up interval is large as the perturbing link will almost continuously be transmitting. One could expect that the required power should grow linearly with the frequency of the wake-ups. Figure 6(b) shows this is true under heavy traffic conditions (PNR) but not under low traffic, whereas frequencies of 8 and 16 Hz have similar power needs. This observation deserves some further investigation.

The last step in our validation tests consisted in comparing latencies and power usage of the four RDC protocols available in Contiki, under three different traffic conditions. In order to be fair, we had to modify the default options in the Contiki implementation of the LPP protocol, as this was the only one that did not use a phase locking mechanism to try to predict when known neighbours would wake up. As the "Encounter Optimization" option is available in Contiki LPP, we enabled it for our comparisons with a wake-up frequency of 8 Hz.

The results presented in Fig. 7 show that RDC protocols trade latency for power. Surprisingly LPP with the encounter optimization shows worse latencies than in our initial experiments in which, by default, encounter optimization was disabled. Encounter optimization should reduce power consumption without affecting latencies.

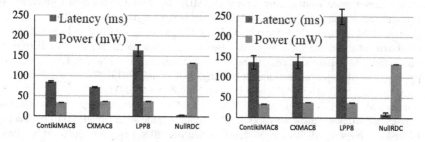

Fig. 7. RDC protocols trade latency for power (a) environment without perturbing traffic (b) with perturbing traffic.

Meanwhile, the responsible bug in the implementation of LPP has been fixed.

4   Conclusions and Future Work

The proposed testbed is versatile and low-cost. Due to the limited radio range of the *black* motes and the much larger range of the *white* ones, networks of any topology and size can be set up. The wireless observer network avoids the burden of using wired monitoring devices.

During the validation experiments, many anomalies observed in earlier tests, such as clustered packet losses in ContikiMAC and unexplained variations in the message latency with ContikiMAC and LPP showed up again, proving that they were not due to experimental artefacts but to undocumented particularities of the Contiki 2.6 implementation of the protocols.

The now validated testbed will enable us to pursue the in-depth study of these protocols. After further identifying the subtle implementation issues and fixing them, we will start with our ultimate goal: understanding in detail the interactions between the routing layer and the RDC-MAC layer.

References

1. Uwase, M.-P., Bezunartea, M., Nguyen, T.L., Tiberghien, J., Steenhaut, K., Dricot, J.-M.: Experimental evaluation of message latency and power usage in WSNs. In: 2014 IEEE International Black Sea Conference on Communications and Networking (BlackSeaCom), pp. 69–72. IEEE (2014)
2. Texas Instruments: Datasheet: CC2420 2.4 GHz IEEE 802.15.4/ ZigBee-ready RF Transceiver. http://www.ti.com/lit/ds/symlink/cc2420.pdf
3. Dunkels, A., Osterlind, F., Tsiftes, N., He, Z.: Software-based on-line energy estimation for sensor nodes. In: Proceedings of the 4th Workshop on Embedded Networked Sensors, pp. 28–32 (2007)
4. Hurni, P., Nyffenegger, B., Braun, T., Hergenroeder, A.: On the accuracy of software-based energy estimation techniques. In: Marrón, P.J., Whitehouse, K. (eds.) Wireless Sensor Networks, pp. 49–64. Springer, Heidelberg (2011)
5. Hergenroeder, A., Wilke, J., Meier, D.: Distributed energy measurements in WSN testbeds with a sensor node management device (SNMD). In: 23rd International Conference on Architecture of Computing Systems (ARCS), pp. 1–7. VDE, Hannover (2010)
6. Buschhoff, M., Günter, C., Spinczyk, O.: MIMOSA, a highly sensitive and accurate power measurement technique for low-power systems. In: Langendoen, K., Hu, W., Ferrari, F., Zimmerling, M., Mottola, L. (eds.) Real-World Wireless Sensor Networks. LNEE, vol. 281, pp. 139–151. Springer International Publishing, Switzerland (2013)
7. Dunkels, A.: The ContikiMAC Radio Duty Cycling Protocol (2011)
8. Buettner, M., Yee, G.V., Anderson, E., Han, R.: X-MAC: a short preamble MAC protocol for duty-cycled wireless sensor networks. In: Proceedings of the 4th International Conference on Embedded Networked Sensor Systems - SenSys 2006, pp. 307–320. ACM Press, New York (2006)
9. Musaloiu-E, R., Liang, C.-J.M., Terzis, A.: Koala: ultra-low power data retrieval in wireless sensor networks. In: 2008 International Conference on Information Processing in Sensor Networks (IPSN 2008) (2008)
10. Beaudaux, J., Gallais, A., Montavont, J., Noel, T., Roth, D., Valentin, E.: Thorough empirical analysis of X-MAC over a large scale internet of things testbed. IEEE Sens. J. **14**, 383–392 (2014)

GOODTECHS

Technology, Citizens and Social Change in the Framework of European Research and Innovation Programmes: Towards a Paradigm Shift

Marta Arniani[✉]

Sigma Orionis, 1240 Route des Dolines, 06050 Valbonne, Sophia Antipolis, France
marta.arniani@sigma-orionis.com

Abstract. In this paper I present the paradigm shift occurred in recent years in the approach to technology development within the European Commission funded Research and Innovation frameworks. This new approach is attentive to social good, societal challenges and bottom-up users and stakeholders, but presents at the same time some limitations. By leveraging Sigma Orionis long-standing experience in European funded projects and highlighting the current trends, challenges and best practices, I identify some avenues for making this approach even more impactful in the coming years.

Keywords: Horizon 2020 · FP7 · European Commission · Social innovation · Communities · Collective Awareness Platforms for Sustainability and Social Innovation (CAPS) · Responsible Research and Innovation (RRI)

1 Introduction

In 1962, Thomas Kuhn released 'The structure of Scientific Revolutions' [1], which contained his most acknowledged contribution to human wisdom: the definition of scientific revolutions as paradigm shift, going against the idea in force until that moment of a cumulative progress of science. In Kuhn's view, progress and innovation happen in an alternation of 'calm' and 'revolutionary' phases (e.g. the shift from Newtonian mechanics to quantum physics), which correspond to great conceptual breakthroughs and lay the foundation for the following phase of 'business as usual'. If we look at European technology R&D agenda under Kuhn's lenses, it seems we are experiencing one of these settlement stages. In a moment where European institutions are vacillating under the threat of the economic crisis and citizens' declining trust, the European Commission Research and Innovation framework named Horizon 2020 (2014–2020) [2] follows up to its predecessor FP7 (2007–2013) and works towards some alternatives to the status quo.

Following the Lisbon European Council (2000) objective for Europe "to become the knowledge-based economy" [3], the focus has indeed progressively shifted from the development of technology for the sake of technology, to an inclusive approach engaging end-users and citizens in the definition of the technology itself and its purposes, completed by a novel attention to the implementation of technology solutions to societal

© ICST Institute for Computer Sciences, Social Informatics and Telecommunications Engineering 2016
B. Mandler et al. (Eds.) IoT 360° 2015, Part I, LNICST 169, pp. 233–238, 2016.
DOI: 10.1007/978-3-319-47063-4_21

challenges. This orientation can be traced in Responsible Research and Innovation (RRI) and Citizen Science fields, in the CAPS (Collective Awareness Platforms for Sustainability and Social Innovation) programme [4], where R&D is for vocation at the service of societal challenges solutions and towards the common good, in the requirement of creating multidisciplinary working groups widespread across all calls, or in the hype around concepts such as open innovation, social innovation, innovation ecosystems.

By leveraging Sigma Orionis experience and active role in several FP7 or H2020 projects at the crossroads of technology, citizens and social changes (PARADISO, CAPS2020, CATALYST, RRI-ICT Forum, FET-ART, MusicBricks), I address in this paper the growing attention given to the development of technology at the service of social good in the framework of Europe's R&D agenda, producing a concise overview of its evolution (it would be impossible to cite here all the programmes and projects concerning the topic), current status and future challenges providing concrete examples from a selection of European funded-projects. I especially focus on the approach and methodologies with which end-users and society are becoming drivers and/or active parts of technology development.

2   ICT: A Societal Issue and Solution

Can Information and Communication Technologies (ICT) contribute to a "better world", characterised by more controlled economic and financial models, by more ambitious solutions to the environmental challenges, and a significant reduction of social inequality? This question, based on the vision of a desirable societal paradigm, was central to the PARADISO project (2007–2011) [5], involving the Club of Rome and Sigma Orionis. In 2009, the explosion of the economic crisis derailed all certitudes. PARADISO and its final reference document captured the spirit of the time by shifting the focus from technology being a value *per se* to a vision of technology being inseparable from its societal implications and motivations: the final recommendations of the project included 'encourage holistic multidisciplinary approaches', 'increase the involvement of users', 'promote values-driven programmes and projects'. Meanwhile, in May 2010, the European Union (EU) was launching the Digital Agenda for Europe [6] flagship initiative, aiming at "rebooting Europe's economy and helping Europe's citizens and businesses to get the most out of digital technologies". The initiative flags up the necessity of exploring the two-way interactions between technology and society, putting the human at the centre of the analysis, and exploring how the digital age can be a success factor not only for EU's competitiveness but also for its values. Today, we can find Responsible Research and Innovation as a cross-cutting issue in the EU Horizon 2020 programme: under this concept the EC defines an inclusive approach to Research & Innovation (R&I), aiming at better aligning both the process and outcomes of R&I with the values, needs, and expectations of the society, notably through reinforcing public engagement, open access, gender dimension, ethical issues, and (formal and informal science) education.

This whole shift is prepared by a broader call into question of Science and Society roles, prompted in the early 2000 by the European Commission's DG Research &

Innovation through its "Science and Society Action Plan" [7] and the working document "Science, Society and the Citizen in Europe" [3] encouraging a better connection between science and European citizens. In the same years, a parallel interest towards the role of technology in the everyday life of European citizens informed the approach to what we call today the Internet of Things (IoT). We have to go back to 2001, when the European Commission launched the Disappearing Computer initiative [8], to see a first attempt to study 'how information technology can be diffused into everyday objects and settings, and to see how this can lead to new ways of supporting and enhancing people's lives that go above and beyond what is possible with the computer today'.

Reading these tendencies with Kuhn's lenses, the beginning of the 21th century sees for EU ICT R&D frameworks the end of the dichotomy between technology, virtual reality, Internet on one side, and on the other, the so-called 'real world', the environment where humans and everyday activities take place. This shift is today far for being granted (the dichotomy between online and offline is still a fashionable one), but a seamless consideration of both aspects is where we are heading to, adjusting our vocabulary and approach (from consumers to prosumers, from top-down to co-creation), and taking into considerations new actors such as makers, hackers and DIY culture representatives.

One of the major manifestations of this shift is that ICT programmes highly focussed on social innovation and addressing grassroots communities and citizens are booming. It is the case of the CAPS one, launched in 2013 (the first dialogue about it took place at the PARADISO final conference). The first batch of projects funded covers and tackles, along with technology, a range of societal issues such as emissions reduction, CSR monitoring, urban accessibility, collective intelligence in online debates, decentralisation of platforms and e-infrastructures. One of these (the Coordination and Support Action Ia4Si), starting from the assumption that social transformations happen through cascades of changes, has created a classification system for such effects, with four main categories (social, economic, political and environmental), whose results will be made available soon [9].

CAPS success - even too much for a relatively small programme, with 193 proposals submitted at the first H2020 call against a budget available for around the 5 % of them - demonstrates the need for and the feasibility of this 'empowering' approach, which can be implemented in similar ways in other EC calls with a social innovation implication. Somehow CAPS 'hacked' the system without quitting it, which is even more remarkable. All CAPS projects and external stakeholders gathered together at CAPS2015 [10], the annual event about CAPS: launched in 2014, the event was a great occasion to see the results of the first round of CAPS projects so far, to cross-pollinate ideas and to involve new actors. Interestingly, despite the CAPS programme being still a novelty, for being just the second edition of the event there was already a generalised urge to go beyond enthusiasm and to share and learn actual best practices. This implies first of all a non-instrumental approach to communities, blurring the line between bottom-up and top-down in favour of a collaborative co-creation. Co-design, and design in general, emerged as important factors for the impact and effectiveness of such initiatives: we are finally talking about 'how' to reach common objectives together supported by technology instead of taking for granted a mechanical and tech-centric view of engagement.

This is most probably why topics such as democracy and collective intelligence where at the centre of the debate, alongside with the need to rethink citizens' sovereignty on their data and privacy, and to set up decentralised structures. This said, turning to communities cannot be the jack of all trades, as they are mostly based on enthusiasm and voluntary engagement, resulting often in immaturity towards their objectives and means to reach them. For the same reason, they can prove 'lazy' towards adopting new means, and prefer to work with known systems and platforms such as Facebook (despite fighting for freedom and privacy). On the other side, it is clear that there is no sense in working for communities without working WITH them. As debated in the framework of the CATALYST CAPS project [11] – focused on developing tools for improving the quality of online conversations and catching the potential of collective intelligence – understanding not only the demand, but also the offer, defining roles and shaping custom tests are central.

So far I mentioned mainly social-driven frameworks, but one should not forget that this collaborative logic applies to business and entrepreneurship as well. There is a broad part of European research that does not hit the ground and does not make it to market (and consequently to society) because all the effort is concentrated on the development and not on the exploitation. As highlighted by the Innovation Radar report [12], a quarter of already mature innovations are not being exploited yet: one of the main barriers to market is that the main focus is on technology aspects, too often at the expense of studying the demand and developing an exploitation strategy. Another interesting data issued by the report is that SMEs and small actors prove to be the most innovative people in the room (they deliver 41 % of innovations despite accounting for the 14 % of the total funding).

If real-world impact and exploitation are key issues lacking adequate approach, as much as new actors are engine for innovation but still far from being valued, can changing attitude towards them be a central component of our new paradigm? In this respect the CONNECT Advisory Forum (CAF) made a groundbreaking work [13], by suggesting to move from Technology Readiness Level (TRL, invented in the 80 s for NASA's rockets, not that applicable to mobile apps) to Market Adoption Readiness Level (MARL): "In addition to the technology readiness levels parameter, this model requires the assessment of three further value parameters: users (numbers of potential early adopters and values associated with feedback loops), data (potential quantity and value of data generated by the system and user interactions at each stage of the process) and the level of risk (assessment of benefits or adverse impacts of the technology on early adopters in various stages of the process)."

As part of our paradigm shift, frequent feedback loops with end-users have started to take over years of closed research in labs: a good example is provided by the #MusicBricks project [14], which is all about the hackathon 'day after'. Music technologies (including gesture sensors for music performance, real-time pitch detention, melody extraction) coming from the best European research centres are made available in the hackathons organised in the framework of events like the Music Hack Day and the Music Tech Fest: a rose of projects conceived during these events get further support (technical, financial and strategic) to make it to the market. It is a win-win situation for researchers - who get feedback from tomorrow's users (they have been seen 'hacking' their own tools during hackathons to make them responsive to the need of the hackers), creatives who may end up starting a new business, and Europe, which desperately need to leverage its talents and resources. Despite of music technology not being directly related to social good, it is interesting to note that among the projects selected so far, many deal with accessibility and healthcare. High Note for instance is a hands-free wireless Midi controller instrument: it uses #MusicBricks technology to sense a range of different motions and mouth-controlled inputs to allow people with limited physical mobility or strength (or people who have their hands otherwise engaged) full participation in musical expression. Using the #MusicBricks R-IoT gesture sensor board, Dolphin is another of these examples, being an accessible gestural interface for controlling music selection & playback using head movements and head gestures. As a platform for interaction, the motion sensitive headphones can be used to track movement in space with respect to the audio played, as well as control that audio.

3   Way Forward: Beyond the End-User Chicken and Egg Situation

Open innovation, social innovation, innovation ecosystems… Innovation has never been so well defined. But to which extent can we frame innovation? Isn't defining something limiting its field of action? And how much is genuine the social aspect of the medal?

The risk here is that of gluing artificially citizens, DYI ambassadors and creatives to pre-determined projects in order to justify their usefulness, similarly to what is happening with revenue based companies hiding behind a sharing claim with accurate 'we-washing' [15]. The first point I would like to make is thus that involving 'unusual suspects' for the sake of doing so does not work: the answers to the questions "who needs to be engaged?" and "why?" must be made clear at the very beginning of any collaborative process. What I want to suggest here as way forward is to forget artificial results, and to focus on quality, dynamisms and inclusiveness. In fact, if the general mind set is starting to change, we are still far for claiming victory: as well explained in 2012 in the paper 'The E-(R)evolution will not be funded' [16], launching frameworks which take into account the social aspects of technology and set out to engage citizens does not imply an immediate effectiveness: the figures presented in the paper are quite demotivating (and in some cases astonishing: the cost of each users' contribution - post or petition's signature - was around 550 euros in the studied platforms). It is when classic concepts and approaches are no longer applicable that we experience the shift to a new paradigm.

Effectiveness and impact come at the cost of real involvement all along the whole process: there is an important difference for instance between calling an artist to illustrate the final results of a research projects, and involving her/him in the research itself. Surely one of the biggest challenges is about fine-tuning co-design: if technology - or at least technology that is supposed to have a social impact - in order to have a real impact is no longer to be developed in the ivory towers of research centres, then, to which extent must the social part be engaged? One of the key aspects of innovation is creating new needs, or at least anticipating them: if users are implied from the very beginning, it means real needs will be taken into account: this could turn out to be a two-faced feature.

The solution to this chicken and egg situation relies most probably in the separation of pure research (abstract, rigorous, anticipating needs), and research explicitly at the service of users and social good. In the second case, seed funds, regular feedback loops, real impact indicators and evaluation, co-creation methodologies, simplification of access barriers (mainly bureaucratic ones) is what we should experiment in the coming years in order to develop technology truly at the service of social good. Public authorities should focus on creating the framework for this to happen, without pre-determining the actors involved and the results. We are no longer talking about research, nor about R&D: we are just at the beginning of the next paradigm mixed playground, where old concepts will be replaced by a bouquet of new ones.

References

1. Kuhn, T.S.: The Structure of Scientific Revolutions. University of Chicago Press, Chicago (1962)
2. Horizon 2020, the EU framework programme for research and innovation. http://ec.europa.eu/programmes/horizon2020/
3. Commission working document: science, society and the citizen in Europe. European Commission (2000)
4. Collective awareness platforms for sustainability and social innovation. http://ec.europa.eu/digital-agenda/en/collective-awareness-platforms-sustainability-and-social-innovation
5. Paradiso Initiative. http://paradiso-fp7.eu/
6. Digital agenda for Europe. http://ec.europa.eu/digital-agenda/
7. Science and society - action plan. Luxembourg: Office for Official Publications of the European Communities (2002)
8. The disappearing computer initiative. http://www.disappearing-computer.eu/index.html
9. Ia4SI. http://ia4si.eu/
10. CAPS2020. http://caps2020.eu/
11. Fledderus, E., et al.: H2020 ICT R&D&I beyond 2015. CAF – CONNECT Advisory Forum (2014)
12. #MusicBricks project. http://musicbricks.net/
13. De Prato, G., Nepelski, D., Piroli, G.: Innovation radar: identifying innovations and innovators with high potential in ICT FP7, CIP & H2020 projects. Science and Policy Report, Joint Research Centre (2015)
14. Huang, L.S.: #WeWashing: when "Sharing" is renting and "Community" is a commodity, Huffington Post (2015). http://www.huffingtonpost.com/leesean-huang/wewashing-when-sharing-is_b_6879018.html
15. Prieto-Martín, P., de Marcos, L., Martínez, J.J.: The e- (R)evolution will not be funded: an interdisciplinary and critical analysis of the developments and troubles of EU-funded eParticipation. Eur. J. ePract. 15, 62–89 (2012)
16. Catalyst project. http://catalyst-fp7.eu/

Understanding the City to Make It Smart

Roberta De Michele and Marco Furini$^{(\boxtimes)}$

Communication and Economics Department,
University of Modena and Reggio Emilia, 42121 Reggio Emilia, Italy
marco.furini@unimore.it

Abstract. Understanding the sentiment of people is a process that may be useful when transforming a city into a smart city. A recent trend is to exploit social media data to infer people sentiments. While many studies focused on textual data, few considered the visual contents. In this paper we investigate whether the images available in the Instagram platform can be useful to understand people sentiments. Through an experimental assessment and two different validation methods, we observed that although the use of images in sentiment analysis can be useful to have insights about people sentiments, the use of Instagram images may be slightly misleading.

Keywords: Smart city · Visual sentiment analysis · Plutchink model

1 Introduction

A Smart city uses digital technology to better manage infrastructure and resources, to improve the services offered to citizens and to address challenges of development and sustainability more efficiently. To truly develop a smart city, citizen should be involved in the process [1], but most of the approaches to build a smart city does not consider the citizens while designing and implementing strategies to transform a city into its smart version [2,3].

A recent approach towards citizens involvement is to exploit the large amount of data available in social media platforms to understand their feelings. Indeed, the idea is to use these information to make more informed decisions that will end in better use of resources, better organization, better citizen lifestyle, better human relations and, eventually, better society.

In literature, many researches on sentiment analysis focused on textual contents (e.g., blogs, forum, tweets) and only recently, researches are trying to exploit the large amount of multimedia contents available in social media platforms to measure people feelings (e.g., [4,5]). The reasons behind this approach is that multimedia contents are more and more produced and shared in social media platforms (e.g., more than one billion of images are shared daily on Facebook, Instagram, Flickr and Whatsapp) and, moreover, these contents are usually produced with a mobile application that couples the pure multimedia content with additional information (e.g., GPS data, users information, etc.) that may be very useful in understanding people feelings.

© ICST Institute for Computer Sciences, Social Informatics and Telecommunications Engineering 2016
B. Mandler et al. (Eds.) IoT 360° 2015, Part I, LNICST 169, pp. 239–244, 2016.
DOI: 10.1007/978-3-319-47063-4_22

In this paper we focus on the Instagram application and we want to investigate whether images shared by people in the Instagram social platform can be useful in the decision making processes that aim at transforming a city into a smart city. Instagram is an online mobile photo-sharing application that enables users to take and share pictures in social platforms. The application is becoming more and more popular among mobile customers (as of December 2014 the platform had over 300 millions of users) and therefore it is possible to publicly access to a huge amount of data.

We perform this investigation in two steps: first we define an area of interest and we access to the Instagram images taken in that area; then we use a psychological model to associate colors to emotions and we compute a low-level color analysis to determine whether the image represents a "positive" or "negative" emotion. By repeating the process for all the images located in the interested area, we can understand what is the people sentiment and how these emotions are distributed in the area. To validate our approach we perform two different validations: ground-truth and users' tag. Results obtained showed that images can be useful in understanding the sentiment of people living in an area of interest, but also showed that Instagram images are slightly affected by the massive usage of filters that modify the original picture.

The paper is organized as follows: in Sect. 2 we present related works in the area of image sentiment analysis; in Sect. 3 we present our study, whereas its evaluation is presented in Sect. 4. Conclusions are drawn in Sect. 5.

2   Background and Related Work

The social web is characterized by an abundance of multimedia resources coupled with many additional information (i.e., metadata) [6]. For instance, an Instagram image is coupled with information about the user, about his/her friends, about its description, tags and location [7,8]. Researchers are trying to exploit these information for many different reasons and one of these is to identify people sentiment. While there are several studies that focused on textual contents (e.g., the ones available in the Twitter platform), the visual sentiment analysis is in its early stage. Examples are the video/image classification and smile detection (e.g., [5,9,10]).

When dealing with emotions, it is necessary to have a psychological model that classifies them. In this paper we focus on the widely used Plutchik model [11]. This model identifies eight basic bipolar emotions (joy, trust, fear, surprise, sadness, disgust, anger, anticipation) that may be extended to 24 emotions by varying the intensity of every basic emotion (e.g., ecstasy $\rightarrow$ joy $\rightarrow$ serenity) and associates a color to each of the 24 emotions as shown in Fig. 1. Therefore, the model connects a color to its emotion (e.g., yellow $\rightarrow$ joy). Looking at the model, we observe that light colors represent positive emotions, whereas dark colors represent negative emotions.

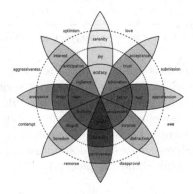

Fig. 1. The Plutchik model: emotions are associated to specific colors. (Color figure online)

3 Our Study

Understanding the sentiments of people living in a city is becoming an important aspect in decision making process and, recently, attention is given to the large amount of multimedia contents available in social media platforms. The motivation behind our study is to investigate whether the huge amount of Instagram images can be useful to understand people sentiments. In particular, our study is composed of three steps: (i) access to Instagram images located in the area one wants to investigate, (ii) mapping the retrieved images into emotions, and (iii) validate the obtained results. By repeating the process for all the images located in the interested area, one can understand the people sentiments and how these emotions are distributed in the area. This should provide useful insights to city administrator, politics, urban designer, etc.

Accessing Instagram Images. To access to Instagram images we develop a Python application that interacts with Instagram API. The application requires to specify a geographical location (latitude and longitude) and gets all the Instagram images located nearby that location (i.e., the distance from the point may vary from the default value of one km to five km). In addition to the image, the application retrieves many other information like comments and tags.

Mapping Images into Emotions. According to the Plutchik model, dark colors correspond to "negative" emotions, whereas light colors correspond to "positive" emotions. To identify whether an image is dark or light, we consider images with 24-bits RGB colors where the lightest color (i.e., white) is defined by the triplet (255, 255, 255) and the darkest color (i.e., black) is defined by the triplet (0, 0, 0).

To determine whether an image is light or dark, we measure the color distance that separates each pixel from the white and black points. The distance is measured through the Euclidean distance (see Eq. 1). Therefore, for each pixel (x, y, z) we know whether it is closer to the white or to the black point. When all the image pixels are analyzed we can call the image as "dark" or "light".

$$\sqrt{(x - bin_r)^2 + (y - bin_g)^2 + (z - bin_b)^2} \tag{1}$$

Validation. One of the most difficult tasks in understanding the insights obtained from the analysis of the data available in social media platforms is the validation process. In this study, we consider two different validation methods: ground-truth (a methodology that requires a group of human beings to say whether an image represents positive or negative emotion) and users' tag (a methodology that analyzes the textual description attached to the image to understand what people think about the picture).

4   Experimental Assessment

To investigate whether Instagram images can be used to determine people sentiments, we set up an experimental scenario where we focus on three towns in the area of our department: Reggio Emilia (where our department is), Modena (30 km east of Reggio Emilia) and Parma (30 km west of Reggio Emilia). And we use the developed python application to build an image dataset for each town. In total, we dataset is composed of around 2,000 images.

Looking at the collected images, we observed a first possible problem in using Instagram images: many images contain textual contents (e.g., logos, flyers or quotes) and/or colored borders (Instagram only handles square images and hence images with different formats are converted using colored borders). Examples of these images are reported in Fig. 2. These images may negatively affect the sentiment results: the color of the borders and the presence of textual contents (which outweigh the colors) may affect the validity of the model. For these reasons, we manually filtered the dataset and we obtained a new dataset composed of 260 images (with no borders or textual contents) for each town.

Fig. 2. Example of images excluded from the dataset: color borders (left) and textual content (right).

We applied the color analysis (defined in the previous section) to get the sentiment of the analyzed images. Results show a predominance of images with a negative connotation for the town of Modena (63 % vs. 37 %), a slight predominance of images with a negative connotation for the town of Parma (56 % vs. 44 %) and an equal distribution between positive and negative images for the

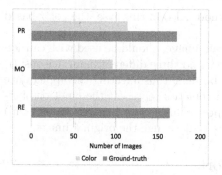 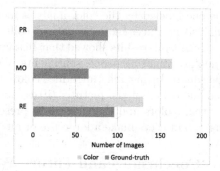

Fig. 3. Ground-truth evaluation: "positive" (left) "negative" (right) images.

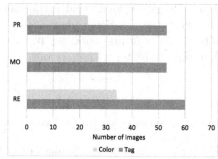 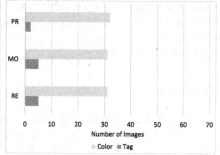

Fig. 4. Users' tags evaluation: images called as "positive" (left) and "negative" (right).

town of Reggio Emilia. By plotting the results on the city map, we can identify areas of the city where people post positive or negative images.

Groud-thruth Evaluation. We asked a group of five people to call either positive or negative every image of the dataset (260 images for each town). In particular, we considered as positive (negative) an image that receives at least three positive (negative) calls. Figure 3 shows that the ground-truth evaluation labeled as "positive" more images than the one labeled by the color analysis method. Needless to say, the color analysis method labeled as "negative" more images than the one labeled by the ground truth evaluation. The results show that the color-based analysis produce more "negative" calls.

Users' Tag. We defined a list of positive tags (e.g., "happy", "beautiful") and a list of negative tags (e.g., "sad", "ugly") and then we filtered the dataset to get only images tagged as "positive" or "negative". The resulting dataset are composed of 65 images for Reggio Emilia (60 positive and 5 negative), 58 for Modena (53 positive and 5 negative) and 55 for Parma (53 positive and 2 negative). Finally, we applied the color-based algorithm. Results presented in Fig. 4 show that the tags evaluation labeled as "positive" more images than the one labeled by the color analysis method. Also in this case, the color-based analysis produces more "negative" calls.

In general, results showed that Instagram images should be used with caution when investigating people sentiments. We found three different main reasons: (i) the square format may introduce colored borders, thus affecting the appearance and the colors of the picture; (ii) textual contents represent the emotions better than colors and therefore their presence nullifies color analysis results; (iii) Instagram users make a large use of filters that change the original image.

5   Conclusions and Future Work

In this paper we investigated whether the Instagram images may be useful to identify people sentiments. Through an experimental assessment and two different validation methods (ground-truth and users' tags) we found that Instagram images may have characteristics that may affect the emotions analysis (e.g., colored borders, textual contents, dark filters). As a future work, we plan to investigate whether it is possible to correlate the used filter with emotions.

References

1. Amaba, B.A.: Industrial and business systems for smart cities. In: Proceedings of EMASC, EMASC 2014, pp. 21–22. ACM, New York (2014)
2. Komninos, N., Tsarchopoulos, P., Kakderi, C.: New services design for smart cities: a planning roadmap for user-driven innovation. In: Proceedings of WiMobCity (2014)
3. Roccetti, M., Marfia, G., Palazzi, C.E.: Entertainment beyond divertissment: using computer games for city road accessibility. Comput. Entertain. 9(2), 10:1–10:9 (2011)
4. Siersdorfer, S., Minack, E., Deng, F.: Analyzing and predicting sentiment of images on the social web. In: International Conference on Multimedia (2010)
5. Abdullah, S., Murnane, E.L., Costa, J.M.R. Choudhury, T.: Collective smile: measuring societal happiness from geolocated images. In: Proceedings of CSCW (2015)
6. Montangero, M., Furini, M.: Trank: ranking Twitter users according to specific topics. In: Proceedings of the 12th International IEEE Consumer Communications and Networking Conference (CCNC 2015), January 2015
7. Furini, M., Tamanini, V.: Location privacy and public metadata in social media platforms: attitudes, behaviors and opinions. Multimed. Tools Appl. 74(21), 9795–9825 (2015)
8. Furini, M.: Users behavior in location-aware services: digital natives vs digital immigrants. Adv. Hum. Comput. Interact. 2014, 23 pages (2014). Article ID 678165
9. Oliveira, E., Martins, P., Chambel, T.: Accessing movies based on emotional impact. Multimed. Syst. 19(6), 559–576 (2013)
10. Furini, M.: Vimood: using social emotions to improve video indexing. In: Proceedings of the 12th International IEEE Consumer Communications and Networking Conference (CCNC 2015), January 2015
11. Plutchik, R.: Emotion: A Psychoevolutionary Synthesis. Harper and Row, New York (1980)

MobilitApp: Analysing Mobility Data of Citizens in the Metropolitan Area of Barcelona

Silvia Puglisi, Ángel Torres Moreira, Gerard Marrugat Torregrosa,
Mónica Aguilar Igartua[✉], and Jordi Forné

Department of Network Engineering, Universitat Politècnica de Catalunya (UPC),
C. Jordi Girona 1-3, 08034 Barcelona, Spain
{silvia.puglisi,monica.aguilar,jforne}@entel.upc.edu,
angel.torres.moreira@gmail.com, gmarrugat@gmail.com

Abstract. MobilitApp is a platform designed to provide smart mobility services in urban areas. It is designed to help citizens and transport authorities alike. Citizens will be able to access the MobilitApp mobile application and decide their optimal transportation strategy by visualising their usual routes, their carbon footprint, receiving tips, analytics and general mobility information, such as traffic and incident alerts. Transport authorities and service providers will be able to access information about the mobility pattern of citizens to offer their best services, improve costs and planning. The MobilitApp client runs on Android devices and records synchronously, while running in the background, periodic location updates from its users. The information obtained is processed and analysed to understand the mobility patterns of our users in the city of Barcelona, Spain.

Keywords: Smart cities · Smart mobility · Mobility pattern recognition · Privacy · Android application

1 Introduction

Mobility and transportation efficiency have always been essential in a city for it to function properly. When the architect Ildefons Cerdà i Sunyer (Spanish urban architect, 1815–1876) drafted his original plan of the extension of Barcelona in the 1850s, he focused on certain key points. Among these the need for seamless movement of people, goods, energy, and information. The extension of the city of Barcelona was conceived along the idea of ensuring more fluid traffic in all directions, above all for public transport. Cerdà wanted to make sure that the steam tram could circulate easily and used its long turning radius to determine the angle of the corners of the buildings.

Smart mobility solutions can provide efficient, safe and comfortable transport services, so that visitors and residents can easily travel across the city. Smart

© ICST Institute for Computer Sciences, Social Informatics and Telecommunications Engineering 2016
B. Mandler et al. (Eds.) IoT 360° 2015, Part I, LNICST 169, pp. 245–250, 2016.
DOI: 10.1007/978-3-319-47063-4_23

mobility services are information driven and rely on technology to provide personalised services to its users. We present a smart mobility platform designed both for urban citizens and transport service providers alike. Our platform is composed by an analytics solution and a client application. The mobile application runs on Android devices, collecting mobility data regarding activities performed by its users. Smart citizens use the application to receive information regarding: their usual routes, their carbon footprint and traffic and incident alerts. Transport authorities can use the analytics solution to provide a clean, efficient and affordable transportation system, analyse mobility pattern of citizens, forecast and prevent network congestions, and general planning and execution.

1.1   State of the Art

The flow of people and goods over the transport network of a city is a complex problem. Transport service providers need to forecast demand around the city and plan long term investment. To provide a more efficient transportation service, authorities in the field analyse data about the mobility patterns of users in metropolitan areas. These analysis are often conducted on partial ticket sales data, surveys and economical models. This information lacks reliability, since it only contains partial mobility samples, not representative enough of a whole metropolitan region. Smart mobility programs and the use of smartphones offer a more efficient and precise way to collect data about transportation usage, while also providing citizens with comprehensive personalised services.

Mobility patterns recognition is the problem of detecting the current mode of transportation of a person. Our approach is to use smartphones to detect mobility patterns. Studies implementing novel accelerometer-based techniques for accurate and fine-grained detection of transportation modes on smartphones [5] have shown promising results to capture key characteristics of vehicular movement patterns. Unfortunately to recognise specific human activities and provide contextual information, a mobile application needs to continuously listen to sensor data from a user's mobile device. Several sensor readings need to be interpreted to produce meaningful data. Frameworks for human activity recognition (HAR) and context aware applications maximising power efficiency have been developed [9] leveraging on topics such as user profile adaptability and variant sensory sampling operations. Activity recognition algorithms and their power consumption, are also further improved by identifying spurious events classification and subsequently pruning a decision tree model on these specific cases [8]. These approaches have shown a 10 % classification improvement in some occasions.

With initiatives like open data, and rising development of open smart city services, urban areas have started to evolve into *open source spaces* where it is possible to design new applications to integrate with existing technologies. Software development kits (SDKs) to develop mobile sensing apps and collect data about smartphones users are already part of most mobile operating systems [1,2,13], turning smart citizens into actual sensors (Fig. 1).

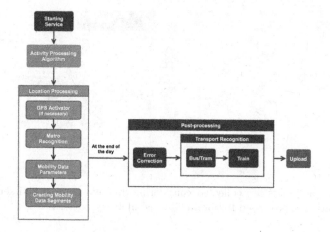

Fig. 1. How users' activities are collected and processed in our MobilitApp application.

It is important to create a mutual relationship between smart city services providers and the actual sensing citizens that contribute with their mobility patterns. More useful and better services are offered, so that the city can gather the necessary data to be more efficient [7]. The importance of smart cities in the end is not merely about efficiency and smart services, as much as enabling people to shape the urban environment. One aspect of this is providing platforms where people would be able to communicate and collaborate. An example of these applications are hyperlocal news and real times updates, connected urban mobility, and what is called grassroots design and city hacking [11,12].

2   Platform Architecture

MobilitApp [3,4] is a smart city platform able to obtain mobility data of the citizens in the metropolitan area of Barcelona, Spain. Our implementation synchronously collects updated geographical position as well as users' current activities. At the end of the day, information is processed and sent to our backend where it is stored and analysed. Our platform, part of the INRISCO project, is designed specifically to provide smart tools to transport authorities and is developed with feedback from ATM (Autoritat del Transport Metropolità). More specifically the MobilitApp platform provides the following functionalities (Fig. 2):

– Traffic information in real-time
– Traffic incidences
– Web app to analyse and filter the collected information on mobility.

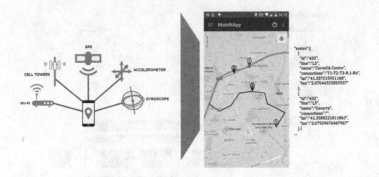

Fig. 2. Users' activities are collected considering different sources and sensors data. This information is processed to obtain citizens' mobility patterns.

2.1 Mobile Application

MobilitApp collects citizens' mobility patterns in the background. MobilitApp uses Google Android APIs to discover the user's positions. This can be considered as a first approach for user's activity detection. The APIs provide a low consumption mechanism to log periodic updates and detected activity types by using mainly the device accelerometer. This information is then processed sample by sample to increase accuracy and efficiency. Our own implementation of the activity detection algorithm consists in calling the Activity APIs and sampling the obtained results every 20 s. Then every 2 min, the algorithm makes a statistical estimation of the most probable result out of the last samples.

To further polish the results obtained we also consider the following factors:

- Accuracy of the GPS: when a device is underground, the GPS accuracy decreases consistently.
- Location of points of interest (POI) to help the algorithm knowing if a user is *close* to a bus stop or a metro station.
- Directions: we use Google Directions APIs to check if there is a known route (using all possible transportation types) between two points.

2.2 Mobility Patterns Recognition

MobilitApp is able to successfully classify between the following activity classes:

- *on foot*: Activity type returned if the citizen is either walking or running.
- *bicycle*: Activity type returned if the citizen is on a bicycle.
- *vehicle*: Activity type returned if the citizen is on a motor vehicle (e.g. car, motorbike, bus,...).
- *still*: Activity type returned if the citizen is not moving.
- *unknown*: Activity type returned if Activity Recognition API is not capable to estimate the actual activity.

A key challenge was to successfully classify different types of vehicles and distinguish between private and public transportation. We use a simplified geofencing technique to identify if the user is using public or private transportation. For example if we observe that a user has lost GPS contact while moving we might assume they have used the metro. Therefore we try to find the closest metro station from the first good GPS sample. The same technique could be applied to bus lines, while also considering other information such as timetables and average speed. However, with this approach we had to listen to GPS data with a very short interval, therefore consuming too much battery. Our next objective is relying more on acceleration data and less on GPS and positioning to identify users' activities. We are also considering the possibility to use alternative information to GPS, to estimate the user's position. We see promising the possibility to cross battery level and consumption information with signal strength and distance from known WIFI/cell access point [6].

2.3   Privacy Conscious Analytics

We are aware that we are collecting sensitive user data constantly and this poses a security and privacy risk for the users participating in the program. We have therefore implemented a number of measures to safely store and analyse user data. We follow the approach of Solove in [10] to classify possible privacy violations in four main categories:

- *Collection*: Surveillance; Information probing; Interrogation.
- *Processing*: Aggregation; Identification; Insecurity; Secondary use; Exclusion.
- *Dissemination*: Breach of confidentiality; Disclosure; Exposure; Increased accessibility; Appropriation; Distortion.
- *Invasion*: Intrusion of someone's private life.

To avoid exposing users to direct threats of *collection* and *processing* of private information, MobilitApp has the option not to supply any personal details to the platform. Users are not obliged to disclose their personal data. To avoid *dissemination* and *invasion*, user data collected by our mobile application is communicated encrypted to the server. We are aware that if an attacker would gain access to the MobiltApp platform they would be able to commit all possible privacy violation on user data. Said this we are continuing researching measures to reduce the users' privacy risk even in these circumstances.

3   Conclusions and Future Work

We are determined to continue developing MobilitApp and improve how we detect the user transportation mode and position. We will especially concentrate on how the phone accelerometer is used to detect the user's activity. More specifically the gravity component provided by the sensor can be estimated by the algorithm and then classified as one of the different mobility indicators that we can use. We want to emphasise that this new improvement will help us distinguish between different motorised transportation modes, which currently represent the main challenge for smartphone-based transportation mode detection. Also, we are considering to implement methods for location discovery without the use of GPS, to reduce device battery consumption. We find promising techniques using the transmitting and receiving power consumption together with distance between the user's device and the base station (access point/mobile cell).

Acknowledgments. This work is supported by the Spanish Government through project INRISCO (INcident monitoRing In Smart COmmunities. QoS and Privacy, TEC2014-54335-C4-1-R). We are also grateful to Xavier Rosselló and Francesc Calvet from the Autoritat del Transport Metropolità de Barcelona for their valuable feedback during different stages of the project.

References

1. DetectedActivity Google APIs for Android. https://developers.google.com/android/reference/com/google/android/gms/location/DetectedActivity. Accessed 18 Aug 2015
2. Funf open sensing framework. http://www.funf.org. Accessed 18 July 2015
3. MobilitApp Android App on Google Play. https://play.google.com/store/apps/details?id=com.mobi.mobilitapp. Accessed 18 July 2015
4. MobilitApp web App. http://mobilitapp.noip.me/. Accessed 18 July 2015
5. Hemminki, S., Nurmi, P., Tarkoma, S.: Accelerometer-based transportation mode detection on smartphones. In: Proceedings of the 11th ACM Conference on Embedded Networked Sensor Systems, p. 13. ACM (2013)
6. Michalevsky, Y., Nakibly, G., Schulman, A., Boneh, D.: PowerSpy: location tracking using mobile device power analysis. arXiv preprint arXiv:1502.03182 (2015)
7. Palazzi, C.E., Teodori, L., Roccetti, M.: Path 2.0: a participatory system for the generation of accessible routes. In: 2010 IEEE International Conference on Multimedia and Expo (ICME), pp. 1707–1711. IEEE (2010)
8. Phan, T.: Improving activity recognition via automatic decision tree pruning. In: Proceedings of the 2014 ACM International Joint Conference on Pervasive and Ubiquitous Computing, pp. 827–832. ACM (2014)
9. Sivakumar, R., Sathyanarayanan, R., Harikrishnan, T.: Battery optimization of Android phones by sensing the phone using hidden Markov model. J. Current Comput. Sci. Technol. **5**(05) (2015)
10. Solove, D.J.: A taxonomy of privacy. University of Pennsylvania law review, pp. 477–564 (2006)
11. Townsend, A.M.: Smart Cities: Big Data, Civic Hackers, and the Quest for a New Utopia. WW Norton & Company, New York (2013)
12. Weber, A.M., Ladstätter, S., Luley, P., Pammer, V.: My places diary: automatic place and transportation-mode detection. In: Proceedings of the 11th International Conference on Mobile and Ubiquitous Systems, pp. 384–386. ICST (2014)
13. Yang, H.C., Li, Y.C., Liu, Z.Y., Qiu, J.: HARLib: a human activity recognition library on android. In: ICCWAMTIP 2014, pp. 313–315. IEEE (2014)

Calibrating Low-End Sensors
for Ozone Monitoring

Óscar Alvear[✉], Carlos Tavares Calafate, Juan-Carlos Cano,
and Pietro Manzoni

Universitat Politècnica de València, 46022 Valencia, Spain
oscar.alvear@alttics.com

Abstract. Performing pollution measurements is a difficult and costly process. On the one hand, specialized laboratories are needed to calibrate sensors and adjust their readings to units that indicate the level of contaminants in the environment, and, on the other hand, measurements depend on the type of sensor. High-end sensors are very accurate but quite expensive, while low-end sensors are more affordable but have less precision and introduce considerable oscillations between readings. This paper presents a methodology to measure ozone pollution data with low-end mobile sensors, focusing on sensor calibration through historical data and the existing environmental monitoring infrastructure. The proposed methodology is developed in three phases: (i) reduction of data measurements variability, (ii) calculation of calibration equations, (iii) and analysis of the spatial-temporal behavior to reduce variations in time produced when data are captured using mobile sensors.

Keywords: Low-end sensor · Sensor calibration · Ozone sensing

1 Introduction

In recent decades, the monitoring of environmental pollutants has become of great importance for governmental institutions and environmental organizations due to the influence of pollution on our lives. There are several institutions worldwide that monitor environmental pollution. In Europe, the European Topic Center on Air Pollution and Climate Change Mitigation (ETC/ACM) brings together 14 European organizations for the analysis and monitoring of climate change. In the United States, the Environmental Protection Agency (EPA) also tracks the evolution of environmental pollution.

There are many studies that analyze ozone levels in cities like Quebec [1] or Toronto [2]. In addition, projects like [3] rely on Waspmote sensors installed in the public transport system of Belgrade, Serbia, to measure the environmental pollution in the city.

In [4], a vehicular ad-hoc network is proposed to monitor different environmental parameters, focusing on the analysis of the data sending rate and the transmission mechanism to minimize the resources consumed.

© ICST Institute for Computer Sciences, Social Informatics and Telecommunications Engineering 2016
B. Mandler et al. (Eds.) IoT 360° 2015, Part I, LNICST 169, pp. 251–256, 2016.
DOI: 10.1007/978-3-319-47063-4_24

In [5], authors propose a system to monitor the concentrations of PM2.5 (particulate matter smaller than 2.5 microns) using crowd-sourcing. This work focuses on the analysis of the mechanical sensor design to optimize the air reception, as well as on data fusion techniques to analyze the data. The calibration of the sensors is achieved by analyzing data produced in the laboratory using neural networks. However, authors do not analyze the variability of the data obtained.

In [6], authors analyze the data obtained from different sources, such as traffic levels, weather conditions and pollution, using different Big Data techniques to infer environmental pollution levels with a better granularity.

Previously described works do quite different types of analysis with the data obtained by the sensors, but they do not analyze the data capture process, neither do they focus on the sensor calibration problem. Hence, in this paper we will address both of these problems, in addition to the time variability of measurements associated to sensor mobility.

In the following sections, we will describe the methodology we propose to solve the aforementioned problems. In Sect. 2, we will discuss the most relevant air pollution monitoring issues, detailing the steps taken in the data capture process. In Sect. 3, we will show captured data and make a comparative analysis against available historical data. Finally, in Sect. 4 we conclude the paper.

2   Pollution Monitoring

The pollution monitoring processes seek to measure pollution levels for a particular contaminant in a specific area by relying on special-purpose sensors. These sensors react by varying their properties when in contact with the element to be monitored, but not other elements.

In general, sensors must have certain characteristics to be considered suitable: (i) being only sensitive to the measured property, (ii) not influencing the measured property, and (iii) having a direct relationship with the measured property. In this regard, the main problems of low-range sensors are that they have a large fluctuation between measurements, and some (e.g. ozone sensors) do not meet all the properties previously described because their measurements are influenced by weather conditions.

In this paper, we have used low-end sensors that can be easily obtained in the market to measure ozone levels. In particular, we used a Waspmote Smart Sense Plug And Environment device, which provides a relatively easy way to measure various environmental parameters. The sensor used is the *Ozone Probe Sensor (MIC-2610)*, which can measure ozone variations ranging between 10*ppb* (parts per billion) to 1000*ppb*. The resistance varies between $11\,k\Omega$ and $2\,M\Omega$, and the input voltage for this sensor is 2.5 V.

2.1   Monitoring Process

The first step to monitoring environmental parameters is to capture data through sensors. However, this is not a simple process since many problems must be solved in order to obtain reliable data about existing pollution levels. In particular, the following issues should be taken into account: (i) sensor output data measurements are highly variable in ranges close to the real values, and so such variability should be reduced; (ii) the sensor outputs should be transformed into the respective units for each pollutant. In our case, the measured resistance value must be converted into particles per billion (ppb); (iii) if mobile elements are used, time-dependent variability must be removed.

Below we detail how each of these issues has been addressed.

Data Reading: Data retrieval processes should eliminate the oscillations associated to sensor readings, and for this purpose we performed the following steps. First, we calculated the average value of 25 samples (n = 25), with an interval of 10 ms between each consecutive sample.

Afterward, since the variability was still very high, we used a low-pass filter for the process of data analysis with α equal to 0.95 to reduce variability.

$$O_i = O_r + \alpha \cdot (O_{i-1} - O_r) \tag{1}$$

In this equation, O_i represents the current ozone level, O_{i-1} represents the ozone level in the previous measurement, O_r represents the filtered ozone value, and α represents the filter coefficient.

At the end of this process, we have measurements without the oscillations introduced at measurement time, reducing the standard deviation by 66 % (from 5.37 to 1.82).

Unit Conversion: For calibrating the sensor we have done several measurements on different days, and under different weather conditions, to get a broad range of values. These data have been linked to the data obtained from the monitoring station located at the Technical University of Valencia (UPV), Spain.

Considering that the measurements have a dependency on ozone levels and temperature, we developed a second degree polynomial regression influenced by the temperature and the resistance obtained by the sensor:

$$O = \alpha + \beta_1 t + \beta_2 r + \beta_3 r^2 \tag{2}$$

In this equation, α is a regression coefficient, β_1 is a temperature coefficient, β_2 is a sensor reading coefficient, β_3 is the reading coefficient squared, t is the measured temperature, and r is the sensor reading (Resistance). The output O is the ozone level measured. Final regression output is shown in Eq. 3.

$$O = -156.27 + 2.84t + 10.2r - 0.14r^2 \tag{3}$$

The adjustment obtained for this regression was $|\overline{R^2}| = 0.63$ and, comparatively with historical data, the values are very similar.

Time Variability Reduction: To cover large areas of land with a fine spatial granularity we use mobile sensors, which can capture data at various points although at different time instants. So, the difference between measurements O have both time $\triangle O_t$, and spatial $\triangle O_s$ dependencies. Since our main goal is to determine differences between ozones levels in a particular area, it is necessary to eliminate the time variation as follows.

$$\triangle O = \triangle O_t + \triangle O_s \qquad (4)$$

$$\triangle O_s = \triangle O - \triangle O_t \qquad (5)$$

For the calculation of the ozone time variations we analyzed data from a monitoring station located at the Technical University of Valencia, focusing on historical data between 2008 and 2014. In the historical data analysis, we analyzed ozone evolution focusing on average monthly measurements between 2008 and 2014. It is noted that the values are higher from April to September, and lower for the remaining months. Figure 1 (right) shows the mean values combined with the standard deviation (shaded area) and the maximum values (line).

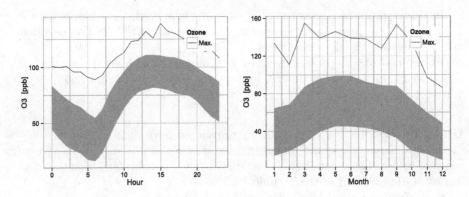

Fig. 1. Ozone evolution in June (left) and the throughout the year (right).

Also, the variation for ozone levels during a representative day of June was analyzed. As shown in Fig. 1 (left), ozone levels reach their lowest value at about 6am, and rise to reach maximum values at 2 or 3 pm, beginning to decline gradually afterward. The behavior for the other months of the year is analogous to the month shown. As a result of the analysis of these data, we can see that ozone has a different behavior during hot periods (from April to September in the northern hemisphere) compared to the other months. During the day, the behavior is very similar to the square logarithmic distribution, with an onset of rapid growth followed by a less pronounced decline. Based on the previous data regarding monthly average values of data between 2008 and 2014, all taken at the monitoring station of the Technical University of Valencia ozone prediction was performed using least-squares logarithmic regression influenced by temperature and season of the year, one for summer, and one for winter. The expression used was:

$$\ln(O_t) = \alpha + \beta_1 s + \beta_2 t + \beta_3 \ln(h) + \beta_4 \ln(h)^2 \tag{6}$$

where h is time of day, s is the season coefficient (3 for winter, 4 for autumn, 7 for sprint and 8 for summer; these values were calculated from the relationship between the means values of ozone), t is the temperature, and the remaining α and β_i values are regression coefficients (β_1 is the season coefficient, β_2 is the temperature coefficient, β_3 is the logarithm of the time of day coefficient, and β_4 is the logarithm of the time of day to the square coefficient).

The values of $|\overline{R^2}|$ range between 0.82 (winter) and 0.91 (summer), showing a behavior very similar to the actual one.

Concerning the procedure followed to correct time-dependent variability, it was: (i) ozone values are calculated at two time instants using Eq. 6; (ii) the difference between the values is obtained; (iii) the calculated variation is reduced from the captured data, according to Eq. 5.

3   Validation

To check the correctness of the proposed methodology, several data collection events took place in different areas of the city of Valencia using the mobile sensor. Different cities areas have been covered, and the data captured was compared against data from the existing public infrastructure.

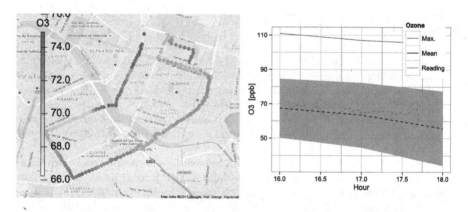

Fig. 2. Data captured (left) and validation expected values for that period (right).

For each route, we have applied the methodology proposed: first, we reduce data oscillation using the low-pass filter (Eq. 1). Next, the readings are adjusted through Eq. 2. Finally, the temporal variation of data is reduced using Eq. 6.

Figure 2 shows data for a particular route and the common values at this time. We can see that ozone levels (reading) are within the range of historical values for the monitored time and close to expected value (mean), which indicates that, with our methodology, we obtain reliable data, allowing to focus our analysis on the spatial variations of pollutants.

4 Conclusions

Environmental pollution monitoring is essential nowadays and, although there are many studies on this topic, few analyze the problems involved in the process of data collection, especially when low-cost mobile sensors are used. In this paper, we have developed a methodology to measure such levels using off-the-shelf sensors to achieve a high spatial granularity compared to that achievable using existing infrastructure.

The proposed process allows measuring and calibrating ozone sensors in a simple and straightforward manner without the need for a specialized laboratory. The data obtained though our method is adjusted to reality using historical data for the target location, and allows analyzing the spatial variability of pollution levels with a small error.

The next steps to be performed include the calculation of the sampling frequency and the spatial granularity of measurements to maintain the evolution of pollution levels in a city under control.

Acknowledgement. This work was partially supported by the *"Programa Estatal de Investigación, Desarrollo e Innovación Orientada a Retos de la Sociedad, Proyecto I+D+I TEC2014-52690-R"*.

References

1. Adam-Poupart, A., Brand, A., Fournier, M., Jerrett, M., Smargiassi, A.: Spatiotemporal modeling of ozone levels in Quebec (Canada): a comparison of kriging, land-use regression (LUR), and combined Bayesian maximum entropy-LUR approaches. Environ. Health Perspect. **122**(9), 970 (2014)
2. Liu, L.-J.S., Rossini, A.J.: Use of kriging models to predict 12-hour mean ozone concentrations in metropolitan toronto-a pilot study. Environ. Int. **22**(6), 677–692 (1996)
3. Brković, M., Sretović, V.: Urban sensing-smart solutions for monitoring environmental quality: case studies from serbia. In: 48th ISOCARP International Congress: Fast Forward: Planning in a (Hyper) Dynamic Urban Context, Perm (2012)
4. Hu, S.-C., Wang, Y.-C., Huang, C.-Y., Tseng, Y.-C.: Measuring air quality in city areas by vehicular wireless sensor networks. J. Syst. Softw. **84**(11), 2005–2012 (2011)
5. Cheng, Y., Li, X., Li, Z., Jiang, S., Li, Y., Jia, J., Jiang, X.: AirCloud: a cloud-based air-quality monitoring system for everyone. In: Proceedings of the 12th ACM Conference on Embedded Network Sensor Systems, pp. 251–265. ACM (2014)
6. Zheng, Y., Liu, F., Hsieh, H.-P.: U-air: when urban air quality inference meets big data. In: Proceedings of the 19th ACM SIGKDD International Conference on Knowledge Discovery and Data Mining, pp. 1436–1444. ACM (2013)

Evaluation of TSCH/IEEE 802.15.4e in a Domestic Network Environment

Luis Pacheco[1], Tom Vermeulen[2], Sofie Pollin[2], and Priscila Solis[1(✉)]

[1] Departamento de Ciência da Computação, Universidade de Brasília,
Caixa Postal 4466, Brasília, DF 70910-900, Brazil
luisbelem@gmail.com, pris@cic.unb.br
[2] Dept. Elektrotechniek-esat-telemic, KU Leuven, Kasteelpark Arenberg, 10,
2444, 3001 Leuven, Belgium
{tom.vermeulen,sofie.pollin}@esat.kuleuven.be

Abstract. The IEEE 802.15.4e standard was published in 2012 as an amendment to the Medium Access Control (MAC) protocol defined by the IEEE 802.15.4-2011 standard. The purpose of this paper is to evaluate the Timeslotted Channel Hopping (TSCH) mode of IEEE 802.15.4e in the context of IoT (Internet of Things) regarding environment and changes in application requirements. A simulation scenario of a typical domestic sensor network is designed to evaluate the TSCH mode in a dynamic environment with the presence of WiFi devices. Also are explored the upper and lower bounds in performance gain due to self-learning. The relatively recent release of such standard accounts for its lack of support in network simulators and this work implements the TSCH in the well known open-source network simulator ns-3. This work enables the preview analysis of TSCH networks, decreasing necessary resources and therefore facilitating the use of such networks for social goods such as health monitoring, The results clearly show that the presence of WiFi signals greatly degrades the IEEE 802.15.4e network performance, in terms of throughput, delay and energy consumption. When applying self-learning techniques to avoid degraded channels, the network can properly function and achieves better performance. Also, a significant decrease in delay is also achieved when adapting the slotframe size according to the number of active devices.

1 Introduction

Wireless sensor networks are composed by several sensor nodes that link the physical with the digital world by transforming the sensed analog information into digital data.

The IEEE802.15.4e Timeslotted Channel Hopping (TSCH) [1] aims to enhance and add functionality to the 802.15.4 MAC layer for better support the industrial markets. This work evaluates the performance of channel hopping (TSCH) operational mode of IEEE 802.15.4e Amendment. Consequently, this work implements the TSCH mode in the ns-3 [5] network simulator. The implementation is verified by known results and a simulation scenario is designed

© ICST Institute for Computer Sciences, Social Informatics and Telecommunications Engineering 2016
B. Mandler et al. (Eds.) IoT 360° 2015, Part I, LNICST 169, pp. 257–262, 2016.
DOI: 10.1007/978-3-319-47063-4_25

to investigate the performance of TSCH under dynamic conditions of channel quality and number of active devices in the network. The paper is organized as follows: Sect. 2 overviews the main features of 802.15.4e, Sect. 3 describes the proposed simulation scenario, Sect. 4 discusses and analyses the results and finally, Sect. 5 concludes this work.

2   IEEE 802.15.4e Amendment

Three new MAC operational modes are defined in this amendment: Low Latency Deterministic Network (LLDN), Deterministic and Synchronous Multi-channel Extension (DSME) and Timeslotted Channel Hopping (TSCH). Channel hopping was introduced to increase network resilience, devices hop among predefined frequency bands, so if there is some interference in a channel, the next one may be in better conditions.

TSCH is a deterministic mode, all communications are previously scheduled during the PAN formation or pre-configured into devices. A slotframe repeats using devices' shared notion of time, each slotframe is composed by timeslots, which contains a link between two devices.

3   Simulation Scenario

The proposed scenario simulates a wireless acoustic sensor network used in a family home. As shown in Fig. 1 the residence dimension's are 8 by 11 m and it has 5 rooms. The sensor network features 16 devices, one as the central sink, which receives and processes all information generated by the other 15 devices.

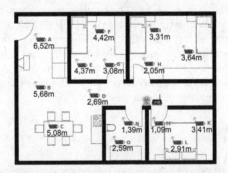

Fig. 1. House schematic used as simulation scenario

The network is configured with one slotframe with 15 timeslots, each timeslot has a length of 10 ms. Sensors produce 114 bytes of data (maximum allowed considering a header of 13 bytes) every 10 ms.

An IEEE 802.11-2007 [6] (WiFi) compliant device is disposed next to the central sink, it is configured with a transmit power of 0.1 W and channel 6 to

Table 1. Activity levels

Activity	Description	Time of the day	Nodes	WiFi activity
Low	Everybody sleeping	23 h to 07 h	3	None
Medium	1 or 2 people present	09 h to 17 h	6	50 %
High	Everybody present	07 h to 09 h and 17 h to 23 h	15	100 %

generate a PSD according to the above mentioned standard. The Friis propagation loss model [15] is used to represent the signal's energy loss during the transmission.

The proposed scenario has a 24 h duration, through the day the number of people in the house changes, as well as the activity of the sensor network and of the WiFi interferer. Table 1 describes the 3 possible activity levels.

4   Results

The presence of a WiFi device in the simulated scenario causes a heavy influence on the sensor network behaviour. Such variance happens due to the attenuation that the WiFi signal suffers along the path to the devices antenna. The graph in Fig. 2 shows the BER observed by the sink node of a transmission performed for each device of the sensor network. As can be seen, the WiFi interferer influences all devices of the network, even the signal from the closer devices are too low compared to the WiFi signal. A BER of 10^{-9} is often considered the threshold as an acceptable condition, Fig. 2 shows that this is only achieved in channels 24, 25 and 26, where there is no WiFi interference, considering that all transmissions in the affected channels would fail or not pass the CCA scheme, only 18,75 % of those transmissions would succeed.

In this study three aspects of the network are analysed: throughput, delay and energy consumption. In order to validate the obtained data a mathematical analysis is performed and compared with the simulation results. Each activity level is analysed for its throughput and then compared with simulated results. Since the slotframe configuration remains the same through all activity levels (with 15 timeslots), there is a different optimal throughput for each one (Table 2).

In Fig. 3 shows the simulated results with and without interference. The results without interference are, as expected, equal to the calculated through-

Table 2. Maximum throughput for each activity level

Activity level	Nodes active	Maximum throughput
Low activity	3	20.32 kbps
Medium activity	6	40.64 kbps
High activity	15	101.60 kbps

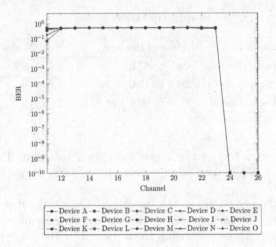

Fig. 2. BER of each channel for each device

puts, this validates the implementation in an ideal scenario where there is no packet loss due to interference.

The first region is relative to a low activity level, which has no WiFi interference, and the maximum throughput of 20.32 kbps is reached. The second region, relative to a high activity level, reaches 18.9 % (19.202 kbps) of the throughput required by the application, this result corresponds to the 18.75 % success rate previously obtained, with transmissions only being successful in 3 of the 16 channels. The third region, relative to a medium activity level, reaches 60 % (24.384 kbps) of the throughput required by the application in this level, considering the WiFi interferer is active during 50 % of the time, in half of this region's

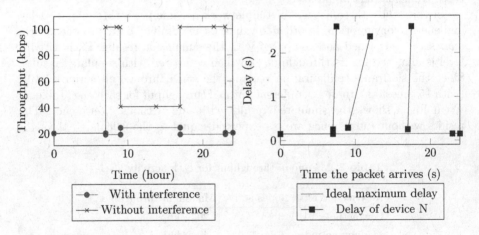

Fig. 3. Simulated throughput with and without interference

Fig. 4. Delay in device N

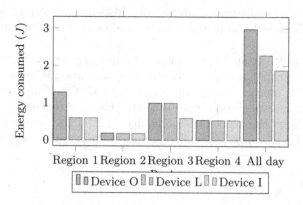

Fig. 5. Energy consumption, in J, of devices O, L and I in each region and throughout the entire simulation

duration the throughput should be as required by the application, in the other half it should be only 18.75 % of the required value, this scheme corresponds to 59.375 % of the required throughput which validates the value obtained by the simulation.

The impact of interference in the network's delay is shown in Fig. 4. The maximum delay without interference is 0.15 s, relative to the length of the slot-frame. In the presence of the WiFi signal, the delay quickly increases going to impractical values. The slope of the line relates with the success rate, in the high activity level the slope is around 77.6° and in the medium activity level the slope is 34.9°.

Using the realistic energy model for TSCH [16], Fig. 5 shows the energy consumption by devices O, L and I in each region of the simulated scenario. Device O represents nodes active through the entire simulation, device L represents nodes active only in regions 2, 3 and 4, and device I represents nodes active only in regions 2 and 4. Since regions 1 and 3 have the same duration, the impact of the WiFi interferer (with a duty cycle of 50 %) in energy consumption can be observed, in region 1 is which device O consumes 1.277 J while in region 3 it consumes 0.989 J.

5   Conclusion

This work analysed the performance of a TSCH network. The results show that in an environment with interference it is indispensable to deploy self-learning techniques. These techniques mainly restrict the channels used by the channel hopping scheme to only the ones with a minimum quality. It was also observed that changing the slotframe size to bear only active devices can bring a huge improvement in the network's delay. This work's analysis was enabled by the TSCH model developed under the ns-3 network simulator, which, for the best of our knowledge, is the first simulator to implement the IEEE 802.15.4e standard.

As a result of the implementation several additions and corrections were also made for the IEEE 802.15.4 model, with the main addition being the interference support.

As future work, certain enhancements can be implemented in the features of TSCH, such as shared timeslots and the synchronization scheme. A full IEEE 802.15.4e model implementation, including other MAC schemes, would provide a tool to assist the evaluation of the entire standard and the development of new proposals made by the academic community. Part of this research was funded under the IWT SBO project Sound INterfacing through the Swarm (SINS).

References

1. I. S. 802.15.4e 2012. Wireless Medium Access Control (MAC) and Physical Layer (PHY) Specifications for Low-Rate Wireless Personal Area Networks (WPANs) Amendment 1: MAC sublayer, IEEE Standard for Information Technology (2012)
2. T. I. E. T. F. (IETF). IPv6 over the TSCH mode of IEEE 802.15.4e, The Internet Engineering Task Force (IETF) (2014)
3. Du, P., Roussos, D.G.: Adaptive time slotted channel hopping for wireless sensor networks. In: Computer Science and Electronic Engineering Conference (CEEC) (2012)
4. Sha, M., Dor, R., Hackmann, G., Lu, C., Kim, T.-S., Park, T.: Self-adapting MAC layer for wireless sensor networks. In: Real-Time Systems Symposium (RTSS) (2013)
5. ns 3 project. ns-3 network simulator. http://www.nsnam.org/
6. I. S. 802.11-2007. Wireless LAN Medium Access Control (MAC) and Physical Layer (PHY) Specifications. IEEE Standard for Information Technology (2007)
7. IEEE, IEEE 802.15 WPANTM Task Group 4 (TG4). http://www.ieee802.org/15/pub/TG4.html. Accessed 09 Apr 2014
8. Information technology - Open Systems Interconnection - Basic Reference Model: The Basic Model (1994)
9. I. S. 802.15.4-2006. Wireless Medium Access Control (MAC) and Physical Layer (PHY) Specifications for Low-Rate Wireless Personal Area Networks (WPANs), IEEE Standard for Information Technology (2006)
10. I. S. 802.15.4-2011. Wireless Medium Access Control (MAC) and Physical Layer (PHY)Specifications for Low-Rate Wireless Personal Area Networks (WPANs), IEEE Standard for Information Technology (2011)
11. Goldsmith, A.: Wireless Communications. Cambridge University Press (2005). ISBN: 0521837162, 9780521837163
12. DARPA. Transmission control protocol, Defense Advanced Research Projects Agency, RFC 793 (1981). http://www.ietf.org/rfc/rfc793.txt
13. Baldo, N., Miozzo, M.: Spectrum-aware channel and phy layer modeling for ns3. In: Spectrum-Aware Channel and PHY Layer Modeling for ns3 (2009)
14. Crecraft, D., Gorham, D..: Electronics. CRC Press (2003). ISBN: 0748770364
15. Kraus, J.D.: Antennas. McGraw-Hill, New York (1950)
16. Vilajosana, X., Wang, Q., Chraim, F., Watteyne, T., Chang, T., Pister, K.S.J.: A realistic energy consumption model for TSCH networks. IEEE Sens. J. 14(2), 482–489 (2014)

A Stochastic Optimization Model for the Placement of Road Site Units

Luis Urquiza-Aguiar[1($\boxtimes$)], Carolina Tripp-Barba[2], and Mónica Aguilar Igartua[1]

[1] Department of Network Engineering, Universitat Politècnica de Catalunya,
C. Jordi Girona 1-3, 08034 Barcelona, Spain
{luis.urquiza,monica.aguilar}@entel.upc.edu
[2] Faculty of Informatics, Universidad Autonóma de Sinaloa (UAS),
De Los Deportes Avenue and Leonismo Internacional, 82107 Mazatlán, Mexico
ctripp@uas.edu.mx

Abstract. In this paper, we propose a simple and scalable optimization model for the deployment of road site units (RSUs). The model takes advantage of the inherent stochasticity provided by the vehicles' movements by using mobility traces to determine which are the best positions to place RSUs to maximize connectivity in a multi-hop VANET scenario and keep the number of RSU as low as possible. Our simulations results validate that the solutions offered by our model are accurate.

Keywords: Stochastic optimization · Vehicular ad-hoc networks (VANETs) · Road site unit (RSU) · RSU deployment

1 Introduction

One of the characteristics that make the study of vehicular ad-hoc networks (VANETs) challenging is the stochasticity introduced by the mobility of the vehicles. In this work, we propose a stochastic optimization model (SOM) [1] for the optimal placement of Road Side Units (RSU) over a geographical area. The aim of our mixed integer linear model is to choose the minimum number of RSU to be deployed in a specific area such that moving vehicles can reach some fixed infrastructure point in a multi-hop fashion regardless their position. To do that, our model does not rely in any deterministic (particular) vehicle distribution to compute the connectivity information between vehicles and RSUs. Instead, our model considers a representative set of different positions of vehicles that can be extracted from real vehicle movements traces as [7], which are more trustful and are becoming more popular among the research community to test their proposals. Therefore, our model provides a solution that is the best for the whole set of movements. Taking uncertainty into account by means of different vehicles positions to compute the connectivity information, gives a solution to the model that is more reliable than only using a deterministic connectivity matrix.

The rest of the paper is organized as follows: Sect. 2 explains the proposed model in detail. Then, the process to obtain the multi-hop connectivity information is described in Sect. 3. After that, Sect. 4 presents results obtained with

© ICST Institute for Computer Sciences, Social Informatics and Telecommunications Engineering 2016
B. Mandler et al. (Eds.) IoT 360° 2015, Part I, LNICST 169, pp. 263–269, 2016.
DOI: 10.1007/978-3-319-47063-4_26

a solution provided by our model in a realistic scenario. Finally, conclusions and future work are drawn in Sect. 5

2   The Problem Formulation

We propose a two-stages stochastic optimization model with recourse [1] to deploy in an optimal way the RSUs over an area. In our problem, the first stage is represented by the subset of RSU that has to be selected prior to know the distribution of vehicles in the area. On the other hand, the best association between vehicles and the chosen RSUs is done in the second stage after the distribution of vehicles is known (when the stochasticity is disclosed). The results of our model are based on the multi-hop connectivity information. In addition, the model considers an approximation of the effective capacity of the wireless channel due to the multi-hop transmission and takes into account the maximum demand that an RSU can serve.

2.1   Parameters of the Model

Our proposal uses connectivity information between vehicles and RSU as input parameter. Let R be the set of candidate RSUs among which our model chooses the most valuable to maximize the packet delivery ratio from vehicles to the RSU deployed. The set R includes an RSU named r_∞ to which every node can connect. If in the solution of the model a vehicle connects to this RSU, it means that this vehicle is disconnected. The use of this artificial RSU simplifies the model. Each RSU $r \in R$ has associated a traffic load capacity C_r and an installation cost $Cost_r$ in the sets C and $Cost$, respectively.

As we anticipated, the model uses a set of observations of vehicles' positions S in order to consider the randomness of this factor. Each observation $s \in S$ is a snapshot of vehicles located at different positions obtained from movement traces. Let V be the set of vehicles considered in the model. In particular V_s is the subset of vehicles which appear in the scenario s. Each vehicle $v \in V_s$ has associated average traffic load $L_{s,v}$. This data set is useful to test different traffic loads among nodes, for instance, the fleet of buses in the city. H represents the set of path lengths allowed by the model to connect nodes with an RSU. In the model, the maximum route length is denoted by $h_{\max} = |H|$, that is the path length from all the vehicles to the artificial RSU. No other RSU is connected to a vehicle by a path of length $h_{\max}$. Related to the set H is the set P, that are the penalty factors since it uses different path lengths. In this work, these factors are the mean numbers of times that a message should be sent to get one successful reception as a function of the number of hops, according to the results obtained in [8]. $P_{h_{\max}}$ is big enough to penalize the fact that a vehicle is not connected to a real RSU.

CVR is the set of tuples $\langle s, h, v, r \rangle$ that provides the information about the connectivity between vehicles V and the set of candidate RSU R. The presence of the tuple $\langle s, h, v, r \rangle$ in the set CVR means that vehicle v can reach RSU r in the scenario s through h hops. Notice that $\langle s, h_{\max}, v, r_\infty \rangle$ for all $v \in V_s$

are always present in the set because we consider that all nodes can reach the artificial RSU.

2.2 Variables of the Model

Our model uses the following variables to determine which gateways should be selected. S is a boolean variable that indicates if an RSU $r \in R$ is chosen for the solution ($S_r = 1$) of the model. The set S is the first stage decision variables in the structure of our stochastic problem.

Rts is a set of variables in the $[0,1]$ domain that associates a portion of the traffic load of a vehicle to an RSU with which it has connectivity. For instance, $Rts_{s,h,v,r} = 0.8$ indicates that the 80% of the traffic load that belongs to vehicle v can be received by RSU r through a route of h hops in the scenario s. Consequently, Rts plays the role of second-stage variables in the stochastic problem, which are decided for each scenario and after that the RSU has been selected.

2.3 The Stochastic Model

The goal of the proposed model is to select the minimum number of RSUs to maximize the multi-hop connectivity between nodes and fixed infrastructure points. The objective function is shown in Eq. (1). The first term of the objective function adds the installation costs of the chosen RSUs, so the model will try to use the minimum number of them. On the other hand, the second term adds the whole traffic generated in the network. The model tries to connect vehicles with RSUs by employing short paths because we are imposing increasing penalty factors as a function of path lengths. Hence, the solution of the model will select RSUs easily reachable from a high number of nodes using the minimum number of hops in the different scenarios. It is worth to mention that if the penalty factor for disconnected ($P_{h_{max}}$) nodes is greater than the maximum installation cost of a gateway, then the model will not leave disconnected nodes to avoid activating RSUs. Moreover, if the specific interest of user's model is to detect the best positions to install the RSUs, regardless the installation cost, then this value must be the same for the whole set of candidate RSUs.

$$\min_{S,Rts} \quad \sum_{r \in R} S_r Cost_r + \sum_{\langle s,h,v,r \rangle \in CVR} Rts_{s,h,v,r} P_h L_{s,v} \tag{1}$$

$$\text{s.t.} \quad \sum_{\substack{h \in H, r \in R: \\ \langle s,h,v,r \rangle \in CVR}} Rts_{s,h,v,r} = 1, \qquad \forall v \in V_s, s \in S \tag{2}$$

$$Rts_{s,h,v,r} \leq S_r, \qquad \langle s,h,v,r \rangle \in CVR \tag{3}$$

$$\sum_{\substack{v \in V, h \in H: \\ \langle s,h,v,r \rangle \in CVR}} Rts_{s,h,v,r} P_h L_{s,v} \leq C_r, \qquad \forall s \in S, \forall r \in R \backslash \{r_\infty\} \tag{4}$$

$$\sum_{r \in R \backslash \{r_\infty\}} S_r \leq \text{Max}_R \tag{5}$$

Constraints from Eqs. (2) to (5) guarantee a proper solution of the problem. The first condition in Eq. (2) states that the traffic load of every vehicle v of the scenarios in S has to be served by some subset of candidate RSUs reachable from the vehicle through multi-hop routing. Notice that in this subset the artificial RSU r_∞ can be included, which is reachable for all vehicles at the maximum number of hops h_{max}. In this case, only the portion of the traffic served by r_∞ will be highly penalized. Also, notice that any $Rts_{s,h,v,r} = 1$ means that the whole traffic of v can be served by a unique RSU r, and this is the closest solution to the real behavior of a VANET, in which balance of traffic loads (fractional values of $Rts_{s,h,v,r}$) is unlikely. The constraint of Eq. (3) is related to the previous constraint and it basically establishes that if a portion of the traffic load of vehicle v is served by the RSU r (i.e., $Rts_{s,h,v,r} > 0$) then the RSU r must be included in the solution $S_r = 1$. This is the condition that forces the model to activate RSUs in the solution and search from the best ones. Best RSUs are those that can receive as much traffic load as possible.

An important constraint of the proposed model provided the realism that it adds to the solution, is written in Eq. (4). This condition imposes that the maximum capacity load of each candidate RSU $r \in R$ can serve, will not be exceeded by the connected vehicles to them. This constraint does not apply to the artificial RSU used by the unserved traffic loads. The last restriction, Eq. (5) sets the maximum number of RSUs (Max_R) that the solution can have. If such limitation is not at stake, it can be removed of the model.

3   Connectivity Information

In this section, we describe how to obtain the input information about multi-hop connectivity through the boolean matrix multiplication of the adjacency matrix among vehicles A_s and the adjacency matrix between vehicles and candidate RSU notated as B_s. Theses matrices represent the connectivity at 1 hop in the network. A non-zero position in this kind of matrices represents that the nodes involved can communicate between them. In particular B_s stores the information on which vehicles can communicate with RSUs directly. The same information for h hops, called $B_{s,h}$, is computed as follows:

$$B_{s,h} = A_s^{h-1} B_s \tag{6}$$

Notice that, $B_{s,h}$ contains information about vehicles that can connect to RSUs using from 1 to h hops. $B_{s,h}$ is the most expensive step in the process with a complexity of $O(n^3 + n^2 m)$ for each hop in each of the scenario, where n is the number of vehicles and m the number of RSUs. The connectivity matrix $C_{s,h}$, which tells us which are the vehicles that are been connected to a RSU using h hops, is obtained as:

$$C_{s,h} = B_{s,h} - B_{s,h-1} \tag{7}$$

Therefore, the position $C_{s,h,v,r}$ of this matrix, which indicates if the vehicle v can reach RSU r will be 1 only the first time that it can communicate with that

RSU and 0 otherwise. The set of tuples of the CVR parameter are constructed from the non-zero positions of $C_{s,h}$ matrices. Notice that $C_{s,1} = B_s$ for each scenario $s \in S$.

4 Results of the Model

We use a synthetic movement trace to determinate which is the best position to locate one RSU among the five candidate positions shown in Fig. 1 within an urban area of Barcelona. Once the model provides a solution, we remove the chosen RSU's position and solve the model again with the remaining set of candidate RSUs until this set is empty. The optimization solver that we use is CPLEX [4]. To test how well the solutions of our model behave, we compare them to simulation results from ten simulations for each one of the candidate RSUs. We use Estinet [2] and C4R [3] to perform this task. The settings of the model and the simulations are depicted in Table 1.

The locations suggested by our stochastic model to install one RSU among the candidate set depicted in Fig. 1 in decreasing order are: *RSU 1, RSU 5, RSU 2, RSU 4, RSU 3*. In fact, our model gives a draw between RSU 2 and RSU 4 (the value of the objective function is the same activating these RSUs). However, the best order revealed by the simulation results showed in Fig. 2 is *RSU 1, RSU 5, RSU 2, RSU 4, RSU 3*. The real order is clearly manifest in both vehicle densities if we look at the performance of the packet delivery ratio (PDR) in Fig. 2a and the average delay in Fig. 2b. On the other hand, the performance difference in the average number of hops, in which our model relies, is not so clear, especially between the results provided by RSU 2 and RSU 4.

The results presented in this section validate the reliability of the solutions of our stochastic model to detect the most suitable locations to install RSUs in a city. Additionally, the results show that badly chosen positions could lead to a very poor PDR and high delays.

Table 1. Simulation settings.

Parameter	Value
Area	1.5 km × 1 km
N° of nodes/RSUs	100 and 150/5
N° hops in model	5 Hops
Simulation time	300 s
N° scenarios in model	20 scn, every 15 s
Transmission range	~400 m (LOS)
Mobility generator	C4R [3]
MAC specification	IEEE 802.11p
Bandwidth	6 Mbps
Packet generation time	$T \sim U(2,6)$ s $E(T) = 4$ s
Packet size	1000 bytes
Routing protocol	MMMR [6]

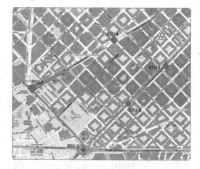

Fig. 1. Considered scenario. Barcelona from OpenStreetMap. 5 candidate *RSUs*.

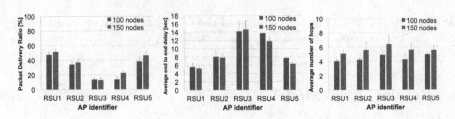

(a) Packet Delivery Ratio (b)   Average   end-to-end (c) Average   number   of
(PDR)   packet delay.   hops.

Fig. 2. Performance metrics results.

5   Conclusions and Future Work

In this paper, we have presented a stochastic optimization model for the optimal
placement of Road Site Units. The proposed model is fed by the multi-hop
connectivity information provided by different vehicles distribution, which can
be obtained from different realistic movement traces. Our tests suggest that our
model detects correctly the most important positions to locate RSUs.

Our model could be used as a second stage in the deployment process of
RSUs to select the most important RSU to be installed in the geographical area.
A first step is to select the candidate positions of the gateways to cover the area.

Our model can be solved for large-scale data sets, which in turns means
big geographical areas through the Benders decomposition method [5]. Future
work includes the formulation and solution of our stochastic model using this
well-known optimization technique and employs real vehicle movement traces.

Acknowledgments. This work was partly supported by the Spanish Government
through the projects TEC 2013-47665-C4-1-R "EMRISCO", TEC2014-54335-C4-1-
R "INRISCO" and by the Universidad Autónoma de Sinaloa (Mexico) through the
project PROFAPI2014/215. Luis Urquiza-Aguiar is the recipient of a scholarship from
SENESCYT and EPN (Ecuador).

References

1. Birge, J.R., Louveaux, F.: Introduction to Stochastic Programming. Springer Series
   in Operations Research and Financial Engineering. Springer, New York (1997)
2. Estinet: EstiNet 8 Network Simulator, July 2015. http://www.estinet.com
3. Fogue, M., Garrido, P., Martinez, F.J., Cano, J.C., Calafate, C.T., Manzoni, P.: A
   realistic simulation framework for vehicular networks. In: 5th International Conference on Simulation Tools and Techniques, pp. 37–46. ACM, Belgium (2012)
4. IBM: ILOG CPLEX Optimizer Studio v 12.5, July 2015. http://www-03.ibm.com/
   software/products/en/ibmilogcpleoptistud
5. Taşkin, Z.C., Cochran, J.J., Cox, L.A., Keskinocak, P.: Benders Decomposition. In:
   Wiley Encyclopedia of Operations Research and. Management Science. Wiley, New
   York (2010)

6. Tripp-Barba, C., Urquiza-Aguiar, L., Aguilar Igartua, M., Rebollo-Monedero, D., de la Cruz Llopis, L.J., Mezher, A.M.: A multimetric, map-aware routing protocol for VANETs in urban areas. Sensors (Basel, Switzerland) **14**(2), 2199–2224 (2014)
7. Uppoor, S., Trullols-Cruces, O., Fiore, M., Barcelo-Ordinas, J.M.: Generation and analysis of a large-scale urban vehicular mobility dataset. IEEE Trans. Mob. Comput. **13**(5), 1061–1075 (2014)
8. Urquiza, L., Tripp, C., Martin, I., Aguilar, M.: Propagation and packet error models in VANET simulations. IEEE Latin Am. Trans. **12**(3), 499–507 (2014)

Can a Game Improve People's Lives? The Case of *Serious Games*

Armir Bujari, Matteo Ciman$^{(\boxtimes)}$, Ombretta Gaggi, and Claudio E. Palazzi

Department of Mathematics, University of Padua, Padua, Italy
{abujari,mciman,gaggi,cpalazzi}@math.unipd.it

Abstract. The popularity of digital games and the wide diffusion of mobile devices with sensors and communication capabilities have led many researchers to think how this technology can be put to good use to improve people's lives and, in general, our society. In this short survey we present an overview on how mobile games can go beyond their entertainment purpose to pursue a service that may be useful to overcome health and accessibility impairments.

Keywords: Serious games · Mobile technologies · Mobile games

1 Introduction

The proliferation of game technology and the commercial success of mobile devices endowed with sensors and communication capabilities is fostering the creation of new software systems able to ubiquitously engage and entertain users. At the same time, the most interesting part of this process is represented by its potential in generating mobile serious games able to amuse players while providing benefits to them or even to larger communities [13,22].

To better understand this scenario and its trends, we overview here some of the most recent and representative examples of mobile serious games devoted to foster physical exercise (Sect. 2), to be employed in the medical field (Sect. 3), and to increase the accessibility in our society for people with impairments (Sect. 4).

2 Exergames

The first category of games that we want to describe, the *Exergames*, use the game paradigm to push users into increasing physical activity. They use sensors to understand users' movement and they use this movement as a form of interaction with the game. In this category, the success of Nintendo's Wii platform is very well known, but also mobile platforms provide the capabilities of exploiting users' real movements as a form of interaction (e.g., rotating the iPhone to have a virtual car steering).

An example of mobile game which aims at increasing people physical activity is *Climb The World* [4], a serious game which uses a machine learning based technique to recognize and count stairsteps. This game aims at persuading people to

© ICST Institute for Computer Sciences, Social Informatics and Telecommunications Engineering 2016
B. Mandler et al. (Eds.) IoT 360° 2015, Part I, LNICST 169, pp. 270–275, 2016.
DOI: 10.1007/978-3-319-47063-4_27

use stairs instead of elevators or escalators. The idea underlying the game is simple: the user has to climb real world buildings, e.g., the Empire State Building or the Eiffel Tower, engaging in physical activity during her/his everyday life. Once started, the game records and analyzes data from the accelerometer and counts the number of stairsteps made by the user. The game performs a fine-grained analysis by exploiting smartphone sensors to recognize single stairsteps. An experiment with a group of 13 users has shown that the engagement of friends in the buildings climb can increase the number of stairsteps made by the users.

The same technology has been exploited to implement pervasive healthcare systems. For instance, wrist rehabilitation is currently accomplished through very expensive and bulky machinery that cannot be moved from hospitals or through exercises that the patient is supposed to perform at home but with no way for the doctor to verify the patient's dedication or performance. Instead, DroidGlove is a serious game for Android and iPhone platforms that proposes to the users several movement tasks [9,10]. The user can perform the exercises anytime and anywhere, the smartphone can remind her/him to exercise with a certain frequency, while the gyroscope is utilized to determine the accuracy of the user's movements so as to assign a score. Both the assigned movement exercises and the accomplished scores can be exchanged in real time between the player and her/his doctor for a comprehensive supervision.

Serious games are also used to train people to do something, for example, in the military field, they are employed to train soldiers using virtual environments that reproduce real-world scenarios. The main scope is to prepare soldiers to situations and obstacles they may encounter in the real world, making them able to take decisions faster and safer. Serious games can be used in the governmental field to simulate the population's reaction to political decisions [3] and in the educational field to increase children' learning abilities, as well as to train employees [29].

3 Serious Games Used in the Medical Field

The second category of games includes games developed to help doctors and patients. The former use the game and train to correctly execute specific procedures or to be exposed to real-life situations [12]. Patients can be pushed into rehabilitative exercises hidden by games, e.g., to perform specific upper limb movements [19] or to offer telerehabilitation to post-stroke patients so that they can perform the long series of exercises at home [11]. Furthermore, games and social communities can improve patients' recovery and motivation [24]. For instance, Re-Mission is a game that improves young patients understanding of cancer by employing game avatars representing drugs which destroy cancer cells, additionally providing a forum where patients can discuss and support each other [18].

PlayWithEyes is a serious game for the early diagnosis of amblyopia in children [8,15]. The authors developed a system for iPad and iPod Touch that uses a serious game to perform an orthoptic test to evaluate children visual acuity.

This project has shown how children find more appealing playing with a game than performing regular tests; their increased attention results in more accurate diagnosis.

Ciman et al. [7] designed a serious game to help the rehabilitation process from CVI (Cerebral Visual Impairment). The game is able to adapt the rehabilitative exercises to each child, also following the improvements of the patient, to reduce the influence of her/his disability in future life. The system also helps doctors to perform a good assessment of a patient and to create a rehabilitation program.

Other examples of serious games used in the medical field regard the use of serious games in identifying the risk of dyslexia in children even at preschool age so as to intervene as soon as possible [16,28]. In particular, in [16] the authors developed a set of serious games that, thanks to a crossplatform approach, can be played both on desktops and on tablets. The set of games share an appealing underwater environment with different sea creatures used to engage the player in activities that stimulate those cognitive capabilities involved in the reading acquisition process. The games are intended to capture children's attention to achieve more accurate measurements than those obtainable with non-entertaining tests.

Similar in spirit to the former works, DYSL-X integrates dyslexia predictors in a tablet game [28]. The authors evaluate several existing games for preschoolers to derive a set of guidelines so as to design an optimal tablet game for 5 years children; then, these guidelines were used to develop Diesel-X, a game about a robot dog (Diesel) which has to fight against a gang of criminal cats.

Instead, Letterprins [27] is a reading game designed to improve the reading development of children with reading disorder through a series of reading tasks. The game requires the children to pronounce letters or words, while a parent or a caregiver has to indicate the correctness of the childs answers. The game allows parents to facilitate the children during the tasks and to record a message to be played at the end of the game.

These examples show that serious games are extremely useful for children since a game can change a boring rehabilitation task into an interesting activity. They can be used during assessment, rehabilitation and telerehabilitation programs. An engaging and easy-to-use interface is a key issue for this kind of games. One solution is to use the so called tangible interfaces, which use physical artifacts for accessing and manipulating information [23]. To this end, Forlines et al. [14] investigated the differences between mouse and direct touch input, both in terms of quantitative performance and subjective preference. The work shows that touch interfaces, even if they may not lead to greater performance, especially for speed and accuracy, are preferable for other considerations like fatigue, spatial memory and simplicity. This is particularly true for children, even called digital native speakers, who find touch interaction very natural, thus avoiding the need for long training sessions to learn how to interact with touch applications.

4   Improving Accessibility Through Serious Games

Mobile serious games could also be used to support people with impairments. In particular, consider social communities composed by thousands (or even much more) of mobile users present in each city. The combination of games with social networks, crowd-sourcing and mobile users with sensor-equipped mobile devices could create a major force able to tackle serious challenges that can be considered too complex for single users and/or difficult to automate. As an example, imagine how a serious game could help visually impaired users. Bringing the Google Image Labeler serious game [2] into the real world, we could design a social community where mobile users are asked to play a game involving the labeling of the surrounding environment (e.g., crossroads, architectural barriers, parks, stores). This way, they will add digital tags to real objects, creating a social community similar to Panoramio [1]. The serious advantage would be that of having a participatory, augmented reality environment where a visually impaired person could perceive the surrounding real world through her/his mobile device able to retrieve the aforementioned digital labels and transform their format (text, image, video, etc.) into audio, thus improving her/his autonomy.

Algorithms supporting mobility-impaired pedestrians have already been proposed by researchers, providing means to generate specific urban routes that consider the accessibility of roads and curbs [5,17]. However, one of the most complex challenges is related to the accessibility assessment of roads and curbs [26]; without this initial assessment, there would be no data to feed to the aforementioned algorithms. To this end, some approaches have focused on the possibility to autonomously and anonymously detect favorite routes chosen by people with a certain impairment (e.g., being on a wheelchair) and consider them as preferable when someone else in the same condition searches for a route in the neighbourhood [6,20]. However, we have to mention that games have been considered as well to involve citizens in playing a mobile serious game whose goal is achieved by labeling as many accessible or non accessible roads, curbs, pedestrian crossing, traffic lights, etc. [21,25]. Aiming at improving as much as possible the inclusion of people with impairments in our society, the best approach is probably a mix between the two approaches: automatic detection and serious game.

5   Conclusion

The combination among digital games and mobile technology is creating unprecedented opportunities in terms of ubiquitous, mobile entertainment. In this paper we have overviewed recent advancements in the field of mobile serious games and shown how they are expected to improve our lives regarding exercise, health and accessibility.

References

1. Panoramio (2006). http://www.panoramio.com/
2. Google image labeler (2007). http://images.google.com/imagelabeler/
3. Practice. Mcgraw-hill education: Government in action (2012). http://www.mhpractice.com/
4. Aiolli, F., Ciman, M., Donini, M., Gaggi, O.: ClimbTheWorld: real-time stairstep counting to increase physical activity. In: Proceedings of the 11th International Conference on Mobile and Ubiquitous Systems: Computing, Networking and Services (Mobiquitous 2014), pp. 218–227, London, UK, December 2014
5. Beale, L., Field, K., Briggs, D., Picton, P., Matthews, H.: Mapping for wheelchair users: route navigation in urban spaces. Cartograp. J. **43**(1), 66–81 (2006)
6. Bujari, A., Licar, B., Palazzi, C.E.: Road crossing recognition through smartphone's accelerometer. In: Proceedings of the IFIP/IEEE Wireless Days 2011 (2011)
7. Ciman, M., Gaggi, O., Nota, L., Pinello, L., Riparelli, N., Sgaramella, T.M.: Helpme! A serious game for rehabilitation of children affected by CVI. In: Proceedings of the 9th International Conference on Web Information Systems and Technologies (WEBIST 2013), pp. 257–262 (2013)
8. De Bortoli, A., Gaggi, O.: PlayWithEyes: a new way to test children eyes. In: Proceedings of the 1st IEEE International Conference on Serious Games and Applications for Health (SeGAH), pp. 1–4, November 2011
9. Deponti, D., Maggiorini, D., Palazzi, C.E.: DroidGlove: an android-based application for wrist rehabilitation. In: Proceedings of the IEEE International Conference on Ultramodern Telecommunications and Workshops (ICUMT 2009) (2009)
10. Deponti, D., Maggiorini, D., Palazzi, C.E.: Smartphone's physiatric serious game. In: Proceedings of the IEEE International Conference on Serious Games and Applications for Health (SeGAH 2011) (2011)
11. Di Loreto, I., Gouaich, A.: Mixed reality serious games: the therapist perspective. In: Proceedings of the IEEE International Conference on on Serious Games and Applicationsm for Health (SeGAH 2011), Braga, Portugal, pp. 1–10 (2011)
12. Esteban, G., Fernandez, C., Matellan, V., Gonzalo, J.: Computer surgery 3D simulations for a new teaching-learning model. In: Proceedings of the IEEE International Conference on on Serious Games and Applicationsm for Health (SeGAH 2011), Braga, Portugal, pp. 1–4 (2011)
13. Ferretti, S., Furini, M., Palazzi, C.E., Roccetti, M., Salomoni, P.: WWW recycling for a better world. Commun. ACM **53**(4), 139–143 (2010)
14. Forlines, C., Wigdor, D., Shen, C., Balakrishnan, R.: Direct-touch vs. mouse input for tabletop displays. In: Proceedings of the SIGCHI Conference on Human Factors in Computing Systems, CHI 2007, pp. 647–656 (2007)
15. Gaggi, O., Ciman, M.: The use of games to help children eyes testing. Multimed. Tools Appl. **75**(6), 3453–3478 (2016)
16. Gaggi, O., Galiazzo, G., Palazzi, C.E., Facoetti, A., Franceschini, S.: A serious game for predicting the risk of developmental dyslexia in pre-readers children. In: Proceedings of the 21st International Conference on Computer Communications and Networking (ICCCN 2012) (2012)
17. Kasemsuppakorn, P., Karimi, H.: Personalized routing for wheelchair navigation. J. Locat. Based Serv. **3**(1), 24–54 (2009)
18. Kato, P.M.: Video games in health care: closing the gap. Rev. Gen. Psychol. **14**(2), 113–121 (2010)

19. Ma, M., Bechkoum, K.: Serious games for movement therapy after stroke. In: Proceedings of IEEE Conference On Systems, Man and Cybernetics, Singapore, pp. 1872–1877 (2008)

20. Palazzi, C.E., Brunati, M., Roccetti, M.: Path 2.0: a participatory system for the generation of accessible routes. In: Proceedings of the IEEE Conference on Multimedia and Expo (ICME 2010) (2010)

21. Palazzi, C.E., Marfia, G., Roccetti, M.: Combining web squared and serious games for crossroad accessibility. In: Proceedings of the IEEE International Conference on Serious Games and Applications for Health (SeGAH 2011) (2011)

22. Palazzi, C.E., Roccetti, M., Marfia, G.: Realizing the unexpected potential of games on serious challenges. ACM Comput. Entertainment **8**(4) (2010)

23. Pittarello, F., Stecca, R.: Querying and navigating a database of images with the magical objects of the wizard zurlino. In: Proceedings of the 9th International Conference on Interaction Design and Children, IDC 2010, pp. 250–253 (2010)

24. Roccetti, M., Casari, A., Marfia, G.: Inside chronic autoimmune disease communities: a social networks perspective to crohn's patient behavior and medical information. In: Proceedings of the IEEE/ACM International Conference on Advances in Social Networks Analysis and Mining (ASONAM 2015) (2015)

25. Roccetti, M., Marfia, G., Palazzi, C.E.: Entertainment beyond divertissment: using computer games for city road accessibility. ACM Comput. Entertainment **9**(2) (2011)

26. Salomoni, P., Prandi, C., Roccetti, M., Nisi, V., Nunes, N.J.: Crowdsourcing urban accessibility: some preliminary experiences with results. In: Proceedings of the ACM CHItaly, 11th Biannual Conference of the Italian SIGCHI Chapter, (CHItaly 2015) (2015)

27. Steenbeek-Planting, E.G., Boot, M., de Boer, J.C., Van de Ven, M., Swart, N.M., van der Hout, D.: Evidence-based psycholinguistic principles to remediate reading problems applied in the playful app letterprins: a perspective of quality of healthcare on learning to read. In: Schouten, B., Fedtke, S., Bekker, T., Schijven, M., Gekker, A. (eds.) Games for Health, pp. 281–291. Springer, Wiesbaden (2013). doi:10.1007/978-3-658-02897-8_22

28. Van den Audenaeren, L., et al.: DYSL-X: design of a tablet game for early risk detection of dyslexia in preschoolers. In: Schouten, B., Fedtke, S., Bekker, T., Schijven, M., Gekker, A. (eds.) Games for Health, pp. 257–266. Springer, Wiesbaden (2013). doi:10.1007/978-3-658-02897-8_20

29. Zapusek, M., Cerar, S., Rugelj, J.: Serious computer games as instructional technology. In: Proceedings of the 34th International Convention MIPRO, pp. 1056–1058 (2011)

About Game Engines and Their Future

Dario Maggiorini[1]([⊠]), Laura Anna Ripamonti[1], and Giacomo Cappellini[2]

[1] University of Milan, Milan, Italy
{dario,ripamonti}@di.unimi.it
[2] Italian National Research Council, Milan, Italy
giacomo.cappellini@idpa.cnr.it

Abstract. In these last few years we are witnessing an increasing adoption of video games in learning and teaching environments. This change is coming thanks to the fact that video games allow students to take a more active role in learning as they develop skills needed to succeed in their professional careers. At the same time, we are also observing a change in the way video games are implemented. Today, the existence of very large teams with a multi-layered organisation calls for the adoption of structured development approaches with associated environments. These environments have been baptised *game engines*. Availability and usability of game engines, in the near future, will positively influence educational activities for the next generations. In this paper, we discuss the general structure of modern game engines and put into question their current architectural approach. Our goal is to raise the attention of the scientific community on the fact that re-baptised software stacks are unlikely, on the long shot, to provide the flexibility and functionalities required by game developers in the coming years. After a detailed discussion of the possible problems on the horizon, an alternative approach for a modular and scalable game engine architecture will also be presented.

Keywords: Game engines architecture · Game development · Scalability · Distributed systems

1 Introduction

In these last years, the way developers implement video games is undergoing a tremendous change. At the beginning of video games history, a very small group – or even a single person – was usually in charge of software production. As a matter of fact, we can see that many block-buster games in the '80s such as *Pitfall!*, *Tetris*, and *Prince of Persia* carry the name of a single developer. Today, with the evolution of the entertainment market and the rise of projects with seven (or eight) figures budget, this situation is changing. In order to (*a*) better allocate competencies and effort, and (*b*) enforce code and resources reusability, video games are now developed on top of software environments defined as *game engines*.

Game engines, as largely discussed in [1], are usually organized as software stacks rooted in the operating system with an increasing level of abstraction

© ICST Institute for Computer Sciences, Social Informatics and Telecommunications Engineering 2016
B. Mandler et al. (Eds.) IoT 360° 2015, Part I, LNICST 169, pp. 276–283, 2016.
DOI: 10.1007/978-3-319-47063-4_28

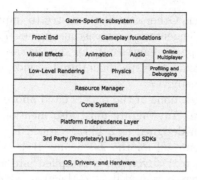

Fig. 1. Summary of a general game engine architecture.

layer-by-layer, up to describing game mechanics. See, as an example, Fig. 1. As it is easy to see from the picture, the adopted architecture is not really different from other solutions adopted in non-gaming environments. As such, given the different application field and performance requirements, a number of limitations may arise for large-scale game development. As we will see, three problems can arise with respect to the produced software: it may be monolithic, it is centralised and may not scale upward, and it may be platform dependent. Despite all the problems we just outlined, the final goal of this paper is not to prove that modern game engines are not fit to the task. Actually, they have demonstrated to be very good tools for the trade. Our aim here is to actually raise the attention of the scientific community that such tools (re-baptized software stacks) are unlikely, on the long shot, to provide the flexibility and functionalities that will be required by game developers in the next generations. We strongly believe that, in order to adapt to future evolutions, game engines should not just target better performances and advanced functionalities, but also provide more adaptable and serviceable internal structures.

2   Related Work

In the past, a fair number of scientific contributions has been devoted to the internal data structures of game engines. Nevertheless, at the time of this writing and to the best of our knowledge, only a very limited number of papers are specifically addressing the engine architecture. The majority of the literature seems to be focused on optimising specific aspects or services, such as 3D graphics (e.g., [2]) or physics (e.g., [3]). Issues related to portability and development have been addressed, among the others, by [4–6]. Authors of [4] propose to improve portability by providing a unifying layer on top of other existing engines. In fact, they extend each architecture with an additional platform-independent layer. Authors of [5] focus on development complexity and propose a solution based on modern model-driven engineering while in [6] an analysis of the open source Quake engine is performed with the purpose to help independent developers contribute to the project. Other contributions try to improve performances by creating distributed implementations of existing engines [7–9]. Unfortunately, all of them aim to increase performances only for specific case studies by applying a distributed system approach to a specific internal service, such as the simulation pipeline or the shared memory.

As it can be observed, none of the papers cited above is pointing to a completely new architecture. Anyway, we must also mention that not all existing game engines have been designed as a library stack. For this, we can address the Inform design system [10] for the Z-Machine [11]. With Inform, the algorithmic description of a text adventure is compiled into a binary package. The binary package is, in turn, executed by a Z-Machine, which is a software available for many hosting platforms. Unfortunately, Inform is limited to text-based adventure games (such as *Zork*) and has never evolved toward modern interface technologies. Nevertheless, we believe that modern game engines should reconsider Inform and Z-Machine as a viable approach.

3   Background on Game Engines

Although game engines have been studied and perfected since mid-'80s, a formal and globally accepted definition is yet to be found for them. Despite this lack of definition, the function of a game engine is fairly clear: it exists to abstract the (sometime platform-dependent) details of doing common game-related tasks, like rendering, physics, and input, so that developers can focus on implementing game-specific aspects. To achieve this goal, game engines are usually divided into two parts: a tool suite and a runtime component. The runtime component assembles together all the internal libraries required for hardware abstraction and to provide services for game-specific functionalities. A variable portion of the runtime is usually linked inside the game or get distributed along with the executable. The tool suite is, on the other hand, a collection of external programs that can be used to manage all the data we feed to the runtime and to manipulate the runtime itself.

Since the tool suit is not part of the internal architecture, in this paper we are going to tackle only on runtime-related issues.

3.1   A Brief History of Game Engines

The first example of game engine dates back to 1984 with the game *Doom*. Doom was not intended to feature a game engine. Nevertheless, it has been designed with a number of software engineering best practices in mind. In particular, we could find a strict separation between software modules and clear distinction from software and data assets. Moreover, a development approach strongly oriented to code reusability was enforced all over the project. To actually see the concept of game engine popping out, we had to wait until mid-'90s for the release of Quake Engine (by IDSoftware) and Unreal Engine (by Epic Games). Starting from this point, games opened up to user customisation and, most important of all, their engines have been regarded by software companies as a separate product to be sold to game developers. As of today, we have companies making games and selling their internal technology (like Epic Games) competing with companies focused only on distributing and supporting a game engine platform (Such as Unity Technologies).

Of course, game engines have not been immune from the *open source movement*. Many open source projects exist; they can provide specialised functionalities (e.g., Ogre3D) or a full application stack (e.g., Cocos2D). On the other side of the spectrum there are proprietary game engines, which are kept secret by gaming companies and are usually born around a specific project. Their architecture can be only guessed. Nevertheless, it is known that engine-focused companies usually fish their architects from gaming companies. Since they are also proposing us a library stack, one may presume that proprietary/private engines are following the same philosophy.

4   Potential Shortcomings of Current Game Engines

As already briefly presented in Sect. 1, creating a software by deploying code on top of a library stack may lead to potential problems when trying to create a video game. In this section we are going to look into these problems in detail and discuss what should be done to overcome them.

4.1   Monolithic Software

Being monolithic means that a gaming software is completely self-contained and developers must rebuild/relink the while project at every change. This global rebuild is required also because, as already mentioned, a portion of the engine is usually distributed together with the game. Since, in modern productions, the size of source code and assets is growing exponentially, a global rebuild might become a significant bottleneck for large projects. Even in small projects, being able to perform global rebuild means to have a clean and well synchronised source tree and requires good coordination among developers to avoid build breaks.

We should provide a way for developers to modify and extend games by means of a plug-in approach with a very fine granularity, even at runtime. This way, only new and changed functionalities will require compilation as standalone components. Moreover, a malfunctioning component is not going to compromise the entire project for other developers.

Technology exists and is already available for a program to load binary code on demand at runtime. All modern languages feature dynamic class loading; moreover, dynamic libraries management facilities are already included in mainstream operating systems. It is technically possible to compile the object code for a game item (only), have the engine recognise it, and finally use the class loader to draw the code inside to be immediately available in the game.

4.2   Centralised Solution

Centralised software is usually difficult to scale upward. Scaling up is required every the computational power required by a software component is exceeding the capacity of the hosting system. This is usually achieved by shedding the offered load between multiple machines. In particular, it is a desired behaviour for online games where many users connect simultaneously to the same (server) engine. In current implementations, the game itself must be aware of the location of a service (on the same machine or elsewhere) and implement a distributed computation. Considering the recent trend in online gaming [12], especially with MMOs (Massively Multiplayer Online games) and MOBAs (Multiplayer Online Battle Arena) ruling the market, the possibility to transparently relocate a component without restarting the server – and interrupting the service – will be an incredible benefit for next generation games. Just consider that the top-tier MOBA *League of Legends* reported, in 2014, 7.5 millions concurrent players at peak time.

Inside a library stack, modules communicate by means of function/method calls. While remote function call is possible in many ways, it is usually bound to a language (e.g., Apache River, only for Java) or a platform (e.g., Microsoft DCOM). An high performance messaging system between modules provided by the engine itself should be considered instead. The engine can simply remap an address from local to remote and vice versa when a component is relocated.

Technologies implementing lightweight and high-performance messages exchange are already available (see, e.g., mbus [13]). Of course, performances may be an issue when relocating a module over the network. Anyway, we already have many time-critical services provided over local area networks with good results (e.g., iSCSI [14]). Moreover, we must remember that relocation is usually performed across a dedicated infrastructures and not over the Internet; cross-traffic is definitely not an issue here.

4.3   Platform Dependency

Even if the engine claims to be multi-platform and uses its lower layers to manage adaptation for vendor-specific hardware, seamless deployment across platforms is not always guaranteed. This behaviour may depend on a number of causes: from undocumented/proprietary APIs preventing actual porting to loss of performances due to a library optimised only for specific hardware. Today, to address this issues, developers are required to write code that, inside the same engine, behave – or compile – differently, based on the underlying platform. As a result, the engine is technically cross-platform, but developer skills and code are likely to be diversified between deployment platforms. Needles to say, this is going to negatively impact team management and production time in many ways.

Once again, a modular architecture may be a viable solution to address the problem we just outlined. Using messages for inter-modular communication can also be beneficial since they can be platform independent and are easier to standardise. Nevertheless, this issue is not purely technical and involves marketing policies from hardware vendors. As a matter of fact, in many cases only vendors can write device drivers, as hardware interface are undisclosed for technical and opportunity reasons. At least, an approach based on software plug-in will help developers to easily modify, upgrade, or deactivate problematic and unsupported software modules.

5 An Alternative Approach

As already discussed in the previous section, potential solutions for each of the envisioned problems are already available. Putting all these solutions together can lead us to propose an alternative architecture for game engines.

We already know that this new architecture should be modular and provide a messaging service between modules. These modules must not be only game-specific but may also implement engine internal services. To achieve this, the engine needs just to implement some sort of sandbox where modules can be efficiently swapped in and out at runtime, plus the messaging system and a basic soft real-time scheduler. Moreover, the messaging system can also be distributed and link engines on different machines to perform transparent load shedding. An existing library stack could be easily transformed in modules inside one or more engines. If we need to preserve the library hierarchy, a message policy subsystem can be easily added.

What we just exposed lies in the middle between a runtime environment (like Java or CLI) and a micro-kernel operating system (such as Amoeba or QNX) with added distributed functionalities. See Fig. 2.

As a matter of fact, since our solution can be obtained from the combination/adaptation of existing technologies, a microkernel game engine seems to be actually implementable. Nevertheless, questions remain open about performances loss and willingness of companies to adopt it. While it is difficult to argue about performances without a working prototype, some considerations can be drawn on a perspective adoption. From an industrial perspective, there is only

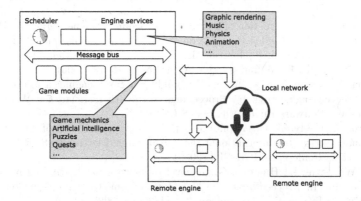

Fig. 2. Possible architecture for a microkernel game engine.

one undesirable constraint: in order to implement an efficient dynamic loader, a reflection/introspection enabled language is required. As of today, for performance reasons, the main development language is in many-cases C++, which does not natively support dynamic class loading. It is possible to add dynamic class loading to C++, with a significative loss in performances. As a result, it will be difficult that the changes we envision will take hold in corporate production pipelines with the current generation of developers, unless the scientific community will be able to provide a solution for a dynamic management of classes inside a sandbox based on C++.

6   Conclusion and Future Work

In this paper we analyzed the current approach for the internal structure of modern game engines. Our intention was to raise the community attention on the fact that this approach is unlikely to provide the flexibility and functionalities required by game developers in the next generations. We believe that, by developing a game on top of a library stack, the resulting software may suffer from being monolithic, centralised, and platform-dependent. We discussed all these issues in detail and it seems that solutions are already available by switching toward a microkernel-like architecture.

In the future, we are planning to create a prototype game engine based on the envisioned architecture and verify if it can be valid substitute for current engines with respect to performance and functionalities. This will be useful to actually deploy widely distributed games such the ones envisioned in [15].

References

1. Gregory, J.: Game Engine Architecture. A. K. Peters/CRC Press, Boca Raton (2014). ISBN 978-1466560017
2. Cheah, T.C.S., Ng, K.-W.: A practical implementation of a 3D game engine. In: International Conference on Computer Graphics, Imaging and Vision: New Trends (2005)
3. Mulley, G.: The construction of a predictive collision 2D game engine. In: Proceedings of the 8th EUROSIM Congress on Modelling and Simulation (2013)
4. Darken, R., McDowell, P., Johnson, E.: Projects in VR: the Delta3D open source game engine. IEEE Comput. Graph. Appl. **25**(3), 10–12 (2005)
5. Guana, V., Stroulia, E., Nguyen, V.: building a game engine: a tale of modern model-driven engineering. In: Proceedings of the 4th International Workshop on Games and Software Engineering, GAS (2015)
6. Munro, J., Boldyreff, C., Capiluppi, A.: Architectural studies of games engines the quake series. In: International IEEE Consumer Electronics Society's Games Innovations Conference, ICE-GIC (2009)
7. Xun, W., Xizhi, L., Huamao, G.: A novel framework for distributed internet 3D game engine. In: Proceedings of the Third International Conference on Convergence and Hybrid Information Technology, ICCIT 2008 (2008)

8. Gajinov, V., Eric, I., Stojanovic, S., Milutinovic, V., Unsal, O., Ayguade, E., Cristal, A.: A case study of hybrid dataflow and shared-memory programming models: dependency-based parallel game engine. In: 26th International Symposium on Computer Architecture and High Performance Computing, SBAC-PAD (2014)
9. Huiqiang, L., Wang, Y., Ying, H.: Design and implementation of three-dimensional game engine. In: Proceedings of World Automation Congress, WAC (2012)
10. Nelson, G.: Natural Language, Semantic Analysis and Interactive Fiction. Whitepaper (2006)
11. The Z-Machine Standards Document version 1.1 (2014). http://inform-fiction.org/zmachine/standards/z1point1/index.html. Accessed 7 Aug 2015
12. Gerla, M., Maggiorini, D., Palazzi, C.E., Bujari, A.: A survey on interactive games over mobile networks. Wirel. Commun. Mob. Comput. 13(3), 212 (2013)
13. Ott, J., Perkins, C., Kutscher, D.: A message bus for local coordination, IETF RFC 3259 (2002)
14. Satran, J., Meth, K., Sapuntzakis, C., Chadalapaka, M., Zeidner, E.: Internet small computer systems interface (iSCSI), IETF RFC 3720 (2004)
15. Maggiorini, D., Quadri, D., Ripamonti, L.A.: Opportunistic mobile games using public transportation systems: a deployability study. Multimedia Syst. J. 20(5), 545 (2014)

Smart Cart: When Food Enters the IoT Scenario

Marco Furini[(⊠)] and Claudia Pitzalis

Communication and Economics Department,
Universty of Modena and Reggio Emilia, 42121 Reggio Emilia, Italy
marco.furini@unimore.it

Abstract. People barely know what they eat and drink: product labels are written with small characters and with a difficult terminology. As a result, people spend too much time reading labels or avoid reading them at all. To connect food data with people we design of a food IoT (Internet of Things) scenario, where a smart cart tells us if the food product we are about to buy meet our preferences or not. In particular, we first perform a real-world study to understand consumers' behavior while they shop; then we design a food IoT scenario and we use current technologies to investigate its feasibility. Results show that people would appreciate a tool able to help them connecting with food data and also show that current technologies are sufficient to create a food IoT scenario.

Keywords: Internet of Things · QR-code · Food shopping

1 Introduction

Today's society is very different from the one of our parents: the advances in technologies changed almost every aspect of our life: from private to public relations, from professional to entertainment activities, from shopping to vacation. We live in a scenario where people and data are more and more linked, where people are informed about everything and in real-time [1–4]. However, if we take a detailed look at the food scenario, we can observe that it is quite similar to the one of our parents: we go to the supermarket (either physically or virtually), we put products in the cart, we check out and pay. Technologies facilitate the payment, allow grocery shopping chains to know consumers, but consumers know almost nothing about the food they buy [5].

The lack of knowledge about the food may lead to health problems: according to the World Health Organization, more than one-third of adults are overweight and several diseases are directly connected to unhealthy diet [6] with people eating too much fat, too much salt, too little fruit and vegetables [7].

In this paper, we imagine a scenario where consumers and food are connected, where food data (e.g., ingredients, nutritional fact, etc.) are easily available to consumers to make them aware of what they buy, eat and drink. In particular, we explore the potential of Internet of Things to make food data easily available to consumers: we want to give them information that may lead to an healthier lifestyle and might prevent health problems.

© ICST Institute for Computer Sciences, Social Informatics and Telecommunications Engineering 2016
B. Mandler et al. (Eds.) IoT 360° 2015, Part I, LNICST 169, pp. 284–289, 2016.
DOI: 10.1007/978-3-319-47063-4_29

Think about the following scenario: Alice is very careful about what she buys because her daughter is allergic to nuts, her husband is on a diet that forbids him to eat food that contains more than 20 % fat, she wants to buy fruits and vegetables produced in area where she lives. Until yesterday, food shopping was a nightmare: for every product Alice had to read the label (sometimes with characters so small that Alice needed to put on her eye glasses), but today Alice is in an IoT food scenario, where things communicate each other through technologies like RFID, NFC and QR-code. In this scenario, Alice uses a smart shopping cart that takes care of everything: it communicates with product labels and, knowing Alice's preferences, it tells Alice whether she should buy or not that product.

The contribution of this paper is twofold: (i) check if the IoT food scenario would be useful to consumers and (ii) design and test an IoT food scenario with current technologies. The former is achieved through a real-world study and the latter is achieved through the employment of QR-code technology and through the development of a prototype application able to connect food data with people. Results obtained from the real-world study show that people are very interested in what's inside a food product, and the developed application shows that current technologies allow connecting food products with consumers. As a result, the designed IoT food scenario will likely increase the knowledge about what people eat an drink and will likely help people to eat healthier.

The paper is organized as follows: in Sect. 2 we present related works in the area of Internet of Things and food; in Sect. 3 we present the real-world study about consumers' behaviors, the IoT food scenario and the prototype application to be used in this scenario. Conclusions are drawn in Sect. 4.

2   Related Work

The Internet of Things will create a huge interconnected ecosystem that will probably cause a profound transformation of human activities and production processes. Several scenarios will be affected by this new technological revolution and the food scenario will likely be one of these [8].

In the literature, different studies focused on IoT food scenario. Fabian et al. [8] considered to couple every object with RFID tags in order to uniquely characterize objects with the idea of building a global network where to retrieve information like nutritional advice. Ren et al. [9] showed that RFID will allow to access messages during the entire life cycle of the product (e.g., state of preservation). Kouma and Liu [10] analyzed possible benefits of using QR-code in food products and depicted a possible scenario where the "on-line" food can be used to prevent obesity. Briseno et al. [7] proposed a mobile health platform intended to increase children's health awareness by using QR-code in food products. Jia and Yang [11] proposed to use IoT to build a food quality supervision platform.

3 Our Smart Cart Proposal

The motivation behind our study is to investigate whether an IoT food scenario would be appreciated and useful to consumers when they buy food. Indeed, nowadays, the only possible connection between food data and consumer is done through the reading of the product label, but this process is time consuming and might be annoying (think of the small character size used in many labels). However, there may be different reasons to read labels: a consumer may be on a particular diet, may want to avoid particular food (e.g., for intolerance reasons, for ethical reasons, etc.) or may want to pay attention to particular ingredients (e.g., saturated fat, sugar, etc.) and the knowledge about the products may result in an healthier eat.

In the following we analyze in details the contributions of this paper: (i) understand consumers' behavior when they shop and (ii) design an IoT food scenario and develop a prototype application to test its feasibility.

3.1 Customers' Behavior

To investigate the customers' behaviors we considered a real-world study and we asked for voluntary participation. We have been contacted by 205 people (76 % women and 24 % men) of different age (35 % of the participants is between 18 and 25 year-old, 43 % is between 26 and 35, 15 % is between 36 and 54 and 7 % is older than 55 year-old).

The first group of questions investigates the reasons people buy specific items. Results (multiple answers were possible), reported in Fig. 1, show that for 69.3 % of the respondents the most important aspect is the price; 50.2 % thinks of ingredients; 49.8 % checks the expiration date; 47.8 % is interested at the product origin; 21 % checks for nutritional value and only 20 % considers the brand.

The second group of questions investigates if people read product ingredients while they shop. Results, reported in Fig. 2 (left), show that 74 % of respondents

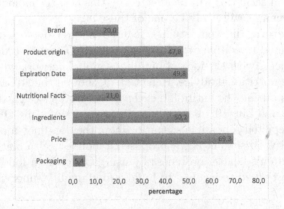

Fig. 1. Main reasons to buy a product (multiple answer were possible).

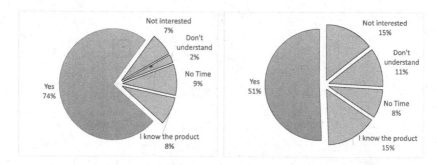

Fig. 2. Label reading: ingredients (left) and nutritional facts (right)

read the product ingredients, whereas the 26 % does not. Among the ones who read labels it emerged that 10.8 % has food intolerances; 15.3 % is on a diet (either for healthy reasons or for some disease) and 67.5 % is concerned about some ingredients (e.g., 3.6 % is concerned about sugar presence; 30.4 % is concerned about vegetable oils; 8 % checks the presence of saturated fat; 58 % wants to avoid specific ingredients like lactose, gluten or aspartame). Among the ones who do not read labels, 38 % of respondents do not have enough time to do that; 34 % already identified the products suited to their needs; 28 % is not interested in what is written on the label, and 10 % do not understand labels.

The third group of questions investigate if people read product nutritional facts while they shop. Results, reported in Fig. 2 (right), show that 51 % of the respondents read these values, whereas the 49 % does not. Among the ones who do not read the nutritional facts, it emerged that 32 % of the respondents already identified the products suitable to them; 32 % is not interested in nutritional facts; 25 % does not understand these data; 19 % does not have enough time to do that.

Finally, we investigated if people would appreciate a tool to help them reading product labels. Results showed that 69 % of respondents would like to have this help and would make use of this device if available.

3.2 Smart Shopping Cart

From the technological point of view, an IoT food scenario can be realized with several different technologies like for example RFID, NFC and/or QR-code. Since the employment of RFID and NFC technologies may require a structural investments (e.g., products equipped with RFID) that may discourage food producers and/or food vendors, we consider the use of QR-code technology. This means that the product producer has to print a QR-code on the label of the product (with product information, or with a link where to find these information, encoded in it) and the food store has to provide a tool (e.g., a smart supermarket cart or a mobile application) able to read the QR-code, to access to the product information and to check if the product meets the consumer's preferences or not.

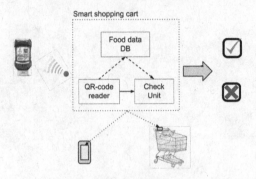

Fig. 3. The smart shopping cart architecture.

Fig. 4. Smart cart: the interface (left), QRcode reading (middle) and app warning (right): the product contains an unwanted ingredient.

To test the feasibility of the IoT food scenario just described, we develop a prototype mobile application in charge of reading the QR-code, accessing the food data, checking the consumer's preferences and suggesting to the consumer whether or not to buy the product.

The IoT food scenario and the prototype architecture are reported in Fig. 3: a QR-code is printed on the product label and a QR-code reader is in charge of accessing to what's inside the product (possibly using an external DB), of checking whether the product characteristics meet the consumer's requirements, and of telling consumer if the product meet his/her preferences.

Figure 4 shows three different screen-shots of the developed prototype application: the left one shows how consumer can create a list of un-wanted ingredients; the middle one shows the QR-code reading operation and the right one shows an example of the output application (in this case the packet of cookies contains a percentage of fat that conflicts with what consumer demands).

The IoT food scenario just designed along with the developed prototype application show that consumers my receive substantial benefits: the automatic filtering of products decreases the time for shopping and increases the purchase of the most suitable products to consumers.

4 Conclusions

In this paper we focused on the opportunities offered by the IoT if applied to the food scenario. We first investigated, through a real-world study, the consumers' behavior while food shopping and we found that people are interested in what's written on product labels and would appreciate a tool able to automatically connect them to the food data. Then, we designed an IoT food scenario using QR-code technology and finally we showed, through the development of a mobile application, its feasibility and effectiveness. The proposed IoT food scenario produces an easy connection between food data and consumers and therefore it may lead to a healthier lifestyle.

References

1. Montangero, M., Furini, M.: Trank: ranking twitter users according to specific topics. In: Proceedings of the 12th International IEEE Consumer Communications and Networking Conference (CCNC 2015), January 2015
2. Furini, M., Tamanini, V.: Location privacy and public metadata in social media platforms: attitudes, behaviors and opinions. Multimedia Tools Appl. **74**(21), 9795–9825 (2015). Springer, US
3. Gerla, M., Maggiorini, D., Palazzi, C.E., Bujari, A.: A survey on interactive games over mobile networks. Wirel. Commun. Mob. Comput. **13**(3), 212–229 (2013)
4. Furini, M.: Users behavior in location-aware services: digital natives vs digital immigrants. Adv. Hum. Comput. Interact. **2014** (2014). Article ID 678165
5. Reitberger, W., Spreicer, W., Fitzpatrick, G.: Situated and mobile displays for reflection on shopping and nutritional choices. Pers. Ubiquit. Comput. **18**(7), 1721–1735 (2014)
6. World Health Organization: Global strategy on diet, physical activity and health. WHO (2014)
7. Vazquez-Briseno, M., Navarro-Cota, C., Nieto-Hipolito, J.I., Jimenez-Garcia, E., Sanchez-Lopez, J.D.: A proposal for using the internet of things concept to increase children's health awareness. In: International Conference on Electrical Communications and Computers, pp. 168–172, February 2012
8. Fabian, B., Günther, O.: Security challenges of the epcglobal network. Commun. ACM **52**(7), 121–125 (2009)
9. Ren, S., Huanliang, X., Li, A., Zhou, G.: Meat-productions tracking and traceability system based on internet of things with RFID and GIS. Trans. Chin. Soc. Agric. Eng. **26**(10), 229–235 (2010)
10. Kouma, J.-P., Liu, L.: Internet of food. In: International Conference on Internet of Things, pp. 713–716 (2011)
11. Jia, B., Yang, Y.: The design of food quality supervision platform based on the internet of things. In: 2011 International Conference on Transportation, Mechanical, and Electrical Engineering (TMEE), pp. 263–266, December 2011

Towards Autonomic Middleware-Level Management of QoS for IoT Applications

Yassine Banouar[1,3(✉)], Saad Reddad[3], Codé Diop[2,3], and Christophe Chassot[2,3]

[1] Université de Toulouse, UPS, Toulouse, France
[2] INSA, Villeurbanne, France
[3] CNRS-LAAS, Toulouse, France
{banouar,reddad,diop,chassot}@laas.fr

Abstract. The Internet of Things is expected to bring large and promising spectrum of social goods in various domains. Several new challenges arise or are to be reconsidered within the IoT systems supporting these goods, among them the Quality of Service (QoS) issue. The goal of this paper is first to introduce our approach for an autonomic Middleware-level QoS management of IoT systems. As a contribution at the second maturity level of the autonomic computing paradigm such as defined by IBM, it is then to propose and validate, within an emulation testbed platform, a proof of concept-oriented architecture of a monitoring component allowing detecting QoS degradation symptoms. We also demonstrate the benefits that could be gained from simple network-inspired QoS-oriented adaptation actions.

Keywords: Internet of Things · Qos · Middleware · Autonomic computing · Monitoring

1 Introduction

Now, the Internet includes not only computers but also all kinds of communicating and more or less smart objects. This new extension is called *Internet of Things* (IoT), it will allow bringing a large and promising spectrum of *social goods* in various domains such as health, safety, etc. Within IoT systems, several challenges are to be considered, among them the *QoS* issue (i.e. the ability of the service to ensure non-functional properties such as bounded response time).

The QoS issue has been addressed many times in the field of the "classical" Internet [1, 2]. This issue becomes again relevant within IoT systems. While conventional services usually involve two end-hosts and intermediate routers, IoT services refer to "activities" involving much many hardware/software entities; their interconnection imposes the use of *communication middleware,* such as the open source *OM2M* platform [5], enabling discovery of connected devices, abstraction of network heterogeneity, etc. Providing such middlewares with QoS-oriented capabilities then becomes a necessity that is still under research study. In this context, the first contribution of this paper is to introduce our vision of an autonomic QoS management at the Middleware level, following the IBM autonomic computing (AC) paradigm [11]. Towards this objective,

© ICST Institute for Computer Sciences, Social Informatics and Telecommunications Engineering 2016
B. Mandler et al. (Eds.) IoT 360° 2015, Part I, LNICST 169, pp. 290–296, 2016.
DOI: 10.1007/978-3-319-47063-4_30

the second contribution takes place at the second level of maturity of the AC such as defined by IBM; it consists of developing monitoring solution aimed at detecting QoS degradations, helping the administrator in his/her decision to execute adaptation actions.

The rest of this paper is organized as follows: Sect. 2 presents the architecture principles towards a QoS-oriented autonomic management of the OM2M middleware. Section 3 details the functionalities and architectural principles of the proposed monitoring solution. Section 4 presents how a "proof of concept" implementation of our monitoring solution has been tested on an emulation platform, together with the benefits that could be gained from a simple network-inspired QoS-oriented action performed by the administrator when a degradation symptom is detected.

2 Architecture Principles Towards QoS-Oriented Autonomic Management of Middleware Layer for IoT Systems

A structured architectural model of an IoT system is proposed in [3, 4], which includes three levels: *Application Level, Network Level* and *Perception Level*. As subpart of the Application level, the *Middleware* level is aimed at hiding the details of various underlying technologies. In an IoT perspective, it abstracts heterogeneity of physical objects by providing homogeneous representation facilitating their handling by IoT applications. It is also aimed at offering several services such as information/services/user access rights/devices management. The contributions exposed in this paper have been done using the ETSI compliant OM2M open source middleware platform [5]. OM2M is a RESTful platform running on the top of the OSGi layer, making it modular and highly extensible via plugins, offering specific ETSI-M2M compliant *service capabilities*.

Managing QoS in dynamic IoT environment contexts is a complex task [6–10], which makes now compulsory autonomous management of QoS-oriented actions. In this context, our final goal consists of upgrading the OM2M platform following the *Autonomic Computing* model defined by IBM [11], based on the MAPE-K cycle (upper part of Fig. 1a). [11] defines five successive levels of maturity to go from a manual management of a given system to a fully autonomic system (Fig. 1b). At the second level, which is targeted in this paper, monitoring tools can be used to collect metrics from the system to detect anomalies (or "symptoms"), helping to reduce the time taken to collect and synthesize information. Human skills are however required to analyze the detected anomalies and execute corrective actions.

Several plans of management have to be considered within OM2M, each one requiring sensors/effectors in order to be monitored/(re)-configured (lower part of Fig. 1a). The first plan deals with the OM2M software: its goal is to collect metrics and to manage actions that could be performed to improve QoS. As OM2M is a JAVA-based platform, the second plan deals with the Java Virtual Machine, which offers all the required resources for OM2M execution (threads, CPU, memory, etc.). The third and fourth plans deal with computing resources and may concern the physical machine level or the virtual machine level in a cloud-based deployment.

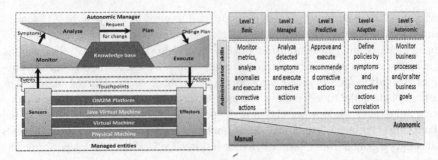

Fig. 1. (a) Autonomic architecture for OM2M QoS management – (b) Maturity levels towards Autonomic behaviour

3   Architectural Principles of the Monitoring Component

The monitoring component is aimed at *collecting metrics* (*events*) and *generating symptoms* identifying QoS degradations. It is based on two main functionalities: the *observation of the monitored system* through sensors, and the *detection of symptoms,* through events aggregation, correlation and filtering actions (Fig. 2).

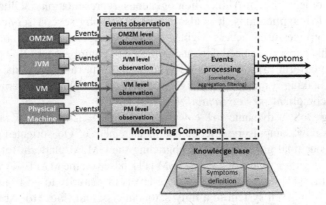

Fig. 2. Architecture of the monitoring component

The *observation function* is performed thanks to logical sensors integrated in the managed entity for events collection. Metrics are collected at four levels; at the OM2M level, such as: execution time, RTT, losses, plugin state, concurrent requests, web server size. At the JVM level (on which OM2M is running), for metrics related to the resources used by the OM2M platform (used memory, used CPU, running threads or number of loaded classes). And at the virtual/physical machine level (on which the JVM is running), with metrics related to machine state, total memory load, CPU load, used disk percentage, etc.

Starting from the events collected by the observation function, the *symptoms detection function* is aimed at detecting *patterns* identifying symptoms that have been pre registered in a knowledge base. To identify these patterns, *complex event processing*

(CEP) is a technique that allows discovering complex events, by deduction, analysis and/or correlation of elementary events. Among the different tools implementing CEP, Esper (http://www.espertech.com/products/esper.php) is an open source Framework that we have used in our study.

4   Validation of the Monitoring Component

4.1   Testbed Platform and Measurement Scenarios

Our validation approach of the monitoring component (that we claim as a basic proof of concept) is based on an *emulation testbed*, which allows testing a real OM2M platform, confronted to an emulated traffic. The emulation platform (Fig. 3) is provided as a set of web services consisting of injectors generating traffic, and of a controller whose main function is to configure the injectors following a defined emulation scenario. To avoid congestions at the sender side, injectors and controllers are launched on different machines. The traffic is sent to a BeagleBone Black gateway executing the OM2M software.

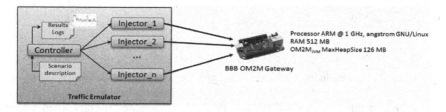

Fig. 3. Overview of the emulation platform

The first injector (Injector_1) is supposed to generate a critical applicative traffic corresponding to the periodic data from a critical sensor in a health care-oriented case study, for which an RTT of 300 ms (threshold value) is required. Due to space limits, we only consider a simple pattern consisting of four successive events indicating an increasing RTT upper than the required threshold value, the last one being twice upper the first one.

An Esper description of the pattern is provided hereafter:

> select * from Event match_recognize (measures A as value1, B as value2, C as value3, D as value4
>   pattern (A B C D) define A as A.value > THRESHOLD, B as (A.value < B.value),
>   C as (B.value < C.value), D as (C.value < D.value) and D.value > (2 * A.value))

The defined scenarios (see Table 1) are aimed at studying the impact of disruptive traffics (Injectors_2 and 3) on the sensitive flow (Injector_1) for which a QoS has to be maintained. Each injector is characterized by a number of HTTP requests (R), a request method (e.g. POST, GET), a destination and a periodicity (P) in second (0 = concurrent requests). Timestamps (t_1, t_2 and t_3 (in seconds)) are collected to evaluate the evolution of the RTT and the remaining inputs.

Table 1. Scenario testbed

Scenario	Controller			Injector 1		Injector 2		Injector 3		Observed metric
	t_1	t_2	t_3	R	P	R	P	R	P	
1	0	–	–	200	0.5	–	–	–	–	RTT_{Inj_1}
2	0	1	–	200	0.5	200	0.5	–	–	RTT_{Inj_1}
3	0	1	1	200	0.5	200	0.5	200	0.5	RTT_{Inj_1}
4	0	20	40	260	0.5	300	0	200	0	RTT_{Inj_1}

4.2   Results Analysis

Scenarios results are provided on Fig. 4. Due to space limits, we focus on the evolution of the RTT_{Inj_1}.

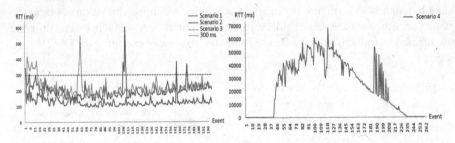

Fig. 4. (a) RTT_{Inj_1} evolution for scenarios 1, 2 and 3 – (b) RTT_{Inj_1} evolution for scenario 4

For the first three scenarios (Fig. 4a), the RTT_{Inj_1} increases slightly when adding disruptive traffic, without leading to degradation symptom detection; only some isolated violation of the required threshold may be observed. Differently, in scenario 4 (Fig. 4b), the RTT_{Inj_1} of the observed traffic reaches much higher and repeated "out of threshold" values that lead to a symptom alert (around the 40th event).

Next section describes the benefits of a simple adaptation action that could be done by the administrator, once notified of this alert.

4.3   Benefits of Adaptation Action in Response to Symptom Detection

Once notified with a QoS degradation symptom, the administrator has to apply QoS-oriented adaptation action(s). Before executing some adequate action(s), he/she has to analyse the potential causes of the observed symptom(s) and then decide about the action(s) to be performed. Let us recall that within a fully autonomic system, such *Analysis* and *Plan* steps should be done by the system itself (transparently for the administrator). These two steps being out of the scope of the AC maturity level targeted in this paper (level two), we suppose here that the administrator has to decide by him/her-self for the execution of a simple adaptation action that consists in activating/de-activating a proxy at the entry of the gateway, allowing discarding part of the incoming traffic (typically the disruptive traffic).

Figure 5 illustrates the benefits of this adaptation action supposed to be performed after the 75th event (the time taken between the symptom detection by the monitoring component - around 40th event - and the execution action of the administrator being not null). At that time, the administrator activates the proxy, in order to discard the traffic coming from the injectors 2 and 3.

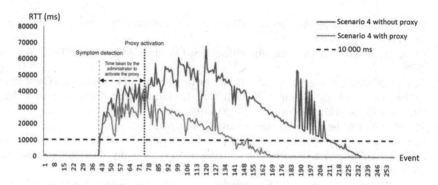

Fig. 5. Comparison of RTT_{Inj_1} without and with the proxy mechanism

Through this scenario, one can notice that the proxy activation leads to a better RTT, still being at a value much higher that the targeted threshold of 300 ms. The targeted RTT is reached around the 169th event, due to the time taken to process the disruptive traffic already in the OM2M gateway when the proxy has been activated.

5   Conclusions and Perspectives

This paper has presented our general vision for an autonomic Middleware-level QoS management of IoT systems. With the aim to target the second maturity level of the AC, the focus has been done on the Monitoring component of the AC paradigm, for which proof of concept implementation principles have been proposed and tested through an emulation platform aimed at stressing the OM2M open source platform. The performed measurements allow concluding that QoS-oriented and resources-oriented symptoms may be detected during execution of the applications (here emulated by traffic injectors), and that simple (network-inspired) adaptation actions allow improving the observed QoS-oriented.

Many perspectives are arising from this work. The enhancement of the set of more complex symptoms is a first perspective. The enhancement of the set of mechanisms to be activated is also under study: instead of activating/de-activating a traffic discarding mechanism, a current improvement of the proposed proxy allows blocking a given percentage of the traffic; similarly, we have also configured a delay-oriented proxy; other mechanisms are going to be proposed, their choice and parameterization depending on the targeted policy and the context. A current study is also to enhance the AC maturity level of our system with the aim (as a first result) to make it transparent to the administrator the step of activating manually the adaptation mechanism to be enforced when a symptom is detected. Finally, enhancing the architectural design of the AC components is also an important perspective towards the deployment of a Middleware-level QoS management system within a real IoT system.

References

1. Braden, R., et al.: Integrated Services in the Internet Architecture: An Overview. RFC 1633, June 1994
2. Black, D., et al.: An Architecture for Differentiated Services. RFC 2475, IETF, December 1998
3. Duan, R., Chen, X., Xing, T.: A QoS architecture for IoT. In: 2011 International Conference on Internet of Things (iThings/CPSCom), and 4th International Conference on Cyber, Physical and Social Computing, pp 717–720 (2011)
4. RICHCLOUD White paper: Internet of things (IOT) (2012)
5. Ben Alaya, M., Banouar, Y., Monteil, T., Chassot, C., Drira, K.: OM2M: extensible ETSI-compliant M2M service platform with self-configuration capability. Proc. Comput. Sci. **32**, 1079–1086 (2011)
6. Skorin-Kapov, L., Matijasevic, M.: Analysis of QoS requirements for e-Health services and mapping to evolved packet system QoS classes. Int. J. Telemed. Appl. (2010)
7. Jin, J., Gubbi, J., Luo, T., Palaniswami, M.: Network architecture and QoS issues in the internet of things for a smart city. In: Proceedings of the ISCIT, pp. 974–979 (2012)
8. Ling, L., Shancang, L., Shanshan, Z.: QoS-aware scheduling of services-oriented internet of things. Indus. Inform. **10**, 1497–1505 (2014)
9. Zhou, M., Ma, Y.: A modeling and computational method for QoS in IoT. In: Proceedings of Software Engineering and Service Science (ICSESS), pp. 275–279, June 2012
10. Ren, W.: QoS-aware and compromise-resilient key management scheme for heterogeneous wireless IoT. Int. J. Netw. Manag. **21**, 284–299 (2011)
11. Kephart, J., Chess, D.: The vision of autonomic comp. Computer **2003**, 41–50 (2003)

Safe Bicycle Parking Platform Based on RFID Technology

Víctor Juan Expósito Jiménez[1]([✉]), Florian Salmhofer[1], Reinhold Frosch[2],
Herwig Zeiner[1], and Werner Haas[1]

[1] Joanneum Research Forschungsgesellschaft mbH, Graz, Austria
victor.expositojimenez@joanneum.at
http://joanneum.at
[2] Freaquent Froschelectronics GmbH, Graz, Austria
http://www.froschelectronics.com/

Abstract. In order to deter bike thieves, we have designed and implemented a theft prevention system for bicycles based on RFID technology. Bikes can be stored in areas monitored by custom designed base stations without the need for visual or contact identification. The system is implemented with Web of Things technology, using a RESTful and a streaming server API, to facilitate communication between the embedded electronics and the back end service. The system is tested by deploying RFID technology in several environments to determine the viability of the platform.

Keywords: RFID · Theft prevention · Mobility · Web of Things · Urban cycling

1 Introduction

As cities put emphasis on bicycles as a modern form of transportation, the safety of cyclists becomes a critical concern, but so does the security of the bicycles themselves. Traditional means of theft mitigation comprise mainly bike locks, or ideally locking the whole bike inside a bike shed. Modern alternatives are bike alarms, as well as personal bike trackers with GPS and GSM functionality to help keep track of a bike in the event of theft. These devices are of course battery powered, and depending on use, have to be recharged within weeks to months of continued use. The fact that only a small percentage of stolen bikes are ever recovered provides a strong argument for the implementation of active measures to prevent bike theft. To supplement the conventional safety precautions currently available to bike owners such as high-quality bike locks, bike theft insurance, coding and registration, etc. the project Safe Bicycle Parking sets out to provide bike owners with yet another anti-theft option. What we are aiming at, is a modern system that utilizes the latest web technologies to create a theft prevention system that allows long battery operation or even battery free operation. For our program, we are using active RFID transponders to provide a stable, long-range solution.

© ICST Institute for Computer Sciences, Social Informatics and Telecommunications Engineering 2016
B. Mandler et al. (Eds.) IoT 360° 2015, Part I, LNICST 169, pp. 297–303, 2016.
DOI: 10.1007/978-3-319-47063-4_31

Inconspicuous and tamper proof mounting solutions are very important for this application, and RFID technology provides a great basis for explorations in this direction, as the necessary transponders can be very small and can be powered by coin cells for months or years. Stem-mounted cases, within handlebars or handlebar grips, inside a saddle or even in bike tires would all be possible places for the transponders.

2   Web of Things Platform: Safe Bicycle Parking

The Web of Things is an effort to create seamlessly interacting embedded devices that are accessible through open web standards to facilitate interconnectedness of sensors, actors and control devices. By relying on radio frequency identification (RFID) technology and Web of Things technology, we aim to make it safer to leave a bike parked in a secure zone. One transponder is securely attached to the bike, another is carried by the person, for example along with the bike lock keys. When entering the parking area, the RFID readers will query both transponders which will trigger the checking-in of the bike. As the person leaves the bike in the parking area, the bike's transponder will be continually monitored. The hardware (transponders, base station) for safe bicycle parking is based on a two-frequency system. The uplink the communication from the base station to the transponder takes place by means of a LF RFID interface at 125 kHz, which has a range of effectiveness that can be adjusted for maximum efficacy and remains largely unaffected by potential electromagnetic disturbances or attenuations caused by metal or by weather conditions. When activated either by means of the uplink through the wireless interface or when a mounting sensor in the transponder detects removal from the bike, the transponder responds to the basis station by means of a UHF signal at 434, 869 or 915 MHz.

The alarm possibilities are versatile and can be adapted for use in diverse places. Additional alarm possibilities include the following:

- Interaction with a local computer system equipped with a camera and the ability to save video or picture files in the case of theft.
- Directly driving an acoustic or visual alarm (sirens, flashing lights)
- Notifications sent to additional people such as doormen, security guards, neighbours, etc.
- Notifications sent to users of social media (Facebook Places, Foursquare) who are currently in the vicinity of the unit.

The software part of the web of things platform is divided into three main parts, namely the base station and the back end services of the Web of Things Platform, including the event manager. The base station software is executed on the base station, the other parts are split into micro services, running in encapsulated containers.

2.1   The Base Station

The purpose of the base station is to read all the transponders that are in the safe area and to forward this information to the event manager. The base station can also trigger a visual and acoustic alarm or signal a CCTV camera to permanently store image data in the event of a bicycle theft. The base station is an outdoor metal enclosure which houses all the electronic hardware required to read transponders and establish a communication with the event manager. Low frequency (LF) and a high frequency (HF) readers are used to read the transponders. As the transponders are active (battery powered) a low frequency (LF) communication is established first to wake the transponder up, and the subsequent data transfer between the transponder and the base station will be carried out through a high frequency (HF) link. The LF system is designed to provide maximum penetration to activate transponders partially occluded by bike frames or other metal parts in the area. The base station reads all transponders that are currently in this area and sends periodic read-outs to the event manager. UMTS communication (3G) is used for data transfer between the base station and the event manager where a wired ethernet connection is not available. In Fig. 1 the base station is depicted with all hardware components labelled.

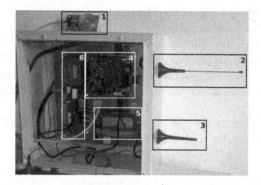

Fig. 1. Development Base Station, Components labelled: 1. Test Low Frequency(LF) antenna, 2. Ultra High Frequency(UHF) antenna, 3. GSM/3G antenna, 4. BeagleBoard, 5. RFID reader, 6. Power supply

2.2   The Event Manager

The event manager is the part which receives all data events and processes them. It is split into several different services, each implemented as a microservice with a common interface. The main program is implemented by using Akka[1]

---

[1] http://akka.io/.

streaming technology which handles all events received from the base stations. Each event contains the base station ID and a list with all serial numbers of all transponders that are currently in the secure area of this base station. It updates the information about which bicycles are parked at a base station based on the submitted information.

All requests to the event manager are made through the RESTful service implemented for this purpose. This RESTful service provides a stateless communication which reduces memory usage and solves the session expiration problems and is easier to support. All of those features are essential for the platform due to the need for reliability, stability and ease of use. The communication is encrypted using Transport Layer Security (TLS) and uses API keys to authenticate the base stations. If an alarm occurs, the event manager notifies the base station and also sends a warning message to the owner via email or SMS. The event manager is also in charge to check the integrity of the actives base stations.

2.3   Web of Things User and Management Interface

In this web interface, the users can manage information associated with their bikes. The user interface shows different information based on the type of profile associated with a user. There are four types of profiles:

– User: Only the information related to this user is shown. The users can see the history of their bicycles and check what the current status of these bicycles is.
– Security Personnel: The people who are associated with this kind of profile can check all data from the base stations they watch. If an alarm is detected, both base station and its associated security personnel will be noticed.
– Company: All bicycles which are included in the fleet of a company are handled through this profile.
– Administrator: This profile has access to all information included in the system. All users, bicycles and base stations can be modified by this kind of profile.

All information is updated in real time through websockets which updates all active clients that are currently viewing the information as soon as any changes occur. This method provides us with a simple and lightweight way to get all clients updated without spending too many resources. More detailed description of system architecture of the underlying Web of Things platform can be found in the recent publication [1].

Additionally, a smartphone application has been created which allows display of the bike status, and checking the bike in or out of the system, with only one transponder mounted to the bike. In Fig. 2, the whole system setup is pictured in an FMC^2 diagram.

---

^{2} http://www.fmc-modeling.org/.

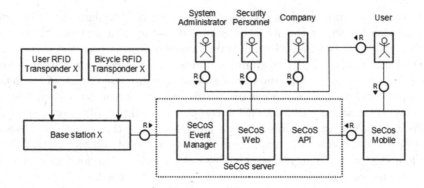

Fig. 2. Diagram of the safe bicycle parking system.

3   Evaluation

First initial tests were performed in April 2015 at the JOANNEUM RESEARCH bicycle parking area with a small group of 20 people. The first tests we encountered some open issues with the communication between the base station and the event manager, but using a RESTful service instead of an SSL socket for communication enabled a stateless communication with the base station which provides us with a more stable and reliable system for the future when the number of base stations grows. After this change the system works stable and is ready for more exhaustive tests. The next step planned for the evaluation is installing the system with more base stations and a few hundred users where more users will test and review the system.

4   Related Work

Early works have already described ways to communicate efficiently with home automation devices [2], but in this work the focus has been put on effortless and hands off operation of the whole system, notwithstanding an initial setup procedure.

Recently, some researchers have proposed an architecture for the Web of Things [3]. The proposed architecture is based on the usage of resource-oriented (REST) principles using HTTP as the application protocol. An HTTP connection is initiated by the client and thus fits the needs of control-oriented applications. However, applications in the Web of Things are often rather monitoring-oriented, which means that connected things will push data to the clients autonomously. Web syndication protocols like Atom have recently been investigated in this context. However, this web of things approach lacks an adequate scalable streaming support.

Complex event processing can also be implemented in a Web of Things platform as is shown in [4]. The paper describes a management system, EcoPark, which is built on combining Event Processing with the EPCGlobal architecture framework. The framework is divided into three parts. The data collection and transmission, in which the RFID sensors collect the data and send it to the system; the application service and event repository, in which the events are handled and transformed into complex events; and the complex sensing event process mechanism, in which the complex events are processed to use in the management platform. Complex event processing can be used in our system design. However, there was no need for such a component in this application.

Related to the event processing on RFID systems, this paper [5] shows a solution for minimizing the impact of out-of-order events on the system. The development of dynamic algorithms that allow the best performance even if there are network problems is the main issue being discussed.

Compared to other Internet of Things platforms [6], our platform fits the general direction other have taken, with the majority employing REST platforms, with only one other platform even utilizing RFID, but without a REST interface, making our platform the first of its kind.

5   Conclusion

As the Web of Things is gaining momentum, creating applications becomes a necessity for facilitating adoption. Our work shows the feasibility of a system in preventing bike thefts. The system is responsive and can alert the bike owner or security personnel to a theft without delay. We have also shown the issues that might come up in an application like this finding and researching new methods to guarantee a secure and reliable system.

Further opportunities for study could be investigations into the desirability of such a system for further applications such as electronic bike identification, providing additional value to businesses that cater to environmentally conscious customers.

References

1. Zeiner, H., Haas, W.: NFC in the K-project secure contactless spheresmart RFID technologies for a connected world. e & i. Elektrotechnik und Informationstechnik **130**(7), 213–217 (2013)
2. Darianian, M., Michael, M.P.: Smart home mobile RFID-based Internet-of-Things systems and servies. In: International Conference on Advanced Computer Theory and Engineering (2008)
3. Guinard, D.: A web of things application architecture-integrating the real-world into the web. Ph.D. thesis. ETH-Zrich., Switzerland (2011)
4. Tseng, C.W., Chang, C.M., Huang, C.H.: Complex sensing event process of IoT application based on EPC global architecture and IEEE 1451. In: 2012 3rd International Conference on the Internet of Things (IOT), pp. 92–98. IEEE, October 2012
5. Mutschler, C., Philippsen, M.: Distributed low-latency out-of-order event processing for high data rate sensor streams. In: Proceedings of 27th International Parallel

and Distributed Processing Symposium, 27th IEEE International Parallel and Distributed Processing Symposium (IPDPS), Boston, Massachusetts, pp. 1133–1144. IEEE Computer Society (2013)

6. Mineraud, J.: A gap analysis of Internet-of-Things platforms. arXiv preprint arXiv:1502.01181 (2015)

CN4IoT

Opportunistic Collaborative Service Networks: The Facilitator for Efficient Data and Services Exchange

Dimosthenis Kyriazis, George Kousiouris, Alexandros Psychas[(✉)],
Andreas Menychtas, and Theodora Varvarigou

National Technical University of Athens, Iroon Polytechniou 9, Athens, Greece
{dimos,gkousiou,alps,ameny}@mail.ntua.gr, dora@telecom.ntua.gr

Abstract. The dynamic rapidly changing and technology-rich digital environment and the market economic constraints shift service provisioning from a pre- and strictly-defined to an on-demand and ad-hoc orientation, where applications depend on dynamic, scarce, distributed resources, which operate at different temporal and spatial scales, have different (potentially conflicting) objectives and are governed under different domains of control. The framework described in this paper aims at enabling the exploitation of all available highly heterogeneous resources (i.e. clouds, communicating objects, sensors and smart devices) by providing a service-based environment that allows for harvesting, dynamically creating and managing these diverse, discrete and distributed resources. Swarms refer to opportunistic service networks, which as new constructs can rapidly emerge in relation either to users and applications requirements or to events and information of great potential for the wider community, coordinated by an open and distributed runtime model.

Keywords: Cloud · IoT · Sensors · Data exchange · Services exchange · Collaborative service networks · Opportunistic service networks · Swarms

1 Introduction

Trends for mobile device market penetration and cities going digital by deploying sensor infrastructures shape a rich and interactive digital environment. According to CISCO [1], during 2008, the number of things connected to the Internet exceeded the number of people on earth and by 2020 there will be 50 billion. Massive scale cloud infrastructures, sensors, intelligent fixed and mobile platforms (e.g. smartphones and tablets) and other network-enabled devices will all need to cooperate and interact to shift efficiency and create value across many sectors [2]. The challenge is for service-based environments to be the enabler for innovation and value creation by supporting the needs of dynamic Future Internet ecosystems and their collaboration models through the exploitation of a combination of technology trends and emerging compute models [3]. The aforementioned ecosystems will be developed and operated on top of the future computing continuum embracing clouds, communicating objects, sensors and smart devices, which will offer the corresponding assets (i.e. resources, services and

© ICST Institute for Computer Sciences, Social Informatics and Telecommunications Engineering 2016
B. Mandler et al. (Eds.) IoT 360° 2015, Part I, LNICST 169, pp. 307–314, 2016.
DOI: 10.1007/978-3-319-47063-4_32

information) by collaborating towards realizing a common goal and providing a common user experience (as also depicted in Fig. 1).

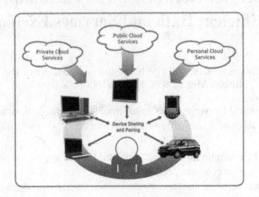

Fig. 1. Intel's view on the Compute Continuum [2]

However, the characteristics of these resources are significantly different to the commoditised and often "infinite" ICT assets offered by cloud infrastructures and some other service platforms today. Real-world resources are often scarce, distributed, governed under different domains of control and incentive schemes, providing unreliable services or information [4]. They are in very large numbers, which makes centralized approaches for their management inefficient [5], while their inherent characteristics and constraints need to be considered by platforms that aim to provide services on top of these resources. Of course it's the community and business structures and behaviours that will exert influence on the organisation of networks with the requirement that services and resources must become increasingly socially and dynamically distributed [6]. The overall goal is to allow for platforms supporting the very large (e.g. clouds) to coexist with platforms supporting the very small (e.g. mobile devices) in loosely coupled dynamic collaborative networks, which as new constructs can rapidly emerge in relation to users and applications requirements (e.g. data sharing in isolated localities such as aircrafts of ships) or when virtual or live events with massive potential generate information of interest for the community (e.g. picture of a football player celebrating a goal score, taken by a spectator sitting in the first row of a football stadium). Such networks can adapt automatically to changing environments, amplifying the collective ability and allowing for the provision of efficient solutions to difficult problems [7]. Nevertheless, their incubation in the Future Internet era faces several challenges.

The rest of the paper is structured as follows: Sect. 2 present the approach taken for the creation of the platform, in Sect. 3 the conceptual architecture is described. A real world application is presented in Sect. 4, while in Sect. 5 the research challenges and technological impact of the proposed approach are analysed. Finally Sect. 6 concludes the paper.

2 Approach

A swarm is a formulated and autonomous opportunistic collaborative service network which consists of voluntary heterogeneous sources that link dynamically and on the fly in order to provide assets (i.e. services, content and resources) to the application and the participants. Swarms are service networks deployed and executed in response to requirements, which may either emerge from application/user requests for services or information, or from opportunities offered in response to data- or event-driven activities. Swarm participants utilize the proposed platform, an open decentralized environment based on a distributed architecture model, in order to achieve the needed levels of logic (abstraction, discovery and participant selection, participation incentives, adaptation, runtime coordination, big data analytics, event identification and delivery patterns) that enable the swarm to perform its functional purpose.

The Platform builds on the notion of Collaborative Networked Organisations [8], which highlights that architecture and governance are influenced by the purpose of networked organisations (see image below Fig. 2).

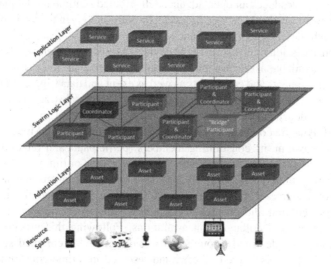

Fig. 2. Platform layers: From resources to collaborative networks

This is important as the platform deals with multiple and aggregated situations of sharing, contributing and co-creating. For "Sharing" a single entity would make assets available. This requires an architecture in which services cater for assets from the single source which may be passed on to many different recipients (services or end-users). For "Contributing" many different entities would make assets available to many recipients. The platform aggregates and collate content from many different sources to be used in many different ways. Ultimately, though, there is also a case where assets from many different sources come together deliberately to form a final, joint output that is "Co-Created".

3 Conceptual Architecture

The platform provides a system and mechanisms that enable the creation, deployment and execution of opportunistic service networks. The platform itself can be seen as a kind of decentralized middleware layer upon which applications are built. This middleware is what we call the swarm logic layer (as depicted in the following Figure) and it allows application service provisioning on top of multiple, diverse, distributed objects, sensors and smart devices. The adaptation layer allows for resources to be exploited both as information or service sources and as processing elements within a swarm. The swarm logic layer enables entities to participate in the service network, as well as management of the established swarm (including processes for monitoring, evaluation, runtime adaptation, etc.). Coordination may be either performed by a swarm entity (based on capacity, location or administration/trust criteria) or be distributed across the participants. Furthermore, participants may be included in swarms, acting as "bridges" so as to develop the required networking topologies that enable participants to be reached within the swarm.

The platform introduces an open advanced distributed runtime model that supports the complete swarm-oriented service lifecycle. Initially and given the available entities, there is a need to describe in a unified and abstract way the features, capabilities, characteristics and accession information of the devices. Moreover, the environment and the corresponding available assets are modelled and analysed with respect to application and system requirements and constraints as well as event and data triggers that may lead to swarm formulation. These requirements are linked to abstract system models described using dependability characterisations, which are used to assess impact in unknown and dynamic contexts for design and runtime operations. Models define the structure of the swarm, its constituting members (participants and relationships) and their roles as well as the swarm characteristics (e.g. location or time).

Furthermore, within this platform are also developed mechanisms that allow for the engagement of resources through approaches to identify, declare and manage different types of social, cultural and economic incentives with respect to service- and data-exchange, financial and collaboration aspirations. Following this process, potential swarm members are identified through real-world knowledge enriched services that allow resources to be discovered, filtered and reserved in a time-constrained way as required by the event- or opportunity- related requirements.

The platform also supports the operation of established swarms through mechanisms to control, influence, monitor and predict ad hoc interactions between swarm members. An open distributed runtime environment for decentralised management and coordination of multiple and diverse devices is developed to overcome inefficiencies of centralized management mechanisms given the number of devices, their locality and the fact that they are governed under different administrative rules and principles. Furthermore, runtime configurable swarm-oriented delivery patterns (e.g. building on top of a P2P concept) are instantiated given that centralized schemes (e.g. server-client) for service delivery is inefficient and in many cases insufficient (e.g. in a stadium with thousands of spectators). Delivery schemes/patterns refer both to the network topologies and communication channels within a swarm and are developed according to application requirements object capabilities and link characteristics. What is more, delivery schemes may affect the swarm formulation since inclusion of a participant as a proxy/bridge may be required to reach a resource. During operation, events are detected and analysed in real-time based on the information being exchanged, triggering actions with respect to resources (e.g. network bandwidth) and services (e.g. frame rate transition rate) provision. The platform provides methods to predict the likelihood of situations based on complex event processing to provide insight into new deployment strategies and the potential future impact of devices contributing to specific swarms (Fig. 3).

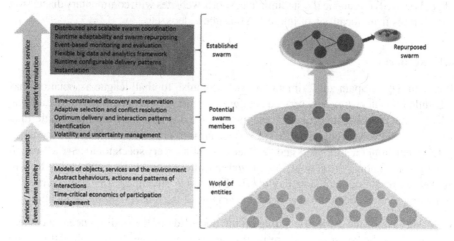

Fig. 3. The swarm formulation process

These tools aim at increasing situational awareness in real-time from information describing dynamic interacting objects based on modelling techniques that can predict the impact of performance and resource consumption under different conditions not known in advance. The platform also delivers mechanisms to handle the amount of structured and unstructured data considering both the location and administrative properties of the resources and the application requirements. Big Data solutions are applied in order to ensure both that the magnitude of data can be stored, retrieved and analysed in an efficient way, and that the object-related information can be utilized during the swarm formulation given that the amount of objects is in the range of millions and the swarm creation must be performed on the fly. Moreover, the techniques used aim at exploiting information out of the data in order to move only the necessary data over the network, thus minimizing redundant or unnecessary network traffic. Considering that valuable assets collected during operation as well as that established collaboration provided added-value, the platform provides mechanisms allowing for network repurposing in order to exploit these assets in new contexts and applications.

4   Applicability to Real World Use Case

This application explores novel ways of enhancing users' multimedia experience, flexible access to interactive and user-centric media and integration of virtual, mixed and augmented realities. The venue is a football stadium with basic IT equipment (e.g. wifi routers, Internet-connected servers, etc.). Furthermore, spectators in the stadium may capture information with their devices (e.g. smart-phones) or consume information and services provided by sources either in the stadium (e.g. infrastructure offering replays of goals scored) or outside the stadium (e.g. sports websites with commentary discussion and pictures from locations of interest, YouTube videos, etc.).

4.1   Scenario

It is Saturday in Spain and Primera Division (Spanish football league association) has scheduled 6 matches. A new service is offered (namely *"ShareYourView"*) by La Liga, which some friends going to watch the match have downloaded from the Google Play website for their Android devices. The service aims to provide an enhanced experience of the event, both for spectators and attendees, enabling every spectator to have a "second screen" for watching the action, *ShareYourView* offers view sharing within the stadium as well as real-time data statistics overlaid on video streaming for the players. The following sections depicts a few typical examples of the *SmartStadium* application:

- Maria (one of the 2 friends) sitting on the north side of the stadium needs a camera view from the south side where the ball is in play and her friends are sitting (she could also obtain the video from other spectators but she does so from her friends since she has added them through the *ShareYourView* application). She opens the application and triggers the request.
- Anastasia (the second friend on the north side) holds a tablet and requests a higher resolution video which can only be offered by a limited number of spectators. Furthermore, Anastasia would like to get players' real-time information overlaid onto the video received from the other side of the stadium. While players' information is offered by the stadium cloud infrastructure, transcoding to enable the overlay cannot be performed in the same infrastructure but only in an external cloud environment.
- A penalty kick is awarded and a spectator sitting just behind the goalposts publishes through the *ShareYourView* application the possibility for others to see his view of the penalty kick. As viewers are now broadcasters, spectators will have access to amateur feeds that capture the authenticity of the live experience, rather than relying on what a director and cameraman focus on More than 10000 spectators express their interest in the specific view, while the view of the penalty kick is also requested by spectators in other locations (i.e. online, in stadiums of other matches). Moreover, advertised entities would like to see the impact of a promotion activity they put in place in all stadiums.

5   Research Challenges and Technological Impact

The proposed solution addresses several research and technical challenges as part of a service-based environment that aims to enable dynamic efficient and reliable service provisioning through the development of collaborative networks exploiting diverse, distributed, remote-located clouds, objects, sensors and devices. Specifically:

- *support opportunistic collaborations* through models of collaborative networks capturing dynamic multi-stakeholder requirements, collaborations classification including abstract behaviours, actions and patterns of interaction, and approaches to manage the economics of participation in order to engage resources, utilize spatial and societal attributes for service optimisation and take actions to encourage the likelihood of contribution to added-value service-based situations;
- *enable efficient and reliable service provision,* through ad-hoc collaborations realizing service networks with optimum delivery schemes and communication patterns to allow for information and service sharing and exchange, while managing uncertainty and creating reliability and dependability from volatile resources;
- *manage heterogeneous device platforms in a decentralized way,* through an event-driven autonomous/self-adaptive coordination of the devices following their role and participation scheme given that control is highly dispersed among the participating entities, and by adapting the collaborative network based on the evaluation of events impact and the anticipated service and information requests; and
- *incorporate scalable data and information management,* through techniques to analyse streaming data from various entities at real-time in order to obtain the potentially valuable knowledge from the information flows, approaches to manage the huge amount of data being generated by various sources, and workload optimized data stores that enable analytics to be performed in a scalable and efficient way (Fig. 4).

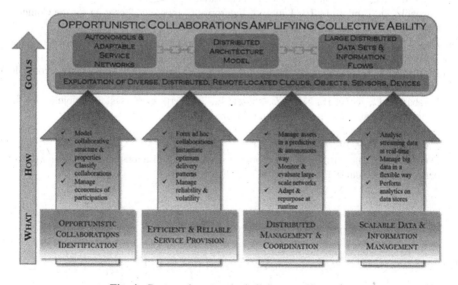

Fig. 4. Proposed approach challenges and impact

6 Conclusions

The dynamic rapidly changing and technology-rich digital environment and the market economic constraints shift service provisioning from a pre- and strictly-defined to an on-demand and ad-hoc orientation, where applications depend on dynamic, scarce, distributed resources, which operate at different temporal and spatial scales.

The presented vision aims at enabling the exploitation of all available highly heterogeneous resources (i.e. clouds, communicating objects, sensors and smart devices) by providing a service-based environment that allows for harvesting, dynamically creating and managing these diverse, discrete and distributed resources. Swarms refer to opportunistic service networks, which as new constructs can rapidly emerge in relation either to users and applications requirements or to events and information of great potential for the wider community, coordinated by an open and distributed runtime model. Time-constrained reservation, adaptive selection, conflict resolution and techniques to consider the volatility and uncertainty need to be developed to enable efficient and reliable service provision, harvest the vast availability of sensors and devices and lead to participatory application schemes of significant societal and economic value.

Acknowledgment. The research leading to these results is partially supported by the European Community's Seventh Framework Programme under grant agreement n609043, in the context of the COSMOS Project.

References

1. CISCO, The Internet of Things, Infographic. http://blogs.cisco.com/news/the-internet-of-things-infographic
2. IPSO Alliance, Smart objects power smart enterprises (2011)
3. Buchholz, D., Dunlop, J.: The Future of Enterprise Computing: Preparing for the Compute Continuum, IT@Intel White Paper, Intel IT (2011)
4. Gupta, A., Kumaraguru, P.: Credibility ranking of tweets during high impact events. In: ACM 1st Workshop on Privacy and Security in Online Social Media (2012)
5. Hofmann, M., Beaumont, L., Kaufmann, M.: Content Networking: Architecture, Protocols, and Practice (2005)
6. Barabási, A.L., Jeong, H., Neda, Z., Ravasz, E., Schubert, A., Vicsek, T.: Evolution of the social network of scientific collaborations. Elsevier Phys. A **311**, 590–641 (2002)
7. Bonabeau, E., Meyer, C.: Swarm intelligence: a whole new way to think about business. Harvard Bus. Rev. **79**, 106–114 (2001)
8. Dutton, W.H.: The wisdom of collaborative network organisations: capturing the value of networked individuals. Prometheus **26**(3), 211–230 (2008)

A Case for Understanding End-to-End Performance of Topic Detection and Tracking Based Big Data Applications in the Cloud

Meisong Wang[1], Rajiv Ranjan[2,5(✉)], Prem Prakash Jayaraman[3],
Peter Strazdins[1], Pete Burnap[4], Omer Rana[4], and Dimitrios Georgakopulos[3]

[1] Australian National University, Canberra, ACT 2601, Australia
dean.wang@gmail.com
[2] Newcastle University, Newcastle Upon Tyne, UK
rranjans@gmail.com
[3] RMIT University, Melbourne 3000, Australia
[4] Cardiff University, Cardiff, UK
[5] CSIRO, Canberra, Australia

Abstract. Big Data is revolutionizing nearly every aspect of our lives ranging from enterprises to consumers, from science to government. On the other hand, cloud computing recently has emerged as the platform that can provide an effective and economical infrastructure for collection and analysis of big data produced by applications such as topic detection and tracking (TDT). The fundamental challenge is how to cost-effectively orchestrate these big data applications such as TDT over existing cloud computing platforms for accomplishing big data analytic tasks while meeting performance Service Level Agreements (SLAs). In this paper a layered performance model for TDT big data analytic applications that take into account big data characteristics, the data and event flow across myriad cloud software and hardware resources. We present some preliminary results of the proposed systems that show its effectiveness as regards to understanding the complex performance dependencies across multiple layers of TDT applications.

Keywords: Cloud computing · Big data · Hadoop map reduce

1 Introduction

Big Data is revolutionizing nearly every aspect of our lives ranging from enterprises to consumers, from science to government. Managing large, heterogeneous and, rapidly increasing volumes of data has long been a challenge. On the other hand, cloud computing [2,13] in recent times has emerged as the platform that can provide an effective and economical infrastructure for collection and analysis of big data produced by data analytics applications such as topic detection and tracking (TDT). TDT applications detect events (such as disease outbreak, sentiments of customers for certain products or movies etc.) by analysing data

© ICST Institute for Computer Sciences, Social Informatics and Telecommunications Engineering 2016
B. Mandler et al. (Eds.) IoT 360° 2015, Part I, LNICST 169, pp. 315–325, 2016.
DOI: 10.1007/978-3-319-47063-4_33

from social media and other online sources. Though big data processing and analytics technologies such as hadoop and mahout have evolved, we still lack orchestration techniques for developing scalable TDT applications in domains such as disease outbreak and sentiment analysis that can elastically scale in response to changing data volume, data velocity, and data variety. Hence, the fundamental challenge is how to cost-effectively orchestrate these TDT applications over cloud-based hardware and software resources for accomplishing big data analytic tasks (e.g. event detection delay) while meeting the new breed of performance Service Level Agreements (SLAs). By the new breed of SLA's we point to the need of future TDT applications that can not be architected to meet the traditional cloud SLA's such as availability and reliability. To the contrary, these new breed of TDT applications need strict SLAs' guarantee on the metrics such as accuracy, precision, and speed of event detection.

To address the above challenges, firstly, it is necessary to establish a taxonomy of performance metrics that can capture the relationship between the applications SLA (e.g., event detection delay, alert generation delay, and alerts sent per second), big data characteristics (e.g. data volume, query rate, and query mix) and resource configuration of the underlying software (e.g., Hadoop, NoSQL, distributed file system, and machine learning library) and hardware (CPU, Storage, and Network). In the literature some performance metric taxonomy and models are available, but they have the following limitations: (i) they target trivial applications (such as "word count") which do not have end-to-end performance management concerns as evident in the complex TDT applications and (ii) most of them are concerned only with the performance modelling the hardware resources while ignoring end-to-end dependencies between the application, software and hardware resource layers. As a consequence, the existing approaches are not appropriate to study the end-to-end performance SLA concerns of the TDT applications. In this vision paper, we propose that a novel, end-to-end taxonomy of performance metrics could be used to develop performance models for studying and analysing the performance SLAs of complex big data applications such as TDT. The novel contributions of this paper include:

- We present a concrete vision statement backed by rigorous analysis of the related work for developing layered and end-to-end performance metric taxonomy for future TDT applications. These performance metrics take into account the data and event flows across multiple software and hardware resource types while considering complex performance dependencies across the layers.
- We present a conceptual architecture for future TDT application which forms the basis for developing the above mentioned performance metrics taxonomy. We also conduct preliminary experimentations for showing the practicality of the proposed approach.

2   Big Data Analytics Application Scenarios

The importance of big data analytics applications such as topic detection [14–17] and tracking has practical values in a variety of fields. Following are some typical application use cases that under take non-real time analysis activities.

1. **Natural Disaster Risk Assessment management application**: By analysing historical data from social media and other sources such as remote sensing satellites and deployed seismic sensors, it is possible to conduct following pre-disaster and post-disaster impact assessment in context of natural disasters such as earthquakes. Historical feeds from social media can be analysed to understand the regions which are most prone to future earthquakes. Such historical feeds can be augmented with crowd sensed data such as high resolution images of public and private infrastructures including buildings, bridges, and roads. These crowd sensed data can be further analysed for pre-assessment of risks and ability of these public and private infrastructures to cope with future earthquakes. The results of such a pre-disaster assessment could be used to evacuate people out of dangerous infrastructures in advance. On the other hand in the post-disaster situations, timely analysis of data from these social media, crowd senses, and other online sources can help rescue teams, medics, and relief workers in planning for future rescue and medical operations.
2. **Traffic pattern analysis application**: By collecting and processing the historical traffic information along with social media feeds, this application can help in meeting the following two goals: Offering the driver the information of the possible traffic congestion; providing advice to the drivers on alternative routes.
3. **Epidemic propagation analysis application**: It is well-known that by carefully analysing the social media feeds related to people's health and well-being could help in learning about past epidemic outbreak. Such data analytic applications can help in improved coordination and deployment of health services.

3   Related Work

The area of performance management of cloud-based big-data processing frameworks have been widely studied. However, understanding and developing an end-to-end performance model of cloud-based big data analytics applications is still in its infancy. In the past several years, Hadoop has been deployed for undertaking batch processing task over large volumes of data (not in real-time). However, most research focus on developing performance model of MapReduce framework only while ignoring the other software and hardware components/resources. In [4] the author describes the complexity of MapReduce (MR) tasks and presents how to model this complexity. Furthermore, the author provides a deep analysis of the working of MapReduce, the interaction and correlation among various steps of MapReduce and the associated costs. The author presents a model to predict the execution time of tasks according to certain cost vectors. The focus of the paper is only on Hadoop more specifically on the MR, HDFS at the IaaS layer. The authors use WordCount, Hive Query Job, and Distributed Pentmino as the usecases for modelling the MapReduce jobs all of whose execution is considerably different from that of analytical machine learning algorithms. *It is well understood that machine learning algorithms generate interactive computations and intermediate data that requires a more concrete formulation of the MR execution strategy.* In [19], the authors focus on the study of tasks assignment issue in Hadoop. The authors prove that the hadoop task assignment process seeking to minimise the total execution time is NP-Complete. However, this paper is completely based on the mathematical formulation of MR and lacks experimental validations in real world cloud environments.

In [5], the authors propose ARIA (Automated Resource Inference and Allocation) framework composed of SLO (Service Level Object) scheduler, slot estimator, job profiler, profile database and slot allocator to address the challenge of resource allocation for MR jobs to meet the required SLOs requirement bound by a job completion deadline. The applications considered include Word count, Sort, Bayesian classification. TF-IDF, WikiTrends and Twitter. Though ARIA address the challenge of estimating performance of application that use machine learning for analysis, it fails to address the following (1) Provide performance insights across each individual cloud layer i.e. IaaS (CPU, Memory, Network) and PaaS (HDFS storage considerations); (2) Employs a simple online greedy algorithm to calculate the *max*, *min* and *mean* of execution time of Map or Reduce tasks to estimate the MR job execution time and (3) Although they employ bayesian classification, the use of it is limited which renders it insufficient to prove that this performance model will be suitable for cloud-based big data analytics systems. In [18] a task scheduling mechanism for runtime performance management of MR framework is proposed. This management scheduler can use two strategies to allocate resources: the *min-scheduler* and the *max-scheduler*. The min-scheduler will give a job minimum resources to meet certain execution time constraint while the max-scheduler will give high priority jobs maximum resources. The proposed model has been evaluated over applications such as word count and table joins using hive. Similarly, in [6], the authors proposed a framework called *MRShare* which can be plugged into any MapReduce system. The *MRShare* is the first framework to analyse the work sharing problem in MapReduce i.e. different jobs might share resources together. A series of experiments were conducted to validate the proposed work sharing approach on Hadoop frameworks (Hadoop HDFS, MapReduce, Hive and Pig) running on Amazon clusters. In [7], the authors proposed a prediction model for MapReduces performance taking into account the I/O congestion and task failure. The authors design a mathematical model to predict the performance of MapReduce, meanwhile they use the Hadoop as the experimental testbed to validate their model. In [8] the author proposes a prediction model based on greedy policy of MapReduce in terms of different configurations (e.g. different MR parameters, different data sizes, different I/O, etc.).

In [9] the authors propose a performance model of Hadoop which describes data flows and cost information. This performance model can be classified into three parts: Map. Reduce and Shuffle. This performance model involves the CPU cost and the I/O cost. In [10], the authors design a model based on historical job execution records adopting locally weighted linear regression (LWLR) technique to predict the execution time of a MapReduce job. Similarly, in [12], the authors propose a performance model of Hadoop. This model takes the network into consideration and proves that network bandwidth plays a vital role in the performance of hadoop system. However, these approach does not provide the metrics required to model the end-to-end performance of big data analytics application. For instance, a ML algorithm like the Naive Bayes classification algorithm will have more than one MapReduce task. Furthermore, some steps (such as serialization, etc.) and relations among different steps (such as parallel or overlap) are not considered in the current performance model presented in the literature. Some of related works also study the performance of MapReduce-based machine learning algorithms complexity. However these focus on the theoretical aspects of the algorithm without any evaluation in real cloud environments to validate the theoretical outcomes [11].

3.1 Summary of Limitations

1. The negligence at the Infrastructure-as-a-Service layer: The influence from the memory has been severely neglected. Most performance models of MapReduce or Hadoop (HDFS and MapReduce) are only related to the CPU and job workload, assuming that memory is a trivial aspect. As a matter of fact, it is the other way around. In actuality, the impact of memory on the speed of processing data in particular in big data TDT application needs to be studied in order to develop an effective performance model (e.g. due to the principal of "Spill" operation in the MapReduce process. The Spill means that the output data would be sent to the memory, and only when the memory is near to be filled (no more memory space for storing the new data), the memory starts transmitting data into storage).

2. The negligence from Platform-as-a-Service layer: Consider the example of Hadoop for processing cloud-based TDT applications. The inaccurate assumption of when the shuffle starts could have a significant impact on the system's performance. Many MapReduce model assume that the shuffle part starts when all the Map tasks have been done. However, it is not always the case. In fact, the shuffle process can start before the end of map process by tuning certain performance parameter or metric. Moreover, many models make a simple assumption to determine the number of mapper based only on the size of input data. However, the number of map tasks is mainly controlled by three parameters which are dfs.block.size, mapred.map.tasks and mapred.min.split.size. Hence, determining the number of mapper is a complex task. Finally, at the application layer such as Mahout machine learning component, there is a clear gap in the existent research with respect to performance modelling. We believe, modelling the end-to-end performance of a TDT application involving machine learning components such as Mahout using only MapReduce performance metrics is not accurate. Our preliminary results validate our proposition.

3. Lack of understanding about the dependencies of each software and hardware resources across TDT stack: Considering the Hadoop MapReduce framework,

the relation between components across layer such as memory, the order of processing the data i.e. sequential or MapReduce and the parameters governing the machine learning component (such as Mahout) needs to be analysed and studied to determine the impact they have on each other's performance. This will help in developing a more concrete and accurate end-to-end performance model.

4   End-to-End Performance Modeling of Cloud-Based Big Data Analytics Applications: Our Vision

4.1   Conceptual Architecture

As new TDT applications start to emerge, there is a need for processing high volume, velocity and heterogeneous variety of data (big data characteristics). We need to develop novel application architecture that builds upon the recent progress made in the domain of cloud datacentres offering hardware resources (CPU, Storage, and Network) and big data processing technologies (e.g. Hadoop, Mahout, S4, Spark, NoSQL, etc.) offering software-based application programming abstractions and operations. To this end, we present the conceptual architecture of such a TDT application in Fig. 1. The conceptual architecture consist of three layers including Software as a Service (SaaS), Platform as a Service (PaaS) and Infrastructure as a Service (IaaS). SaaS represents the TDT application, PaaS includes the big data processing technologies or software resources, and IaaS has the cloud datacentre hosted hardware resources.

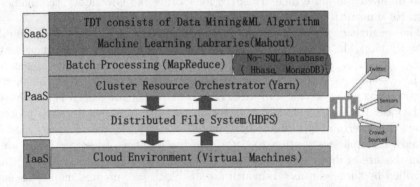

Fig. 1. The conceptual architecture of big data analytics application

4.2   Performance Metric Selection: Preliminary Exploration

Table 1 lists the various high-level parameters that we consider at each layer to build the proposed end-to-end TDT-based big data application performance model. These parameters have been developed taking into consideration the

Table 1. Big data analytics application (TDT) performance metrics for each layer

Layer		Metric
SaaS		Precision and Recall
PaaS	MapReduce	Number of Map tasks, Number of Reduce tasks, the total size of input data, the size of splitting data, the scheduling mechanism, the format of file
	HDFS	The architecture of HDFS like the number of Datanodes, the resources possessed by each node (Namenode and Datanode), the replication number
IaaS		CPU utilization, Memory utilization, Network Bandwidth

conceptual architecture presented in Fig. 1 typical cloud-based batch processing system such as Hadoop.

In the SaaS layer, recall and precision will be impacted considerably due to the different types of data mining algorithms adopted and the variation in data. E.g. considering the naive bayes algorithm, the training part is implemented using four MapReduce steps. However, the testing process consist of only one MapReduce job called *BayesClassifierDriver*. The PaaS layer for the frameworks such as Hadoop has two software components, namely, MapReduce and HDFS. For the MapReduce operation, we will use the number of maps and reducers, the total size of input data, the size of splitting data, the scheduling mechanism (there are three popular kinds of scheduling algorithms which are FIFO - First in First Out, capacity and fair), and file format. For HDFS, we are mainly concerned with the architecture of HDFS. The different architectures of HDFS lead to changes in data storage efficiency that influence the number of replications and storage locations. Another important factor at the HDFS layer is the block size. The block size will directly affect the number of mappers. At the IaaS layer, we consider configurations [20] of CPU, memory and network. The number of CPUs on the shared cluster and the speed of each CPU core has significant impact on the modelling the execution time. Further, memory also plays a pivotal role in determining the execution speed.

5   Preliminary Experimental Outcomes

In this section, we present preliminary experimental trials conducted to validate and verify the correctness of the identified metrics at each layer. The evaluation was conducted using Hadoop 2.4.1 and Mahout 1.0 systems. The performance metric configurations of these system are presented in the Table 2.

In order to validate and verify the identified parameter's influence on various hardware and software components across the layers of a TDT application, we conducted 4 preliminary experiments. Our input dataset is a collection of Tweets related to Flu collected by COSMOS project (www.cs.cf.ac.uk/cosmos/) at Cardiff University. We employ the Naive bayes classification technique to match tweets to topics i.e. *"related to FLU"* and *"not related to flu"*.

Table 2. Experiment test bed configuration

Node	Configuration
Master Node	4 Intel(R) Core(TM) CPU T7700 2.40 GHz 8 GB 10 GB Ubuntu 14
Name Node 1	4 2 Intel(R) Core(TM) CPU T7700 2.40 GHz 4 GB 10 GB Ubuntu 14
Name Node 2	2 Intel(R) Core(TM) CPU T7700 2.40 GHz 4 GB 10 GB Ubuntu 14

In our experiments, we extended the naive bayes implementation provided by the Apache Mahout (mahout.apache.org). Apache Mahout is a scalable machine learning library built on Hadoop Map Reduce framework.

5.1 Experiment 1: Influence of Data Size

In this experiment, we fix the hadoop cluster configuration, while changing the volumes of input Tweet data. We compute and measure the execution time for the following operations (1) converting tweet data into vectors (a requirement for Mahout to process the data) to be consumed by the naive bayes algorithm and (2) training the data for naive bayes classification. The result of this experiment is shown in Table 3.

Table 3. Experiment 1: influence of data size

Data size	Operation	Execution time
0.316 GB	Text vectorisation	4.025 min
	Naive Bayes training	1.444 min
78.34 MB	Text vectorisation	3.98 min
	Naive Bayes training	1.4077 min

5.2 Experiment 2: Changing Hadoop Map Reduce Configuration

Secondly, we conduct experiments with 0.316 GB data keeping the CPU configuration fixed (shown in Table 2) while changing the numbers of mappers and reducers. The result is shown in Table 4 dealing with the execution time of training model.

5.3 Experiment 3: Changing Hadoop Map Reduce Configuration

In this experiment, we use 2 different machine learning algorithms namely the Naive Bayes and C Naive Bayes. The data size used for the experiment is 0.316 GB. The hadoop map reduce layer is configured with 1 mapper and 1 reducer. Table 5 shows the values for Precision and Recall.

Table 4. Experiment 2: changing MR configuration

Mappers	Reducers	Execution time
1	1	1.441 min
2	1	1.219 min
3	3	1.433 min

Table 5. Experiment 3: different machine learning algorithms

Algorithm	Precision	Recall
C-Bayes	59.22 %	61.08 %
Naive-Bayes	57.20 %	60.40 %

Table 6. Experiment 4: changing VM configuration

VM Configuration	Execution time
MapMemory: 1600 Mb; ReduceMemory: 3072 Mb; SortMemory: 512 Mb	1.3328 min
MapMemory: 512 Mb; ReduceMemory: 1024 Mb; SortMemory: 286 Mb	1.4441 min

5.4 Experiment 4: Changing CPU (VM) Configuration

In this experiment, we use 2 different VM configurations for hadoop name and data nodes. The data size used for the experiment is 0.316GB. The hadoop map reduce layer is configured with 1 mapper and 1 reducer and the Mahout layer runs the C-Bayes algorithm. Table 6 shows the outcome of this experiment.

5.5 Experimentation Summary

The experimental outcomes verify the interdependencies between the various components of a big data analytics system across each layer of the cloud and their impact on system's performance. In particular, results of experiment 2 further validates our vision in developing an end-to-end performance model as with more mapper and reduces, the system's performance degraded for an identical dataset and machine learning algorithm.

6 Conclusion

In this paper, we presented our vision and challenges of designing of a generic TDT application (that has non real-time data analytics requirement) based on integrating hardware (CPU, Storage, and Network) and software (batch processing system, NoSQL system, Machine Learning system) resources. We further considered and analysed the new performance challenges arising in such TDT applications due to integration of multiple resource types and processing of heterogeneous data flows. Next, we developed taxonomy of performance metrics relevant to hardware and resource types. Finally, we conducted small scale experiment based on real-world implementation to study the performance of flu detection TDT application based on varying workload and resource configurations.

In the future work, we will extend our conceptual architecture and performance metric taxonomy to include real-time processing requirements. At the same time we will work on generalizing our taxonomy to include the features of other classes of big data systems such as Apache Spark, and Apache SAMOA (online machine learning library).

References

1. Lara Yejas, O.D., Zhuang, W., Pannu, A.: Big R: large-scale analytics on hadoop using R. In: IEEE International Congress on Big Data (BigData Congress), 27 June-2 July, pp. 570–577 (2014)
2. Yang, X., Sun, J.: An analytical performance model of MapReduce. In: IEEE International Conference on Cloud Computing and Intelligence Systems (CCIS), 15–17 September, pp. 306–310 (2011)
3. Costa, F., Silva, L., Dahlin, M.: Volunteer cloud computing: MapReduce over the Internet. In: 2011 IEEE International Symposium on Parallel and Distributed Processing Workshops and Phd Forum (IPDPSW), 16–20 May, pp. 1855–1862 (2011)
4. Lin, X., Meng, Z., Xu, C., Wang, M.: A practical performance model for Hadoop MapReduce. In: IEEE International Conference on Cluster Computing Workshops (CLUSTER WORKSHOPS), pp. 231–239 (2012)
5. Verma, A., Cherkasova, L., Campbell, R.H.: ARIA: automatic resource inference and allocation for mapreduce environments. In: Proceedings of the 8th ACM International Conference on Autonomic Computing (ICAC 2011), pp. 235–244. ACM, New York (2011)
6. Nykiel, T., Potamias, M., Mishra, C., Kollios, G., Koudas, N.: MRShare: sharing across multiple queries in MapReduce. Proc. VLDB Endow. **3**(1–2), 494–505 (2010)
7. Cui, X., Lin, X., Hu, C., Zhang, R., Wang, C.: Modeling the Performance of MapReduce under resource contentions and task failures. In: 2013 IEEE 5th International Conference on Cloud Computing Technology and Science (CloudCom), 2–5 December 2013, vol. 1, pp. 158–163 (2013)
8. Xu, L.: MapReduce framework optimization via performance modeling. In: 2012 IEEE 26th International Parallel and Distributed Processing Symposium Workshops & PhD Forum (IPDPSW), 21–25 May, pp. 2506–2509 (2012)
9. Herodotou, H.: Hadoop performance models. Technical report, CS-2011-05, Computer Science Department, Duke University
10. Khan, M., Jin, Y., Li, M., Xiang, Y., Jiang, C.: Hadoop performance modeling for job estimation and resource provisioning. IEEE Trans. Parallel Distrib. Syst. **27**, 441 (2015)
11. Tamano, H., Nakadai, S., Araki, T.: Optimizing multiple machine learning jobs on MapReduce. In: IEEE Third International Conference on Cloud Computing Technology and Science (CloudCom), 29 November–1 December, pp. 59–66 (2011)

12. Han, J., Ishii, M., Makino, H.: A Hadoop performance model for multi-rack clusters. In: 2013 5th International Conference on Computer Science and Information Technology (CSIT), 27–28 March, pp. 265–274 (2013)
13. Alhamazani, K., Ranjan, R., Mitra, K., Jayaraman, P.P., Huang, Z., Wang, L., Rabhi, F.: CLAMS: cross-layer multi-cloud application monitoring-as-a-service framework. In: IEEE International Conference on Services Computing (SCC), 27 June–2 July, pp. 283–290 (2014)
14. Liu, B., Blasch, E., Chen, Y., Shen, D., Chen, G.: Scalable sentiment classification for big data analysis using Nave Bayes classifier. In: 2013 IEEE International Conference on Big Data, 6–9 October, pp. 99–104 (2013)
15. Amayri, O., Bouguila, N.: Online news topic detection and tracking via localized feature selection. In: The 2013 International Joint Conference on Neural Networks (IJCNN), 4–9 August, pp. 1–8 (2013)
16. Huang, J., Zhao, H., Zhang, J.: Detecting flu transmission by social sensor in China. In: 2013 IEEE and Internet of Things (iThings/CPSCom), IEEE International Conference on Green Computing and Communications (GreenCom), and IEEE Cyber, Physical and Social Computing, 20–23 August, pp. 1242–1247 (2013)
17. Wu, Z., Liao, J., Zhang, L.: Predicting on retweeting of hot topic tweets in microblog. In: 2013 5th IEEE International Conference on Broadband Network & Multimedia Technology (IC-BNMT), 17–19 November, pp. 119–123 (2013)
18. Berliska, J., Drozdowski, M.: Scheduling divisible MapReduce computations. J. Parallel Distrib. Comput. **71**(3), 450–459 (2011). doi:10.1016/j.jpdc.2010.12.004
19. Fischer, M.J., Su, X., Yin, Y.: Assigning tasks for efficiency in Hadoop: extended abstract. In: Proceedings of the Twenty-Second Annual ACM Symposium on Parallelism in Algorithms and Architectures (SPAA 2010), pp. 30–39. ACM, New York (2010)
20. Zhang, M., Ranjan, R., Nepal, S., Menzel, M., Haller, A.: A declarative recommender system for cloud infrastructure services selection. In: Vanmechelen, K., Altmann, J., Rana, O.F. (eds.) GECON 2012. LNCS, vol. 7714, pp. 102–113. Springer, Heidelberg (2012). doi:10.1007/978-3-642-35194-5_8

On Security SLA-Based Monitoring as a Service

Dana Petcu[1,2(✉)], Silviu Panica[1,2], Bogdan Irimie[1,2], and Georgiana Macariu[1]

[1] Institute e-Austria Timişoara, Timişoara, Romania
petcu@info.uvt.ro
[2] West University of Timişoara, Timişoara, Romania

Abstract. Client-driven monitoring of security service level agreements is not available nowadays in the market of Cloud services. Supposing that security obligations associated with a service will be available soon in the service level agreements, we designed such a monitoring service that can be deployed on Cloud provider premises or as external service. It is a stand-alone component of a larger system that allows the negotiation of service level agreements and their enforcement. The concepts, design and architecture of the proof-of-concept service are presented in this paper.

Keywords: Cloud · Security · SLA · Monitoring

1 Introduction

Resources deployed in a cloud environment grow day by day as companies and governments move from on premises model to the Cloud. Moving to the Cloud implies less responsibilities for the client as the Cloud provider manages different aspects of the infrastructure [1]. However, monitoring responsibilities should not be delegated completely to the Cloud provider, and monitoring from the user perspective should be implemented. The monitoring tools should allow clients to check that the quality of services they agreed with the Cloud provider is maintained. They can provide insights on the security of the system through the specification by the client of security parameters of interest. Such parameters can be the status of the ports or the services running on a specific host.

Client-driven security monitoring in Cloud environments is laging behind other client-driven operational monitoring, like performance monitoring. This fact is sustained by the absence of security obligations associated with a service in current service level agreements (SLAs), hindering the Cloud providers capacity to offer trustworthy services [2]. Currently, the only service aspect included in SLAs is service availability [3]. However, cloud services provider contracts are expected to provide soon detailed and substantial security SLAs [4,5].

In this context, we are interested to provide an open-source SLA-based Cloud security monitoring system that can act as Monitoring-as-a-service. It is deployed together with a customer application on a Cloud provider premises providing infrastructure-as-a-services (IaaSs), resides on the Cloud provider resources, or is offered on third party premises. The role of such an SLA-based Cloud security

© ICST Institute for Computer Sciences, Social Informatics and Telecommunications Engineering 2016
B. Mandler et al. (Eds.) IoT 360° 2015, Part I, LNICST 169, pp. 326–336, 2016.
DOI: 10.1007/978-3-319-47063-4_34

Table 1. Challenges, barriers, models, metrics

Category	Short description
Challenges	Mapping between low-level metrics and application-based SLA parameters
	Ability to monitor SLA parameters to multiple Cloud layers (IaaS, PaaS)
	Uncertainty of Cloud environments in event observation (rate of probes)
	Cloud agnosticism (tightly coupling of monitoring tools to the services)
	Big data security is time consuming, instant reaction difficult to achieve
Barriers	Security SLAs are not in place
	Privacy laws that are restricting instant monitoring by Cloud providers
	Security metrics are still vagues
	Virtualization makes monitoring harder
	The ability to monitor services is considered a security risk
Models	Multi-layer model (facility, network, hardware, OS, middleware, appl, user)
	Cloud security control domains (application, interfaces, identity, access etc.)
Metrics	Cloud service measure &metric (scenarios, measure, metric, measurement)
	Service measurement index (category Security and Privacy)
	Security indicators (e.g. rate of compliance with a catalogue of criteria)
	Cloud security properties (core elements: identifier, definition, attributes)
	Security parameters for monitoring (incident, data, change, log, isolation, etc.)

monitoring service in a larger framework, named SPECS, was exposed in [6]: a security SLA (Sec-SLA) that is negotiated with a IaaS provider will be monitored for compliance and alerts will be generated in case of security changes or in case of Sec-SLA violations (leading to its enforcement).

We identified recently in [7] the challenges, barriers, models and metrics for building a SLA-based Cloud security monitoring system. Table 1 summarizes our conclusions. Other opinions related to the challenges of security monitoring in Cloud environment are presented in [8].

In this paper we present the core and support services of the proposed service. The next section is referring to related work and our motivation. The third section is dedicated to core services, while the fourth to support services. The last section is dedicated to conclusions.

2   Related Work

Analyzing the reports about the academic prototypes or commercial services that are available for SLA monitoring or security monitoring in Clouds, we identified in [9] the fact that there is no report until date of an Sec-SLA based Cloud monitoring service. We mention here only few of the monitoring tools that were identified. There are several open-source SLA-oriented Cloud monitoring tools like CloudCompas (available on github.com), or Everest/SLA@SOI (on sourceforge.net), as well as open-source Cloud security monitoring tools like Snorby (on github.com). Commercial Cloud monitoring tools are many, e.g. SLA-oriented ones from nimsoft.com or site24x7.com, or security-oriented ones from ciphercloud.com, cloudflare.com, cloudpassage.com, splunk.com or threatstack.com. Often Cloud monitoring tools are relying upon the services of open-source general monitoring tools, like collectl, Ganglia, Nagios (all three on sourceforge) or MonALISA (monalisa.caltech.edu). A comprehensive study of the Cloud monitoring systems is available in [10].

Security parameters for monitoring systems were classified in [11,12], along with methods and techniques for measuring parameters in practice. Thresholds were established also to indicate when to trigger an event. However, security indicators (observable characteristic that correlates with a desired security property) were not provided. To overcome this problem, a step forward was made in [13] by providing an attribute-based security property vocabulary (security properties in abstract terms and as a properties with a set of defined attributes).

Cloud security monitoring is currently done on-premises, on the monitored infrastructure, or via a SaaS. In the case of monitoring on-premises, a security tool is able to make use of specific APIs as well as to collect logs from Cloud services. In the second case, of monitored IaaS, a security tool is loaded directly into an IaaS (no high bandwidth requirement, possible some high storage costs). In the third case, monitoring data is obtained from the Cloud service (if available), and hand it to a managed security service provider. We are interested to offer a deployable service that supports client-driven monitoring and can be mapped to all three cases.

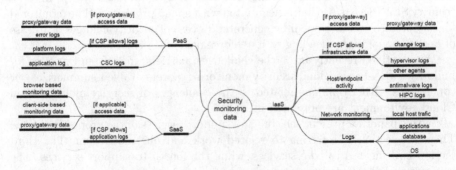

Fig. 1. Security monitoring data

We proposed recently in [14] a taxonomy for the SLA-based monitoring of cloud security. We reproduce here in Fig. 1 the class related to security monitoring data. Note that monitoring specific utilities for collecting information about security are referring to software vulnerabilities or bugs (OS/middleware layer), IDS or firewalls (network), authentication systems or surveillance (facility), workload, voltage or temperature, memory or CPU (hardware).

3 SPECS Monitoring

Monitoring is highly important for SPECS framework. The features offered by its platform(-as-a-service) rely on the information processed by the monitoring module (whether we are talking about to overall platform functional process or about the end-users SLAs that need to be fulfilled).

Monitoring as a Module in the SPECS Framework. The SPECS monitoring module addresses the problem of using monitoring for the fulfillment of security-related user requirements. It enables the users to continuously keep an eye on their applications with respect to certain security properties that might be of interest to them. The module monitors the resources and services and notifies events considered of relevance (according the SLAs) to an enforcement module. The module integrates existing and custom monitoring tools/agents to gather information on SLO metrics, in order to help the enforcement module to detect possible alerts and violations.

Once signed a SLA enters the observed state in which dedicated monitoring agents keep collecting information with regards to the execution of the negotiated services, continuously checking in that way the fulfillment of the specified service level objectives (SLOs). The module focuses on SLO metrics, i.e. the measurable part of the SLAs. This assumption keeps the monitoring and enforcement (diagnosis) functionalities separated, and improve the scalability of the approach in presence of a large number of SLAs to follow. We assume the existence of a monitoring services repository that contains a static mapping between possible SLO metrics and available monitoring components able to gather data on those metrics. An enforcement planning component performs a lookup in such repository to retrieve the monitoring services to activate. Such services are then deployed, configured and activated by an enforcement implementation component. The configuration of the monitoring systems includes setting proper thresholds, intervals and values for the related SLO metrics according to what has been specified in the SLA. The activation of the monitoring components is carried out by a platform functionality (see next section).

Monitoring Workflow. The module deals with large amount of information that needs to be collected, filtered or routed to other components. The monitoring data volume depends on the number of metrics that need to be monitored together and the number of users the platform need to deal with.

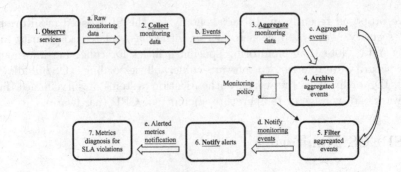

Fig. 2. Simplified monitoring workflow

The monitoring workflow include the following tasks (described in Fig. 2):

observe and collect: the targeted services are continuously monitored and specific data is collected directly from the services log files; this data is then sent to the core monitoring infrastructure from where it is routed to dedicated components that need to analyze the data;

aggregate: the monitoring information is used to compute some statistic data regarding different targeted service behaviour; this aggregation is made based on predefined or dynamically defined aggregation rules described in monitoring policies that are continuously updated during the platform runtime;

filter: the monitoring data received from the targeted services is filtered and routed to specialized services that needs the data to analyze;

archive: all the monitoring data is archived for later use, for example in case of historical statistical computation of some defined metrics;

notify: send out external notifications in case of broken filtering rules set for the monitored metrics.

The monitoring data is split into two types: the *raw monitoring data*, collected by the monitoring adapters from the targeted services and *monitoring events*, the data that is send through the monitoring infrastructure. The raw monitoring data collected by the monitoring adapters is mapped into a standard message called the event format. The event format uses a simple but general structure (Table 2) in order to allow any type of raw monitored data to be mapped. In this way the monitoring core services are independent from the platform and can be reused while not being tied up to a specific set of services that can be monitored.

Core Services. The components of the SPECS monitoring core services are:

Event Archiver: aims to retain all the monitoring data for a defined period of time for later data preprocessing;

Event Aggregator: is responsible with point-in-time observations, transformations of events by showing the global status of the monitored system;

Table 2. Monitoring event format

Field	Description
component	Identifier of the component instance generating the event (i.e., a VM)
object	Hierarchical string pointing event source that generated the event
labels	Hierarchical string that provides a way to give a context to the event
type	Hierarchical string representing the type of event
data	Concrete information specific for each type of event
timestamp	Time of the event, in seconds
token	(optional) Used by some monitoring component for a specific purpose

Event Hub: acts as a router between the monitoring adapters and the other monitoring components; it uses filters to route the monitoring data among the components;

Monitoring Adapter: collects the raw data from the targeted services and sends out the data to the monitoring core in form of monitoring events;

Monitoring Policy Filter: filters the aggregated events and searches for possible violation or alerts of the monitored metrics;

SLO Metrics Exporter: notifies the others platform components in case of violations or alerts set for the monitored metrics.

The Event Hub receives the events collected by the various Monitoring Adapters and routes them towards the Event Aggregator, Event Archiver and the Monitoring Policy Filter (Fig. 3). There are several important sub-components. A HTTP Mux implements an HTTP interface through which the Monitoring Adapters publish events to the Event Hub and clients like the MoniPoli Filter can receive desired events. A Router Multi-Decoder, which accepts as input events

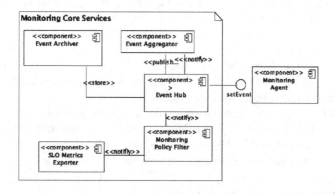

Fig. 3. SPECS monitoring core services architecture

and transforms them into a format which can be handled by the Mozilla Heka[1] stream processing and routing system, used internally by the Event Hub. A Router Multi-Encoder encodes the Hub's internal messages back as events, represented in the platform's internal format (Table 2). A Router Output, together with the HTTP Mux sub-component, streams events to all interested parties. An Archive Output call the Event Archiver in order to store routed events. A Heka Router forwards internal messages to any filter of the Event Hub and to the Router Output and Archive Output sub-components. A Router Input uses the Router Multi-Decoder for decoding received events and delivers the decoded internal messages to the Heka router. Sieve Filters group events based on information contained in them. For example, one may define a filter for grouping all events related to CloudWatch[2] and use this in order to stream all these events to the MoniPoli Filter.

The Event Aggregator consumes events and pushes out the data back into the Event Hub for further consumption. Based on various aggregation rules, it aggregates the events. To fulfill the usual statistical measurements (like min, max, average, standard deviation, etc.) a basic aggregator implementation is currently implemented. More sophisticated, implementations could be implemented to support more complex measurements like identifying trends through various methods like statistical or neural networks. At runtime there can be multiple instances of the same event aggregator implementation, with different aggregation rules, especially for scalability purposes.

The Monitoring Policy Filter has three main components. The Event Filter registers itself to the Event Hub to receive all the stream of events labeled with the security metric labels reported in the corresponding label attribute of the policy. The MoniPoli Rule Filter applies the rule at runtime and export them, through the MoniPoli Output interface. The MoniPoli Rule generator accepts as input a new SLAs and generates new rules, according to the algorithms proposed in the MoniPoli section, communicating them to the MoniPoli Rule Filter.

The Event Archiver retains the monitoring data and events for a defined period of time (when an SLA finished its execution or it is terminated then all the associated archived monitoring data and events are disposed). The communication interface is based on a REST API that supports PUT, GET and DELETE actions (store data and events; retrieves the data from the archiver database at query like event attribute and a time interval; erases the data from the database on query); operation handlers are the actual functions that perform a specific operation. A request pool handles multiple requests that need to be routed to specific internal handlers. A distributed object-store database is used for storing the monitoring data and events.

The SLOM Exported receives only the monitoring events that should be notified. MoniPoli Filter makes the selection of the events and forwards them to the SLOM Exporter. The Exporter generates an XML representation of the monitoring event, made in agreement with the SLA XML framework. It uses the

---

[1] https://github.com/mozilla-services/heka.
[2] https://aws.amazon.com/cloudwatch/.

SPECS's SLA Platform API in order to notify the event, in the right format to the enforcement module.

The Monitoring Adapter sends out the events to the Event Hub and receives data from Monitoring Agents. The format of this data depend on the type of agent, and the data is transformed by the Monitoring Adapter into the platform internal format to represent events that are finally sent to the Event Hub.

Monitoring Agents. Two agents were tested in SPECS context: OpenVAS, a vulnerability scanner and Nmap, a network security scanner. Three others are on the list for the next integration steps, to prove the concepts feasibility: OSSEC, a host intrusion detection and prevention system, Snort, a network intrusion detection system, and Monit, a general purpose monitoring tool[3]. Security metrics that can be monitored by Nmap, for example, are status of ports, service version, guess OS, time since last restart, ciphers used by TLS Ciphers used by servers that offer TLS.

We proposed in [16] a monitoring system (agent in SPECS context, despite the agent-less internal architecture) based on Nmap that allows to execute multiple Nmap instances at the same time to provide efficiency and fault tolerance. As number and type of resources that should be monitored can quickly become very large, a monitoring system should be scalable, provide small overhead and fault tolerance. The tests performed on Google Compute Engine premises showed the scalability of the proposed system. The event message mentioned in Table 2 includes in this case, as component, the UUID of the component that creates the message, as object, nmap, as labels, client id and job id, as type, metric, as data, Nmap results after they have been processed, and as timestamp, the time when the event message was created.

4   SPECS Enabling Platform

The Enabling Platform creates the execution environment for the SPECS' platform that hosts the SLA services. This component is a bootstrap service that transforms a standard resource (e.g. a Cloud virtual machine, a VM, with an Linux OS) into an execution environment ready to host other resources. The other resources have some special requirements in terms of local libraries or software packages and services or to remote resources to interact with. The Enabling Platform solves this issue and it is also able to acquire the compute resources, from various Cloud providers, where the SPECS Platform is hosted.

The Enabling Platform consists of several core components (Fig. 4):

– *resource allocator*, a standalone service able to acquire resources from the cloud providers based on a resource descriptor document where the end-user specifies the requirements and constraints for platform deployment;

---

[3] OpenVas: openvas.org; NMAP: nmap.org; OSSEC: ossec.net; Snort: snort.org; Monit: mmonit.com/monit/.

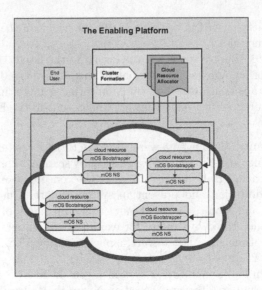

Fig. 4. Enabling platform architecture

– *cluster formation service*, an orchestrator service able to manage the resources scheduling based on the definition given by the end-user (resource descriptor);
– *mOS node bootstrapper*, a simple and autonomous resource clustering solution that transform a standard operating system into a specialized environment that is able to host the platform resources (mOS stands for multi-purpose OS); it uses Chef service-client architecture for package deployment;
– *mOS naming service*, a distributed resource management service able to offer resource management features like resource registration and retrieval in a heterogeneous distributed system.

We focus here on cluster formation service, mOS bootstrapper and naming service (NS), as having the particular ability (not yet encountered in literature) to transform a set of simple Cloud resources (acquired by the resource allocator) into an execution environment ready to host complex applications and services.

The cluster formation service takes a resource descriptor from the user or a third party service and tries to interpret it. The result is a bootstrap configuration that contains, among others, the number of resources that need to be acquired and for each resource a bootstrap plan that mOS node bootstrapper needs to apply on the acquired Cloud resources. The latest is a package that is deployed on the target VM, as a system service that will transform the VM, based on the bootstrap plan, into an execution environment that will host the target platform. It relies on Chef[4] technology for package deployment and on mOS NS for distributed resource identification. Chef server-client architecture is complex to configure in an unattended manner as it implies a lot of security

---

[4] www.chef.io.

and resource information to be exchanged between the clients and the server. Using the mOS NS service the clients can automatically find the Chef server contact information (like IP address, chef services ports and registration URLs used by the clients to get registered in the Chef server database). When the Chef cluster is setup the mOS node bootstrapper will tell to the Chef server to apply deployment plan on each client based on the initial implementation plan.

mOS naming service is a distributed resource management service that uses a distributed system as an engine based on Paxos algorithm described in [15]. The package is started on each targeted node and the distributed system will be automatically be created based on standard network discovery protocols (multicast or broadcast). When the nodes are synchronised they can start exchange and store information. Each time a Chef client will install a service a trigger is activated and mOS NS client will register the service together with some additional information (IP address, port number or other distinctive information) required for resource discovery. On the other hand when a node needs a specific resource to consume it will query the service to find out if such a service is already registered and what are the details of it. In this way the Chef server-client architecture can be deployed unattended and further the entire platform as well in the same manner. The naming service can be also used by any other resource that needs to store or retrieve other resource information because it offers a standard communication interface (REST).

5 Conclusions

The motivation, the concepts and implementation of a SLA-based Cloud security monitoring system were exposed in this paper. Special particularities are its modularity and ability to integrate external security scanners. The proposed software prototype is a proof of the fact that a interoperability layer can be used in Cloud security monitoring to interconnect various existing tools. The presentation focused on the component design and we neglected the description of the entire SPECS framework which can be found in previous reports.

Acknowledgments. This work is partially supported by the European Commission under grant agreement FP7-610795 (SPECS). We thank also Ciprian Crăciun for his consistent contributions to the design of the core services.

References

1. Spring, J.: Monitoring cloud computing by layer, Part 1. IEEE Secur. Priv. 9(2), 66–68 (2011)
2. Bernsmed, K., Jaatun, M.G., Meland, P.H., Undheim, A.: Security SLAs for federated cloud services. In: 6th ARES, pp. 202–209 (2011)
3. Ouedraogo, M., Mignon, S., Cholez, H., Furnel, S., Dubois, E.: Security transparency: the next frontier for security research in the cloud. J. Cloud Comput. Adv. Syst. Appl. 4(12), 1–14 (2015). doi:10.1186/s13677-015-0037-5

4. Wagner, R., Heiser, J., Perkins, E., Nicolett, M., Kavanagh, K.M., Chuvakin, A., Young, G.: Predicts 2013: cloud and services security. Technical report, Gartner ID:G00245775 (2012)

5. Casola, V., De Benedictis, A., Rak, M.: On the adoption of security SLAs in the cloud. In: Felici, M., Fernández-Gago, C. (eds.) A4Cloud 2014. LNCS, vol. 8937, pp. 45–62. Springer, Heidelberg (2015). doi:10.1007/978-3-319-17199-9_2

6. Rak, M., Luna, J., Petcu, D., Casola, V., Suri, N., Villano, U.: Security as a service using an SLA-based approach via SPECS. In: CloudCom 2013, pp. 1–6 (2013)

7. Petcu, D.: SLA-based cloud security monitoring: challenges, barriers, models and methods. In: Lopes, L., et al. (eds.) Euro-Par 2014, Part I. LNCS, vol. 8805, pp. 359–370. Springer, Heidelberg (2014). doi:10.1007/978-3-319-14325-5_31

8. Mazhar, A., Khan, S.U., Vasilakos, A.V.: Security in cloud computing: opportunities and challenges. Inf. Sci. **305**, 357–383 (2015)

9. Petcu, D., Craciun, C.: Towards a security SLA-based cloud monitoring service. In: 4th CLOSER, pp. 598–603 (2014)

10. Aceto, G., Botta, A., De Donato, W., Pescape, A.: Cloud monitoring: a survey. Comput. Netw. **57**(9), 2093–2115 (2013)

11. Hogben, G., Dekker, M.: Procure secure: a guide to monitoring of security service levels in cloud contracts. Technical report, ENISA (2012)

12. Rahulamathavan, Y., Pawar, P. S., Burnap, P., Rajarajan, M., Rana, O.F., Spanoudakis, G. Analysing security requirements in cloud-based service level agreements. In: 7th SIN, pp. 73–76 (2014)

13. Pannetrat, A., Hogben, G., Katopodis, S., Spanoudakis, G., Cazorla, C.S.: Security-aware SLA specification language and cloud security dependency model. Technical report, CUMULUS (2013)

14. Petcu, D.: A taxonomy for SLA-based monitoring of cloud security. In: 38th COMPSAC, pp. 640–641 (2014)

15. Lamport, L.: Paxos made simple, fast, and byzantine. In: OPODIS, pp. 7–9 (2002)

16. Irimie, B.C., Petcu, D.: Scalable and fault tolerant monitoring of security parameters in the cloud. In: 17th SYNASC (2015, in print)

Security and IoT Cloud Federation: Design of Authentication Schemes

Luciano Barreto[1], Antonio Celesti[2], Massimo Villari[2], Maria Fazio[2(✉)], and Antonio Puliafito[2]

[1] Federal University of Santa Catarina, Florianópolis, Brazil
lucianobarreto@das.ufsc.br
[2] Università Degli Studi di Messina, Messina, Italy
{acelesti,mvillari,mfazio,apuliafito}@unime.it

Abstract. The advent of both Cloud computing and Internet of Things (IoT) is changing the way of conceiving information and communication systems. Generally, we talk about IoT Cloud to indicate a new type of distributed system consisting of a set of smart devices interconnected with a remote Cloud infrastructure, platform, or software through the Internet and able to provide IoT as a Service (IoTaaS). In this paper, we address such a challenging paradigm focusing on security in IoT Cloud Federation. In particular, we discuss several authentication schemes fitting different types of scenarios.

Keywords: Cloud federation · IoT · Authentication scheme

1 Introduction

Nowadays, in the Internet of Things (IoT) panorama, the number of smart devices that can be integrated in different physical environments is rapidly growing. Considering such a context, smart devices can be deployed for collecting sensing data (e.g., temperature, pressure, etc.) and to perform (actuate) actions (e.g., turn on/off a light, send an alert, etc.). The success of IoT is due to the recent investments on both hardware and software technologies that are allowing IoT infrastructure, platform and applications to quickly evolve. Another factor that is contributing to the rapid evolution of IoT is its combination with the Cloud computing paradigm that is pursuing new opportunities in delivering services, representing a strategic approach for IT operators of increasing their business. The emerging business perspectives coming from IoT are pushing private, public, and hybrid Cloud providers to integrate their system with smart devices (including sensors and actuators) in order to provide together with the traditional Infrastructure, Platform, and Software as a Services (IaaS, PaaS, SaaS) even a new type of transversal service level, that is *IoT as a Service* (IoTaaS). An *IoT Cloud* represents a new type of distributed system consisting of several smart devices interconnected with a remote Cloud infrastructure, platform, or software through the Internet that is able to provide IoTaaS. We believe that the

© ICST Institute for Computer Sciences, Social Informatics and Telecommunications Engineering 2016
B. Mandler et al. (Eds.) IoT 360° 2015, Part I, LNICST 169, pp. 337–346, 2016.
DOI: 10.1007/978-3-319-47063-4_35

near future evolution of IoT Clouds will be the establishment of federated environments, in order to extend context-based capabilities and increase flexibility in IoTaaS provisioning. In a federated scenario, how to access IoT devices and services in a secure way is a very big concern. In this paper, we address security issues in federated IoT Clouds, specifically focusing on authentication strategies, presenting a new system model for secure IoT Cloud Federation and discussing several authentication schemes that allow users and manufacturers to access IoT devices and IoTaaS in a secure way. In particular, our use cases are based on the Identity Provider/Service Provider (IdP/SP) and Trusted Computing models.

The paper is organized as follows. Section 2 briefly describes the state of the art of IoT Cloud security. In Sect. 3, we provide an overview on IoT Cloud federation, specifically focusing on IoT resources and identity federation. In Sect. 4, we present a system model for IoT Cloud federation. In Sect. 6, we describe several authentication schemes for IoT Clouds and the resulting protocol flows formalized by means of different sequence diagrams. Section 7 concludes the paper.

2   Related Work

Cloud federation is a topic that has been studied for years and several experiences in this research area have been discussed n literature. One of the first scientific works on Cloud federation was presented in [1], where a federation of Clouds was described as a model of multiple providers aimed at resource sharing. Users are associated with a provider that is responsible for fulfilling all customer requests. Similar approaches can be found in [2,3]. All these models are based on a central Cloud broker, that looks for and allocate resources into the Clouds. Some security concerns on Cloud federation were presented in [4], where the authors defined authentication protocols.

Recent scientific works on the integration of IoT devices and Cloud computing providers was presented in [5], where protocols and use cases on how to integrate IoT devices with a Cloud computing provider were described. In [6], the authors present a system model for the development of applications for processing sensing data collected by IoT devices. The main idea is that the processing system runs over the Cloud, and IoT devices are exclusively exploited to collect sensing data. Another example of integration between IoT and Cloud computing is described in [7], where the authors describe an hybrid storage system specifically aimed to store Big Data collected for smart environment monitoring.

Regarding IoT Cloud security, in [8,9] the authors discussed how to perform a self-identification process in order to achieve a secure auto-configuration of IoT devices joining the Cloud. In [10] the authors present the challenges of integrating IoT devices with the Cloud (Cloud of Things as defined by the authors). The authors present a business model for this kind of architecture as well as the limitations and issues related to the security of IoT devices.

The limited number of scientific works focusing IoT and Cloud Federation security proves how currently this topic is still at an early stage and needs to be investigated with more attention.

3 IoT Cloud Federation Overview

Cloud federations has been widely discussed in terms of federation of datacenters [4,11]. In such a distributed system model, Clouds and, hence, related providers connect to each other in order to share their resources, typically Virtual Machines (VMs). Interactions among providers are based on pre-established trust relationships, so that they share their resources with other trusted providers.

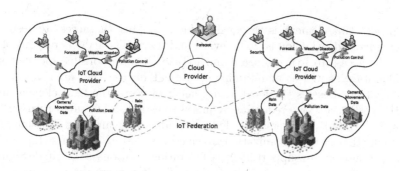

Fig. 1. IoT federation overview

Following the same idea, it is possible to think to share IoT devices as resources. We define IoT Cloud federation as a mesh of IoT Cloud providers that are interconnected to provide a wide decentralized sensing and actuating environment where everything is driven by agreements in a ubiquitous infrastructure. In such an environment, smaller, medium, and large IoT Cloud providers can federate themselves to gain economies of scale and an enlargement of their sensing and actuating capabilities, in order to arrange more flexible IoTaaS. Providers managing IoT devices make them available to other federated providers and their users. This allows users to access different kinds of data from different sensors, possibly deployed in different geographical regions. Figure 1 shows an example of such a scenario, where several providers share their IoT devices, allowing external users to collect data coming from different locations. From a business perspective, IoT Clouds can elastically enlarge the set of available IoT devices to deliver advanced IoTaaS to their users.

4 System Model for Federated IoT Clouds

In order to design authentication schemes, in this Section, we present a basic system model for IoT Cloud federation. As shown in Fig. 2, the model includes several components. The main building block represents an IoT Cloud and, in our model, the federation involves many IoT Clouds. At the high-level, each IoT Cloud is basically composed by two elements: the Cloud Provider and the Identity and Access Management (IAM) system. The *Cloud Provider* is a piece of middleware that manages the IoT resources of an administrative domain.

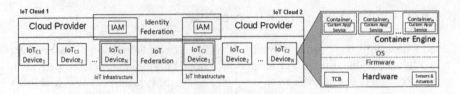

Fig. 2. Model overview of IoT federation

In addition, this element is responsible for managing the access to resources among federated IoT Clouds, IoT device, and users. The IAM is responsible to secure the access to IoT resources and IoTaaS. It is responsible for managing user identities, as well as maintaining secure IoT devices that are connected to the IoT Cloud. Besides the local management of users, the IAM element manages the authentication credentials required to establish federated relationships among IoT Cloud providers. The federated identity management is based on agreements that enable organizations to share their users' identities [12]. A challenging mechanisms to support identity federation solutions is the Single Sign-On (SSO) [13], that allows users to pass through the authentication process once accessing to different trusted service providers.

At the low level of the system model depicted in Fig. 2, there are several IoT devices. Each IoT device component exploits a relatively new technology, i.e., Container Virtualization. The concept of container applied to computers is currently object of studies in IoT devices. Following the same concept applied to computers, using containers in IoT devices means abstracting hardware resources creating virtual execution environments. Pushing containers into IoT devices is a very innovative approach and more and more manufactures are looking at container engines to simplify the packaging, distribution, installation and execution of complex applications on IoT devices. For example, a popular emerging solution consists in deploying Docker [14] on multi-core Raspberry PI devices.

The IoT device model adopted in this paper is shown on the right part of Fig. 2. We can break up the device into three layers: Container Engine, OS/Firmware and Hardware. The *Container Engine* is a software layer that enables the deployment and execution of containers. Cloud users can request to instantiate a container on a device to perform a specific task/application. Several Container per user can be instantiated on the same IoT devices thanks to isolation mechanisms, that is a Container is accessible only by its owner. In this sense, authentication and authorization controls must be enforced for accessing containers. The *Firmware* layer in the IoT device manages hardware resources. It abstracts hardware resources and provides an interface to control them. In addition, the firmware can be updated to provide new features or for bug correction. Therefore, the firmware of an IoT device is critically important because possible failures can compromise the behavior of the whole IoT device. The firmware can be either integrated as part of the Operating System (OS) (e.g., in Raspberry) or independent (e.g., in Arduino Yun). Given the importance of this layer in the IoT device, the access must be completely secured. In our proposal, only two entities may have access to this software layer: the Cloud provider, that controls and manages the device, and the manufacturer, that produced it. At the hardware layer, there are two main elements: *sensors/actuators* and the *Trusted Computing Base (TCB)* [15]. The latter allows IoT devices to be identified only by the Cloud provider and ensures that malicious entities do not have corrupted the hardware/software configurations. The TCB can be a Trusted Platform Module (TPM), a FPGA Boards, or an USB Crypto Token. The latter is a technology that is really promising for IoT devices security [5].

5   IoT Resource and Identity Federation

As highlighted in Fig. 2, the authentication schemes proposed in this paper address two main aspects of IoT Cloud federation, i.e., *Identity Federation* and *Resource Federation*.

IoT Resource Federation is aimed at sharing IoT devices among IoT Cloud providers. Each IoT Cloud provider manages accesses to its own IoT devices. Moreover, it has an updated list of external IoT devices belonging to other federation providers and can ask for temporary access to these devices on demand. Thus, for example, a user can request through is provider data from an IoT device belonging to a federated IoT Cloud in a transparent way. In addition, IoT Cloud federation allows providers to arrange new IoTaaS that they could not provide only using their own infrastructures, i.e., an IoTaaS can be composed combining features from different federated IoT devices. A preliminary requirement for the federation establishment is the creation of trust relationships among providers according to particular Service Level Agreements (SLAs). After that, the design and implementation of an infrastructure that allows the management of federated IoT devices is required. Such an infrastructure may involve mechanisms for resource discovery, resource allocation, identity management, and so on.

IoT Identity Federation allows IoT Cloud users to access IoT devices and IoTaaS belonging to a federated Cloud environment by forwarding the request to the federated provider. Thence, the authentication process should be extended beyond the administrative domain of a single provider. Identity federation allows users to access other IoT Cloud provider in a transparent way through a SSO authentication process. In particular, a user, with single assertion or authentication token can access the IoT devices belonging to different trusted federated IoT Cloud providers. The main advantage of this kind of federation is that the user does not need to keep multiple accounts for different providers. Generally, the identity federation requires one or more trusted Identity Providers, which manage users' credentials and a Certification Authority responsible for issuing digital certificates needed for authentication.

6   Users, Roles, and Authentication Schemes

According to the previously described IoT Cloud federation system model, different types of entities need to access IoT devices for different purposes. In this

Section, we describe several authentication schemes addressing different scenarios. We remark that in this paper we focus on authentication, instead authorization and auditing are out of the scope of this paper.

6.1 Maintenance and Container Setup

The piece of firmware of an IoT device can be upgraded for multiple reasons, e.g., to offer new software capabilities, for bug fixing, and so on. Only authorized *Manufacturers* and *Cloud Providers* that manage these IoT devices must be able to perform such types of critical operations, because unauthorized users could corrupt IoT devices with serious risks for the security of the whole system. We define Cloud Providers and Manufactures as kinds of super users who hold the rights to performs the aforementioned operations on IoT devices through a direct access. Figure 3(a) shows the interaction required to install a digital certificate in the TCB of the IoT device in order to make it trusted with a Cloud provider/Manufacturer. In step 1, a Cloud Provider (CP1) starts a setup process contacting the $IoTdevice_{CP1}$ that in turn, in step 2, contacts the IAM_{CP1} requesting a digital certificate. In step 3, the IAM_{CP1} requests identification info from the $IoTdevice_{CP1}$ that is sent back in step 4. In step 5 the IAM_{CP1} generates a certificate that is sent to the $IoTdevice_{CP1}$ and installed. In step 6 $IoTdevice_{CP1}$ is ready for further configuration.

In our Cloud federation model, the Cloud provider acts also as *Container Manager*. In fact, it is able to manage containers on IoT devices along with other storage, processing, and networking resources of the datacenter in order to arrange IoTaaS. Therefore, a safe access to the container engine of IoT devices is required. The authentication process required to instantiate a new container on the IoT device is shown in the sequence diagram of Fig. 3(b). In step 1, $CP1$ sends an access request to the $IoTDevice_{CP1}$, that in step 2, sends an authentication request to IAM_CP1. In step 3 IAM_CP1 sends a credentials request to $CP1$. Credentials are sent to the IAM_CP1 in step 4. In step 5, the $IoTDevice_{CP1}$ is informed that $CP1$ is authenticated. In step 6 $CP1$ is notified that it can control

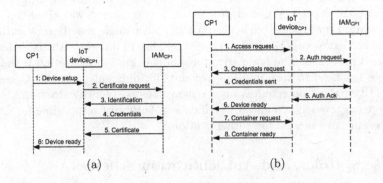

(a)   (b)

Fig. 3. (a) Sequence diagram of digital certificate setup process. (b) Sequence diagram of a container instantiation process.

$IoTDevice_{CP1}$. In step 7 $CP1$ sends a container request to $IoTDevice_{CP1}$ that instantiates it. In step 8, $CP1$ is informed that it can use the new container.

6.2   Accessing IoT Devices

In this Section, we present two main user roles for accessing IoT devices: *Basic User* and *Advanced User*. A Basic User can access sensing data through the IoT Platform offered by Cloud Provider, whereas an Advanced User is able to perform a direct access to the IoT device in order to manage containers. Moreover, we consider both roles acting in local and in a federated Cloud.

Basic Local and Federated Users. A Basic User is a user who only needs sensing data coming from IoT devices. The user gets sensing data through the IoT Platform APIs supplied by a Cloud Provider. In this case, the Cloud Provider accesses the IoT device on behalf of the user and the IoT device is transparent for the user. The user is defined "local" when he/she accesses his/her own Cloud provider and "federated" when it access another Cloud that is federated with his/her Cloud provider.

Figure 4(a) shows the sequence diagram of a Basic Local User authentication. In step 1, the user sends an access request to $CP1$ in order to access his/her IoT Platform. In step 2, an authentication request is sent IAM_{CP1}. In step 3 credentials are requested to the $user_1$ and in step 4, they are sent to the IAM_{CP1} that authenticates the user. In step 5, an authentication acknowledgement is sent to $CP1$ and in step 6 $user_1$ is informed that he/she got grant access rights to access the $CP1$ IoT Platform. In step 7, a sensing data request is sent to $CP1$ IoT

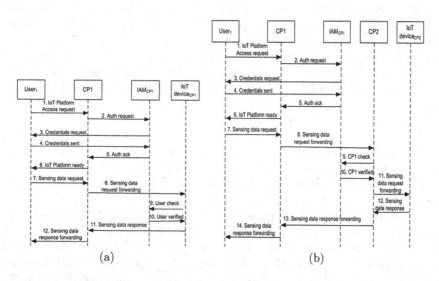

(a)   (b)

Fig. 4. (a) Sequence Diagram of Basic Local User Access. (b) Sequence Diagram of Basic Federated User Access.

Platform that is forwarded to $IoTDevice_{CP1}$ in step 8. In step 9, $IoTDevice_{CP1}$ checks if $user_1$ is authenticated, and since an authentication assertion already exist, exploiting the well-known concept of Single Sign On (SSO), in step 10, IAM_{CP1} notifies that he/she is already authenticated. In step 11, a sensing data response is sent to $CP1$ IoT Platform. Finally, in step 12, such a response is forwarded to $user_1$.

Figure 4(b) shows the sequence diagram for the Basic Federated User authentication. In this scenario, we consider two federated Cloud providers: CP_1 and CP_2. Let us assume that $user_1$ belonging to CP_1 wants to access sensing data supplied by the CP_2 Iot Platform. For this purpose, a federated SSO authentication process is required. Thanks to the concept of federated identity, $user_1$ can access the IoT Platform APIs of CP_2. Step 1, 2, 4, 5, 6, and 7 are similar to the Basic Local User authentication sequence diagram previously described. In step 8, a sensing data request is forwarded to the CP_2 IoT Platform. In step 9, a federated authentication process is performed. In this example, we assume that IAM_{CP1} acts as federated Identity Provider (IdP) and that $CP2$ is trusted with it, but it is also possible to consider either another trusted third party or a federated network of different IdP(s). In particular, $IoTDevice_{CP1}$ checks if $CP1$ is authenticated, and since an authentication assertion already exist, in step 10, exploiting the well-known concept of SSO, IAM_{CP1} notifies that it is already authenticated. In step 11, the sensing data request is forwarded to $IoTDevice_{CP2}$. In the end, pieces of sensing data are forwarded back to $user_1$ in steps 12, 13, 14.

Advanced Local and Federated Users. The Advanced User needs a direct access to IoT devices in order to customize them, control the container engine, manage containers, collect raw data and set actuators. Compared to the Basic Local User, the authentication is quite different. The user is defined "local" when he/she accesses his/her own Cloud provider and "federated" when it access another federated Cloud. Figure 5(a) shows the sequence diagram of an Advanced Local User authentication. Steps from 1 to 6 are similar to the sequence diagrams previously described. In step 7 the $user_1$ requests a direct access to $IoTDevice_{CP1}$. In step 8, an authentication process is performed between $user_1$ and $IoTDevice_{CP1}$. In particular, $IoTDevice_{CP1}$ checks if $user_1$ is authenticated, and since an authentication assertion already exist, in step 9, exploiting the well-known concept of SSO, IAM_{CP1} notifies that it is already authenticated. In step 10 $user_1$ gains the control of $IoTDevice_{CP1}$, e.g., from now on he/she can instantiate containers. In this case, sensing data are directly sent to $user_1$.

Figure 5(b) shows the sequence diagram of an Advanced Federated User authentication. Steps from 1 to 6 are similar to the sequence diagrams previously described. In step 7, $user_1$ sends a request to access the $CP2$ IoT Platform and such a request is forwarded to $CP2$ in step 8. In steps 9 and 10 $CP2$ verifies that a valid authentication assertion exists for $user_1$ in the trusted third party (i.e., IAM_{CP1} in this example). In step 11, $user_1$ gain the access to the $CP2$

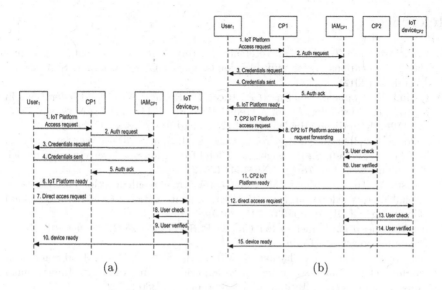

Fig. 5. (a) Sequence Diagram of Advanced Local User Access. (b) Sequence Diagram of Advanced Federated User Access.

IoT Platform. In step 12, $user_1$ sends a direct access request to $IoTDevice_{CP2}$. In steps 13 and 14 $IoTDevice_{CP2}$ verifies that a valid authentication assertion exists for $user_1$. Finally, $user_1$ gains the direct control of $IoTDevice_{CP2}$ in step 14.

7   Conclusion

In this paper, we combined several cutting-age topics, that are IoT, Cloud computing, and federation. In particular, we focused on security proposing several authentication schemes for IoT Cloud federation. From our study, we can conclude that designing and developing authentication schemes in emerging IoT Cloud scenarios is not trivial at all due to the current technological limitations. In fact, the real obstacle in the development of our scenario is represented by the development of TPB and related software features in IoT devices. In this regard, even though the Trusted Computing Group has recently started to look at IoT, at the time of writing of this paper, there are not concrete implementations yet. In this scientific work, we hope we succeeded in stimulating the interest of researchers and developers towards this topic.

Acknowledgements. The research leading to the results presented in this paper has received funding from the European Union's FP7 2007–2013 Project frontierCities under grant agreement number 632853.

References

1. Calheiros, R.N., Toosi, A.N., Vecchiola, C., Buyya, R.: A coordinator for scaling elastic applications across multiple clouds. Future Gener. Comput. Syst. **28**(8), 1350–1362 (2012)
2. Carlini, E., Coppola, M., Dazzi, P., Ricci, L., Righetti, G.: Cloud federations in contrail. In: Alexander, M., et al. (eds.) Euro-Par 2011, Part I. LNCS, vol. 7155, pp. 159–168. Springer, Heidelberg (2012). doi:10.1007/978-3-642-29737-3_19
3. Villegas, D., Bobroff, N., Rodero, I., Delgado, J., Liu, Y., Devarakonda, A., Fong, L., Masoud Sadjadi, S., Parashar, M.: Cloud federation in a layered service model. J. Comput. Syst. Sci. **78**(5), 1330–1344 (2012)
4. Celesti, A., Tusa, F., Villari, M., Puliafito, A.: How to enhance cloud architectures to enable cross-federation. In: 2010 IEEE 3rd International Conference on Cloud Computing (CLOUD), pp. 337–345 (2010)
5. An Authentication Model for IoT Clouds, Paris, France, 26–27 August 2015, IEEE Computer Society (2015, in press)
6. Rao, B.B.P., Saluia, P., Sharma, N. Mittal, A., Sharma, S.V.: Cloud computing for Internet of Things & sensing based applications. In: 2012 Sixth International Conference on Sensing Technology (ICST), pp. 374–380 (2012)
7. Fazio, M., Celesti, A., Puliafito, A., Villari, M.: Big data storage in the cloud for smart environment monitoring. Procedia Comput. Sci. **52**, 500–506 (2015)
8. Villari, M., Celesti, A., Fazio, M., Puliafito, A.: A secure self-identification mechanism for enabling IoT devices to join cloud computing. In: Giaffreda, R., Cagáňová, D., Li, Y., Riggio, R., Voisard, A., Cagánová, D., Cagánová, D. (eds.) IoT 2014. LNICST, vol. 151, pp. 306–311. Springer, Heidelberg (2015). doi:10.1007/978-3-319-19743-2_41
9. Barreto, L., Celesti, A., Villari, M., Fazio, M., Puliafito, A.: Authentication models for IoT clouds. In: International Symposium on Foundations of Open Source Intelligence and Security Informatics FOSINT-SI. IEEE Computer Society (2015)
10. Parwekar, P.: From internet of things towards cloud of things. In: Computer, pp. 329–333 (2011)
11. Rochwerger, B., Breitgand, D., Levy, E., Galis, A., Nagin, K., Llorente, I.M., Montero, R., Wolfsthal, Y., Elmroth, E., Caceres, J., Ben-Yehuda, M., Emmerich, W., Galan, F.: The reservoir model and architecture for open federated cloud computing. IBM J. Res. Dev. **53**(4), 1–11 (2009)
12. Sharma, A.K., Lamba, C.S.: Survey on federated identity management systems. In: Meghanathan, N., Boumerdassi, S., Chaki, N., Nagamalai, D. (eds.) NeCoM 2010. CCIS, vol. 90, pp. 509–517. Springer, Heidelberg (2010). doi:10.1007/978-3-642-14493-6_52
13. Maler, E., Reed, D.: The Venn of identity: options and issues in federated identity management. IEEE Secur. Priv **6**, 16–23 (2008)
14. Zheng, C., Thain, D.: Integrating containers into workflows: a case study using makeflow, work queue, and docker. In: Proceedings of the 8th International Workshop on Virtualization Technologies in Distributed Computing, VTDC 2015, pp. 31–38. ACM (2015)
15. Rushby, J.: A trusted computing base for embedded systems. In: Proceedings of the 7th Department of Defense/NBS Computer Security Conference, pp. 294–311 (1984)

When the Cloud Goes Pervasive: Approaches for IoT PaaS on a Mobiquitous World

Luiz Angelo Steffenel[1][(⊠)] and Manuele Kirsch Pinheiro[2]

[1] Université de Reims Champagne-Ardenne Laboratoire CReSTIC, Reims, France
luiz-angelo.steffenel@univ-reims.fr
[2] Université Paris 1 Panthéon-Sorbonne, Centre de Recherche en Informatique,
Paris, France
manuele.kirsch-pinheiro@univ-paris1.fr

Abstract. Today, IoT applications are heavily dependent on public cloud computing services to perform data storage and analysis. Unfortunately, the cloud computing paradigm is unable to meet the requirements of critical applications that require low latency or enhanced privacy levels. The deployment of private cloud services on top of pervasive grids represent an interesting alternative to traditional cloud infrastructures, allowing the use of near-environment resources for IoT data analysis tasks. In this work we discuss the challenges associated with the deployment of IoT services over pervasive environments, and present a study case deployed over CloudFIT, a computing middleware for pervasive systems. Hence, we evaluate the behavior of a data-intensive application under volatility and heterogeneity constraints, bringing to light to the use of low-end devices that are usually located at the proximity to IoT sensors/actuators.

Keywords: IoT · Pervasive environments · PaaS · Cloud computing

1 Introduction

According to [1], in the next 25 years, most of the things and devices we interact with will be linked to a global computing infrastructure. This massive integration of communicating capabilities on physical objects symbolize the advent of IoT. The Internet of Things (IoT) represents a new tendency on IT industry, in which physical environment is populated by interconnected and communicating objects, capable of interacting with each other and with the environment itself. The strength of this concept lies in the seamlessly integration of sensors, actuators and other devices in the environment in a large scale, allowing interacting and collecting information from this.

Several factors are contributing the increasing development of IoT, among them the cost of sensors, bandwidth and processing power that have decline in the last years [5]. Thanks to current technology and its reducing costs, IoT is already becoming a reality. Nowadays, it is possible to put a wireless interface on

© ICST Institute for Computer Sciences, Social Informatics and Telecommunications Engineering 2016
B. Mandler et al. (Eds.) IoT 360° 2015, Part I, LNICST 169, pp. 347–356, 2016.
DOI: 10.1007/978-3-319-47063-4_36

almost all every day object, making possible interaction between them [9]. Such communicating capabilities open countless opportunities in different application domains, like health-care and smart cities, just to name a very few.

However, the full potential of IoT will only be reached if the data collected by IoT devices can be analyzed and explored. As suggested by Jones [5], big data analytics is making IoT possible. Indeed, only collecting data from the environment is not enough without an appropriate computing analysis allowing actions and decisions to be made based on these data.

Currently, computing IoT data is been performed mostly on cloud computing infrastructures. Different authors [2,3,6] have been pointing the integration with cloud infrastructures as a key aspect for IoT platforms, since storage and computing power of IoT devices is often limited. Indeed, cloud computing are offering powerful and flexible capabilities for running IoT data services and applications by using Internet infrastructure [12]. By using cloud platforms, it is possible to analyze increasingly volume of data, following an on-demand model, in which new resources can be easily allocated according application needs.

Despite its advantages, cloud platforms have also some important drawbacks. Among these, we may cite security and privacy concerns, as well as network latency [4]. Indeed, the transfer of large volume of data from IoT environments to cloud platforms may be significantly costly and time consuming, and it may also expose private data to a public infrastructure. Such drawbacks may prevent the use of public cloud infrastructures on IoT applications particularly concerned by privacy issues or by the transfer of large volume of data. In order to overcome these limitations, the use of private cloud have been considered. Further, most of private cloud platforms suppose the availability of dedicated resources, such as a cluster, which represent an important investment for concerned organizations.

In this paper, we explore a different approach for IoT applications concerned by these issues. We consider, in this paper, the deployment of IoT applications over pervasive grids. Pervasive grids represent the extreme generalization of grid platforms, in which heterogeneous resources may dynamically and opportunistically integrate (or leave) the platform [8,13]. Pervasive grids allow exploring under-utilized resources available on the near environment for IoT data analysis tasks, reducing the need for expensive data transfers and costly computing infrastructures. We propose here the deployment of the CloudFIT platform, a private PaaS (Platform as a Service) cloud, over a pervasive grid and discuss challenges and opportunities this deployment offers for IoT applications.

This paper is organized as follows: Sect. 2 presents related works on cloud platforms for IoT processing. Section 3 discusses opportunities and challenges of using pervasive grids for IoT processing. Section 4 introduces the platform CloudFIT as a private PaaS platform for IoT, while Sect. 5 analyses experimental results of CloudFIT on pervasive grids. Finally, Sect. 6 presents our conclusions and future works.

2   Related Works

One of the most important outcomes of IoT is the possibility of creating an unprecedented amount of data, which has to be stored and used intelligently for smart monitoring and actuation [3]. This ability of sensing physical phenomena or triggering actions on the physical reality is what differentiates IoT from traditional networked systems. IoT focus is on data and information, since, from the conceptual standpoint, IoT is about entities acting as providers and/or consumers of data related to the physical world [6].

In this context, cloud platforms may act as a receiver of data from the IoT environment, offering computer power to analyze and interpret the data [3]. Different cloud-based platforms have been proposed for distribute and manage IoT applications and data. Villalba et al. [15] proposes a scalable platform for IoT data storage and processing in the cloud, named ServIoTicy, which focus on data stream processing, offering IoT applications data store and access facilities through a REST based API. Similarly, Fazio et al. [2] focus on data storage services, proposing a monitoring-oriented cloud architecture for storage of big data. These authors propose a platform offering services for managing and querying data of different kinds, from simple measures performed by sensing devices up to complex multimedia objects.

Serrano et al. [12] share a similar focus, by considering IoT Cloud service data management based on annotated data of monitored Cloud performance and user profiles. They consider enabling management systems to use shared public infrastructures and resources in order to provide an efficient deployment mechanism for IoT services and applications. By this mechanism, these authors focus indeed on enabling elasticity of IoT Cloud services. Similarly, the Aneka platform [3], a .Net based PaaS (Platform as a Service) platform, offers cloud management services and support resources coming from other private and public cloud platforms, such as Microsoft Azure.

Finally, Mulfari et al. [7] propose a message-oriented middleware for cloud, named MOM4C, which allows composing cloud facilities according to client requirements. This platform offers services to dynamically deploy applications running on smart objects by means of container-based virtualization techniques. Virtualization isolates applications from heterogeneity of IoT environment, but, in the case of MOM4C, this also limits targets objects to those based on Linux, preventing other smart kinds of objects to contribute with the platform.

Establishing on-demand cloud services on top of existing resources is also alternative to the complete externalization of services in a cloud. For example, [10] explore the limitations of mobile devices through the use of Cloudlets, i.e., virtual machines deployed on-demand in the vicinity of the demanding devices. Using cloudlets deployed as Wi-Fi hotspots in coffee shops, libraries, etc., the authors of [10] suggest a simple way to offer enough computing power to perform complex computations (services) all while limiting the service latency. This idea of consuming proximity resources is also explored by pervasive grids, which promote the use of heterogeneous devices in an opportunistic way. Next section discusses the use of such grids for IoT applications.

3   Pervasive Grids for IoT

Previous section demonstrated how cloud platform can significantly contribute to IoT applications. Such platforms are commonly used for distributing processing and storage capabilities necessary to IoT applications. Although advantageous, cloud platforms have also important drawbacks that may limit their adoption by some IoT applications. First of all, public cloud platforms are prone to privacy and security concerns. Public cloud providers do not offer sufficient protection for organizations that depend upon classified or proprietary information [4]. Schadt et al. [11] also underline important privacy issues related to medical or biometric data. Besides, network latency may have an important impact on the transfer of large volume of data to cloud platforms. Indeed, even high-speed connections have a limited bandwidth that can be overloaded by the transfer of important volume of data. As applications make even-more intense use of large volume of data, data transfer poses an increasing bottleneck [4].

In these cases, an alternative for IoT application can be the use of pervasive grids. Pervasive grids seamlessly integrate pervasive sensing/actuating instruments and devices together with classical high performance systems [8]. These grids lie on the use of idle and under-explored resources as a dynamic computing platform. In the context of IoT, pervasive grids represent an opportunity to deploy computing tasks, and notably data analysis ones, in computing resources available around IoT devices, minimizing data transfer over distant network. Pervasive grids offer the possibility of consuming computing power and storage from any available resources, independently of its nature, from small Raspberry Pi devices up to virtual machines deployed on cluster infrastructures.

Nevertheless, the use of pervasive grids raises important challenges, related to the dynamic nature of these environments. Among these challenges, two of them, heterogeneity and volatility, are quite related to IoT applications, which also have to cope with mobility and network volatility, and by consequence, with temporary unavailability of objects and resources [9]. Handling heterogeneity means to be able to seamlessly integrate resources of different natures in the same computing environment. Whatever it nature is, a resource should be able to contribute with computing tasks assigned to the grid, according its own capabilities. Considering volatility, it comes from the dynamic nature of the resources composing these grids. A pervasive grids rely on volatile resources that may appear and disappear from the grid, according their availability [13]. It can be a laptop that come and go, according its owner's moving, or a Raspberry Pi that switches off due to a low battery condition. Pervasive grids platforms have to deal with this volatility, allowing resources to seamlessly leave the grid or new ones to join it, without a significant impact on tasks execution. Application executing on pervasive grids might keep executing despite this volatility, taking advantage from the resources while they are available.

4   CloudFIT as a PaaS

As stated in the previous section, one of the major concerns on the design of a pervasive platform is to be able to ensure the execution of an application in spite of failures, a constraint that requires the use of decentralized coordination, fault tolerance and replication techniques.

CloudFIT [13] is a P2P distributed computing middleware structured around collaborative nodes connected over an overlay network (Fig. 1) and based on the FIIT (Finite Independent Irregular Tasks) paradigm. CloudFIT was designed to be independent of the underlying overlay, and the current version supports both FreePastry and TomP2P overlay networks, as well as their respective DHT services. While initially designed for computing intensive applications (combinatorial problems, etc.), the association with the storage capabilities from DHTs offer interesting possibilities for the big data and data analysis for IoT.

As previously presented in [14], we believe that CloudFIT can be used to provide a pervasive PaaS for IoT applications. Indeed, CloudFIT can be deployed on heterogeneous devices, from dedicate servers to Rapsberry PI-like devices, and is supported on both Android, Linux, Windows or MacOS. While this flexibility allows CloudFIT to be run directly on some recent IoT devices, the limited resources from these nodes make this approach very unreliable. A better approach, instead, is to use CloudFIT as a computing backend for IoT devices and applications. This mixed architecture, as illustrated in the left side of Fig. 1, allows an IoT application connected to CloudFIT network to act as an interface to gather data and launch computing tasks according to the application needs.

The development of an interface for IoT devices can be provided through *REST* calls or even a direct a connection to the devices via Bluetooth or Wi-Fi, but such development is outside the scope of this paper. Instead, the next section

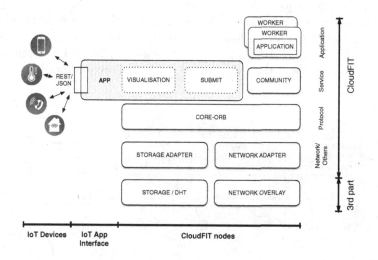

Fig. 1. CloudFIT architecture stack

analyzes the deployment of a data intensive application over a pervasive cluster using CloudFIT, with a special attention to both volatility and heterogeneity aspects of the execution.

5   Experiments

The experiments in this paper presents the deployment of a Map-Reduce application over a cluster of nodes running CloudFIT. As in a previous work [14] we compared the performance of CloudFIT against the well-known Hadoop framework, this paper focus on the impact volatility and heterogeneity on the behavior of CloudFIT.

5.1   Impact of Volatility

This first experiment presents the deployment of a WordCount application with a total of 1 GB of data, split in blocks of 64 MB. Figure 2 shows the Gantt diagram for an execution with no failures (for clarity, we limit each node to one single execution core). Indeed, we observe the deployment of several map tasks (with variable execution lengths), plus a reduce task at the end.

Here, we can observe the basic scheduling mechanism implemented on Cloud-FIT, developed to be totally decentralized and fault tolerant. For instance, when an application is deployed, a list of tasks is distributed among the nodes. Each node rearranges the list of tasks in a random order. When node picks a task tagged as *available*, it changes its status to *in execution* and advertises this to the others nodes. When a task is *completed*, its status is broadcasted to the other nodes and its status is updated. If all tasks marked as *available* were picked, a node may start computing other tasks marked as *in execution*.

This scheduling algorithm ensures that all tasks will be computed with little coordination between the nodes. We can easily recover tasks from failed nodes or perform speculative executions on tasks that take too long due to a slow processor, for example. Also, when a node joins the CloudFIT community, it receives an update about the tasks current status and the working data, allowing

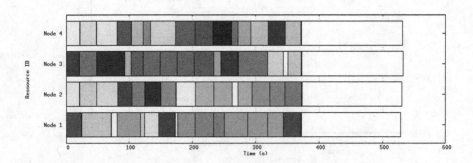

Fig. 2. Regular execution of WordCount (1 GB, 64 MB data blocks)

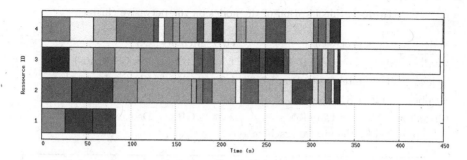

Fig. 3. WordCount execution when one node fails (1 GB, 64 MB data blocks)

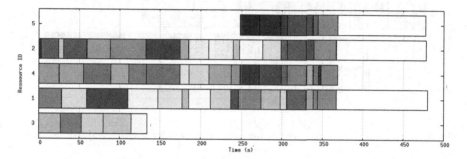

Fig. 4. Execution when a node joins after another failed (1 GB, 64 MB data blocks)

it to start working on available (incomplete) tasks. Figures 3 and 4 respectively illustrate a situation where one node fails and another where a failed node is replaced by a new node.

One eventual drawback of the totally decentralized scheduler is the fact that a task may be launched by multiple nodes simultaneously. This is indeed the reason why our experiments show several nodes executing the reduce task. Please note that CloudFIT allows users to develop additional scheduling algorithms that respond to specific need. Currently we are studying how to integrate context-awareness to incorporate additional parameters such as CPU speed, available memory and network speed in order to optimize the execution of the applications.

5.2   Impact of Heterogeneity

This second experiment aims at observing the impact of node heterogeneity when running CloudFIT, as our proposal relies on the association of nodes with different characteristics to offer PaaS on a pervasive system. For instance, we interconnected four nodes with different specifications (cf. Table 1). As in the precedent experiment, we limit to one core per node to simplify the visualization.

We also modified the experiment parameters to perform over 512 MB of data split in chunks of 2 MB each, as we believe that this configuration is closer to the patterns from current IoT devices (each sensor/node generating a limited data

Table 1. Specification of the nodes on the pervasive cluster

Node	Processor	GHz	Memory	OS
MacBook Air	Intel Core i7-4650U	1.7	8 GB	MacOS 10.10.5
Lenovo U110	Intel Core2 Duo L7500	1.6	4 GB	Ubuntu Linux 15.4
Raspberry Pi 2	ARM Cortex-A7	0.9	1 GB	Raspbian Linux Wheezy
Virtualbox VM	Intel Core i7*	2.2*	1 GB	Debian Linux 8.2

*values provided by the virtual machine guest

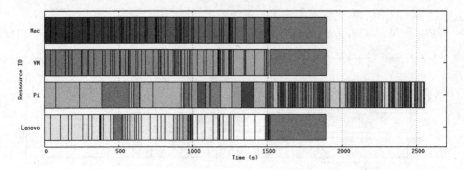

Fig. 5. WordCount execution on an heterogeneous network (512 MB, 2 MB data blocks)

amount). Also, this allows less powerful nodes to contribute with some tasks. Figure 5 shows the Gantt diagram for an execution on such scenario.

While the tasks distribution among the laptops and the virtual machine presents no distinctive difference, we observe without surprise that the Raspberry Pi does not perform as fast as the other nodes (as illustrated by the average task length on the first half of the execution). In addition, we observe that this node misses several status update messages and does not detects the end of the map phase and keeps trying to launch completed tasks. Unfortunately, this proves unsuccessful as the results are already in the DHT (the reason why the latter tasks take so little time).

This result does not refrain us from targeting small, less-powerful devices but, on the contrary, challenges us to understand and attack the causes of these problems. Up to now we identified that the DHT replication algorithm is one of the major factors affecting low-end devices. For instance, small devices have slow and limited memory/storage capacity (only a few hundred MBs of RAM, SD cards, etc.), and they expend a lot of resources trying to keep up with the replication process. As a consequence, this overhead interferes both with the computing performance and the message delivery between nodes, as observed in our experiment. We are currently investigating alternative techniques to integrate such nodes to the computing network without the burden of managing the DHT. Further developments, configuration and experiments with other DHT and overlays shall allow us to address these issues.

A complementary approach consists on developing context-aware schedulers so that small devices could contribute to tasks/jobs corresponding to their capabilities. This way, applications with specific needs such as response time, complex data transfer patterns or huge storage needs could be preferentially directed to nodes corresponding to these attributes, without overloading the small devices. As stated in the previous section, we are currently developing context-aware schedulers that eventually will perform such distinction among the nodes.

6   Conclusions and Future Work

IoT environments are the next important step towards the establishment of mobiquitous systems. Currently, computing IoT data is been performed mostly on cloud computing infrastructures, which are not always adapted to the needs from IoT devices. Indeed, moving data to distant platforms for filtering, analysis and decision-making is both expensive, time consuming and prone to security flaws, not always corresponding to the requirements from IoT applications.

In this paper, we explore a different approach for IoT applications concerned by these issues. Such approach relies on the deployment of IoT applications over pervasive grids, allowing the use of near-environment resources for IoT data analysis tasks. This way, we reduce the need for expensive data transfers and costly computing infrastructures, and are able to delimit the diffusion of the data. We present how CloudFIT can be used to create private PaaS clouds at the proximity of the demanding IoT devices. Using a P2P overlay, CloudFIT offers both storage and computing capabilities on top of pervasive networks.

As pervasive systems are characterized by strong volatility and heterogeneity of the resources, this paper analysis the CloudFIT behavior through the deployment of a data-intensive application under such constraints. With these experiments, we bring to light to the use of low-end devices like Raspberry Pi. These devices are usually located at the closest-area to IoT sensors/actuators, offering both interconnection and elemental processing capabilities.

Of course, the possibilities that CloudFIT offers to IoT are not limited to MapReduce applications. The CloudFIT API and its distributed computing model allow many other usages, as devices can use the platform as a storage support, data analysis support, intensive computing support, etc. By coordinating activities over CloudFIT, IoT devices and applications can elaborate a supply chain from data gathering to reasoning and actuation.

References

1. Broy, M., Schmidt, A.: Challenges in engineering cyber-physical systems. Computer **47**(2), 70–72 (2014)
2. Fazio, M., Celesti, A., Puliafito, A., Villari, M.: Big data storage in the cloud for smart environment monitoring. Procedia Comput. Sci. **52**, 500–506 (2015). The 6th International Conference on Ambient Systems, Networks and Technologies (ANT-2015), the 5th International Conference on Sustainable Energy Information Technology (SEIT-2015)

3. Gubbi, J., Buyya, R., Marusic, S., Palaniswami, M.: Internet of things (IoT): a vision, architectural elements, and future directions. Future Gener. Comput. Syst. **29**(7), 1645–1660 (2013)
4. Hofmann, P., Woods, D.: Cloud computing: the limits of public clouds for business applications. IEEE Internet Comput. **14**(6), 90–93 (2010)
5. Jones, M.: Internet of things: shifting from proprietary to standard. ValueWalk, July 2014. http://www.valuewalk.com/2014/07/internet-of-things-iot/
6. Miorandi, D., Sicari, S., Pellegrini, F.D., Chlamtac, I.: Internet of things: vision, applications and research challenges. Ad Hoc Netw. **10**(7), 1497–1516 (2012)
7. Mulfari, D., Fazio, M., Celesti, A., Villari, M., Puliafito, A.: Design of an IoT cloud system for container virtualization on smart objects. In: Celesti, A., Leitner, P. (eds.) ESOCC 2015 Workshops. CCIS, vol. 567, pp. 33–47. Springer, Heidelberg (2016). doi:10.1007/978-3-319-33313-7_3
8. Parashar, M., Pierson, J.M.: Pervasive grids: challenges and opportunities. In: Li, K.C., Hsu, C.H., Yang, L.T., Dongarra, J., Zima, H. (eds.) Handbook of Research on Scalable Computing Technologies, pp. 14–30. IGI Global (2010)
9. Paridel, K., Bainomugisha, E., Vanrompay, Y., Berbers, Y., Meuter, W.D.: Middleware for the internet of things, design goals and challenges. ECEASST **28** (2010). http://journal.ub.tu-berlin.de/index.php/eceasst/article/view/392
10. Satyanarayanan, M., Bahl, P., Caceres, R., Davies, N.: The case for VM-based cloudlets in mobile computing. IEEE Pervasive Comput. **8**, 14–23 (2009)
11. Schadt, E.E., Linderman, M.D., Sorenson, J., Lee, L., Nolan, G.P.: Computational solutions to large-scale data management and analysis. Nat. Rev. Genet. **11**(9), 647–657 (2010)
12. Serrano, M., Le-Phuoc, D., Zaremba, M., Galis, A., Bhiri, S., Hauswirth, M.: Resource optimisation in IoT cloud systems by using matchmaking and self-management principles. In: Galis, A., Gavras, A. (eds.) FIA 2013. LNCS, vol. 7858, pp. 127–140. Springer, Heidelberg (2013). doi:10.1007/978-3-642-38082-2_11
13. Steffenel, L., Flauzac, O., Charao, A., Barcelos, P., Stein, B., Cassales, G., Nesmachnow, S., Rey, J., Cogorno, M., Kirsch-Pinheiro, M., Souveyet, C.: MapReduce challenges on pervasive grids. J. Comput. Sci. **10**(11), 2194–2210 (2014)
14. Steffenel, L.A., Pinheiro, M.K.: CloudFIT, a PaaS platform for IoT applications over pervasive networks. In: 3rd International Workshop on Cloud for IoT (CLIoT 2015), Taormina, Italy September 2015
15. Villalba, Á., Prez, J.L., Carrera, D., Pedrinaci, C., Panziera, L.: servioTicy and iServe: a scalable platform for mining the IoT. Procedia Comput. Sci. **52**, 1022–1027 (2015). The 6th International Conference on Ambient Systems, Networks and Technologies (ANT-2015), the 5th International Conference on Sustainable Energy Information Technology (SEIT-2015)

Coordinating Data Analysis and Management in Multi-layered Clouds

Ioan Petri[1]([✉]), Javier Diaz-Montes[2], Omer Rana[1], Yacine Rezgui[4],
Manish Parashar[2], and Luiz F. Bittencourt[3]

[1] School of Computer Science and Informatics, Cardiff University, Cardiff, UK
petrii@cardiff.ac.uk
[2] Rutgers Discovery Informatics Institute, Rutgers University, New Brunswick, USA
javidiaz@rdi2.rutgers.edu
[3] Institute of Computing, University of Campinas, Campinas, Brazil
bit@ic.unicamp.br
[4] School of Engineering, Cardiff University, Cardiff, UK
RezguiY@cardiff.ac.uk

Abstract. We introduce an architecture for undertaking data processing across multiple layers of a distributed computing infrastructure, composed of edge devices (making use of Internet-of-Things (IoT) based protocols), intermediate gateway nodes and large scale data centres. In this way, data processing that is intended to be carried out in the data centre can be pushed to the edges of the network – enabling more efficient use of data centre and in-network resources. We suggest the need for specialist data analysis and management algorithms that are *resource-aware*, and are able to split computation across these different layers. We propose a coordination mechanism that is able to combine different types of data processing capability, such as *in-transit* and *in-situ*. An application scenario is used to illustrate the concepts, subsequently evaluated through a multi-site deployment.

Keywords: Distributed clouds · Cloud computing · Data analytics · CometCloud

1 Introduction

With increasing deployment of sensors to measure physical phenomenon, there has been interest in recent years in standardising sensor device types, communication protocols and their data exchange formats. This has resulted in various attempts to define interoperability specifications for Internet-of-Things (IoT) – which according to NIST (as part of their "Cyber-Physical Systems" programme), is "a global network infrastructure, linking physical and virtual objects through the exploitation of data capture and communication capabilities" [7]. Recent efforts at the IEEE, such as P2413 [8], also attempt to define an architectural framework for IoT, indicating that "most current standardization activities are

© ICST Institute for Computer Sciences, Social Informatics and Telecommunications Engineering 2016
B. Mandler et al. (Eds.) IoT 360° 2015, Part I, LNICST 169, pp. 357–366, 2016.
DOI: 10.1007/978-3-319-47063-4_37

confined to very specific verticals and represent islands of disjointed and often redundant development" in the IoT area. The P2413 architectural framework "will promote cross-domain interaction, aid system interoperability and functional compatibility."

Understanding how data collected from IoT-based devices can be channelled for analysis into a Cloud-based system remains an important research area. Although significant work exists in offloading computation from mobile devices to Cloud-based systems [15], better understanding how to divide data processing across IoT-based devices (which can have on-board computational capability, e.g. through the use of Arduino or Raspberry Pi-based deployments) and Cloud-based infrastructure has received limited attention. Recent efforts in creating an open source "IoTCloud" (providing sensors-as-a-service) [13] and middleware oriented efforts in European Open IoT project [14] indicate significant interest in this area from the academic community. In the same context, HTTP/REST-based APIs, such as Xively (previously Pachube) [9], Open Sen.se [10], Think Speak [11] and Pacific Control Gateways [12], indicate strong commercial interest, in applications ranging from smart cities to intelligent homes.

We describe how IoT-based devices and Clouds can be integrated using a multi-layered architecture. The basis of this comes from the observation that not all data collected through IoT-based devices needs to be channeled to a Cloud platform. Current practice is primarily to stream or batch-collect all data from devices and carry out subsequent analysis via a Cloud platform. However, this is often unnecessary (and may involve costly data transfers across networks with varying characteristics, in terms of bandwidth, cost of access, availability and latency) as only a subset of the data may actually contribute to the analysis being performed. Similarly, partial data processing may be carried out directly on the devices or through intermediate collection gateways (that are situated between the devices and the Cloud platform). We therefore propose a coordination model where the Cloud platform, intermediate gateway devices and IoT-based devices need to work collectively to carry out data processing. Such coordination takes account of constraints of the devices (e.g. limited network and battery power) and optimisation criteria of Cloud platforms (e.g. improve throughput and reduce execution time). Section 2 describes the overall systems architecture, and the various layers involved from data collection to processing. Section 3 outlines a coordination mechanism that enables the data processing to be split across multiple layers, followed by an example scenario in Sect. 4 and evaluation in Sect. 5. We conclude with a general discussion in Sect. 6.

2   Approach and Architecture

The distributed system architecture presented in Fig. 1 consists of three main layers: (i) L3: data capture point, (ii) L2: gateway nodes (in practice, multiple levels may exist) and (iii) L1: data centre/computing cluster. At L1 various data capture devices, such as sensors, mobile phones (with human input) record values based on an observed phenomena. These devices capture data with a pre-defined frequency (often dictated by the rate of change of the phenomenon

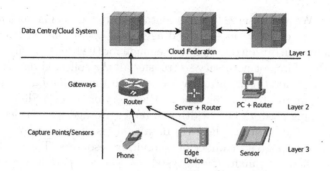

Fig. 1. Conceptual (system) architecture

being observed), depending on the capacity of the device to record/collect data and also based on specific system requirements that need to be satisfied. L2 involves the use of multiple gateways, which may be realised in practice using network switches and routers, fronted by OpenFlow software (for instance) or network processor-based hardware, which enables such network components to be remotely managed. However, such gateways may also be computational devices that aggregate data from a variety of L3 sensors. Finally, L1 contains more complex computing clusters, where greater computational and storage capability is made available to application users, enabling more complex, generally long running, simulations to be carried out on the data.

Devices at L2 can carry out various operations on the raw data collected at L3 – such as performing stream operations (average, min, max, filtering, aggregation etc.) on a time/sample window of data, carrying out encryption of an incoming data stream or a variety of other data encoding/transcoding operations before forwarding this data for subsequent analysis to L1. Hence, devices at L2 retrieve data but can also perform some preliminary analysis. We envision a distributed Cloud to be composed of devices at all of these levels, and with a need to coordinate work across these levels to achieve particular data analysis and performance targets. Each level also has its own objective function which influences the types of operations carried out. For instance, L3 generally consists of resource constrained devices (i.e. limited battery power, network range, etc.) which must carry out operations in the context of these constraints. Similarly, L2 consists of various network elements or computing nodes that need to be shared across multiple concurrent data flows, requiring any analysis to be constrained by the number of flows and time constraints in carrying out the filtering/pre-analysis. Operations at L1 are based on pre-agreed targets between a client and a data centre provider, such as throughput, response time, cost, etc. Understanding how an application hosted on a Cloud at L1 can interact and coordinate with L3 and L2 (either directly or via L2) is a key research challenge in such systems, particularly for real time, streaming applications.

Distributing analysis of data across these different levels can improve the overall system performance and reduce the load on L1 infrastructure and the core network. We also observe that raw data collected at L3 may not necessarily be needed (in its entirety) at L1 – and aggregate operations on the data (e.g. average, summation/fusion, etc.) may be enough for the type of analysis required at L1. It is therefore not necessary to transfer all the collected data to the data centre (as often undertaken currently – even with the availability of recent systems such as Amazon Kinesis [3], Google BigQuery or Apache Flink for streaming data), wasting network bandwidth and buffer/storage space at levels L2 and L1. We identify the following classes of data analysis: In-situ analysis: is carried out at L1, on a pre-agreed number of computing resources. This is the current mode of operation with many Cloud systems – whereby data is aggregated at a central site prior to analysis. In streaming systems (e.g. Amazon Kinesis), data sharing is carried out prior to transfer of this to Amazon VM instances hosted at a particular data centre. This approach can have major disadvantages in terms of load and response time, as collection at a central server can be time consuming (and sometimes not necessary). Data-drop analysis: After data values are collected by edge devices, and sent over the network, the actual data analysis process starts when the data sets are dropped into a specific folder. Data-drop analysis is the ability to trigger on-demand analysis making use of elastic computing resources available at L1 (at the data centre). A key challenge in this type of analysis is to predict the number of computing resources needed (as data is dynamically made available) based on heuristics or prior execution history. This type of analysis can suffer from the same QoS limitations as In-situ analysis, as it still requires data to be shipped over the network from L3 to L1 infrastructure. In-transit data analysis: Identifies the type of distributed analysis carried out at L3 and (more generally) L2. In-transit analysis makes use of capability available in software defined networks to undertake partial analysis while the data is in transit from source (L3) to the data processing engine (generally L1). This approach can significantly improve overall analysis time (and limit use of resources at L1), as pre-analysis can help identify what needs to be carried out at L1. In-transit analysis therefore makes more effective use of computing capability available at L2.

3   Multi-Layered Coordination

A coordination mechanism should enable selection of the type of analysis (as discussed in Sect. 2) to be carried out at a particular level (sensor, gateway or data centre). The coordination mechanism also needs to take account of application specific constraints (hosted at the data centre). We consider an overall quality of service metric – associated with an application – to be composed of three individual layer metrics:

$$QoS_T = QoS_T^{L1} \bigoplus QoS_T^{L2} \bigoplus QoS_T^{L3} \tag{1}$$

where QoS_T represents the total quality of service that the system needs to support to meet application requirements, $\bigoplus$ represents the aggregation operator (and may be min or max, depending on the QoS parameter being considered), QoS_T^{L1} represents the quality of service for the clouds/data centre layer, QoS_T^{L2} is the quality of service at the gateway layer and QoS_T^{L3}, the quality of service at the sensors layer, respectively. Each QOS_T^x is influenced by constraints within that layer, for instance:

1. Sensor/device Level (L3): battery power, network coverage, on-board memory available, type of sensing (for a multi-purpose sensor) etc.
2. Gateway Level (L2): data storage, network bandwidth, operations supported (influenced by window or sample size for incoming data), number of concurrent streams processed, sample rate, etc.
3. Cloud/data centre Level (L1): throughput, response time, execution time per application, number of concurrent applications (for multi-tenancy), cost of access etc.

The coordination mechanism is, given particular constraints, attempting to improve QoS_T over a given time frame. Such a mechanism could be realised in practice by using a controller at each layer in Fig. 1, which aims to learn potential control actions. For instance:

– QoS_T – minimise response time for a particular application job running at L3, which could be achieved by: (i) reduce the size of data transfered from L2 to L1, (ii) reduce sampling interval at L3, (iii) increase number of VMs at L1. The same outcome could be realised by: (i) pre-process data at L2 and L3; (ii) increase number of VMs at L1.
– QoS_T – increase accuracy of analysis at a particular budget, which would lead to: (i) identify number of VMs within budget constraints at L1; (ii) identify data size needed from L2 to maximise VM utilisation at L1; (ii) vary sampling rate at L3 based on network capability between L2, L3 and L1, L2, etc.

Each of these application requirements could therefore be expressed as a set of min/max constraints, leading to potential control actions carried out to realise the outcome.

4   Application Scenario

To demonstrate the use of our multi-layered approach, we consider a scenario in the construction/built environments domain focusing on energy flow analysis within a building using EnergyPlus [1]. Consider a user job to be defined as: $[input, obj, deadline]$, where $input$ data is represented as $[IDF, W, [param]]$, where IDF represents the building model to be simulated, W represents the weather file required for the simulation, $[param]$ defines the parameter ranges associated with the IDF file that need to be optimised $[param] = [r_i \rightarrow (x_m, x_n)]$. We consider an optimisation $objective : [outVarName, min/max]$, defining the name of the output variable to be optimised $outVarName$ and the target of the optimisation process min/max, min:minimising the $outVarName$

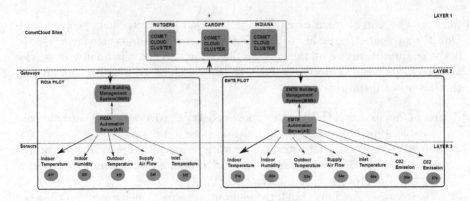

Fig. 2. Application scenario

or max:maximising the $outVarName$.$Deadline$ is a parameter defining the time interval associated with the job submitted. We make use of CometCloud [2] as our Cloud platform.

A job contains a set of tasks $N = \{t_1, t_2, t_3, ..., t_n\}$ mapped into tuples within the CometCloud tuple-space. Each task t_i is characterised by two parameters $t_i \rightarrow [ID, data]$ with the first parameter being a task identifier and $data$ represents one set of results (given a particular parameter range). The simulation output represents an optimum setpoint to be implemented within the building using suitable actuation mechanisms. We use sensor data from the $SportE^2$ project pilot called FIDIA[1] and EMTE[2] – both public sports buildings in Rome, Italy and Bilbao, Spain, respectively (Fig. 2).

Based on the layers in Fig. 1, at layer 3, each sensor in our pilot can either connect via a gateway or directly to an Automation Server (AS). Sensors are generally battery powered meters which can measure: (i) indoor temperature and air temperature inlet – via a Modbus IP protocol connected to the AS gateway; (ii) water temperature using a regular I/O operation to the AS gateway; (iii) indoor humidity – communicating to the AS gateway; (iv) supplied air flow rate measured with a velocity sensor and using I/O operations to the AS gateway. Additional details of the sensors can be found in [5].

4.1 Level 2: Building Management System and Automation Server

There are two distinct gateways: (i) Building (Energy) Management System (BMS) and (ii) Automation Server (AS) – each acting as an autonomous system. The BMS gateway is a server machine that controls the activities and spaces within the building. In addition to controlling the building's internal environment, BMS systems are sometimes linked to access control (turnstiles and access doors controlling who is allowed access to the building) or other security systems such as closed-circuit television (CCTV) and motion detectors. The AS

---

[1] http://www.asfidia.it.
[2] http://www.emtesport.com/.

gateway is a hardware-based server that is factory programmed with Struxure-Ware Building Operation software (for instance). In small installations, an AS may act as a stand-alone server, mounted with its I/O modules. In medium and large installations, functionality is distributed over multiple Automation Servers (ASs) that communicate over TCP/IP. An AS can deliver data directly to an analysis system or to other servers throughout the site. The AS can run multiple control programs, manage local I/O, alarms, and users, handle scheduling and logging, and communicate using a variety of protocols.

4.2   Level 1: CometCloud Sites Level

At this level, we have a CometCloud-based federation of resources [4,6], where each site has access to a set of heterogeneous and dynamic resources, such as public/private clouds, supercomputers, etc. Each site decides on the type computation it runs, as well as the prices based on various decision functions that include factors such as availability of resources, computational cost, etc. This federation is dynamically created at runtime where sites can join or leave at any given time. Notably, this requires a minimal configuration at each site that amounts to specifying the available resources and access credentials. We consider three sites in this scenario: at Cardiff, Rutgers, and Indiana Universities. Each site provides the following resources: Cardiff: has a virtualized cluster-based infrastructure with 12 dedicated physical machines. Each machine has 12 CPU cores at 3.2 GHz. Each virtual machine (VM) uses one core with 1 GB of memory. The networking infrastructure is 1Gbps Ethernet with a measured latency of 0.706 ms on average. Rutgers: has a cluster-based infrastructure with 32 nodes. Each node has 8 CPU cores at 2.6 GHz, 24 GB memory, and 1Gbps Ethernet connection. The measured latency on the network is 0.227 ms on average. FutureGrid: make use of an OpenStack cloud deployment at Indiana University. We have used instances of type medium, where each instance has 2 cores and 4 GB of memory. The measured latency of the cloud virtual network is 0.706 ms on average. Based on the use of CometCloud [2], each site has a master process that receives task requests from other sites, and is able to forward requests to other sites. Each site also has multiple worker processes that carry out actual task executions on locally available resources. In this application scenario, each worker is responsible for executing an EnergyPlus [1] simulation with a different input parameter range.

5   Evaluation

In our experiments we use two different configurations – (a) Cloud level analysis where the tasks are executed exclusively at the cloud level with two configurations: (i) single cloud context where all the tasks have to be processed locally (within the local site) and (ii) federated cloud context where the sites have the option of outsourcing tasks to remote sites and (b) distributed Cloud analysis where the tasks are executed on a multi-cloud infrastructure – i.e. making use of gateway nodes alongside the CometCloud deployment.

5.1 Distributed Clouds Analysis

In use case (b) above, information collected by sensors will be processed in-transit in the Gateway layer (i.e. L2) to filter out various sensor information (e.g. values out of range or certain combination of parameters that cannot lead to reasonable results) and then create jobs to be sent to sites at L1. An example of filtering at gateway layer is the average of the temperature values that are recorded at various zones of a building(north, south, etc.). Often, although significant to record these value across all the zones of a building for maintaining the optimization accuracy, it is useful to use an average of these temperature values not only to reduce the total number of EnergyPlus simulations at cloud layer but also to have a more comprehensive view of the overall building behaviours. Through such pre-filtering, we are able to reduce the computational requirement at L1. We explore the benefit of in-transit data analysis by comparing differences between these two scenarios in terms of the total cost for each site to compute all jobs, the overall time spent and number of jobs completed successfully.

We consider sensors in two geographically distributed buildings that are collecting information about the status of the building and sending this information to gateways (at L2). In order to better explore the behavior of in-transit data analysis and task distribution, we emulate the execution of the tasks and use a Poisson distribution to periodically generate sensor collected information every 100 min. A job is generated after the gateway has received data from sensors. One job will produce multiple EnergyPlus computation sub-tasks. All three sites bid for computing those jobs based on their available resources and the number of sub-tasks they can finish before the deadline. No single winner will get all the sub-tasks. Instead, these sub-tasks will be distributed to all bidder sites based on their estimation of job completion deadline. Each site will get $bidNum/allSitesTotalBidNum$ sub-tasks to compute. We allocate two local and two external workers to each site. Once a site consumes a list of sub-tasks, these tasks will be sent to workers to finish computation. *No filtering:* sensor outputs include four types of parameters which then gives a combination of 16 EnergyPlus sub-tasks per job. Each EnergyPlus sub-task takes 30 min to compute on all three sites. In Fig. 4, we observe that due to resource limitation, some jobs are rejected because these sub-tasks cannot be completed before the deadline by these three sites. Among the accepted jobs, *Not 100 % Completed* jobs are those whose sub-tasks were not completed within the given deadline. This may occur due to the availability of limited network bandwidth, scheduling constraints, placing multiple bids without knowing results of previous auctions, etc. Conversely, *100 % Completed* jobs have all sub-tasks completed on time. *With filtering:* After analysis of sensor data, we can filter out the data received from sensors, with the number of sub-tasks for each job being reduced to eight.

In order to better compare this use case with the previous one, in this experiment we assume that jobs are generated following the same process as the previous experiment. This means the total number of jobs are the same, only the number of sub-tasks per job is smaller. Figure 4 shows the number of rejected jobs, reduced after filtering. From Fig. 3a, the total execution time for completing

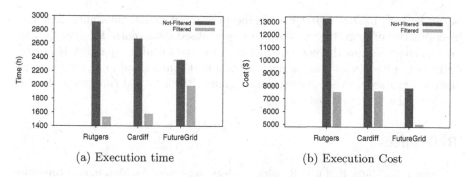

(a) Execution time

(b) Execution Cost

Fig. 3. Summary of experimental results for use cases with filter and without filter – 3a shows total execution time and 3b the total cost spent on computing all jobs

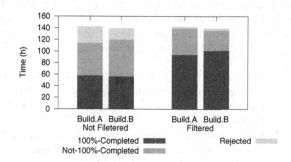

Fig. 4. Shows the number of rejected, fully & partially completed jobs

all jobs also decreases, along with reduction in total execution cost in Fig. 3b. This is mainly due to the number of sub-tasks per job, being reduced from 16 to 8 after filtering. This demonstrates the benefit of undertaking in-transit analysis via L2.

6   Conclusions

We demonstrate the benefit of supporting multi-layered Clouds, whereby computation can be distributed across multiple layers of a data capture and computation infrastructure. Each layer offers specific capabilities and constraints, and we discuss the need to support resource-aware computation to be combined across multiple layers. With increasing availability of devices that support standardised access protocols, as proposed in recent developments towards specifying IoT standards, we discuss the benefit of combining these devices with resources at federated data centres, enabling data analysis to be split across multiple layers based on a coordination mechanism. A building energy simulation scenario is used to illustrate the concept. Edge devices can range in capability – from sensing devices within limited battery power and on-board memory, to large scale scientific instruments that have significant computational capability. The current practice of migrating all data to a centralised data centre for analysis may be inefficient in how the network capacity and data centre capability is utlised. In the experiments section we demonstrate that multi-cloud analysis and coordination can reduce the total execution time with tasks and can greatly lead to reducing the execution cost.

References

1. Fumo, N., Mago, P., Luck, R.: Methodology to estimate building energy consumption using EnergyPlus benchmark models. Energy Buildings **42**(12), 2331–2337 (2010). Elsevier
2. CometCloud Project. http://nsfcac.rutgers.edu/CometCloud/. Accessed Jul 2015
3. Amazon Kinesis. http://aws.amazon.com/kinesis/. Accessed Mar 2014
4. Petri, I., Beach, T., Zou, M. et al.: Exploring models, mechanisms for exchanging resources in a federated cloud. In: International Conference on Cloud Engineering (IC2E 2014), pp. 215–224. IEEE Computer Society, Boston (2013). ISBN: 978-1-4799-3766-0
5. Petri, I., Rana, O., Yacine, R., Li, H., Beach, T., Zou, M., Diaz-Montes, J., Parashar, M.: Cloud supported building data analytics. In: 14th IEEE/ACM International Symposium on Cluster, Cloud, Grid Computing (CCGrid), 26–29 May 2014, pp. 215–224 (2014). doi:10.1109/CCGrid.2014.29
6. Diaz-Montes, J., Xie, Y., Rodero, I., Zola, J., Ganapathysubramanian, B., Parashar, M.: Exploring the use of elastic resource federations for enabling large-scale scientific workflows. In: Proceedings of Workshop on Many-Task Computing on Clouds, Grids, and Supercomputers (MTAGS), pp. 1–10 (2013)
7. National Institute of Standards and Technology (NIST): Cyber Physical Systems. http://www.nist.gov/cps/. Accessed Jul 2015
8. IEEE: P2413 IoT Architectural Framework. https://standards.ieee.org/develop/project/2413.html. Accessed Jul 2015
9. Xively. http://xively.com. Accessed Jul 2015
10. Open Sen.se/Internet of Everything. http://open.sen.se/. Accessed Jul 2015
11. Think Speak. https://thingspeak.com/. Accessed Jul 2015
12. Pacific Controls Gateway. http://pacificcontrols.net/products/galaxy.html. Accessed Jul 2015
13. IoT Cloud. http://sites.google.com/site/opensourceiotcloud/. Accessed Jul 2015
14. Open IoT. http://www.openiot.eu/. Accessed Jul 2015
15. Fernando, N., Loke, S.W., Rahayu, W.: Mobile cloud computing. Future Gener. Comput. Syst. **29**(1), 84–106 (2013)

Foundations for Simulating IoT Control Mechanisms with a Chemical Analogy

Gabor Kecskemeti$^{(\boxtimes)}$ and Zsolt Nemeth

Institute for Computer Science and Control, Hungarian Academy of Sciences,
Kende u. 13-17, Budapest 1111, Hungary
kecskemeti.gabor@sztaki.mta.hu

Abstract. The emergence of IoT systems introduced new kind of challenges for the designers of such large scale highly distributed systems. The sheer number of participating devices raises a crucial question: how they can be coordinated. Engineers often opt for using a simulator to evaluate new approaches or scenarios in various environments. This raises the second crucial question: how such a large system can be simulated efficiently. Existing simulators (even if they are IoT focused) are often focused on some particular scenarios and not capable to evaluate coordination approaches. In this paper we propose a chemical coordination model and a new extension to the DISSECT-CF cloud simulator. We expect that their combination on one hand ensures a distributed adaptive coordination on the other hand allows the separation of simulation problems into manageable sizes; these enable the analysis of large scale IoT systems with decentralized coordination approaches.

Keywords: IaaS · Internet of Things · Simulation · Actuator · Sensor · Smart object · Chemical coordination

1 Introduction

As the world gets more and more connected, the mere number of devices suggests that decentralized coordination approaches are going to be more prominent in the future. Compared to traditional distributed systems where computing resources are shared and coordinated to rapidly and efficiently reach a shared goal, internet of things (IoT) introduces new kind of resources (e.g., sensors and actuators) and goals [1]. These new resource types have remarkably different properties compared to past resource types. Such new properties demand alternative coordination mechanisms in order to enable the collaboration of these new resources with traditional distributed systems.

Smart objects (e.g., smart-phones, integrated computing facilities in actuators and sensors) in the IoT concept allow computation to be executed as near as possible to the sensing and actuating objects in the system. These smart objects are on the edge of the distributed computing infrastructure and they allow intelligent behavior of many localized IoT systems (e.g., smart homes) even without

© ICST Institute for Computer Sciences, Social Informatics and Telecommunications Engineering 2016
B. Mandler et al. (Eds.) IoT 360° 2015, Part I, LNICST 169, pp. 367–376, 2016.
DOI: 10.1007/978-3-319-47063-4_38

outsourcing computing activities (like behavior modeling and analysis, data mining of sensor data and decision making based on the results of the data mining operation). To provide better and more resilient services it was identified that advanced computational intelligence was lacking in current IoT systems [2–4].

This paper introduces a nature inspired, chemical analogy for decentralized coordination of IoT systems. Unfortunately, the nascent state of IoT systems does not allow the real life experimentation for identification of concerns and possible improvements. To overcome this issue this paper also introduces the design of an extension of the DISSECT-CF cloud and distributed systems simulator [5] which would allow its users to freely alter the rules and axioms of the chemical analogy. We expect that utilizing this extension will enable new IoT scenarios to be rapidly evaluated in such large scale distributed environments that was previously not possible.

The next sections of the paper are organized as follows: first, in Sect. 2, we introduce the related works that already have some success of introducing simulation techniques for IoT systems. Next, in Sect. 3, we show how can a chemical analogy help us improve the coordination and computational intelligence in IoT systems. The section also provides an overview of the chemical computing models and the ways one can customize such models to better fit to new previously unexplored scenarios. Finally, Sect. 4 shows how the chemical model can be applied in an advanced simulation toolkit (i.e. DISSECT-CF). The section also provides an overview on the necessary extensions for the simulator and the ways the simulation can be distributed to better model the non-centralized system view available most IoT systems.

2 Related Works

In [6], I. Moschakis and H. Karatza, introduces several simulation concepts for IoT systems. First, they show how the interfacing between the various cloud providers and IoT systems could be modeled in a simulation. Next, they provide a novel model for IoT related workloads where data is processed from sensors taking part in the IoT system. Unfortunately, their work do not consider actuators, and mainly discusses the behavior of cloud systems that support the processing of data originated from the IoT system. In contrast, the our simulation concepts put more emphasis on how sensors actuators and smart objects on the edges of clouds would interface with each other and with the cloud systems.

[7] introduces SimIoT, which is derived from the SimIC simulation framework [8]. SimIoT provides a deeper insight into the behavior of IoT systems, but still restrains itself to the basic sensor-data processing scenario. Compared to the previously introduced work by Moschakis et al., this simulator introduces several techniques (e.g. a broker) that simulates the communication between an IoT sensor and the cloud. Alongside, SimIoT the authors introduce a new – more interactive – user concept as well which is significantly different from the widely accepted big data processing model. Compared to this work, SimIoT is limited by its compute oriented activity modeling.

While the previous simulation approaches were focusing on larger scale systems, [9] addresses IoT simulation from a completely different perspective. Simulations in that paper are visual, allow the observation of the behavior of the simulated system in real time and are more similar to industrial modeling tools than the previously mentioned simulators. Such simulators allow precise modeling of actuator and smart object operations depending on the sensor's output – because of their detailed models such simulations are more useful for smaller systems (like evaluating IoT behavior in a factory or allowing student experiments with self-built systems). In this paper, we aim at introducing a simulation framework that allows to incorporate as much detail as possible while it still allows to model the size of amount of resources necessary for sufficient evaluation of new IoT coordination models based on the chemical analogy.

Amongst recent works, [10] is one of the few which deals with the dynamic nature of IoT systems namely, it investigates fault behaviors and introduces a fault model for such systems. Although faults are important part of dependability and IoT, the scalability of the introduced fault behaviors and concepts (e.g., the applied use case scenario in their paper is home automation just like in [11]) are not sufficient for modeling large enough systems that would benefit from the decentralized control mechanisms we envisioned in this paper.

Finally, [11,12] both introduce novel infrastructure coordination techniques that support the use of larger scale IoT systems. In both cases the authors evaluate their approaches with a simulation framework. In [11], CloudSim [13] is used to model a community cloud based on residential infrastructures. On top of CloudSim the authors provide customizations that are tailored for their specific home automation scenarios and therefore limit the applicability of their extensions for evaluating new IoT coordination approaches. These papers are also limited on sensors/smart objects thus not allowing to evaluate a wide range of IoT scenarios that are expected to rise to widespread use in the near future [1].

With respect to the chemical model proposed in this paper, the γ-family (the chemical calculus and the related languages) has already been investigated in various scenarios, like self-organizing systems [14] where a self-healing, self-optimizing and self-protecting mail system is studied; enacting workflows on-the-fly with strong emphasis on dynamicity [15], modeling self-developing secure virtual organizations [16] and dynamic service composition [17] and many others.

3   Chemical Analogy for IoT Control

A brief introduction to chemical computing. Most algorithms are described as a series of computational steps, operations applied to data elements and computing is governed by a control thread. The chemical paradigm radically obliterates this notion rather, a program is conceived as a chemical solution where data and procedures are molecules floating around and computation is a series of reactions between these molecules. This vision of chemical computing is formalized in the γ-calculus [18] as (without the chemical guise) a declarative functional computational model where terms are commutative and associative.

The fundamental data structure in the γ-calculus [18] is the multiset that are affected by so called reactions taking place independently and potentially simultaneously, according to local and actual conditions yielding a multiset rewriting system. There is no centralized control, ordering, serialization, rather the computation is carried out in an indeterministic, inherently parallel, self-evolving way. Molecules, i.e. γ-terms are variables, γ-abstractions (procedure definitions) and solutions (separated by membranes). Juxtaposition of γ-terms is commutative and associative realizing the 'Brownian-motion', the free distribution and unspecified reaction order among molecules that is a basic principle in the chemical paradigm. γ-abstractions are the reactive molecules that can take other molecules and transform them by reduction; molecules of a reaction are extracted by pattern matching. The semantics of a γ-reduction is very similar to that of λ-calculus. Reactions may depend on certain conditions and can also capture multiple molecules in a single atomic step. Besides the associativity and commutativity, reactions are governed by: (i) law of locality, i.e. if a reaction can occur, it will occur in the same way irrespectively to the environment; and (ii) membrane law, i.e. reactions can occur in nested solutions, solutions may contain sub-solutions separated by a membrane. The γ-calculus is a *higher order* model, where abstractions – just like any other molecules – can be passed as parameters or yielded as a result of a reduction. The Higher Order Chemical Language (HOCL) [18] is a language realized on the principles of the γ-calculus.

The concept of IoT coordination based on the chemical computing model. An IoT scenario can be seen as a large set of various entities, notably sensors, actuators and smart objects. Sensors and actuators are the gateways between the physical and the virtual world: sensors provide data such as temperature or speed whereas actuators realize some physical transformations according to decisions such as increase heating or apply brakes. Smart objects furthermore, have the capability to compute and communicate. There are some goals predefined to be fulfilled and can be achieved by the interaction of these entities – we are aimed at providing a nature inspired coordination mechanism to facilitate these interactions.

To create such a model we set up the following assumptions and requirements. (i) entities are independent from each other and can perform their activities concurrently. (ii) entities do not have any predefined pattern for their interaction other than their goal and the conditions how to reach it (iii) entities may change their functional and non-functional characteristics of their services any time, even abruptly. (iv) entities can select the cooperating entities (either as consumer or provider) at their discretion. (v) the state of the entity can be changed by their interacting parties only and unaffected by others. (vi) entities must accommodate to local and actual conditions.

To facilitate the flexible and adaptive yet predictable interaction of entities, we envision a chemical metaphor where entities correspond to molecules dissolved in a solution. Molecules also represent data or intermediate control information provided by the entities. Molecules thus, can move freely which, on one hand models their mobility, on the other hand the Brownian motion ensures engaging in reactions in their vicinity. A molecule has its chemical properties that determine which other molecules can react with and in what conditions – this corresponds to the conditions an entity must fulfill before it can perform its activities. The series of reactions transform the molecules and reactions are possible until a molecule becomes inert. At this point the entity modeled by the molecule namely, an actuator or a smart object is triggered accordingly. Each reaction transforms the molecules closer to their inert state yet, there is no pre-defined order or governing of reactions other than the chemical properties of the molecules. Entities could be self-evolving towards a state when they are enabled to perform their tasks, constantly accommodating to local and actual conditions.

In this very simple vision we may express the followings. (i) Molecules pre-cisely define the entity and also define the conditions that must be fulfilled before the goal can be reached. These conditions determine the matching mole-cules and the types of reactions that can transform the molecule towards its inert state. Some molecules may act as catalysts: they must be present in the reaction (enabling a transformation) but remain intact afterwards. (ii) There can be global conditions that must be kept satisfied, they can model certain bound-aries of the IoT environment such as overall energy consumption. (iii) Sensors and smart objects insert molecules into the virtual solution, this way the phys-ical world is converted into the virtual chemical world where the coordination takes place. (iv) In contrast, an inert molecule triggers an action in the physi-cal world via smart objects or actuators. Note, that the chemical model is not applied for problem solving but solely *coordinates* the execution. Reaching an inert state is an exit point form the coordination level. (v) Reactions are affected by local and actual conditions. Since changes in the world are represented in the virtual chemical solution, the coordination mechanism adapts to the changing conditions.

4   Simulation Approach Towards the Chemical Analogy

4.1   The DISSECT-CF Cloud Simulator

DISSECT-CF [5,19] is a compact, highly customizable open source[1] cloud sim-ulator with special focus on the internal organization and behavior of IaaS sys-tems. Figure 1 presents its architecture (as of version 0.9.6). The figure groups the major components with dashed lines into subsystems. Each subsystem is implemented as independently from the others as possible. There are five major subsystems each responsible for a particular aspect of internal IaaS function-ality: (i) event system – for a primary time reference; (ii) unified resource sharing – to resolve low-level resource bottleneck situations; (iii) energy mod-eling – for the analysis of energy-usage patterns of individual resources (e.g., network links, CPUs) or their aggregations; (iv) infrastructure simulation – to model physical and virtual machines as well as networked entities; and finally (v) infrastructure management – to provide a real life cloud like API and encapsulate cloud level scheduling (the target of improvements presented here).

---

[1] Available from: https://github.com/kecskemeti/dissect-cf.

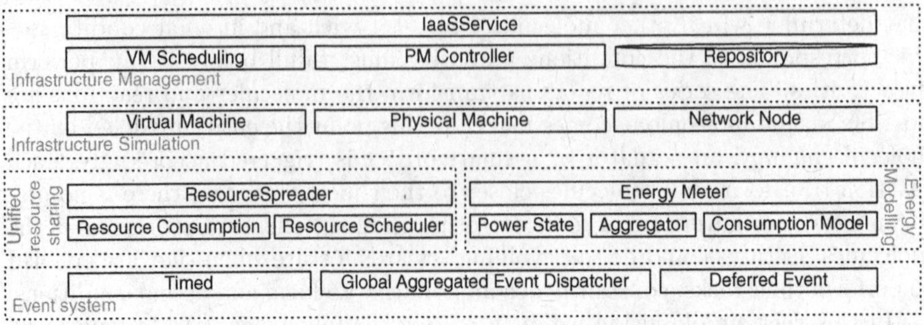

Fig. 1. The architecture of the DISSECT-CF simulator

4.2 New IoT Related Simulation Constructs

As we aim at supporting the simulation of hundreds of millions of devices participating in previously unforeseen IoT scenarios, the high performance of the simulator's resource sharing mechanism is essential therefore, we have chosen to use the DISSECT-CF simulator because of its unified resource sharing foundation. Building on this foundation it is possible to implement the basic constructs of IoT systems (e.g., smart objects, sensors or actuators) and keep the performance of the past simulator. In the following, we list the four main entities in our extension and we show how they participate in an IoT simulation:

- *Sensors.* These passive entities in the simulated system have four major features: (*i*) their performance is limited by their connectivity and maximum update frequency; (*ii*) they can provide historical data (preloaded from a file and offered based on the time and situation of the sensor query); (*iii*) they can offer dynamic data based on user provided custom algorithms that alter the sensor's reported metrics; and finally (*iv*) in some cases replicating data from sensors of the real world would help to steer the rest of the simulator's sensors (e.g., a few sensors could bridge with the real world).
- *Actuators.* Although DISSECT-CF is aimed at simulating the properties of computing systems both sensors and actuators could extend these properties further. Therefore, the simulator allows its users to integrate with third party libraries and also allows the dynamic sensor behavior to be updated via the actuator interface (i.e. acting like some of the physical properties around the sensor really changed). Similarly to sensors, these interfaces are limited by their network connectivity and reaction time (e.g., how long does it take to actually perform an actuation action). Actuators also have the unique feature that allow the changing of the locations of others (except the central services).
- *Smart objects* are simulated as localized and significantly limited computing and storage resources that might be coupled with some sensors and actuators and that might perform regular activities arriving from their coupled counterparts. With these objects local goals of the particular IoT system can often be achieved. Also the chemical analogy might coordinate several smart objects

in the vicinity to work together in order to achieve the local goals without turning to the central services. These coordination steps might be needed for long delays experienced with central services or because privacy concerns, etc.

– *Central computing services*. These computing services provide the large scale background processing and storage capabilities some big data applications building on the other actors might need. In the chemical analogy, these services are expected to be used only if unavoidable.

In all cases, dynamic location information is offered with the actors. Allowing one of the most crucial information and behavior (i.e., the brownian motion and membrane formation) to be simulated for the chemical analogy. Failures of the actors are also modeled on two levels: location based resource availability (e.g., an action cannot be taken because the actuator cannot reach the particular location) and physical device degradation (e.g., an actuator is no longer capable to accomplish its tasks). Users are free to provide failure models for both cases.

4.3   The Role of the Chemical Model in IoT Simulations

As we aim at simulating millions of sensors/actuators/smart objects, it can be foreseen that the simulations cannot be run on a single host (e.g. mainly because of memory constraints – e.g., a single sensor might consume only a dozen or so bytes of memory but modeling messages and activities between them could introduce several orders of magnitude more memory requirements). On the other hand, the chemical model has both the locality principle and the separation of the solutions by a membrane. Therefore, we propose to divide the DISSECT-CF simulations into simulation of localities or sub-solutions – this separation is shown in Fig. 2 with separate boxes per membrane (i.e., per simulator host). These membranes on one hand may be permeable and allow the molecules to move across the boundary, on the other hand they significantly limit the number of actors to be simulated at a time.

Although in most cases the time in the various simulations can be kept diverging (because of the lack of chemical control across membrane boundaries), during the contact of the central computing services a clock synchronization must occur between the various simulation cores. This clock synchronization ensures the happened before relations of the various simulation events can be ensured even across membrane boundaries. The clock synchronization mechanism is also ensuring that simulations of network communications between the membranes are possible and incoming/outgoing network links from/to membranes are ensured to be working according to the resource sharing rules in the simulator by the new cross membrane network synchronization component.

Next, the original main simulator functionalities are executed on top of the central DISSECT-CF core. Within this simulation we evaluate the big data processing and storage operations. Here the user of the simulator can define the large scale computing operations as well as the capabilities of the centralized infrastructure. In case of commercial IoT applications this centralized infrastructure could be simulated as a private cloud hosted on the company's premises.

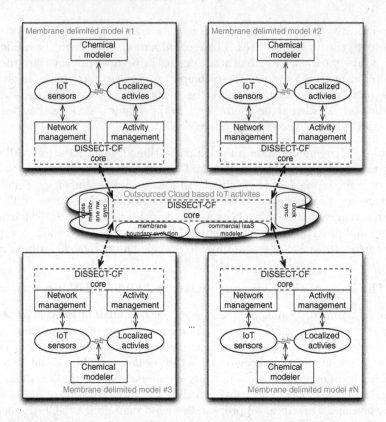

Fig. 2. Multi host IoT simulation for localized chemical solutions and centralized outsourcing capabilities

Finally, inside the membranes operations of actors in the simulation will take place as coordinated by the chemical modeler. This component guarantees the Brownian motion based quasi-random activity to sensor/actuator mapping. Thus, the chemical modeler will be the main user of the membrane level DISSECT-CF core components by instructing the actors for their tasks and ensuring that localized goals within the membrane are met according to the chemical ruleset (e.g. possible reactions, available catalysts). The simulator allows the customization of this ruleset thus, allows the evaluation of multiple organization strategies even at the lowest level of the simulations.

5   Conclusions

In this paper we have introduced a new simulation technique for IoT systems. This technique has built on two existing concepts and solutions: (*i*) coordinating distributed systems through a chemical analogy and (*ii*) simulating centralized cloud components and low level IoT concepts with the help of the unified resource sharing foundation of the DISSECT-CF simulator. The chemical model allows the separation of actors in a controlled way and keeping the size of each such partition (sub-solution separated by membranes) proper for efficient simulation. We expect that with the help of these DISSECT-CF extensions future research will be capable of analyze new decentralized coordination approaches in IoT systems. In our future works, we plan to further investigate the possible chemical to IoT entity mappings and the ways they can alter our thinking about IoT systems and their coordination.

Acknowledgements. This paper was partially supported by the János Bolyai Research Scholarship of the Hungarian Academy of Sciences, by the COST Program Action IC1304: Autonomous Control for a Reliable Internet of Services (ACROSS) as well as the European Unions Horizon 2020 research and innovation programme under Grant Agreement No. 644179 (ENTICE).

References

1. Miorandi, D., Sicari, S., De Pellegrini, F., Chlamtac, I.: Internet of things: vision, applications and research challenges. Ad Hoc Netw. **10**(7), 1497–1516 (2012)
2. Tsai, C.-W., Lai, C.-F., Vasilakos, A.V.: Future internet of things: open issues and challenges. Wirel. Netw. **20**(8), 2201–2217 (2014)
3. Baresi, L., Mottola, L., Dustdar, S.: Building software for the internet of things. IEEE Internet Comput. **2**, 6–8 (2015)
4. Karatza, H.D., Mavromoustakis, C.X.: Special issue on simulation-based performance evaluation of infrastructures for the internet of things: connectivity and resource considerations in the mobility Era. Simul. Model. Pract. Theory **34**, 157–158 (2013)
5. Kecskemeti, G.: DISSECT-CF: a simulator to foster energy-aware scheduling in infrastructure clouds. Simul. Model. Pract. Theory **58**, 188–218 (2015)
6. Moschakis, I.A., Karatza, H.D.: Towards scheduling for internet-of-things applications on clouds: a simulated annealing approach. Concurrency Comput. Pract. Experience **27**(8), 1886–1899 (2015)
7. Sotiriadis, S., Bessis, N., Asimakopoulou, E., Mustafee, N.: Towards simulating the internet of things. In: 2014 28th International Conference on Advanced Information Networking and Applications Workshops (WAINA), pp. 444–448. IEEE (2014)
8. Sotiriadis, S., Bessis, N., Antonopoulos, N., Anjum, A.: Simic: designing a new inter-cloud simulation platform for integrating large-scale resource management. In: 2013 IEEE 27th International Conference on Advanced Information Networking and Applications (AINA), pp. 90–97. IEEE (2013)
9. Dhoutaut, D., Piranda, B., Bourgeois, J.: Efficient simulation of distributed sensing and control environments. In: Green Computing and Communications (GreenCom), 2013 IEEE and Internet of Things (iThings/CPSCom), IEEE International Conference on and IEEE Cyber, Physical and Social Computing, pp. 452–459. IEEE (2013)
10. Silva, I., Leandro, R., Macedo, D., Guedes, L.A.: A dependability evaluation tool for the internet of things. Comput. Electr. Eng. **39**(7), 2005–2018 (2013)

11. Khan, A.M., Navarro, L., Sharifi, L., Veiga, L.: Clouds of small things: Provisioning infrastructure-as-a-service from within community networks. In: 2013 IEEE 9th International Conference on Wireless and Mobile Computing, Networking and Communications (WiMob), pp. 16–21. IEEE (2013)

12. Manate, B., Fortis, T.-F., Negru, V.: Optimizing cloud resources allocation for an internet of things architecture. Scal. Comput. Pract. Experience 15(4), 345–355 (2015)

13. Calheiros, R.N., Ranjan, R., Beloglazov, A., De Rose, C.A., Buyya, R.: CloudSim: a toolkit for modeling and simulation of cloud computing environments and evaluation of resource provisioning algorithms. Softw. Pract. Experience 41(1), 23–50 (2011)

14. Banâtre, J.-P., Fradet, P., Radenac, Y.: Programming self-organizing systems with the higher-order chemical language. Int. J. Unconventional Comput. 3(3), 161–177 (2007)

15. Caeiro, M., Németh, Z., Priol, T.: A chemical model for dynamic workflow coordination. In: PDP, pp. 215–222 (2011)

16. Arenas, A.E., Banâtre, J.-P., Priol, T.: Developing autonomic and secure virtual organisations with chemical programming. In: Guerraoui, R., Petit, F. (eds.) SSS 2009. LNCS, vol. 5873, pp. 75–89. Springer, Heidelberg (2009)

17. Banâtre, J.-P., Priol, T.: Chemical programming of future service-oriented architectures. JSW 4(7), 738–746 (2009)

18. Banâtre, J.-P., Fradet, P., Radenac, Y.: Generalised multisets for chemical programming. Math. Struct. Comp. Sci. 16, 557–580 (2006)

19. Kecskemeti, G., Ostermann, S., Prodan, R.: Fostering energy-awareness in simulations behind scientific workflow management systems. In: The 7th IEEE/ACM International Conference on Utility and Cloud Computing (UCC), pp. 29–38. IEEE Computer Society, London, December 2014

Towards Urban Mobile Sensing
as a Service: An Experience from Southern Italy

Marco Zappatore[1,2(✉)], Antonella Longo[1,2], Mario A. Bochicchio[1], Daniele Zappatore[1],
Alessandro A. Morrone[1], and Gianluca De Mitri[1]

[1] Department of Innovation Engineering, University of Salento,
via Monteroni sn, 73100 Lecce, Italy
{marcosalvatore.zappatore,mario.bochicchio,
antonella.longo}@unisalento.it,
{danielemario.zappatore,alessandroantonio.morrone,
gianluca.demitri}@studenti.unisalento.it
[2] Alba Project s.r.l., via Don Luigi Sturzo 36, 73100 Lecce, Italy
{marco.zappatore,antonella.longo}@albaproject.it

Abstract. A considerable amount of research activities deals with Internet of Things and Smart Cities, by leveraging the continuously growing usage of cloud computing solutions and mobile devices. The pervasivity of mobiles also enables the Mobile Crowd Sensing paradigm, which aims at using mobile-embedded sensors to ease the monitoring of multiple phenomena. The combination of these elements has recently converged into a new sensing model: Sensing as a Service (S^2aaS), which is expected to offer novel monitoring approaches in the next years. In this paper, we propose a platform to pave the way for applying S^2aaS in urban scenarios by considering both noise and electromagnetic field exposure. Design and implementation choices are discussed, along with privacy-related issues and preliminary monitoring tests conducted at a city in Southern Italy, in order to demonstrate the suitability of our approach.

Keywords: Mobile crowd sensing · Sensing as a service · Noise monitoring · Electromagnetic monitoring · Data warehouse · FIWARE

1 Introduction

Both the *Internet of Things* (IoT) and the *Smart Cities* (SCs) terms are nowadays largely adopted: the former one refers to technological advancements that offer unprecedented levels of connectivity to both users and machines, whilst the latter one identifies urban scenarios where city problems are tackled with novel IT solutions. They both mostly leverage the enormous diffusion of Cloud Computing (CC) and mobiles (e.g., smartphones, tablets), boosted by the mobile broadband (MBB) technology, which currently represents one of the most dynamic market segments worldwide. Higher data rates, more reliable coverage and improved Quality of Service determined a penetration rate of 47 % for MBB and an overall network coverage of 69 % of the world population (89 % if we consider the urban population only) for the year 2015 [1]. The trend for the year 2020

© ICST Institute for Computer Sciences, Social Informatics and Telecommunications Engineering 2016
B. Mandler et al. (Eds.) IoT 360° 2015, Part I, LNICST 169, pp. 377–387, 2016.
DOI: 10.1007/978-3-319-47063-4_39

envisions that worldwide mobile subscriptions will amount 9.2bn (6.1bn for smart-phones) [1] while currently they are 7.1bn (2.6bn for smartphones). The expected number of connected devices will skyrocket, reaching nearly 30bn entities in 2020.

In this highly dynamic scenario, a new paradigm is emerging, known as *Sensing as a Service (S^2aaS)* [2], which aims at solving typical SC challenges by exploiting CC and IoT infrastructures and by offering multiple sensing capabilities in order to satisfy heterogeneous sensing requests coming from different geographical areas. Mobiles, along with their rich set of embedded (or pluggable external) sensors and their high pervasivity, represent at the moment the most suitable way to offer such sensing capabilities on a large scale without revolving to traditional Wireless Sensor Networks (WSNs) approaches. Therefore, S^2aaS is firmly rooted on the Mobile Crowd Sensing (MCS) paradigm [3], which allows collecting data directly from mobiles and overcomes typical limitations of WSNs (thanks to wider coverage areas, high number of deployable nodes, more reliable communication and connectivity). Users can choose monitoring modalities (*participatory sensing*) or delegate their mobiles to send data automatically (*opportunistic sensing*). Both the approaches can be combined properly in S^2aaS to satisfy different needs, such as directly requesting mobile owners to perform measurements or simply sending automatic sensing tasks to mobiles in a given area.

Urban scenarios offer a promising arena for MCS applications, where citizens can consume/provide information about specific situations occurring around them. We believe that this can improve the S^2aaS paradigm, that we can define as *Urban Mobile Sensing as a Service (UMS^2aaS)* to point out how it is deeply tailored on SCs challenges and issues. Citizens could be dynamically scattered across huge areas with multiple sensing purposes and they could acquire contextual awareness from the surrounding environment [4]. Similarly, they could be engaged in collaborative, large-scale monitoring experiences that widen the scope of traditional sensing campaigns [5].

In this paper, we propose a platform capable of paving the way for the deployment of UMS^2aaS solutions by: (1) identifying noise and electromagnetic (EM) monitoring as suitable urban sensing scenarios; (2) proposing a mobile app for gathering data from sensors and optional users' comments; (3) proposing a cloud-based data management system; (4) estimating platform data growth.

As for a technical point of view, we designed, developed and tested (at a city in Southern Italy) a system prototype that gathers data from mobiles and sends them to a context broker application, which forwards them to a Hadoop-based server farm. Then, a complete ETL (Extract-Transform-Load) pipeline elaborates measurements in a Data Warehouse (DWH) system: they are aggregated w.r.t. sensing location, device type, timestamp, serving network type/provider. These functionalities are achieved by merging a set of components from FIWARE middleware [6] with our platform.

The paper is organized as it follows: Sect. 2 briefly examines MCS paradigm and our research purposes; the proposed platform is detailed in Sect. 3; discussions about the platform prototype are presented in Sect. 4; Section 5 enlists conclusions.

2   State-of-the-Art and Research Purposes

MCS is the enabling element for S^2aas and UMS^{2}aaS paradigms and it actually helps addressing multiple urban monitoring issues such as traffic and road safety [3]; air [7] and water [8] pollution; noise [9]; flooding [10]; earthquakes [11], large-scale events [12]. Let us now consider the two identified monitoring scenarios for our research. As for noise monitoring, the majority of MCS applications are for personal use only: they mimic Sound Level Meters (SLMs) interfaces and allow users to check how loud much their surrounding environment is (e.g., Advanced Decibel Meter[1], Sound Meter Pro[2]). However, they do not provide data aggregation on a geographical/temporal basis. Very few research works address urban noise mapping, such as the "Ear-Phone" project [9] where smartphones are used to predict outdoor sound levels or the "2Loud?" project [13] that uses iPhones to assess nocturnal indoor noise near highways in Australia.

Conversely, a comparable diffusion of MCS solutions for EM field level assessment is not yet available. The majority of them only refers to Wi-Fi indoor coverage analysis [14] or outdoor Access Points (APs) localization [15], with very few proposals considering 3G/4G systems, specifically tailored to evaluate traffic data for network operators rather than users [16] or quantifying signal strength for single devices [17].

MCS-based noise and EM monitoring currently suffer from a series of limitations: (1) absence of functionalities tailored to city managers for improving citizens' life quality; (2) users' involvement as mere data collectors, without providing them with educational outcomes or trying to raise awareness; (3) lack of extensive monitoring purposes. Our platform aims at filling these gaps. Firstly, we want to increase users' awareness about phenomena under observation by adding educational contents in the mobile app. Secondly, we aim at complying with S^2aaS by adopting proper architectural design solutions and a general-purpose data modelling approach, easily customizable for different sensing scenarios. Thirdly, our platform will act as a preliminary, low-cost, large-scale and sufficiently accurate monitoring tool for locating areas with potential pollution risks where more accurate sensing campaigns can be performed.

We referred to noise and EM monitoring to test our platform, since European citizens are particularly concerned about these topics. Urban noise is considered one of the most relevant factors of life quality condition worsening [18] (due to congested roads, high-traffic, wrong or obsolete urban planning) and still very few interventions are made by city managers and local administrations to reduce citizenship's noise exposure [19]. Several scientific research works examining the correlations between health effects and noise enforce the necessity of proper monitoring, since noise exposure may determine progressive hearing losses, stress, distraction, sleep fragmentation, socio-behavioral changes, hypertension and other long-term or chronic diseases [20].

---

[1] https://itunes.apple.com/us/app/advanced-decibel-meter/id595718101?mt=8.
[2] https://play.google.com/store/apps/details?id=com.soundmeter.app&hl=it.

Similarly, EM pollution concern is due to the increasing number of base stations that are installed across our cities. However, whilst citizens can perceive quite easily their exposure to noise by referring to the "loudness" of the surrounding emitting sources, the exposure to EM fields is even more difficult to be evaluated. Despite this inherent complexity, and although no scientific research works have yet determined a direct correlation between EM fields and medium/long-term health effects, public opinion is becoming more and more sensitive to this problem [21]. From a monitoring point of view, whilst mobile-embedded microphones can provide sufficient accuracy in assessing noise levels, EM fields cannot be sensed so easily: mobile internal antennas provide neither broadband metering nor a direct quantification of the effective electric field levels in a given point (they can assess the received signal strength from their serving cell). Therefore, we performed an accurate selection of the physical quantities under observation and we introduced some error-mitigation policies (Subsect. 4.2).

3 The Proposed System

3.1 Adopted Quantifiers for Noise and Signal Strength Exposure

Our system provides both noise and signal strength opportunistic measurements. Noise measurements can be also achieved in a participatory way. As for the noise exposure quantification, we adopted the well-known A-weighting scale, which measures the Sound Pressure Level (*SPL*) in units of *dB(A)* [22] and allows assessing the dependence of perceived loudness w.r.t. frequency. The *SPL* is an instantaneous measurement, therefore actual noise regulations require to consider also the Equivalent Sound Level $L_{EQ(T)}$ [22] quantity to cope effectively with sounds varying in time and having different durations. The $L_{EQ(T)}$ averages, in *dB(A)*, *SPL* values measured during a given time window *T* (which ranges typically from 30 s to 24 h), thus smoothing spikes and outliers. Despite mobile-embedded microphones differ from professional sound metering equipment due to a series of limitations (e.g., optimization for voice reception rather than environmental noise; reduced sensitivity; heterogeneous usage conditions, etc.), several recent studies demonstrated the effectiveness of MCS applications for noise monitoring scenarios, by assessing mismatches between ± 1.5 dB and ± 5 dB [23].

Signal strength measurements estimate the power level received by mobile antennas and can be used as a quantifier for electric field exposure in the range 0.9-2.4 GHz, even if they are not as accurate as broadband field probes. For both UMTS and LTE networks, we refer to the RSSI (Received Signal Strength Indicator) quantity [24], which expresses in *dBm* the total received power over the carrier frequency. The RSSI includes: signals from the co-channel serving cell, interferences from non-serving neighboring cells, thermal noise, etc. However, each mobile is able to provide RSSI from just its serving network provider, therefore RSSI is always a portion of the overall signal power available in a given location (since signals from other providers are also present but not sensed by that mobile) and this casts the need of post-processing analyses (Subsect. 3.3). Additionally, we refer to RSRP (Reference Signal Received Power), for both UMTS and LTE. It represents the linear average over the power contributions in Watt of the resource elements carrying cell-specific reference signals along carrier frequency (therefore

RSRP is always lower than RSSI). RSRP expresses, in *ASU* (i.e., Arbitrary Strength Unit, which is an integer value proportional to the received signal strength), the contribution of the pilot channels compared to RSSI.

3.2 Data Modeling

Data coming from sensors are multidimensional [25], thus a typical solution for dealing with them is to follow a DWH approach [26], according to which data are processed in an ETL pipeline, thus allowing us to clean, transform and store measurements before aggregating and making them available to final users. We adopted the Dimensional Fact Model (DFM) [26], which is a graphical conceptual model based upon the *fact* entity (i.e., any concept evolving in time, relevant to decision-making processes). We identified two facts: noise (Fig. 1A) and signal strength measurements (Fig. 1B). Facts (the central rounded boxes) are described qualitatively by *fact attributes* and quantitatively by *fact measures* (i.e., numerical properties or calculations, enlisted in the bottom part of the fact). Noise *fact measures* are *SPL* and current/max/min/average $L_{EQ(T)}$, both in *dB(A)*. Similarly, signal strength *fact measures* are *RSRP* value (in *ASU*) and current/max/min/average *RSSI* value (in *dBm*). Each analysis coordinate of a fact is called a *dimension* and it consists of several *dimensional attributes* organized as a directed tree departing from the fact (the attributes are the circles connected by lines to the fact; the dimension is the root circle). Dimensional attributes qualify the finite domain of their dimension along with its different degrees of granularity (e.g., the temporal dimension can vary from seconds to days, weeks, months; a product is described by its name, series, brand, etc.). The dimensions shared among multiple facts are the *conformed hierarchies*: time (timestamp, date/month/year); position (latitude, longitude, town, province, region, country); sensor type (external or embedded); device type (model and brand) and outlier condition. The device type also stores the IMEI (International Mobile Equipment Identity) code, which univocally identifies each mobile. The signal strength fact also has the following dimensions: MNC (Mobile Network Code, i.e. the network provider) and network (e.g., GSM, UMTS, LTE). The noise fact also has an optional dimension

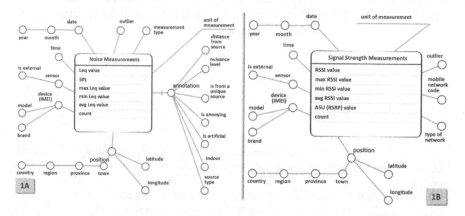

Fig. 1. DFM representation: noise (on the left) and signal strength (on the right) measurements.

representing user's annotations about the source (e.g., type, annoyance, distance, etc.). Unit of measurement is the *descriptive attribute* (depicted as a simple line departing from the fact) for both the facts.

3.3 Platform Architecture and ETL Pipeline

Our platform consists of a mobile sensing app and of a cloud-based system tasked to data management. The app works on Android mobile devices (and exploits Android 4.2 APIs[3]; the app mimics a professional SLM user interface and collects peak, average and current values of *SPL* and $L_{EQ(T)}$ on customizable temporal windows, as required by EU and Italian noise regulations. It also collects *RSSI* and *RSRP* values that assess the power of the signal received by the mobile. Measurements are stored locally (short-term history) and sent to the cloud-hosted system for data aggregation and filtering. The data brokering functionality is achieved by using Orion[4], a Generic Enabler (GE) from FIWARE middleware [6] that provides publishing and subscribing operations on collected data. Another FIWARE GE, Cosmos[5], offers the HDFS-based persistent storage (but other solutions are under examination at the moment). Orion data are persisted in Cosmos thanks to the FIWARE Cygnus[6] connector. Figure 2 depicts the proposed three-layer logical architecture. The first layer consists of non-persistent sensor data storage on mobiles (implemented via SQLite), of persistent storage on the cloud (implemented via Apache Hive) and of relational DBs for law regulations, device technical specifications and administrative divisions. The second layer has context-brokering capabilities for managing multiple sensors as well as data filtering (thanks to Pentaho CE[7], a freeware ETL application), integration and reporting functionalities. The third layer offers a Web app for accessing data reporting and integration results. Mobiles and a limited number of fixed monitoring stations represent data sources. We also developed a Web app for data visualization purposes, according to requirements elicited from users (i.e., city managers, citizens, students).

The ETL pipeline is responsible for data management, outlier identification and removal process as well as for the *RSSI* aggregation of measurements from mobiles served by different network providers but located in the same area in a relatively short time window. By doing so, it is possible to achieve a more realistic evaluation of the overall received power in a given area, since each mobile is able to quantify only the RSSI provided by its serving network operator.

---

[3] Android 4.2 APIs (Level 17): http://developer.android.com/about/versions/android-4.2.html.
[4] Orion: http://catalogue.fiware.org/enablers/publishsubscribe-context-broker-orion-context-broker.
[5] Cosmos: http://catalogue.fiware.org/enablers/bigdata-analysis-cosmos.
[6] Cygnus Connector: https://github.com/telefonicaid/fiware-cygnus#section1.
[7] Pentaho Community Edition: http://community.pentaho.com/projects/data-integration/.

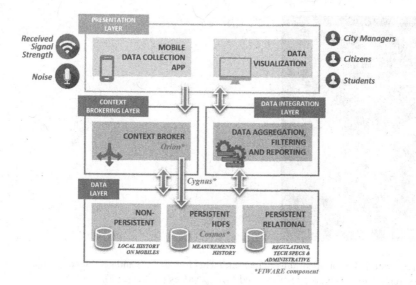

Fig. 2. Platform logical architecture.

4   Prototype Platform Analysis

4.1   On-Site Trials

A group of students from our University tested the platform in a central area of the city of Lecce (Southern Italy). The selected area presents high-traffic hotspots (two round-abouts and two 4-lane roads) and two base stations hosting multiple antennas from different network providers (on the rooftop of two multi-storey buildings).

As for the mobile app usage test, we evaluated the opportunistic sensing mode by collecting measurements in 1-hour time windows by walking across the area. Once started, the app does not require any further intervention by the user, who can examine measurements at any time, as indicated in Fig. 3A (app overall page for opportunistic measurements). Both $L_{EQ(T)}$ and SPL values are reported and plotted on a XY graph. Additionally, selected observation time window T, actual $RSSI$ and serving network type are indicated. The user can stop the sensing session with a dedicated button (page bottom). The participatory sensing mode allows users to decide when performing a measurement and whether enriching it with comments assessing noise sources w.r.t. location (indoor/outdoor), nature (artificial/natural), estimated distance from the observer, typology (amongst a set of predefined values). It is also possible to quantify perceived nuisance levels (by activating a slider on a 10-value scale) and to add free-text comments. This mode is available for noise measurement only, since the assessment of EM emitting sources is much more difficult for unskilled users.

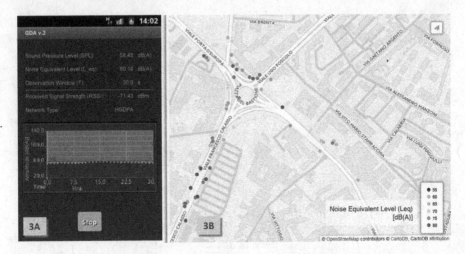

Fig. 3. Mobile UI for opportunistic measurements (on the left) and georeferenced map of noise measurement locations along with sensed $L_{EQ\,(30s)}$ values (on the right).

Users can benefit from a Web application for georeferencing and visualizing measurements coming from a given area as points on a map with a colour ramp directly proportional to measured values: both $L_{EQ(T)}$ and *RSSI* values can be plotted on this map. Figure 3B reports the $L_{EQ\,(30s)}$ values sensed across the selected area. Measurements can be interpolated as well, thus achieving an *intensity map*, which is a surface map where adjacent measurements are interpolated according to a given algorithm in order to compute values also for those points where no measurements were actually performed. Intensity maps are extremely useful for understanding how measured levels are distributed throughout the urban environment. Map renderings are achieved by forwarding data, after the ETL process, towards a CartoDB[8] instance, an open-source, Software as a Service cloud platform for GIS map storage and Web visualization.

4.2 Measurement Accuracy and Privacy Concerns

One of the most relevant issues about MCS is the measurement accuracy, since mobile-embedded sensors are typically less accurate than professional metering equipment. We tackled this aspect in a two-fold way: on the one hand, noise measurements have been validated instrumentally against a known sound sample thanks to a professional SLM; on the other hand, both noise and signal strength measurements are examined during the ETL pipeline in order to remove outliers. The instrumental validation involved a 30 s steady, mid-level, broadband noise source against which measurements gathered from different smartphone models and from a professional, portable, Class-1 SLM (i.e., DeltaOhm HD9019) have been compared. After these trials, we achieved acceptable accuracy, with average ±5 dB bias between MCS and SLM measurements, thus confirming smartphone amenability to be used as preliminary monitoring tools. The

---

[8] CartoDB: https://cartodb.com.

outlier detection is perfomed thanks to a univariate algorithm removing measurements with excessive amplitude in a given temporal window. We opted for a slightly modified version of the Tukey's method [27], which is simple and quite effective with datasets following both a normal distribution and a not highly skewed lognormal distribution.

We also considered privacy issues, for reducing users' concerns about their potential tracking or identification. Any information or metadata capable of identifying the device owner is discarded and users are notified about this when they start the app for the first time. Mobile devices are only indexed thanks to their IMEI code, which do not allow going back to respective owners (therefore, mobiles are traceable but their owners are unknown to both platform managers and other application end users).

4.3   Data Estimation for a Smart City Scenario

The proposed platform exploits mobile devices and their embedded sensors, therefore the number of prospected users is significant and it can be considered as a real Smart City scenario, where several hundreds of data providers can be enrolled on a very large geographical scale. This subsection is devoted to estimate the data occupancy growth for our platform. Firstly, we estimated the average storage occupation of a single sensor data measurement in nearly 4 kB. Then, by considering energy consumption issues and typical users' behaviors, we hypothesized that a plausible data collection pattern would consist of 30 raw measurement per hour, over a time window of 6 h per day. We also hypothesized 20 days of usage per month and 10 months of usage per year. Finally, if we estimate to involve 5000 users during the first year of deployment and to double this quantity each year, we have the estimations reported in Table 1, according to which the DWH storage will grow of 30 GB per month and 314 GB per year in the third year after the system deployment.

Table 1. Data growth estimations up to 3 years.

Parameter	Year 1		Year 2		Year 3	
	per month	per year	per month	per year	per month	per year
Involved users growth (%)	–	0	–	100	–	100
Number of involved users	–	5000	–	10000	–	20000
DWH occupation [GB]	4.58	45.29	15.71	157.69	31.14	314.15

5   Conclusions and Further Developments

In this paper, we examined how the Mobile Crowd Sensing (MCS) paradigm can be exploited as an enabling factor for the fulfilment of the so-called Sensing as a Service model (S^2aaS) in a urban context, thus aiming at reaching a Urban Mobile Sensing as a Service (UMS^{2}aaS) model. Two monitoring scenarios have been identified, related to typical life quality concerns of European citizens: noise and EM field exposure. Therefore, we designed, developed and preliminarily tested a mobile app allowing us to gather (1) noise measurements by using smartphone-embedded microphones and (2) received signal power levels (RSSI) by using smartphone internal antennas. The platform also consists of a DWH system for managing sensing data and of a web app providing users with multiple views about collected measurements. The platform exploits some components of the FIWARE middleware for data brokering and storage functionalities. Preliminary tests have been performed in a central area of the city of Lecce demonstrating its suitability in assessing both noise levels and RSSI. A series of improvements are currently under evaluation, such as introducing other sensing tasks and providing the system with publishing/subscribing functionalities, in order to schedule and request sensing tasks to mobile devices scattered across a given geographical area. We will also study proper policies to address energy consumption issues, in order to make the platform capable of sending the requested sensing tasks only to those devices having enough energy to fulfill them for a sufficient lapse of time.

Acknowledgement. This research activity has been partially funded within the EU FIWARE accelerator "frontierCities" (Grant agreement n. 632853, sub-grant agreement n. 021).

References

1. Ericsson: Ericsson Mobility Report. EAB-15:026112 Rev. A, Stockholm, SWE (2015)
2. Sheng, X., Xiao, X., Tang, J., Xue, G.: Sensing as a service: a cloud computing system for mobile phone sensing. In: IEEE Sensors 2012, pp. 1–4. IEEE (2012)
3. Ganti, R.K.: Mobile crowdsensing. IEEE Commun. Mag. **49**(11), 32–39 (2011)
4. Heggen, S.: Integrating participatory sensing and informal science education. In: 2012 ACM Conference on Ubiquitous Computing (UbiComp 2012), pp. 552–555 (2012)
5. Guo, B., et al.: From participatory sensing to mobile crowd sensing. In: 2nd IEEE International Workshop on Social and Community Intelligence, pp. 593–598 (2014)
6. FIWARE. https://www.fiware.org/our-vision/. Accessed 2015
7. Leonardi, C., et al.: SecondNose. In: NordiCHI 2014, pp. 1051–1054 (2014)
8. Minkman, E., et al.: Citizen science in water quality monitoring: mobile crowd sensing for water management in the Netherlands. In: EWRI 2015, pp. 1399–1408 (2015)
9. Rana, R.K., et al.: Ear-Phone. In: IPSN 2010, pp. 105–116 (2010)
10. Degrossi, L.C., et al.: Flood citizen observatory. In: SEKE 2014, pp. 1–6 (2014)
11. Faulkner, M., et al.: Community sense and response systems: your phone as quake detector. Commun. ACM **57**(7), 66–75 (2014)
12. Stopczynski, A., et al.: Participatory Bluetooth Sensing. In: PerCom'13, pp. 242–247 (2013)
13. Leao, S., Ong, K.L., Krezel, A.: 2Loud?: community mapping of exposure to traffic noise with mobile phones. Envion. Monit. Assess. **186**, 6193–6206 (2014)
14. Radu, V., Kriara, L., Marina, M.K.: Pazl: a mobile crowdsensing based indoor WiFi monitoring system. In: CNSM 2013, pp. 75–83 (2013)
15. Farshad, A., Marina, M.K., Garcia, F.: Urban WiFi characterization via mobile crowdsensing. In: NOMS 2014, pp. 1–9 (2014)
16. Weisi, G., Hagler, L., Siyi, W.: Mobile crowd-sensing wireless activity with measured interference power. IEEE Wirel. Commun. Lett. **2**(5), 539–542 (2013)
17. Kaibits Software: Network Signal Info Pro (2015). http://www.kaibits-software.com/
18. TNS Opinion and Social: Attitudes of Europeans towards urban mobility. Survey Special Eurobarometer 406/Wave EB79.4, European Commission (DG-MOVE) (2013)
19. European Environment Agency: Noise in Europe 2014. EEA Report No. 10/14 (2014)
20. Goines, L., Hagler, L.: Noise pollution: a modern plague. South. Med. J. **100**, 287–294 (2007)

21. Blake Levitt, B., Lai, H.: Biological effects from exposure to EM radiation emitted by cell tower base stations and other antenna arrays. Environ. Rev. **18**, 369–395 (2010)
22. Alton Everest, F., Pohlmann, K.C.: Master Handbook of Acoustics, 5th edn. McGraw-Hill, San Francisco (2009)
23. Kardous, C.A., Shaw, P.B.: Evaluation of smartphone sound measurement application. J. Acoust. Soc. Am. **135**(4), 186–192 (2014)
24. Wong, K.D.: Fundamentals of Wireless Communication Engineering Technologies, 1st edn. Wiley, New York (2012)
25. Burke, J., et al.: Participatory sensing. In: WSW 2006, pp. 117–134 (2006)
26. Golfarelli, M., Rizzi, S.: Data Warehouse Design, 1st edn. McGraw-Hill, New York (2009)
27. Hoaglin, D.C., Iglewicz, B., Tukey, J.W.: Performance of some resistant rules for outlier labeling. J. Am. Stat. Assoc. **82**, 1147–1149 (1986)

On the Minimization of the Energy Consumption in Federated Data Centers

Alexis I. Aravanis[✉], Panagiotis Karkazis,
Artemis Voulkidis, and Theodore Zahariadis

Synelixis Solutions Ltd., Athens, Greece
{aravanis,pkarkazis,voulkidis,zahariad}@synelixis.com

Abstract. As cloud services are becoming increasingly popular, the number of operating data centers is accordingly increasing, together with the need of implementing federated data centers and clouds. In this context, we consider a framework for achieving energy efficiency in federated clouds, by means of continuous monitoring and SLA renegotiation, coupled with the operation of prediction and multi-layered optimization components. In this paper, relevant prediction and optimization components, based on Support Vector Regression and Bin-Packing solving heuristics, operating at local data center level are examined and the experimental results of their deployment in a real-life testbed are presented and discussed.

Keywords: Federated data centers · Energy minimization · Optimization · Support vector regression · Bin-packing problem

1 Introduction

The ever increasing demand for computing capacity and the resulting burgeoning of large scale Data Centers (DCs), which constitute huge energy sinks, have a direct impact on the ICT related energy consumption. This huge energy consumption poses a great challenge for the energy sector and the problem is further intensified by the volatility of the energy markets and the inability of Smart Grids to follow the electricity demand-response model, which impedes the seamless integration of large scale DCs to the energy network. Thus, Smart Grid operators need to address on the one hand the immense energy consumption of DCs and on the other hand the erratic operation of Smart Grids, caused by the inability to follow the demand-response paradigm.

To elaborate on the first of the two problems, the increase of DCs, which is accompanied by huge electricity consumption and sub-optimal energy management, directly affects their energy footprint and the environmental conditions. It is well known that the average server utilization in DCs is low, often below 30 % of the maximum server load [1, 2] and only 10 % in case of facilities that provide interactive services [3]. This low utilization is primarily due to two reasons: (i) the provisioning of a DC is done based on the expected peak load, rather than the average load. For interactive services, peak utilization often exceeds the average utilization by more than a factor of three [3]; and

© ICST Institute for Computer Sciences, Social Informatics and Telecommunications Engineering 2016
B. Mandler et al. (Eds.) IoT 360° 2015, Part I, LNICST 169, pp. 388–398, 2016.
DOI: 10.1007/978-3-319-47063-4_40

(ii) in order to provide redundancy in the event of failure. DC operators deploy more systems than are actually needed. The over-design and over-provisioning of DCs and the increased number of low utilized servers, have significantly increased the waste of energy. In the last couple of years, the electricity consumed by DCs has doubled, representing an aggregate annual growth rate of 16.7 % per year worldwide [4]. Approximately 80 % of this growth is caused by the increased electricity used by servers, 10 % by the growth in electricity used for DC communications and around 10 % by the growth in electricity by storage equipment.

Besides electricity consumed for supporting the computational operation of the servers, a huge amount of energy is also consumed for the cooling of DC servers. To lower this waste of energy, DC containment strategies (both hot aisle and cold aisle) are widely regarded as the starting point for energy-efficiency best practices. Moreover, the so called "Green DCs" aim to use a number of green electricity sources (e.g. photovoltaic cells, geothermal power, hydroelectric energy, etc.), for normal operations and cooling purposes. The results are, in many cases, impressive, but they still represent a minority of the deployed DCs and even in those cases the intermittent nature of green electricity sources make the need for integration of green energy sources to the energy network and for stable Smart Grid operation more actual than ever.

As already highlighted above, this additional problem, that is the instability of the Smart Grids and the difficulty to follow the electricity demand-response model constitutes a major problem in the energy sector. In particular, as Europe shifts away from fossil fuels, electricity is becoming an even more important energy vector and the seamless integration of renewable energy sources to the energy network becomes imperative. More than 29 European countries have targets for a share of renewable energy in the range of 10–33 % until 2020. Achieving these goals is vital for the EU internal energy market, as it will lower the dependency on importing oil and it will help towards a more sustainable growth. The implementation of more intelligent and active transmission, distribution and supply systems in the form of Smart Grids is central to the success of such a development. Thus, Smart Grids are very high on the agenda of the European energy and ICT sector. However, the problem is that Smart Grids have difficulty in following the electricity demand-response model. The introduction of Smart City technology is also being developed as a mechanism to enable intelligence in buildings, city blocks and regions. As a result, we need solutions, which can support the features of the Smart Grid, coupled with the capabilities of Smart Cities, in order to carefully manage the energy profile of DCs, especially under periods of increased demand.

Recent literature suggests that the problem of optimizing and coordinating the energy consumption of federated Data Centers and its alignment with the Smart Grid stabilization needs, is actively researched. In [23], a survey on the existing techniques utilizing geographical load balancing for optimizing the energy consumption of Data Centers in the context of a Smart Grid is presented. The optimization may have different targets, including absolute energy consumption with respect to QoS guarantees [25], cost [24] and carbon footprint [26], the techniques employed varying among Mixed Integer Programming, Dynamic Programming, heuristics through Genetic Algorithms etc. [23]. Load balancing of Data Centers in the context of the Smart Grid are also investigated in [30], where the authors present a two-stage framework for modelling the relevant interactions and formulate a cost-minimization problem based on linear programming. Similarly, the authors of [29] present a cooperation scheme between Smart Grids and Data Centers, with the aim to maximize the share of renewables in the energy mix used for Data Center operation. The problem of optimal load (VM) allocation in federated Data Centers is also tackled in [28], where a greedy heuristic is presented with a view towards minimizing the carbon dioxide emissions due to Data Center operation. Finally, in [27], an in-depth survey of existing algorithms and techniques for orchestrated energy management and energy sustainability in federated clouds is presented.

In the direction of tackling the above problems and significantly contributing toward improving the energy efficiency of DCs and stabilizing Smart Grids, the present paper introduces a holistic approach interconnecting networks of DCs and Smart Grids, addressing both problems in a complementary way. Specifically, in the context of smart city and Smart Grid integration, a network of synergetic DCs can adjust its operation shifting load to regions of renewable energy surplus, playing a key role toward Smart Grid stabilization and "Green" operation of modern DCs. Moreover, the proposed approach can be seamlessly integrated to legacy DC equipment discounting any capital expenditure employing solely the software defined networking (SDN) and software defined infrastructures (SDI) of legacy DC equipment. The proposed framework, developed in the context of the European Union project: "Data centres Optimization for energy-efficient and enviromentalLy Friendly iNternet (DOLFIN)" [5], facilitates therefore the integration of a federated DC network to the Smart Grid within a Smart City exchange network, allowing the optimal allocation of the cumulative load, based on predictive optimization techniques, that will be presented hereafter. The efficacy of these will be further corroborated by the actual results obtained by the in-house micro DC, presented herein.

The remainder of the paper is organized as follows. Section 2 presents the DOLFIN approach, exploiting SDN to seamlessly integrate the Smart Grid and DC networks in a Smart City agglomeration. Thus, counteracting the adverse effect of erratically operating Smart Grids and allowing for the energy efficient operation of DCs. Section 3 introduces the predictive optimization techniques employed by the DOLFIN ecosystem, in order to implement the proposed approach. Section 4 presents the preliminary results obtained by our in-house micro DC, after the employment of the predictive optimization techniques described in Sect. 3. Finally, Sect. 5 concludes the paper and presents relevant perspectives.

2   DOLFIN Flexible Approach

Modern DCs are part of computing and storage clouds, offering their customers Virtual Machines (VMs) as a virtual operating environment. Exploiting this virtualization of modern DCs and capitalizing on the benefits of SDN, the present approach focuses on modelling, monitoring, and measuring the energy consumption of VMs. This real time monitoring allows for the seamless, autonomic migration of VMs between servers of the same DC or across a group of Energy-conscious, Synergetic DCs, aiming to (i) optimize the overall energy consumption by dynamically changing the percentage of active versus stand-by servers and the load per active server in a DC, and (ii) stabilize the Smart Grid energy distribution, under peak load and increased demand, by dynamically changing the energy consumption/production requirements of the local DCs.

To elaborate, the leeway provided by the independent management of VMs allows for the optimal allocation of the computing load. On the one hand the optimal allocation of VMs within the same DC could lead to the VM consolidation in favor of significant energy savings emerging from the hibernation of inactive servers. On the other hand the optimal allocation of VMs across synergetic DCs could allow for DCs to adjust their operation in accordance with the Smart Grid needs, moving VMs to DCs where energy is cheaper or abundant either due to the time difference of the respective DCs or due to the existence of renewable energy surplus, generated by renewable energy sources in the vicinity of the destination DC. The high-level architecture of such a network of synergetic DCs interacting with the energy network is depicted in Fig. 1.

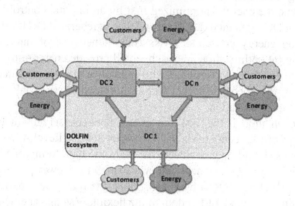

Fig. 1. Network of synergetic DCs interacting with the energy network.

Evidently, the stabilizing effect of the proposed paradigm allows the seamless integration of renewable energy sources (RES) to the energy network, counteracting the adverse effect of the intermittent green energy generation. In particular, occasional peaks and troughs of green energy generation, leading to inverse power flow or reduced system inertia can be balanced by the demand response of federated DCs, mitigating electrical grid instabilities and system outage or blackout threats.

The above energy consumption optimization approach, revolves around three main pillars, underpinning the DOLFIN ecosystem:

(a) Energy-conscious Synergetic DC-level: optimizing the energy consumption within the limits of a single DC, based on system virtualization and the optimal distribution of VMs. This is coupled with the dynamic adaptation of active and stand-by servers and the load optimization per active server. Utilizing a monitoring framework to measure the energy consumption per server module/networking component and activate low-power states on devices.

(b) Group of Energy-conscious Synergetic DCs-level: optimizing the cumulative energy consumption in a group of DCs, based on optimal distribution of VMs across all of the servers that belong in the group of DCs using load prediction methods for the standalone DCs and the group of DCs. Measuring and predicting the energy consumption on the DC level and achieving a decreased cumulative power consumption across the whole group of DCs.

(c) Smart City-level: optimizing the energy consumption at the smart city level and providing stabilization of the local Smart Grid, based on distribution of VMs across the servers that are part of a group of DCs, following an electricity demand-response approach. In order to stabilize the Smart City Energy consumption, the percentage of active versus stand-by servers per DC is dynamically changed and the load per active server is optimized.

The above hierarchical classification gives rise to four different optimization levels that should be dealt with. In this course, a distributed spiral optimization process is assumed dealing with these four levels of optimization. Specifically, during a single optimization cycle the energy is optimized first by an internal control loop at servers rack level, next at DC segment or DC level and then at federated DC level allowing load relocation among energy conscious DCs. Thus, a network of interconnected DCs employing the spiral optimization approach, could provide energy-efficient DC operation in the context of a fully elastic cloud, while playing a key role in a Smart Grid energy network balancing the stochastic energy surplus provided by renewable energy sources, through efficient load relocation.

Moreover, even though the VM movement between servers in geographically distributed groups of DCs is not trivial, as very strict Service Level Agreements (SLAs) to the DCs' clients should be guaranteed, the real time monitoring of SLAs described above ensures that the VM movement will only exploit the leeway provided not leading to any Quality of Service (QoS) breakage. Thus, the real time monitoring of SLAs provides an additional degree of freedom to the flexible VM management allowing the exploitation of the SLA margin to its fullest.

Having outlined the optimization levels of the DOLFIN approach pertaining to the optimal VM allocation at four different levels, the relevant optimization problems need to be formally formulated, whereas the predictive optimization techniques employed for the problems in hand, need to be thoroughly described as well. In this course, the VM optimization problem and the predictive optimization techniques employed are presented hereafter.

3   Predictive Optimization

The employment of load prediction methods for the efficient prediction of the standalone DC load, the synergetic DC load and the user load is of paramount importance for the efficient optimization of the load allocation to the synergetic DCs. Such methods provide energy predictions based on the user habits, the behavior and the workload patterns as well as the weather forecast, allowing the devise of predictive energy patterns. Subsequently, based on these a priori devised energy patterns the relevant optimization modules can devise relevant plans optimizing the VM /load allocation to standalone and synergetic DCs, based on the Smart Grid status.

A number of techniques have been proposed for forecasting aggregated and correlated energy consumption inspired by machine learning, and have passed from linear regression and autoregressive moving average models [6] to neural networks [7] and boosting approaches [8] and finally to the Support Vector Machine For Regression (SVR) that is a state of the art forecasting method [9–11]. The SVR uses the same principles as the Support Vector Machine (SVM) for classification, but as output instead of a real number, which has infinite possibilities, it returns a margin of tolerance, to minimize error.

The SVR method is employed by DOLFIN for energy consumption forecasting, as it combines several desirable properties compared with other existing techniques: it has a good behavior even if the ratio between the number of variables and the number of observations becomes very unfavorable, with highly correlated predictors, it makes possible to construct a nonlinear model without explicitly having to produce new descriptors (the famous "kernel trick"), while a deeply study of the characteristics of the method allows to make comparison with penalized regression such as ridge regression [12], whereas a number of pre-calibrated SVR toolkits can be found online [13], facilitating the easier fine-tuning of the SVR.

Having fine-tuned the SVR parameters for the load prediction at DC and user level an appropriate optimization algorithm must be selected in order to efficiently employ the SDI (through cloud managers such as OpenStack [14], OpenNebula [15] and Eucalyptus [16]) in order to minimize the reserved physical resources and the implicit operating cost. In practice, VMs reserve virtual shared CPU and shared storage, whereas the only physical resource reserved in a stringent way is the server physical memory. Thus, the problem of optimal VM allocation across the network of synergetic DCs is reduced to that of allocating the aggregate server memory to VMs, based on their forecasted load and availability.

The above problem can be reduced to a "bin packing" problem [17] and has been formally formulated by the authors in [18]. In particular, "the problem of VM allocation can be considered as a "bin packing" problem, where given a finite set $U = \{u_1, u_2, ..., u_n\}$ of "items"(i.e. VMs) and a rational "size" (i.e. memory) $s(u)$ for each item $u \in U$ a partition of U into disjoint subsets $U_1, U_2, ..., U_k$ must be found such that the sum of the sizes of the items in each subset U_i is no more than a respective "bin size"(i.e. server memory) Si and such that k is as small as possible. Thus, VMs of memory s need to be allotted to servers of memory S, while reserving the minimum number of servers, whereas a memory granularity of 512 MB can be assumed which is a typical value encountered in practice."

The above problem constitutes an NP-hard problem [17], however a number of approximation and heuristic techniques can be employed to provide solutions to the problem. The Best Fit Decreasing Algorithm (BFD) [17] constitutes one of the best approximation algorithms for the "bin packing" problem and it can be employed to achieve a consolidated VM allocation. As stressed by the authors in [18] in the direction of employing the BFD "the DC servers are indexed based on their energy-efficiency, with energy-efficient servers being assigned a lower index. Subsequently, "items" (i.e. VMs) are placed into "bins"(i.e. servers) in order of increasing index. As a result, energy-efficient servers are assigned a higher priority and for instance servers of a Green Room are reserved first, or servers of the same DC segment are reserved prior to remote DC servers in order to allow remote DC servers to hibernate, providing substantial energy savings. Next, "items" in U are sorted by size and reindexed so that $s(u_1) \geq s(u_2) \geq \cdots \geq s(u_n)$. "Items" are then placed in order of increasing index, first into the occupied "bins" of lower available capacity and then, in case they do not fit into the occupied "bins", or in case of a tie, "items" are placed in order of increasing index into the lower indexed "bin" they fit."

Thus, the documented success of the BFD approximation solution can be exploited to initialize the search of an appropriate heuristic approach. Specifically, the above solution is used as an initial seed to initialize the search of a Genetic Algorithm (GA) approach [19]. The GA constitutes one of the most successful heuristics [19], however, a number of factors hinder the convergence of GA when the latter is applied to grouping problems such as the "bin packing" problem in hand. In particular, grouping problems – aiming either to find a good partition of a set or better yet to group together the members of a set - challenge the cornerstone of the GA, namely the principal of minimal redundancy of each solution[1], as different encodings and different permutations of the groups may refer to the same solution. Also, solution clustering into groups hinders the passing of useful (i.e. standalone) information to the next generation through the crossover and mutation operators of the GAs [20–22].

In this course, the Grouping Genetic Algorithms (GGA) have been proposed [20] allowing the encoding of grouping problems like the one in hand, by using groups or in our case "bins" as the GA building blocks on which GA operators are applied. One could envisage a GGA as a simple GA where each gene of a GAs' chromosome corresponds to a tuple of elements corresponding to the "items" of each "bin", whereas the "bins" are the building blocks evolved by the employment of the GAs. This approach alters all GA operators significantly, however this approach outperforms the standalone GA substantially when applied to grouping problems.

The employment of the GGA, initialized by the BFD, for the optimal VM allocation, allows for the consolidated allocation of VMs at an intra-DC level as well as an inter-DC level, whenever a VM consolidation is imposed by the Smart Grid operation. Thus, the distributed application of the above optimization algorithm on DC sites, when that is deemed necessary based on the SVR load predictions, could yield significant energy savings as well as reliable Smart Grid operation.

In order to validate the efficiency of the proposed approach and the feasibility and applicability of the DOLFIN approach employing solely the SDI, the preliminary results of the optimized VM allocation are tested on our in-house micro DC and the obtained data corroborating the substantial benefits arising from the proposed approach are presented hereafter.

---

[1] The principal of minimal redundancy refers to the necessary one to one relation between each encoded solution and each member of the search space.

4 Experimental Results

In the process of developing and fine-tuning the prediction engine and optimization module of the DOLFIN ecosystem a number of attested scenarios were used as benchmark to quantify the convergence of the developed optimization algorithms and the accuracy of the developed prediction models. These optimized test scenarios to which the predictive optimization converged to, were then implemented based on the SDI of a small scale testbed, as a proof of concept, employing OpenStack for the actuation of these scenarios. The testbed consists of 4 low consumption blade servers (less than 50 W of energy consumption at average load, simultaneously underclocking idle cores) which run artificial loads to emulate the operation of a commercial DC.

The performance of the implemented prediction engine is depicted in Fig. 2, where the load (power) prediction is plotted against the real power demand values. The training set of the prediction engine spanned two months of data. The Root Mean Squared Error between the actual power demand values and the predicted ones is 74.3 which is considered acceptable for our value range, granted the limited training set volume; further training of the prediction engine is required in order to acquire more accurate results.

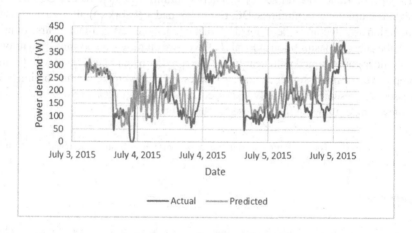

Fig. 2. Prediction engine performance

In the same context, Fig. 3 presents the outcome of the load optimization on the aforementioned test setup. Specifically, under random load and granted relevant predictions from the prediction engine, the optimization component was able to reorganize the existing load in such a way that the energy consumption dropped by approximately 15 %, exhibiting that through proper management, the energy consumption of DCs can be significantly lowered, to help towards assisting the operation of Smart Grids. Moreover, when considering the ability to relocate loads to geographically distant DCs when intra-DC optimization is unable to accommodate the load inside the DC boundaries, the coordination of DC loads with the Smart Grid demand response plans, is expected to contribute substantially to the achievement of Smart Grid stability.

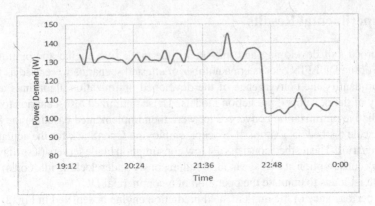

Fig. 3. Test optimization scenario result

5 Conclusions

In this paper, a framework for achieving energy optimization in federated DCs has been presented, employing continuous DC resources and network monitoring and scalar optimization architectures operating at local and federated levels. In the course of mini-mizing the energy consumption at local DC level, we employ load optimization through load re-allocation, coupled with near future load predictions, implemented with the help of support vector regression techniques. The results of the prediction and optimization processes are presented and briefly discussed, indicating significant power savings may be achieved by employing the proposed architecture.

Acknowledgments. The work presented in this paper was partially supported by the EU-funded Project FP7 ICT-609140 DOLFIN.

References

1. Bash, C., Forman, G.: Cool job allocation: measuring the power savings of placing jobs at cooling-efficient locations in the Data Centre. In: Proceedings of the 2007 USENIX Annual Technical Conference, January 2007
2. Bohrer, P., Elnozahy, E., Keller, T., Kistler, M., Lefurgy, C., Rajamony, R.: The case for power management in web servers. Power Aware Comput. January 2002
3. Fan, X., Weber, W.-D., Barroso, L.A.: Power provisioning for a warehouse-sized computer. In: Proceedings of the 34th Annual International Symposium on Computer Architecture (2007)
4. Koomey, J.G.: Worldwide electricity used in Data Centres. Environ. Res. Lett. **3**, 034008 (2008). IOP Publishing
5. Dolfin.: Project Number: 609140; Strategic objective: FP7-SMARTCITIES-2013 (ICT-2013.6.2). http://www.dolfin-fp7.eu/
6. Taylor, J.W.: Triple seasonal methods for short-term electricity demand forecasting. Eur. J. Oper. Res. **204**(1), 139–152 (2010)

7. Hippert, H.: Neural networks for short-term load forecasting: a review and evaluation. IEEE Trans. Power Syst. (2001)
8. Taieb, S.B., Hyndman, R.J.: A gradient boosting approach to the Kaggle load forecasting competition. Int. J. Forecast. (2013)
9. Chen, B.-J., Chang, M.-W., Lin, C.-J.: Load forecasting using support vector machines: a study on EUNITE competition 2001. IEEE Trans. Power Syst. **19**(4), 1–7 (2004)
10. Sapankevych, N., Sankar, R.: Time series prediction using support vector machines: a survey. IEEE Comput. Intell. Mag. **4**(2), 24–38 (2009)
11. Humeau, S., Wijaya, T., Vasirani, M., Aberer, K.: Electricity load forecasting for residential customers: exploiting aggregation and correlation between households. In: IEEE Sustainable Internet and ICT for Sustainability (SustainIT), Palermo, 30–31 October 2013
12. Christianni, N., Taylor, J.S.: An Introduction to Support Vector Machines and Other Kernel-Based Learning Methods. Cambridge University Press, New York (2000). Sect. 6.2.2
13. Scikit-learn. http://scikit-learn.org/stable/index.html
14. Openstack. http://www.openstack.org/
15. Opennebula. http://opennebula.org/
16. Eucalyptus. https://www.eucalyptus.com/
17. Garey, M., Johnson, D.: Computers and Intractability. A Guide to the Theory of NP-Completeness. W.H. Freeman and Company, New York (1979)
18. Aravanis, A., Velivassaki, T.H., Voulkidis, A., Zahariadis, T., Cottis, P.: Federated data centers as smart city stabilizing factors. In: The 3rd IEEE ISCC 2015 International Workshop on Smart City and Ubiquitous Computing Applications, July 2015
19. Talbi, E.G.: Metaheuristics From Design to Implementation. Wiley, Hoboken (2009)
20. Emanuel, F., Alain, D.: A genetic algorithm for bin packing and line balancing. In: Proceedings of the IEEE 1992 International Conference on Robotics and Automation (RA 1992), 10–15 May 1992, Nice, France (1992)
21. Emanuel, F.: The grouping genetic algorithms - widening the scope of the GAs in JORBEL. Belgian J. Oper. Res. Stat. Comput. Sci. **33**(1, 2), 79–102 (1993)
22. Emanuel, F.: New representation and operators for GAs applied to grouping problems. Evol. Comput. **2**(2), 123–144 (1994)
23. Rahman, A., Liu, X., Kong, F.: A survey on geographic load balancing based data center power management in the smart grid environment. IEEE Commun. Surv. Tutorials **16**(1), 214–233 (2014)
24. Rao, L., Liu, X., Ilic, M.D., Liu, J.: Distributed coordination of internet data centers under multiregional electricity markets. Proc. IEEE **100**(1), 269–282 (2012)
25. Rao, L., Liu, X., Xie, L., Liu, W.: Minimizing electricity cost: optimization of distributed internet data centers in a multi-electricity market environment. In: Proceedings of International Conference on Computer Communications, pp. 1–9. IEEE (2010)
26. Zhang, Y., Wang, Y., Wang, X.: GreenWare: greening cloud-scale data centers to maximize the use of renewable energy. In: Kon, F., Kermarrec, A.-M. (eds.) Middleware 2011. LNCS, vol. 7049, pp. 143–164. Springer, Heidelberg (2011)
27. Giacobbe, M., Celesti, A., Fazio, M., Villari, M., Puliafito, A.: Towards energy management in Cloud federation: a survey in the perspective of future sustainable and cost-saving strategies. Comput. Netw. **91**, 14 (2015)
28. Giacobbe, M., Celesti, A., Fazio, M., Villari, M., Puliafito, A.: An approach to reduce carbon dioxide emissions through virtual machine migrations in a sustainable cloud federation. In: Sustainable Internet and ICT for Sustainability (SustainIT), 2015, pp. 1–4, 14–15 April 2015

29. Niedermeier, F., et al.: Increasing data centre renewable power share via intelligent smart city power control. In: Proceedings of the 2015 ACM Sixth International Conference on Future Energy Systems. ACM (2015)
30. Wang, H., et al.: Exploring smart grid and data center interactions for electric power load balancing. ACM SIGMETRICS Perform. Eval. Rev. **41**(3), 89–94 (2014)

Towards Enabling Scientific Workflows for the Future Internet of Things

Attila Kertesz[1,2(✉)] and Tamas Pflanzner[1]

[1] University of Szeged, Dugonics ter 13, Szeged 6720, Hungary
{keratt,tampfla}@inf.u-szeged.hu
[2] MTA SZTAKI, P.O. Box 63, Budapest, Hungary

Abstract. Cloud computing offers on-demand access to computational, infrastructure and data resources operated from a remote source. This novel technology has opened new ways of flexible resource provisions for businesses to manage applications and data responding to new demands from customers. In the current web application scenario a rapidly growing number of powerful devices join the Internet, significantly impacting on the global traffic volume and foreshadowing a world of smart devices, or things in the Internet of Things (IoT) perspective. This trend calls for an ecosystem that provides means to interconnect and control these devices. In this position paper we envision the integration of IoT into Cloud-enabled scientific workflows to support the proliferation of IoT with the help of cloud technologies. These enhanced workflows will enable the creation and management of user applications that bring clouds and IoT closer to users by hiding the complexity and cumbersome utilization of virtualized resources, data sources and things. The goal of this approach is to ease the lives of users and foster scientific work by engaging the Internet of Things.

Keywords: Cloud computing · Scientific workflows · Internet of Things

1 Introduction

Cloud computing is a diverse research area that encompasses many aspects of sharing software and hardware solutions, including computing and storage resources, application runtimes or complex application functionalities. Cloud computing offers on-demand access to computational, infrastructure and data resources operated from a remote source. This novel technology has opened new ways of flexible resource provisions for businesses to manage Information technology (IT) applications and data responding to new demands from customers. The concept of cloud computing has been pioneered by commercial companies with the promise to allow elastic construction of virtual infrastructures, which attracted users early on. Its technical motivation has been introduced in [1,4]. Cloud solutions enable businesses with the option to outsource the operation and management of IT infrastructure and services, allowing the business and its employees to concentrate on their core competencies. As new products and

© ICST Institute for Computer Sciences, Social Informatics and Telecommunications Engineering 2016
B. Mandler et al. (Eds.) IoT 360° 2015, Part I, LNICST 169, pp. 399–408, 2016.
DOI: 10.1007/978-3-319-47063-4_41

technologies are offered in the near future, Gartner estimated that till 2015 $112 billion would be spent by businesses and individuals on cloud computing offerings from service providers such as Amazon, IBM and Microsoft [2].

In the current worldwide Information and Communications Technology (ICT) scenario a growing number of powerful devices (smartphones, household appliances, etc.) join the Internet, significantly impacting on the global traffic volume (e.g. by data sharing, voice, multimedia) and foreshadowing a world of smart devices, or things in the Internet of Things (IoT) perspective. The Cluster of European Research Projects on the Internet of Things considers the Internet of Things as a vital part of Future Internet and they defined it as a dynamic global network infrastructure with self configuring capabilities based on standard and interoperable communication protocols. Things in this network interact and communicate among themselves and with the environment by exchanging data and information sensed, and react autonomously to events and influence them by triggering actions with or without direct human intervention [8]. According to another Gartner report there will be 30 billion devices always online and more than 200 billion devices discontinuously online by 2020 [3]. These trends and estimations call for an ecosystem that provides means to interconnect and control these devices.

Nowadays cloud computing has reached a maturity state and high level of popularity that various cloud services have become a part of our lives. These services are offered at different cloud deployment models ranging from the lowest infrastructure level to the highest software or application level. Within Infrastructure as a Service (IaaS) solutions we can differentiate public, private, hybrid and community clouds according to recent reports of standardization bodies. The previous two types may utilize more than one cloud system, which is also called as a cloud federation [7]. Such federations can be good candidates to serve as a base for the envisioned ecosystem. With the help of cloud solutions, user data can be stored in a remote location, and can be accessed from anywhere. Therefore mobile devices can also benefit from these cloud services: the enormous data users produce with these devices are continuously posted to online services, which may require the use of several Cloud providers at the same time to efficiently store and retrieve these data.

Gubbi et al. [6] have identified that to support the IoT vision, the current computing paradigm need to go beyond traditional mobile computing scenarios and cloud computing has the potential to address these needs, and it is able to hide data generation, processing and visualization tasks. Assuncao et al. [5] also highlighted that there are many open challenges in applying clouds for Big Data management. By addressing some of these challenges, the goal of our proposed approach is to support the proliferation of IoT with the help of cloud technologies, thus to integrate IoT into a cloud ecosystem, a complex system of interdependent components that work together to enable the creation and management of user applications in the form of heterogeneous service mashups or workflows. In this paper we present a vision to create such an integrated ecosystem, and discuss the main requirements for enabling this vision.

The remainder of this paper is as follows: Sect. 2 presents a survey of related works in the corresponding categories, and Sect. 3 presents the vision and requirements of our proposed approach to engage things in scientific workflows. Finally, the contributions are summarized in Sect. 5.

2 Related Works

Most of current cloud computing offerings still lock customers into a single cloud infrastructure, platform or application, preventing the portability of data or software created by them. Even if portability is supported, it is barely used by customers due to its complexity and high switching costs. The European Network and Information Security Agency (ENISA) has also recognized the lock-in problem as a high risk that cloud infrastructures entail [9]. The increasing competition between the leading vendors in the cloud market, such as Amazon, Microsoft, Google and SalesForce, each of which promotes its own, incompatible cloud standards and formats [10], prevents them from agreeing on a widely accepted, standardized way to utilize cloud details and specifications. However, an interoperable cloud environment would benefit customers, as they could migrate their virtual machines, data and applications between cloud providers without setting data at risk. Nevertheless there are promising approaches that work for enabling interoperability: DeltaCloud [11] is an open source software that moves towards standard public/hybrid cloud interaction APIs, with an emphasis on compute and VM-based IaaS, and has been submitted to DTMF. OCCI [12] is a family of specifications and standards for cloud interfaces, geared towards interoperability and extensibility, by means of a definition of a Core model, and a suite of already developed documents, falling under two categories, Renderings and Extensions, the former aimed at definition and description of interaction methods and APIs for extending the model with new resource types, attributes, and available actions. The need for intermediary components (coordinators, brokers, exchange) is explained in [13], where the authors outline an architecture for a federated network of clouds. Federation issues in cloud environments have been considered in some research projects, such as mOSAIC [26] and OPTIMIS [27].

In the field of resource abstraction for IoT, good efforts have been made towards the description and implementation of languages and frameworks for efficient representation, annotation and processing of sensed data. There are several standardization bodies, such as the OGC Sensor Web Enablement [14] that develops languages and semantic annotations for abstracting sensors and sensor networks. It has taken important steps towards enabling the web-based discovery, exchange, and processing of sensor observations. Web service interface specifications such as the Sensor Observation Service [15] facilitate the discovery, access and search over the sensor data, and it provides means to integrate data from heterogeneous sources in a standard format accessible to internet users. The W3C Semantic Sensor Network Incubator Group [16] has also been established, aiming at extending this syntactic level interoperability to a semantic level, through the investigation of two separate but closely related tasks:

the development of an ontology for describing sensors and sensor data, and the development of an annotation framework for using semantic metadata.

Concerning virtualization for IoT, Alam et al. [18] propose an Internet of Things (IoT) virtualization framework to support connected objects sensor event processing and reasoning by providing a semantic overlay of underlying IoT cloud. The framework uses the sensor-as-a-service notion to expose IoT clouds connected objects functional aspects in the form of web services. The framework uses an adapter oriented approach to address the issue of connectivity with various types of sensor nodes. Virtual sensor networks have also been proposed towards virtualization in order to offer a new and dynamic collaboration paradigm that requires accommodating multiple logical network instances over a single physical network infrastructure with the ultimate goal to support applications with different requirements and to utilize in an efficient manner the available network resources.

The integration of IoT and clouds has been envisioned by Botta et al. [23] by summarizing their main properties, features, underlying technologies, and open issues. A solution for merging IoT and clouds is proposed by Nastic et al. [24]. They argue that system designers and operations managers face numerous challenges to realize IoT cloud systems in practice, due to the complexity and diversity of their requirements in terms of IoT resources consumption, customization and runtime governance. They propose a novel approach to IoT cloud that encapsulates fine-grained IoT resources and capabilities in well-defined APIs in order to provide a unified view on accessing, configuring and operating IoT cloud systems, and demonstrate the framework for managing electric fleet vehicles.

Integrating sensor network approaches to clouds has been investigated by Hassan et al. [17]. They proposed a framework of sensor-cloud integration, in which they introduced a publish/subscribe based model to simplify the integration of sensor networks with cloud-based community-centric applications. The core component to manage subscriptions is the publish/subscribe Broker, which is responsible for monitoring, processing and delivering events to registered users through SaaS applications. In [19] an infrastructure called Sensor-Cloud infrastructure is proposed, that can manage physical sensors on IT infrastructure. The Sensor-Cloud infrastructure virtualizes a physical sensor as a virtual sensor on the cloud computing and dynamic grouped virtual sensors on cloud computing can be automatic provisioned when the users need them. Combining sensors with cloud computing has been addressed by Mitton et al. [25]. They state that the constantly growing number of powerful devices join the Internet significantly impacting data traffic. Heterogeneous resources can be aggregated and abstracted according to tailored thing-like semantics, thus enabling a cloud of Things. They say that in the Future Internet initiatives, sensor networks will assume even more of a crucial role, especially for making smarter cities. Smart sensors are very heterogeneous in terms of communication technologies, sensing features and elaboration capabilities. They also propose an architecture based on standard specifications, and define an approach by the phrase Sensing and Actuation as a Service (SAaaS). It envisages new scenarios and innovative, ubiquitous, value-added applications, disclosing the sensing and actuation world to any user, a customer and at the same time a potential provider as well, thus enabling an open marketplace of sensors and actuators. In this paper we also follow and build on this definition.

Gesing et al. [20] states that in the last decades many mature workflow engines and workflow editors have been developed to support primarily scientific communities in managing workflows. While there is a trend followed by these workflow managers to ease the creation of workflows tailored to their specific workflow system, the available tools still require much understanding of the workflow concepts and languages. They propose an approach targeting various workflow systems and building a single user interface for editing and monitoring workflows under consideration of aspects such as optimization and provenance of data. They envision a workflow dashboard offered in a web browser and connecting seamlessly to available workflow systems and external resources like cloud infrastructures. In this paper we plan to follow a similar vision by enabling the combination of various cloud, social networking and IoT services to workflows in a simple way, similarly to the approach followed by ITTT [21] that enables interconnecting web-based services by so-called, predefined channels. DashMash [22] also follows a web service composition approach that is easy to grasp by users. They propose a web platform that allows end users to develop their own mashups making use of an intelligible paradigm that abstracts from technical variables. They use also-called recommendation mechanisms that take into account quality variables to help end users select data sources, components and composition patterns specifying also non-functional user requirements.

Apart from these research approaches our vision is to combine cloud computational and data services, and IoT capabilities into an ecosystem. This vision brings these technologies closer to users, and provides a simple way to form general purpose mashups or workflows of these services in order to ease their everyday lives, and scientific works. In this way their own mobile devices can be used to participate in this ecosystem, and they can be interlinked with their data of interest either coming from social media sites, other public sources or personal cloud storages, and their required data manipulation or processing can be computed dynamically in infrastructure clouds, or fed to traditional web services.

3   An Approach for Enabling Workflows for IoT

3.1   A Vision for Integrating Clouds and IoT Services in an Ecosystem

An overview of our approach is shown in Fig. 1, representing an ecosystem of compute, data, networking and sensing resources (computers, disks, mobile or other sensing devices (i.e. things)) in the cloud belonging to separate administrative domains, managed according to the policies by the local systems. In order to create and manage such a cloud ecosystem, we need to use or enable the abstraction and virtualization these heterogeneous resources and provide customization features for encapsulating them into services. We use the following naming conventions for these resource groups:

- Infrastructure as a Service (IaaS): represents cloud compute and data services in Virtual Machines (VMs) offered or managed by public or private clouds. In the ecosystem it is possible to use heterogeneous providers both from industrial and academic providers.
- Storage as a Service (STaaS): represents online data storage services such as Personal Clouds (e.g. DropBox, Google Drive).
- Data as a Service (DaaS): this category represents data sources for user communities covering big and small data. Social networking (e.g. Twitter or Facebook) and social media sites (e.g. YouTube) are one of the main sources, but traces from workload or experiment archives/provenances can also be made available through these services.
- Sensing and Actuation as a Service (SAaaS): this category brings the Internet of Things to the ecosystem and provides access to various devices and their sensors (e.g. mobile phones, tablets, smart televisions as well as their sensors such as thermometer, GPS, microphone or camera).
- Web Service (WS): represents the traditional web services covering various areas, e.g. business processes, compute services, travel planners, data analyzers or search engines.

In our vision resources from these categories are encapsulated to services (some are already available), and these services are composed into a dynamic workflow forming a unique application to be executed within the ecosystem. These services can be put together just like pieces of a puzzle, and this composition should be done in a straightforward and user friendly web-based graphical environment.

The main goals of this vision are:

- to create a straightforward, easy to use web-based graphical environment for users to use and manage this ecosystem;
- to bring clouds and IoT closer to users by hiding the complexity and cumbersome utilization of virtualized resources and data sources;
- and to open the world made available by this cloud ecosystem to non-expert users as well as to the scientific community – to enable the combination of social networking, cloud computing and the Internet of Things.

3.2   Requirements to Enable the Proposed Vision

In order to realize this vision, the following issues should be addressed by bringing innovation to current state of the art:

- Sensor abstraction: sensing and actuation resources and devices have to be abstracted and encapsulated to services, providing a homogeneous view of heterogeneous sensors and actuators hosted by both mobiles and sensor networks, also providing adequate hardware contextualization and isolation features.

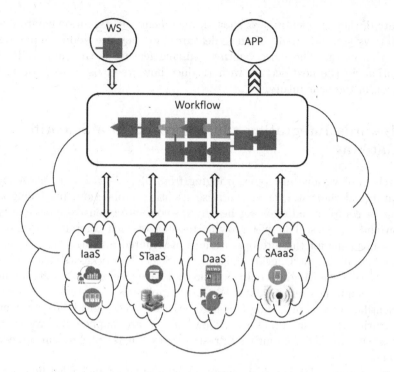

Fig. 1. Workflow applications on top of a cloud ecosystem

- Cloud service management: adequate mechanisms and tools have to be provided in order to manage a cloud provider subscription, and implementing and enforcing policies merging device owner and cloud provider objectives.
- Workflow management and orchestration: facilities for enabling higher level features for integrating cloud, IoT and social networking services into mashups, and enhanced services/APIs have to be provided, also in terms of methods and processes for software development and management applying software engineering principles. All these necessary mechanisms and tools have to implement basic functionalities that are easily customizable and extensible, also adaptive to changes such as load fluctuations.
- Straightforward, easy-to-use application development: There is a need to bring cloud technologies closer to users, and provide a simple way to form general purpose mashups of these services in order to ease their lives, everyday works. In our vision user devices can be interlinked with their data of interest either coming from social media sites, other public sources or personal cloud storages, and their required data manipulation or processing can be computed dynamically in infrastructure clouds.
- Security: effective mechanisms are required to provide identity management, privacy, trustiness, resources and metadata protection and integrity. We plan to provide specific policies that preserve user privacy and conformation to national legislation for data processing.

State-of-the-art scientific workflow development and execution environments or gateways support many of these features, so they are good candidates to realize this vision. The most wanting, missing feature is the support for IoT integration. In the next section we introduce how we envision to perform this extension in the near future.

4   Towards Integrating the Approach to a Scientific Gateway

Researchers of various disciplines ranging from life sciences and astronomy to computational chemistry, create and use scientific applications producing large amount of complex data relying heavily on compute-intensive modeling, simulation and analysis. The ever growing number of such computation-intensive applications calls for the interoperation of distributed infrastructures including private and public clouds, grids and clusters. Scientific workflows have become a key paradigm for managing complex tasks and have emerged as a unifying mechanism for handling scientific data. Workflow applications capture the essence of the scientific process, providing means to describe it via logical data- or control-flows. During the execution of a workflow, its jobs are mapped onto resources of concrete Distributed Computing Infrastructures (DCIs) to perform large-scale experiments.

One of the popular workflow execution environments and scientific gateways is the WS-PGRADE/gUSE portal environment [29] that is capable of executing scientific workflows in an interoperability way, through multiple DCIs. Recently a new feature has been introduced in this gateway by enabling a new type of workflow called infrastructure-aware workflow [28]. These are scientific workflows extended with new node types that enable the on-the-fly creation and destruction of the required infrastructures in the clouds. The paper also describes the semantics of these new types of nodes, how these new type of workflows can be implemented by a new service called as One Click Cloud Orchestrator, and how this service can be integrated with the WS-PGRADE/gUSE portal to provide the required functionalities.

By following this approach we plan to develop an IoT-aware workflow, which is a scientific workflow extended with new resource adaptor node types. These special nodes will be used to encapsulate sensors and things by realizing a SAaaS call in the workflow to send or receive data to/from entities of the IoT world.

5   Conclusions

In this paper we envisioned a future ecosystem integrating IoT, web and cloud-based services. The goal of our proposed approach is to support the proliferation of IoT with the help of cloud technologies. In this complex system interdependent components can work together to enable the creation and management of user applications in the form of heterogeneous service mashups or workflows.

These enhanced workflows will enable the creation and management of user applications that bring clouds and IoT closer to users by hiding the complexity and cumbersome utilization of virtualized resources, data sources and things. Our future work will address the development of this approach in a real-world workflow execution environment.

Acknowledgment. The research leading to these results has received funding from the European COST programme under Action identifier IC1304 (ACROSS), and it was supported by the Janos Bolyai Research Scholarship of the Hungarian Academy of Sciences.

References

1. Buyya, B., Yeo, C.S., Venugopal, S., Broberg, J., Brandic, I.: Cloud computing and emerging it platforms: vision, hype, and reality for delivering computing as the 5th utility. Fut. Gener. Comput. Syst. **25**(6), 599–616 (2009)
2. Pring, B., et al.: Forecast: public cloud services, worldwide and regions, industry sectors, 2009–2014. Gartner report, June 2010. http://www.gartner.com/Display-Document?ref=clientFriendly-Url&id=1378513
3. Mahoney, J., LeHong, H.: The Internet of Things is coming, Gartner report, September 2011. https://www.gartner.com/doc/1799626/internet-things-coming
4. Vaquero, L.M., Rodero-Merino, L., Caceres, J., Lindner, M.: A break in the clouds: towards a cloud definition. SIGCOMM Comput. Commun. Rev. **39**(1), 50–55 (2008)
5. Assuncao, M.D., Calheiros, R.N., Bianchi, S., Netto, M.A.S., Buyya, R.: Big data computing and clouds: challenges, solutions, and future directions, December 2013. arXiv:1312.4722
6. Gubbi, J., Buyya, R., Marusic, S., Palaniswami, M.: Internet of Things (IoT): a vision, architectural elements, and future directions. Fut. Gener. Comput. Syst. **29**(7), 1645–1660 (2013)
7. Kertesz, A.: Characterizing cloud federation approaches. In: Mahmood, Z. (ed.) Cloud Computing - Challenges, Limitations and R&D Solutions. Springer Series on Computer Communications and Networks, pp. 277–296. Springer, New York (2014)
8. Sundmaeker, H., Guillemin, P., Friess, P., Woelffle, S.: Vision, challenges for realising the Internet of Things. CERP IoT - Cluster of European Research Projects on the Internet of Things, CN: KK-31-10-323-EN-C, March 2010
9. Catteddu, D., Hogben, G., Cloud Computing-Benefits, risks and recommendations for information security, ENISA report (2009)
10. Machado, G.S., Hausheer, D., Stiller, B.: Considerations on the Interoperability of, between Cloud Computing Standards. In: 27th Open Grid Forum (OGF27), G2CNet Workshop: From Grid to Cloud Networks, Banff, Canada (2009)
11. Apache Deltacloud website. http://deltacloud.apache.org/developers.html. Accessed December 2014
12. OCCI-Open Cloud Computing Interface. http://occi-wg.org/. Accessed December 2014
13. Buyya, R., Ranjan, R., Calheiros, R.N.: InterCloud: utility-oriented federation of cloud computing environments for scaling of application services. In: Hsu, C.-H., Yang, L.T., Park, J.H., Yeo, S.-S. (eds.) ICA3PP 2010. LNCS, vol. 6081, pp. 13–31. Springer, Heidelberg (2010). doi:10.1007/978-3-642-13119-6_2

14. Reed, C., Botts, M., Davidson, J., Percivall, G.: OGC Sensor Web Enablement: Overview and High Level Architecture. IEEE Autotestcon (2007)
15. Open Geospatial Consortium Inc.: Sensor Observation Service. Document: OGC 06–009r6, Version: 1.0, Category: OpenGIS Implementation Standard (2007)
16. Neuhaus, H., Compton, M.: Ontology, the semantic sensor network: a generic language to describe sensor assets. AGILE Workshop Challenges in Geospatial Data Harmonisation (2009)
17. Hassan, M.M., Song, B., Huh, E.: A framework of sensor-cloud integration opportunities and challenges. In: Proceedings of the 3rd International Conference on Ubiquitous Information Management and Communication, pp. 618–626. ACM, New York (2009)
18. Alam, S., Chowdhury, M.M.R., Noll, J., SenaaS: an event-driven sensor virtualization approach for internet of things cloud. In: Proceedings of the 1st IEEE International Conference on Networked Embedded Systems for Enterprise Applications, November 2010
19. Yuriyama, M., Kushida, T.: Sensor-cloud infrastructure: physical sensor management with virtualized sensors on cloud computing. In: Proceedings of the 13th International Conference on Network-Based Information Systems, Gifou, Japan, September 2010
20. Gesing, S., Atkinson, M., Filgueira, R., Taylor, I., Jones, A., Stankovski, V., Liew, C.S., Spinuso, A., Terstyanszky, G., Kacsuk, P.: Workflows in a dashboard: a new generation of usability. In: Proceedings of the 9th Workshop on Workflows in Support of Large-Scale Science (WORKS 2014), pp. 82–93. IEEE Press, Piscataway (2014)
21. ITTT website. https://ifttt.com/wtf. Accessed December 2014
22. Cappiello, C., Matera, M., Picozzi, M., Sprega, G., Barbagallo, D., Francalanci, C.: DashMash: a mashup environment for end user development. In: Auer, S., Díaz, O., Papadopoulos, G.A. (eds.) ICWE 2011. LNCS, vol. 6757, pp. 152–166. Springer, Heidelberg (2011)
23. Botta, A., de Donato, W., Persico, V., Pescape, A.: On the integration of cloud computing and internet of things. In: The 2nd International Conference on Future Internet of Things and Cloud (FiCloud-2014), August 2014
24. Nastic, S., Sehic, S., Le, D., Truong, H., Dustdar, S.: Provisioning software-defined IoT cloud systems. In: The 2nd International Conference on Future Internet of Things and Cloud (FiCloud-2014), August 2014
25. Mitton, N., Papavassiliou, S., Puliafito, A., Trivedi, K.S.: Combining Cloud and sensors in a smart city environment. EURASIP J. Wirel. Commun. Netw. **2012**, 247 (2012)
26. mOSAIC website: Open Source API and Platform for multiple Clouds. http://www.mosaic-cloud.eu. Accessed December 2014
27. OPTIMIS website. http://www.optimis-project.eu. Accessed December 2014
28. Kacsuk, P., Kecskemeti, G., Kertesz, A., Nemeth, Zs., Visegradi, A., Gergely, M.: Infrastructure aware scientific workflows and their support by a science gateway. In: 7th International Workshop on Science Gateways, Budapest, Hungary (2015)
29. gUSE science gateways (2015). http://www.guse.hu/portals/sg

Cloud Computing-Based Marketplace for Collaborative Design and Manufacturing

Ashis Gopal Banerjee, Benjamin Beckmann, John Carbone, Lynn DeRose,
Annarita Giani$^{(\boxtimes)}$, Peter Koudal, Patricia Mackenzie, Joseph Salvo,
Dan Yang, and Walter Yund

Complex Systems Engineering Laboratory, General Electric,
Niskayuna, NY 12309, USA
annarita.giani@gmail.com

Abstract. This paper introduces an open-source, interoperable platform for real-time collaboration in complex product lifecycle development across multiple companies. Each segment of the lifecycle, including
product conception, design, analysis, prototyping, component sourcing,
manufacturing and assembly, logistics and delivery, and services from
installation to maintenance, repair and overhaul, can benefit from this
collaboration through easy access, development, deployment, and integration of heterogeneous models and data. The platform is built on an
elastic cloud-computing environment, which provides efficient scaling of
computational performance needs to support the collaboration platform.
We believe that this platform will enable organizations of all sizes to enter
a new digital age of integrated product design, manufacturing and service
systems.

Keywords: Cloud computing · Industrial internet · Internet of things ·
Digital manufacturing · Collaborative design · Lifecycle · Supply chain ·
Crowd-sourcing · Cloud-based design and manufacturing

1 Introduction

General Electric (GE) is one of the founding members of the Industrial Internet
Consortium (IIC) [1] created in 2014 to accelerate the advancement and adoption
of the Industrial Internet [2] (II). The Industrial Internet brings together industrial engineering, sensors, software, and big data analytics to create a networked
system of brilliant machines. The term II was created to further expand the
scope of the existing paradigm of the Internet of Things (IoT) to industrial systems. An exercise from [4] highlights that if the Industrial Internet boosted US
labor productivity by about 1.5 % and by half that value in the rest of the world,
Global Gross Domestic Product (GDP) output would be $15 trillion higher by
2030. This translates to an increase of 15 % over baseline projection [4].

While several Industrial Internet technologies are focused on developing connected machines and advanced analytics, new solutions are required to address

© ICST Institute for Computer Sciences, Social Informatics and Telecommunications Engineering 2016
B. Mandler et al. (Eds.) IoT 360° 2015, Part I, LNICST 169, pp. 409–418, 2016.
DOI: 10.1007/978-3-319-47063-4_42

the problems associated with storage, access, and computing needs of heterogeneous and distributed models across the product lifecycle. Such models are used in one or more of the segments of the product lifecycle including conception, design, analysis, prototyping, component sourcing, manufacturing, assembly, logistics and distribution, and services from installation to maintenance, repair and overhaul. The output of one model typically impacts the parameters of other models. For example, part geometry affects the choice of manufacturing process which in turn is constrained by what is available in the actual factories involved at the original equipment manufacturer and suppliers. However, these impacts are frequently not considered due to a lack of interaction among the model developers, users, and owners with inherently different skill sets and performance goals. This leads to many repetitive and cumbersome iterations before a successful product is built or a failed product is abandoned [5].

Hence, there is an acute need for real-time collaboration among the different model stakeholders to reduce the overall product development cost, time, and failure rate. Cloud-Based Design and Manufacturing (CBDM) [6] offers a promising solution to this need. Cloud computing is emerging as one of the major enablers for the manufacturing industry; it transforms the traditional manufacturing business model, helps it to align product innovation with business strategy, and creates intelligent factory networks that encourage effective collaboration [20]. With cloud computing, users have access to Hardware/Software as a Service (XaaS) on a pay-as-you-go basis. Thus, there is no need for capital expenditure. Storage capacity is unlimited. Backing up data and restoring it is easy. Thus, it affords a natural service for collaboration and crowdsourcing, where a group of people within and across companies can work on the same project with access to unlimited information and the ability to connect to the Industrial Internet on a global scale.

Cloud-Based Design and Manufacturing refers to a networked design and manufacturing model that exploits on-demand access to a shared collection of diversified and distributed resources to enhance efficiency, reduce product lifecycle costs, and allow for optimal resource allocation in response to variable demand [6]. References [6,7] compare Cloud-Based Design and Manufacturing (CBDM) with traditional collaborative design and distributed manufacturing systems.

In addition, cloud computing enables scale and elasticity, two essential elements of the evolving nature of the Industrial Internet. To address the computing and networking needs of many engineering organizations, manufacturers, suppliers, and other stakeholders, cloud computing offers an affordable and efficient strategy to ensure a continued competitive edge. A summary of benefits and limitations of cloud computing for cloud manufacturing is presented in [19].

This paper introduces a platform called Digital Manufacturing Commons (DMC) [8] that uses the cloud as the infrastructure to integrate design and manufacturing models. The DMC provides an open-source platform for real-time collaboration during the design-to-manufacturing process. This new system requires a cultural change in the manufacturing industry that we believe is the key for growth opportunities. This project builds upon a previous Defense Advanced Research Projects Agency (DARPA)-sponsored General Electric/Massachusetts Institute of Technology joint effort called Crowd-driven Ecosystem for Evolutionary Design (CEED) [10]. The vision is to build a crowd-driven ecosystem for evolutionary design that connects data, design tools and simulation models in a collaborative environment to accelerate the design and development of highly complex industrial systems.

The rest of the paper is organized as follows. Section 2 presents the limits of the current manufacturing paradigm together with emerging solutions. Section 3 outlines the architecture, cloud deployment, and cyber security aspects of the Digital Manufacturing Commons. We conclude by summarizing the benefits of the proposed system in Sect. 4.

2   Design and Manufacturing Trends

Manufacturing has faced a number of significant challenges recently. In a consumer driven world, manufacturers need to manage fast paced innovation. Traditional ways of building things must be replaced by more flexible approaches. But often manufacturing organizations, particularly Small and Medium size Enterprises (SMEs) are not ready for this change, limiting their participation to a few segments of the product lifecycle instead of the entire lifecycle chain.

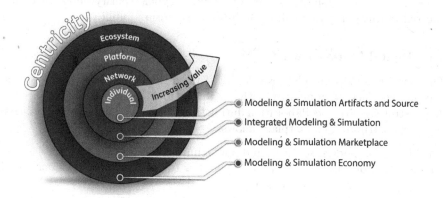

Fig. 1. Evolving paradigms for digital manufacturing

A shift in manufacturing that can help SMEs is co-development and crowdsourcing. With co-development, more participants can contribute ideas to the product development process. Figure 1 shows how modeling for design and manufacturing is evolving from stand-alone tools to an interconnected ecosystem. Metcalfe's law [11] establishes a critical mass after which networking and collaboration bring increasing value as exemplified by consumer and social networks. The revolution now is about industrial networks. Traditional models, where only employees and suppliers provide services and ideas, are augmented by the crowds global knowledge base. In this new environment, organizations expand their processes with capabilities from a globally distributed community rather than just from their own employees or suppliers. This new mode of manufacturing is embraced by the DMC.

The DMC is a key to digital manufacturing innovation because it allows the integration of engineering models across the digital thread [12]. The digital thread is the concept defined by the integration of information through an enterprise's value chain, from planning to disposal. Key advantages of the DMC include: establishment of an online community that may be accessed to cooperatively develop products. Organizations can bring better products to the market at a lower cost and SMEs have access to resources that would be unaffordable otherwise.

The main contribution of our framework compared to current practice is the enablement of users to combine distributed open source and proprietary tools and models. With the Digital Manufacturing Commons proprietary manufacturing models can be made available in a manner that allows others to run the models while keeping the underlying code hidden.

3   DMC Platform Technical Details

We now present the collaboration marketplace, architecture and cloud deployment of the DMC. Aspects related to stability, cyber security and privacy are omitted in this paper and will be addressed in a future publication.

3.1   Digital Marketplace

The DMC is a software platform delivered via a networked system of systems. The marketplace is populated with an initial foundational set of models to demonstrate real-time collaboration during the design-to-manufacturing process. The new distributed marketplace allows:

– Exchange of models, services, and opportunities
– Integration of nontraditional team members to freely express opinions, vote, test, and distribute information
– Management of reputation building to identify high-performance individuals
– Fostering of a healthy ecosystem through an iterative system of controlled selection pressure events that weed out poor designs and select for robust yet unforeseen and unplanned features
– Facilitation of the democratization of hardware design

The marketplace, Fig. 2, consists of three different parts.

1. *Design*: In the DMC, users search for services that drive model execution, integrate and execute them. The users judge model accuracy and send feedback to the designer. In this way manufacturers can not only consume prebuilt models but may also sell them.

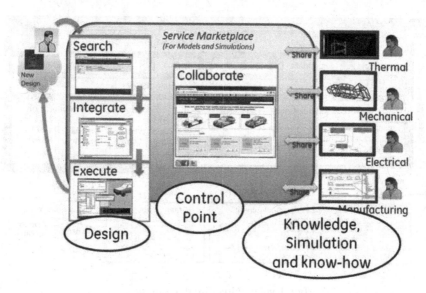

Fig. 2. Digital design and manufacturing marketplace

2. *Knowledge simulation and know-how*: Through the DMC, different communities of design and manufacturing engineers and other personnel can create and share projects from the most diverse domains. Complex systems can be realized by integrating disciplines into a team effort that allows an integrated design to become a part, sub-system or product. The marketplace combines information that users all over the world share.

3. *Control point*: The DMC platform facilitates the collaboration between two parties that jointly benefit from the interaction. In two-sided marketplaces customer's participation generates economic value. In fact, the DMC marketplace value depends on the number of users who publish models and users who use models. The two-sided platform is a broker through which publishers can closely interact with their customers.

3.2   DMC Platform Architecture

The DMC platform architecture is both *distributed* and *federated*. As expected in a distributed model, users may select whether data and models are stored locally or remotely. The DMC platform is able to connect these models so that assemblages of data and models can be linked seamlessly. The federated design of the DMC platform permits users to finely control data access permissions. DMC users are able to publish dataset metadata while maintaining restricted access to the same datasets.

The DMC platform architecture is *cloud-based*. It has automated geographically dispersed failover protection. It is able to run on an International Traffic in Arms Regulations (ITAR)-compliant cloud. The DMC platform architecture

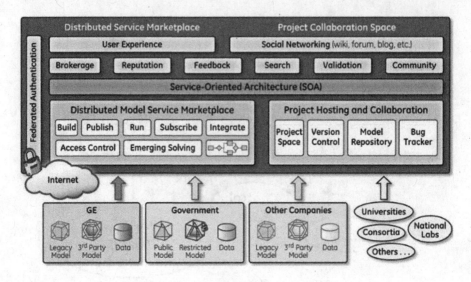

Fig. 3. High-level architecture diagram of the DMC

enables cloud-based execution of user generated code in a fashion which enables users to upload scripts (e.g. Python), executable files and data. It also enables users to automate and batch processes.

A high-level architecture diagram of the DMC is depicted in Fig. 3. Authentication services provide service access via a Service Oriented Architecture (SOA). This platform is an example of how SOA and cloud computing complement each other. Cloud computing provides resources to host data services and processes on demand.

The Distributed Object-based Modeling Environment (DOME) [15] is used for the creation and orchestration of models. DOME supports transparent, decentralized integration of models built using a wide variety of application tools and operating system platforms [16].

The DMC platform provides user access to externally hosted software applications through mechanisms that ensure interoperability between various data model types. The DMC platform architecture includes a data repository capable of storing and organizing data streamed from the internet of things. This data repository also allows users to store content including data and executables. In summary the DMC platform architecture enables a true 'Commons' for the design-to-make process so that:

– Users can share reusable data and executable models
– Owners of data and executable models retain rights when sharing, if desired
– Users can search for data and models
– Quantitative metrics such as availability, consistency and usage are tracked and visible
– Qualitative metrics such as community defined reputation are tracked and visible

3.3   DMC Cloud Deployment

An early version of the DMC was the first commercial application deployed on Amazon Web Services GovCloud [17]. The cloud environment provides an easy, low cost solution to deploy applications.

The DMC is deployed using multiple protective measures designed to secure sensitive data. Some of these measures are shown in Fig. 4. Users connect to the DMC through the internet. Public and private subnets are used to isolate internet facing services from the rest of the system. Tailored security groups are assigned to each machine instance that is deployed. Each security group restricts network traffic to specific ports from known source and destination machines. A Virtual Private Network (VPN) gateway allows communication between instances and an organization's private network.

Elasticity is another useful feature of a cloud environment. This feature allows individual subsystems to expand and contract to handle varying load levels. The DMC uses auto scaling groups to ensure a sufficient number of resources are available to handle the system load. It is possible to specify the minimum and

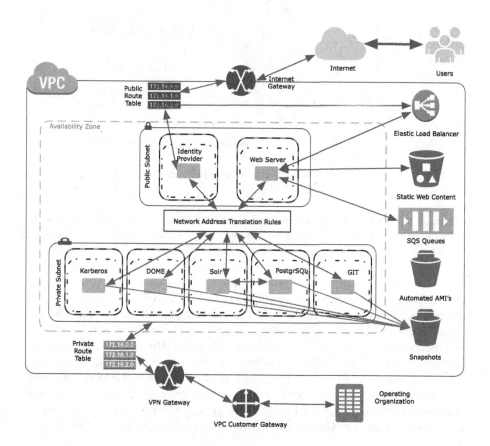

Fig. 4. Cloud deployment of the DMC

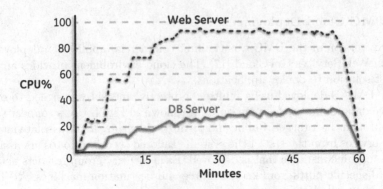

Fig. 5. Static system deployment

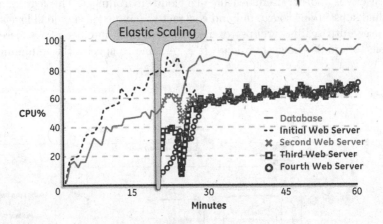

Fig. 6. Elastic system deployment

maximum number of instances in each auto scaling group to manage costs. In addition, scaling policies are assigned to each auto scaling group. These policies define when and how the scaling events occur.

Figures 5 and 6 show the results of load tests performed on a DMC deployment hosted in Amazon Web Services. Figure 5 shows the results of a load test performed on static deployment, using a single web server and database server, where all scaling events were disabled. In this experiment, increasing load was applied to the web server, as shown by the blue line. The load was generated using prerecorded site activity that was replayed using LoadRunner [18]. This experiment provides a baseline for the capacity of the web server and database server in a static environment. In comparison, Fig. 6 shows the results of a load test, using the same configuration, with web server scaling events enabled. Specifically, when a web server experiences a CPU utilization greater than 80 % for a five minute time window other web servers were created to manage the load. In Fig. 6, this scaling event is triggered and new web servers are created which lowers the CPU utilization of a web server from greater that 80 % to approximate 60 %.

4   Conclusions

The overarching benefit of the DMC is the creation of an industrial commons around digital manufacturing, where software-based manufacturing services can be exchanged, and where technology development is pulled by the market rather than pushed by vendors and technologists. Small and large manufacturers can work together, sharing models and expertise. With this form of industrial networking, productivity will increase, global economy will improve and new products will be created to better serve the Industrial Internet.

The DMC is currently used within GE. A team of engineers is working on enhancing the platform with the goal of having more than 100,000 users from companies, universities, research institutes, and entrepreneurs by 2017 [9]. We are now populating the marketplace with an initial set of representative design-manufacturing models. We are also working on improving the user interface (UI) and user experience (UX), and developing educational material for widespread dissemination. Rigorous security assessment and functionality testing are also being performed to ensure the platform's readiness for release to the user community.

Acknowledgement. This work was supported in part by the US Defense Advanced Research Projects Agency (DARPA)/Contracts Management Office (CMO) Contract No. HR0011-11-C-0092 and Digital Manufacturing Design Innovation Institute Agreement (DMDII) No. 2014-434.

References

1. Industrial Internet Consortium. http://www.iiconsortium.org/
2. GE, Accenture: Industrial Internet Insights Report for 2015. https://www.gesoftware.com/sites/default/files/industrial-internet-insights-report.pdf
3. The Economist: Wealth without workers, workers without wealth. http://www.economist.com/news/leaders/21621800-digital-revolution-bringing-sweeping-change-labour-markets-both-rich-and-poor
4. Evans, P.C., Annunziata, M.: Industrial internet: pushing the boundaries of minds and machines, GE White Paper, November 2012
5. DARPA AVM Program. http://cps-vo.org/group/avm
6. Wu, D., Rosen, D.W., Wang, L., Schaefer, D.: Cloud-based design and manufacturing: a new paradigm in digital manufacturing and design innovation. Comput.-Aided Des. **59**, 1–14 (2015)
7. Red, E., French, D., Jensen, G., Walker, S.S., Madsen, P.: Emerging design methods and tools in collaborative product development, ASME. J. Comput. Inf. Sci. Eng. **13**(3), 031001 (2013)
8. Digital Manufacturing Common. http://dmdii.uilabs.org/the-institute/dmc
9. Business Wire. GE's Digital Marketplace to Revolutionize Manufacturing. http://www.businesswire.com/news/home/20150602006480/en/#.VY2of03bLcs

10. Cao, Q., Wallace, D., Beckmann, B., Citriniti, T., Chigani, A.: Crowd-Driven ecosystem for evolutionary design, Final Report, General Electric Global Research/Massachusetts Institute of Technology, vehicleforge.mil_Team, 28 July 2012
11. Shapiro, C., Varian, H.R.: Information Rules. Harvard Business Press, Cambridge (1999)
12. NIST: Digital Thread for Smart Manufacturing. http://www.nist.gov/el/msid/syseng/dtsm.cfm
13. grabCAD. https://grabcad.com/
14. Linthicum, D.: Cloud computing and SOA Convergence in your Enterprise. Addison-Wesley Professional, Boston (2009)
15. Senin, N., Wallace, D., Borland, N.: Distributed object-based modeling in design simulation marketplace. Trans. ASME 125(1), 2–13 (2003)
16. Kraines, S., Wallace, D.: Urban sustainability technology evaluation in a distributed object-based modeling environment. Comput. Environ. Urban Syst. 27(2), 143–161 (2003)
17. Amazon Web Services GovCloud. https://aws.amazon.com/govcloud-us/
18. HP LoadRunner. http://www8.hp.com/us/en/software-solutions/loadrunner-load-testing/
19. Wang, P., Gao, R., Fan, Z.: Cloud computing for cloud manufacturing: benefits and limitations. ASME J. Manuf. Sci. Eng. 59, 1–14 (2015)
20. Xu, X.: From cloud computing to cloud manufacturing. Robot. Comput.-Integr. Manuf. 28(1), 75–86 (2012)

Towards Defining Families of Systems in IoT: Logical Architectures with Variation Points

Simone Di Cola[✉], Kung-Kiu Lau, Cuong Tran, and Chen Qian

School of Computer Science, The University of Manchester,
Manchester M13 9PL, UK
{dicolas,kung-kiu,ctran,cq}@manchester.ac.uk

Abstract. In system design, the distinction between a logical architecture at design level and the corresponding physical distributed architecture at implementation level is recognised as good practice. In this paper we show how we can define logical architectures in which variation points can be defined explicitly. Such architectures define families of systems, and should therefore be useful for defining such families in IoT.

Keywords: Software architecture · Product families · Component model · Variability

1 Introduction

The distinction between a *logical* architecture and its physical counterpart, a *physical* distributed architecture, is well-known in system design and is deemed good practice. A logical architecture can be regarded as a *design*, with the corresponding physical architecture as its *implementation*. For example, in [4] Broy describes different architecture levels for cars (Fig. 1): at design level he identifies a logical architecture which, at platform level, is mapped to its corresponding hardware architecture.

In the provisioning of Cloud services, the architecture of software and hardware components is a very challenging task [11]. Specifically, a software architecture S is a kind of logical architecture, since S is normally regarded as a design level artefact[1]. However, in our view, S often looks more like a physical architecture, particularly when the level of abstraction is low [3].

At a low abstraction level, architectural units (with ports) defined by ADLs (architecture description languages) [21] can appear to resemble chips (with pins). Consequently, an ADL architecture (containing architectural units connected together via their ports) is similar to a circuit boards (containing chips wired together via their pins). This physical resemblance can suggest that a software architecture is not a logical architecture, but a physical one. More importantly, this resemblance also seems to carry over into certain architectural properties of an ADL-defined software architecture.

---

[1] Notwithstanding Broy's view of software architectures as task level artefacts, as reflected by the automotive software standard AUTOSAR (www.autosar.org).

© ICST Institute for Computer Sciences, Social Informatics and Telecommunications Engineering 2016
B. Mandler et al. (Eds.) IoT 360° 2015, Part I, LNICST 169, pp. 419–426, 2016.
DOI: 10.1007/978-3-319-47063-4_43

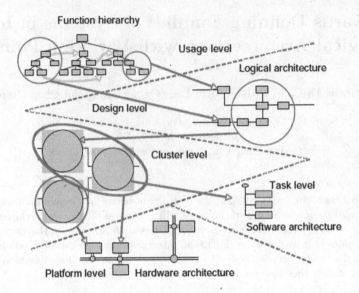

Fig. 1. Broy's architecture levels for cars [4].

The property we want to focus on is the ease of explicitly defining variation points, as in a feature model[2] [17] in family of systems [5,24] for IoT. On a circuit board, switches can direct flow in various directions; correspondingly, in some ADLs (e.g. Koala [28]) switches are used to guide (and configure) bindings between architectural units. However, switches do not fully define variation points in the sense of feature models, namely *optional*, *alternative* (exclusive 'or'), and *or* (inclusive 'or'). At best, switches can be used to create templates for generating different behaviours (code fragments) that correspond to *optional* or *alternative* features. Moreover, a feature model can also define more general dependencies between features as *composition rules* (e.g. feature A *requires/excludes* feature B), but switches cannot define such rules.

In this paper we briefly show how we define logical architectures in which we can explicitly define the full set of variation points; the latter are thus first-class citizens in our architectures. We can also handle composition rules.

2   Related Work

Our work in this paper is on the topic 'Variability and architecture description'.

A key observation in [12] is that "variability is often not explicitly described in software architectures". Our work (partially) addresses this issue: we show how we can define logical architectures with explicit variation points.

Existing approaches that also define explicit variation points include the ADLs Koala [28], xADL [9], and Mae [27]. In terms of variation points, the

---

[2] A hierarchical representation of a product family in terms of features.

difference between these approaches and ours is that they only define *optional* and *alternative* variation points, whereas we define all possible variation points.

In Koala, an *alternative* variation point is defined by a special construct called `switch`, which routes connections among component interfaces, according to input coming from a special component called `module`. A Koala architecture is a template, and a module is used to configure its instances. To generate a particular instance, the Koala compiler removes unconnected components.[3]

Koala also allows variation within a component via a `diversity interface` (a special kind of required port). However, a diversity interface only provides a general parameterisation mechanism, which allows any kinds of variations that are possible at component code level. So it does not define variation points at architecture level.

In xADL, architectures are modelled as instances of predefined XML schemas. At architectural level, an *optional* variation point is expressed by the `optional` tag. Like a Koala diversity interface, a `variant` tag defines variation within a component. Both tags are guarded by user-defined Boolean expressions, which must respect their semantics. For instance, a `variant` tag only specifies alternatives if the user defines guard expressions which are mutually exclusive.

As a predecessor of xADL, Mae also has a textual language to define architectures with variability. Architectural elements can be included, or excluded by evaluating the associated *name/value* pairs.

Other ADLs, like MontiArc[HV][14] and Plastic Partial Component [23], do not define variation points explicitly, but only place-holders for different realisations of a named but otherwise unspecified feature. Like in Koala, an architecture in these ADLs is a template that needs to be configured in order to derive its instances.

3 Defining Logical Architectures with Variation Points

Before we describe our approach, we need to be precise about what we mean by logical architectures. We follow the definition given in [25]:

> "The *logical architecture* is a breakdown of the functionality into interacting logical components. It represents the functional decomposition of a system into functional components, as well as the behaviors of these components at the logical level. The functional components provide the functionalities described in the requirements model."

A logical architecture is thus the logical view of a system architecture [18].

Clearly ADLs, or more generally, component models [19,20] can be used to define logical architectures. However, for reasons mentioned earlier, and judging by existing work, it seems that it is not straightforward to define variation points in ADL-defined software architectures. Consequently, we decided to use a component model [7] to define logical architectures, and in our model, we have defined variation points explicitly.

---

[3] Extensions to Koala for configuration definition and generation are provided by Koalish [2] and Kumbang [1].

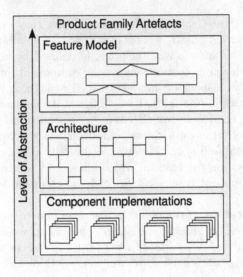

Fig. 2. Levels of abstraction in product family artefacts [26].

Our motivation is to define logical architectures for Cloud systems that will be as close a match as possible to feature models, rather than ADL-defined architectures, in the context of product family artefacts (Fig. 2). Supporting the development of family of services is very useful for the production of IoT (Internet of Things) oriented applications, where services are related to context based information [10]. However, this means we have to define logical architectures as trees, since feature models are trees.

Our approach is based on a component model (X-MAN [15]) useful to develop also Cloud systems [8], that constructs logical architectures as trees. In X-MAN, components can be atomic or composite, and architectures are built by hierarchically composing components using connectors that implement coordination mechanisms. Thus an architecture is a tree of coordinated components, both atomic and composite. In Fig. 3, `AverageMPH`, `AverageMPG`, `Maintenance`, `Monitoring`, `FrontDetection`, and `BackDetection` are atomic components, whereas `AutoCruiseControl` and `AutoBrakeBackDetection` are composite components. The insets show these composite components as trees.

However, X-MAN does not define variation points, and therefore it cannot define product families. Hence, we expanded it with variation operators and family connectors; together they realise the variability expressed by variation points in a feature model. Variation operators are applied to X-MAN architectures to generate variations which are tuples of X-MAN architectures. Family connectors are applied to these tuples to generate product families. Thus the expanded model (FX-MAN [7]) creates architectures with a full set of variation points. Such architectures are product families described by feature models.

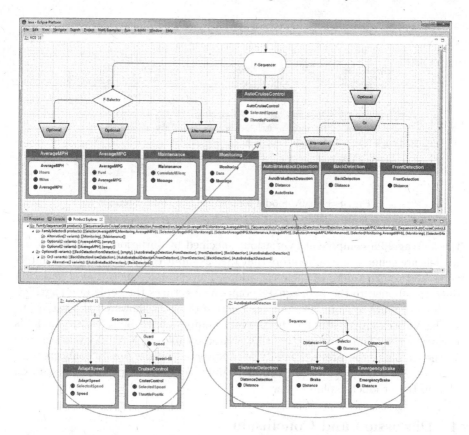

Fig. 3. Logical architecture for Vehicle Control Systems.

An example[4] of a logical architecture is shown in Fig. 3. It is the logical architecture of a product family of vehicle control systems (VCS), whose feature model is shown in Fig. 4.

As can be seen in Fig. 3, in a logical architecture the first-class citizens are: X-MAN architectures, variation operators and family connectors. X-MAN architectures appear at the bottom, and variation operators appear on top of these architectures. In Fig. 3 there are three *Optional*, two *Alternative* and one *Or* variation operators. Variation operators can be nested like variation points in feature models; in Fig. 3 an *Optional*, an *Alternative* and an *Or* variation operators are nested. Family connectors appear on top of variation operators, or X-MAN architectures which are mandatory; in Fig. 3 there are one *F-Selector*, and one *F-Sequencer* which connects to a mandatory X-MAN architecture `AutoCruiseControl`.

Clearly the logical architecture of VCS mirrors the tree structure of its feature model (Fig. 4). Indeed, the leaves of the feature model are implemented by X-MAN architectures. For instance, the `AverageMPH` feature is implemented by

---

[4] The example has been created using our FX-MAN Eclipse tool.

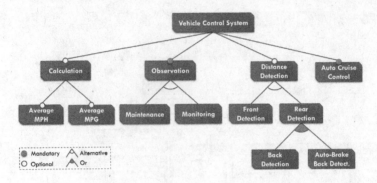

Fig. 4. Feature model for Vehicle Control Systems.

the `AverageMPH` component. Variations specified by variation points in feature models are generated by operators that take as input tuples of X-MAN architectures and return tuples of their variations. For example, an *Optional* variation operator applied to the `AverageMPH` component returns the tuple ⟨`AverageMPH`, ∅⟩. The product explorer view at the bottom of Fig. 3 shows all the variations in the VCS example. Finally, the product family defined by a feature model is constructed by family connectors that compose tuples of X-MAN architectures. In the example, the product family is constructed by the family connectors *F-Selector* and *F-Sequencer*. The product family contains 48 products, as can be seen in the product explorer view.

4   Discussion and Conclusion

Our logical Cloud architecture is executable: all the products in the product family it defines are composed from executable X-MAN components. This is in contrast to the general nature of a logical architecture as merely a logical representation (of the decomposition) of the function hierarchy (Fig. 1), i.e. a structure without behaviour. Executability means our logical architecture can realise not only the feature model (except for non-functional features) but also the functional model of the domain (which defines the behaviour of all possible products in the domain). We are currently examining suitable formulations of the functional model for facilitating the validation of its realisation.

Our logical architecture is a tree, so in terms of levels of abstraction for product family artefacts, it is closer to a feature model than an ADL-defined architecture (Fig. 2). This means that in practice the construction of a product family architecture, which is currently a difficult challenge [6,13], can be closely guided by the feature model. Moreover, since it can also realise the functional model, a logical architecture constructed this way can be a reference architecture for the domain, the construction of which is currently also a difficult challenge [22]. It will be interesting to investigate these issues further.

Although ADL-defined architectures can also serve as logic architectures, current ADLs do not define all possible variation points as first-class citizens.

For instance, Koala, xADL, and Mae do not define the *Or* (inclusive 'or') variation point at architecture level. However, some ADLs provide variation mechanisms at component code level. Such variations are internal to components and can be defined in arbitrary manners. This can be done in Koala via a `diversity interface` and in xADL via a `variant` tag. By contrast, our approach defines the full set of variation points as first-class citizens, with fixed semantics. Our experience provides some evidence that it is easier to define variation points using our logical architectures.

With variation points as first-class citizens our logical architecture explicitly contains all the members of a product family. This means that all the products can be extracted directly, rather than configured individually. Furthermore, composition rules can be realised by filters applied to the whole product family.

Returning to Fig. 1, for a chosen platform our logical architecture can be deployed to a physical architecture. In this regard, it maybe advantageous to transform our logical architecture into an equivalent ADL one, especially when the last resembles a hardware architecture, e.g. [16].

Finally, since our work has been done in the component-based development community, we would really appreciate any feedback from the Cloud architecture community.

References

1. Asikainen, T., Männistö, T., Soininen, T.: Kumbang: a domain ontology for modelling variability in software product families. Adv. Eng. Inf. **21**, 23–40 (2007)
2. Asikainen, T., Soininen, T., Xu, Y.: A koala-based approach for modelling and deploying configurable software product families. In: van der Linden, F.J. (ed.) PFE 2003. LNCS, vol. 3014, pp. 225–249. Springer, Heidelberg (2004)
3. Bass, L., Clements, P., Kazman, R.: Software Architecture in Practice. SEI Series in Software Engineering, 3rd edn. Addison-Wesley, Boston (2012)
4. Broy, M.: Challenges in automotive software engineering. In: Leon, J., Osterweil, H., Rombach, D., Soffa, M.L. (edr.) 28th International Conference on Software Engineering, pp. 33–42. ACM (2006)
5. Clements, P., Northrop, L.: Software Product Lines: Practices and Patterns. Addison-Wesley, Boston (2002)
6. Clements, P.: Biglever newsletter: from the ple frontline - paul's three surprises: part 3
7. Cola, S.D., Lau, K.-K., Tran, C., Qian, C., Arshad, R., Christou, V.: A component model for software product families. In: Paper submitted to the 18th International ACM Sigsoft Symposium on Component-Based Software Engineering (2015)
8. Cola, S., Tran, C., Lau, K.-K., Celesti, A., Fazio, M.: A heterogeneous approach for developing applications with FIWARE GEs. In: Dustdar, S., Leymann, F., Villari, M. (eds.) ESOCC 2015. LNCS, vol. 9306, pp. 65–79. Springer, Heidelberg (2015). doi:10.1007/978-3-319-24072-5_5
9. Dashofy, E.M., van der Hoek, A., Taylor, R.N.: A comprehensive approach for the development of modular software architecture description languages. ACM Trans. Softw. Eng. Methodol. (TOSEM) **14**, 199–245 (2005)
10. Fazio, M., Celesti, A., Puliafito, A., Villari, M.: An integrated system for advanced multi-risk management based on cloud for IoT. In: Re, G.L. (ed.) Advances onto the Internet of Things. AISC, vol. 260, pp. 253–269. Springer, Heidelberg (2014)

11. Fazio, M., Puliafito, A.: Cloud4sens: a cloud-based architecture for sensor controlling and monitoring. IEEE Commun. Mag. **53**(3), 41–47 (2015)

12. Galster, M., Avgeriou, P., Weyns, D., Männistö, T.: Variability in software architecture: current practice and challenges. SIGSOFT Softw. Eng. Notes **36**(5), 30–32 (2011)

13. Garlan, D.: Software architecture: a travelogue. In: Proceedings of the on Future of Software Engineering, FOSE, pp. 29–39. ACM, New York (2014)

14. Haber, A., Rendel, H., Rumpe, B., Schaefer, I., Van Der Linden, F.: Hierarchical variability modeling for software architectures. In: 15th International Software Product Line Conference (SPLC), pp. 150–159. IEEE (2011)

15. He, N., Kroening, D., Wahl, T., Lau, K.-K., Taweel, F., Tran, C., Rümmer, P., Sharma, S.: Component-based design and verification in X-MAN. In: Proceedings of Embedded Real Time Software and Systems (2012)

16. Tran, C., Saudrais, S., Lau, K.-K., Štěpán, P., Tchakaloff, B.: A holistic (component-based) approach to autosar designs. In: Proceedings of 39th EUROMICRO Conference on Software Engineering and Advanced Applications, pp. 203–207. IEEE (2013)

17. Kyo, C., Kang, J.L., Donohoe, P.: Feature-oriented product line engineering. IEEE Softw. **19**(4), 58–65 (2002)

18. Kruchten, P.: The Rational Unified Process: an Introduction. Addison-Wesley Professional, Boston (2004)

19. Lau, K.-K., Wang, Z.: Software component models. IEEE Trans. Softw. Eng. **33**(10), 709–724 (2007)

20. Lau, K.: Software component models: past, present and future. In: Proceedings of the 17th International ACM Sigsoft Symposium on Component-based Software Engineering, pp. 185–186. ACM (2014)

21. Medvidovic, N., Taylor, R.N.: A classification and comparison framework for software architecture description languages. IEEE Trans. Softw. Eng. **26**(1), 70–93 (2000)

22. Nakagawa, E.Y.: Reference architectures and variability: Current status and future perspectives. In: Proceedings of the WICSA/ECSA 2012 Companion Volume, WICSA/ECSA 2012, pp. 159–162. ACM, New York (2012)

23. Pérez, J., Díaz, J., Costa-Soria, C., Garbajosa, J.: Plastic partial components: a solution to support variability in architectural components. In: Joint Working IEEE/IFIP Conference on Software Architecture, & European Conference on Software Architecture, WICSA/ECSA, pp. 221–230. IEEE (2009)

24. Pohl, K., Böckle, G., Van Der Linden, F.: Software Product Line Engineering: Foundations, Principles, and Techniques. Springer, Berlin (2005)

25. Pretschner, A., Broy, M., Kruger, I.H., Stauner, T.: Software engineering for automotive systems: a roadmap. In: Future of Software Engineering, FOSE 2007, pp. 55–71. IEEE Computer Society, Washington (2007)

26. Sinnema, M., Deelstra, S., Nijhuis, J., Dannenberg, R.B.: COVAMOF: a framework for modeling variability in software product families. In: Nord, R.L. (ed.) SPLC 2004. LNCS, vol. 3154, pp. 197–213. Springer, Heidelberg (2004)

27. van der Hoek, A., Mikic-Rakic, M., Roshandel, R., Medvidovic, N.: Taming architectural evolution. In: Proceedings of the 8th European Software Engineering Conference Held Jointly with 9th ACM SIGSOFT International Symposium on Foundations of Software Engineering, ESEC/FSE-9, pp. 1–10. ACM, New York (2001)

28. van Ommering, R., van der Linden, F., Kramer, J., Magee, J.: The Koala component model for consumer electronics software. IEEE Computer (2000)

HealthyIoT

An Overview on the Internet of Things for Health Monitoring Systems

Mobyen Uddin Ahmed[✉], Mats Björkman, Aida Čaušević, Hossein Fotouhi, and Maria Lindén

Mälardalen University, Västerås, Sweden
{mobyen.ahmed,mats.bjorkman,aida.causevic,hossein.fotouhi,
maria.linden}@mdh.se

Abstract. The aging population and the increasing healthcare cost in hospitals are spurring the advent of remote health monitoring systems. Advances in physiological sensing devices and the emergence of reliable low-power wireless network technologies have enabled the design of remote health monitoring systems. The next generation Internet, commonly referred to as Internet of Things (IoT), depicts a world populated by devices that are able to sense, process and react via the Internet. Thus, we envision health monitoring systems that support Internet connection and use this connectivity to enable better and more reliable services. This paper presents an overview on existing health monitoring systems, considering the IoT vision. We focus on recent trends and the development of health monitoring systems in terms of: (1) health parameters and frameworks, (2) wireless communication, and (3) security issues. We also identify the main limitations, requirements and advantages within these systems.

1 Introduction

According to the Eurostat population projection, by 2030 just in the European Union, the percentage of elderly people (65 years old and older) will increase with 6.1 %, compared to 2008, with the assumption that the growth will continue in the future [11]. At the same time, we are facing the problem of birth rates that are below the level needed for a sustained population. This results in a growing need for healthcare, and reduces the ability to financially support it. In 2008, four persons of working age were supporting one person aged 65 or older, while projection shows that by 2030 the number of working persons will decrease to 2.5. This calls for less expensive solutions in healthcare that will utilize the benefits of modern technology, providing distance monitoring of elderly, and avoiding hospitalization when it is possible.

Technical advances in physiological sensing devices and wireless connectivity provided by the IoT can enable dramatic changes in the ways health monitoring and remote healthcare will be performed in the future. However, for such changes to take place, the enabling technologies must be employed with the well-being

© ICST Institute for Computer Sciences, Social Informatics and Telecommunications Engineering 2016
B. Mandler et al. (Eds.) IoT 360° 2015, Part I, LNICST 169, pp. 429–436, 2016.
DOI: 10.1007/978-3-319-47063-4_44

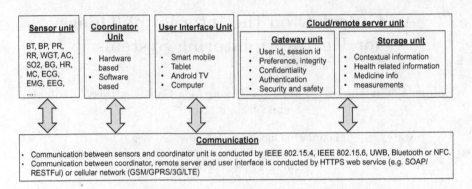

Fig. 1. A system-level framework for health monitoring systems.

of the patient in focus, since neither individuals nor society would accept IoT solutions that mismatch the standards of current best practice in healthcare.

IoT for health monitoring systems can enable new possibilities not available to patients today, especially to those not ill enough to be admitted to a hospital. By providing low-cost solutions to in-home monitoring, IoT can enable monitoring of such patients, enabling early detection of signs of deteriorating health, allowing for earlier responses and treatment. In order for in-home monitored patients to feel safe and secure when staying at their homes, the IoT solutions used must guarantee safety and security at a more technical level. Hence, one important focus of this overview is the security of the health monitoring systems studied.

In this paper, we are targeting health monitoring issues by considering the IoT vision. Section 2 provides an overview on the relevant parameters and frameworks. In Sect. 3, we explain the most common wireless standards and technologies for remote health monitoring. Section 4 continues with relevant security issues and challenges in this area. Finally, we conclude the paper in Sect. 5.

2   Parameters and Frameworks for Health Monitoring

Remote health monitoring systems support monitoring a number of physiological parameters. Most common parameters included in health monitoring systems are vital signs, such as: Body Temperature (BT), Blood Pressure (BP), Pulse Rate (PR), and Respiratory Rate (RR) [2,4]. Beside these parameters, there are some other parameters defined as; Weight (WGT), Activity (AC), Oxygen Saturation (SO2), Blood Glucose (BG), Heart Rate (HR), and Medication Compliance (MC) [26]. Some systems facilitate remote monitoring of Electrocardiography (ECG) and Electromyography (EMG) [24], while few are looking forward to develop electroencephalogram (EEG) [25]. Some health parameters are measured sparsely, such as BP, BG, WGT, BT, while HR, PR, RR. EEG, EMG and ECG are measured continuously at specific time periods. There are different ways for sensor data management, considering IoT and most common components that are presented in a block diagram — see Fig. 1.

Main components in health monitoring systems are: (1) sensor unit, (2) coordinator unit, (3) remote server unit, (4) user interface unit, and (5) communication unit. A sensor unit contains a set of sensors for different health parameters that typically are battery powered, together with a microcontroller for data processing, and an antenna for communication purposes. According to the literature, most of the systems use commercially available and CE[1] certified sensors, while few of them use sensors that are under development within academia. The coordinator unit is developing in two directions; (1) hardware direction, and (2) software direction. The main hardware parts are processor, memory, radio and relevant sensor(s) [19], while the software direction is an application, performing on a host platform, e.g. an Android operating system that collects different measurements from sensors [2,4]. A remote server is placed in the cloud, which usually consists of a Gateway and a storage. The Gateway that delivers data from one wireless domain to another, focuses on security, safety and privacy issues, and it manages users and user requests in term of data management. The storage stores all user related information together with health measurements. Moreover, it also provides import and export facilities, while enabling data encryption. Most of the existing user interfaces are implemented either for smartphones or tablets [2,24,26], or in laptop-based platforms [25], with exception of a smart TV-based implementation [19]. The data communication is considered in two aspects: local and global. The local communication is between sensor and coordinator units, which is normally obtained by either Bluetooth [13] or IEEE 802.15.4, which will be further discussed in Sect. 3. The global communication provides connection between the coordinator, remote server and user interface and is established via either HTTPS web service (e.g. SOAP/RESTFul) or cellular networks. In [3], the authors proposed a generic system-level framework for health monitoring systems, where they tried to combine several available techniques.

3   Wireless Communication in Health Monitoring

The use of wireless sensing devices on the human body is attracting the healthcare and wireless communities. However, there are still many open issues that need further investigation within the wireless domain. For instance, which wireless technologies and standards are appropriate enablers for different healthcare scenarios? Is it feasible to employ multiple Low-Power Wireless Network (LPWN) technologies in a healthcare system? How can health monitoring systems provide IoT requirements? In this section, we investigate various wireless technologies and their main features, followed by providing a generic system model for the health monitoring applications.

---

[1] The CE marking is the manufacturers' declaration that the product meets the necessary requirements.

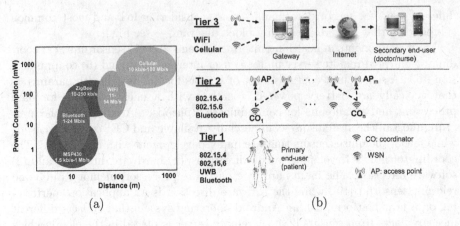

Fig. 2. Wireless communication for healthcare: (a) comparing different wireless technologies in terms of transmission power, transmission range and data rate, and (b) categorizing wireless technologies at each tier.

LPWN contains a group of wireless standards/technologies that support low-power radios, such as IEEE 802.15.4 (ZigBee [5]), IEEE 802.15.1 (Bluetooth [13]), IEEE 802.15.6 (UWB), Radio Frequency Identification (RFID) [21], and IPv6 over Low-Power Wireless Personal Area Networks (6LoWPAN) [22]. Internet Protocol (IP)-based LPWNs are becoming increasingly important for many applications. From the aforementioned LPWN standards/technologies, 6LoWPAN supports IPv6 over IEEE 802.15.4 based networks that guarantees some security levels. The IP-based addressing provides smooth integration of LPWNs within other wireless technologies, such as WiFi and cellular network. This integration provides the possibility of connecting sensing devices to cloud-based services, allowing extensive information processing for early diagnosis.

The use of LPWNs for critical applications is very challenging. LPWNs operate at a very low data rate and transmission power, aiming at a prolonged lifetime. Figure 2(a) shows a comparison of power consumption of wireless transceivers and a microprocessor in different wireless systems. The maximum transmission power of a regular LPWN device (e.g. TelosB with MSP430 microprocessor [7]) is 1 mW, while in WiFi access points is in the range of 30 mW to 800 mW and in cellular networks from 500 mW in smartphones to $\approx 10^5$ mW in base stations. Providing reliable data transmission between sensing devices with extremely low-power radios in a noisy environment is very challenging. This requires considering various parameters, such as link quality estimation, time synchronization, collision avoidance and mobility management when designing a data communication protocol.

There are various system architectures for communication in different health monitoring applications [16,17,27]. In this paper, we present a generic system that covers all the related works — see Fig. 2(b). It shows three tiers based on using appropriate wireless technologies. *Tier* 1 requires LPWNs for communicating between sensing devices and the coordinator[2]. One of the sensing devices or an additional device is usually devised to collect data from all sensors. This level of communication consists of multiple physiological sensing devices that are capable to sample the vital signs, process data and communicate through a wireless medium. These devices should be carefully placed on the human body by either direct attachment on the body skin, or placing in special clothes, or implanting inside the body. *Tier* 2 provides the possibility of communication between coordinators and fixed set of sensor nodes, known as Access Points (APs) [8,9]. This would benefit elderly people by avoiding the necessity of holding smartphones for collecting data. Finally, *Tier* 3 is devised for relaying data from LPWN toward the secondary end-user for further processing. In this level, health monitoring systems gain from the existing WiFi and cellular infrastructure.

4   Security in Health Monitoring

In pervasive healthcare that assumes an IoT-based environment, it is important to ensure basic security services such as: *privacy* (patient identity protection); *confidentiality* (protecting medical information of patients, as well as medical staff information); *integrity* (protection of data alternation during the transmission by any adversary); *authentication* (making sure that the data is sent from a trusted source); *data freshness* (preventing an adversary to capture transmitted data and later replay it, causing possible confusion in the system); etc. These services are required by existing legislatives such as European directive 95/46 [18] on data protection and HIPAA [6] in the United States, and should ensure guarantees of patient's safety and privacy. IEEE 802 has established a working group for standardization of Wireless Body Area Networks (WBAN) that produced IEEE 802.15.6 standard [12]. The standard establishes foundation for low-power in-body/on-body nodes to serve a number of different applications, including health monitoring application in a secure and safe way.

Any security mechanism in sensor-based systems should be fit with existing system requirements such as energy efficiency, memory restrictions, minimum possible computational and communication resource consumption, fast operation mode in order to avoid any delays of critical data, and high level of scalability. One has to bear in mind that the growth in number of connected devices in IoT brings larger number of possibilities for attacks on personal data. Also, communication is extended far outside of local networks, which requires strong authentication and authorisation protocols to be defined. The existing security-related solutions in many cases are not able to cope with all these requirements to their full extend and therefore more research in this area is required.

There is a number of research projects that aim at addressing security-related challenges. In [23], authors address patient's privacy as one of the main challenges when providing efficient and effective service in e-healthcare. Haque et al.

---

[2] The coordinator is a regular sensor device that is assigned for collecting data from other sensors.

describe open security issues in pervasive computing and emphasise the importance and the role of strong authentication in pervasive environments that is applicable to healthcare in IoT [14]. In [15], authors describe an authentication mechanism based on correct calculation of a Message Authentication Code, that is used to identify data as being sent by a trusted participant. As a way to achieve data confidentiality a light-weight data encryption model is proposed [20]. Garcia-Morchon et al. describe a security framework that combines strong security primitives such as public-key cryptography with light-weight cryptographic primitives, providing a trade-off between security, availability and efficiency that is followed by privacy-aware user identification in the system [10]. Nguyen et al. describe challenges and limitations of existing secure communication protocols for IoT [1]. They provide a novel classification of existing protocols based on their bootstrapping approach to establish a secure communication channel, and point out the performance challenges with respect to the use of these protocols.

5   Conclusions

This paper presents an overview on health monitoring systems in a daily life considering the IoT for health. Here, we reviewed the main aspects related to health, focusing on recent trends and development of the health monitoring systems through IoT. A number of recent health monitoring systems have been reviewed in terms of health parameters, frameworks, wireless communication and security issues. We presented the motivation for considering the IoT for interoperability between different devices, networks and applications. According to the observations, the development and the trend of the research on IoT in the area is growing, however, many issues are not tackled yet. Considering unreliable links in LPWNs and coexistence of interference from high-power wireless networks working in the same frequency band, risk factor analysis and user evaluation, based on primary and secondary end-users, can extend the study, which is our future focus.

Acknowledgments. This work is funded by Knowledge Foundation's research profile Embedded Sensor System for Health (ESS-H) and the distributed environment Ecare@Home.

References

1. Survey on secure communication protocols for the internet of things. Ad Hoc Netw. (2015)
2. Ahmed, M.U., Banaee, H., Loutfi, A., Rafael-Palou, X.: Intelligent healthcare services to support health monitoring of elderly. In: HealthyIoT (2014)
3. Ahmed, M.U., Björkman, M., Lindén, M.: A generic system-level framework for self-serve health monitoring system through internet of things (iot). In: pHealth (2012)

4. Ahmed, M.U., Espinosa, J.R., Reissner, A., Domingo, À., Banaee, H., Loutfi, A., Rafael-Palou, X.: Self-serve ict-based health monitoring to support active ageing. In: HEALTHINF (2015)
5. Alliance, Z.: Zigbee specification (2006). http://zigbee.org/
6. Congress, U.S.: Health insurance portability and accountability act (1996). http://www.gpo.gov/fdsys/pkg/PLAW-104publ191/html/PLAW-104publ191.htm
7. Crossbow Technology, Inc.: Telosb datasheet, December 2014. http://www.willow.co.uk, http://www.willow.co.uk/TelosB_Datasheet.pdf
8. Fotouhi, H., Moreira, D., Alves, M.: mRPL: boosting mobility in the internet of things. Elsevier Ad-Hoc Netw. **26**, 17–35 (2015)
9. Fotouhi, H., Zuniga, M., Alves, M., Koubaa, A., Marrón, P.: Smart-HOP: a reliable handoff mechanism for mobile wireless sensor networks. In: Picco, G.P., Heinzelman, W. (eds.) EWSN 2012. LNCS, vol. 7158, pp. 131–146. Springer, Heidelberg (2012)
10. Garcia-Morchon, O., Falck, T., Heer, T., Wehrle, K.: Security for pervasive medical sensor networks. In: 6th Annual International on Mobile and Ubiquitous Systems: Networking Services, MobiQuitous 2009 (2009)
11. Giannakouris, K.: Population and social conditions, regional population projections europop2008: most eu regions face older population profile in 2030. Eurostat: Statistics in focus (2010)
12. Group, W.W.P.A.N.W.W.: Ieee standard for local and metropolitan area networks - part 15.6: wireless body area networks (2012). http://standards.ieee.org/about/get/802/802.15.html
13. Haartsen, J.C.: The bluetooth radio system. IEEE Pers. Commun. **7**, 28–36 (2000)
14. Haque, M.M., Ahamed, S.I.: Security in pervasive computing: current status and open issues. Int. J. Netw. Secur. **3**, 203–214 (2006)
15. Kumar, P., Lee, Y.D., Lee, Y.D.: Secure health monitoring using medical wireless sensor networks. In: NCM (2010)
16. Liang, X., Li, X., Barua, M., Chen, L., Lu, R., Shen, X., Luo, H.: Enable pervasive healthcare through continuous remote health monitoring. IEEE Wirel. Commun. **19**, 10–18 (2012)
17. Mitra, U., Emken, B.A., Lee, S., Li, M., Rozgic, V., Thatte, G., Vathsangam, H., Zois, D.S., Annavaram, M., Narayanan, S., et al.: Knowme: a case study in wireless body area sensor network design. IEEE Commun. Mag. **50**, 116–125 (2012)
18. European Parliament and of the Council: Directive 95/46/ec of the european parliament and of the council on the protection of individuals with regard to the processing of personal data and on the free movement of such data (1995). http://eur-lex.europa.eu/LexUriServ/LexUriServ.do?uri=CELEX:31995L0046:en:HTML
19. Parra, J., Hossain, M.A., Uribarren, A., Jacob, E.: Restful discovery and eventing for service provisioning in assisted living environments. Sensors **14**, 9227–9246 (2014)
20. Rekha, N.R., PrasadBabu, M.: Secured framework for pervasive healthcare monitoring systems. IJSCAI **2**, 39–47 (2013)
21. Roberts, C.M.: Radio frequency identification (RFID). Elsevier Comput. Secur. **25**, 18–26 (2006)
22. Shelby, Z., Bormann, C.: 6LoWPAN: The Wireless Embedded Internet. Wiley, Chichester (2011)
23. Sun, J., Fang, Y., Zhu, X.: Privacy and emergency response in e-healthcare leveraging wireless body sensor networks. IEEE Wirel. Commun. **17**, 66–73 (2010)
24. Tomasic, I., Avbelj, V., Trobec, R.: Smart wireless sensor for physiological monitoring. Stud. Health Technol. Inform. **211**, 295–301 (2014)

25. Xavier, B., Dahikar, P.: A perspective study on patient monitoring systems based on wireless sensor network, its development and future challenges. Int. J. Comput. Appl. **65**, 35–38 (2013)
26. Yang, G., Xie, L., Mantysalo, M., Zhou, X., Pang, Z., Da Xu, L., Kao-Walter, S., Chen, Q., Zheng, L.R.: A health-iot platform based on the integration of intelligent packaging, unobtrusive bio-sensor, and intelligent medicine box. IEEE Trans. Ind. Inform. **10**, 2180–2191 (2014)
27. Yuce, M.R.: Implementation of wireless body area networks for healthcare systems. Elsevier Sens. Actuators A: Phys. **162**, 116–129 (2010)

An Adaptive QoE-Based Network Interface Selection for Multi-homed eHealth Devices

Sami Souihi[✉], Mohamed Souidi, and Abdelhamid Mellouk

Image, Signal and Intelligent Systems Lab (LiSSi), Network and Telecoms Dept,
IUT CV, University of Paris-Est Crteil Val de Marne (UPEC),
122 rue Paul Armangot, 94400 Vitry sur Seine, France
{sami.souihi,mohamed.souidi,mellouk}@u-pec.fr

Abstract. Conventional network control mechanisms are no longer suitable for Internet of Things (IoT) because they don't allow scalability with a guarantee of Quality of Experience (QoE) especially when it comes to the health sector characterized by its real time and critical life aspects. That's why we need to think differently about control. One aspect consists of improving the network accessibility by considering Multi-homed terminals using multiple network access points simultaneously. In this paper we present a new Q-Learning-based adaptive network interface selection approach. Experimental results show that the proposed approach involve QoE compared to a simple linear programming approach. *abstract* environment.

Keywords: Reinforcement Learning · Q-learning · Quality of Experience · Mean Opinion Score (MOS) · Multi-homed devices · ICT health · Internet of Things (IoT)

1 Introduction

ICT health is a part of a new paradigm called the Internet of Things (IoT) [1]. The role of IoT in the current networks are expanding in terms of communicating things such as smart devices, gadgets, on-body sensors, cameras, and also in terms of applications and services (see Fig. 1).

Therefore, conventional network control mechanisms are no longer suitable because they don't permit scalability with a guarantee of Quality of Experience (QoE) especially when it comes to the health sector, which is characterized by its real time and critical life aspects. That's why we need to think differently about control mechanisms and protocols in the perspective of adaptive and autonomous aspects, that guarantee the high QoE. To achieve this goal, we shall improve the network accessibility by considering Multi-homed terminals using multiple network access points simultaneously (see Fig. 2). The Multi-homed methodology [2] provides the flexibility to select the best available network access points (e.g. wired or wireless include WiFi, 3G, 4G, WLAN, Satellite, etc.) for efficiently transport of information data. In such environment, the major issue is Always

© ICST Institute for Computer Sciences, Social Informatics and Telecommunications Engineering 2016
B. Mandler et al. (Eds.) IoT 360° 2015, Part I, LNICST 169, pp. 437–442, 2016.
DOI: 10.1007/978-3-319-47063-4_45

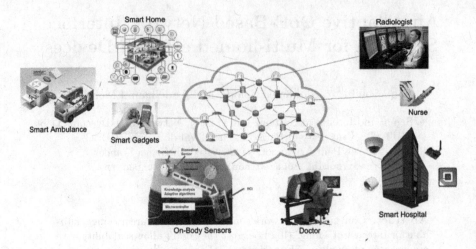

Fig. 1. IoT health network

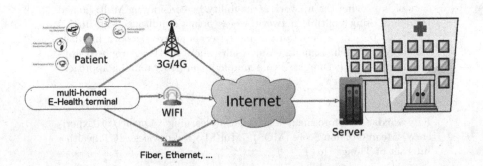

Fig. 2. Multi-homed IoT health device

Best Connected (ABC), which means that the mobile nodes rank the network interfaces and select the best one at anytime and anywhere. In this article, we present an adaptive ABC approach depending on QoE.

This paper is organized as follows: (i) The next section defines the ABC problem and describes a simple solution to address it. (ii) Then, Sect. 3 explains the proposed adaptive ABC approach depending on an estimated Mean Opinion Score (MOS) based on real time network measurements. (iii) Finally, the last section summarizes the evaluation results and demonstrates the performance of the proposed adaptive approach.

2   The ABC Problem

The evolution of mobile terminals with multiple access network interfaces give mobile users the possibility of being "Always Best Connected", where mobile users can switch between different network technologies, and connect to the best one that satisfies their service requirements at anytime and anywhere. In case of eHealth application, disaster or emergency situations, the Multi-homed method is an efficient solution to overcome the shortage of limited network access points. In fact, it is not always possible for patients to be whiting a healthcare facility due to several factors such as, emergency, remote location, limited mobility, being part of daily routine (patients with chronic conditions), or simply because it is a tedious expensive task for some simple procedures; this is where e-health fits in, with a multi-homed, easy-to-use, wearable devices in order to check blood pressure, heart rate, blood glucose level, oxygen levels, weight and health status, and sends the data to the server for doctor's diagnosis.

A simple solution to solve ABC problem is a Linear programming (LP; also called linear optimization). It is consist of a method to achieve the best outcome (such as maximum profit or lowest cost) [3]. Linear programming is a special case of mathematical programming (mathematical optimization). More formally, linear programming is a technique for the optimization of a linear objective function, subject to linear equality and linear inequality constraints. Its feasible region is a convex polyhedron, which is a set defined as the intersection of finitely many half spaces, each of which is defined by a linear inequality. Its objective function is a real valued affine function defined on this polyhedron. A linear programming algorithm finds a point in the polyhedron where this function has the smallest (or largest) value if such a point exists. In our case, the objective function consist of maximizing MOS by selecting the most suitable network interface. The problem of this method is that a choice made at time "t" may be inappropriate at time "t+1". That's why an adaptive model is needed.

3   An Adaptive Approach to Address the ABC Problem

Our proposed adaptive approach to address ABC problem is based on Reinforcement Learning (RL) which is an area of machine learning inspired by behaviorist psychology, concerned with how software agents ought to take actions in an environment so as to maximize some notion of cumulative reward.

Q-learning [4] is a model-free reinforcement learning technique (see Fig. 3). Specifically, Q-learning can be used to find an optimal action-selection policy for any given (finite) Markov decision process (MDP). It works by learning an action-value function that ultimately gives the expected utility of taking a given action in a given state and following the optimal policy thereafter. When such an action-value function is learned, the optimal policy can be constructed by simply selecting the action with the highest value in each state. One of the strengths of Q-learning is that it is able to compare the expected utility of the available actions without requiring a model of the environment. Additionally, Q-learning can handle problems with stochastic transitions and rewards, without requiring any adaptations. It has been proven that for any finite MDP, Q-learning eventually finds an optimal policy.

The algorithm therefore has a function which calculates the Quality of a state-action combination: Before learning has started, Q returns an (arbitrary)

$$Q_{t+1}(s_t, a_t) = \underbrace{Q_t(s_t, a_t)}_{\text{old value}} + \underbrace{\alpha_t(s_t, a_t)}_{\text{learning rate}} \times \left[\underbrace{R_{t+1}}_{\text{reward}} + \overbrace{\underbrace{\gamma}_{\text{discount factor}} \quad \underbrace{\max_a Q_t(s_{t+1}, a)}_{\text{estimate of optimal future value}}}^{\text{learned value}} - \underbrace{Q_t(s_t, a_t)}_{\text{old value}} \right]$$

Fig. 3. Q-learning equation

fixed value, chosen by the designer. Then, each time the agent selects an action, and observes a reward and a new state that both may depend on both the previous state and the selected action. The core of the algorithm is a simple value iteration update. It assumes the old value and makes a correction based on the new information. In our case the states are the current interface and the reward is the estimated MOS.

4   The Evaluation of Network Interface Selection Approches

In order to evaluate our work, we emulated the network behavior by varying the main network metrics based on realistic models. For the packet loss, we used a gilbert eliot loss model [5], for the latency we used a normal distribution model [6] and for bandwidth we used a random variation model. We connect our

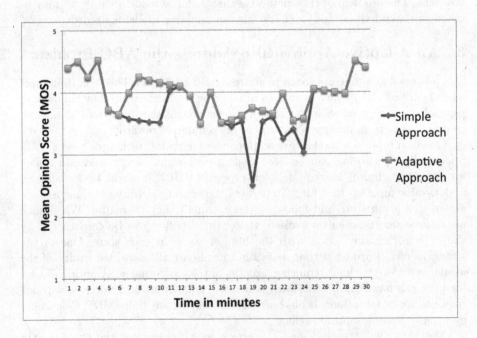

Fig. 4. Network interface selection approches

multi-homed box to network emulator throw three interfaces that represented three kind of network accesses: Wi-Fi, Ethernet and 3G/4G. In addition, we implemented in this box a module that continuously measures the delay, the bandwidth and the packet loss in order to estimate the MOS. To switch from one interface to another, the system takes only few milliseconds (around 30 ms). This lost time is nothing comparing to the gain made by changing the interface. The total experimentation duration is 30 min.

Figure 4 show the experimentation results. It represents the MOS variation through time and compares the score obtained by the simple approach based on Linear programming (LP) to the one obtained by our adaptive approach based on Q-learning. Indeed, the simple approach consists in selecting the best interface (based on MOS) and continues with that interface independently of network parameters evolution while the adaptive selection algorithm changes the network interface based on the estimated MOS calculated from the current network metrics values. The proposed algorithm gives the same score when the first interface selected gives the best score, otherwise, the proposed algorithm gives the best measured score.

5   Conclusion

Selecting the network over which data should be sent is important, and it depends on multiple criteria. In case of a patient with a chronic condition, periodic vital signs measurements are needed, and network with average bandwidth/delay is suitable for such a situation, where a sudden rise in those signs should be reported in real time through a high bandwidth/low delay network. In this paper, we present an adaptive approach to address the "Always Best Connected" issue. Experimental results show that this approach, based on a Q-Learning model, improves Quality of Experience compared to a simple non adaptive approach.

As a perspective, we intend to improve the information transportation in an efficient manner without changing the existing hardware components of the core network. To address this challenge, we think to use a new paradigm called Software Defined Networking (SDN).

References

1. Gubbi, J., Buyya, R., Marusic, S., Palaniswami, M.: Internet of Things (IoT): a vision, architectural elements, and future directions. Future Gener. Comput. Syst. **29**(7), 1645–1660 (2013)
2. Mitharwal, P., Lohr, C., Gravey, A.: Survey on network interface selection in multihomed mobile networks. In: Kermarrec, Y. (ed.) EUNICE 2014. LNCS, vol. 8846, pp. 134–146. Springer, Heidelberg (2014)
3. Souidi, M., Souihi, S., Hoceini, S., Mellouk, A.: An adaptive real time mechanism for IaaS cloud provider selection based on QoE aspects. In: IEEE International Conference on Communications (ICC), London, United Kingdom, 8–12 June 2015. (confrence de rfrence dans le domaine des rseaux)

4. Mellouk, A., Tran, H.A., Hoceini, S.: Quality-of-Experience for Multimedia. Wiley-ISTE, October 2013. ISBN: 978-1-84821-563-4
5. Goncalves, V., Ballon, P.: Adding value to the network: mobile operators experiments with Software-as-a-Service and Platform-as-a-Service models. Telematics Inform. **28**(1), 12–21 (2011)
6. Proko, E., Ninka, I.: Analysis and strategy for the performance testing in cloud computing. Global J. Comput. Sci. Technol. Cloud Distrib. **12**(10), 11–14 (2012)

An Internet-Based Tool for Pediatric Cardiac Disease Diagnosis Using Intelligent Phonocardiography

Arash Gharehbaghi[✉] and Maria Lindén

Department of Innovation, Design and Technology,
Mälardalen University, 72123 Västerås, Sweden
{Arash.ghareh.baghi,Maria.linden}@mdh.se

Abstract. This paper suggests an internet-based tool for cardiac diagnosis in children. The main focus of the paper is the intelligent algorithms for processing heart sounds that are implementable on an internet platform. The algorithms are based on the statistical classification methods, tailored for the heart sound signal processing. The algorithms, applied to 55 healthy and 45 children with congenital heart diseases. The accuracy of the algorithm is estimated to be 86.0 % in screening the children with pathological murmurs, and 95.7 %, 92.9 % and 91.4 % in detecting the children with aortic stenosis, pulmonary stenosis and mitral regurgitation, respectively, showing an acceptable performance to be employed as a decision support tool.

Keywords: Heart sounds · Phonocardiogram · Intelligent phonocardiography · Artificial intelligence

1 Introduction

Timely assessment of a pediatric heart disease plays an important role in the disease management. The assessment is firstly performed by physicians using heart sound auscultation. Then, the diseased children are often supervised by pediatric cardiologists for finding appropriate therapeutic procedure after being precisely investigated. Phonocardiogram is a recording of the acoustical wave, emanating from heart, so called heart sound. Heart sound auscultation is a complicated task which needs expertise and experiences especially in children with high heart rate. However, access to expert cardiologists is not easy especially in the developing countries and rural places. This makes development of an internet-based decision support system been sophisticated for pediatric cardiac disease, a priority by which the screening, assessments and supervision is remotely feasible. The key part of such a system is the automatic algorithm for processing heart sounds that attributes intelligence to the system. Our long term studies on heart sound signals revealed that screening of congenital heart disease with sufficient accuracy and sensitivity is possible [1, 2]. The studies have been continued toward extracting diagnostic features from the heart sound which may eventually lead to an automatic system for the disease diagnosis [3–5].

This paper presents an internet-based tool for timely screening of pediatric heart disease using heart sound signal. The main focus of the paper is on the automatic

© ICST Institute for Computer Sciences, Social Informatics and Telecommunications Engineering 2016
B. Mandler et al. (Eds.) IoT 360° 2015, Part I, LNICST 169, pp. 443–447, 2016.
DOI: 10.1007/978-3-319-47063-4_46

processing algorithms for screening diseased children and extracting pathological signs from the heart sounds. The resulting system, which we call the intelligent phonocardiography, offers a noninvasive, inexpensive and easy-to-use approach for cardiac diagnosis, employable by the nurses, practitioner or family doctors in primary healthcare centers to increase diagnosis accuracy, as studies showed that the screening accuracy is still low in these centers [6, 7]. This causes a large number of the children with normal heart to be referred to the referral hospitals, and on the other hand a number of the diseased children to be overlooked, during cardiac auscultation in the primary healthcare centers. The proposed system can drastically decrease unnecessary echocardiography, which is by far a more expensive approach.

2   Backgrounds

Phonocardiogram is a rhythmic signal, characterized as having two basic sounds; the first heart sound (S1) and the second heart sound (S2). The rhythm frequency and the cycle period are termed as the "heart rate" and "cardiac cycle", respectively. S1 is a result of the closure of the mitral and tricuspid valves, where the tricuspid component follows the mitral ones. Closure of the aortic and pulmonary valves, creates the second heart sound. In contrary to the basic sounds, there may be extra sounds in each cycle, heard between the basic sounds. The temporal interval between S1 to S2 is called "systolic phase" while the one between S2 to S1 is termed by "diastolic phase". An extra sound can be considered as a sign of the cardiac abnormality; however, the presence of the extra sounds is not necessarily a sign of the disease. The extra sounds, caused by the heart defects, are called pathological sounds, in contrast with the physiological ones, which are initiated by a healthy heart. Prevalence of the physiological murmurs can be as high as 70 % [6, 7]. Heart murmur is a group of the extra sounds that can be heard either in systolic or in diastolic phase. Systolic murmur is by far the most important extra sounds as can be considered either as a physiological sound, called innocent murmur, or as a pathological sound in valvular or septal defects. Auscultating and interpreting heart sounds along with the discrimination between pathological and physiological murmurs, are complicated tasks.

3   Methods

The method is based on performing a first level of analysis, aimed to detect the presence of a pathological murmur. The phonocardiogram (PCG) with a detected pathological sign is sent to the server where an expert physician investigates the PCG using our complementary intelligent methods. Figure 1 illustrates functional block diagram of the tool. The PCG signal is automatically segmented, where the S1, S2 along with the systolic and diastolic phases are annotated on the recording. Details of our automatic algorithms for PCG segmentation can be found in [8, 9]. The segmented PCG is processed through our unique intelligent method based on the combination of the neural network and discriminant analyses. This method which has been internationally patented (patent publication number: US 2011/0021939 A1, PCT number: PCT/EP09/51410) performs a binary classification on the segmented PCG and sends the pathologically detected recording to the server for the further analysis. Details of the method are found in [1]. The transferred recording is investigated by the physicians who use our complementary intelligent analysis to explore the presence of the valvular diseases, by invoking temporal and spectral representation of the recording. This level of processing is preferred to be performed by a physician who is accustomated to the phonocardiogram, as the outcomes convey medical information regarding the pathology. Accurate interpretation of these signs, and sometimes proper employment of the proposed methods [10–13], needs some extent of the medical background.

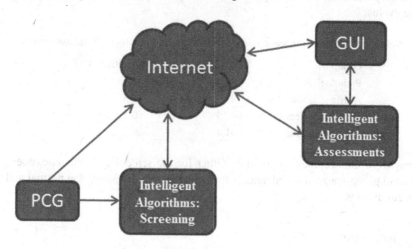

Fig. 1. Block diagram of the tool.

4   Data Preparation

PCG signals of 10 s duration were acquired from the referrals to the Children Medical Center of Tehran University. All the referrals or their legal guardians gave their informed consent for record and use of the data prior to undergoing echocardiography, according to the guidelines of the University which are in compliance with the Declaration of Helsinki. A WelchAllyn Meditron Analyzer electronic stethoscope together with a Dell laptop equipped with 16 bit soundcard was used for data acquisition. The characteristics of the patient population are listed in Table 1.

Table 1. The patient characteristics.

Condition	Number	Age (year)
Normal	30	3–15
Innocent murmur	25	2–14
Aortic stenosis	15	1–8
Pulmonary stenosis	15	1–10
Mitral regurgitation	15	4–18

5   Results

Performance of the intelligent methods was differently evaluated using the leave-one-out method where accuracy and sensitivity were considered as the performance measures. In the leave-one-out method, one patient is employed for testing and the rest for training the method. This procedure is repeated N times, with each single patient used only once for testing, where N is the total number of the patients. The accuracy and sensitivity were defined as the percentage of the total referrals and unhealthy patients which were correctly classified by the method, respectively. Table 2 demonstrates results of the evaluation.

Table 2.   Results of the leave-one-out validation for the screening and assessment.

Group	Accuracy (%)	Sensitivity (%)
Pathological murmurs	86.0	86.7
Aortic stenosis	95.7	93.3
Pulmonary stenosis	92.9	86.7
Mitral regurgitation	91.4	80.0

Remark.   In the accuracy calculation, either for the screening or the assessment, an abnormal group was compared against the healthy group including the normal and the innocent murmur.

6   Discussion

This study suggested the use of the modern artificial intelligence method for cardiac diagnosis in children, where an internet platform serves as the communication tool providing a connection among the patient, nurse and cardiologist. Results showed that the constituted tool, which we call intelligent phonocardiography, has the potential to be employed in the clinical settings as a decision support system for an enhanced diagnosis, as the accuracy of the intelligent algorithms show superior performance comparing to the physicians. However, unlike the screening task, the ultimate assessment for the management should be performed by the cardiologists who use echocardiography, due to complexities in the management and disease control. Nevertheless, the intelligent methods provide important clues even for the cardiologists.

References

1. Sepehri, A.A., Hancq, J., Dutoit, T., Gharehbaghi, A., Kocharian, A., Kiani, A.: Computerized screening of children congenital heart diseases. Comput. Methods Programs Biomed. **92**, 186–192 (2008)
2. Kocharian, A., Sepehri, A.A., Janani, A., Malakan-Rad, E.: Efficiency, sensitivity and specificity of automated auscultation diagnosis device for detection and discrimination of cardiac murmurs in children. Iran J. Pediatr. **23**, 445–450 (2013)

3. Gharehbaghi, A., Ask, P., Lindén, M., Babic, A.: A novel model for screening aortic stenosis using phonocardiogram. In: Mindedal, H., Persson, M. (eds.) 16th Nordic-Baltic Conference on Biomedical Engineering. IFMBE Proceedings, vol. 48, pp. 48–51. Springer, New York (2014)

4. Gharehbaghi, A., Ask, P., Babic, A.: A pattern recognition framework for detecting dynamic changes on cyclic time series. Pattern Recogn. **48**, 696–708 (2015)

5. Gharehbaghi, A., Borga, M., Janerot-Sjöberg, B., Ask, P.: A novel method for discrimination between innocent and pathological heart murmurs. Med. Eng. Phys. **37**, 674–682 (2015)

6. Watrous, R.L.: Computer-aided auscultation of the heart: from anatomy and physiology to diagnostic decision support. Conf. Proc. IEEE Eng. Med. Biol. Soc. **1**, 140–143 (2006)

7. Watrous, R.L., Thompson, W.R., Ackerman, S.J.: The impact of computer-assisted auscultation on physician referrals of asymptomatic patients with heart murmurs. Clin. Cardiol. **31**, 79–83 (2008)

8. Gharehbaghi, A., Dutoit, T., Sepehri, A., Hult, P., Ask, P.: An automatic tool for pediatric heart sounds segmentation. Comput. Cardiol. **38**, 37–40 (2011)

9. Sepehri, A.A., Gharehbaghi, A., Dutoit, T., Kocharian, A., Kiani, A.: A novel method for pediatric heart sound segmentation without using the ECG. Comput. Methods Programs Biomed. **99**, 43–48 (2010)

10. Gharehbaghi, A., Ekman, I., Ask, P., Nylander, E., Janerot-Sjöberg, B.: Assessment of aortic valve stenosis severity using intelligent phonocardiography. Int. J. Cardiol. **198**, 58–60 (2015)

11. Gharehbaghi, A., Dutoit, T., Ask, P., Sörnmo, L.: Detection of systolic ejection click using time growing neural network. Med. Eng. Phys. **36**, 477–483 (2014)

12. Gharehbaghi, A., Ask, P., Nylander, E., Janerot-Sjöberg, B., Ekman, I., Lindén, M., Babic, A.: A hybrid model for diagnosing sever aortic stenosis in asymptomatic patients using phonocardiogram. In: Jaffray, D.A. (ed.) World Congress on Medical Physics and Biomedical Engineering. IFMBE Proceedings, vol. 51, pp. 1006–1009. Springer, New York (2015)

13. Gharehbaghi, A., Sepehri, A.A., Kocharian, A., Lindén, M.: An intelligent method for discrimination between aortic and pulmonary stenosis using phonocardiogram. In: Jaffray, D.A. (ed.) World Congress on Medical Physics and Biomedical Engineering. IFMBE Proceedings, vol. 51, pp. 1010–1013. Springer, New York (2015) ·

Non-contact Physiological Parameters Extraction Using Camera

Hamidur Rahman(✉), Mobyen Uddin Ahmed, and Shahina Begum

School of Innovation, Design and Engineering, Mälardalens University, Västerås, Sweden
{rahman.hamidur,mobyen.ahmed,shahina.begum}@mdh.se

Abstract. Physiological parameters such as Heart Rate (HR), Beat-to-Beat Interval (IBI) and Respiration Rate (RR) are vital indicators of people's physiological state and important to monitor. However, most of the measurements methods are connection based, i.e. sensors are connected to the body which is often complicated and requires personal assistance. This paper proposed a simple, low-cost and non-contact approach for measuring multiple physiological parameters using a web camera in real time. Here, the heart rate and respiration rate are obtained through facial skin colour variation caused by body blood circulation. Three different signal processing methods such as Fast Fourier Transform (FFT), independent component analysis (ICA) and Principal component analysis (PCA) have been applied on the colour channels in video recordings and the blood volume pulse (BVP) is extracted from the facial regions. HR, IBI and RR are subsequently quantified and compared to corresponding reference measurements. High degrees of agreement are achieved between the measurements across all physiological parameters. This technology has significant potential for advancing personal health care and telemedicine.

Keywords: Heart rate · Respiration rate · Inter-Bit-Interval · Camera

1 Introduction

The ability to monitor physiological signals by a remote, non-contact methods include lasers Doppler [1], microwave Doppler radar [2], and thermal imaging [3, 4], but these systems are very expensive and require complex hardware. Using photoplethysmography (PPG) to measure BVP and then Heart-rate-variability (HRV) has been widely used in clinics and research labs, due to its simplicity, convenience and accuracy. The principle of PPG method is to illuminate the skin with a light-emitting diode (LED) and then measure the amount of light reflected or transmitted to a photodiode. In the past few years several papers proposed colour-based methods for remote heart rate measurement using ordinary commercial cameras [5, 6]. Poh et al. [7] explored the possibility to measure HR from 1-minute face videos recorded by a web-cam.

In this paper, a new framework for non-connected physiological parameters measurement is proposed which can work for any length of time. The information of the heart rate and respiration rate is obtained through facial skin colour variation caused by body blood circulation. Three different signal processing methods such as Fast Fourier

© ICST Institute for Computer Sciences, Social Informatics and Telecommunications Engineering 2016
B. Mandler et al. (Eds.) IoT 360° 2015, Part I, LNICST 169, pp. 448–453, 2016.
DOI: 10.1007/978-3-319-47063-4_47

Transform (FFT), Independent Component Analysis (ICA) and Principal Component Analysis (PCA) have been applied on the colour channels in video recordings and the Blood Volume Pulse (BVP) is extracted from the facial regions. The outcomes of the system using three methods are compared with existing ECG and respiration sensors system named cStress[1]. The paper is organized as: the measurement methods, its application and a real-time measurement system are described is chapter 2, Verification and validation of the designed real time measurement system is presented in chapter 3. Finally, the paper is summarized.

2   Materials and Methods

Data acquisition is conducted using 9 participants of different genders (3 females, 6 males), ages (25 to 40 years) and skin colours. The experiments are conducted indoors and with a varying amount of ambient sunlight entering through windows as the only source of illumination. Two out of nine experiments were conducted in artificial light environment and the result does not change so much. The test subjects were asked to sit without any movement. Participants are informed the aim of the study and they seated at a table in front of a laptop at a distance of approximately 0.5 m from the built-in webcam (HP HD webcam). During the experiment, participants are asked to keep still, breathe spontaneously, and face the webcam while their video was recorded for 10 min. All videos are recorded in colour (24-bit RGB) at 30 frames per second (fps) with pixel resolution of 640×480 and saved in AVI format in the laptop. Simultaneously HR, RR and IBI are also recorded using ECG sensors and cStress system.

All the videos and physiological recordings are analysed offline using custom software written in MATLAB 2013b. After extracting all the frames from the video automatic face detection is used using Viola and Jones methods [11] to identify the coordinates of the face location in the first frame and a boosted cascade classifier is used for the x and y-coordinates along with the height and width that define a box around the face. We select the centre 60 % width and full height of the box as the region of interest (ROI) for our subsequent calculations. The ROI is then separated into the three RGB channels and spatially averaged over all pixels in the ROI to yield a red, blue, and green measurement point for each frame and form the raw signals respectively. Each trace is 10 min long. The raw traces are detrended using a procedure based on a smoothness priors approach [12] and normalized. The normalized RGB traces are sent to three different algorithms ICA [8], PCA [9] and FFT [10] to quantify HR, RR and IBI.

For the ICA, the normalized raw traces are decomposed into three independent source signals using ICA based on the joint approximate diagonalization of Eigen matrices (JADE) algorithm [12]. ICA is able to perform motion-artifact removal by separating the fluctuations caused predominantly by the BVP from the observed raw signals. However, the order in which ICA returns the independent components is random. Thus, the component whose power spectrum contained the highest peak was then selected for further analysis. Similarly the normalized raw traces are also

---

[1] http://stressmedicin.se/neuro-psykofysilogiska-matsystem/cstress-matsystem/.

decomposed by PCA to find the principal components. This transformation is defined in such a way that the first principal component has the largest possible variance (that is, accounts for as much of the variability in the data as possible), and each succeeding component in turn has the highest variance possible under the constraint that it is orthogonal to the preceding components. The resulting vectors are an uncorrelated orthogonal basis set. The principal components are orthogonal because they are the eigenvectors of the covariance matrix, which is symmetric. PCA is sensitive to the relative scaling of the original variables. Finally, the Fast Fourier Transform (FFT) is applied on the selected source signal to obtain the power spectrum. The pulse frequency was designated as the frequency that corresponded to the higst power of the spectrum within an operational frequency band.

As the frame rate of the video is 30 fps so every 30 image frames are passed together through the algorithm to find the physiological parameters for one second. In this way all the image frames are passed as a bundle of 30 images to calculate physiological parameters for whole session and the extracted data are saved in an excel file which are used later for further analysis. Before applying PCA, ICA and FFT the RGB signal is filtered by Hamming window (128 point, 0.6-4 Hz, Heart rate 36–240) for heart rate extraction and Hamming window (64 points, 0.15–0.5 Hz, respiration rate 9–30) for the RR. Then the HR is calculated as HR = $60*f_h$ and RR = $60*f_r$ where f_h is the extracted frequency of the Heart rate and f_r is the extracted frequency of respiration rate. IBI is calculated from the number of peak points in which HR is calculated.

3 Experimental Works

The physiological parameters are extracted from 7 out of 10 min (first 2 and last 1 min are excluded) for all the 9 test persons using webcam and cStress system. For the first two minutes it is observed how the system works properly and the last minute is also deducted because of preparation of shutting down the system. For the statistical analysis minimum, maximum, average, median and standard deviations are calculated for both the web camera and cStress data. Finally, calculating Root Mean Square (RSQ) value and slope compares both the statistical values. The statistical analyses of HR, IBI, and RR for the 9 test subjects are presented in Table 1.

As can be seen from Table 1, both the RSQ and Slope values are close to 90 % or more than 90 %. Here, RSQ and Slope values represent the Goodness-of-fit or correlation co-efficient compare to the reference measurements, where 1 means 100 % accuracy. The average RSQ and Slope of 9 subjects are also calculated for HR, IBI and RR by applying three methods presented through bar charts as Figs. 1, 2 and 3. According to the Figures, PCA method shows its best performance compare to the other methods.

Table 1. Statistical analysis of HR, IBI and RR

Subject	Criteria	HR			IBI			RR		
		FFT	PCA	ICA	FFT	PCA	ICA	FFT	PCA	ICA
1	RSQ	0.98	0.99	0.98	0.96	0.98	0.95	0.89	0.91	0.86
	SLOPE	0.97	0.95	0.91	0.94	0.95	0.92	0.90	0.92	0.89
2	RSQ	0.99	0.99	0.95	0.93	0.97	0.90	0.91	0.95	0.90
	SLOPE	0.94	0.93	0.92	0.93	0.96	0.91	0.92	0.96	0.89
3	RSQ	0.95	0.99	0.96	0.90	0.91	0.88	0.89	0.95	0.88
	SLOPE	0.96	0.95	0.95	0.91	0.93	0.90	0.92	0.94	0.90
4	RSQ	0.99	0.99	0.98	0.93	0.98	0.89	0.93	0.95	0.91
	SLOPE	0.92	0.98	0.95	0.93	0.96	0.90	0.92	0.97	0.90
5	RSQ	0.99	0.99	0.98	0.91	0.94	0.88	0.91	0.95	0.88
	SLOPE	0.86	0.94	0.95	0.94	0.95	0.91	0.88	0.93	0.88
6	RSQ	0.99	0.99	0.97	0.90	0.96	0.86	0.89	0.93	0.90
	SLOPE	0.91	0.97	0.95	0.93	0.95	0.89	0.90	0.96	0.88
7	RSQ	0.99	0.99	0.98	0.92	0.93	0.89	0.91	0.95	0.90
	SLOPE	0.90	0.96	0.95	0.95	0.99	0.91	0.92	0.96	0.91
8	RSQ	0.99	0.99	0.99	0.90	0.95	0.88	0.91	0.95	0.90
	SLOPE	0.88	0.94	0.93	0.93	0.96	0.91	0.90	0.92	0.90
9	RSQ	0.99	0.99	0.99	0.93	0.99	0.91	0.89	0.91	0.88
	SLOPE	0.82	0.92	0.93	0.91	0.96	0.89	0.88	0.92	0.87

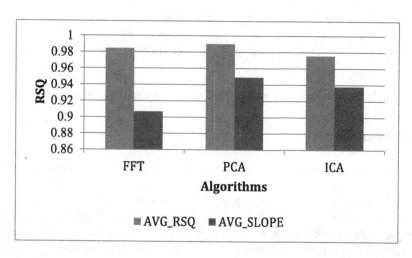

Fig. 1. Comparison between FFT, PCA and ICA methods considering HR

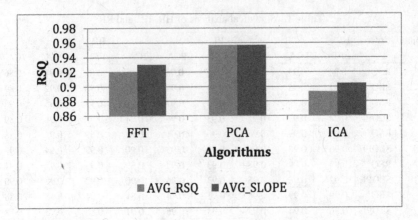

Fig. 2. Comparison between FFT, PCA and ICA methods considering IBI

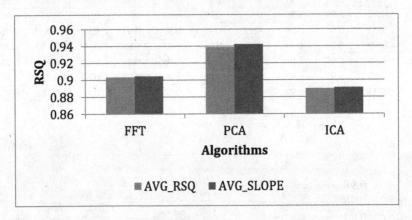

Fig. 3. Comparison between FFT, PCA and ICA methods considering RR

4   Conclusion

An easy to implement, low cost and non-contact physiological parameters detection method based on facial video image processing technology and blind source component technologies are described in this paper. Here, the methodology for recovering the cardiac pulse rate from video recordings of the human face and an implementation using a simple webcam with ambient daylight providing illumination are demonstrated. According to the experimental works, both the RSQ and slope values shows highest closeness (i.e. > 94 %) with the reference measurements while considering PCA methods for all the parameters. From the table and the figures presented in earlier chapter it is noted that RSQ gives better result than Slope and among the three methods PCA works the best and FFT works better. Given the low cost and widespread availability of webcams, this technology is promising for extending and improving access to medical care if the experiment is done by more test subjects and more verifying systems.

Although this paper only addressed the recovery of the cardiac HR, RR, IBI but many other important physiological parameters such as, heart rate variability and arterial blood oxygen saturation can potentially be estimated using the proposed technique. Creating a real-time, multi-parameter physiological measurement platform based on this technology will be the subject of future work.

Acknowledgement. The authors would like to acknowledge the Swedish Knowledge Foundation (KKS), Swedish Governmental agency for innovation Systems (VINNOVA), Volvo Car Corporation, The Swedish National Road and Transport Research Institute, Autoliv AB, Hök instrument AB, and Prevas AB Sweden for their support of the research projects in this area.

References

1. Ulyanov, S., Tuchin, V.: Pulse-wave monitoring by means of focused laser beams scattered by skin surface and membranes. In: Proceedings of the SPIE, Los Angeles, CA, pp. 160–167 (1884)
2. Greneker, E.: Radar sensing of heartbeat and respiration at a distance with applications of the technology. In: Proceedings of Conference on RADAR, Edinburgh, U.K., pp. 150–154 (1997)
3. Garbey, M., Sun, N., Merla, A., Pavlidis, I.: Contact-free measurement of cardiac pulse based on the analysis of thermal imagery. IEEE Trans. Biomed. Eng. **54**(8), 1418–1426 (2007)
4. Fei, J., Pavlidis, I.: Thermistor at a distance: Unobtrusive measurement of breathing. IEEE Trans. Biomed. Eng. **57**(4), 988–998 (2009)
5. Zhang, Q., Xu, G., Wang, M., Zhou, Y., Feng, W.: Webcam based non-contact real-time monitoring for physiological parameters of drivers. In: The 4th Annual IEEE International Conference on Cyber Technology in Automation Control and Intelligent Systems, Hong Kong, China, pp. 4–7 (2014)
6. Guo, Z., Jane, Z., Shen, Z.: Physiological Parameter monitoring of drivers based on video data and independent vector analysis. In: IEEE Int. Conf. on Acoustic, Speech and Signal Processing (ICASSP), pp. 4374–4378 (2014)
7. Poh, M.Z., McDuff, J.D., Picard, R.W.: Advancement in noncontact, multiparameter physiological measurement using a webcam. IEEE Trans. Biomed. Eng. **58**(1), 7–11 (2011)
8. Comon, P.: Independent component analysis, a new concept. J. Trans. Signal. Process. **36**, 287–314 (1994)
9. Krammer, M.A.: Nonlinear principal component analysis using autoassociative neural networks. AICHE **37**(2), 233–243 (1991)
10. Veenkant, R.L.: A serial-minded FFT. IEEE Trans. Audio Electroacoust. **20**, 180–185 (1972)
11. Viola, P., Jones, M.: Rapid object detection using a boosted cascade of simple features. In: Proceedings of the 2001 IEEE Computer Society Conference on Computer Vision and Pattern Recognition CVPR 2001, vol. 1, pp. I–511. IEEE (2011)
12. Tarvainen, M.P., Ranta-Aho, P.O., Karjalainen, P.A.: An advanced detrending method with application to HRV analysis. IEEE Trans. Biomed. Eng. **49**(2), 172–175 (2002)

Security Analysis of an IoT Architecture for Healthcare

M. Teresa Villalba, Manuel de Buenaga, Diego Gachet^(✉), and Fernando Aparicio

Universidad Europea de Madrid, 28670 Villaviciosa de Odón, Spain
{maite.villalba,buenaga,diego.gachet,fernando.aparicio}@uem.es

Abstract. Security issues of IoT devices are increasing with their massive use in healthcare. Recollection of data from devices is not clear to the users so far, and different problems arise including confidentiality, integrity and availability of the information. We analyze security issues mainly related to IoT data storage and transmission in our proposal of healthcare system architecture including cloud services and big data processing of information. We identify protocols needed and security problems including authentication, transmission of data to the cloud, as well as their insufficient anonymization process and the opaque procedure for users in order to control the storage of their data.

Keywords: Internet of Things · Security · Privacy · Wearable · Healthcare

1 Introduction

Nowadays society is demanding new services and technology allowing citizens to better manage their own health and disease, resulting in more cost effective healthcare systems and alleviating the issues of an increasing aging population. New emerging technologies can be combined with other widely deployed ones to develop such next-generation healthcare systems.

According to World Health Organization, chronic diseases are the leading cause of death worldwide, as they cause more deaths than all other causes together. While these diseases have reached epidemic proportions, they could be reduced significantly by combating the risk factors and applying early detection, the indoor and outdoor monitoring joined with prevention measures and a healthier life style. For both chronic and pre-chronic people several dangerous clinical situations could be avoided or better monitored and managed with the participation of the patient, their caregivers and medical personnel [1].

In this paper we present main issues in the security analysis of an IoT architecture for healthcare in the framework of the project IPHealth [2], including key aspects of security in the Internet of Things in healthcare, the description of our system architecture proposal with a significant focus on IoT elements, and the analysis of security key aspects of main IoT components.

© ICST Institute for Computer Sciences, Social Informatics and Telecommunications Engineering 2016
B. Mandler et al. (Eds.) IoT 360° 2015, Part I, LNICST 169, pp. 454–460, 2016.
DOI: 10.1007/978-3-319-47063-4_48

2   Security in the Internet of Things in Healthcare

According to Gartner, wearable fitness and personal health devices will be $5 billion market by 2016 [3]. In spite of this expected growth, just as "Fifth Annual Benchmark Study on Privacy & Security of Healthcare Data" [4] reveals, the majority of healthcare organizations do not spend enough resources to protect patient data. Moreover, the last "Internet Security report of Symantec" estimates a 125 % growth in healthcare cyber-attacks over the past five years, and reported that a 37 % of security incidents affected to healthcare organizations [5], with the largest number of data breaches for the fourth year in a row. The huge amount of personal information coupled with this lack of resources to protect them, turn health data into an attractive and lucrative objective.

Currently the devices being used in healthcare to collect biometric data are usually smartphones with sensors or specific wearable devices. Both of them are commonly combined with apps to process data, interpret the signals, and show statistics to users. These apps carry out simple processing, so the functionality is sometimes extended by transferring the data to the cloud to be processed with complex algorithms. Security issues in this scenario can be categorized into three major areas: security, or as is widely accepted confidentiality, integrity, and availability; privacy or the appropriate use of the information; and legal issues, i.e. security concerns related to laws. Regarding security, three points of risks can be identified in the general architectures previously shown: device, data transmission (sensor to smartphone and smartphone to cloud) and cloud storage.

– Devices are individual and personal, so the motivation for data theft is smaller. Still malware can be used to automate the task of enabling a massive theft of data. Moreover the physical device can be stolen or lost. Wearable sensors do not include protection, and mobiles need to be configured by users (phone locking, tracking …). Mobile devices use apps to extend functionality to users. Symantec reviewed 100 health apps finding that 20 % transmit user credentials without encryption, 52 % not use any privacy policies and each one connects with an average of 5 websites while using usually with advertisement and analytics services [5].
– During transmission, data can be captured by using different attacks in the same way than in other architectures. The solution is to use strong encryption to avoid reading the data if they are capture, and authentication to confirm that data are sent to the true receptor. But there are some issues related to encryption and strong authentication to be solved, such as they slow down data transfer, are difficult to use, and are heavy energy-consumers.
– Finally, cloud computing architectures store data on database. Cloud services are provided by third party vendors who are exposed to attacks from insiders. But in addition, these databases are exposed to the Internet network in order to receive data from users. So the risks are similar to other similar databases, and depend on the configuration. Solutions involve multi-factor authentication, access control methods, strong passwords, etc. Again these methods make the systems more difficult to use and slower.

3   IoT Architecture Proposal for Healthcare

Our proposal of architecture for collecting data in order to promote wellbeing and physical activity is based on the need for a scalable data storage and high-performance computing infrastructure for efficiently storing, processing and sharing of health and activity sensor data. With this situation in mind we propose a simple and coherent activity monitoring solution. That solution takes into account several factors like using noninvasive sensors, allowing the processing of high volumes of data coming from them (including information from other sources as for example clinical texts); searching and retrieval of medical related information from forums, and designing appropriate visualization interfaces for each user type (patients, healthcare professionals, caregivers, relatives, etc.)

According to the above features, our general architecture for activity monitoring as well as its associated services are presented in Fig. 1: the components shown are being developed under the project ipHealth [2]. The architecture allows monitoring of both chronic and non-chronic patients, as well as healthy people that need to be monitored by different circumstances in both, home and external environment. Moreover it allows interaction with their family, the emergency systems and the hospitals through the application of Cloud computing, Big Data and Internet of Things approaches. IoT plays a key role in our architecture allowing users benefit from the utilization of different wearables and sensors devices.

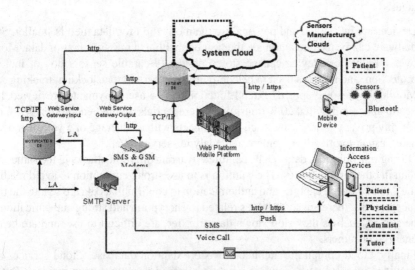

Fig. 1. Proposed architecture for patients monitoring

The architecture includes as main elements the following: smart mobile phones which in turn accepts data from wearable vital signs or activity sensors, a cloud based (public as Amazon Web Service or private) infrastructure for data store and an analytic module for activation of alarms to be sent to the patient and/or patient's caregivers, access to the different sensors of cloud manufacturers, an interoperability and messaging platform for delivery of information to all involved actors in the system, and a website platform that allows to consult the associated patient information from desktop computer as well as from mobile devices.

4   Security Analysis of the Architecture

For our system, health and activity data are mainly taken from the clouds of sensor's manufacturers using different APIs that allow developers to establish a connection between applications and health data generated by users with their products. At present time we are conducting tests for monitoring physical activity and cardio-vascular status using iHealth BP7 bluetooth enabled blood pressure sensors, iHealth PO3 pulse oximeters, and Fitbit flex wristbands. Since the other components of the architecture here presented are common to other Internet connected architectures and, due to space limitations, in this paper we will focus on the wearables segment of the architecture. Specifically we will take FitBit as a representative element of wearable.

FitBix Flex [6] is a wrist monitor with a MEMS 3-axis smart accelerometer that collects data about user's movement such as steps taken, distance walked, and calories buried. Collected data are sent to a cloud to provide more detailed information to users through an online website. A free app, FitBit, extend the functionality syncing the sensor statistics with the mobile through BLE (Bluetooth Low Energy) 4.0 among others. An API to integrate third-party applications getting and modifying user's data from Fitbit.com is provided. Moreover, the user can create an account to keep in touch with other users.

Figure 2 shows the specific architecture of Fitbit. We separate the different components according to the division mentioned in Sect. 2: (1) and (3) devices, (2) and (4) data transmission, and (5) cloud storage.

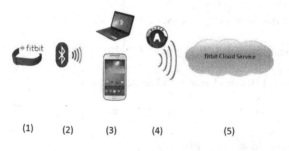

(1)	(2)	(3)	(4)	(5)

Fig. 2. Fitbit architecture

Regarding the device, logs stored in the mobile phone with more data than shown to users were found in [7], in contrast to what they declare in their privacy policy [6]. Moreover, more data than needed are requested to users, for example date of birth instead to only the year. On the other hand, the provided API uses OAuth 1.0 (version 2.0 is in beta state) which has several discovered vulnerabilities [8].

Otherwise, synchronization between Fitbit and mobile devices or personal computers is done over BLE 4.0. BLE supports encryption and authentication.

In addition, it provides a mechanism which allows a device to use and change private addresses as frequently as needed to avoid tracking [9]. However, Fitbit does not take advantage of this feature, and consequently it is possible to track activities of specific users, even when the user has the location functions inactivated. Additionally, BLE credentials are sent to the mobile device in plaintext over TLS [7]. Finally, in [9] it has been reported that none of the pairing methods used by BLE protects against passive eavesdropping, although in the BLE specification claims its future versions will resolve this issue [12].

Regarding the data transmission between the mobile device and the cloud, during the connection the mobile device notifies to the server all the Fitbit devices within the range [7]. This can lead to privacy issues by providing more information than necessary.

Fitbit provides access to its social network to share results with friends. As the same of other social networks, privacy preferences should be well configured in order to preserve data privacy. Although the privacy preferences are right configured, a social engineering attack is possible too. Education and awareness of users are the only way here to avoid these kinds of attacks.

On the other hand, the Fitbit privacy policy just claims to use a combination of security technical controls, so users cannot know the level of protection of their data neither of the stored data in the device nor the cloud [6]. They declare that the users will be notified if their data would be made publish, but they do not let users the option of

Table 1. Summary of compliance for privacy and security properties

Security and privacy properties [13]	Fitbit compliance (yes/no/ partially/not informed)	References
P1. Inform Patients about collected and stored data (what, why, where, who can access, …)	Partially	[6, 7]
P2. Enable Patients to review storage and use of their PHI	Yes	
P3. Enable Patients to control, through informed consent	No	[6]
P4. Provide access to PHI to read, modify and delete their registers	Partially	
P5. Provide easy-to-use interfaces to review and control all their data	Partially	
P6. Limit collection and storage of PHI	No	[7, 9]
P7. Limit use and disclosure of PHI to those purposes previously specified	No	[6]
P8. Ensure quality of PHI (freshness, integrity, completeness and authenticity)	Partially	[9, 10]
P9. Hide Patient identity	Partially	[10]
P10. Support accountability through robust mechanisms	Not informed	
P11. Support mechanisms to remedy effects of security breaches or privacy violations	Not informed	

objecting. Moreover, they claim to use anonymization techniques for some data (do not specify which ones), and that they can share or sell those anonymized data without option for user to participate in the decision. However, anonymization techniques have proved to be insecure [11, 12]. In addition, Fitbit does not provide users any control of their data stored in the cloud [6]. Table 1 shows a summary of the privacy and security according to the properties following the model defined in [13].

5 Conclusions and Future Work

We have studied main issues in the security analysis of an IoT architecture for healthcare in the framework of the project IPHealth. Common IoT architectures involve as main security vulnerability issues the storage in device (sensor and/or smartphone), data transmission (sensor to smartphone and smartphone to cloud) and cloud storage. As wearables are being connected to social networks, the risks to reveal private and sensitive information are higher. It is important to identify vulnerabilities of these devices in order to avoid attacks.

As a reference to carry out the security analysis, we have presented our architecture involving IoT devices, cloud architectures and big data components. Using FitBix Flex as representative of the sensors manufacturers we integrate, we have eventually found several important security risks and vulnerabilities impacting to nowadays users. After the analysis and following a common model of privacy and security properties, a table with the compliance of Fitbit to these properties is provided. The results show that the privacy provided by Fitbit is clearly insufficient.

Although more devices need to be analyzed, this results make us suspect that there is a long way to go in regards to security of the devices used in healthcare, here analyzed.

References

1. Gachet, D., Aparicio, F., de Buenaga, M., Padrón, V.: Personalized health care system with virtual reality rehabilitation and appropriate information for seniors. Sensors **12**(5), 5502–5516 (2012)
2. Gachet, D., Aparicio, F., de Buenaga, M., Ascanio, J.R.: Big data and IoT for chronic patients monitoring. In: Hervás, R., Lee, S., Nugent, C., Bravo, J. (eds.) Ubiquitous Computing and Ambient Intelligence. Personalization and User Adapted Services. LNCS, vol. 8867, pp. 416–423. Springer, Heidelberg (2014)
3. Angela McIntyre, J.E.: Gartner, Market Trends: Enter the Wearable Electronics Market with Products for the Quantified Self, July 2013
4. Ponemon Institute LLC: Fifth Annual Benchmark Study on Privacy & Security of Healthcare Data (2015)
5. Symantec: Internet Security Threat Report (2015). http://www.symantec.com/security_response/publications/threatreport.jsp
6. FitBit: FitBit Flex (2015). http://www.fitbit.com/es/flex. Accessed June 2015
7. Cyr, B., Horn, W., Miao, D., Specter, M.: Security Analysis of Wearable Fitness Devices (Fitbit). Massachusetts Institute of Technology (MIT), December 2014

8. Hsu, Y., Lee, D.: Authentication and authorization protocol security property analysis with trace inclusion transformation and online minimization, pp. 164–173 (2010)
9. Gomez, C., Oller, J., Paradells, J.: Overview and evaluation of bluetooth low energy: an emerging low-power wireless technology. Sensors **12**, 11734 (2012)
10. The Bluetooth Special Interest Group: Specification of the Bluetooth System, Covered Core Package, Version: 4.0. Kirkland, WA, USA (2010)
11. Backstrom, L., Huttenlocher, D., Kleinberg, J., et al.: Group formation in large social networks: membership, growth, and evolution, pp. 44–54 (2006)
12. Sweeney, L.: K-anonymity: a model for protecting privacy. Int. J. Uncertainty Fuzziness Knowl.-Based Syst. **10**, 557–570 (2002)
13. Avancha, S., Baxi, A., Kotz, D.: Privacy in mobile technology for personal healthcare. ACM Comput. Surv. **45**, 31–354 (2012)

A Cooperative Decision Support System for Children's Neurodevelopment Monitoring

María-Luisa Martin-Ruiz[1(✉)], Miguel-Angel Valero[1,2],
Ana Gómez[1], and Carmen Torcal[3]

[1] Department of Telematic and Electronic Engineering, Technical University of Madrid,
Carretera de Valencia KM7, Madrid, Spain
{marisam,mavalero,agomez}@diatel.upm.es
[2] Visiting Professor at Mälardalen University, Högskoleplan 1,
Västerås, Sweden
[3] Legamar School, Madrid, Spain
infantiluno@colegiolegamar.es

Abstract. Decision Support Systems can enhance e-Health monitoring and IoT scenarios on the early detection of neurodevelopmental disorders in children. Thus, Ambient Intelligence could support innovative application domains like motor or cognitive impairments' detection at the home environment. The paper describes the design of an innovative cooperative system (Galatea) that supports the refinement process of a Knowledge Base expressed as an OWL ontology. The ontology supports decision-making process and is the core of: (1) a Web-Based Smart System aimed to enhance the screening of language disorders at medical centers and schools by fostering the identification of a developmental disorders before 4 years old of age; (2) a set of child smart care services that use Ambient Intelligent paradigm for early attention of motor impairments in children who are often not diagnosed or treated by health care entities.

Keywords: E-health · Smart systems · Disabilities · Healthcare services

1 Introduction

Detection of neurodevelopmental disorders in early childhood remains an outstanding task. In fact, current rates of detection of development disorders are lower than their real incidence [1]. Pediatricians and education professionals can play a valuable role in early detection during their routine interactions with a child. However, the lack of resources to perform individualized exhaustive evaluations of all children makes the use of efficient and reliable methods of detection necessary [2]. On the one hand, the availability of smart monitoring solutions at home can provide medical doctors, physiotherapists and health professionals with reliable data about people's health status [3]. On the other, since early childhood educators are considered, along with parents, leading observers in child development, the availability of this system in the nursery will facilitate early detection of possible pathologies in the development of children in the 0-3 year stage [4].

© ICST Institute for Computer Sciences, Social Informatics and Telecommunications Engineering 2016
B. Mandler et al. (Eds.) IoT 360° 2015, Part I, LNICST 169, pp. 461–466, 2016.
DOI: 10.1007/978-3-319-47063-4_49

Gades [5] is a Web Based Support System (WBSS) developed with the primary purpose of serving as an automatic tool to improve the efficient screening of language disorders at the early stages of a child's development. This decision support system, developed with the collaboration of a multidisciplinary team of professionals, defined a few questions to evaluate the degree of language acquisition in children. To achieve a consistent system operation was necessary to provide Gades with a questions refining process to make it more reliable according to the criteria of the team professionals. Hence, Galatea is an innovative Cooperative Decision Making (CDM) system that supports the refinement process of the knowledge base (expressed as an ontology) of Gades WBSS. This solution paves the way for EDUCERE project to support adaptable home healthcare services by embedding sensors on toys and pieces of furniture according to the Internet of Things (IoT) paradigm. In this way, it aims to smart cooperative prevention and early attention of motor and language impairments by monitoring and stimulating children's activities.

The core of this Healthcare Cooperative System that incorporates previous Galatea work and EDUCERE project is a rules-based ontology that integrates children's developmental items according to the age. The ontologies also support the communication between all professionals involved in the system construction, allow reuse domain knowledge and facilitate recovery, integration and interoperability between heterogeneous sources of knowledge. Furthermore, the ontology was created using as a representation language OWL-DL.

This paper describes the design and deployment of a tool for refinement process of the ontology in a collaborative way in order to fasten the correct evolution of the Decision Support System (DSS) [6] developed under an IoT based children's development model.

2 Methods

A multidisciplinary team of 10 people (2 neonatologists, 3 psychologists, 2 educators and 3 engineers) developed Gades. This WBSS was validated starting from an analysis of 237 children enrolled along two years in a nursery school.

The improvement of the decisions gathered from the sensors embedded Smart Toys (developed by EDUCERE project) and Gades WBSS require an ontology refinement process to improve language evaluations at daily routine with the therapist and educators, both at the nursery school and the health care unit. It could be performed through a manual process or by using the Galatea System. Ontology evolution process does not require generating new knowledge as experts have this knowledge.

The new system must focus on knowledge agreements coming from the experts' experience. Hence, the ontology should dynamically evolve to achieve efficient and effective Decision Systems and Smart Toys performance.

Figure 1 shows the interaction process between the children, the IoT based in smart toys, Gades Web Based Decision Support System, the Galatea Web platform and the health professionals, aimed to achieve the better health prescription as possible.

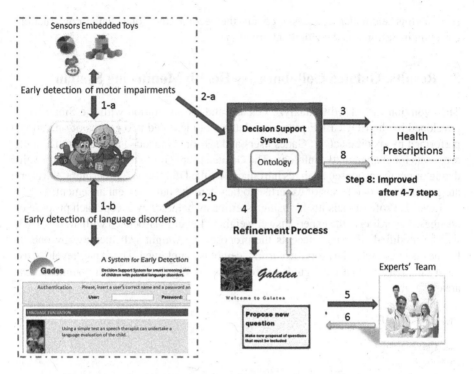

Fig. 1. Functional architecture of the smart children's monitoring system

As Fig. 1 shows, it is possible to improve the results provided by the developed early detection systems in order to detect both motoric disorders (steps 1-a, 2-a) and language disorders (steps 1-b, 2-b). By steps 4–7 the team of experts will be able to facilitate a refinement process in the ontology core of the Decision Support Systems developed. In fact, health recommendations provided by the Smart Toys will be more accurate after the execution of existing steps between step 3 and step 8.

Furthermore, the CDM process carried out by Galatea involves the cooperation of a group of people through technological tools that support joint decisions [7].

In collaborative decision, several individuals make a decision among a number of valid alternatives. Galatea system supports to the WBSS and the sensors embedded toys developed with two main tasks: Task 1. Generate suggestions for improvement of professionals who work with the WBSS and the smart toys through the introduction, modification or elimination of questions or items in the ontology (developed in the first stage of Galatea System construction). Task 2. Acceptance or rejection of proposed improvements introduced in previous step to be performed by a group of experts in neurodevelopmental disorders who are grouped according to their experience levels. After a telematics consensus mechanism experts grouped at least in two level of experience provide clear and well-structured information changes proposed on the ontology for the IoT/items model. This telematics consensus process was accepted by the professional team who participated in the validation process outlined at the beginning of this section (this telematics consensus covers the second stage of Galatea construction, currently in design and development process).

3   Results: Galatea Collaborative Health Monitoring System

The evolution model led to analyze Galatea and its integration with the Smart Toys developed by the EDUCERE project. Galatea tool identified two groups of operations performed by specific actors: Gades users and sensors embedded toys users that make proposals for change in the ontology. The Galatea users groups are responsible for validating or not the proposed changes introduced by the DSS users. Furthermore, the users are grouped into two levels of expertise to facilitate the ontology enhancement:

Level 1: Professionals justify using assertions whether they accept each propose of changes. According to the expert answer weighing Level 1, associated with the proposal, will be modified. If expert accepts the proposal the weight will increase by one. If he/she disagrees with the proposal current weight is maintained. The expert level 1 must justify the reasons that have guided its decision, as Fig. 2 shows with comments text area.

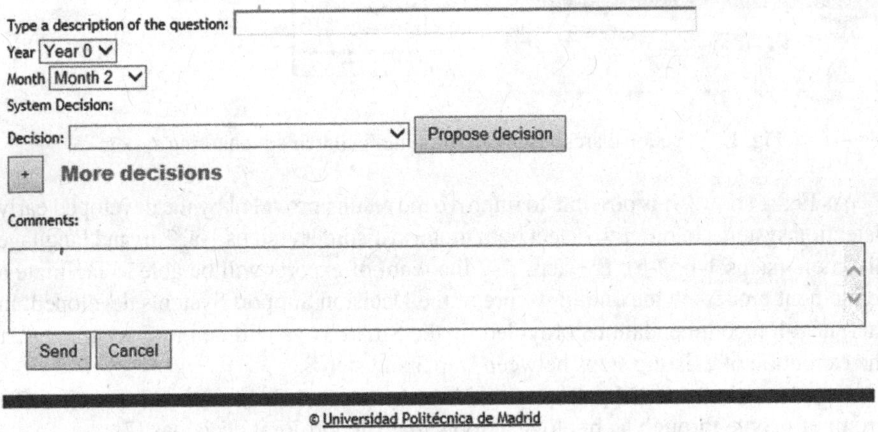

© Universidad Politécnica de Madrid

Fig. 2. Galatea-propose of new question/developmental item

Level 2: Experts are responsible for making the final decision for each of the proposals. Therefore, they are based on their expertise and the information provided by level 1 experts. They use weights and level 1 expert's assertions. Besides, the proposal has an associated weight related to these level experts' decisions: the weight of level 2 experts. The way to manage it is similar to level 1 experts. When a level 2 expert accepts the proposal then he/she increases the level 2 weights by one. If he/she disagrees with the proposal current weight is maintained. Then, the level 2 expert must justify the decision to accept or reject the change.

Galatea allows the evolution through the consensus techniques implemented inside. Furthermore, these techniques provide information to users as a flowchart graphic.

This method eases the understanding of a discussion about specific topics. The flowchart and consensus techniques have been developed taking into account the behavior, needs and activity of experts during the manual refinement process. Finally, the consensus technique will be developed in a completely usable way. This method will allow a process of debate necessary to achieve the refinement of the ontology core in the DSS.

4 Conclusions

Gades validation stage showed that open web applications allowed the easy utilization and refinement of ontologies by different kinds of professionals (educators, psychologists, therapists, etc.). EDUCERE smart toys such us the stackable cubes help to register, obtain and provide dynamic information about children's development. Galatea system facilitates the automation process of refining the DSS ontology for an IoT cooperative system.

The design task of the Galatea system has involved a multidisciplinary team of 10 experts. They have positively validated the decisions taken and the design of the user interface and most important they proposed ideas that will achieve a faster consensus in decision-making process to improve both Gades ontology and the integration of the IoT smart toys monitoring service.

Acknowledgments. This article is part of research conducted under EDUCERE project (Ubiquitous Detection Ecosystem to Care and Early Stimulation for Children with Developmental Disorders; TIN2013-47803-C2-1-R), supported by the Ministry of Education and Science of Spain through the National Plan for R + D + I (research, development, and innovation). Thanks to the Swedish Knowledge Foundation for supporting the research profile ESS-H and R&D work as MDH Visiting Professor.

References

1. Council on Children with Disabilities, Section on Developmental Behavioral Pediatrics, Bright Futures Steering Committee, and Medical Home Initiatives for Children with Special Needs Project Advisory Committee: Identifying infants and young children with developmental disorders in the medical home. Pediatrics **118**, 405–415 (2006)
2. Prior, M., Bavin, E., Ong, B.: Predictors of school readiness in five-to six-year-old children from an Australian longitudinal community sample. Educ. Psychol. **31**, 3–14 (2011)
3. Valero, M.A., Linden, M., Velasco, J.R., Björkman, M.: Big data and IoT for chronic patients monitoring. In: Hervás, R., Lee, S., Nugent, C., Bravo, J. (eds.) Ubiquitous Computing and Ambient Intelligence. Personalization and User Adapted Services. LNCS, vol. 8867, pp. 476–479. Springer, Heidelberg (2014)
4. Ygual-Fernández, A., Cervera-Mérida, J.F., Baixauli-Fortea, I., et al.: Protocolo de observación del lenguaje para maestros de educación infantil. Eficacia en la detección de dificultades semánticas y morfosintácticas. Rev. Neurol. **52**, 127–128 (2011)
5. Martín Ruiz, M.L., Valero Duboy, M.A., Torcal Loriente, C., Pau de la Cruz, I.: Evaluating a web-based clinical decision support system for language disorders screening in a nursery school. J. Med. Internet Res. **16**, 1–13 (2014)

6. Burstein, F., Holsapple, C. (eds.): Handbook on Decision Support Systems. Springer, Berlin (2008)
7. Martín Ruiz, M.L, Valero Duboy, M.A., Pau de La Cruz, I., Peñafiel Puerto, M., Torcal Loriente, C. A supervised cooperative learning system for early detection of language disorders. In: Proceedings of International Work-Conference on Bioinformatics and Biomedical Engineering, pp. 766–777 (2014)

Can the Regression Trees Be Used to Model Relation Between ECG Leads?

Ivan Tomasic[1(✉)], Roman Trobec[2], and Maria Lindén[1]

[1] Biomedical Engineering Research Group, Mälardalen University,
Box 883 721 23 Västerås, Sweden
{ivan.tomasic,maria.linden}@mdh.se
[2] Department of Communication Systems, Jožef Stefan Institute,
Jamova Cesta 39, 1000 Ljubljana, Slovenia
roman.trobec@ijs.si

Abstract. Presented is a preliminary study that investigates regression trees application for the purpose of mapping relationship between three differential ECG leads and leads of the 12-lead ECG. The approach was evaluated on a single ECG measurement on which it was superior to two syntheses performed by universal and personalized linear transformations, in terms of correlation coefficients between the synthesized and measured leads. A prominent imperfection however is that the regression trees can output only a limited number of values equal to the number of leaf nodes. The paper indicates some ideas on how to overcome this deficiency.

Keywords: ECG · Leads synthesis · Derived electrocardiograms · Regression trees · Differential leads · Electrocardiography · Wireless electrodes

1 Introduction

Both linear and nonlinear methods have been used before to model relation between electrocardiographic (ECG) leads for the purpose of leads' syntheses [1, 2]. Among the nonlinear methods mostly neural networks were used [3], whereas for the linear mapping, linear regression is the most often used method. Recent publications in addition to multiple linear regression [4], report using state-space model [5], support vector regression [6], multi-scale linear regression [7], and combination of methods [8, 9] for the ECG leads synthesis. In this work we will investigate the usage of regression trees for the same purpose.

In our previous studies, we have shown that it is possible to synthesize high quality 12-lead ECGs from three differential leads (DLs) [10]. Differential leads are bipolar leads that measure the potential between two closely placed body-surface electrodes. DL measurements can be obtained by so called wireless body electrodes (WBEs) – novel devices that enable minimal obtrusion and wireless transmission of recorded signals [11].

By using the algorithm for selection of optimal DLs [10], we have identified optimal universal positions of three DLs (see Fig. 1) from which 12-lead ECG can be synthesized

© ICST Institute for Computer Sciences, Social Informatics and Telecommunications Engineering 2016
B. Mandler et al. (Eds.) IoT 360° 2015, Part I, LNICST 169, pp. 467–472, 2016.
DOI: 10.1007/978-3-319-47063-4_50

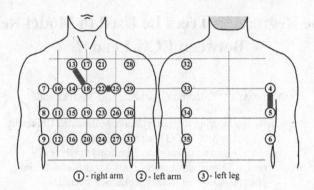

Fig. 1. Schematic locations of multichannel ECG (MECG) electrodes on the chest (left) and the back (right). The *gray lines* represent the calculated optimal universal leads for the 12-lead ECG synthesis: $\{(13, 18), (22, 25), (4, 5)\}$.

by employing universal or personalized linear transformations [12] that map the three DLs to the leads of the 12-lead ECG. In this study we investigate how regression trees can be used to map the same relation.

2   Methods

2.1   Studied Data

A single MECG measurement was obtained from a patient scheduled for a coronary artery bypass surgery. The data recording device and data acquisition procedure is described in [13]. The measurement was obtained during our previous study [14]. The positions of MECG electrodes are specified in Fig. 1.

The length of the measurement was 360 s. The measurement was processed using MATLAB (MathWorks, Inc.) where first the baseline wander was removed by interpolating a cubic spline through the isoelectric points of each MECG lead and subtracting it from the corresponding lead.

Subsequently, 10-second interval was randomly extracted from the MECG measurement and associated target 12-lead ECG obtained simultaneously. The extracted interval was filtered by a low-pass filter with a cutoff frequency of 40 Hz, an attenuation of 60 dB, and a stop frequency of 100 Hz. First seven seconds subinterval of the extracted interval was used for building the regression trees, whereas the remaining three seconds were used for the evaluation.

2.2   Regression Trees

Regression trees are simple but effective method of fitting a set of numeric input variables to a single numeric output variable. The general concept of regression trees is to partition the space defined by input variables and fit a simple model (usually a constant) in each one of the partitions [15]. In addition to regression trees, which give numeric responses, there are also classification trees, which give responses that are nominal, such as *true* or *false*.

To create regression trees between the three optimal DLs and the 12-lead ECG we have used MATLAB's Statistics and Machine Learning Toolbox™ trees which are binary. The details of how MATLAB creates trees can be found in the MATLAB's documentation [16]. All the parameter of function that creates trees were left on default values.

2.3 Experimental Procedure

The three optimal differential leads were calculated from the input MECG data (10 s intervals) by taking differences between appropriate MECG unipolar leads, e.g. DL (13, 18) is obtained as a difference between MECG leads 13 and 18. A regression tree was then built between the three DLs and each of the leads of the 12-lead ECG which makes 12 trees all together. The trees were examined for the number of nodes created.

To evaluate the performance of the created trees they were used to synthesize the 12-lead ECG (in regression trees terminology: "predict the response") on the evaluation three second subintervals. The linear correlation coefficients (CCs) between the 12-lead ECG synthesized by using trees, and the measured target 12-lead ECG, were compared to the CCs obtained by the universal and personalized transformation matrix. The synthesized 12-lead ECG was also compared to the target measured 12-lead ECG visually.

3   Results

Table 1. shows the CCs between the synthesized and measured (target) leads for the tree synthesis methods on the evaluation interval. Additionally, the synthesized 12-lead ECG obtained from the regression trees, are compared with the measured 12-lead ECG, graphically in Fig. 2. whereas a closer look on a segment from lead I is presented in Fig. 3.

Table 1. Correlation between the synthesized leads and the measured leads for universal linear transformation, for personalized linear transformation, and for regression trees.

Lead	Universal transformation	Personalized transformation	Regression trees
I	0.9543	0.9940	0.9920
II	0.9446	0.9485	0.9610
III	0.8716	0.9885	0.9889
aVR	0.9644	0.9918	0.9903
aVL	0.9332	0.9933	0.9919
aVF	0.6133	0.9473	0.9686
V1	0.9668	0.9796	0.9918
V2	0.9604	0.9943	0.9946
V3	0.9087	0.9876	0.9968
V4	0.8447	0.9718	0.9939
V5	0.8967	0.9681	0.9912
V6	0.9752	0.9823	0.9894

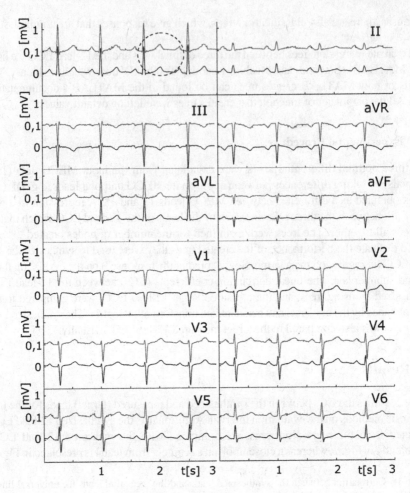

Fig. 2. Target (below) and synthesized (above) 12-lead ECG. On lead I, a T-wave that is zoomed in on Fig. 3., is approximately marked with a dashed ellipse.

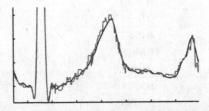

Fig. 3. Target (smooth) and synthesized (coarse) signals on a segment form lead I approximately marked in Fig. 2. (The two signals were moved one on top the other for easier comparison.).

4   Discussion

Table 1. reveals that even though the CCs between the synthesized and the measured leads are high for all the leads and all three synthesis methods, the synthesis with the regression trees is still superior to the other two methods. In only three leads has personalized transformation outperformed the regression trees (leads I, aVR, aVL) but in those situations the CCs for both methods are larger than 0.99.

In Fig. 2 the leads synthesized by regression trees seem almost identical to the measured leads of the 12-lead ECG, but a closer inspection (Fig. 3) reveals that the synthesized leads are coarser that the measured leads. This is because the output from regression trees can take only limited number of values, i.e. the number of output values is equal to the number of leafs a tree has. In our experiment the trees had number of leafs in a range from 1302 to 1374.

The possibilities for improving the synthesis output form the regression trees would be to increase the number of output leafs which will in turn increase the number of levels the predicted value can obtain, and/or to use a filter to smooth the output of the synthesis.

5   Conclusion

We have used regression trees to map relations between three DLs and the leads of the 12-lead ECG, for the purpose to synthesize the 12-lead ECG. The approach was evaluated by using one MECG measurement and has shown to be superior to the universal and personalized linear transformations used in previous investigations.

This is a preliminary research which shows that the regression trees have a potential in modeling relations between ECG leads. Further work is needed to investigate their performance on more measurements from different subjects, and to find satisfying solution for smoothing the output of regression trees.

The proposed synthesis of the 12-lead ECG from the 3 DLs enables new applications of the WBEs in Internet of Things (IoT) supported long-term remote health monitoring, because it enables a significant data reduction since only three leads have to be communicated, instead of eight independent leads in the standard 12-lead ECG.

Acknowledgments.   This work was supported by the Swedish Knowledge Foundation (KKS) financed research profile Embedded sensor systems for health (ESS-H), and by the distributed environment Ecare@Home (2015-2019) funded also by KKS.

References

1. Tomasic, I., Trobec, R.: Electrocardiographic systems with reduced numbers of leads-synthesis of the 12-Lead ECG. IEEE Rev. Biomed. Eng. **7**, 126–142 (2014)
2. Vozda, M., Cerny, M.: Methods for derivation of orthogonal leads from 12-lead electrocardiogram: a review. Biomed. Sig. Process. Control **19**, 23–34 (2015)

3. Atoui, H., Fayn, J., Rubel, P.: A novel neural-network model for deriving standard 12-lead ECGs from serial three-lead ECGs: application to self-care. IEEE Trans. Inf. Technol. Biomed. **14**, 883–890 (2010)

4. Figueiredo, C.P., Mendes, P.M.: Towards wearable and continuous 12-lead electrocardiogram monitoring: synthesis of the 12-lead electrocardiogram using 3 wireless single-lead sensors. In: International Conference on Biomedical Electronics and Devices (BIODEVICES), pp. 329–332 (2012)

5. Lee, J., Kim, M., Kim, J.: Reconstruction of precordial lead electrocardiogram from limb leads using state-space model. IEEE J. Biomed. Health Inform. **20**, 818–828 (2015)

6. Yodjaiphet, A., Theera-Umpon, N., Auephanwiriyakul, S.: Electrocardiogram reconstruction using support vector regression. In: IEEE International Symposium on Signal Processing and Information Technology (ISSPIT), pp. 269–272. IEEE (2012)

7. Nallikuzhy, J.J., Dandapat, S.: Enhancement of the spatial resolution of ECG using multi-scale Linear Regression. In: Twenty First National Conference on Communications (NCC), pp. 1–6. IEEE (2015)

8. Acharyya, A., Schiariti, M., Puddu, P.E.: Personalized reduced 3-lead system formation methodology for remote health monitoring applications and reconstruction of standard 12-lead system. Int. Arch. Med. **8**, 1–15 (2015)

9. Hsu, C., Wu, S.: Robust signal synthesis of the 12-lead ECG using 3-lead wireless ECG systems. In: First IEEE International Conference on Communications (ICC), pp. 3517–3522 (2014)

10. Trobec, R., Tomašić, I.: Synthesis of the 12-lead electrocardiogram from differential leads. IEEE Trans. Inf. Technol. Biomed. **15**, 615–621 (2011)

11. Tomasic, I., Avbelj, V., Trobec, R.: Smart wireless sensor for physiological monitoring. In: Studies in Health Technology and Informatics, pHealth 2015, pp. 295–301. IOS Press (2015)

12. Tomasic, I., Frljak, S., Trobec, R.: Estimating the universal positions of wireless body electrodes for measuring cardiac electrical activity. IEEE Trans. Biomed. Eng. **60**, 3368–3374 (2013)

13. Avbelj, V., Trobec, R., Gersak, B., Vokac, D.: Multichannel ECG measurement system. In: Proceedings of the 10th IEEE Symposium on Computer Based Medical Systems, pp. 81–84 (1997)

14. Frljak, S., Avbelj, V., Trobec, R., Meglic, B., Ujiie, T., Gersak, B.: Beat-to-beat QT interval variability before and after cardiac surgery. Comput. Biol. Med. **33**, 267–276 (2003)

15. Hastie, T., Tibshirani, R., Friedman, J.: Tree-based methods. The Elements of StatisticalLearning: Data Mining, Inference, and Prediction, 2nd edn., pp. 305–317. Springer Science & Business Media (2009). doi:10.1007/b94608. ISBN: 978-0-387-84857-0

16. ©The MathWorks Inc.: Classification Trees and Regression Trees. In: Statistics and Machine Learning Toolbox™ Documentation (R2014a) (2015)

Elderly Monitoring System with Sleep and Fall Detector

Abdulakeem Odunmbaku[1(✉)], Amir-Mohammad Rahmani[1,2],
Pasi Liljeberg[1], and Hannu Tenhunen[1,2]

[1] Department of Information Technology, University of Turku, Turku, Finland
{abadod, amirah, pakrli}@utu.fi, hannu@kth.se
[2] Department of Industrial and Medical Electronics,
KTH Royal Institute of Technology, Stockholm, Sweden

Abstract. Monitoring of elderly people has drawn attention of healthcare and medical professionals. Various health problems have been attributed to either fall or lack of sleep in the context of elderly people. Falling and sleep problems on a long term basis could eventually lead to sharp deteriorate in health, poor state of health and high cost for covering their health care. In this paper a new accurate and convenient while cost-efficient implementation of a monitoring system is presented. The use of an accelerometer based system was utilized in this work. The targeted device fit for this implementation is a smart watch. The algorithm of both the fall detector and sleep monitor presented in this work have been implemented and tested on multiple subjects. It also includes a database backend which is used to save the information collected from the system for further analysis and can provide healthcare professional with more insight of the person's life and can help more on further health medication being given to the person.

Keywords: Fall detector · Sleep monitor · Healthcare · Internet-of-Things

1 Introduction

Elderly people are a significant section of the society, with the rise in their population, many organizations are concerned about managing the quality of life being lived by this large population. The average population of this group (age 60 and above) is estimated to be 1.2 billion by 2025 and is expected to rise to about 2 billion by 2050 [10]. A custom way of monitoring the activity of a section of the elderly people's population, who cannot take care of themselves properly in every situation, is the employment of caregivers. However, it is unlikely that a larger amount of caregivers also can cater for continuous monitoring and if that is provided, it overburdening the caregiver and in turn drive up cost [1]. There are different existing solutions to assist the elderly people such as remote robot assistance, entertainment services, and reminder services just to mention a few [1, 2]. Unfortunately it is very difficult to estimate the amount of activities that an elderly person experiences during the night or the rate at which they fall during the day due to their weak leg frame or health status. The researches selection of either a fall detector or sleep monitoring is as a result of surveys

© ICST Institute for Computer Sciences, Social Informatics and Telecommunications Engineering 2016
B. Mandler et al. (Eds.) IoT 360° 2015, Part I, LNICST 169, pp. 473–480, 2016.
DOI: 10.1007/978-3-319-47063-4_51

on the elderly. Examples of simple diagnosis that can be detected by the monitoring sleep pattern in elderly people, long terms of poor sleep time can lead to extensive health problem such as high-blood pressure [3]. In addition to critical conditions that can arise due to falling, fall detecting is a monitoring process that should be taken seriously when the section of our population the elderly.

In papers that have proposed monitoring of elderly people, the approaches have focused most often solely either on the fall detector or sleep monitor. The architecture of our monitoring approach is to combine both the fall detector and sleep monitoring. The fall detector proposed in this work offers accurate detection taking into advantage of existing solutions, as it has three methods to determine a fall event. Our sleep monitoring system also offers accurate results with little or no input from the user. Existing sleep monitoring system detect sleep pattern by attaching sensors to the body, which could actual cause discomfort during sleep and affect the accuracy of the results and quality of sleep.

2 Related Works

An asynchronous temporal contrast (ATC) vision sensor that is capable of reporting pixel changes with latency of milliseconds are used to determine fall events is presented in [11]. This ATC image sensor is placed on the perimeter walls of the enclosure. It extracts change in motion events pixels for the background and reports the temporal contrast in manner of milliseconds, which is also equivalent to image reflective change when the lighting effect is constant. However, this approach requires complex installations and is expensive.

Sleep monitoring based on real-time implementation of obtaining the respiration rhythm and pulse rate of a subject using an air-free water filled vinyl tube under the pillow of the subject during the sleep time is presented in [12]. The obtained data is compared to a peak detection system already pre-defined in their algorithm. A sensor unit is placed under the subject's pillow to detect the pressure changes beneath the head area. The pressures components within the tubes are conditioned and connected to embed catheters. A downside of this system is that, if the sensor plate if not correctly placed beneath the pillow of the subject, pressure variation cannot reach the sensor plate appropriately to give readings and the system is complex.

3 System Implementation

Implementation of the system consists of both sleep monitor and fall detector for elderly people in the same device. A pre-made device was preferred option to combination of different sensor component to implement this work. This enables us to create a cost efficient and flexible approach. Furthermore, the user can also utilize the device for other purposes as per individual needs. Also the consideration of having a back-end that would be able to receive processed data was included as a part of this work.

The essential component used in this system is an accelerometer. Accelerometers are used in many applications such as prosthetic limbs, drones and the game industry. The emergence of micro-electro mechanical-systems (MEMS) based accelerometers have revolutionizes this technology by changing the structure of components to micrometer scale. The measurement of this accelerometer is based on the movement of a small structure component due to vibration stress on it, the acceleration of the component can then be converted into different forms depending on the function it will be applied [5, 6].

3.1 Fall Detector

Implementing fall detector involves several steps. Firstly the accelerometer sensor axes data is extracted and represented in form of sine wavelet. The less significant part of the signals is separated, and only the important part of data is utilized. Discrete Wavelength Transform (DWT) is applied to the data, to yield a representation of the discrete data signal, a mother wavelength Ψ is selected and from the mother wavelength, filters h and g will be determined. The wavelength coefficients for the discrete signals are calculated at first scale, these signals are then passed through a first filter to eliminate noise and further passed through another filter. These filters eliminate the noise and effect of gravitational pull on the accelerometer ball (1) and (2).

$$a_n = \sum_{k=-\infty}^{\infty} x[k]h[n-k] = (x * h)[n]. \tag{1}$$

$$d_n = \sum_{k=-\infty}^{\infty} x[k]g[n-k] = (x * g)[n]. \tag{2}$$

From the entire signal frequency of the accelerometer data, an approximated coefficient and detailed coefficient constitutes of about half of the signal frequency. To eliminate the effect of error in the signals, each reading of the accelerometer is calculated to produce the approximated coefficient. This is done by using the previous coefficients to calculate the next ones, this process is done repeatedly therein forming a filter bank for the frequency signals. The subsequent coefficients are shown below in (3) and (4);

$$a_{s+1}[n] = \sum_{k=-\infty}^{\infty} \bar{a}_s[k]h[n-k] = (\bar{a}_s * h)[n]. \tag{3}$$

$$d_{s+1}[n] = \sum_{k=-\infty}^{\infty} đ_s[k]g[n-k] = (đ_s * g)[n]. \tag{4}$$

The $\bar{a}_s$ is the subsequent approximate coefficient while the $đ_s$ is the subsequent detail coefficient. These are performed on all the three axes of the accelerometer, and subsequently used to calculate the acceleration of the accelerometer and will be used in eventually for the fall detection. Below are the equations to validate the three axis of the accelerometer in (3), (4) and (5);

$$\alpha = (X - X_{old}). \tag{5}$$

$$\beta = (Y - Y_{old}). \tag{6}$$

$$\gamma = (Z - Z_{old}). \tag{7}$$

When calculating the acceleration, new data acquired from the accelerometer are used in a way to favor of the previous data. This would eliminate the error in calculation due to incorrect data selection. In the equation, α represents the X axis, β represents the Y axis, γ represents the Z axis, X_{old} represents the previous data of the X-axis, Y_{old} represents the previous data Y-axis and Z_{old} represents the previous data of the Z-axis. The acceleration is shown in (8) and δ, represents the acceleration of the accelerometer.

$$Acce(\delta) = \sqrt{\alpha^2 + \beta^2 + \gamma^2}. \tag{8}$$

For fall to be determined the system undergoes four stages. Firstly is the threshold calculation, which involves the calculation of a threshold t. The threshold is to be compared to the acceleration which is constantly computed. After comparison, the system determines if there is a fall activity or not. The expression which explains the comparison is shown in (10). The threshold is calculated by randomly simulating fall activities while collecting their accelerations, the minimum peak values are rounded up and the average is calculated. Secondly is the data acquisition and system calibration which involves the collection of system data. Thirdly is the feature extraction which involves: (i) extraction of the accelerometer axes positions before and after a fall phase, (ii) registering dynamic and static acceleration and (iii) current physical body orientation. For a fall event to be detected by the system, the four stages have to be fulfilled [7, 8].

3.2   Sleep Monitor

The method used in the sleep monitor to collect the accelerometer data is same as the one discussed in the fall detector, indicated in Eqs. (4), (5) and (9). The principle employed in the sleep monitoring is as such that, activity of the brain is equivalent to the motion produced by the body during sleep. With the accelerometer attached to the body at sleep, these motions can be easily detected. There are three distinct state than need to be differentiated here; the awake state, when the subject is in constantly movement and awake, the light sleep state, when there is reduced motion of the body that is asleep when compared to the awake state. The third is the deep sleep state, there is minimum amount of body movement. During the sleep period, the acceleration is bounded between 0m/s^2 to 1.5m/s^2 according to vibration on a bed and the sleep states are represented on different acceleration values between the boundaries [9]. The duration of each sleep states and body movements are collected and used in deriving the sleep quality index. The sleep quality index takes into account also the time of going to bed to wake up time.

$$Sleep\ Efficiency = \frac{A.T + L.S}{T_b^a} * 100\%. \tag{9}$$

$A.T$, represents the awake state times, $L.S$, represents the awake state coefficient and T_b^a, represents the total time the subject is at sleep from start point a, to stop time b.

4 System Architecture

The system allows the option of choosing either the fall detector or the sleep monitor. As mentioned, collected data is passed through the filter bank. The data from the filter bank are used to calculate the acceleration, and can be used in any of the monitoring process. In the example implementation Simvalley Mobile AW-414 smart watch is utilized. The system architecture is shown in Fig. 1.

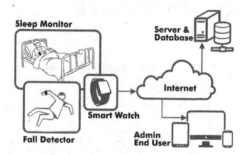

Fig. 1. The system architecture.

The system comes with a complementary event-based back-end database system. At each event change in the monitoring system, the information of the system is collected with timestamp of the event and tag of the user. This information is sent to the database for further analysis. On the user side of the system, an internet TCP protocol ensures that the phone is connected. At each change in event, an internet connection will be made to the database. At the administartion side of the system, the terminal is enabled with WebSocket and HTML enabled browser that can be used to access the database information of the users in real time.

5 Result

The fall detector was evaluated in a controlled room environment with simulated fall by three subjects, a 26 year old, 1.73 meters tall male volunteer, a 30 year old, 1.80 meters tall male volunteer and a 23 year old 1.62 meters tall female volunteer for ten times on five different occasions. For the tests result, the sensitivity and the specificity (9) and (10) of the fall detector was calculated using the following parameters; True positive (TP) which means that during test, fall happened and the algorithm is able to detect it successfully. False positive (FP), is when a there is no fall activity detected and the algorithm records it as a fall detected. True Negative (TN), is the daily activities of the algorithm that goes undetected and False Negative (FN), is when a fall occurs and the algorithm fails to detect that a fall actually occurred.

The fall parameters were collected and on the first three set of falls, few falls (i.e. FN) were not detected, see Table 1. On the fourth set of fall simulation, the accuracy of the fall detection is noticed to have increased linearly, while in the fifth set of, all falls were detected (i.e. TP) at 100 %, while NF is zero. The success and failure rate of the tests were computed and the sensitivity and the specificity of the tests were evaluated using Eqs. (10) and (11). The accuracy of the tests was also calculated using the success and failure rate to be 95 % of the fall simulated by the test subjects.

$$Sensitivity = \frac{TP}{TP + FN}. \tag{10}$$

$$Specificity = \frac{TN}{TN + FP}. \tag{11}$$

Table 1. Results of fall activities test.

Falls	Subject									
	Simulated Fall Activity									
	1		2		3		4		5	
	TP	FN	TP	FN	TP	FN	TP	FN	TP	FN
1	10	0	10	0	9	1	91	1	10	10
2	9	1	9	1	9	1	9	1	10	0
3	8	2	9	1	10	0	10	0	10	0
Total	27	3	28	2	28	2	29	1	30	0
	Success rate = 142, Fail = 8; Sensitivity = 95 %, Specificity = 100 %; Accuracy = 94.7 %									

Our result was compared with a tri-axial accelerometer-based fall detector described in [13]. The detector in [13] is also based on a 3D accelerometer that uses FPGA for the computation and ZigBee module to transmit data. The tri-axial based fall detector offers higher sensitivity than our prorposed fall detector, but has lower specificity. The specificity rate shows that there are misses in the data collection rate from the accelerometer which in our system prove to better specificity as shown in Table 2.

Table 2. Fall detection result comparison.

	Sensitivity (%)	Specificity (%)
Purposed Fall-detector	95.0	100
Tri-axial fall detector [13]	97.7	94.8

Evaluation of the sleep monitor was carried out by placing the device next to the pillow of the subject, by this the movement of the subject can be easily tracked as the bed and pillow moves. This evaluation was also carried out with the same three test subjects by monitoring their sleep over the night. The movement of the accelerometer ball, as a result of the body movement, are translated into graphical representation and plotted in real-time against the time of the sleep. At the end of the monitoring the sleep quality is computed (9) and sent to the database for further analysis. The result of the sleep monitor can vary from person to person, and the data can also be retrieved from the database and can be viewed in real time. The information can be further analyzed and possible causes of health problems can be identified and attended to in time.

6   Conclusion

Design and implementation of monitoring system architecture for monitoring elderly people activity both during day and at night was presented. The combination of two implementations, i.e. fall detector and sleep monitor, were explored and it turned out to be successful. Most of the existing implementation has custom made devices which turned out to be expensive to build a prototype, but the focus of this work is to have a reasonable priced device that can is readily available. The choice of using a smart watch was perfect for the aim of the work, as it is ready available in the market.

References

1. Hossain, M.A., Ahmed, D.T.: Virtual caregiver: an ambient-aware elderly monitoring system. IEEE Trans. Biomed. Eng. **16**(6), 102–103 (2012)
2. Peng, Y.-T., Lin, C.-Y., et al.: Multimodality sensor system for long-term sleep quality. IEEE Trans. Biomed. Circ. Syst. **3**, 217–227 (2007)
3. Sposaro, F., Tyson, G.: iFall: an Android application for fall monitoring and response. In: IEEE Conference Publications, pp. 6119–6122, 3–6 September 2009
4. Prado-Velasco, M., Rio-Cidoncha, D., et al.: The inescapable smart impact detection system (ISIS): an ubiquitous and personalized fall detector based on a distributed "divide and conquer strategy". In: 30th Annual International Conference of the IEEE, pp. 3332–3335, 20–25 August 2008
5. Cao, R., Chen, Y., et al.: Failure mechanism analysis of quartz accelerometer under vibration condition. In: IEEE Conference Publications, pp. 1–5 (2011)
6. Alwan, M., Rajendran, P.J., et al.: A Smart and passive floor-vibration based fall detector for elderly. In: IEEE Conference Publications, pp. 1003–1007 (2006)
7. Soaz, C., Lederer, C., et al.: A new method to estimate the real upper limit of the false alarm rate in a 3 accelerometry-based fall detector for the elderly. In: IEEE Conference Engineering in Medicine, pp. 244–247, 28 August 2012–1 September 2012
8. Rescio, G., Leone, A., et al.: Support vector machine for tri-axial accelerometer-based fall detector. In: IEEE Conference Publications, pp. 25–30 (2012)
9. Scholz, U., Bianchi, A.M., Cerutti, S., Kubicki, S.: Vegetative background of sleep: spectral analysis of the heart rate variability. Physiol. Behav. **62**, 1037–1043 (1997)

10. Hossain, M.A., Ahmed, D.T.: Human caregiver support system in elderly monitoring facility. In: IEEE Trans. Biomed. Eng. **16** (2012)
11. Fu, Z., Delbruck, T., et al.: An address-event fall detector for assisted living applications. IEEE Trans. Biomed. Circ. **2**, 88–96 (2008)
12. Zhu, X., Chen, W., et al.: Real-time monitoring of respiration rhythm and pulse rate during sleep. In: IEEE International Conference on Circuits and Systems, December 2006
13. Rescio, G., Leone, A., et al.: Support vector machine for tri-axial accelerometer-based fall detector. In: 5th IEEE International Workshop for Sensors, pp. 25–30 (2013)

Health Sensors Information Processing and Analytics Using Big Data Approaches

D. Gachet Páez[✉], M.L. Morales Botello, E. Puertas, and M. de Buenaga

Universidad Europea de Madrid, 28670 Villaviciosa de Odón, Spain
{gachet,mariadelaluz.morales,enrique.puertas,buenaga}@uem.es

Abstract. In order of maintain the sustainability of the public health systems it is necessary to develop new medical applications to reduce the affluence of chronic and dependent people to care centers and enabling the management of chronic diseases outside institutions Recent advances in wireless sensors technology applied to e-health allow the development of "personal medicine" concept, whose main objective is to identify specific therapies that make safe and effective individualized treatment of patients based for example in remote monitoring. The volume of health information to manage, including data from medical and biological sensors make necessary to use Big Data and IoT concepts for an adequate treatment of this kind of information. In this paper we present a general approach for sensor's information processing and analytics based on Big Data concepts.

Keywords: Big data · Internet of things · Cloud computing · Elderly · Sensors

1 Introduction

The rapidly growing popularity of health care and activity monitoring applications for smart mobile devices like smart phones and tablets provide new ways to collect information about people health status, both manually and automatically. Also, there are appearing new COTS (*Commercial Off-The-Shelf*) wearable medical sensors that can easily connect with the smart phones or tablets via Bluetooth and transfer the sensing measures directly to a public or private cloud infrastructure. This has provided a more efficient and convenient way to collect personal health information like blood pressure, oxygen saturation, blood glucose level, pulse, electrocardiogram (ECG), etc., that can be analyzed for generating alarms or furthermore, it would also be possible to track the patient's behaviors on a real-time basis and over long periods, providing a potential alert for signs of physical and/or cognitive deterioration [1].

Medical and bio-signal sensors are also commonly used in Intensive Care Units (ICU) at hospitals and the information provided by them can be used for example to develop methods for patient-specific prediction of in-hospital mortality. Sensors used in ICUs can provide precise, heterogeneous and continuous information about clinical condition of a patient as for example heart rate, invasive mean arterial blood pressure, invasive diastolic arterial blood pressure, invasive systolic arterial blood pressure, etc. All this data can be processed and analyzed in order to predict special clinical situation or as above mentioned in-hospital mortality.

© ICST Institute for Computer Sciences, Social Informatics and Telecommunications Engineering 2016
B. Mandler et al. (Eds.) IoT 360° 2015, Part I, LNICST 169, pp. 481–486, 2016.
DOI: 10.1007/978-3-319-47063-4_52

2 Big Data Processing and Analysis

One of the most important aspects when we are dealing with health monitoring is how the data generated by the sensor and medical devices is processed and analyzed. The first thing we have to think about is the goal, that is, we need to establish what we want to do before thinking about how we are going to achieve it. Health data mining approaches are similar to standard data mining procedures, and is performed basically in five stages [2].

Data acquisition and preprocessing. The three most important data sources are experimental data, public datasets, and simulated data. In the first scenario, data is usually gathered from a set of wearable devices that are monitoring a group of test users. Public datasets are those that have been made publicly available in sites like UCI ML Repository or Kaggle.com. When data is gathered from many heterogeneous wearable devices or sources, a normalization of data step is required. Data preprocessing involves data cleaning for removing noise and data interpolation for mitigate the effects of missing values.

Data Transformation. When there are a big number of attributes, dimensionality reduction is a required step because it improves efficiency and reduces over fitting. There are usually two ways to do this task: feature selection and feature extraction [3].

Modeling. This stage, applies knowledge discovery algorithms to identify patterns in the data or predict some variables, at this point we can apply several algorithms as for example Rule induction learners, Decision trees, Probabilistic Learners, Support Vector Machines (SVM), Hidden Markov Models (HMM), etc.

Evaluation. The effectiveness of learning algorithms systems is measured in terms of the number of correct and wrong decisions. Some of the metrics used for evaluating the modes are recall and precision. Recall is defined as the proportion of class members assigned to a category by a classifier. Precision is defined as the proportion of correctly assigned documents to a category.

3 Processing Cardiovascular Data

As use case for data processing and analytics we use real data set obtained from Physionet Computing in Cardiology Challenge 2012: Predicting Mortality of ICU Patients [4]. The origin of data were the hospital medical information systems for Intensive Care Unit (ICU) patients with ICU stays lasting at least 48 h. The dataset consisted of Set A and Outcome-related descriptors (csv) text file. Set A was composed of four thousand records (text files) corresponding to the four thousand ICU stays (patients), and each record was composed of up to 37 time series variables (such as Heart Rate, Weight, pH, SysABP, DiasABP, Urine, ...) which could be observed once, more than once, or not at all in some cases (not at all records), and could be recorded at regular intervals (hourly, daily) or at irregular intervals. The time stamps of the measurement indicated the elapsed time since admission to the ICU. In addition to the previous variables, each record included six general descriptors collected at the time the patient was admitted in ICU (RecordID, Age, Gender, Height, ICUType, and Weight). These descriptors appeared at the beginning of each record (time 00:00). In correspondence with Set A, the Outcomes was a file composed by four thousand rows, where each row contained six outcome-related descriptors for each record (patient). These descriptors were: RecordID, SAPS-I score [5], SOFA score [6], Length of stay (days), Survival (days) and In-hospital death (0 indicated survival and 1 indicated in-hospital death).

All valid values for general descriptors, time series variables, and outcome-related descriptors were non-negative (≥ 0). A value of -1 indicated missing or unknown data. The four thousand records of individual patients that make up the Set A were joined together resulting in a file next to 2 million of rows (1885594 rows). This amount of data cannot be processed by many conventional analysis tools. In order to process and analyze this big amount of data, we used R, an open source software for statistical computing [7]. In this work, we used the tools of R to perform a predictive model from the cardiovascular data described previously.

3.1 Predictive Modelling with R

The aim of the model is to predict in-hospital mortality (0: survival, or 1: in-hospital death) of each patient from the corresponding variables and descriptors. The first step for building a predictive model about the patient's mortality in UCU is to perform data formatting and pre-processing. The text file of 1885594 rows (and four columns: RecordID, Time, Variable, Value), which contained the complete time series variables of the four thousand patients, was saved as a "data table" in R. This allowed us to process big data with high speed. In order to get static variables, that is, in order to work with a unique value for each time series variable, for each patient (record) we calculated the median of the measurements for each variable.

Then, we constructed a structure where the (37) variables are the columns and the 4000 patients (RecordID) are the rows. As well as, we added 8 columns corresponding to the following general and outcomes-related descriptors: RecordID, Age, Gender, Height, ICUType, SAPS.I, SOFA and InHospitalDeath.

Before using these data for the logistic regression model, we carried out a data pre-processing, which consisted of:

1. Replacing invalid physiological values with valid values in the descriptor Height (for example, height value of 13 cm probably corresponds to 130 cm).
2. Assigning NA (Not Acknowledge) to both outlier and invalid values of the following variables: pH, NISysABP, NI DiasABP, DiasABP, MAP (for example, a value of 0 in NISysABP);
3. Replace -1 with NA from missing or unknown data (which were indicated with -1 in the original dataset).

Logistic regression is a common analysis technique for situations with binary outcome data [8, 9]. This method has been employed by several participants of the Physionet Challenge 2012 to produce predictions of the binary variable "InHospital-Death" [10, 11]. In this work, we used the same method to predict survival or in-hospital death using the statistical software R. The logistic regression was performed using the function "glm" included in "stats" package of R. The dependent variable of the model was InHospitalDeath and the independent variables will be the rest of the columns (pre-processed variables and descriptors) previously presented. Due to the logistic model in R deletes the missing observations, we only used as independent variables the variables or descriptors in which missing data were present in less than 10 % of patients. In addition, we deleted the rows (patients) with missing data in any column (796 of 4000 rows). We applied repeatedly the model in order to select the more significant variables, and only the variables with a statistical significance level (p < 0.001) were included in the final model. For training the logistic regression model we used the 60 % of the patients (training dataset, 1922 patients) and the remaining 40 % (testing dataset, 1282) was used to test the model. The variables finally considered for inclusion in the logistic regression model are presented in Table 1.

Table 1. The first column shows the variables that were selected for the model according to a few missing values. The second column shows the variables finally used by the model based on the higher significance.

All Variables	Model Var.
BUN Blood urea nitrogen	X
Creatinine	
GCS Glasgow Coma Score	X
Glucosa Serum glucose	X
HCO3 Serum bicarbonate	
HCT Hematocrit	X
HR Heart rate	X
K Serum potassium	
Lactate	
Mg Serum magnesium	X
Na Serum sodium	
Platelets	
Temp Temperature	X
Urine	
Urine.Sum	X
WBC White blood cell count	
Weight	
Age	X
Gender	
ICUType	
SAPS.I	
SOFA	

We used the function "predict" included in "stats" package in R to predict the probability of death of the testing dataset patients using the model obtained with the training dataset patients. The predicted outcome is a value between 0 and 1. In order to get a binary outcome, that is, to predict survival (0) or in-hospital death (1), we assigned 0 to the predicted value when the probability predicted was lower than 0.5, and in otherwise, we assigned 1 to the predicted value.

For model evaluation we take into account the official metric used for Physionet Challenge 2012, score 1 (s1), defined as the minimum value between Sensitivity (Se) and Positive Predictivity (P^+):

$$S_e = \frac{TP}{TP + FN} \tag{1}$$

$$P^+ = \frac{TP}{TP + FP} \tag{2}$$

TP is the number of true positives, FP is the number of false positives and FN is the number of false negatives. True positive indicates that the model predicts 1 when InHospitalDeath is 1, false positive indicates that the model predicts 1 when InHospitalDeath is 0, and false negative indicates that the model predict 0 when InHospitalDeath is 1. Therefore, the Se value quantifies the fraction of in-hospital deaths that are predicted, and P^+ quantifies the fraction of correct predictions of in-hospital deaths.

4   Conclusion and Future Work

We obtained a fraction of correct predictions of in-hospital deaths, P^+ of 0.455. The fraction of in-hospital deaths that are predicted, Se, was 0.006. Therefore, the score s1 obtained by our model was of 0.006. Our fraction of correct predictions was higher than the s1 value obtained by the winners of Challenge 2012 [12] using Set A. This result suggests us that the fraction of correct predictions of in-hospital deaths given by our model is relatively good. However, the fraction of in-hospital deaths predicted by our model was small. A possible cause is that many variables (22 physiological variables) were not taken into account by the model due to frequent missing data. However, frequent missing data does not imply a minor relation between the variables and the patient death. An information gain analysis performed between the median of each variable and the in-hospital death variable (results not shown) revealed that variables which were in the variable group with longer weights, i.e., the variables better related with the death of the patient (such as PaCo2, Bilirubin, Albumin and AST) were rejected by high missing observations.

Other aspects that could affect to the results of our model are the diverse population with a wide variety of life-threatening conditions, with frequent missing and occasionally incorrectly recorded observations, idiosyncrasies of care administration, and highly unbalanced class sizes that make up the dataset. Whatever the cause, our logistic regression model can be improvable, however, the aim of this work was not to get the best model, but carry out a R implementation of a predictive model based on cardiovascular (big) data. Despite of poor performance, the methodology proposed in this research using the statistical package R can be used for analyzing other biomedical datasets. R has thousands of libraries that can help to analyze and visualize complex datasets, and it lets researchers to deal with big data, providing libraries and functions for cleaning and analyzing large volumes of data produced by medical devices and sensors.

Acknowledgments. This work is still being developed with funds granted by the Spanish Ministry of Economy and Competitiveness under project iPHealth (TIN-2013-47153-C3-1).

References

1. Fundación Vodafone: Innovación TIC para las personas mayores. Situación, requerimientos soluciones en la atención integral de la cronicidad y la dependencia (2011). http://www.vodafone.es/static/fichero/pro_ucm_mgmt_015568.pdf
2. Sow, D.M., Turaga, D.S.: Schmidt: mining of sensor data in healthcare: a survey. In: Aggarwal, C.C. (ed.) Managing and Mining Sensor Data, pp. 459–504. Springer, Berlin (2013)
3. Apiletti, D., Baralis, E., Bruno, G., Cerquitelli, T.: Real-time analysis of physiological data to support medical applications. Trans. Inf. Tech. Biomed. **13**, 313–321 (2009)
4. Physionet 2012 Cardiovascular Challenge. http://physionet.org/challenge/2012/
5. Le Gall, J.R., Loirat, P., Alperovitch, A., Glaser, P., Granthil, C., Mathieu, D., Mercier, P., Thomas, R., Villers, D.: A simplified acute physiology score for ICU patients. Crit. Care Med. **12**(11), 975–977 (1984)
6. Ferreira, F.L., Bota, D.P., Bross, A., Mélot, C., Vincent, J.L.: Serial evaluation of the patients. JAMA **286**(14), 1754–1758 (2001)
7. R project: http://www.r-project.org/
8. Hosmer, D.W., Lemeshow, S.: Applied Logistic Regression, 2nd edn. Wiley, New York (2000)
9. Hamilton, S.L., Hamilton, J.R.: Predicting in-hospital-death and mortality percentage using logistic regression. Comput. Cardiol. **39**, 489–492 (2012)
10. Vairavan, S., Eshelman, L., Haider, S., Flowers, A., Seiver, A.: Prediction of mortality in an intensive care unit using logistic regression and hidden Markov model. Comput. Cardiol. **39**, 393–396 (2012)
11. Bera, D., Nayak, M.M.: Mortality risk assessment for ICU patients using logistic regression. Comput. Cardiol. **39**, 493–496 (2012)
12. Johnson, A.E.W., Dunkley, N., Mayaud, L., Tsanas, A., Kramer, A.A., Clifford, G.D.: Patient specific predictions in the intensive care unit using a Bayesian ensemble. Comput. Cardiol. **39**, 249–252 (2012)
13. GachetPáez, D., Aparicio, F., de Buenaga, M., Ascanio, J.R.: Big data and IoT for chronic patients monitoring. In: Hervás, R., Lee, S., Nugent, C., Bravo, J. (eds.) UCAmI 2014. LNCS, vol. 8867, pp. 416–423. Springer International Publishing, Cham (2014)
14. Sahoo, S.S., Jayapandian, C., Garg, G., Kaffashi, F., Chung, S., Bozorgi, A., et al.: Heart beats in the cloud: distributed analysis of electrophysiological big data using cloud computing for epilepsy clinical research. J. Am. Med. Inform. Assoc. **21**(2), 263–271 (2014)
15. Chandola, V., Banerjee, A., Kumar, V.: Anomaly detection: a survey. ACM Comput. Surv. **41**, 15:1–15:58 (2009)

Leveraging IoT Device Data
for Emotional Health

Hariprasad Anumala$^{(\boxtimes)}$, Shiva Murthy Busetty, and Vishal Bharti

Samsung Research Institute India, Bengaluru, India
{hariprasad.a,shiva.m22,visu.bharti}@samsung.com

Abstract. Recent evolution of wearable devices is primarily focused on physical health and fitness but ignore emotional health aspects of an individual. Current health services help user define goals "Reduce weight" but do not provide interfaces for users to define goals as "Stay Happy". Lot of existing research has focused on sensing user mood classification based on device data but there is limited research that has focused to diagnose and heal depression. A conventional method of doctors detecting depression is based on Hamilton scale of depression with a set of questions and is an intrusive method to probe depression patients. IoT devices are slowly gaining popularity and huge data that is generated from these devices can be leveraged to determine user emotional health. Proposed method attempts to analyze IoT device data and calculate user depression scale and recommends relevant social communication with user social contacts (Friends, Family Members). Identifying precise social contacts and recommending actions and content to recover from early stages of depression is one of the goals of the proposed system. Method recommends relevant social contacts based on current depression score. Proposed system tries to monitor user's emotional state and more tries to act as preventive health assistant to correct emotional states in early stages and avoids user moving to advanced stages of depression.

Keywords: IoT · Healthcare · Depression · Emotional health

1 Introduction

Emotional Health is defined as 'a positive sense of wellbeing which enable an individual to be able to function in society and meet the demands of everyday life; people in good mental have the ability to recover effectively from illness, change or misfortune'. It encompasses mental health issues like depression, anxiety, bipolar disorder, addiction, and other conditions. Depression is a condition that reportedly affects 1 in 10 Americans at one point or another. Over 80 % of the people that have symptoms of clinical depression are not receiving any specific treatment for their depression. The number of patients diagnosed with depression increases by approximately 20 % per year [1]. Long time very severe depression might lead to suicidal tendencies. So it is very important to identify person's depression state in early stages. Suicide is the 12th leading cause of death in the United States [2].

© ICST Institute for Computer Sciences, Social Informatics and Telecommunications Engineering 2016
B. Mandler et al. (Eds.) IoT 360° 2015, Part I, LNICST 169, pp. 487–501, 2016.
DOI: 10.1007/978-3-319-47063-4_53

This paper presents the method to quantify the depression level based on data streams from IoT devices. As lot of devices are getting connected in IoT space users emotional data can be derived based on his interaction with smart devices. Proposed method uses user's IoT device data, message conversations, call logs, browsing history, social activity data, photos, videos etc. to calculate emotional state of a user. It then tries to map user's emotional data to Hamilton depression scale. The Hamilton Rating depression scale abbreviated as HAM-D [4] is the most widely used clinician-administered depression assessment scale. HAM-D is a multiple item questionnaire used to provide an indication of depression, and as a guide to evaluate recovery. The questionnaire is designed for adults and is used to rate the severity of their depression by probing mood, feelings of guilt, suicide ideation, insomnia, agitation or retardation, anxiety, weight loss and somatic symptoms. There are 17 items present which are used to calculate depression scale. Table 1 represents key parameters referred in questionnaire. Four other questions are not added to total score and are used to provide other clinical information. Each item on the questionnaire is scored on a 3 or 5 point scale, depending on the item, and the total score is compared to the corresponding descriptor. Assessment time is estimated at 20 min.

Data from IoT devices and smartphone can be correlated to determine HAM-D Score. New devices like Sensiotec and Affectiva provide new sources of data.

Table 1. HAM-D params

HAM-D params	Mobile data params	IoT devices data	Fitness wearable data
Depressed mood	Call logs – low voice Message Social activity – Depressed content posted Images – Depressed face	Emospark(device) detects sadness	Low sleep Low food intake Weight loss Less Active
Feelings of guilt		Cry detection	
Anxiety	Images	Emergency Alerts, IFTTT Events (Kid Not reached home, Thief at Home)	BP data (low blood pressure), Anxiety data from Affectiva
Anxiety somatic		Jawbone UP paired with Smart things/Nest Hub	Sleep data (less sleep)
Suicide	Browsing data		
Insomnia late	More browsing/social activity while still at bed		
Work and activities			Activity monitoring (Less, Average, High)
Retardation: Psychomotor	Call content/Messaging		
Agitation	Images	Sensiotec	Stress data, Heartrate data, sweating (from wearables)
Somatic symptoms (Gastrointestinal)			Food data collected from Apps
Somatic symptoms general			Exercise Activity data
Loss of weight			Accessories (OMRON etc.), Apps(S Health etc.)
Insight	Depression App usage		

Sensiotec developed a device which can calculate person's agitation [8]. Affectiva developed a wearable device which can calculate anxiety [9].

1.1 Abbreviations and Acronyms

IoT-Internet of Things
IFTTT-If This Then That
IoHT-Internet of Health things
.

2 IoT Health Devices and Impact of Device Data

IoT Device Data: IoHT includes implantable devices surgically implanted by physicians, such as pacemakers, which are configured and managed externally using Bluetooth or other wireless technology. It can also include external devices that are plugged into our bodies to administer medications such as insulin pumps.

IoHT includes wearable devices that can clip to our belts, be sported on an armband or embedded into our watches or eyeglasses to measure our activity or heart rates.

IoHT includes remote monitoring devices that can be installed in a patient's home to track blood pressure, weight, blood glucose levels and other important health data. This would also include consumer electronic devices such as smartphones and tablets that run specialty health apps or are integrated into health solutions.

IoHT includes the back-end systems built to power these mobile and remote monitoring health solutions, including cloud and Big Data infrastructures and our legacy infrastructure of classical health IT systems.

Current paper focusses on wireless implantable devices, wearable devices, remote monitoring devices and IoT hubs that can be connected to smart phone over short range connectivity protocols like BT/BLE/ZigBee/Ant+. Recent evolution of home automation hubs like Nest Thermostat and SmartThings hub play important role for realizing health use cases.

Devices like Kiband, Child Angel alert parents when kids are outside proximity ranges of some meters. Also IoT Health devices like "Mimo" send parents real-time information on their baby's breathing, skin temperature, sleeping position, and activity level. Similarly IFTTT kind of automation platforms help user defines recipes (When thief at home alerts me where ever I am). Motion, smoke Detector, Door/window Sensor, Glass Break Sensor and Indoor/Outdoor Camera provide important sources of IoT data that can impact an individual emotional level. In emerging countries like India gas leak detection is a major safety concern.

Also lot of effort is going on in the development of new medical IoT devices. UroSense™ urine management system provides real-time awareness to caregivers enabling them to mitigate health and safety issues associated with catheterized patients while realizing substantial cost savings. UroSense™ provides fill level and core body temperature (CBT) data directly to a monitor or nursing station wirelessly. Also devices like Philips medical dispenser which help seniors manage on time medications when tied with other devices can generate meaningful IoT notifications to other devices. For example missed medication alerts can be sent to family member devices (Table 2).

Table 2. Different IoT device data

IOT Devices	Data inputs for emotional Health
Mimo	Temperature, sleep, breathing
Milk nanny	Milk consumption data
Listnr	Baby's cry detection
Sproutling	Heartrate, Temperature
Temp Traq	Temperature
Owlet baby care	Oxygen level, heart rate
Sensible baby	Movement, temperature, breathing
Withings home	Analyzes local sound for signs of distress
Pacif-i	Temperature, Boundary check for kid
Emospark	Emotion text and content analysis
EAR-IT	Acoustic event detection

A lot of such IoT devices and wearables help user to define automation rules like "If event X occurs trigger action A". Though these event action platforms are primarily meant to trigger critical alerts and can help them manage their day to day activities easily, they can also act as key inputs that cause anxiety which is one of emotional health parameters. Careful analysis of above data can help to measure events that can make user anxious and repeated occurrence of such events can lead to mild and severe depression.

2.1 IoT Data Processing

As explained in Fig. 3 IoT Event Action Map consists of set of IoT events coupled with space and time context. IoT Events are "Kid Missing" and "Sudden hike in BP Level of father" generated from IoT devices (Ex: kiband) and Wearable BP Monitor. Corresponding IoT Actions in such context could be to trigger real time interface to "call user X" or "Notify user Y".

Figure 1 represents flow of events. IoT Event Analyzer disseminates appropriate events and sends it to "Event to Alert Mapper" module. Alert Mapper module maps events to critical Alerts. These Alerts are then correlated using correlation engine which classifies alerts based on emotional parameters associated with the alert data and generates set of IoT Actions.

Figure 2 represents architecture of emotional health assistant platform. Various IoT Streams of data are locally analyzed to build an emotional profile. Depression or Emotion Monitor consists of IoT Event Analyzer, Event to Alert Mapper, Correlation Engine Modules se.

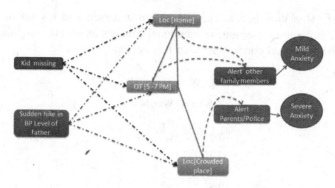

Fig. 1. IoT event action map

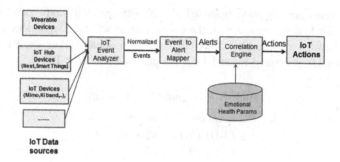

Fig. 2. IoT event data processing

2.2 Calculating Depression Score with Device Data

There are numerous IoT devices and each of these devices will generate many events. System shall determine critical events and assigns weightage and validity for each of the events. Validity here means duration till the event for which an IoT action is valid. Table 3 shows top 8 events sorted in the order of weightage.

Table 3. Weightage and validity for events

IOT Devices	Events	weightage	Validity in hrs
D1	E1	w_e^1	V1
D1	E2	w_e^2	V2
D2	E3	w_e^3	V3
D3	E4	w_e^4	V4
D4	E5	w_e^5	V5
D4	E6	w_e^6	V6
D4	E7	w_e^7	V7
D5	E8	w_e^8	V8

A list of association is maintained between a person and his set of emotional contacts. Table 4 shows user top six emotional contacts along the weightage. Weight represents the emotional connect between that person and user.

Table 4. Weightage and persons

Contacts	Weightage
P1	w_p^1
P2	w_p^2
P3	w_p^3
P4	w_p^4
P5	w_p^5
P6	w_p^6

When events are triggered from IoT devices, system will know person to event association. To find the criticality of the event, system will take sum of wex and wpx. [Table 5] shows 5 sample events sorted based on criticality. For ex: P1-D1-E1-T1 means device D1 generated event E1 for the person P1 at time T1.

Table 5. Event order and its weight

Event order	Score(S)
P1-D1-E1-T1	$w_p^1 + w_e^1$
P3-D2-E2-T2	$w_p^3 + w_e^2$
P2-D4-E5-T3	$w_p^2 + w_e^5$
P4-D5-E8-T4	$w_p^4 + w_e^8$
P6-D5-E10-T4	$w_p^6 + w_e^{10}$

Table 6. Score calculation for device data

Call variance	Message variance	Social activity variance	Image variance	DMS value
Val >=70	val <=100	val <=100	val <=20	0
val >=52	val <=200	val <=200	val <=40	1
val >=34	val <=300	val <=300	val <=60	2
val >=17	val <=400	val <=400	val <=80	3

If two events are generated at same time as shown in above table at time T4, then wp4, we8, wp6 and we10 are added to the total weight. The system will maintain the event, its generated time and validity in our system. When time elapsed more than the validity, the event will be removed.

In Fig. 3, at 1:00 h event E1 occurred having validity 5 h and at 3:00 h event E2 occurred with validity 8 h. This time validity of E1 is reduced by 2 h. More than one event can occur at same time as shown above at 12:00. At any point of time weightage is calculated as sum of weights of all the events exists in the system.

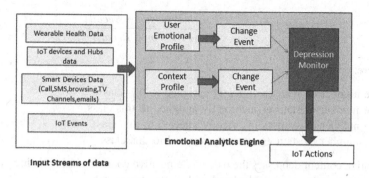

Fig. 3. Emotional health architecture

Score from the weights is calculated as below:

Events and persons are divided into 4 groups each and sum of weights for all the combinations of events and persons in each group are calculated. If present weight falls under first group then user's score for IoT device data is 4, else if present weight falls under second group then user's score for IoT device data is 3 and so on.

Call logs: From the whole call log data only favourite social contact log data is segregated. Further Variance in favourite call log data is analyzed for any change in call log durations. Variance is now associated with identifying "Depressed mood" parameter. This parameter ranges from 0–4 scale. Following formula will be used to get "Depressed mood" scale (DMS).

Call Variation = Average favorite call duration for previous 180 days/Average call duration for last week * 100.

Messages: The research paper "Social Networks" Text Mining for Sentiment Classification: The case of Facebook' statuses updates in the "Arabic Spring" Era" [4] mines the messages and tells the sentiment of that message. This system will use same method for text mining. This research is divided into 5 steps: raw data collection, lexicon development, data preprocessing, feature extraction and sentiment classification. Lexicon development phase parses the messages and finds out emoticons like "☺,:P,☹, : > , …", Interjections like "wow, oh dear, Thank you…" and Acronyms like "LOL, GR8…". To evaluate the performance of sentiment classification, they used following formulas: The accuracy (1), the precision (2), the recall (3) and the F-measure (4).

$$Accuracy = \frac{(a+d)}{(a+b+c+d)} \tag{1}$$

$$Precision = \frac{a}{(a+d)} \tag{2}$$

$$Recall = \frac{a}{(a+c)} \tag{3}$$

$$F - measure = \frac{(2 * Precision * Recall)}{(Precision + Recall)} \qquad (4)$$

Where:

- a: the number of statuses correctly assigned to this class.
- b: the number of statuses incorrectly assigned to this class.
- c: the number of statuses incorrectly rejected to this class.
- d: the number of statuses correctly rejected to this class.

Negative content depresses the user while positive content makes him happy. DMS for message content can be calculated with below formula.

Message Variation Last Week = No. of negative messages in last week/Total no. of messages in last week. MessageVariationLast6Months = No. of negative messages in last 6 months/Total no. of messages in last 6 months.

Message Variation = MessageVariationLastWeek/MessageVariationLast6Months * 100.

Social activity: Similar to messages, system can find out whether social media content user posted or received is negative or positive. DMS for social media activity can be calculated with below formula.

SocialVariationLastWeek = No. of negative messages in last week/Total no. of messages in last week.

SocialVariationLast6Months = No. of negative messages in last 6 months/Total no. of messages in last 6 months.

SocialVariation = SocialVariationLastWeek/SocialVariationLast6Months * 100.

Images: There are many face detection algorithms which tells whether a person is feeling happy, sad, exited etc. For example Face.com – a face detection and recognition service will analyze the images and tells whether person is Happy, Sad, Surprised, Angry and Neutral. These services will be used for finding the emotional score of a user. DMS for image content can be calculated with below formula.

ImageVariation = No. of sad images/Total no. of images * 100. So DMS for mobile data will be (DMSforCall + DMSforMessages + DMSforSocialActivity + DMSforImages)/4.

Similarly, the score can be calculated for all the remaining 16 params in HAM-D and adding all the values will give us user's emotional score.

Apart from above mobile data, physical health data like sleep, Heartrate, Calorie intake, Calorie burnt, Blood glucose, Blood pressure, Stress will help in finding emotional score of the user.

2.3   Test Setup

Test bed shall consist of android phone running Android version 4.3 with an application build on android platform. Android phone is assumed to have aggregated data from all IoT devices and wearable devices. System is trained with 6 months of simulated data as in schema listed in Table 7. Table 8 represents actual simulated data used for building prototype. Figures 4 and 5 shows an individual data with severe depression. Score is calculated as explained in detail in Table 6. As shown in graph IoT data plays a key role in evaluation of depression data.

Table 7. Simulated data structure

Tables	Columns
Critical IoT alerts	Event: Event details Device: Device name from which event is generated Person: Name of the person this event is related to Validity: Validity of the event Time: Time when event is occurred Weight: Weightage given to the event
Contacts	Number: Number of contact Name: Contact name Favorite: Favorite or not
Call logs	Number: Number of the caller Name: Name of the caller Date: Date and time of the call Type: Incoming or outgoing Call duration: Call duration in mins
Messages	Number: Number of the sender/receiver Name: Name of the sender/receiver Subject: Message subject Content: Message content Date: Date and time of the message Type: Incoming or outgoing State: Whether message sentiment is +ve or -ve
Social activity	ID: Number of the sender/receiver Name: Name of the sender/receiver Subject: Message subject Content: Message content Date: Date and time of the message Type: Incoming or outgoing State: Whether message sentiment is +ve or -ve
Images	Path: Image path in mobile CreateTime: Image creation time UpdateTime: Image updation time Tags: Names of the persons present in image State: Whether user is happy or sad

3 Evaluations

Emotional score can vary from 0–53 based on Hamilton scale of depression. Based on this score, system can tell whether person is mildly depressed or moderately depressed or severely depressed or very severely depressed. System updates emotional score when user experiences any aggressive behaviour during call, when his face has

Table 8. Simulated data

Device data	Last 6 months avg.	Last week avg.
Call duration in mins	118.87	50.53
Positive message count	8.75	2.8
Negative message count	1.8	3.64
Positive social media count	67.74	20.8
Negative social media count	17.2	35.6
Calorie intake in kcal	1923	1042
Calorie burnt in kcal	458	156
Sleep duration in hrs.	8.25	4.1
Weight in kgs.	72	66
Heart rate in bpm	74	88
Stress level from 1–10	3	7
Blood glucose before meals in mmol	5.1	5.1
Blood glucose after meals in mmol	7.2	7.2
Blood pressure in mmHg	130/90	145/98
Depression app usage duration in mins	0	30

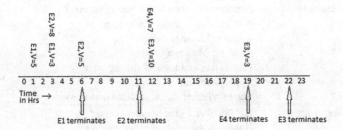

Fig. 4. Timeline for simulated events

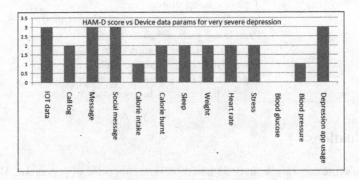

Fig. 5. Score for device data

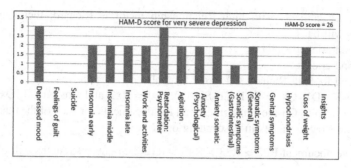

Fig. 6. Score for HAM-D params

depression feelings in the pictures taken, when he receives negative content through messages, when he posts depressed content in social media, when he searches negative content in internet. Similarly system improves emotional score when user experiences long smooth calls, when his face tells good feelings in the pictures taken, when he receives positive content through messages, when he posts happy content in social media, when he searches positive content in internet.

As per NIMH guidelines one can recover from depression by

"Try to be active and exercise. Go to a movie, a ballgame",

"Try to spend time with other people and confide in a trusted friend or relative. Try not to isolate yourself, and let others help you."

Based on user emotional state system recommends suitable activities to user. Like when user depression level is mild system recommends user to have good sleep and maintain proper food timings. When user is moderately depressed system recommends user to do regular exercises as this improves both physical and mental health. When user is severely depressed system recommends communication with relevant contacts as determined from his communication data. Recommended contacts could be a friend or a family member. When user is very severely depressed system will alert his friends/family about user so that they can give proper advice.

Based on user current depression score appropriate actions are recommended to the user which will help him to recover from his depression state. User interests are mined using Vector Space Model (VSM) [6]. VSM calculates term frequency (tf) and inverse document frequency (idf) for all the communication data (SMS, IoT Rules and Alerts, SNS posts) stored in document format. Query on system computes cosine similarity value for each of the document. Query contains all the combinations of favorite contacts with high relationship factor, all the games, and synonyms of enjoy, like, good, etc. Synonyms are identified by word net search [7]. After finding cosine similarity value for each of the document for all the queries, system will identify queries which have more cosine similarity value and suggest that activity to the user with that person (if person exists in that query).

Ex: Below are the messages posted by user

D1: After a long time our team played good cricket.

D2: Today's cricket was very good.

D3: Played football with Richard.

If suppose contacts with high Relationship factor is Richard, then our sample queries will be

Q1: good cricket Richard

Q2: good cricket

Q3: good football Richard Q4: good football

Let $CosSin(D1, Qx) = Rx1$, $CosSin(D2, Qx) = Rx2$ and $CosSin(D3, Qx) = Rx3$. [Table 9] shows Cosine similarity for all the documents for each of the query sorted based on CosSin values in descending order

In above document $R22 > R33 > R43 > R12$ then query strengths will $q2 > q3 > q4 > q1$.

Table 9. Cosine similarity values for queries

Query	CosSin value	Query	CosSin value	Query	CosSin value	Query	CosSin value
Q1	R12	Q2	R22	Q3	R33	Q4	R43
Q1	R13	Q2	R21	Q3	R32	Q4	R42
Q1	R11	Q2	R23	Q3	R31	Q4	R41

So, possible recommended IoT Actions could be "play cricket" or "play football with Richard".

Table 10 shows set of possible recommended IoT Actions based on user interest analysis.

Table 10. Recommended IoT actions

Recommended activities based on user's depression
Listening to music
Watching movie with A
Watching good TV shows
Showing good past moments from mobile images/videos
Suggesting to take a walk outside with B
Playing game X with C
Playing indoor sport Y with D
Suggesting to have good sleep
Suggesting to have good food habits
Doing meditation
Practicing yoga or exercise
Suggesting to read books
Suggesting gardening
Suggesting to take a short trip with group F
Take out the dog for 30 min with G
Using mobile apps
Speaking with friend H/family I
Suggesting to consult doctor

A, B, C... are user's friends/family who has done these activities or with whom user's social relationship is good. During severe depression, system will suggest very close person to the user to speak where in mild depression, system will suggest a person who is moderately close. This closeness factor can be calculated as below.

For Severe depression, system will suggest favorite contacts with higher relationship strength factor Table 11. Contacts could be family or friends. For Very Severe depression, along with suggesting contacts with higher relationship strength factor with their location, system will suggest doctors to consult and alert family members about user's emotional state.

Table 11. Favorite contacts with their relationship strength factor

Contacts	Relationship	Call duration	Message count	Social activity messages	Social activity score	Relationship strength factor
C1	Family	1739	142	1235	17.31	0.086
C2	Family	1423	104	1563	17.16	0.085
C3	Friend	1780	150	1823	20.85	0.104
C4	Friend	1041	62	963	11.47	0.057
C5	Friend	1081	89	853	11.23	0.056
C6	Others	222	21	163	2.25	0.011

3.1 Experiments

A survey was conducted on 663 random people with the age group of 20 to 45 to validate the claim as listed in Sect. 3. Set of questions were prepared to collect users' feedback. Questionnaire consists of finding user preferred mode of sharing emotions, happiness levels, sleep disturbances and user activities to recover from depression levels. Out of 663, 363 participants responded that they would talk to their friends or family members when they are depressed. In the survey taken, out of 663 participants 109 participants were Happy, 277 participants were Satisfactory and 277 participants were disappointed about their life.

Figure 6 shows survey results for participants who are not happy in their life and who are happy in their life. Figure 6(a), (c), (e) indicates 73 % of people who face high sleep disturbances, 58 % of people who never do exercise and 50 % of people who prefer not to share their emotions are unhappy in the life. Figure 6(b), (d), (f) indicates 57 % of people who are happy in their life have no sleep disturbances, 55 % people who are happy in the life do regular exercise and 72 % of people who are happy in the life speak with friends/family regularly. Survey results were indicative that good sleep, Regular exercise and speaking with friends/family keeps the participants happy. This data substantiates the claims made in the proposed system those recommendations actions as listed in Table 10 can create a positive effect on users negative emotional state.

HAM-D score is derived with inputs from survey data. Data associated with sleep, exercise data and communication patterns was extrapolated to determine score. Accuracy achieved was 55 %.

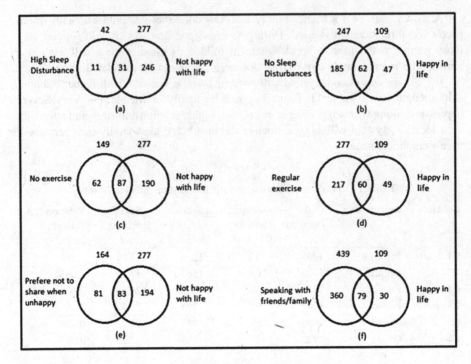

Fig. 7. Survey results

4 Conclusion

This paper analyzes the users' data from various IoT devices, evaluates the person's depression state and suggests actions then helps recover from early stages of depression. As lot of health and home automation devices get connected over IoT Networks and users' engagement on this devices increases, system can apply the above method to develop a user emotional and depression profile. Proposed method after learning about user social interactions determines the set of key emotional contacts and associated actions. We also look forward for doing further research on IoT data on cloud networks to infer more appropriate IoT Actions that can heal people suffering from mental health problems and help them lead better and happy life.

References

1. http://www.healthline.com/health/depression/statistics-infographic, pp. 68–73
2. https://en.wikipedia.org/wiki/Suicide_in_the_United_States
3. Baldonado, M., Chang, C.-C.K., Gravano, L., Paepcke, A.: The Stanford Digital Library Metadata Architecture. Int. J. Digit. Libr. **1**, 108–121 (1997)
4. Social Networks' Text Mining for Sentiment Classification: The case of Facebook' statuses updates in the "Arabic Spring" Era

5. https://en.wikipedia.org/wiki/Hamilton_Rating_Scale_for_Depression
6. https://en.wikipedia.org/wiki/Vector_space_model
7. http://www.nimh.nih.gov/health/publications/depression/index.shtml?rf=3247
8. http://sensiotec.com/
9. http://www.imedicalapps.com/2011/10/wearable-sensor-by-affectiva-can-measure-anxiety-and-is-helping-autism-research/

SMARTA: Smart Ambiente and Wearable Home Monitoring for Elderly

Paolo Perego[1](✉), Marco Tarabini[2], Marco Bocciolone[2],
and Giuseppe Andreoni[1]

[1] Design Department, Politecnico di Milano, 20158 Milano, Italy
`paolo.perego@polimi.it`
[2] Mechanical Engineer Department, Politecnico di Milano, 23900 Lecco, Italy

Abstract. The last two decades show that population is continuously and gradually aging; in Italy, the percentage of over-sixties has increased since 1980 by more than 50 % while the over-eighties by more than 150 %. Aging causes a consequent psycho-physical decline which in many cases requires specific care and precautions by relatives. However, as can be easily inferable from the percentage of elderly just shown, today the national health-care systems are not able to manage and take charge of all these elders. More and more seniors are choosing to live alone, with all the problems related to emergencies and urgencies cases that can occur due to poor health status related to aging (falls, cardiovascular events, neurological events). In this case, providing health-care initiates to have its new challenges. One of the worst possible case of emergency in elderly living alone is bad injury within the home without the possibility for seeking a help. This paper presents a work related to this issue; project SMARTA, focused on biomedical and environmental monitoring for the active aging. The project is based on the use of biomedical sensors and sensorized garments for health status and cardio-monitoring, and accelerometers fixed on the floor for activity and fall detection. All this sensors are integrated in a system that is used for monitoring elderly both indoor and outdoor during their daily life thanks also to the connection over the Internet.

Keywords: Home monitoring · Fall detection · Wearable device · Accelerometers · Elderly · Active aging

1 Introduction

Data from the Eurostat estimations [1] shows that European population is constantly and progressively aging due particularly to low birth rates, ageing "baby-boomers" and rising life expectancy [2]:

- between 2010 and 2060, the number of people over 65 will grow from 17.4 % to 29.5 % of the total population. The number of people over 80 will nearly triple to 12 %;

© ICST Institute for Computer Sciences, Social Informatics and Telecommunications Engineering 2016
B. Mandler et al. (Eds.) IoT 360° 2015, Part I, LNICST 169, pp. 502–507, 2016.
DOI: 10.1007/978-3-319-47063-4_54

- during the same time, the working age population in the EU is expected to decline by 14.2 %.

Pensions, health care and long-term care systems risk becoming unsustainable, with a shrinking labour force no longer able to provide for the needs of the growing number of older people. This aging population bring to an increase of request for medical care and hospitalization which bring the cost for the National Health-care System to grow; in 2006 the average hospitalization cost for one day amount to 674€ [3]. With this trend in population aging and health-care system cost rising, a new approach for the care of elderly people is mandatory in order to avoid a collapse of the National Health-care System. For these reason many countries are trying to find alternatives and strategies based on early de-hospitalization, tele-medicine and home-care services In this frame, assistive technology represents one of the best choice which allows for taking the cure, and especially the prevention, to the home of the patient. In fact prevention is the main strategy to be pursued in different disease at various age. It fits particularly with the concept of "active aging" that the European Union is promoting as a means of controlling health care costs and increase the quality of life [4]. Moreover active aging allows for reducing the risk of bad events like fall which in many case cause very serious consequences; among the elderly hospitalized after a fall, only half survive more than a year, while the multiple drops and instability precipitated admission to nursing home [5]. Project SMARTA has the aim to develop an integrated system which completes personal signals and data with environmental variables, thanks to wearable sensors and environmental sensors, for the fulfillment of a service/system which allows for:

- Monitoring vital signs and lifestyle (e.g. daily number of steps, sedentary, minutes of walk, heart-rate, glycemia, weight);
- Monitoring the rehabilitation process (e.g. monitoring of exercise);
- Detecting safety problem (e.g. falls and stumble detections).

On this way, the elderly alone at home is constantly monitored both from the physiological and environmental point of view. This monitoring gives the possibility to elderly to live a safer and active life, and to the caregivers (relatives and/or medical staff) to be able to intervene promptly in case of need, even if the senior is unable to ask for help.

2   SMARTA Project

The SMARTA system has an architecture composed by three main parts:

- The biomedical monitoring subsystem;
- The accelerometer based environmental subsystem;
- The hub for collecting, processing and visualizing data.

Figure 1 shows the main components of the system architecture with their relative puroposes and features.

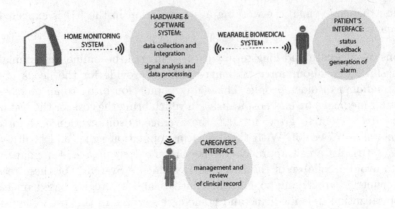

Fig. 1. Description of the SMARTA system.

2.1   Biomedical Monitoring System

The biomedical monitoring system is composed by different sensors for different measurement which data are aggregated by means of the hub. The sensors can be divided into two typologies: wearable sensors and non-wearable sensors. The wearable sensors are:Pulse oxymeter, Sensorized garment for ECG, Fall sensor. The pulse oxymeter is a commercial one which is able to transmit the spot acquire data to the hub wireless. The sensorized garment is composed by a belt with three textile electrodes. This kind of electrodes need neither for conductive gel nor adhesive: for this reason they are very useful for application with elders because they don't affect the skin or cause discomfort. The three electrodes allows for acquiring single lead ECG (Einthoven Lead I). The signal is acquired by a small device, shown in Fig. 2 at a sample frequency FS = 512 Hz with 24bit. The raw signal and the data processed can be stored in an internal flash memory or streamed trough Bluetooth connection. The same device has also a three axes accelerometer which is used for wearable fall detection. In this way the elderly is continuously monitored both in the house and outside. Figure 2 shows the three sensorized belts developed. The belts differ only for the material they are built; these belts are used in order to study both the quality of the signal both the comfort based on the material. Figure 2 reports the quality of the ECG signal recorder with the same electronics in the same condition; the first belt report a smaller signal then the second and the third (0.2 mV respect respectively to 0.5 mV and 0.6 mV); but quality is almost the same and allows for correctly processing the signal to extract the heart-rate [6]. The non-wearable sensors are instead commercial device like smart scales, gluco-meter, etc. that can be connected to the hub via Bluetooth connection in order to record all the data in the same database. The integration of this sensors is thought to be scalable; the subject can use one, two o no sensors according to his/her requirements.

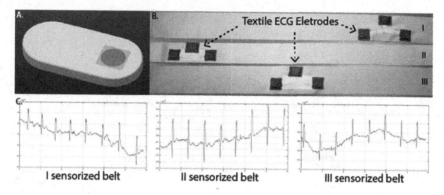

Fig. 2. The wearable system: A. The wearable device developed for the project; B. The three sensorized belts; C. The three ECG signals recorded using each belt.

2.2   Enviromental Monitoring System

The environmental monitoring system supports the biomedical monitoring system in the detection of ADL (Activities of daily living) also when the wearable devices are not used. The main idea of the environmental monitoring system is to use different vibration sensors located on the ground and to identify the type of activity starting from the vibration signals. At the current state of the art [7], there are different issues preventing the detection of ADL and elders fall from vibration signals: the first related to the force generated by subjects fall, which has only been studied by simulating falls of healthy subjects. The fall of elder people is expected to be very different, owing to their limited muscular force and to their reduced mental alertness. The second derives from the transmissibility of vibration trough the different kinds of residential floors, which has never been studied in the literature; since the position of the event (activity or fall) is unknown, the measured signal strongly depends not only on the activity but also on the floor mechanical characteristics. Finally, it is necessary to reduce the amount of information deriving from the vibration signal by using classifiers capable of distinguishing between ADL, falls and other possible events. We assume the floor response to vibration is linear in order to predict the vibration at any measurement position by characterizing separately the vibration transmissibility and the force generated by ADL and falls. The proposed approach is summarized in Fig. 3.

The ground vibration transmissibility has been experimentally identified in more than 30 rooms of residential buildings. Results showed that the transmissibility is averagely lower than one and depends on the ground covering (parquet/tiles) and on the room geometrical characteristics. The time history of the force generated by falls of subjects and of a crash test dummy has been characterized on a force platform. The acceleration of different points of the platform has been measured as well.

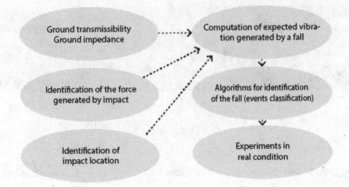

Fig. 3. Summarized proposed project protocol for the environmental subsystem.

2.3   The Hub

The hub is composed by two parts: the smart-phone and the server. The smart-phone has a triple purpose, the collection of the data from Bluetooth devices (like the wearable garment, the smart scale, etc.), the transmission of the data to the central server (Fig. 1) and the generation of alarm, the visualization of the state of health for the elderly users. The server gathers all the data, process it and eventually transmit the alarm directly to the elderly and to the care-givers. Both the smart-phone and the server are connected over the Internet; this approach allows to keep the connection with the care-givers always on. All the collected data are transmitted to the server which stores them in order to create an historical. The history an all the generated alarm can be visualized online by the care-givers.

3   Conclusion

The technical tests to match textile sensors (belt) and wearable device were successful. Subjects wore the three belts in a random order and without gel on the sensors. ECG tracks were clearly detected and waveform preserved (2). The HR computation as requested by clinicians was available for most of the time and comparable to previous literature findings [6]. The belts have different elasticity and transpiration characteristics but same textile sensors. The preliminary wearability judgements on short duration test were comparable. A light preference for the belt III was expressed but this need to have confirmation with 1-week test in the clinical trial setting. To have immediate best results in terms of electrode-skin coupling, a second test was carried out by wetting the electrodes of the belt with few drops of water before wearing them. The noise on the ECG tracks reduced significantly as expected. This effect is usually produced by skin perspiration in few minutes after belt is worn by people. This effect will be evaluated during the next long term test in the future clinical trial.

Technical in-lab test for the environmental subsystem evidenced that the peak force ranges between 2 and 10 times the static weight of the subject; this could be useful for discriminating between falls and normal activities. Preliminary tests outlined that the difference between the measured acceleration and the acceleration predicted using the fall force and the platform impedance is averagely lower than 20 %. Furthermore, the simultaneous usage of three or more accelerometers allow locating the position of the subject, allowing a more robust identification of the type of the event.

Even this sub-system, and the integration with the hub/server and the usability test with elderly users during different scenarios (nursing home, rehab center), will be evaluated during the next clinical trial.

Acknowledgment. Authors thanks in particular all partners of the project (www.smarta-project.it): DATAMED S.r.l., FLEXTRONICS DESIGN S.r.l., ARGONET S.r.l., SOFTWARE TEAM S.r.l., EELECTRON, Fondazione Don Carlo Gnocchi Onlus, UNIMI Dipartimento di Informatica, CoDeBri. This research has been supported by Lombardy Region in the frame cluster of research for Smart Cities and Communities.

References

1. Report on demography, In 2012, for every person aged 65 or older, there were 4 people of working age in the EU27. Eurostat (2013)
2. Marsili, M., Sorvillo, M.P.: Previsioni della popolazione residente per sesso, eta e regione dal 1.1.2001 al 1.1.205. Istituto Nazionale di Statistica, ISTAT, Roma (2002)
3. European Commission. Directorate-General for Economic, Economic Policy Committee of the European Communities. The impact of aging on public expenditure: projections for the EU-25 Member States on pensions, healthcare, long-term care, education and unemployment transfers (2004–50). Office for Official Publications of the European Communities (2006)
4. European Innovation Partnership on Active and Healthy Ageing. http://ec.europa.eu/research/innovation-union/index_en.cfm?section=active-healthy-ageing
5. Da Silva Gama, Z.A., Gmez-Conesa, A.: Risk factors for falls in the elderly: systematic review. Rev. Sade Pblica. **42**(5), 946–956 (2008)
6. Andreoni, G., Fanelli, A., Witkowska, I., Perego, P., Fusca, M., Mazzola, M., Signorini, M.G.: Sensor validation for wearable monitoring system in ambulatory monitoring: application to textile electrodes. In: Proceedings of the 7th International Conference on Pervasive Computing Technologies for Healthcare. ICST (Institute for Computer Sciences, Social-Informatics and Telecommunications Engineering), pp. 169–175 (2013)
7. Alwan, M., Rajendran, P.J., Kell, S., Mack, D., Dalal, S., Wolfe, M., Felder, R.: A smart and passive floor-vibration based fall detector for elderly. In: 2nd Information and Communication Technologies, ICTTA 2006, vol. 1, pp. 1003–1007. IEEE (2006)

A Labview Based Ubiquitous Telehealth System for the Elderly

M.W. Raad$^{(\boxtimes)}$ and Tarek Sheltami

King Fahd University of Petroleum and Minerals KFUPM,
Box # 1874, Dhahran 31261, Saudi Arabia
raad@kfupm.edu.sa

Abstract. Chronic diseases are becoming the world's leading causes of death and disability, and are predicted to account for almost three quarters of all deaths by 2020. A Graphical User Interface (GUI) based telemedical system has been developed using LabView instrumentation software for real time analysis of vital signs captured for elderly patients suffering from Arrhythmia. The developed system includes a suit of signal processing algorithms for the detection of severe cases of Arrhythmias in elderly patients. In particular, we used time frequency distributions and wavelets to estimate a number of features from ECG traces which are then used in classification. The performance of the system was tested on simulated data and the real data from MIT, and our own collected data with very satisfactory results. A questionnaire was conducted with physicians and health practitioners to study the feasibility of implementing a Tele-health system at the KFUPM Medical Center.

Keywords: Telehealth · Ubiquitous · Electrocardiogram · Arrhythmia

1 Introduction

The world's population is aging. In Japan, for example, a quarter of the population will soon be older than 65 years. As we age, the incidence and prevalence of chronic illness continue to rise. Chronic diseases are becoming the world's leading causes of death and disability, and will account for almost three-fourth of all deaths by 2020. Demographic trends indicate rapidly aging population throughout the world, particularly in Europe. In many societies the proportion of elderly population larger than 60 by 2050 is expected to double from 11 %–22 %. [1]. This is one reason why expenditure on healthcare is skewed: in most healthcare delivery systems, 5 % of patients are responsible for 50 % of costs. These patients are at the heart of crisis in healthcare costs that is beginning to occupy the policy discussions of most governments in the industrialized world. Telehealth clearly has a role in the case of emergencies in remote environments such as the Antarctic and in ships or aeroplanes, where it may be difficult, if not impossible, to get medical care to the patient in time. On the other side, home telehealth as a definition is intended to indicate the use of telehealth techniques in a non-institutional setting at home, or in an assisted-living facility. Physiological monitoring leads to richer data and therefore to improved decision making. Giving patients access to their own physiological data leads to improved self-care. In some

© ICST Institute for Computer Sciences, Social Informatics and Telecommunications Engineering 2016
B. Mandler et al. (Eds.) IoT 360° 2015, Part I, LNICST 169, pp. 508–516, 2016.
DOI: 10.1007/978-3-319-47063-4_55

cases, patients are so enthusiastic that they purchase the equipment with their own money. The use of home telehealth thus allows patients to be monitored at home, nurses to visit in person less often and better management of chronic disease [2, 3].

ECGs are a well-established and widely accepted method for monitoring the electrical activity of the heart. Numerous ECG monitoring devices have been developed and marketed for the sports industry. Athletes needs have been targeted so that they can be monitored under conditions that are physically stressful. Ambulatory elder patients have significantly different needs.

One of the first prototypes for monitoring arrhythmia is the arrhythmia monitoring system (AMS), which is a wireless telemetry system developed at NASA. Next generation cardiac monitoring systems makes available continuous monitoring to patients whenever necessary. It consists of wearable wireless biomedical sensors (for measuring 3 lead ECG, spo2, heartbeat, and blood pressure) which constantly communicate to the monitor, a unit about the size of a mobile phone or PDA. The monitor is battery powered and equipped with signal processing/conditioning module, memory, and different wireless interfaces and radios [4].

The implications of wearable health monitoring technologies are paramount, since they could: (1) enable the detection of early signs of health problems; (2) notify healthcare providers in critical situations; (3) find correlations between lifestyle and health; (4) bring healthcare to remote locations and developing countries, and help doctors and researchers with accessing multi-sourced real-time physiological data [5]. With the advent of advanced telecommunication technology, long-term home care of the elderly or what we call telehealth is becoming a rapidly growing area of healthcare industry. Lately, many researchers have begun investing their time into the research of wireless telehealth systems. Proponents of wireless systems claim that the increased mobility and the lower cost of the systems are highly beneficial to telehealth. Mobility and lower cost healthcare solutions are benefits of new telecommunications technologies [6]. Telehealth has the potential of improving the quality of delivered health services and reducing total healthcare costs by avoiding unnecessary hospitalisations and ensuring the fast delivery of healthcare. In addition to cost-effective telehealth, remote health monitoring can significantly contribute to the enhancement of disease prevention, early diagnosis, disease management, treatment and home rehabilitation [7, 8]. Furthermore, a number of researchers have investigated the feasibility and success factors of implementing telehealth and its cost effectiveness in delivering healthcare including the financial relevance and patient satisfaction [9].

This paper is based on our previous published research for an integrated portable wireless ECG sensor used in home telehealth for monitoring the vital signs of Elderly, particularly the ECG for the purpose of arrhythmia early detection in KFUPM [10]. See Fig. 1. The current research focuses on simulation of ECG signals captured from elderly patients using Labview as well as using Wavelet transform approach for filtering data for patients to satisfy the vast need for the telehealth solution in Saudi Arabia. The paper is organized as follows. Section 2 describes the simulation of ECG using Labview. Section 3 presents the feasibility study of implementing Telehealth in KFUPM.

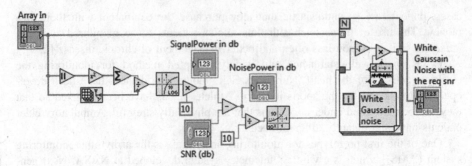

Fig. 1. White Gaussian Noise block diagram (Labview) with required SNR

2 Simulating the ECG Signal Using Labview

Prior to the capturing an actual ECG signal, National Instruments software Labview is used for the simulation and analysis of the ECG signal. For this purpose, Simulation ECG Labview palette is used as shown below. Using the simulate ECG signal, a lot of parameters could be controlled like the beats per minutes (bpm), P-QRS delay, QRS-T delay, amplitude of ECG, number of samples etc. Also, three different scenarios could be selected from Atrial Tachycardia, Hyperkalemia and normal ECG signal. To this simulated ECG, white Gaussian noise was added programmatically with a controlled signal to noise ratio. See Fig. 1.

2.1 Data Collection

ECG data is collected from the university community comprising of youth, middle-aged and elderly faculty and staff. These data are recorded as txt files with 2000 Hz sampling rate in the first phase and then using 250 Hz for rest of the data. In all, about sixty five ECG signals (fifty-five samples from students and ten samples from elderly faculty and staff) comprise our ECG signal databank. Few ECG data has also been taken from the university clinic in our databank for analysis.

2.2 Filtering the Signal

The next challenge faced during its implementation was the filtering of the signal for extracting the characteristics of signals. As seen from the above sample, the recorded ECG is often contaminated by noise. So we need to preprocess the signal to remove this inherent noise. Contamination of ECG signal can come from the following sources:

- Power-line interference
- Baseline wandering
- Contact noise
- Patient-electrode motion
- Electromyographic noise

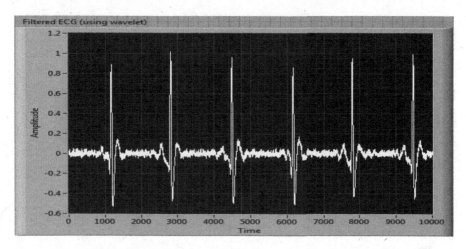

Fig. 2. ECG waveform filtered using the wavelet approach

The first two being the most common type of contaminations that can strongly affect the ECG signal.

In our case we try to minimize the baseline wandering of the ECG signal. Following are the two methods used to remove the baseline wandering. Baseline wandering usually comes from respiration at frequencies wandering between 0.15 and 0.3 Hz and we can use high pass digital filter or we can use the wavelet transform by eliminating the trend of the ECG signal.

Wavelet Transform Approach.

Another effective approach learned from literature is using the wavelet transform approach as follows. Using the Labview ASPT (Advanced Signal processing Toolkit), WA detrend VI, the low frequency trend of the signal can be removed. We use daubechies6 (db06) wavelet which is similar the real ECG signal for removing the trend using the following formula for establishing the trend level. Figure 2 shows the implementation of wavelet transform approach and its result. When we compare the output, we see that the trend or the baseline wandering has been removed and has retained most of the characteristics of the original signal. This approach is much better when compared to the digital filter approach.

Then the next step is to remove other type of noise so that the features extraction of the ECG signal is possible. To remove these wideband noises, wavelet denoise express VI is used as follows.

This express VI first decomposes the EC signal into several subbands by applying the wavelet transform, and then modifies each wavelet coefficient by applying a threshold or shrinkage function, and finally reconstructs the denoised signal. Figure 3 shows an example of applying the undecimated wavelet transform (UWT) to the ECG signal.

The UWT has a better balance between smoothness and accuracy than the discrete wavelet transform (DWT). By comparing the denoised ECG signal with the non-denoised ECG signal, we find that the wideband noises are strongly suppressed while almost all the details of the ECG signal are kept invariant.

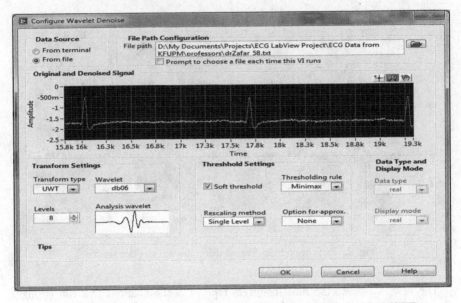

Fig. 3. ECG waveform denoised using undecimated wavelet transform (UWT)

3 ECG Peak Detection

The procedure is that we first identify the peaks and valleys within the ECG signal and then identify these peaks and valleys as R, P, T, Q and S points within our plot. Then other feature extraction is done. For the QRS duration the difference in the values of the S point and Q point gives us the no of samples and dividing them by the no of samples gives is the duration. For the P and T duration, few samples are collected around the P and Q duration and a second order polyfit analysis is done to extract the duration of the P and T waves. For obtaining the heart rate in bpm, the R-R duration is extracted and divided by the sampling rate to give us the value. See Figs. 4 and 5.

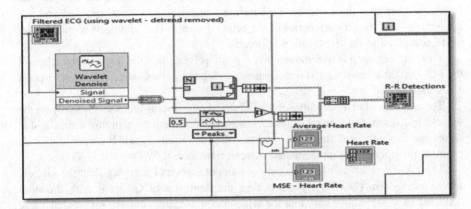

Fig. 4. ECG R-R peak detection Labview block diagram

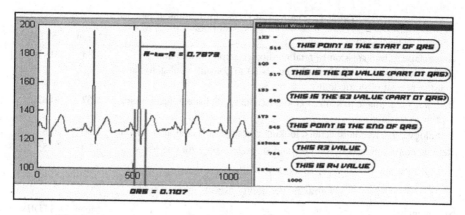

Fig. 5. A sample shows both QRS and R-to-R intervals with their values

4 Feasibility of Implementing Telehealth at the KFUPM Medical Centre

Conducting a careful planning and readiness study is critical before developing and implementing a telehealth system. A questionnaire survey on a likert scale of '1' to '5', where '1' represents least important and '5' represents most important, was used to collect the data and descriptive analysis was performed. The questionnaire raises many vital issues that were identified. The purpose of the study is to investigate the feasibility of implementing telehealth in the KFUPM medical centre and the readiness of the physicians to use telehealth. The questionnaire was developed in collaboration with a cardiologist working at the KFUPM medical centre. The questionnaire was distributed to 17 physicians working at the KFUPM medical centre. To examine respondent's specific view on the evaluation of telehealth feasibility, a detailed item list is presented to them on various issues of implementing telehealth at the medical centre. Regarding the feasibility of implementing telehealth in clinical practice, the results show that the transmission of foetal cardiotograph information to consultant is the most important mean (4.83), followed by radiology transmission to a remote specialist e.g. head injury prior to transfer mean (4.67), pathology e.g. a remote specialist looking at a slide on a computer screen mean (4.5), remote consultation and routine remote consultation between GPs and specialists on a routine basis mean (4.5). See Table 1. There are a few components that contribute to efficient implementation of telehealth that were inves-tigated in the research. The list of items is presented in Table 2, together with the analysis of importance level. Regarding the impact of travelling and distance problems on telehealth, the majority of physicians agreed that telehealth is critical for disabled patients and patients in remote areas of the country with a mean of (4.67) and 4.33) respectively. Regarding the readiness of the medical centre physicians to implement telehealth the majority agreed that telehealth would increase the number of patients in his/her practice with a mean (4.67). The study also showed that most of them were ready to adopt new technology with a mean of (4.83). Regarding the role of telehealth in follow-up care it took the highest score mean (5.5), followed by applying telehealth

Table 1. The role of telehealth in clinical practice

Type of medical care	Mean	STDEV
Antenatal e.g. transmission of fetal cardiotocograph information (obtained by midwives doing home visits) to consultant obstetricians at the nearest obstetric unit	4.83	0.41
Radiology e.g. image transmission to a remote specialist e.g. head injury prior to transfer	4.67	0.82
Pathology e.g. a remote specialist looking at a slide on a computer screen	4.50	0.84
Remote consultation between GPs and specialists on a routine basis	4.50	0.55

Table 2. Feasibility aspects in Telehealth

Statement	Mean	STDEV
The need to attend lectures/courses in Telehealth if they were offered	5.00	0.00
Readiness to adopt promising new technologies	4.83	0.41
The readiness to use telehealth for the following applications:		
a- Initial office visits	3.33	1.63
b- Follow-up care	4.50	0.84
Patients are likely to receive better quality care when they see the specialist in person	4.67	0.82
Plan to use telehealth in practice	4.67	0.52
Telehealth might be effective for the following types of care:		
a- Chronic condition management	4.67	0.52
b- Home health care	4.67	0.52
c- Preventive services	4.33	0.82
d- Emergency care	3.33	1.63
e- Acute non-emergency care	3.33	1.63
An adequate physical exam cannot be conducted without the patient being present physically	4.17	0.98
Telehealth combined with easy public access to health information and advice will make for a healthier population in the future	4.50	0.84
Use of Telehealth will blur the distinction between primary and secondary healthcare by improving the links between patients, nurses, GPs and consultants	4.00	0.89
Use of Telehealth could encourage more team working in healthcare	4.50	0.84
Use of Telehealth could make the distribution of healthcare more even with more emphasis on prevention	4.50	0.84

for initial office visits a mean of (3.33). Regarding the effect of telehealth on various types of healthcare, the study showed that the chronic condition management of patients and the home health care were among the most critical factors in determining the need for telehealth with a mean of (4.67), followed by preventive services a mean of (4.33), post surgical follow-up mean of (3.83), emergency care and acute none-mergency care both with mean of (3.33). Many of the physicians believed that telehealth combined with easy public access to health information and advice will make for a healthier population in the future in addition to encouraging more team working in healthcare with a mean of (4.5). Nevertheless, some of the physicians believed that an adequate physical exam cannot be conducted without the patient being present physically with a mean of (4.17). The study also showed that some physicians believe that more research has to be made on the effectiveness of telehealth before they can refer patients for teleconsultation with a mean of (3.50).

5 Conclusion

A graphical user interface (GUI) based telehealth system has been developed using Labview instrumentation software. The purpose of the developed system is real time analysis of the vital signs captured from elderly suffering from arrhythmia. The Matlab & Labview simulation results were used to validate the real data captured from volunteers using ECG sensors. The successful implementation and utilization of the wireless ECG system in the KFUPM clinic, has paved the way for establishing a ubiquitous mobile telehealth which proved to be a cost effective solution for patients suffering from severe arrhythmia. The deployed system provides a big hope for patients with chronic diseases and could therefore avoid catastrophic results in the future by providing immediate medical care in the field. The system will also open new opportunities for further research in the area of biomedical signal and image processing. The use of Telehealth will provide higher-quality service and increased efficiency to the practice of medicine. Emergency and critical response professionals can be given immediate access to a wealth of vital information, particularly for the elderly and disabled. It also becomes possible to observe and deliver care to patients while living in their homes, instead of spending months or even years in the hospital. As a result of the feasibility study conducted in KFUPM medical center, many of the physicians believed that telehealth combined with easy public access to health information and advice will make for a healthier population in the future in addition to encouraging more team working in healthcare with a mean of (4.5).

Acknowledgements. The authors would like to acknowledge the support of King Fahd University of Petroleum & Minerals for this research.

References

1. Bujnowska-Fedak, M.M., Grata Borkowska, U.: Use of telemedicine based care for the aging and elderly: promises and pitfalls. Smart Homecare Technol. Telehealth **3**, 91–105 (2015)
2. Wootton, R., Dimmick, S.L., Kvedar, J.C.: Home Telemedicine: Connecting Care Within the Community. Royal Society of Medicine Press Ltd., London (2006)
3. Wootton, R., Craig, J., Patterson, V.: Introduction to Telemedicine. Royal Society of Medicine Press, London (2006)

4. Kumar, S., Kambhatla, K., Hu, F., Lifson, M., Xiao, Y.: Ubiquitous computing for remote cardiac patient monitoring: a survey. Int. J. Telemed. Appl. **2008**, 1–19
5. Oliver, N., Mangas, F.F.: HealthGear: a real-time Wearable System for monitoring and analyzing physiological signals. Technical report MSR-TR-182 (2005)
6. Xiao, Y., Chen, H.: Mobile Telemedicine: A Computing and Networking Perspective. CRC Press, Boca Raton (2008)
7. http://www.suunto.com
8. http://www.bodymedia.com
9. Trobec, R., Stanic, U.: Telehealth: a myth or reality? In: MIPRO, 2011 Proceedings of 34th International Convention, Opatija, Croatia, pp. 295–300
10. Raad, M.W., et al.: A ubiquitous telehealth system for the elderly. In: 1st International Conference on IOT Technologies for Healthcare, 28–29 October 2014, Rome, Italy

Context-Aware Early Warning System for In-Home Healthcare Using Internet-of-Things

Arman Anzanpour[1]([✉]), Amir-Mohammad Rahmani[1,2], Pasi Liljeberg[1], and Hannu Tenhunen[1,2]

[1] Department of Information Technology, University of Turku, Turku, Finland
{armanz,amirah,pakrli}@utu.fi
[2] Department of Industrial and Medical Electronics,
KTH Royal Institute of Technology, Stockholm, Sweden
hannu@kth.se

Abstract. Early warning score (EWS) is a prediction method to notify caregivers at a hospital about the deterioration of a patient. Deterioration can be identified by detecting abnormalities in patient's vital signs several hours prior the condition of the patient gets life-threatening. In the existing EWS systems, monitoring of patient's vital signs and the determining the score is mostly performed in a paper and pen based way. Furthermore, currently it is done solely in a hospital environment. In this paper, we propose to import this system to patients' home to provide an automated platform which not only monitors patents' vital signs but also looks over his/her activities and the surrounding environment. Thanks to the Internet-of-Things technology, we present an intelligent early warning method to remotely monitor in-home patients and generate alerts in case of different medical emergencies or radical changes in condition of the patient. We also demonstrate an early warning score analysis system which continuously performs sensing, transferring, and recording vital signs, activity-related data, and environmental parameters.

Keywords: Early warning score · Internet-of-Things · e-Health · Remote patient monitoring

1 Introduction

Internet of Things (IoT), the world of connected devices, is expanding and hence soon it will step into every area of our life. The presence of this concept in the field of healthcare leads to a new communication channel between health professionals and patients. Several sensors can be attached to patient's body to form a wireless body area network (WBAN) to record medical parameters and patient's vital signs and transfer them by benefiting IoT to a cloud system via Internet [1].

It has been reported that the number of patients with critical illnesses are increasing every year [2] and the patients who leave the intensive care unit are

© ICST Institute for Computer Sciences, Social Informatics and Telecommunications Engineering 2016
B. Mandler et al. (Eds.) IoT 360° 2015, Part I, LNICST 169, pp. 517–522, 2016.
DOI: 10.1007/978-3-319-47063-4_56

still subjected to deterioration. There are some abnormalities in patient's vital signs several hours before deterioration happens. Based on this fact, an early warning score (EWS) system has been developed for early deterioration detection in hospitals. In this system, nurses record the vital signs of patient to find the abnormalities. EWS is often done in a paper-based fashion using manual procedures in hospitals which sometimes leads to misdiagnose or late warning. It is also slow and time consuming which tends hospitals towards using automated electronic early warning systems [3]. IoT-based solutions for remote patient monitoring bring an opportunity to extend the use of EWS beyond hospitals. EWS systems in hospitals monitor patients who are mostly located in a standard environment. However, there are several parameters that affect the value of vital signs outside the hospital (e.g., patient's activities, room temperature, barometric pressure) which should be considered to reach a more complete picture [4]. Moreover, the quality of the environment in which a patient is receiving care and remote monitoring services should be ensured to be almost the same as clinical standards.

In this paper, we propose and demonstrate a context-aware EWS system using a set of medical, activity, and environmental sensors to detect an in-home deterioration prior serious consequences. It reinforces our earlier EWS system presented in [5] with context-awareness features. Therefore, our main objective in this paper is to develop an intelligent and portable IoT-based early warning system considering all affecting parameters around the patient such as environmental and daily activity information.

2   Early Warning Score

Early Warning System is a set of instructions and algorithms for estimating the risk of health deterioration before it happens to reduce the complications or sudden hospitalization. It has designed based on the fact that patients often have signs of clinical deterioration up to 24 h before it happens [7]. In this system instruction and algorithms are based on a process called Early Warning Score (EWS) to assign a value, a score, representing patient medical status according to his/her vital signs. Table 1 shows a typical early warning score model.

The overall score of a patient, even if not be high-enough to trigger an alarm, affects to the treatment orders and recording intervals to be updated. The idea of

Table 1. A typical early warning score model [6]

Physiological parameters	3	2	1	0	1	2	3
Respiration rate (breaths per minute)	≤8		9-10	12-20		21-24	≥25
Oxygen saturation (%)	≤ 91	92-93	94-95	≥96			
Temperature (oC)	≤35.0		35.1-36.0	36.1-38.0	38.1-39.0	≥39.1	
Systolic BP (mmHg)	≤90	91-100	101-110	111-219			≥220
Heart rate (beats per minute)	≤40		41-50	51-90	91-110	111-130	≥131
Level of consciousness				A*			V,P or U*

early warning score was presented in 1997 [8]. Earlier versions of the score were simply calculated with five parameters: heart rate, blood pressure, respiration rate, body temperature, blood oxygen saturation and level of consciousness. Further enhancements led to a modified early warning system (MEWS), a standardized early warning system (SEWS), and national early warning system (NEWS). They were mostly different because of the number of medical parameters used in score calculation and the range limits for each parameter. Beside many benefits of using early warning system in hospital to save lives and reducing healthcare costs, there are also some reports regarding misdiagnosis and mistakes due to imprecise recorded data which force the hospitals to move towards electronic early warning solutions [3].

There are some solution commercially available for electronic early warning system in hospitals [9,10]. However, they are designed for in-hospital scenarios and do not provide remote in-home patient monitoring services. The novelty of our solution comes from the development of an IoT-based EWS method for in-home patients with the support of supplementary information such as patient activity and environmental information.

3   System Architecture

The architecture of our proposed IoT-based EWS system is shown in Fig. 1. The system consists of three layers.

At the first layer, there exist a network of sensors which record several types of signals. There are three groups of sensors at this layer: (i) medical sensors which are used to record the patient's vital signs such as heart rate, respiration rate, blood pressure, blood oxygen level and body temperature sensor, (ii) activity sensors which record the movement, sleep time, posture, daily step count and sudden falls, and (iii) environmental sensors which record parameters such as room temperature, light, and humidity. Most of the sensors at this layer are low resolution sensors, while there are also some high resolution sensors such as ECG (Electrocardiogram) and respiration rate sensors (Fig. 2).

The second layer consists of a gateway which collects data from several types and groups of sensors. The task of the gateway is to unify the received data and

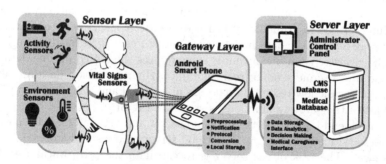

Fig. 1. Architecture of the proposed IoT-based clinical early warning system

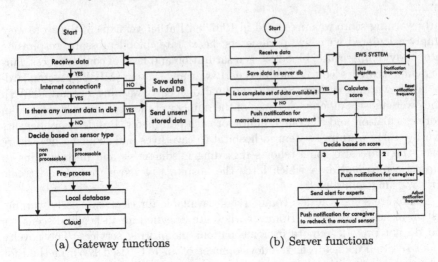

(a) Gateway functions   (b) Server functions

Fig. 2. EWS system flowcharts

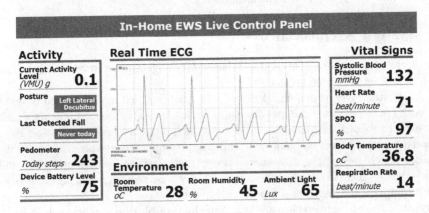

Fig. 3. Live control panel web interface

prepare them to be transferred to a cloud server using some protocol conversion, data compression, and offline storage. It can also handle the situation where there is no Internet access available. When the Internet connection is not available, the gateway records the data from sensors and stores it in its local database and when the gateway is on-line again, it synchronizes the stored off-line data with the cloud and resume sending real-time data. High resolution data are always sent directly while low resolution data are first stored and then sent as a packet. Flowchart of the gateway functions is shown in Fig. 3(a).

The back-end layer consists of a cloud server and user interface for patients, caregivers and medical experts. The cloud server receives and stores data from the gateway. The task of the server is to calculate the early warning score in specific intervals. The frequency of early warning score calculation depends on the patient's medical history and earlier scores. As there are also some manual measurements such as blood pressure and blood glucose, the server is also responsible for sending a notification to patients to enter the manually measured values to the system. The final calculated score shows the status of patient and if an abnormality is detected, the system decides to reconfigure the measurement frequency or fire an emergency alarm. Cloud server also provides an administering panel which provides access to real-time medical, activity, and environmental information of the patient for health professionals. The flowchart of the cloud server functions is shown in Fig. 3(b).

4   Demonstration and Evaluation

Our EWS system prototype consists of a set of sensors, gateway and cloud server. The main sensor for collecting the patient data is the Bioharness 3 [11] device which is a Bluetooth-based wearable chest strap sensor pack. We use this device to collect heart rate, respiration rate, body temperature, patient's activity, daily steps, and posture. A pulse oximeter fingertip grip is used to record the blood oxygen saturation. To measure the blood pressure, we use a Bluetooth-based upper arm blood pressure monitor (iHealth BP5) which can be controlled remotely through Bluetooth communication. Also a Texas Instruments' ADS1192 analog front end is used to read ECG signal. To gather context-related data, we use a DHT11 sensor which senses the temperature and humidity and a photocell to read the ambient light.

The collected data from all sensors are sent to the gateway and cloud server using both Bluetooth and Wi-Fi communication protocols. We send the output data of Bioharness 3 device together with the results of iHealth BP5 blood pressure monitor device via Bluetooth to an Android smart-phone that acts as a gateway. We develop an Android mobile application for patient's smart phone or tablet that operate as the gateway for data transmission between the sensor network and cloud server. It also alerts the patient or caregivers regarding the time for blood pressure measurement. Other low resolution sensors send data is sent directly to the cloud server using ESP8266 [12] Wi-Fi module. This module works originally with Attention (AT) commands, but we made a custom firmware for this module to enable continuous data reading from serial input and sending via Wi-Fi using UDP protocol. The high resolution ECG sensor uses RTX4140 which is a more powerful Wi-Fi module for data transmission with UDP protocol.

Currently our cloud server is a virtual private server with four 3.30 GHz Intel Xeon CPUs and 4 GB RAM. On this server, CentOS Linux runs a web server using Apache which is responsible for storing data in a MySQL database and the EWS score calculation using PHP. When all medical and environmental parameters are available in the database, an EWS algorithm on the server calculates the patient's warning score based on the thresholds of each parameter. Then, according to score results, the server sends notifications to an android device and the web control panel. The web server also provides the administration control panel to display real-time data and reports. There is a UDP server on this Linux machine operated with *Node.js* to receive data from sensors and the Android gateway. The *Node.js* server also sends real-time data to browsers using WebSocket. Our in-home EWS live control panel is shown in Fig. 3. The user interface is divided into four parts: it streams the real-time ECG signal in the middle, patient's vital signs in the right sidebar, patient activity in the left sidebar, and environment properties in the footer section. The data reported in the Fig. 3 was captured from a 34 years old healthy male volunteer during walking, sitting and lying on the left side.

5   Conclusions and Future Work

In this paper, we presented a context-aware Early Warning Score (EWS) system using an IoT-based solution. We showed the feasibility of implementing an EWS method for in-home patients while monitoring the activity level of patients and environmental properties to ensure that patients are given care in a standard situation and the EWS scoring data is captured in a suitable condition. We demonstrated an IoT-based EWS system for collecting, transferring, and displaying patient's information including vital signs, activity level and environment attributes. The collected information is used to calculate the early warning score in an automated and realtime fashion. In the future, the aim is to make the system more intelligent and autonomic. In addition, we intend to integrate the body area sensors network in an all-in-one wearable device to be conveniently used by different patients. We plan to validate the system for different kind of illnesses to validate the EWS algorithm in a real field trial.

References

1. Istepanian, R.S.H., et al.: Internet of m-health Things "m-IoT". In: IET Seminar on Assisted Living, pp. 1–3 (2011)
2. Wu, S.-Y., et al.: Projection of Chronic Illness Prevalence and Cost Ination. RAND Health, Santa Monica (2000)
3. Zarabzadeh, A., et al.: Features of electronic early warning systems which impact clinical decision making. In: CBMS International Symposium, pp. 1–4 (2012)
4. Taylor, C.: Fundamentals of Nursing Art & Science of Nursing Care. LIPPIN-COTT, Philadelphia (2005)
5. Anzanpour, A., et al.: Internet of things enabled in-home health monitoring system using early warning score. In: MobiHealth 2015 (2015)
6. Georgaka, D., et al.: Early warning systems. Hosp. Chronicles **7**, 37–43 (2012)
7. McGaughey, J., et al.: Outreach and early warning systems (ews) for the prevention of intensive care admission and death of critically ill adult patients on general hospital wards. Cochrane Database Syst. Rev. **18**(3), CD005529 (2007)
8. Morgan, R.J.M., et al.: An early warning scoring system for detecting developing critical illness. Clin. Intensive Care **8**(2), 100 (1997)
9. Bellomo, R.: Austin Hospital, Melbourne, Australia. Well-implemented early warning scores can help rapid response teams in improving outcomes (2012)
10. Siemens Healthcare Diagnostics Inc. http://usa.healthcare.siemens.com
11. Zephyr Technology Corp. http://zephyranywhere.com
12. Espressif Systems. http://espressif.com/en/products/esp8266

On Evaluating Blood Pressure
Through Photoplethysmography

Giovanna Sannino[✉], Ivanoe De Falco, and Giuseppe De Pietro

ICAR-CNR, Via P. Castellino 111, 80131 Naples, Italy
{giovanna.sannino,ivanoe.defalco,giuseppe.depietro}@na.icar.cnr.it

Abstract. This paper investigates the hypothesis that a nonlinear relationship exists between photoplethysmography (PPG) and blood pressure (BP) values. Trueness of this hypothesis would imply that, instead of measuring a patient's BP in an invasive way, this could be indirectly measured by applying a wearable PPG sensor and by using the results of a regression analysis linking PPG and BP. Genetic Programming (GP) is well suited to find the relationship between PPG and BP, because it automatically evolves the structure of the most suitable explicit mathematical model for a regression task. In this paper, for the first time, some preliminary experiments on the use of GP to explicitly relate PPG and BP values have been performed. For both systolic and diastolic BP values, explicit nonlinear mathematical models have been achieved, involving an approximation error of less than 3 mmHg in both cases.

Keywords: Blood pressure · Wearable sensors · Photoplethysmography · Regression · Genetic programming

1 Introduction

Arterial blood pressure can be continuously measured in real time and with no patient's body cannulation by means of the continuous non-invasive arterial pressure (CNAP) method. This method shows the positive features of two clinical "gold standards": firstly, the Blood Pressure (BP) is continuously measured in real time as it takes place in the invasive arterial catheter system, and secondly it is non-invasive as it is the case for the standard procedure based on upper arm sphygmomanometer.

Currently a high demand exists for accurate and easy-to-use CNAP-systems. Because of this, there is an increasing focus on these devices. The development of efficient BP measurement instruments is facilitated by the use of small yet powerful microcomputers, and by that of digital signal processors as well. Small, cheap devices of this kind allow for an easy processing of complex and computationally intensive mathematical functions.

This paper hypothesizes the existence of a nonlinear relationship between PPG and BP values. Trueness of such a hypothesis would imply that, instead of measuring a patients BP in an invasive way, both systolic and diastolic BP

© ICST Institute for Computer Sciences, Social Informatics and Telecommunications Engineering 2016
B. Mandler et al. (Eds.) IoT 360° 2015, Part I, LNICST 169, pp. 523–529, 2016.
DOI: 10.1007/978-3-319-47063-4_57

values could be indirectly measured by applying a wearable wireless PPG sensor to patients finger and by making use of the results of a regression analysis linking PPG and BP values. Genetic Programming (GP) [1] is well suited to find the relationship between PPG and BP, because it automatically evolves the structure of the most suitable explicit mathematical model for a regression task.

An analysis of the related scientific literature shows that this is the first attempt to explicitly relate PPG and BP values through GP. Some papers exist in which the aim is the investigation of the relationship between the blood pressure and some other variables, for example [2–6]. Very recently, we proposed a noninvasive approach relying on the hypothesis of the existence of a nonlinear relationship between PPG and heart activity (and thus ECG and Heart Rate Variability -HRV- parameters), and BP [7]. GP was used to find this explicit relationship. Results were very promising, the approximation error on unseen data being slightly lower than 2 % for both BP values. With respect to that paper, the novelty in the current paper is that just one PPG sensor is used, aiming at improving non-invasiveness and ease of use.

2   The Study

To realize the mathematical model, a study has been conducted on a group of 11 healthy subjects, with a mean age of 34.18 years (range 28–54 years), enrolled in accordance with the following selection criteria, namely that they were:

- not suffering from any pathological cardiovascular conditions, neurological or psychiatric disorders or other severe diseases;
- not taking any medication at the time of the study;
- had not taken any caffeine or had not smoked any cigarette in the 2 h prior to the measurements.

During the study, a PPG signal was monitored using a wearable oximeter sensor, the NONIN 9560 onyx 2 Bluetooth finger pulse oximeter. The BP values were measured with a digital sphygmomanometer, the A&D Medical Upper Arm Blood Pressure Monitor UA-767PBT-Ci, with the left arm comfortably positioned on a horizontal surface and the cuff positioned at the level of the heart at about 2 cm from the inner side of the elbow.

The experiments were carried out in a quiet room, with dimmed lighting and a comfortable temperature of about 23 °C. During the study the volunteers were invited to sit in a comfortable position, without crossing their legs, for 5 consecutive minutes. During this phase, systolic and diastolic BP was recorded five times, with a 60 s interval, and the PPG was continuously recorded during these 5 min. The acquired PPG signal is processed using a Matlab script developed by us to automatically calculate the minimum and the maximum values from the PPG waveform, as shown in Fig. 1.

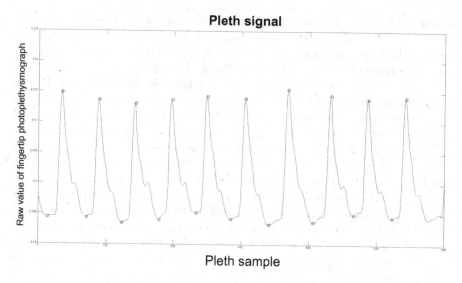

Fig. 1. An example of a record contains the PPG waveform: blue circles indicate the maximum PPG values, and red circles the minimum PPG values.

2.1 The Database

Our database contains the BP measurements and the PPG measurements. It is composed by 10 instances for each subject. Each instance i makes reference to 30 s, and is constituted by the following information:

- sub_id: a number value to identify the subject;
- $SBP(i)$: the Systolic BP value measured in the i-th 30-s time slot;
- $DBP(i)$: the Diastolic BP value measured in the i-th 30-s time slot;
- $Pl_M(i)$: the average of the maximum values of PPG signal computed in the i-th 30-s time slot;
- $Pl_m(i)$: the average of the minimum values of PPG signal computed in the i-th 30-s time slot;

Both systolic and diastolic BP values were recorded with a 60–s interval, due to inflation/deflation times of the sphygmomanometer cuff, whereas database items make reference to 30–s intervals. Therefore each recorded value is assigned to a pair of consecutive items.

In this paper we have enrolled 11 patients, six female and five male, so our database contains 110 instances in total.

3   Experiments

For the experiments described in this paper GPTIPS [8], a GP tool working under MATLAB, has been used. To create the regression functions, a set of 11 elementary functions has been considered, including the four arithmetical ones ($+$, $-$, $\cdot$, $/$), two trigonometric ones (sin, cos), hyperbolic tangent (tanh), the exponential (exp), the square value (sqr), the protected square root (psqroot) and the protected logarithm (plog) (see [7] for details).

The database has been divided into train, validation, and test sets. The train set contains the items onto which the approximation of the actual output values will be carried out in the learning phase. The generalization ability of the model achieved is, instead, evaluated on the validation set. Finally, the real evaluation of algorithms performance is carried out over the test set. For each patient, each item has been randomly and exclusively assigned to one of the three sets in this way: 44 % for the train set, 24 % for the validation set, and 32 % for the test set.

GP is a nondeterministic algorithm, which means that its execution and its results depend on the initial value assigned to a random seed. In order to get rid of this feature, the GP algorithm has been run over the database 25 times. Among the 25 runs, we consider as the best one that in which the lowest Root Mean Square Error (RMSE) value over the validation set has been achieved. In fact, the model found in that run shows the best ability to correctly get totally unknown data, so it has the highest generalization capability.

The formula achieved in the best run for the systolic blood pressure is:

$$
\begin{aligned}
SBP = {} & 21.75 \cdot sin(sin((12.79 \cdot Pl\_M)/Pl\_m)) \\
& - 12.52 \cdot sin((12.92 \cdot plog(tanh(Pl\_M)))/Pl\_m^2) \\
& - 5188.0 \cdot cos(-Pl\_M^2 + plog(Pl\_m) + plog(Pl\_m - 82.88)) \\
& - 4403.0 \cdot tanh(sin(cos(plog(Pl\_M)))) - 2201.0
\end{aligned}
$$

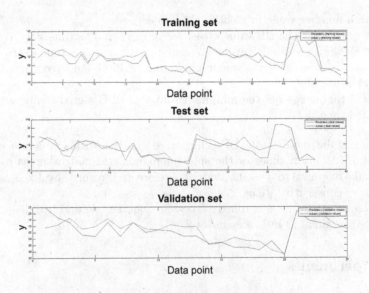

Fig. 2. Results for the systolic blood pressure.

Figure 2 reports how this formula allows fitting the real systolic BP values. The top pane shows the behaviour over the train set, the middle pane that over the test set, and the bottom pane that over the validation set.

The results over the test set, i.e. over data never learned by the GP algorithm, are very good, and the RMSE is 8.49. This means that, on average, over previously unseen data any actual systolic BP value and the corresponding computed one differ by $\pm\sqrt{8.49} = \pm 2.91$ mmHg, which is a good approximation.

The formula achieved in the best run for the diastolic blood pressure is:

$$DBP = 88.3 - 27.74 \cdot psqroot((Pl_m - sin(Pl_M))/sqr(sqr(Pl_m)))$$
$$- 5.97 \cdot plog(((Pl_m - sqr(Pl_M)) \cdot (Pl_m - Pl_M))/sqr(Pl_m))$$
$$- (196.4 \cdot (Pl_m - sin(Pl_M)) \cdot (sqr(Pl_m) + sqr(Pl_M))^2)/(Pl_M - sin(Pl_m))$$
$$- 127.7 \cdot psqroot(Pl_M + plog(Pl_m) + Pl_m \cdot Pl_M)$$

Figure 3 reports how this formula allows fitting the real diastolic BP values. The top pane describes the behaviour over the train set, the middle pane that over the test set, and the bottom pane refers to the validation set.

For the diastolic pressure the results over the test set, never learned by the GP algorithm, yield an RMSE value of 6.66. In this case the approximation of any actual diastolic blood pressure value with its corresponding computed value over previously unseen data is even better than that for the systolic case, since their difference is now equal to $\pm\sqrt{6.66} = \pm 2.58$ mmHg.

Summarizing the results from these preliminary experiments, PPG values are very important to indirectly estimate BP values.

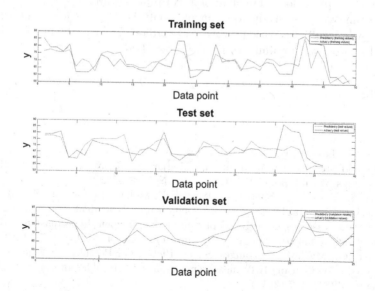

Fig. 3. Results for the diastolic blood pressure.

The comparison of these results against those achieved in our previous paper [7], in which both PPG and HRV values were used to evaluate blood pressure values, is very interesting. In fact, in that paper slightly lower RMSE values were achieved on both systolic and diastolic values, leading to approximations of ± 1.83 mmHg and ± 1.63 mmHg respectively. Nonetheless, to obtain those approximations we had to use one PPG sensor and one ECG sensor. Here instead, the approximations are a bit higher, i.e. ± 2.91 mmHg and ± 2.58 mmHg, but to obtain these approximate values we need just one PPG sensor. This makes the approach much easier, less invasive, and cheaper.

4   Conclusions and Future Work

This paper has tested the hypothesis that a nonlinear relationship exists between PPG and BP values. Genetic Programming (GP) is well suited to find the relationship between PPG and BP, because it automatically evolves the structure of the most suitable explicit mathematical model for a regression task.

Preliminary experiments on a real-world database have been performed. The numerical results achieved have confirmed that this non-linear relationship indeed exists, and GP has been able to find a mathematical model expressing it. This implies that, instead of measuring a patient's BP in an invasive way, both systolic and diastolic BP values could be indirectly measured by applying a wearable wireless PPG sensor to patient's finger and by making use of the results of a regression analysis linking PPG and BP values. For both systolic and diastolic cases this method involves an approximation error of less than 3 mmHg. Although this model could be difficult to understand for medical personnel who always seeks a physiological explanation, it results accurate.

Unfortunately, this study could involve only healthy subjects. As a future work we will enroll also patients with real cardiovascular problems, in order to test and improve the preliminary results shown here.

References

1. Koza, J.: Genetic Programming: On the Programming of Computers by Means of Natural Selection. MIT Press, Cambridge (1992)
2. Meigas, K., Lass, J., Karai, D., Kattai, R., Kaik, J.: Pulse wave velocity in continuous blood pressure measurements. In: Magjarevic, R., Nagel, J.H. (eds.) IFMBE Proceedings, vol. 14, pp. 626–629. Springer, New York (2007)
3. Najjar, S., Scuteri, A., Shetty, V., Wright, J., Muller, D., Fleg, J., Spurgeon, H., Ferrucci, L., Lakatta, E.: Pulse wave velocity is an independent predictor of the longitudinal increase in systolic blood pressure and of incident hypertension in the baltimore longitudinal study of aging. J. Am. Coll. Cardiol. **51**(14), 1377–1383 (2008)
4. Sannino, G., Melillo, P., Stranges, S., De Pietro, G., Pecchia, L.: Blood pressure drop prediction by using HRV measurements in orthostatic hypotension. J. Medical Systems. **39**(11), 1–7 (2015)

5. Inajima, T., Imai, Y., Shuzo, M., Lopez, G., Yanagimoto, S., Iijima, K., Morita, H., Nagai, R., Yahagi, N., Yamada, I.: Relation between blood pressure estimated by pulse wave velocity and directly measured arterial pressure. J. Robot. Mechatron. **24**(5), 811–821 (2012)
6. Gesche, H., Grosskurth, D., Kuechler, G., Patzak, A.: Continuous blood pressure measurement by using the pulse transit time: comparison to a cuff-based method. Eur. J. Appl. Physiol. **112**, 309–315 (2012)
7. Sannino, G., De Falco, I., De Pietro, G.: Non-invasive estimation of blood pressure through genetic programming: preliminary results. In: 8th International Conference on Biomedical Electronics and Devices, pp. 241–249. Scitepress (2015)
8. Searson, D.: GPTIPS: Genetic Programming and Symbolic Regression for MATLAB (2009). http://gptips.sourceforge.net

An Inhaler Dose Recording Service Designed for Patients Who Need Chronic Respiratory Disease Control

Shu-Hui Hung[1]([✉]), Hsin-Hung Lin[1], Chin-Shian Wong[1], Ian Kuo[2], and James Pang[2]

[1] National Applied Research Laboratories, NCHC, Taichung 40763, Taiwan
{bonitahung,jonathan,fed}@nchc.org.tw
[2] BalDr Strategic Consulting (Hong Kong) Ltd., Taiwan Branch, Taipei 115, Taiwan
{Ian.kuo,James.pang}@baldr-consulting.com

Abstract. The paper introduces a completely integrated and developed care cycle for patients with chronic respiratory disease who need to take inhaler drugs twice a day. Because patients may simply forget to take an inhaler dose or take the wrong inhaler medication. Inconsistent and mistaken inhaler medications may cause problems for diseases control. The system contains a main website for medical experts and caregivers to manage patients' health information from clinics. It also provides an off-site APP that allows patients to download the program to their mobile phones to monitor the inhaler dose they should be using. The APP connects to a smart inhaler device that has been patented in Taiwan. In this study, we implemented it as a cap for the metered dose in the medicine cylinder for the first experimental stage. We randomly selected 16 patients with asthma for the prototype face-to-face usage interview. Feedback from users was significantly positive.

1 Introduction

The World Health Organization (WHO) reports that the worldwide mortality rate from lower respiratory infections has rapidly increased [1]. During the past few years, we have used Internet Communication Technology (ICT) to create and deploy a few system platforms for pulmonary disease care management for asthma, chronic obstructive pulmonary disease (COPD), etc. [2–4].

Our experience with such systems indicates that physicians and caregivers are usually satisfied with the outcomes of using them; nevertheless, collecting historical data on medicine taken and inhaler doses missed is difficult. Inhalation medications often contain drugs that taking overdoses or under-doses of might jeopardize a patient's health, for example, steroid and bronchodilator components for asthma and COPD. In practice, many patients often do not precisely comply with physicians' recommendations. For example, patients might not regularly use prescribed medications, because they are afraid of the side effects, or they might simply forget. Additionally, our experimental experience tells us that at least 70 % of patients need follow-up education to ensure that they properly comply with their prescribed medical regimen. In other cases, some patients might not remember the last time they took the medication, and so they might unnecessarily repeat a dose.

© ICST Institute for Computer Sciences, Social Informatics and Telecommunications Engineering 2016
B. Mandler et al. (Eds.) IoT 360° 2015, Part I, LNICST 169, pp. 530–535, 2016.
DOI: 10.1007/978-3-319-47063-4_58

Other studies report that mistakenly using the wrong inhaler drug might cause a patient's condition to worsen. Approximately 4–9 % of patients who use inhalers do so incorrectly [5, 6]. Moreover, misusing metered doses might also unnecessarily increase medical expenses: "…this applies equally to metered dose inhalers and dry powder inhalers and leads to poor disease control and increased healthcare costs" [7].

At present, many inhaler medicines show the number of doses (baseline maximum and number of doses taken) on the container (e.g., "60/120"), and once a medicine dose is taken, the metered counter number decreases by 1. Physicians normally recommend that patients take their prescribed medication at a certain frequency, e.g., twice a day. Thus, a dose inhaler with 60 doses per fill can be used for as long as 1 month.

Our goal in this experiment was to provide patients taking inhaler medications an easy-to-use method for correctly using their inhalers. Using the current ICT method and the Internet of Things (IOT) concept, we implemented a service called "MDP" (metered-dose plus) as a smartphone plug-in subsystem that contains both APP software and a cap device (Fig. 1). To design a convenient and extendable service that records the number of inhaler doses taken supports consistent and safe drug use by patients. We hope that this kind of system will not only improve patient health because it efficiently monitors and reminds patients of their correct drug doses and frequencies, but also suggests to manufacturers to consider in greater detail how to develop inhalers and other commercial personal drug delivery systems that are significantly more user-friendly.

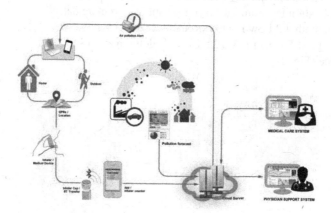

Fig. 1. The complete workflow of service for our MDP chronic respiratory pulmonary disease care platform.

2   Methods

The technology of high-tech devices is changing rapidly, and the mobility functions of devices connected using sensors and wireless access to the Internet or a private network have blossomed in today's market [8]. A systematic platform also becomes part of an information platform that allows data mining and analysis in the current health-conscious climate [9–11]. "A mobile patient monitoring system [uses] mobile computing and wireless communication technologies [to measure and analyze the] biosignals of a mobile patient. In [many trials,] these systems have [proved to be user-friendly, convenient, and effective, both for] patients and [for] healthcare professionals" [12]. Mobility, as in "mobile APPs", is becoming a key for the healthcare industry, not only for controlling disease, but also for being a reminder of healthcare activities, like taking one's medications on time, and for being a safety monitor [13].

2.1 System Architecture

The MDP incorporates three major components: a remote server, a mobile application, and a smart inhaler. The user-enabled application (APP) provides end-to-end service for disease control, and it computes and stores corresponding data on remote servers. The inhaler is paired automatically with the APP via a BLE GATT service. Once the inhaler is triggered, data with a pre-defined BLE service and characteristics are extracted by the application as a dosage record.

   Glossary:

- COMM: Communication Block for HTTP/Socket data handling.
- UI: Mobile User Interface for care service delivery flow.
- Engine: Back-end computing and management module.
- Database: Relational database of user data.
- API: Application Program Interface for capturing remote data.
- BLE: Bluetooth 4.0 Low Energy protocol.
- BLE GATT: BLE Generic Attribute Profile defining corresponding BLE data schema and service (Fig. 2).

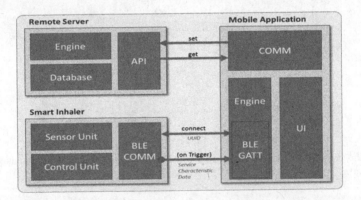

Fig. 2. The system architecture of MDP service.

2.2 MDP Prototype Description

The MDP service provides alerts, records, and easy-to-submit functional information, like the patient's posture, the time an inhaler dose was taken, and the number of doses left in the patient's medication container. Moreover, if an incorrect dose is taken, a red-light alert will show on the cap device to warn the patient of the error. When the patient is using the dose inhaler, a start circuit is initiated to detect the time the inhaler dose is taken. When the patient presses the inhaler's trigger, a sensor chip determines whether the pressure exceeds the acceptable threshold, a timer generates time data, a counter generates frequency data, and a memory chip simultaneously stores and submits the data.

3 Results

The MDP service provided a total mobile and web solution both for patients and for physicians, and it rendered the following benefits: increased patient dose compliance and life-style control; made patients more aware of their disease control progression; gave them a greater understanding of how to control their disease; established a synchronized information-sharing connection between the patient and their physicians; and increased the effectiveness of their current treatment. These are all qualitative judgments, of course.

The MDP device could be recycled simply by unplugging it from the used inhalant. The cap helped physicians (i) better understand and evaluate each patient's personal progress using specific medication, (ii) proactively rectify patient doses, (iii) build up each patient's self-awareness and knowledge of medication and patient health, and (iv) subsequently improved their quality of life (Fig. 3).

Fig. 3. The output of the prototype MDP service.

4   Discussion and Conclusions

Sixteen patients who were taking inhaler medicine were selected to participate in the experiment and to express their opinions of the development of the MDP service. Thirteen (81 %) of the 16 patients were satisfied with the service. A second trial can be planned for the near future to test the MDP service for at least 3-6 months with randomly selected patients who have been diagnosed with appropriate respiratory diseases (asthma or COPD).

We also learned from the Internet, that there is a similar device now on the market that retails for US$39.99 [14]. This device stores data on an individual item without wireless access or data analysis feedback messages. The smart inhaler device contains a BLE chip, which makes it expensive; therefore, how to improve the user interface and reduce the price of the device will be our next challenge.

Acknowledgments. We thank Professor Han-Pin Kuo, MD, Chang Gung University College of Medicine, and his medical team members from Chang Gung Memorial Hospital, Linkou, for graciously supporting this experiment.

References

1. WHO Media Centre: the 10 leading causes of death in the world, 2000 and 2012. (Updated May 2014). http://www.who.int/mediacentre/factsheets/fs310/en/. Accessed 3 June 2015
2. Hung, S.H., Tseng, H.C., Tsai, W.H., Lin, H.H., Cheng, J.H., Chang, Y.M.: COPD endurance training via mobile phone. In: AMIA Annual Symposium Proceedings, Chicago (2007)
3. Liu, W.T., Wang, C.H., Lin, H.C., Lin, S.M., Lee, K.Y., Lo, Y.L., Hung, S.H., Chang, Y.M., Chung, K.F., Kuo, H.P.: Efficacy of a cell phone-based exercise programme for COPD. Eur. Respir. J. **32**, 651–659 (2008)
4. Shark, A.R., Toporkoff, S. (eds.): EHealth: A Global Perspective, pp. 57–68. Public Technology Institute & Items International, Washington, D. C. (2010). Chapter 5: ISBN 978-1451540291
5. Giraud, V., Roche, N.: Misuse of corticosteroid metered-dose inhaler is associated with decreased asthma stability. Eur. Respir. J. **19**, 246–251 (2002)
6. Lavorini, F., Magnan, A., Dubus, J.C., Voshaar, T., Corbetta, L., Broeders, M., Dekhuijzen, R., Sanchis, J., Viejo, J.L., Barnes, P., Corrigan, C., Levy, M., Crompton, G.K.: Effect of incorrect use of dry power inhalers on management of patients with asthma and COPD. Respir. Med. **102**, 593–604 (2008)
7. Inhaler Error Steering Committee, Price, D., Bosnic-Anticevich, S., Briggs, A., Chrystyn, H., Rand, C., Scheuch, G., Bousquet, J.: Inhaler competence in asthma: common errors, barriers to use and recommended solutions. Respir. Med. **107**, 37–46 (2013)
8. 10 Wearable Health Tech Devices To Watch: InformationWeek. http://www.informationweek.com/mobile/10-wearable-health-tech-devices-to-watch/d/d-id/1107148?page_number=5. Accessed 1 June 2015
9. Niesink, A., Trappenburg, J.C., de Weert-van Oene, G.H., Lammers, J.W., Verheij, T.J., Schrijvers, A.J.: Systematic review of the effects of chronic disease management on quality of life in people with chronic obstructive pulmonary disease. Respir. Med. **101**, 2233–2239 (2007)

10. Holden, R.J., Karsh, B.T.: The technology acceptance model: its past and it future in health care. J. Biomed. Inform. **43**, 159–172 (2010)
11. Ferguson, G., Quinn, J., Horwitz, C., Swift, M., Allen, J., Galescu, L.: Towards a personal health management assistant. J. Biomed. Inform. **43**, S13–S16 (2010)
12. Pawar, P., Jones, V., van Beijnum, B.J., Hermens, H.: A framework for the compassion of mobile patient monitoring system. J. Biomed. Inform. **45**, 544–556 (2012)
13. Klasnja, P., Pratt, W.: Health care in the pocket: mapping the space of mobile-phone health interventions. J. Biomed. Inform. **45**, 184–198 (2012)
14. e-pill INHALER Puffer Alarm. http://www.amazon.com/e-pill-INHALER-MONITOR-DOSER-Inhalers/dp/B002X0DJ5S/ref=sr_1_14?ie=UTF8&qid=1432899851&sr=8-14&keywords=doser. Accessed 11 June 2015

A Novel Approach to Unify Robotics, Sensors, and Cloud Computing Through IoT for a Smarter Healthcare Solution for Routine Checks and Fighting Epidemics

Arijit Sinharay[✉], Arpan Pal, Snehasis Banerjee, Rohan Banerjee,
Soma Bandyopadhyay, Parijat Deshpande, and Ranjan Dasgupta

TCS Innovation Labs, Kolkata, India
{arijit.sinharay,arpan.pal,snehasis.banerjee,rohan.banerjee,
soma.bandyopadhyay,parijat.deshpande,ranjan.dasgupta}@tcs.com

Abstract. This paper attempts to project a novel concept where medical sensors, cloud computing and robotic platform are unified to offer state-of-the-art healthcare solutions to a wide variety of scenarios. The proposed solution is most effective if there is scarcity of healthcare providers or if putting them in the field expose them into a high risk environment such as fighting epidemics. In addition, the proposed system will also benefit routine checks in quarantine wards of hospitals where human reluctance of performing routine task by the healthcare providers can be avoided. Finally, it can also assist a doctor as a decision support system by using machine's capability of number crunching while it examines through patient's complete history, goes through every medical test reports and then applies data mining for catching possible ailments from his/her symptoms.

Keywords: Robot · IoT · Cloud · Healthcare · Sensing

1 Introduction

Using robots in healthcare is becoming more and more popular every day. Robots carrying out surgery [1], nano-bots delivering drugs inside human body [2], or therapeutic usage [3] are already in place. Similarly, using IoT for telemedicine and tele-pathology [4] or cloud computing for context based data mining are all nothing but a reality today [5]. These demonstrate a tremendous potential of today's technology and if all these technologies are clubbed into a single system, then it can bring us to the next-generation healthcare solution.

In this paper, we propose a methodology to unify all the above mentioned technologies in a single platform to have a powerful system that can move, measure, analyze and infer medical condition of patients without or with minimal human intervention. This can come handy in situations like epidemic outbreaks where robots can be deployed in contagious areas, collect samples, analyze the results and send the diagnosis to doctors for their advice. These robots can also be deployed in quarantine wards in hospitals for regular and effective patient monitoring. In contrast to these high risk scenarios, doctors can use this system for their everyday out-patient chambers to take advantage of the number crunching power of machines to eliminate any missed instances in patient's

© ICST Institute for Computer Sciences, Social Informatics and Telecommunications Engineering 2016
B. Mandler et al. (Eds.) IoT 360° 2015, Part I, LNICST 169, pp. 536–542, 2016.
DOI: 10.1007/978-3-319-47063-4_59

medical records as well as getting inference about the ailment in fraction of a second. In fact, we have already worked on building innovative and portable digital medical gadgets (ideal for easy mobility with robots), a framework for cognitive engine, and robotics that are supported by a wide range of publications in recent years. To be specific, we have exploited smartphone camera and microphone to extract blood pressure (BP), heart rate (HR) and heart rate variability (HRV) [6, 7]. In addition, we also exploited LED based reflective photoplethysmography (PPG) sensor to extract blood pressure information from wide variety of body positions that supports wearable sensing [8]. In our lab, we have developed an algorithm to enable a robot to identify sound source from 3D augmentation obtained from a camera and an array of microphones [9], Moreover, we worked on building a cognitive engine that addressed smart city public alerting system having novel features like stream windowing, incremental reasoning etc. [10–12]. Although the system was trained for smart-city use case, it can be re-trained for healthcare applications as discussed in Sect. 3. Furthermore, we have also investigated medical data compression techniques and came up with a novel adaptive approach that is best suited for preserving critical information related to abnormalities in the medical data [13]. Finally, our lab has developed a cloud hosted IoT PAAS solution named TCS Connected Universe Platform (TCUP)[1] that provides a set of restful services to manage devices, to store sensor data, to do complex event processing, to run analytics and to develop IoT applications. We are now integrating all those in a single platform to come up with our first prototype of the envisioned healthcare system, an early version of which is presented in this paper.

We describe need of such system in Sect. 1.1, the proposed system architecture in Sect. 2, and our initial implementation and result in Sect. 3. Finally, we summarize our work along with scope of future improvements in Sect. 4.

1.1 Why It Is Important

It is a grim reality that at the time of Ebola attack in 2012 [14], healthcare providers were reluctant to go to the field and help patients because of the possibility of getting infected. An IoT-enabled robotic solution would have helped the scenario dramatically as the robots could have been deployed in the field and performed both physiological and pathological tests and sent the results to remote healthcare team for further diagnosis, since now-a-days connected digital medical instruments are readily available [15]. Similarly, healthcare workers in quarantine wards in hospitals may feel fatigue to perform periodic routine checks specially to take adequate measures like disinfecting the area, putting mask etc. every time they enter the ward. This situation can also be helped by robotic solutions. In addition to many such scenarios a variant of the proposed system can also be useful for healthcare in sparsely populated areas. For example, in sparsely populated countries where a family doesn't have neighbor in a few square km of area, it is very difficult for them to get medical attention in case of emergency. Here, a drone robot could fly to the patient, take measurements and inform the hospitals about patient's condition. While there are limitless possibilities and use cases, one common

---

[1] http://tcup.web2labs.net/tcup/assets/TCUPWebpages-Kol-v1.4/TCUP-Mainpage.html.

factor in all would be to use computing capabilities of the cloud connected robot to conduct machine-assisted diagnostics. To summarize, it can be foreseen that a system incorporating computing power of a cloud, measuring capability of digital connected instruments, and mobility capability by robotic platforms along with the intelligence to understand the medical knowledge from web can have tremendous potentials in health-care. Neither such complete end-to-end system exists nor has it been conceptualized.

2   Proposed System Architecture/Methodology

In this section, we would present the end-to-end system architecture and operational methodology to describe how to actually instantiate such a system. Figure 1 depicts the proposed system architecture. It mainly has three different functional components. The first layer is composed of digital medical devices both for physiological and pathological sensing, a second layer is composed of alert generation system (on finding anomaly/abnormality in the measurements) and finally a third layer is composed of cloud based cognitive engine that maps abnormalities to disease and send the report to a doctor/caregiver. The measuring instruments are carried by a sophisticated robotic platform capable of movement as well as fine mechatronics. The cognitive engine is connected to this robotic platform via internet for real-time data exchange.

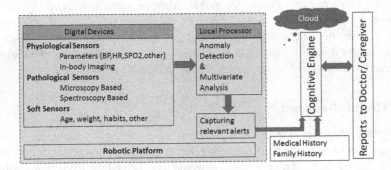

Fig. 1. System architecture and working methodology.

The robot first comes to the patient and takes measurements through the compre-hensive medical sensors consist of physiological, pathological and in-body imaging. This is to note that in-body imaging system (say, ultrasound imaging) with robotic arm could be far more efficient than usual manual scans as robotic arm can conduct very precision movements for scanning. Although only a few parameters like BP, HR etc. are highlighted in the figure they are just indicative placeholders and the actual set can include all sorts of other parameters. Similarly, auto-analyzer[2] based measurements can include a large set of pathological tests including detection of virus/bacteria, blood glucose level, cholesterol etc. [15]. All these measurements are fed to the anomaly detection module that derives critical information mostly related to abnormalities of the

---

[2] http://hydrology1.nmsu.edu/teaching/soil698/student_material/AutoAnalyzer.

measurements with reduced false positives and negative. Only these relevant anomalies are then sent to cognitive engine that resides on the cloud. The job of this cognitive engine is to relate this set of anomalies to possible disease and send the report to doctors/ hospitals for their use. This is to note that the reasoning section (i.e. mapping anomalies to disease) requires lot of computational power as one needs to build the knowledgebase by going through the vast digital knowledge available in the web. Moreover, since the medical information is always updated in the web, the cognitive engine needs to update its rules continuously much like how IBM Watson[3] learns and updates itself. An in-depth understanding of such Big Data analytics on healthcare system can be found in our published work in 2012 [16].

3   Initial Implementation and Result

In our initial work, we use our smartphone based BP, HR, HRV solutions [6, 7] along with off-the-shelf available eHealth[4] sensor to additionally include breathing rate, ECG, SPO2, temperature and blood glucose measurements. Smartphones are particularly attractive for its wireless connectivity and multipurpose sensing capabilities via built-in sensors and readily available attachments like flir[5], lens[6], etc.

An Arduino board, connected to the iPhone via blue-tooth and connected to eHealth sensors through eHealth shield, is used for sensor data acquisition. It then sends the data to a PC via USB connection for alert generation (Fig. 2a). At this stage, we built the anomaly detection layer as well as a cognitive engine both hosted in a PC. Although, implementation of the cognitive engine for healthcare is still in progress, we briefly outline our design approach. The cognitive engine is based on deriving meaningful actionable inferences by reasoning on the combined knowledge of static facts (like user profile), ontologies (like disease taxonomy) and dynamic facts (like sensed data) [10] as depicted in Fig. 2b. For handling streaming data, a snapshot of it is usually used for reasoning, the snapshot window being determined by various strategies [11]. Sensed data is put in a queue and processed by Data Handler (that performs tasks like data filtering and transformation) before being put into Working Memory where matching rules are fired and registered queries are triggered at specified intervals to produce results. The above module is developed by extending Apache Jena[7] and is based on Semantic Web framework. The rules are being written in a triple format and so is the query in SPARQL, for knowledge clubbing. Rules are written from medical books and consultation with doctors. A sample rule is to entail stress condition of a patient based on heart rate and blood pressure readings: *(?patient <p:hasHeartRate> <s:high>) (?patient <p:hasBloodPressure> <s:high>) -> (?patient <p:possibleDiagnosis> <d:Stress>).*

---

[3] http://www.ibm.com/smarterplanet/us/en/ibmwatson.
[4] https://www.cooking-hacks.com/documentation/tutorials/ehealth-biometric-sensor-platform-arduino-raspberry-pi-medical.
[5] http://www.flir.com/flirone/.
[6] http://www.instructables.com/id/10-Smartphone-to-digital-microscope-conversion/.
[7] https://jena.apache.org/.

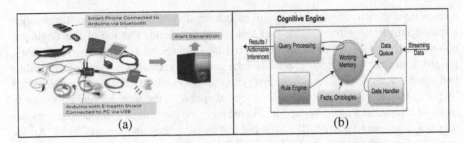

Fig. 2. (a) Initial implementation, and (b) working principle of cognitive engine

A sample query is: *select ?disease where {<u:user123> <p:possibleDiagnosis> ? disease}.*

We report successful measurement of BP and HRV parameters when tried on 10 participants following our earlier work [6, 7]. For example, mean error for diastolic (Pd) and systolic pressure (Ps) are under 5 % when validated against Omron sphygmoman- ometer[8]. Similarly, the maximum error in HRV parameters (RMSSD, SDSD, SDNN, nn50, pnn50, nn20, pnn20) are also found to be under 14 % when validated against HRV calculated from AliveCor ECG[9] data. The rest of the sensing is done with e-Health medical grade sensors and hence, reporting measurement accuracy is not required. These measures are then fed to anomaly detection to raise alert. For example, Fig. 3b depicts successful detection of anomalies (shown in red) from ECG dataset[10] based on Brute Force Discord Discovery (BFDD) [17]. The anomaly detection algorithm was executed on the web hosted dataset as all our measurements taken from our colleagues came out to be normal.

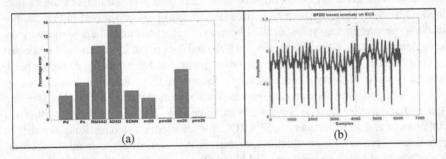

Fig. 3. (a) Error in BP, HRV measurement (b) BFDD based anomaly detection in ECG data

4 Summary

Our preliminary work supports feasibility of automatic alert generation by measuring healthcare parameters through portable digital gadgets. In addition, if a robotic platform

---

8 http://omronhealthcare.com/blood-pressure/upper-arm/.

9 http://www.alivecor.com/.

10 http://www.cs.ucr.edu/~eamonn/discords.

comes into place to actually carry the sensors then this proposed system would cater for a variety of situation in healthcare that would otherwise be difficult to be handled by humans. Specially, the robotic platform will reduce or even eliminate the need for humans to come close to patients in high risk environments like contagious virus attacks. Alternatively, it can also address the problem of unavailability of trained healthcare workers in remote villages of under developed countries or for countries with sparsely populated areas. Moreover, the cloud hosted cognitive engine may assist the doctors by checking detailed patient's history and medical reports that would have been left unattended due to human limitation in terms of their memory and processing ability. Our future work would include hosting the cognitive engine on TCUP as well as choosing a robotic platform to carry the sensors.

References

1. Kwoh, Y.S., Hou, J., Jonckheere, E., Hayati, S., et al.: A robot with improved absolute positioning accuracy for CT guided stereotactic brain surgery. IEEE Trans. Biomed. Eng. **35**(2), 153–160 (1988)
2. Yadav, A., Ghune, M., Jain, D.K.: Nano-medicine based drug delivery system. J Adv. Pharm. Educ. Res. **1**, 201–213 (2011)
3. Kwakkel, G., Kollen, B.J., Krebs, H.I.: Effects of robot-assisted therapy on upper limb recovery after stroke: a systematic review. Neurorehabil. Neural Repair **22**, 111–121 (2007)
4. Della Mea, V.: Internet electronic mail: a tool for low-cost telemedicine. J. Telemed. Telecare **5**(2), 84–89 (1999)
5. Cao, H., Jiang, D., et al.: Context-aware query suggestion by mining click-through and session data. In: Proceedings of SIGKDD, pp. 875–883. ACM (2008)
6. Banerjee, R., et al.: Noise cleaning and Gaussian modeling of smart phone photoplethysmogram to improve blood pressure estimation. In: ICASSP. IEEE (2015)
7. Misra, A., Banerjee, R., Choudhury, A.D., Sinha, A., Pal, A.: Novel peak detection to estimate HRV using Smartphone audio. In: BSN. IEEE (2015)
8. Nasimuddin, A., et al.: Feasibility analysis for estimation of blood pressure and heart rate using a smart eye wear. In: Proceedings of the WearSys 2015, pp. 9–14 (2015)
9. Reddy, V.R., Deshpande, P., Dasgupta, R.: Robotics audition using kinect. In: Proceedings of ICARA 2015, pp. 34–41. IEEE (2015)
10. Mukherjee, D., Banerjee, S., Misra, P.: Towards efficient stream reasoning. In: Demey, Y.T., Panetto, H. (eds.) OTM 2013. LNCS, vol. 8186, pp. 735–738. Springer, Heidelberg (2013). doi:10.1007/978-3-642-41033-8_97
11. Banerjee, S., Mukherjee, D.: Windowing mechanisms for web scale stream reasoning. In: Proceedings of Web-KR (CIKM Workshop), San Francisco, USA (2013)
12. Banerjee, S., Mukherjee, D., Misra, P.: What affects me?': a smart public alert system based on stream reasoning. In: Proceedings of ACM ICUIMC (2013)
13. Ukil, A., Bandyopadhyay, S., Sinha, A., Pal, A.: Adaptive sensor data compression in IoT systems: sensor data analytics based approach. In: IEEE ICASSP (2015)
14. Preston, R.: The hot zone: the terrifying true story of the origins of the Ebola virus. Anchor, Hamburg (2012)
15. Beyette Jr., F.R., Kost, G.J., Gaydos, C., Weigl, B.H., et al.: Point- of-care technologies for health care. IEEE Trans. Biomed. Eng. **58**(3), 732–735 (2011)

16. Mukherjee, A., Pal, A., Misra, P.: Data analytics in ubiquitous sensor-based health information systems. In: Proceedings of NGMAST. IEEE (2012)
17. Chuah, M.C., Fu, F.: ECG anomaly detection via time series analysis. In: Thulasiraman, P., He, X., Xu, T.L., Denko, M.K., Thulasiram, R.K., Yang, L.T. (eds.) ISPA 2007. LNCS, vol. 4743, pp. 123–135. Springer, Heidelberg (2007). doi:10.1007/978-3-540-74767-3_14

Author Index

Printed in the United States
By Bookmasters